SELECTED
LETTERS OF
OSCAR
WILDE

SELECTED LETTERS OF OSCAR WILDE

EDITED BY

RUPERT HART-DAVIS

Oxford New York Toronto Melbourne

OXFORD UNIVERSITY PRESS

1979

Oxford University Press, Walton Street, Oxford OX2 6DP

OXFORD LONDON GLASGOW
NEW YORK TORONTO MELBOURNE WELLINGTON
KUALA LUMPUR SINGAPORE JAKARTA HONG KONG TOKYO
DELHI BOMBAY CALCUTTA MADRAS KARACHI
NAIROBI DAR ES SALAAM CAPE TOWN

The Letters of Oscar Wilde first published by Rupert Hart-Davis
Ltd (London) and Harcourt Brace & World, Inc. (New York), 1962.
This selection first published as an Oxford University Press
paperback and simultaneously in a clothbound edition by
Oxford University Press, Oxford, 1979.

British Library Cataloguing in Publication Data

Wilde, Oscar
    Selected letters of Oscar Wilde.
    I. Hart-Davis, Rupert
    826'.8   PR5812

    ISBN 0-19-212205-3
    ISBN 0-19-281218-1 (Pbk)

Printed in Great Britain by
Lowe & Brydone Printers Limited, Thetford, Norfolk

THIS SELECTION
IS DEDICATED BY ITS EDITOR
WITH GRATITUDE AND AFFECTION
TO THE MEMORY OF VYVYAN HOLLAND

CONTENTS

CONTENTS

PREFACE

This selection has been made from *The Letters of Oscar Wilde* (1962), which is now out of print and unavailable. That volume necessarily contained, besides much repetition, a large number of letters which were included for biographical or other factual reasons and are now on the record. Moreover it was, for those days, expensive, and its size and price may have deterred many who would have enjoyed it.

For this selection I have chosen a representative group of letters from each period of Wilde's life, giving preference to those of literary interest, to the most amusing, and to those that throw light on his life and work. I have again printed in its entirety the long letter to Lord Alfred Douglas, usually known as *De Profundis*, because it is the most important letter that Wilde ever wrote, and it can be fully appreciated only in its entirety.

In *The Letters* I gave details of the provenance of each letter, including the location of the manuscript. Where it had not been possible to trace the manuscript I used such sources, identified in each case, as printed texts (books about Wilde, memoirs, and sale catalogues), typescript and manuscript copies. The texts of all letters to periodicals were taken from the periodicals. In this selection I have not thought it necessary to repeat all this information, which is available in the full edition. An asterisk in front of the heading to a letter indicates that the text is *not* taken from the manuscript; all letters not preceded by an asterisk have been taken from the manuscript or from a facsimile.

Since *The Letters* a number of manuscripts have come to light and in this edition I am able to provide accurate and complete texts for letters to Waldo Story (p. 53), Lily Langtry (p. 54), H. C. Marillier (p. 64), Thomas Hutchinson (p. 73), Arthur Fish (p. 83), and Frances Forbes-Robertson (p. 351). All these letters are now in the collection of Mrs Mary Hyde, to whom, as to her late husband Donald, my debt, if unpayable, is at least deeply and warmly appreciated. I have also been able to give slightly fuller texts from typescript copies in the William Andrews Clark Memorial Library, Los Angeles, of the letter to Lady Wilde (p. 1), and that to Leonard Smithers (p. 339). The originals of letters to Norman Forbes-Robertson have also been made available by Mr Donald J. Kaufmann, but no textual changes are necessary.

With these few exceptions the texts of the letters have been taken from

The Letters, incorporating corrections made in the fourth impression of 1963. As I explained in the Introduction to that edition, I have corrected Wilde's occasional misspellings, and tidied up his punctuation. Except for two omissions all these letters are printed exactly as Wilde wrote them. Ten words of unimportant gossip which might give pain to descendants have been omitted from the letter on p. 141. To save space I have cut out of the letter to Robert Ross of 6 April 1897 a passage about Wilde's legal and financial worries (printed in full in the complete edition) which is an almost exact repetition of the letter of 1 April 1897.

Wilde seldom dated his letters. All dates editorially supplied are enclosed within square brackets: doubtful ones are preceded by a query. Postmarks are indicated, but in most cases I have not repeated the full detail provided in the complete edition to substantiate the dating. In a few places later information has enabled me to correct a date. I have not usually identified the source of letters or other documents quoted in the footnotes, since this information is available in the complete edition, where can also be found full bibliographical references to the Collected Edition of Wilde's works edited by Robert Ross in 1908, and the Bibliography compiled by Stuart Mason in 1914. I have included a modicum of cross-reference to assist the reader, but he will have to rely largely on the index, where the first page-number after each person's name indicates the position of his main biographical particulars.

I should like to renew my thanks to everyone listed in *The Letters*: the owners of original letters; those who generously gave permission for reproduction of copyright material; the many people who provided personal reminiscences and specialised information, or lent books, papers and photographs. By helping with the original work they have also made an indispensable contribution to this selection. I should like as well to thank those people who wrote to me after the appearance of the 1962 volume and provided corrections which appear in this volume.

I am very grateful for the kindness I received from all my benefactors. The first and greatest of these was Vyvyan Holland, the son of Oscar Wilde, who helped me throughout with encouragement, information and forbearance. He approved the idea of this selection, but alas did not live to see it realised.

In the quest for footnote information I originally had the benefit of the researches of a small group of friends. I should like to repeat my thanks to them for all their labours on my behalf. In the preparation of this new volume I have been immeasurably assisted by Owen Dudley Edwards and by Joyce and Ernest Mehew, who by their unsparing assiduity and exactitude have saved me countless hours of checking and rearrangement.

RUPERT HART-DAVIS

Marske-in-Swaledale
    July 1978

BIOGRAPHICAL TABLE

1854	October 16	Oscar Wilde born at 21 Westland Row, Dublin
1855		Family moves to 1 Merrion Square North
1864–71		At Portora Royal School, Enniskillen
1871–74		At Trinity College, Dublin
1874	October	Goes up to Magdalen College, Oxford, as Demy
1875	June	Travels in Italy with Mahaffy
1876	April 19	Death of Sir William Wilde
	July 5	First in Mods
1877	March–April	Visits Greece with Mahaffy, returning *via* Rome
1878	June 10	Wins Newdigate Prize with *Ravenna*
	July 19	First in Greats
	November 28	B.A. degree
1879	Autumn	Takes rooms with Frank Miles at 13 Salisbury Street, London
1880	August	Moves with Miles to Keats House, Tite Street, Chelsea
1881	June ?30	*Poems* published
	December 24	Embarks for U.S.A.
1882		Lectures in U.S.A. and Canada all the year
1883	January–?May	In Paris, Hôtel Voltaire
	?July	Moves into rooms at 9 Charles Street, Grosvenor Square
	Aug–Sept	Visits New York briefly for production of *Vera*
	September 24	Begins lecture-tour in U.K., which lasts off and on for a year
	November 26	Engaged to Constance Lloyd
1884	May 29	Married to Constance Lloyd in London
	May–June	On honeymoon in Paris and Dieppe
1885	January 1	Moves into 16 Tite Street
	June 5	Cyril Wilde born

xi

1886		Meets Robert Ross
	November 3	Vyvyan Wilde born
1887		Undertakes editorship of the *Woman's World*
1888	May	*The Happy Prince and other Tales* published
1889	July	"The Portrait of Mr W. H." published in *Blackwood's*
	October	Gives up editorship of the *Woman's World*
1890	June 20	*The Picture of Dorian Gray* published in *Lippincott's*
1891	?January	Meets Lord Alfred Douglas
	January	*The Duchess of Padua* produced in New York as *Guido Ferranti*
	February	*The Soul of Man under Socialism* published in *Fortnightly*
	April	*The Picture of Dorian Gray* published in book form
	May 2	*Intentions* published
	July	*Lord Arthur Savile's Crime and Other Stories* published
	November	*A House of Pomegranates* published
	Nov–Dec	Writes *Salome* in Paris
1892	February 20	*Lady Windermere's Fan* produced
	May 26	Limited edition of *Poems* published
	June	*Salome* banned by Lord Chamberlain
	July	Takes cure at Homburg
	Aug–Sept	Writes *A Woman of No Importance* in Norfolk
	November	Takes Babbacombe Cliff, near Torquay
1893	February 22	*Salome* published in French
	March 5	Leaves Babbacombe
	April 19	*A Woman of No Importance* produced
	June–October	At The Cottage, Goring-on-Thames
	October	Takes rooms at 10 and 11 St James's Place
		Writes *An Ideal Husband* there
	November 9	*Lady Windermere's Fan* published
1894	February 9	*Salome* published in English, illustrated by Beardsley
	May	In Florence with Douglas
	June 11	*The Sphinx* published
	Aug–Sept	Writes *The Importance of Being Earnest* at Worthing
	October 9	*A Woman of No Importance* published
	October	At Brighton with Douglas

1895	January 3	*An Ideal Husband* produced
	January 17–31	Visits Algiers with Douglas
	February 14	*The Importance of Being Earnest* produced
	February 28	Finds Queensberry's card at Albemarle Club
	March 1	Obtains warrant for Queensberry's arrest
	March 9	Queensberry remanded at Bow Street for trial at Old Bailey
	March	Visits Monte Carlo with Douglas
	April 3	Queensberry trial opens
	April 5	Queensberry acquitted. Wilde arrested
	April 6–26	Imprisoned at Holloway
	April 26	First trial opens
	May 1	Jury disagree. New trial ordered
	May 7	Released on bail
	May 20	Second trial opens
	May 25	Sentenced to two years' hard labour and imprisoned (after two days in Newgate) at Pentonville
	July 4	Transferred to Wandsworth
	September 24	First examination in Bankruptcy
	November 12	Second examination in Bankruptcy
	November 20	Transferred to Reading
1896	February 3	Death of Lady Wilde
	February 11	*Salome* produced in Paris
1897	January–March	Writes *De Profundis*
	May 18	Transferred to Pentonville
	May 19	Released. Crosses to Dieppe by night boat
	May 26	Moves from Dieppe to Berneval-sur-Mer
	August ?28–29	Meets Douglas at Rouen
	September 4–11	At Rouen
	September 15	Leaves Dieppe for Paris
	September 20	Arrives at Naples
	September ?27	Moves to Villa Giudice, Posilippo
	October 15–18	Visits Capri with Douglas
	December	Visits Sicily
1898	January	Moves to 31 Santa Lucia, Naples
	February ?13	Moves to Hôtel de Nice, Paris
	February 13	*The Ballad of Reading Gaol* published
	March *c.* 28	Moves to Hôtel d'Alsace
	April 7	Death of Constance Wilde
	June–July	At Nogent-sur-Marne
	August	At Chennevières-sur-Marne
	December 15	Leaves for Napoule, near Cannes
1899	February	*The Importance of Being Earnest* published

1899	February	Leaves Napoule for Nice
	February 25	Leaves Nice for Gland, Switzerland
	April 1	Leaves Gland for Santa Margherita
	April–May	Returns to Paris, Hôtel de la Neva
	May	Moves to Hôtel Marsollier
	June 23–26	At Trouville and Le Havre
	July	*An Ideal Husband* published
	July	At Chennevières-sur-Marne
	August	Moves back to Hôtel d'Alsace
1900	April 2–10	At Palermo
	April 12–	
	May ?15	In Rome
	May	Ten days at Gland
	May–June	Returns to Paris
	October 10	Operated on
	November 30	Dies in Hôtel d'Alsace

PART ONE

OXFORD · 1875-1878

Oscar Wilde was born on 16 October 1854 at 21 Westland Row, Dublin, and on 26 April 1855, in the neighbouring church of St Mark, he was christened Oscar Fingal O'Flahertie. In his youth he added the name Wills, which his father also used. His brother Willie was born in 1852 and his sister Isola in 1859. She died in 1867.

Their father, Sir William Wilde (born 1815), was a leading oculist and ear-surgeon who had built and equipped his own hospital in Dublin. He published books on aural surgery, topography, Dean Swift, and an immense medical report on the 1851 census. He was knighted in 1864.

In 1851 he married Jane Francesca Elgee (born about 1824), who had played a leading part in the Young Ireland movement of the 1840's, writing inflammatory poems and articles in the *Nation* under the name Speranza. She published books in prose and verse, including *Sidonia the Sorceress* (1849), a translation from the German of *Sidonia von Bork* (1847) by Wilhelm Meinhold (1797–1851), which William Morris reprinted at the Kelmscott Press in 1893.

In 1855 the Wilde family moved to 1 Merrion Square North, and in 1864 Oscar was sent to Portora Royal School, Enniskillen, where he stayed until 1871. From Portora dates the first letter which has survived (if the writer had dated and addressed all his letters as scrupulously, his editor's task would have been lighter):

*8 September 1868   *Portora School*
Darling Mama, The hamper came today, I never got such a jolly surprise, many thanks for it, it was more than kind of you to think of it. Don't please forget to send me the *National Review* . . . The flannel shirts you sent in the hamper are both Willie's, mine are one quite scarlet and the other lilac but it is too hot to wear them yet. You never told me anything about the publisher in Glasgow, what does he say? And have you written to Aunt Warren on the green note paper?

In 1871 he won an entrance scholarship at Trinity College, Dublin, and went there armed with an exhibition from Portora. During the next three years he won many prizes for classics, including a foundation scholarship and the Berkeley Gold Medal for Greek. He also came strongly under the influence of the Rev. John Pentland Mahaffy (1839–1919). This remarkable man (who later became Provost of the College, and was knighted in 1918) was then Professor of Ancient History. His passion for all things Greek, his study of the art of conversation, and his social technique all left their mark on his pupil.

In 1874, at the age of twenty, Wilde crowned his academic success by winning a Demyship at Magdalen College, Oxford. It was worth £95 a year for four years, and in October he took up residence in the rooms known as Chaplain's I (2 Pair Right). A year later he moved into Cloisters VIII (Ground Room Right). During his first summer vacation he travelled to Italy, where the letters begin.

To Lady Wilde

Thursday [and Friday, 24 and 25 June 1875]   *Milan*

I believe you left me last looking at the moon from the Piazza San Marco. With difficulty we tore ourselves away to the hotel. Next morning we went up the Grand Canal in a gondola. Great palaces on each side with huge steps leading down to the water, and all round big posts to moor the gondolas to, coloured with the arms of the family. Wonderful colour everywhere—windows hung with striped yellow awnings, domes and churches of white marble, campaniles of red brick, great gondolas filled with fruit and vegetables going to the Rialto where the market is. Stopped to see the picture gallery which, as usual, was in a suppressed monastery. Titian and Tintoretto in great force. Titian's *Assumption* certainly the best picture in Italy. Went to a lot of churches, all however in extravagant "baroque" style—very rich in worked metal and polished marble and mosaic but as a rule inartistic. In the picture gallery besides the Titians there are two great pictures; one a beautiful Madonna by Bellini, the other a picture of Dives and Lazarus by Bonifazio containing the only *lovely* woman's face I have seen in Italy.

Spent the day in gondolas and markets; in the evening a great band and promenade of all the swells of Venice in the Piazza San Marco. Every woman, nearly, over thirty powdered the front of her hair; most wore veils but I see that bonnets are now made with very high crowns and two wreaths, one under the diadem and one round the crown.

After marriage the Italian women degenerate awfully, but the boys and girls are beautiful. Amongst married women the general types are "Titiens" and an ugly sallow likeness of "Trebelli Bettini."[1]

[1] Thérèse Tietjens or Titiens (1831–77) and Zélie Trebelli (1838–92), who married Alexander Bettini, an Italian tenor, were prima donnas of ample proportions who had regularly sung in Dublin with J. H. Mapleson's Italian Opera Company in the 1860's and 1870's.

2

In the morning breakfasted on board the P. & O. steamer *Baroda*. I was asked by the doctor, a young Dublin fellow called Fraser. Left for Padua at twelve o'clock. Believe me, Venice in beauty of architecture and colour is beyond description. It is the meeting-place of the Byzantine and Italian art—a city belonging to the *East* as much as to the West.

Arrived at Padua at two o'clock. In the middle of a rich vineyard stands the Baptistery, the great work of Giotto; the walls covered entirely with frescoes by him; one wall the life of Mary, the other the life of Christ; the ceiling blue with gold stars and medallion pictures; the west wall a great picture of Heaven and Hell suggested to him by Dante who, weary of trudging up the steep *stairs*, as he says, of the *Scali*geri when in exile at Verona, came to stay at Padua with Giotto in a house still to be seen there.[1] Of the beauty and purity of sentiment, the clear transparent colour, bright as the day it was painted, and the harmony of the whole building, I am unable to tell you. He is the first of all painters. We stayed over an hour in the Baptistery filled with wonder and reverence and above all love for the scenes he has painted.

Padua is a quaint town with good colonnades along each street, a university like a barracks, one charming church (Sant' Anastasia) and a lot of bad ones, and the best restaurant in Italy, where we dined.

Arrived at Milan in a shower of rain; went in the evening to the theatre and saw a good ballet.

This morning the Cathedral. Outside most elaborate in pinnacles and statues awfully out of proportion with the rest of the building. Inside most impressive through its huge size and giant pillars supporting the roof; some good old stained glass and a lot of hideous modern windows. These moderns don't see that the use of a window in a church is to show a beautiful massing together and blending of colour; a good old window has the rich pattern of a Turkey carpet. The figures are quite subordinate and only serve to show the sentiment of the designer. The modern fresco style of window has *suâ naturâ* to compete with painting and of course looks monstrous and theatrical.

The Cathedral is an awful failure. Outside the design is monstrous and inartistic. The over-elaborated details stuck high up where no one can see them; everything is vile in it; it is, however, imposing and gigantic as a failure, through its great size and elaborate execution.

From Padua I forgot to tell you we went to Verona at six o'clock, and in the old Roman amphitheatre (as perfect inside as it was in the old Roman times) saw the play of *Hamlet* performed—and certainly indifferently—but you can imagine how romantic it was to sit in the old amphi-

---

[1] Cf. Dante, *Paradiso*, xvii, 59–60:

> *com' è duro calle*
> *Lo scendere e il salir per l'altrui scale*

and the opening of Wilde's sonnet "At Verona," published in *Poems* (1881):

> How steep the stairs within Kings' houses are
> For exile-wearied feet as mine to tread.

He had already used the first line in his *Ravenna* (1878).

3

theatre on a lovely moonlight night. In the morning went to see the tombs of the Scaligeri—good examples of rich florid Gothic work and ironwork; a good market-place filled with the most gigantic umbrellas I ever saw—like young palm trees—under which sat the fruit-sellers. Of our arrival at Milan I have told you.

Yesterday (Thursday) went first to the Ambrosian Library where we saw some great manuscripts and two very good palimpsests, and a bible with Irish glosses of the sixth or seventh century which has been collated by Todd and Whitley Stokes and others;[1] a good collection of pictures besides, particularly a set of drawings and sketches in chalk by Raffaelli—much more interesting I think than his pictures—good Holbeins and Albrecht Dürers.

Then to the picture gallery. Some good Correggios and Peruginos; the gem of the whole collection is a lovely Madonna by Bernardino standing among a lot of trellised roses that Morris and Rossetti would love; another by him we saw in the library with a background of lilies.

Milan is a second Paris. Wonderful arcades and galleries; all the town white stone and gilding. Dined excellently at the Biffi Restaurant and had some good wine of Asti, like good cider or sweet champagne. In the evening went to see a new opera, *Dolores*, by a young maestro called Auteri; a good imitation of Bellini in some parts, some pretty rondos; but its general character was inharmonious shouting.[2] However, the frantic enthusiasm of the people knew no bounds. Every five minutes a terrible furore and yelling of *Bravas* from every part of the house, followed by a frantic rush of all the actors for the composer, who was posted at the side-scenes ready to rush out on the slightest symptom of approval. A weak-looking creature who placed his grimy hand on a shady-looking shirt to show his emotion, fell on the prima donna's neck in ecstasy, and blew kisses to us all. He came out no less than nineteen times, and finally three crowns were brought out, one of which, a green laurel one with green ribbons, was clapped on his head, and as his head was very narrow it rested partly on a very large angular nose and partly on his grimy shirt-collar. Such an absurd scene as the whole thing was I never saw. The opera except in two places is absolutely devoid of merit. The Princess Margherita was there, very high-bred and pale.[3]

I write this at Arona on the Lago Maggiore, a beautiful spot. Mahaffy

---

[1] This document is not a bible and has no Irish glosses. It is a service-book, known as the Antiphonary of Bangor, and is perhaps the oldest known Irish manuscript. James Henthorn Todd (1805–69) and Whitley Stokes (1830–1909), both of Trinity College, Dublin, were two of the ablest Irish antiquarian scholars of their time.

[2] *Dolores* by Salvatore Auteri-Manzocchi (1845–1924) was performed first in Florence earlier in 1875, and on 24 June at the Teatro dal Verme in Milan. It was revived at the Scala in 1878.

[3] Margherita Teresa Giovanna, Princess of Savoy-Genoa (1851–1926), married (1868) her cousin, the Prince of Piedmont, who became the second King of Italy as Humbert I (1878). Her only son became King Victor Emmanuel III.

and young Goulding[1] I left at Milan and they will go on to Genoa. As I had no money I was obliged to leave them and feel very lonely. We have had a delightful tour.

Tonight at twelve o'clock the *diligence* starts. We go over the Simplon Pass till near Lausanne; eighteen hours *en diligence*. Tomorrow night (Saturday) I get to Lausanne. Yours   OSCAR

To Reginald Harding[2]

Wednesday [5 July 1876]   *Magdalen College, Oxford*

My dear Kitten, I am very sorry to hear you did not meet the poor Bouncer Boy;[3] see what comes of having rowdy friends fond of practical jokes. I had an awful pencil scrawl from him yesterday, written sitting on the rocks at Lundy. I hope nothing will happen to him.

I had a very pleasant time in Lincolnshire, but the weather was so hot we did nothing but play lawn tennis, as probably Bouncer will tell you when you see him next (I wrote a full account to him). I examined schools in geography and history, *sang* glees, *ate* strawberries and argued fiercely with my poor uncle,[4] who revenged himself on Sunday by preaching on Rome in the morning, and on humility in the evening. Both very " nasty ones" for me.

I ran up to town yesterday from Lincoln and brought Frank Miles[5] a great basket of roses from the Rectory. I found him sketching the most

---

[1] Probably William Joshua Goulding (1856–1925), later director of many Irish companies, Baronet 1904, Privy Councillor 1917. He was certainly a friend of Mahaffy, but his descendants have no record of their travelling abroad together.

[2] Richard Reginald Harding (1857–1932), Magdalen Commoner 1875–79. Everyone at Magdalen had a nickname (Wilde's was Hosky) and Harding's came from a popular music-hall song which began:

> "Beg your parding, Mrs Harding,
> Is my kitting in your garding?"

His elder brother James was known as Puss and his sister Amy as Miss Puss. Harding was a member of the London Stock Exchange from 1895 until his death.

[3] William Welsford Ward (1854–1932) went up to Magdalen from Radley as a Classical Demy in 1873. First in Mods 1874. His nickname came from *Little Mr Bouncer and his Friend Verdant Green* (1873), the last of a series of comic Oxford novels by Cuthbert Bede (Edward Bradley, 1827–89). Wilde's drawing inscribed "Little Mr Bouncer" can still be seen scratched on the window of the room they successively occupied in the college. Ward went down at the end of 1876 and, after a five-months tour of the continent, followed his father as a solicitor in Bristol. His short "Oxford Reminiscence" of Wilde was published as an appendix to *Son of Oscar Wilde* by Vyvyan Holland (1954).

[4] The Rev. John Maxwell Wilde, Sir William's elder brother. He was Vicar of West Ashby, Lincolnshire, from 1866 to 1885.

[5] George Francis Miles (1852–91), son of the Rev. Robert Henry William Miles (1819–83), Rector of Bingham, Notts, 1845–83, was a popular artist in the early 80's: his many drawings of Lily Langtry did much to enhance her popularity. After he had shared two sets of rooms with Wilde in London they quarrelled and separated. Miles spent the last four years of his life in an asylum.

lovely and dangerous woman in London—Lady Desart. She is very fascinating indeed.[1]

I came down Monday night to read for *viva voce*, but yesterday morning at ten o'clock was woke up by the Clerk of the Schools, and found I was in already. I was rather afraid of being put on in Catullus, but got a delightful exam from a delightful man—not on the books at all but on Aeschylus *versus* Shakespeare, modern poetry and drama and every conceivable subject. I was up for about an hour and was quite sorry when it was over. In Divinity I was ploughed of course.

I am going down to Bingham with Frank Miles and R. Gower[2] on Saturday for a week. They have the most beautiful modern church in England, and the finest lilies. I shall write and tell you about it.

Being utterly penniless I can't go up to town till Friday. It is very slow here—now that Bouncer is gone. But tonight the Mods list comes out so I will have some excitement being *congratulated*—really I don't care a bit (no one ever does now) and quite expect a Second *after* my Logic, though *of course much the cleverest man in*. (Such cheek!)

You will probably see the list on Thursday or Friday; if I get a Second mind you write and condole with me awfully, and if I get a First say it was only what you expected.

See the results of having nothing to do—ten pages of a letter! Yours ever

OSCAR F. O'F. WILLS WILDE

My address will be The Rectory, Bingham, Notts after Saturday. I hope you will write a line and tell me all extra news about Bouncer.

PS no. 2. The paper enclosed in Bouncer's letter was *not dirty*.

To William Ward

[*Postmark 10 July 1876*]   *4 Albert Street, S.W.*

My dear Boy, I know you will be glad to hear I have got my First all right.[3] I came up from Lincolnshire to town on Monday and went down that night to Magdalen to read my Catullus, but while lying in bed on Tuesday morning with Swinburne (a copy of) was woke up by the Clerk of the Schools to know why I did not come up. I thought I was not in till Thursday. About one o'clock I *nipped* up and was ploughed immediately in Divinity and then got a delightful *viva voce*, first in the *Odyssey*, where we discussed epic poetry in general, *dogs*, and women. Then in Aeschylus

---

[1] Maria Emma Georgina (Minnie) Preston married the fourth Earl of Desart (1845–98) in 1871 and was divorced by him in 1878. The co-respondent, whom she later married, was the actor Charles Sugden (1850–1921).

[2] Lord Ronald Sutherland-Gower (1845–1916), younger son of the second Duke of Sutherland, was sculptor, politician, author and art-critic. On 4 June 1876 he wrote in his diary: "By early train to Oxford with F. Miles . . . There I made the acquaintance of young Oscar Wilde, a friend of Miles's. A pleasant cheery fellow, but with his long-haired head full of nonsense regarding the Church of Rome. His room filled with photographs of the Pope and of Cardinal Manning."

[3] Wilde's First in Classical Moderations (Mods) was announced on 5 July and listed in *The Times* on 6 July.

where we talked of Shakespeare, Walt Whitman and the *Poetics*. He had a long discussion about my essay on Poetry in the Aristotle paper and altogether was delightful. Of course I knew I had got a First, so swaggered horribly.

The next day the B.C.'s and myself were dining with Nicols in Christ Church[1] and the list came out at seven, as we were walking up the High. I said I would not go up to the Schools, as I knew I had a First etc., and made them all very ill, absolutely. I did not know what I had got till the next morning at twelve o'clock, breakfasting at the Mitre, I read it in *The Times*. Altogether I swaggered horribly, but am really pleased with myself. My poor mother is in great delight and I was overwhelmed with telegrams on Thursday from everyone I know. My father would have been so pleased about it. I think God has dealt very hardly with us.[2] It has robbed me of any real pleasure in my First, and I have not sufficient faith in Providence to believe it is all for the best—I know it is not. I feel an awful dread of going home to our old house, with everything filled with memories. I go down today for a week at Bingham with the Mileses. I have been staying here with Julia Tindal[3] who is in great form. Yesterday I heard the Cardinal at the Pro-Cathedral preach a charity sermon.[4] He is more fascinating than ever. I met MacCall[5] and Williamson there who greeted me with much *empressement*. I feel an impostor and traitor to myself on these occasions and must do something decided.

Afterwards I went to the Zoo with Julia and the two Peytons[6]—Tom is nearly all right. Young Stewy dined with us on Saturday. He said he was afraid he must have jarred you by his indecencies and was going to reform. Altogether I found out we were right in thinking that set a little jarred about our carelessness about them. Next term I shall look them up.

I hope you will see the Kitten. I got a very nice letter from him about Mods. Miss Puss has fallen in my estimation if she is fetched with Swan[7]—who to men is irritable, but to women intolerable I think. Write

---

[1] Possibly Edward Richard Jeffereys Nicolls, Christ Church undergraduate 1876–79. Wherever possible I have briefly identified Wilde's Oxford friends: those without footnotes I have failed to trace.

[2] Sir William Wilde had died on 19 April.

[3] Nickname of Charles Harrison Tindal (1851–1930). He was a Magdalen undergraduate 1870–74, took his B.C.L. at Oxford 1877, and was called to the Bar, Lincoln's Inn, 1878.

[4] The Church of Our Lady of Victories in High Street, Kensington, was used as Pro-Cathedral until the consecration of Westminster Cathedral in 1903. Cardinal Manning preached there on Sunday, 9 July 1876. Henry Edward Manning (1808–92), originally an Anglican clergyman, became a Roman Catholic in 1851. He was created Archbishop 1865 and Cardinal 1875.

[5] Archibald Noel Locke MacCall (1852–1926), Magdalen undergraduate 1874–76, became a Roman Catholic 1875. Member of the London Oratory 1876–91, Canon of Southwark 1916.

[6] Algernon Francis Peyton (1855–1916) succeeded his father as sixth Baronet 1888. His brother Thomas Thornhill Peyton (1856–1927) became Rector of St Mary's, March, Cambridgeshire 1882, Rural Dean 1909, Canon of Ely 1915.

[7] Charles Arthur Swan (1854–1941), an Etonian, was a Magdalen Demy 1874–77. Became regular soldier, commanding the 3rd Battalion, the Lincolnshire Regiment.

soon to Bingham Rectory, Nottinghamshire. Ever yours

OSCAR O'F. W. WILDE

To William Ward

Wednesday [26 July 1876. Postmark 27 July 1876]

1 Merrion Square North, Dublin

My dear Boy, I confess not to be a worshipper at the Temple of Reason. I think man's reason the most misleading and thwarting guide that the sun looks upon, except perhaps the reason of woman. Faith is, I think, a bright lantern for the feet,[1] though of course an exotic plant in man's mind, and requiring continual cultivation. My mother would probably agree with you. Except for the *people*, for whom she thinks dogma necessary, she rejects all forms of superstition and dogma, particularly any notion of priest and sacrament standing between her and God. She has a very strong faith in that aspect of God *we* call the Holy Ghost—the divine intelligence of which we on earth partake. Here she is very strong, though of course at times troubled by the discord and jarring of the world, when she takes a dip into pessimism.

Her last pessimist, Schopenhauer, says the whole human race ought on a given day, after a strong remonstrance *firmly but respectfully* urged on God, to walk into the sea and leave the world tenantless, but of course some skulking wretches would hide and be left behind to people the world again I am afraid.

I wonder you don't see the beauty and necessity for the *incarnation* of God into man to help us to grasp at the skirts of the Infinite. The atonement is I admit hard to grasp. But I think since Christ the dead world has woke up from sleep. Since him we have lived. I think the greatest proof of the Incarnation aspect of Christianity is its whole career of noble men and thoughts and not the mere narration of unauthenticated histories.

I think *you* are bound to account (psychologically most especially) for S. Bernard and S. Augustine and S. Philip Neri—and even in our day for Liddon and Newman[2]—as being good philosophers and good Christians.

---

[1] "Thy word is a lantern unto my feet" are the opening words of the portion of the Psalm (CXIX, verse 105) for Morning Prayer on the twenty-sixth day of the month. It seems possible that Wilde had either been to Matins or had read the Prayer-book for the day.

[2] The Rev. Henry Parry Liddon (1829–90), Ireland Professor of Biblical Exegesis at Oxford 1870–82, Canon of St Paul's Cathedral from 1870, and last of the great pulpit orators of the English Church, was a strong defender of the High Church, Tractarian, or Oxford Movement. The Rev. John Henry Newman (1801–90), the original leader of the movement, turned Roman Catholic. He was not created Cardinal till 1879. In a letter to Ward a week earlier Wilde had written:

> About Newman I think that his higher emotions revolted against Rome but that he was swept on by Logic to accept it as the only rational form of Christianity. His life is a terrible tragedy. I fear he is a very unhappy man. I bought a lot of his books before leaving Oxford.

That reminds me of Mallock's *New Republic* in *Belgravia*; it is decidedly clever—Jowett especially. If you have the key to all the actors please send it to me.[1]

I send you this letter and a book together. I wonder which you will open first. It is *Aurora Leigh*, which I think you said you had not read.[2] It is one of those books that, written straight from the heart—and from such a large heart too—never weary one: because they are sincere. We tire of art but not of nature after all our aesthetic training. I look upon it as much the greatest work in our literature.

I rank it with *Hamlet* and *In Memoriam*. So much do I love it that I hated the idea of sending it to you without marking a few passages I felt you would well appreciate—and I found myself marking the whole book. I am really very sorry: it is like being given a bouquet of plucked flowers instead of being allowed to look for them oneself. But I could not resist the temptation, as it *did* instead of writing to you about each passage.

The only fault is that she overstrains her metaphors till they snap, and although one does not like polished emotion, still she is inartistically rugged at times. As she says herself, she shows the mallet hand in carving cherry-stones.[3]

I hope you will have time to read it, for I don't believe your dismal forebodings about Greats.

I wrote to Kitten for your address, and his letter and yours arrived simultaneously. His thoughts and ink rarely last beyond one sheet.

I ride sometimes after six, but don't do much but bathe, and although always feeling slightly immortal when in the sea, feel sometimes slightly heretical when good Roman Catholic boys enter the water with little amulets and crosses round their necks and arms that the good S. Christopher may hold them up.

I am now off to bed after reading a chapter of S. Thomas à Kempis. I think half-an-hour's warping of the inner man daily is greatly conducive to holiness.

[1] William Hurrell Mallock (1849–1923), a nephew of J. A. Froude, the historian, and Newman's friend, Hurrell Froude, had come down from Balliol in 1874, having won the Newdigate Prize in 1871. His Peacockian novel *The New Republic, or Culture, Faith and Philosophy in an English Country House*, was serialised anonymously in *Belgravia* from June to December 1876. In book form it was published, still anonymously, in two volumes in March 1877. Clearly its authorship was known from the beginning, at any rate in Oxford. All the characters were portraits: the main ones Ruskin, Jowett, Matthew Arnold, Huxley and Walter Pater.

[2] A novel in verse by Elizabeth Barrett Browning (1857). This copy, inscribed "W. W. Ward from Oscar F. O'F. Wilde. 1 Merrion Square. July 25th '76," was at one time in the possession of Vyvyan Holland.

[3] I wrote tales beside,
Carved many an article on cherry-stones
To suit light readers,—something in the lines
Revealing, it was said, the mallet-hand,
But that, I'll never vouch for.

Aurora Leigh, Third Book

Pray remember me to your mother and sisters. Ever yours

OSCAR F. O'F. WILLS WILDE

Post Scriptum[1]

You don't deserve such a long letter, but I must tell you that I met Mr Rigaud (the gentleman who met with that sad accident in early youth) and his brother the General swaggering up Grafton Street here yesterday.[2] I had a long talk with them and the General told me yarns by the dozen about the time he was quartered here "with the 16th Battalion, sir! Damme, sir! We were the best corps in the Regiment! Service gone to the dogs! Not a well drilled soldier in the country, sir!"

To Reginald Harding

Wednesday [?*16 August 1876*]   *Moytura House*[3] [*Cong, Co. Mayo*]

Dear Kitten, Have you fallen into a well, or been mislaid anywhere that you never write to me? Or has one of your nine lives gone?

Frank Miles and I came down here last week, and have had a very royal time of it sailing. We are at the top of Lough Corrib, which if you refer to your geography you will find to be a lake thirty miles long, ten broad and situated in the most romantic scenery in Ireland. Frank has done some wonderful sunsets since he came down; he has given me some more of his drawings. Has your sister got the one he calls "My Little Lady"—a little girl's face with a lot of falling hair? If she has not got it I would like to send it to her in return for her autograph on the celebrated memorial.

Frank has never fired off a gun in his life (and says he doesn't want to) but as our proper sporting season here does not begin till September I have not taught him anything. But on Friday we go into Connemara to a charming little fishing lodge we have in the mountains where I hope to make him land a salmon and kill a brace of grouse. I expect to have very good sport indeed this season. Write to me there if your claws have not been clipped. Illaunroe Lodge, Leenane, Co. Galway.

Best love to Puss. I hope he is reading hard. Ever yours

OSCAR F. O'F. WILLS WILDE

To William Ward

[*Postmark 28 August 1876*]   *Illaunroe Lodge, Connemara*

Dear Bouncer, I am very glad you like *Aurora Leigh*. I think it simply "*intense*" in every way. I am deep in a review of Symonds's last book

---

[1] This postscript has become detached from its letter, but it was clearly written from Dublin at the end of a comparatively long letter to Ward.

[2] Major-General Gibbes Rigaud (1821–85) had served in the Kaffir War (1851–1853) and in China (1860). His brother, the Rev. John Rigaud (1823–88), was at various times Fellow, Senior Dean of Arts, Bursar, Vice-President, Dean of Divinity, and Librarian, of Magdalen.

[3] Built by Sir William Wilde, two miles from Cong, with a fine view over Lough Corrib, about which he published a successful book in 1867.

whenever I can get time and the weather is too bright for fishing. Mahaffy has promised to look it over before publication.[1] Up to this however I am glad to say that I have been too much *occupied with rod and gun for the handling of the quill* (neat and Pope-like?).

I have only got one salmon as yet but have had heaps of sea-trout which give great play. I have not had a blank day yet. Grouse are few but I have got a lot of hares so have had a capital time of it. I hope next year that you and the Kitten will come and stay a (lunar) month with me. I am sure you would like this wild mountainous country, close to the Atlantic and teeming with sport of all kinds. It is in every way magnificent and makes me years younger than actual history records.

I hope you are reading hard; if you don't get your First the examiners ought to be sent down.

Write like a good boy to Moytura House, Cong, County Mayo, as I will be leaving here this week.

With kind regards to your mother and sisters, ever yours

OSCAR F. O'F. WILLS WILDE

I have Frank Miles with me. He is delighted with all.

To William Ward

[*Week ending 3 March 1877*]   [*Oxford*]

[*A letter of four double sheets, the first of which is missing*]

Webbe and Jack Barrow,[2] and is blossoming out into the fast man: however his career has been cut short by the Dean refusing to let him take his degree through his late hours in lodgings! *Wee! Wee!* is Mark's expression in consequence.

The freshmen *in it* are Gore,[3] a great pal of Tom Peyton's lot, Grey a nice Eton boy[4]—and we have all suddenly woke to the idea that Wharton[5] is charming. I like him very much indeed and ran him in for the Apollo lately. I also ran in Gebhardt[6] with whom I have had several rows through

---

[1] John Addington Symonds (1840–93) published the second and final volume of his *Studies of the Greek Poets* in 1876. Wilde's review is not known to have been published. In a letter from Dublin earlier this month Wilde had written:

I am with that dear Mahaffy every day. He has a charming house by the sea here, on a place called the Hill of Howth (one of the crescent horns that shuts in the Bay of Dublin), the only place near town with fields of yellow gorse, and stretches of wild myrtle, red heather and ferns.

He had been helping Mahaffy with the proofs of his *Rambles and Studies in Greece* (1876).

[2] John Burton Barrow (b. 1855), Magdalen undergraduate 1874–78, became a barrister.

[3] Frederick St John Gore (b. 1857), Magdalen undergraduate 1877–80.

[4] John Chipchase Grey (1857–1946), Magdalen undergraduate 1877–80, became a clergyman.

[5] John Henry Turner Wharton (1857–1944), Magdalen undergraduate 1876–80, rowed in university eight 1879–80; became a solicitor in Southampton.

[6] Thomas Gebhardt (b. 1855), Magdalen undergraduate 1875–78.

his *drunken-noisy-Jewish ways*—and two freshmen Vinton[1] and Chance[2] both of them very casual fellows indeed. I have got rather keen on Masonry lately and believe in it awfully—in fact would be awfully sorry to have to give it up in case I secede from the Protestant Heresy.[3] I now breakfast with Father Parkinson,[4] go to St Aloysius, talk sentimental religion to Dunlop[5] and altogether am caught in the fowler's snare, in the wiles of the Scarlet Woman—I may go over in the vac. I have dreams of a visit to Newman, of the holy sacrament in a new Church, and of a quiet and peace afterwards in my soul. I need not say, though, that I shift with every breath of thought and am weaker and more self-deceiving than ever.

If I *could hope* that the Church would wake in me some earnestness and purity I would go over *as a luxury*, if for no better reasons. But I can hardly hope it would, and to go over to Rome would be to sacrifice and give up my two great gods "Money and Ambition."

Still I get so wretched and low and troubled that in some desperate mood I will seek the shelter of a Church which simply enthrals me by its fascination.

I hope that now in the Sacred City you are wakened up from the Egyptian darkness that has blinded you. *Do* be touched by it, *feel* the awful fascination of the Church, its extreme beauty and sentiment, and let every part of your nature have play and room.

We have had our Sports and are now in the midst of Torpids[6] and tomorrow the pigeons are shot.[7] To escape I go up to town to see the Old Masters[8] *with the Kitten!* who is very anxious to come. Dear little Puss is up, and looks wretched, but as pleasant and bright as ever. He is rather keen on going to Rome for Easter with me, but I don't know if I can afford it, as I have been elected for the St Stephen's and have to pay £42. I did not want to be elected for a year or so but David Plunket ran me in

---

[1] Frank Jones Vinton (b. 1857), Magdalen undergraduate 1877–80.

[2] Henry Featherstone Chance (b. 1859), Magdalen undergraduate 1877–80, became a member of Lloyd's.

[3] Wilde was admitted to the thirty-third degree of the Scottish Masonic rite at the Oxford University chapter on 27 November 1876.

[4] The Rev. Thomas B. Parkinson, S.J., was the Superior at St Aloysius, the Roman Catholic church in St Giles, Oxford, from 1875 to 1888. The church was built 1874–75; the architect was Joseph Aloysius Hansom (1803–82), who invented the hansom cab. Wilde was much interested in the church, and was present when Cardinal Manning preached at the dedication service on 23 November 1875. Gerard Manley Hopkins, the poet, was an assistant priest at St Aloysius 1878–79.

[5] Archibald Claude Dunlop (1858–1924) became a Catholic while a Magdalen undergraduate. Later he lived and worked in Southampton, where he acted as Consul for several foreign countries and built St Boniface's Catholic church, largely at his own expense.

[6] The Lent Term rowing-races at Oxford.

[7] The shooting of pigeons in Oxford college gardens is not done at any particular time, but only when the birds become too great a nuisance.

[8] In January and February 1877 the Royal Academy held its usual exhibition of "Old Masters and Deceased Masters of the British School" at Burlington House.

in three weeks some way rather to my annoyance.[1]

I would give worlds to be in Rome with you and Dunskie.[2] I know I would enjoy it awfully but I don't know if I can manage it. You would be a safeguard against Dunskie's attacks.

I am in for the "Ireland" on Monday.[3] God! how I have wasted my life up here! I look back on weeks and months of extravagance, trivial talk, utter vacancy of employment, *with feelings so bitter that I have lost faith in myself*. I am too ridiculously easily led astray. So I have idled and won't get it and will be wretched in consequence. I feel that if I had read I would have done well up here but I have not.

I enjoy your rooms awfully.[4] The inner room is filled with china, pictures, a portfolio and a piano—and a grey carpet with stained floor. The whole get-up is much admired and a little made fun of on Sunday evenings. They are more delightful than I ever expected—the sunshine, the cawing rooks and waving tree-branches and the breeze at the window are too charming.

I do nothing but write sonnets and scribble poetry—some of which I send you—though to send anything of mine to Rome is an awful impertinence, but you always took an interest in my attempts to ride Pegasus.

My greatest chum, except of course the Kitten, is Gussy[5] who is charming though not educated well: however he is *"psychological"* and we have long chats and walks. The rest of Tom's set are capital good fellows but awful children. They talk nonsense and smut. I am quite as fond of the dear Kitten as ever but he has not enough power of character to be more than a pleasant affectionate boy. He never exerts my intellect or brain *in any way*. Between his mind and mine there is no *intellectual friction to rouse me up to talk or think*, as I used when with you—especially on those dear rides through the greenwood. I ride a good deal now and the last day rode an awful brute which by a skilful buckjump threw me on my head on Shotover. I escaped however unhurt and got home all safe.

The Dean comes sometimes and we talk theology, but I usually ride by myself, and have got such new trousers—quite the dog! I have written a very foolish letter; it reads very rambling and absurd, but it is so delightful writing to you that I just put down whatever comes into my head.

[1] St Stephen's is a "Conservative and Constitutional" Club on Victoria Embankment, Westminster, established in 1870. Wilde's proposer was probably the Hon. David Robert Plunket (1838–1919), third son of the third Lord Plunket and Conservative M.P. for Dublin University from 1870 to 1895, when he was created Lord Rathmore.

[2] The nickname (from Dunskey, his Galloway home) of David Hunter-Blair (1853–1939), a contemporary and friend of Wilde at Magdalen. A Roman Catholic convert in 1875, he entered the Benedictine Order in 1878, was ordained priest in 1886, and was Abbot of Fort Augustus 1913–17. In 1896 he succeeded his father as fifth Baronet. He published several volumes of reminiscences, of which *In Victorian Days* (1939) contains a chapter "Oscar Wilde as I knew him."

[3] In 1877 the examination for the annual Ireland Scholarship in "classical learning and taste" began on Monday, 5 March. Wilde was unsuccessful.

[4] When Ward went down Wilde moved into his rooms on the Kitchen Staircase (1 Pair Left), overlooking the Cherwell.

[5] Perhaps the nickname of Cresswell Augustus Creswell (1856–1935), Magdalen undergraduate 1875–79, who became a London stockbroker.

13

Your letters are charming and the one from Sicily came with a scent of olive-gardens, blue skies and orange trees, that was like reading Theocritus in this grey climate. Goodbye. Ever, dear boy, your affectionate friend

OSCAR WILDE[1]

I have a vacant page.

I won't write to you theology, but I only say that for *you* to feel the fascination of Rome would to me be the greatest of pleasures: I think it would *settle me.*

And really to go to Rome with the bugbear of formal logic on one's mind is quite as bad as to have the "Protestant jumps."

But I know you are keenly alive to beauty, and do try and see in the Church not man's hand only but also a little of God's.

To Reginald Harding

<table>
<tr><td>[Late March 1877]</td><td align="right">Magdalen College</td></tr>
</table>

My dear Kitten, I start for Rome on Sunday; Mahaffy comes as far as Genoa with me: and I hope to see the golden dome of St Peter's and the Eternal City by Tuesday night.

This is an era in my life, a crisis. I wish I could look into the seeds of time and see what is coming.

I shall not forget you in Rome, and will burn a candle for you at the Shrine of Our Lady.

Write to me like a good boy, Hôtel d'Angleterre, Rome. Yours ever

OSCAR

To the Rev. H. R. Bramley[2]

<table>
<tr><td>2 April 1877</td><td align="right">Hotel St George, Corfu</td></tr>
</table>

My dear Mr Bramley, My old tutor Mr Mahaffy, Fellow of Trinity College Dublin, met me on my way to Rome and insisted on my going with him to Mykenae and Athens. The chance of seeing such great places—and in such good company—was too great for me and I find myself now in Corfu. I am afraid I will not be able to be back at the beginning of term. I hope you will not mind if I miss ten days at the beginning: seeing Greece is really a great education for anyone and will I think benefit me greatly, and Mr Mahaffy is such a clever man that it is quite as good as going to lectures to be in his society.

---

[1] At this time, Wilde dropped his other names and initials from his signature.

[2] Henry Ramsden Bramley (1833–1917) was a Tutor of Magdalen 1858–68 and 1871–83. He was also Dean of Arts 1871–82. A great favourite in the College, he was a Tractarian, a Jacobite, the editor of several collections of carols, and claimed to be "in favour of progress, but of progress backward." He was Canon and Precentor of Lincoln 1895–1902.

14

We[1] came first to Genoa, which is a beautiful marble city of palaces over the sea, and then to Ravenna which is extremely interesting on account of the old Christian churches in it of enormous age and the magnificent mosaics of the *fourth century*. These mosaics were very remarkable as they contained two figures of the Madonna enthroned and receiving adoration; they completely upset the ordinary Protestant idea that the worship of the Virgin did not come in till late in the history of the Church.

I read the book you kindly lent me with much interest; the Roman Catholics certainly do seem to confuse together Catholic doctrines which we may all hold and the supremacy of the Pope which we need not hold.

I hope your health has been good this Easter. We expect to be in Athens by the 17th and I will post back to Oxford immediately. Yours very truly

OSCAR WILDE

To Reginald Harding

Tuesday [May 1877]   *1 Merrion Square North*

My dear Boy, Thanks for your letter: I had made out the facts by a careful study of the statutes going up to town, but it was comforting all the same to have it confirmed by such an authority as the Schools Clerk.[2]

I had a delightful time in town with Frank Miles and a lot of friends and came home on Friday. My mother was of course awfully astonished to hear my news and very much disgusted with the wretched stupidity of our college dons, while Mahaffy is *raging*! I never saw him so indignantly angry: he looks on it almost as an insult to himself.

The weather is charming, Florrie[3] more lovely than ever, and I am going to give two lectures on Greece to the Alexandra College girls here, so I am rapidly forgetting the Boeotian ἀναισθησία[4] of Allen[5] and the wretched time-serving of that old woman in petticoats, the Dean.

---

[1] Besides Mahaffy, the party consisted of his friend Goulding (see note 1, p. 5) and George Macmillan (1855–1936), a member of the publishing family and one of the founders of the Hellenic Society in 1879. His elder brother Malcolm disappeared from the top of Mount Olympus in 1889.

[2] As a punishment for coming up to Oxford a month late after his journey to Greece, Wilde was fined £47.10 (half his Demyship for the year) and rusticated, i.e. sent down for the rest of the term. The money was paid back to him in 1878. Years later Charles Ricketts reported his saying: "I was sent down from Oxford for being the first undergraduate to visit Olympia."

[3] Florence Anne Lemon Balcombe (1858–1937), daughter of a retired lieutenant-colonel living at 1 Marino Crescent, Clontarf, Dublin. He had fought in the Crimea, and it seems likely that Florence was named after Miss Nightingale. A drawing of her by Wilde is reproduced in Vyvyan Holland's *Son of Oscar Wilde* (1954). George du Maurier is said to have considered her one of the three most beautiful women he had ever seen.

[4] Boorish insensitiveness.

[5] The Rev. William Dennis Allen (1848–1923), Fellow of Magdalen 1871, Classical Tutor 1873–81, Vicar of Findon, Sussex, 1881.

As I expected, all my friends here refuse to believe my story, and my brother[1] who is down at Moytura at present writes me a letter marked "*Private*" to ask "what it *really* is all about and *why* have I been rusticated," treating my explanations as mere child's play.

I hope you will write and tell me all about the College, who is desecrating my rooms and what is the latest scandal.

When Dunskie comes tell him to write to me and remember me to Dick and Gussy and little Dunlop and everyone you like or I like. Ever yours

OSCAR

I am going down I hope for my May fishing soon, but I am overwhelmed with business of all kinds.

Get *Aurora Leigh* by Mrs Browning and read it carefully.

To Lord Houghton[2]

[*Circa 16 June 1877*]   *1 Merrion Square North*

Dear Lord Houghton, Knowing your love and admiration for John Keats I venture to send you a sonnet which I wrote lately at Rome on him: and should be very glad to know if you see any beauty or stuff in it.

Someway standing by his grave I felt that *he too* was a Martyr, and worthy to lie in the City of Martyrs. I thought of him as a Priest of Beauty slain before his time, a lovely Sebastian killed by the arrows of a lying and unjust tongue.

Hence—my sonnet. But I really have other views in writing to you than merely to gain your criticism of a boyish poem.

I don't know if you have visited Keats's grave since a marble tablet in his memory was put up on the wall close to the tomb. There are some fairly good lines of poetry on it, but what is really objectionable in it is the bas-relief of Keats's head—or rather a *medallion profile*, which is *extremely ugly*, exaggerates his facial angle so as almost to give him a hatchet-face and

[1] William Charles Kingsbury Wilde (1852–99). After coming down from Trinity College, Dublin, he was called to the Bar, but soon became a journalist. He wrote for the *World* and *Vanity Fair* and was for many years a leader-writer on the *Daily Telegraph*. He was once briefly engaged to the composer Ethel Smyth. He lived with his mother until he married Mrs Frank Leslie, a rich American widow and newspaper-owner. The marriage was not a success, and Willie turned to alcohol. Later he married an Irish girl, Sophie (Lily) Lees, who bore him a daughter, Dorothy Ierne (Dolly), who died in 1941.

[2] Richard Monckton Milnes (1809–85), poet, politician and philanthropist. His *Life, Letters and Literary Remains of John Keats* had appeared in 1848 and his edition of the *Poetical Works*, with a memoir, in 1854. He had been created Lord Houghton in 1863, and had visited Ireland in October and November 1876. Many phrases in this letter occur in Wilde's article "The Tomb of Keats" which appeared with the sonnet in *The Irish Monthly* for July 1877. The sonnet was revised and reprinted in *Poems* (1881). Wilde also sent copies of the article to W. M. Rossetti and H. Buxton Forman. Wilde had paid his first visit to Rome on his way home from Greece.

instead of the finely cut nostril, and Greek sensuous delicate lips that he had, gives him thick almost negro lips and nose.[1]

Keats we know was lovely as Hyakinthos, or Apollo, to look at, and this medallion is a very terrible lie and misrepresentation. I wish it could be removed and a tinted bust of Keats put in its place, like the beautiful coloured bust of the Rajah of Koolapoor at Florence.[2] Keats's delicate features and rich colour could not be conveyed I think in plain white marble.

In any case I do not think this very ugly thing ought to be allowed to remain: I am sure a photograph of it could easily be got, and you would see how horrid it is.

Your influence and great name could achieve anything and everything in the matter, and I think a really beautiful memorial might be erected to him. Surely if everyone who loves to read Keats gave even half-a-crown, a great sum of money could be got for it.

I know you always are engaged *in Politics and Poetry*, but I feel sure that with your name at the head of the list, a great deal of money would be got: in any case the ugly libel of Keats could be taken down.

I should be very glad to hear a line from you about it, and feel sure that you will pardon my writing to you on the subject. For you are fitted above all others to do anything for Keats's memory.

I hope we will see you again in Ireland: I have very pleasant memories of some delightful evenings passed in your society. Believe me yours truly

OSCAR WILDE

KEATS' GRAVE

Rid of the world's injustice and its pain
He rests at last beneath God's veil of blue;
Taken from life while life and love were new
The youngest of the Martyrs here is lain,
Fair as Sebastian and as foully slain.
No cypress shades his tomb, nor funeral yew,
But red-lipped daisies, violets drenched with dew,
And sleepy poppies, catch the evening rain.
O proudest heart that broke for misery!
O saddest poet that the world hath seen!

[1] The medallion by John Warrington Wood (1839–86) was unveiled on 21 February 1876 by Major-General Sir Vincent Eyre (1811–81), who also wrote the acrostic poem engraved beneath:

Keats! if thy cherished name be "writ in water,"
Each drop has fallen from some mourner's cheek:
A sacred tribute, such as heroes seek,
Though oft in vain, for dazzling deeds of slaughter.
Sleep on! not honoured less, for epitaph so meek.

[2] A coloured and gilt bust of Rajaram Chuttraputti, Maharajah of Koolapoor, who died in 1870, in his twenty-first year, while passing through Florence on his way home to India. It forms part of an elaborate memorial marking the site of his funeral pyre in the Cascine, the public park of Florence.

O sweetest singer of our English land!
Thy name was writ in water on the sand,
But our tears shall keep thy memory green,
And make it flourish like a Basil-tree.

Rome: 1877.   OSCAR WILDE

To Reginald Harding

[*Circa 16 June 1877*]   1 *Merrion Square North*

My dear Kitten, Many thanks for your delightful letter. I am glad you are
in the midst of beautiful scenery and *Aurora Leigh*.

I am very much down in spirits and depressed. A cousin of ours to
whom we were all very much attached has just died—quite suddenly from
some chill caught riding. I dined with him on Saturday and he was dead
on Wednesday.[1] My brother and I were always supposed to be his heirs
but his will was an unpleasant surprise, like most wills. He leaves my
father's hospital about £8,000, my brother £2,000, and me £100 on condition of my being a Protestant!

He was, poor fellow, bigotedly intolerant of the Catholics and seeing
me "on the brink" struck me out of his will. It is a terrible disappointment
to me; you see I suffer a good deal from my Romish leanings, in pocket
and mind.

My father had given him a share in my fishing lodge in Connemara,
which of course ought to have reverted to me on his death; well, even this
I lose "if I become a Roman Catholic for five years" which is very infamous.

Fancy a man going before "God and the Eternal Silences" [2] with his
wretched Protestant prejudices and bigotry clinging still to him.

However, I won't bore you with myself any more. The world seems
too much out of joint for me to set it right.

I send you a little notice of Keats's grave I have just written which may
interest you. I visited it with Bouncer and Dunskie.

If you would care to see my views on the Grosvenor Gallery[3] send for
the enclosed, and write soon to me. Ever yours   OSCAR WILDE

I heard from little Bouncer from Constantinople lately: he said he was
coming home. Love to Puss.

---

[1] The "cousin" was in fact Wilde's half-brother, one of Sir William's bastards.
He was Dr Henry Wilson, Fellow of the Royal College of Surgeons of Ireland. He
died of pneumonia on Wednesday, 13 June 1877, aged thirty-nine. Oscar and his
brother Willie were the chief mourners at the funeral.

[2] Perhaps an echo of Alfred de Vigny's "*silence éternel de la Divinité*" (from '*Le
Mont des Oliviers*' in *Les Destinées*, 1864) or of Carlyle's "brief Life-transit to all the
Eternities, the Gods and Silences" (*Past and Present*, book iv. ch. iv).

[3] Wilde's notice of the first exhibition at the Grosvenor Gallery in London, which
opened on 1 May 1877. It appeared in the July issue of the *Dublin University*

To Florence Balcombe

[*April 1878*]   *Royal Bath Hotel, Bournemouth*

My dear Florrie, I send you a line to wish you a pleasant Easter. A year ago I was in Athens and you sent me I remember a little Easter card—over so many miles of land and sea—to show me you had not forgotten me.

I have been greatly disappointed in not being able to come over, but I could only spare four days and as I was not feeling well came down here to try and get some ozone. The weather is delightful and if I had not a good memory of the past I would be very happy.

I have a delightful friend (a *new* friend) with me and have written *one* sonnet, so am not so misanthropic as usual. I hope you are all well especially Gracie: Willie's success in the North is most encouraging.[1]

I send you an account of Bournemouth. Ever yours   OSCAR

To Marian Willett[2]

Monday, 13 May [*1878*]   *Magdalen College*

Dear Miss Willett, I send you the magazine you kindly wished to see. I have tried, in the metre as well as the words, to mirror some of the swiftness and grace of the springtime.[3]

And though I know but too well that in this, like in everything that I do, I have failed, yet after all Nature lies out of the reach of even the

---

Magazine. He was very proud of the fact that it brought him the following letter from Walter Pater (1839–94), Fellow and Tutor of Brasenose College:

July 14   *Bradmore Road, Oxford*
Dear Mr Wilde, Accept my best thanks for the magazine and your letter. Your excellent article on the Grosvenor Gallery I read with very great pleasure: it makes me much wish to make your acquaintance, and I hope you will give me an early call on your return to Oxford.

I should much like to talk over some of the points with you, though on the whole I think your criticism very just, and it is certainly very pleasantly expressed. It shows that you possess some beautiful, and, for your age, quite exceptionally cultivated tastes: and a considerable knowledge also of many beautiful things. I hope you will write a great deal in time to come. Very truly yours
                                                WALTER PATER

[1] Gracie and Willie were Florence's sister and brother. Gracie married the novelist Frankfort Moore (1855–1931).

[2] Marian Fitzgerald Willett (1853–1916) was living in Oxford with her stepfather, the Rev. James Legge (1815–97), who had been appointed first Professor of Chinese in 1876. An undergraduate, Bertram Hunt (1856–95), fell in love with her in the train, but could find no means of being introduced to her until one day on the towpath he saw her talking to Wilde, who gave a tea-party for them both at Magdalen. They were married at Oxford in 1880. Hunt became a doctor and helped to discover the anti-diphtheria serum. Wilde sent Miss Willett an inscribed copy of *Ravenna*.

[3] In his poem "Magdalen Walks," which had appeared in the *Irish Monthly* of April 1878. From 1875 poems by Wilde had begun to appear in magazines.

19

greatest masters of song. She cannot be described, she can only be worshipped: and there is more perfection of beauty, it seems to me, in a single white narcissus of the meadow than in all the choruses of Euripides, or even in the *Endymion* of Keats himself.

If you care to keep the magazine it will give me great pleasure—still more if my verses can recall to you any of the loveliness of that time of the year, which, though I have failed to describe, I at least have loved. Believe me, truly yours   OSCAR WILDE

To William Ward

[Circa 20 July 1878]   *Magdalen College*

My dear old Boy, You are the best of fellows to telegraph your congratulations: there were none I valued more.[1] It is too delightful altogether this display of fireworks at the end of my career. I cannot understand my First except for the essays which I was fairly good in. I got a very complimentary *viva voce*.

The dons are "astonied" beyond words—the Bad Boy doing so well in the end! They made me stay up for the Gaudy and said nice things about me. I am on the best terms with everyone including *Allen!* who I think is remorseful of his treatment of me.

Then I rowed to Pangbourne with Frank Miles in a birchbark canoe! and shot rapids and did wonders everywhere—it was delightful.

I cannot, I am afraid, yacht with you. I am so troubled about my law suit, which I have won but find my own costs heavy, though I was allowed them.[2] I have to be in Ireland.

Dear old boy, I wish I could see you again. Ever yours   OSCAR

To Florence Balcombe

Monday night [late 1878][3]   *I Merrion Square North*

Dear Florrie, As I shall be going back to England, probably for good, in a few days, I should like to bring with me the little gold cross I gave you one Christmas morning long ago.

[1] Wilde's First in Greats was announced on 19 July 1878 and listed in *The Times* on 20 July. Another success was the award of the Newdigate Prize to his poem *Ravenna* on 10 June 1878. Its author recited parts of it before the Vice-Chancellor and other notables in the Sheldonian Theatre on 26 June.

[2] A case, heard in Dublin, concerning some house property Wilde had inherited from his father.

[3] Florence Balcombe was married on 4 December 1878 at St Anne's Church, Dublin, to Bram Stoker (1847–1912), a young Irish civil servant with literary and dramatic interests. He had done much to promote Irving's triumphal visit to Dublin two years earlier, and in October 1878 Irving appointed him business manager of the Lyceum Theatre, the management of which Irving had just taken over from Mrs Bateman. Stoker's horrific novel *Dracula* was published in 1897. See also p. 28.

I need hardly say that I would not ask it from you if it was anything you valued, but worthless though the trinket be, to me it serves as a memory of two sweet years—the sweetest of all the years of my youth—and I should like to have it always with me. If you would care to give it to me yourself I could meet you any time on Wednesday, or you might hand it to Phil,[1] whom I am going to meet that afternoon.

Though you have not thought it worth while to let me know of your marriage, still I cannot leave Ireland without sending you my wishes that you may be happy; whatever happens I at least cannot be indifferent to your welfare: the currents of our lives flowed too long beside one another for that.

We stand apart now, but the little cross will serve to remind me of the bygone days, and though we shall never meet again, after I leave Ireland, still I shall always remember you at prayer. Adieu and God bless you.

OSCAR

---

[1] Florence's sister Philippa, who did not marry till 1881.

PART TWO

LONDON I · 1879-1881

After Wilde's academic triumphs in the summer of 1878 Magdalen renewed his Demyship for a further (fifth) year. On 22 November he satisfied the examiners in the Rudiments of Religion, and on 28 November took his degree as Bachelor of Arts. It is not known how much of the year he spent in Oxford—presumably in lodgings, since he no longer had rooms in college—but it seems probable that he was mostly in London, learning to charm Society with his conversation and developing his aesthetic tastes.

*To Helena Sickert [1]

[*2 October 1879*]   *Thames House, 13 Salisbury Street*[2]

Dear Miss Nellie, Though you are determined to go to Cambridge, I hope you will accept this volume of poems by a purely *Oxford* poet. I am sure you know Matthew Arnold already but still I have marked just a few of the things I like best in the collection, in the hope that we may agree about them. "Sohrab and Rustum" is a wonderfully stately epic, full of the spirit of Homer, and "Thyrsis" and "The Scholar Gipsy" are exquisite

[1] Helena Maria Sickert (1864–1939), writer, lecturer and untiring advocate of women's rights. Younger sister of W. R. Sickert (see note 1, p. 43). She went up to Girton College, Cambridge, in 1882 and took a degree in Moral Science. In 1888 she married F. T. Swanwick, and always wrote as H. M. Swanwick. She was a prominent suffragist, the first president of the Women's International League (British Section) and was made C.H. in 1931. In her autobiography *I Have been Young* (1935) she described Wilde's friendship with her family: "He was the first of our friends to call me Miss Nellie . . . He discussed books with me and gave me my first volume of poetry, *Selected Poems of Matthew Arnold*, marking his favourites."

[2] Wilde and Frank Miles shared rooms at this address, off the Strand, till August 1880. I have been unable to discover when they went there.

23

idylls, as artistic as "Lycidas" or "Adonais:" but indeed I think all is good in it, and I hope you will accept it, φιλίας μνημόσυνον,[1] from your sincere friend   OSCAR WILDE

To Reginald Harding

[*28 November 1879*]   *St Stephen's Club, Westminster*

Dear Reggie, I was only in Cambridge for the night with Oscar Browning[2] (I wish he was *not* called Oscar) and left the next morning for the Hicks-Beach's in Hampshire, to kill time and pheasants and the *ennui* of not having set the world quite on fire as yet.

I will come some day and stay with you, though your letters are rather what boys call "Philippic."

I am going to night with *Ruskin* to see Irving as Shylock,[3] and afterwards to the *Millais* Ball.[4] How odd it is. Dear Reg, ever yours   OSCAR

Remember me to Tom Peyton.

*To Oscar Browning

[? *January–February 1880*]

Will you do me a good service, and write me a testimonial of what you think my ability for a position in the Education Office or School Inspectorship would be? Rents being as extinct in Ireland as the dodo or moly, I want to get a position with an assured income, and any Education work

---

[1] "As a memento of friendship."

[2] 1837–1923. Eton master 1860–75, Cambridge don and "character" 1876–1909 (George Curzon, Arthur Balfour and Austen Chamberlain were all his pupils). Author of many books, mainly historical.

[3] Henry Irving (stage-name of John Henry Brodribb, 1838–1905) had gone on the stage in 1855, and in 1871 joined the company at the Lyceum. He began his triumphant management of the Lyceum in 1878. His production of *The Merchant of Venice* opened on 1 November 1879. This visit may have been Wilde's first meeting with Irving (although he saw his *Macbeth* in 1876). "Portia," Wilde's sonnet to Ellen Terry, appeared in the *World* on 14 January 1880, and he was a guest at the Lyceum banquet to celebrate the hundredth performance on 14 February.

[4] John Everett Millais, English painter (1829–96), R.A. 1863, Baronet 1885, P.R.A. 1895, married (1855) Euphemia (Effie) Chalmers Gray, whose marriage to Ruskin had been annulled in 1854. Their daughter Effie married Captain James of the Scots Greys on 28 November 1879. "Wisely and thoughtfully," according to *Vanity Fair* of 6 December, "Mr and Mrs Millais abstained from giving that most tiresome of all things, a wedding breakfast; they did much better by giving in its stead a ball in the evening ... There were notable artists (with their wives in Grosvenor Gallery dresses), notable actors and actresses and notable persons of the smarter sort, all met together like a happy family." For Wilde's memories of Ruskin see p. 71.

would be very congenial to me, and I have here good opportunity of studying the systems of France and Germany. I think your name would carry a good deal of weight with it in a matter of this kind. The Duke of Richmond is the President of the Council in whose hands the appointments rest.[1]

OSCAR WILDE

*To Genevieve Ward[2]

[*April–May 1880*]   *St Stephen's Club*

Dear Miss Ward, I suppose you are very busy with your rehearsals. If you are not too busy to stop and drink tea with a *great* admirer of yours, please come on Friday at half-past five to 13 Salisbury Street. The two beauties—Lady Lonsdale[3] and Mrs Langtry[4]—and Mamma, and a few friends are coming. We are all looking forward to *L'Aventurière* so much: it will be a great era in our dramatic art.[5] Yours most sincerely

OSCAR WILDE

[1] The sixth Duke of Richmond (1818–1903) was President of the Council 1874–80.

[2] Genevieve Teresa Ward (1838–1922), an American, began as an opera singer but lost her singing voice and became an actress. As a girl she was married in St Petersburg, almost at pistol-point, to a Russian Count, whom she never saw after the ceremony. She made her English début in 1873 as Lady Macbeth, which in 1878 she played in French in Paris. In August 1879 at the Lyceum she scored a great hit in *Forget-Me-Not* by Herman Merivale and F. D. Grove, which was revived at the Prince of Wales's Theatre in February 1880, and which she afterwards acted all over the world. In 1893–96 she appeared with Irving in *Henry VIII*, *Richard III* and Tennyson's *Becket*. Beerbohm Tree described her as "an old iron-clad."

[3] Constance Gladys (1859–1917), daughter of the first Baron Herbert of Lea and sister of the thirteenth Earl of Pembroke, married the fourth Earl of Lonsdale in 1878. After his death in 1882 she married Lord de Grey, who succeeded his father as second Marquess of Ripon in 1909. Wilde dedicated *A Woman of No Importance* to her.

[4] Emily Charlotte Le Breton (1852–1929), who came from Jersey and was considered the most beautiful woman of her generation, married in her teens Edward Langtry, an Irish widower of thirty. He brought her to London, where she quickly became a leading figure in Society and a friend of the Prince of Wales. She was painted by Whistler, Poynter, Watts, Burne-Jones, Leighton, and particularly Millais, whose portrait of her, called *The Jersey Lily*, was the origin of her nickname. Wilde's friend Frank Miles did many drawings of her. Wilde's poem to her, "The New Helen," appeared in *Time* for July 1879 and was reprinted, with revisions, in *Poems* (1881). In Mrs Langtry's copy of this book Wilde wrote: "To Helen, formerly of Troy, now of London." In 1899 she married Hugo Gerald de Bathe (1871–1940), who succeeded his father as fifth Baronet in 1907. Vincent O'Sullivan records Wilde as saying in 1899: "The three women I have most admired are Queen Victoria, Sarah Bernhardt, and Lily Langtry. I would have married any one of them with pleasure."

[5] During the run of her perennial *Forget-Me-Not* Genevieve Ward gave a performance in French of Emile Augier's *L'Aventurière* on 10 May 1880 at the Prince of Wales's Theatre. Two of the cast were French, the others (including Beerbohm Tree) English. The Prince and Princess of Wales were in the audience.

To Mrs Alfred Hunt[1]

Dear Mrs Hunt, It was so good of you to take the trouble of sending me such a long account of your little village.[3] I have been hoping to go every week, but have had so many engagements that it has been out of my power; which, believe me, is no small disappointment. I should like so much to be with you all.

And now I am trying to settle a new house, where Mr Miles and I are going to live. The address is *horrid* but the house very pretty. It is much nearer you than my old house, so I hope we shall often, if you let me, have "dishes of tea" at one another's houses.

I have broken a promise shamefully to Miss Violet about a poem I promised to send her. My only excuse is that nowadays the selection of colours and furniture has quite taken the place of the cases of conscience of the middle ages, and usually involves quite as much remorse. However I send her one I have just published. I hope she will see some beauty in it, and that your wonderful husband's wonderful radicalism will be appeased by my first attempt at political prophecy, which occurs in the last verse.[4] If she will send me a little line to say what she thinks of it, it will give me such pleasure.

I hope she has been writing herself. After all, the Muses are as often to be met with in our English fields as they ever were by Castaly, or Helicon, though I have always in my heart thought that the simultaneous appearance of *nine (unmarried)* sisters at a time must have been a little embarrassing.

Please remember me *most* kindly to your husband, and all yours, and believe me very truly yours   OSCAR WILDE

---

[1] Margaret Raine (1831–1912), the original of Tennyson's "Margaret," married the landscape painter Alfred William Hunt in 1861, and for many years they lived at Tor Villas, Campden Hill. She was a voluminous and successful novelist under her married name. Her daughter Violet Hunt (1862–1942) was also the author of many novels.

[2] Wilde and Frank Miles had recently moved into rooms at No 1 Tite Street. This southern end of the street had been called Calthorpe Place until 1875, when it was renamed in honour of the architect Sir William Tite (1798–1873). (The northern end of the street, which Wilde was later to inhabit, was built between 1877 and 1887.) A Miss Elizabeth Skeates had lived in the southern part of the street from 1814 to 1821, and it was probably Skeates House that Wilde's poetic imagination quickly transformed into Keats House.

[3] Mrs Hunt was staying at Warkworth in Northumberland.

[4] "Ave Imperatrix," described as "A Poem on England," appeared in the *World* on 25 August 1880. Its last stanza runs:

> Yet when this fiery web is spun,
>   Her watchmen shall descry from far
> The young Republic like a sun
>   Rise from these crimson seas of war.

To Ellen Terry[1]

[*Circa September 1880*]   *Tite Street*

Dear Miss Ellen Terry, Will you accept the first copy of my first play, a drama on modern Russia.[2] Perhaps some day I shall be fortunate enough to write something worthy of your playing.

We all miss you so much, and are so jealous that the provinces should see you in all the great parts you are playing before we do.

So please come back quite soon. Believe me, yours sincerely

OSCAR WILDE

To George Lewis Junior[3]

[*Postmark 1 November 1880*]   *Tite Street*

My dear George, I send you by this post a little pencil-case as a present, in order that you may take down everything that Mr Jacobs[4] says, and that when you go to the Lyceum you may be able to make notes in a wise manner on the side of your programme, like all the dramatic critics. I hope you will like it: if it gives you half as much pleasure to receive as it gives me to send it to you I feel sure you will. Believe me, your affectionate friend   OSCAR WILDE

Who is this?[5]

[1] Ellen Alice Terry (1847–1928), after making her stage début at the age of nine and acting with the Keans and the Bancrofts, had been engaged by Irving as his leading lady at the Lyceum in 1878. This partnership continued till 1902. She toured the provinces in the second half of 1880.

[2] A copy of the first, privately printed, edition (1880) of *Vera; or, The Nihilists*, a drama in four acts, which Wilde had had specially bound in dark red leather, with Ellen Terry's name stamped in gold on the binding. The book is inscribed "From her sincere admirer the Author." Only two other copies are known to survive.

[3] George James Graham Lewis (1868–1927) later succeeded his father (see note 1, p. 31) as second Baronet and head of the firm of Lewis & Lewis, solicitors.

[4] Joseph Jacobs (1854–1916), an Australian Jew, author and editor of many books on religion, folklore and other subjects, who occasionally gave lessons to the Lewis children.

[5] The Lewis family were all great admirers of Irving.

To Ellen Terry

[*3 January 1881*]   *Tite Street, Chelsea*

My dear Nellie, I write to wish you *every success* tonight.[1] *You* could not do anything that would not be a mirror of the highest artistic beauty, and I am so glad to hear you have an opportunity of showing us that passionate power which *I know you have.* You will have a great success—perhaps one of your greatest.

I send you some flowers—two crowns. Will you accept one of them, whichever you think will suit you best. The other—don't think me treacherous, Nellie—but the other please give to Florrie *from yourself.* I should like to think that she was wearing something of mine the first night she comes on the stage, that anything of mine should touch her. Of course if you think—but you won't think she will suspect? How could she? She thinks I never loved her, thinks I forget. My God how could I!

Dear Nellie, if you can do this—in any case accept these flowers from your devoted admirer, your affectionate friend   OSCAR WILDE

To Matthew Arnold[2]

[*June–July 1881*]   *Keats House, Tite Street*

Dear Mr Arnold, Will you accept from me my first volume of poems . . . of the constant source of joy and wonder that your beautiful work was to all of us at Oxford . . . for I have only now, too late perhaps, found out how all art requires solitude as its companion, only now indeed know the splendid difficulty of this great art in which you are a master illustrious and supreme. Still, such as it is, let me offer it to you, and believe me in all affectionate admiration, truly yours   OSCAR WILDE

To James Knowles[3]

[? *Late 1881*]   *Keats House, Tite Street*

Dear Mr Knowles, I send you a—rather soiled—copy of my mother's pamphlet on the reflux wave of *practical* republicanism which the return

---

[1] Tennyson's verse play *The Cup* was produced at the Lyceum on 3 January 1881, with Irving, Ellen Terry and William Terriss in the leading parts. One of the "Priestesses and Attendants in the Temple" was Florence Balcombe. Wilde wrote a sonnet to Ellen Terry called "Camma" (her part in the play): it was published in *Poems* (1881).

[2] 1822–88. Wilde's *Poems* were published by David Bogue *c.* 30 June 1881. Five editions (each of 250 copies) were issued within a year. Wilde paid all the expenses of publication. He also sent copies to Robert Browning, and to Gladstone.

[3] Architect and editor (1831–1908), friend of Tennyson, with whom he started the Metaphysical Society in 1869. Designed Tennyson's house, Aldworth, in Surrey, and the gardens in Leicester Square, London. He was editor of the *Contemporary Review* from 1870 to 1877, when he founded and edited the *Nineteenth Century*. Knighted 1903.

of the Irish emigrants has brought on Ireland. It was written three years ago nearly, and is extremely interesting as a political prophecy.[1] You probably know my mother's name as the "Speranza" of the *Nation* newspaper in 1848. I don't think that age has dimmed the fire and enthusiasm of that pen which set the young Irelanders in a blaze.

I should like so much to have the privilege of introducing you to my mother—all brilliant people should cross each other's cycles, like some of the nicest planets. In any case I am glad to be able to send you the article. It is part of the thought of the nineteenth century, and will I hope interest you. Believe me, truly yours   OSCAR WILDE

---

[1] Probably *The American Irish*, which was published in New York *circa* 1879.

PART THREE

AMERICA · 1882

Gilbert and Sullivan's *Patience* was first produced by Richard D'Oyly Carte (1844–1901) at the Opera Comique, London, on 23 April 1881, and on 10 October was moved to the Savoy Theatre, which Carte had just built. The opera satirised contemporary aestheticism, and the character of Bunthorne, the Fleshly Poet, though perhaps intended for Rossetti, was generally taken as a caricature of Wilde. *Patience* opened in New York on 22 September, and Col. W. F. Morse, Carte's American representative, thought that the appearance of Wilde himself might provide useful publicity. He was accordingly booked to give a series of lectures, sailed on the *Arizona* on 24 December 1881, and landed at New York on 2 January 1882.

His first lecture, at the Chickering Hall, New York, on 9 January, was on "The English Renaissance." His other principal lecture was on the subject of house decoration.

To Mrs George Lewis[1]

[*Circa 15 January 1882*]   [*New York*]

My dear Mrs Lewis, I am sure you have been pleased at my success! The hall had an audience larger and more wonderful than even Dickens had. I was recalled and applauded and am now treated like the Royal Boy.[2] I

---

[1] Betty Eberstadt (1844–1931) married (1867) George Henry Lewis (1833–1911), head of the firm of Lewis & Lewis, solicitors. He was knighted in 1893 and made a baronet in 1902. Elizabeth Robins reports Wilde's saying of him in 1888: "George Lewis is the best [solicitor] in London. Brilliant. Formidable. A man of the world. Concerned in every great case in England. Oh, he knows all about us—and forgives us all." See also p. 169.

[2] Popular nickname for the Prince of Wales, later King Edward VII.

have several "Harry Tyrwhitts" as secretaries.[1] One writes my autographs all day for my admirers, the other receives the flowers that are left really every ten minutes. A third whose hair resembles mine is obliged to send off locks of his own hair to the myriad maidens of the city, and so is rapidly becoming bald.

I stand at the top of the reception rooms when I go out, and for two hours they defile past for introduction. I bow graciously and sometimes honour them with a royal observation, which appears next day in all the newspapers. When I go to the theatre the manager bows me in with lighted candles and the audience rise. Yesterday I had to leave by a private door, the mob was so great. Loving virtuous obscurity as much as I do, you can judge how much I dislike this lionizing, which is worse than that given to Sarah Bernhardt I hear.[2]

For this, and indeed for nearly all my successes, I have to thank your dear husband. Pray give Mr Lewis my most affectionate remembrances, also to the Grange,[3] and believe me, very sincerely yours   OSCAR WILDE

To Archibald Forbes[4]

[20 January 1882]   Arlington Hotel, Washington

Dear Mr Forbes, I felt quite sure that your remarks on me had been misrepresented. I must however say that your remarks about me *in your*

---

[1] The Hon. Harry Tyrwhitt (1854–91), eldest son of Sir Henry Tyrwhitt, Bart., and Baroness Berners. Assumed the additional surname of Wilson in 1876. Equerry in Waiting to the Prince of Wales from 1881.

[2] The great French actress (1844–1923) had made her début at the Comédie Française in 1862, paid her first visit to London in 1879, when Wilde is said to have welcomed her with an armful of lilies, and to New York in 1880.

[3] The London home of Edward Burne-Jones the painter (1833–98). The two families were close friends.

[4] British war correspondent and author (1838–1900). He was also lecturing in the States at this time, wearing all his medals, and had small sympathy with Wilde's ideas of aesthetics and dress reform. It had been reported that Wilde would attend Forbes's lecture at Baltimore on 19 January, but the two men quarrelled on the train from Philadelphia, and Wilde went straight on to Washington without stopping at Baltimore. Both Forbes and the leaders of Baltimore Society were offended. The passage in Forbes's lecture to which Wilde objected described a visit to the Czar in war-torn Bulgaria:

> I glanced down at my clothes, which I had not changed for a fortnight, and in which I had ridden 150 miles. Now I wish it understood that I am a follower, an humble follower, of the aesthetic ecstasy, but I did not look much like an art object then. I did not have my dogskin knee breeches with me, nor my velvet coat, and my black silk stockings were full of holes. Neither was the wild, barren waste of Bulgaria congenial to the growth of sunflowers and lilies.

An acrimonious correspondence followed in the course of which Forbes referred to Wilde's "utterly mercenary" motives in lecturing. Wilde replied on 29 January:

> As regards my motive for coming to America, I should be very disappointed if when I left for Europe I had not influenced in *however* slight a way the growing

lecture may be regarded as giving *some* natural ground for the report. I feel bound to say quite frankly to you that I do not consider them to be either in good taste or appropriate to your subject.

I have something to say to the American people, something that I know will be the beginning of a great movement here, and all foolish ridicule does a great deal of harm to the cause of art and refinement and civilisation here.

I do not think that your lecture will lose in brilliancy or interest by expunging the passage, which is, as you say yourself, poor fooling enough.

You have to speak of the life of action, I of the life of art. Our subjects are quite distinct and should be kept so. Believe me, yours truly

OSCAR WILDE

To Oliver Wendell Holmes[1]

[? *29 January 1882*]   *Vendome Hotel, Boston*

Dear Doctor Holmes, Will you accept from me a copy of my poems as a small token of the pleasure and the privilege I had in meeting you. I will be in Boston for a few days and will look forward to the chance of finding you at home some afternoon.

Pray remember me most kindly to your son, and to that Penelope of New England whose silken pictures I found so beautiful, and believe me most truly yours   OSCAR WILDE

To Colonel W. F. Morse[2]

[? *26 February 1882*]   *St Louis* [*Missouri*]

Dear Colonel Morse, Will you kindly go to a good costumier (theatrical) for me and get them to make (you will not mention my name) two coats, to wear at matinées and perhaps in evening. They should be beautiful;

---

spirit of art in this country, very disappointed if I had not out of the many who listen to me made one person love beautiful things a little more, and very disappointed if in return for the dreadfully hard work of lecturing—hard to me who am inexperienced—I did not earn enough money to give myself an autumn at Venice, a winter at Rome, and a spring at Athens; but all these things are perhaps dreams.

[1] American writer and physician (1809–94). In 1856–57 he was a co-founder of the *Atlantic Monthly*, and made its name (as well as his own) with his series of papers, *The Autocrat of the Breakfast Table*, which were published as a book in 1858. Later the *Autocrat* was followed by the *Professor* and the *Poet*. In a letter to Mrs Lewis of 12 February describing his "immense success" in Boston, Wilde proudly related that he had "dined with Oliver W. Holmes, breakfasted with Longfellow." Earlier in January he had visited Walt Whitman.

[2] D'Oyly Carte's representative in America and manager of Wilde's tour.

tight velvet doublet, with large flowered sleeves and little ruffs
of cambric coming up from under collar. I send you design and
measurements. They should be ready at *Chicago* on Saturday for matinée
there—at any rate the black one. Any good costumier would know what
I want—sort of Francis I dress: only knee-breeches instead of long hose.
Also get me two pair of grey silk stockings to suit grey mouse-coloured
velvet. The sleeves are to be flowered—if not velvet then plush—stamped
with large pattern. They will excite a great sensation. I leave the matter
to you. They were dreadfully disappointed at Cincinnati at my not wearing
knee-breeches. Truly yours   OSCAR WILDE

*To Joaquin Miller[1]

28 February 1882   *St Louis*

My dear Joaquin Miller, I thank you for your chivalrous and courteous
letter to me published in the *World*. Believe me, I would as lief judge of
the strength and splendour of sun and sea by the dust that dances in the
beam and the bubble that breaks on the wave,[2] as take the petty and profitless vulgarity of one or two insignificant towns as any test or standard of
the real spirit of a sane, strong and simple people, or allow it to affect my
respect for the many noble men and women whom it has been my privilege
in this great country to know.

For myself and the cause which I represent I have no fears as regards
the future. Slander and folly have their way for a season, but for a season
only; while, as touching either the few provincial newspapers which have
so vainly assailed me, or that ignorant and itinerant libeller of New
England who goes lecturing from village to village in such open and
ostentatious isolation, be sure I have no time to waste on them. Youth
being so glorious, art so godlike, and the very world about us so full of
beautiful things, and things worthy of reverence, and things honourable,
how should one stop to listen to the lucubrations of a literary *gamin*, to the
brawling and mouthing of a man whose praise would be as insolent as his

---

[1] Pen-name of American poet, playwright, lawyer and journalist, Cincinnatus
Hiner (or Heine) Miller (1837–1913). His best-known book of poems was *Songs of
the Sierras* (1869). He had lectured in London, dressed as a cowboy and very
much the literary backwoodsman. Rossetti took a fancy to him and he came to be
known as "the American Byron." Wilde had met him in New York, whence on 9
February he had written a letter apologising to Wilde for the behaviour of some
Americans and for the attacks in the "Philistine Press." It concluded:
    So go ahead, my brave youth, and say your say if you choose. My heart is with
    you; and so are the hearts of the best of America's millions. Thine for the
    Beautiful and True   JOAQUIN MILLER
The *New York World* published this letter on 10 February under the heading
THE SINGER OF THE SIERRAS SMITES THE PHILISTINES, and Wilde's answer on 3
March.
    [2] This sentence from "judge" to "wave" is a quotation from Wilde's lecture
"The English Renaissance."

34

slander is impotent, or to the irresponsible and irrepressible chatter of the professionally unproductive?

" 'Tis a great advantage, I admit, to have done nothing, but one must not abuse even that advantage!"[1]

Who, after all, that I should write of him, is this scribbling anonymuncule in grand old Massachusetts who scrawls and screams so glibly about what he cannot understand?[2] This apostle of inhospitality, who delights to defile, to desecrate, and to defame the gracious courtesies he is unworthy to enjoy? Who are these scribes who, passing with purposeless alacrity from the police news to the Parthenon, and from crime to criticism, sway with such serene incapacity the office which they so lately swept? "Narcissuses of imbecility," what should they see in the clear waters of Beauty and in the well undefiled of Truth but the shifting and shadowy image of their own substantial stupidity? Secure of that oblivion for which they toil so laboriously and, I must acknowledge, with such success, let them peer at us through their telescopes and report what they like of us. But, my dear Joaquin, should we put them under the microscope there would be really nothing to be seen.

I look forward to passing another delightful evening with you on my return to New York, and I need not tell you that whenever you visit England you will be received with that courtesy with which it is our pleasure to welcome all Americans, and that honour with which it is our privilege to greet all poets. Most sincerely and affectionately yours   OSCAR WILDE

To Mrs George Lewis

Tuesday, 28 February [1882]   *Grand Pacific Hotel, Chicago*

Dear Mrs Lewis, I send you a line to say that since Chicago I have had two great successes: Cincinnati where I have been invited to lecture a second time—this time to the workmen, on the handicraftsman—and St Louis. Tomorrow I start to lecture eleven consecutive nights at eleven different cities, and return here on Saturday week for a second lecture. I go to Canada then, and also return to New England to lecture. Of course I have much to bear—I have always had that—but still as regards my practical influence I have succeeded beyond my wildest hope. In every city they start schools of decorative art after my visit, and set on foot public

---

[1] *"C'est sans doute un terrible avantage que de n'avoir rien fait, mais il ne faut pas en abuser"* (*Le Petit Almanach de nos Grands-hommes*, 1788, by Antoine de Rivarol, 1753–1801).

[2] This was generally believed to refer to Thomas Wentworth Higginson (1823–1911) of Cambridge, Mass., who had been a prominent anti-slavery reformer, a Colonel in the Civil War, was a keen advocate of Women's Suffrage, and a prolific author. He had denounced Wilde's poems as "immoral" and suggested he be socially ostracised.

museums, getting my advice about the choice of objects and the nature of the building. And the artists treat me like a young god. But of this I suppose little reaches England. My play will probably come out,[1] but this is not settled, and I will be back about May I hope.

Pray remember me most affectionately to Mr Lewis, and believe me very truly yours   OSCAR WILDE

To James McNeill Whistler [2]

[? *Early March 1882*]   *Chicago*

My dear Jimmy, Your abominable attempt at literature has arrived: I don't believe that my lovely and *spirituelle* Lady Archie[3] ever signed it at all. I was so enraged that I insisted on talking about you to a reporter. I send you the result.   OSCAR WILDE

To Colonel W. F. Morse

[*Early March 1882*]   *Bloomington, Illinois*

Dear Colonel Morse, The mail has just arrived: I hope California can be arranged. These small towns should not be taken without guarantee: it's so depressing and useless lecturing for a few shillings.

Kindly send enclosed telegram.[4]

[1] D'Oyly Carte arranged for a new, revised, edition of *Vera* (see note 2, p. 27) to be printed and copyrighted in America during Wilde's visit. Wilde sent it round to various theatrical managers. For its eventual production see p. 50.
[2] American artist (1834–1903), after studying in Paris, in 1862 settled in England and spent the rest of his life there. His methods of painting and opinions on art roused a storm of protest from conservative critics (including Ruskin) and from the public. At the beginning of their friendship, he and Wilde got on very well.
[3] Janey Sevilla Callander (d. 1923) married (1869) Lord Archibald Campbell, younger son of the eighth Duke of Argyll. She was a close friend of Whistler.
[4] In answer to a communication dated 4 February 1882, signed with Whistler's butterfly, and reading:

Oscar! We of Tite Street and Beaufort Gardens joy in your triumphs, and delight in your success, but—we think that, with the exception of your epigrams, you talk like Sidney Colvin in the Provinces, and that, with the exception of your knee-breeches, you dress like 'Arry Quilter.
Signed J. McNeill Whistler, Janey Campbell, Mat Elden, Rennell Rodd
New York papers please copy.

Both Lady Archie Campbell and Rennell Rodd (see p. 45) lived in Beaufort Gardens, Chelsea. This letter, with minor variations of wording (including S— C— for Sidney Colvin), was printed in the *World* of 15 February, over Whistler's signature only. In the issue of 22 February Whistler protested at the editor's caution: "My dear Atlas, if I may not always call a spade a spade, may I not call a Slade Professor Sidney Colvin?"
Sidney Colvin (1845–1927), Slade Professor of Fine Arts at Cambridge 1873–

Wilde, New York	Whistler, Tite Street, Chelsea, London

I admit knee-breeches, and acknowledge epigrams, but reject Quilter and repudiate Colvin.

I hope I am to lecture again in New York—and in Boston. Yours truly

OSCAR WILDE

The most lying telegrams are being sent to the *Daily News* of London every day about me. Who does it? I can guess.[1]

To Mrs George Lewis

[? *Circa 20 March 1882*]   [? *Sioux City*]

Dear Mrs Lewis, I am sure you will be interested to hear that I have met Indians. They are really in appearance very like Colvin, when he is wearing his professorial robes: the likeness is quite curious, and revived pleasant literary reminiscences. Their conversation was most interesting as long as it was unintelligible, but when interpreted to me reminded me strangely and vividly of the conversation of Mr Commissioner Kerr.[2]

I don't know where I am: somewhere in the middle of coyotes and cañons: one is a "ravine" and the other a "fox," I don't know which, but I think they change about. I have met miners: they are big-booted, red-shirted, yellow-bearded and delightful ruffians. One of them asked me if I was not "running an art-mill," and on my pointing to my numerous retinue, said he "guessed I hadn't need to wash my own pans," and his "pardner" remarked that "I hadn't need to sell clams neither, I could toot my own horn." I secretly believe they read up Bret Harte privately; they were certainly almost as real as his miners, and quite as pleasant. With my usual passion for personality I entertained them, and had a delightful time, though on my making some mention of early Florentine art they unanimously declared they could neither "trump or follow it."

Weary of being asked by gloomy reporters "which was the most beautiful colour" and what is the meaning of the word "aesthetic," on my last Chicago interview I turned the conversation on three of my heroes, Whistler, Labouchere,[3] and Irving, and on the adored and adorable

1885, Director of Fitzwilliam Museum 1876–84, Keeper of Prints and Drawings in the British Museum 1884–1912, knighted 1911, friend and editor of Robert Louis Stevenson, biographer of Keats. The origin of Wilde's dislike of him is not known.

Harry Quilter (1851–1907), English barrister, author and art-critic, was Whistler's "arch-enemy" and butt.

[1] Archibald Forbes.

[2] Robert Malcolm Kerr (1821–1902), Scottish judge of the City of London Court, 1859–1901. He was a strict teetotaller.

[3] Henry Du Pré Labouchere (1831–1912). Radical M.P. for Northampton 1880–1905. Founded *Truth* 1876. He was responsible for inserting into the Criminal Law Amendment Act (1885) the clause under which Wilde was convicted. After Wilde's conviction Labouchere wrote in *Truth* that he was sorry his original maximum penalty had been reduced from seven to two years.

Lily.[1] I send you them all.

I hope you are all well. Pray remember me to your husband, and to the Grange when you visit there next.

Colvin in a blanket has just passed the window: he is decked out with feathers, and wants me to buy bead slippers; it is really most odd, and undoubtedly Colvin, I could hardly be mistaken.

Give my love to Katie[2] please!!! and believe me, most sincerely and truly yours   OSCAR WILDE

To Emma Speed[3]

21 March 1882   [*Omaha, Nebraska*]

What you have given me is more golden than gold,[4] more precious than any treasure this great country could yield me, though the land be a network of railways, and each city a harbour for the galleys of the world.

It is a sonnet I have loved always, and indeed who but the supreme and perfect artist could have got from a mere colour a motive so full of marvel: and now I am half enamoured of the paper that touched his hand, and the ink that did his bidding, grown fond of the sweet comeliness of his charactery, for since my boyhood I have loved none better than your marvellous kinsman, that godlike boy, the real Adonis of our age, who knew the silver-footed messages of the moon, and the secret of the morning, who heard in Hyperion's vale the large utterance of the early gods, and from the beechen plot the light-winged Dryad, who saw Madeline at the painted window, and Lamia in the house at Corinth, and Endymion ankle-deep in lilies of the vale, who drubbed the butcher's boy for being a bully, and drank confusion to Newton for having analysed the rainbow. In my heaven he walks eternally with Shakespeare and the Greeks, and it may be that some day he will lift

---

[1] Mrs Langtry, whose husband had lost his money, had gone on the stage and was planning an American tour. In an interview at Halifax, Nova Scotia, in October Wilde said: "I would rather have discovered Mrs Langtry than have discovered America," and when she arrived he met her with lilies at the boat.

[2] Mrs Lewis's daughter Katherine (1878–1961).

[3] 1823–83. Wife of Philip Speed and daughter of George Keats, the poet's younger brother, who had emigrated to America in 1818 and made a fortune out of timber. She lived at Louisville, Kentucky, as her father had done, and after Wilde had lectured there on 21 February she invited him home and showed him her Keats letters and manuscripts. On 12 March she sent him the manuscript of Keats's "Sonnet on Blue," which he had quoted in his lecture. Wilde's account of this incident appeared in the *Century Guild Hobby Horse* for July 1886 (together with a facsimile of the manuscript). At the forced sale of Wilde's belongings on 24 April 1895 lot 122, "An etching of a lady, by Menpes after W. Graham Robertson, and a Manuscript Poem, by Keats, framed," was knocked down to a Mr Shaw for 38/-.

[4] Cf. Sappho (Lobel & Page, no. 156).

"his hymenaeal curls from out his amber gleaming wine,
With ambrosial lips will kiss my forehead, clasp the hand of noble love in
mine."[1]

Again I thank you for this dear memory of the man I love, and thank you
also for the sweet and gracious words in which you give it to me: it were
strange in truth if one in whose veins flows the same blood as quickened into
song that young priest of beauty, were not with me in this great renaissance
of art which Keats indeed would have so much loved, and of which he,
above all others, is the seed.

Let me send you my sonnet on Keats's grave, which you quote with such
courteous compliment in your note, and if you would let it lie near his own
papers it may keep some green of youth caught from those withered leaves
in whose faded lines eternal summer dwells.

I hope that some day I may visit you again at St Louis,[2] and see the
little Milton and the other treasures once more: strange, you call your
house "dingy and old," ah, dear Madam, fancy has long ago made it a
palace for me, and I see it transfigured through the golden mists of joy.
With deep respect, believe me, most truly yours   OSCAR WILDE[3]

To Norman Forbes-Robertson[4]

29 March 1882   *San Francisco*

My dear Norman, Here from the uttermost end of the great world I send
you love and greeting, and thanks for your letters which delight me very
much. But, dear boy, your hair will lose its gold and your cheek its roses
if you insist on being such a chivalrous defender of this much abused
young man. It is so brave and good of you! Of course I will win: I have
not the slightest intention of failing for a moment, and my tour here is
triumphal. I was four days in the train: at first grey, gaunt desolate plains,
as colourless as waste land by the sea, with now and then scampering herds
of bright red antelopes, and heavy shambling buffaloes, rather like Joe
Knight[5] in manner and appearance, and screaming vultures like gnats
high up in the air, then up the Sierra Nevadas, the snow-capped mountains

---

[1] A slightly altered quotation from Wilde's poem "Flower of Love," published
in *Poems* (1881).

[2] A slip for Louisville.

[3] Enclosed was a handwritten copy of Wilde's sonnet "The Grave of Keats"
(see p. 17).

[4] 1859–1932. Younger brother of the actor-manager Johnston Forbes-Robertson
(1853–1937). He acted as Norman Forbes and wrote several plays.

[5] Joseph Knight (1829–1907), English dramatic critic. Editor of *Notes and
Queries* from 1883. Wilde slated his *Life of Dante Gabriel Rossetti* in the *Pall Mall
Gazette* of 18 April 1887 under the heading "A Cheap Edition of a Great Man,"
describing the book as "just the sort of biography Guildenstern might have written
of Hamlet," and Knight in his turn scoffed at *Lady Windermere's Fan* in 1892.
Norman's actor brother Ian Forbes-Robertson (1857–1936), whom Wilde visited
in New York, was married to a daughter of Joseph Knight.

shining like shields of polished silver in that vault of blue flame we call the sky, and deep cañons full of pine trees, and so for four days, and at last from the chill winter of the mountains down into eternal summer here, groves of orange trees in fruit and flower, green fields, and purple hills, a very Italy, without its art.

There were 4,000 people waiting at the "depot" to see me, open carriage, four horses, an audience at my lecture of the most cultivated people in 'Frisco, charming folk. I lecture again here tonight, also twice next week; as you see I am really appreciated—by the cultured classes.[1] The railway have offered me a special train and private car to go down the coast to Los Angeles, a sort of Naples here, and I am fêted and entertained to my heart's content. I lecture here in California for three weeks, then to Kansas; after that I am not decided.

These wretched lying telegrams in the *Daily News* are sent by Archibald Forbes, who has been a fiasco in his lecturing this season and is jealous of me. He is a coward and a fool. No telegram can kill or mar a man with anything in him. The women here are beautiful. Tonight I am escorted by the Mayor of the city through the Chinese quarter, to their theatre and joss houses and rooms, which will be most interesting. They have "houses" and "persons."[2]

Pray remember me to all at home, also to that splendid fellow Millais and his stately and beautiful wife.

Love to Johnston. Ever yours   OSCAR WILDE

(My new signature—specially for California)

*To Mrs Bernard Beere[3]

[*17 April 1882*]   *Kansas City, Missouri*

My dear Bernie, I have lectured to the Mormons. The Opera House at Salt Lake is an enormous affair about the size of Covent Garden, and holds with ease fourteen families. They sit like this

---

[1] Wilde lectured in Platt's Hall, San Francisco, on March 27 and 29, and on April 1 and 5.

[2] Presumably brothels and their inhabitants.

[3] English actress (1856–1915). Originally Fanny Mary Whitehead, she married three times, but always acted under her second married name. She made her début at the Opera Comique in London in 1877. All arrangements had been made for her to play the principal part in Wilde's *Vera* at the Adelphi Theatre on 17 December 1881, but three weeks beforehand the production was cancelled, "considering the present state of political feeling in England." The Czar Alexander II had been assassinated in March, and the new Czarina was the Prince of Wales's sister-in-law.

and are very, very ugly. The President, a nice old man, sat with five wives in the stage box. I visited him in the afternoon and saw a charming daughter of his.[1]

I have also lectured at Leadville, the great mining city in the Rocky Mountains. We took a whole day to get up to it on a narrow-gauge railway 14,000 feet in height. My audience was entirely miners; their make-up excellent, red shirts and blonde beards, the whole of the first three rows being filled with McKee Rankins of every colour and dimension.[2] I spoke to them of the early Florentines, and they slept as though no crime had ever stained the ravines of their mountain home. I described to them the pictures of Botticelli, and the name, which seemed to them like a new drink, roused them from their dreams, but when I told them in my boyish eloquence of the "secret of Botticelli" the strong men wept like children. Their sympathy touched me and I approached modern art and had almost won them over to a real reverence for what is beautiful when unluckily I described one of Jimmy Whistler's "nocturnes in blue and gold." Then they leaped to their feet and in their grand simple way swore that such things should not be. Some of the younger ones pulled their revolvers out and left hurriedly to see if Jimmy was "prowling about the saloons " or "wrestling a hash" at any eating shop. Had he been there I fear he would have been killed, their feeling was so bitter. Their enthusiasm satisfied me and I ended my lecture there. Then I found the Governor of the State[3] waiting in a bullock *wagon* to bring me down the great silver-mine of the world, the Matchless. So off we drove, the miners carrying torches before us till we came to the shaft and were shot down in buckets (I of course true to my principle being graceful even in a bucket) and down in the great gallery of the mine, the walls and ceilings glittering with metal ore, was spread a banquet for us.

---

[1] John Taylor (1808–1887). He accompanied Brigham Young on the mass migration to Utah, became acting President on Brigham Young's death in 1877, and officially third President of the Church of Jesus Christ of Latter-day Saints in October 1880. He had seven wives who bore him thirty-four children. In Wilde's lecture "Personal Impressions of America" he said:

Salt Lake City contains only two buildings of note, the chief being the Tabernacle which is in the shape of a soup-kettle ... The building next in importance is called the Amelia Palace, in honour of one of Brigham Young's wives. When he died the present President of the Mormons stood up in the Tabernacle and said that it had been revealed to him that he was to have the Amelia Palace, and that on this subject there were to be no more revelations of any kind.

[2] Arthur McKee Rankin (1842–1914), American actor-manager, had appeared at Sadler's Wells in *The Danites in the Sierras*, a sensational melodrama about the Mormons by Joaquin Miller, in April 1880.

[3] Horace Austin Warner Tabor (1830–99), miner, politician and "bonanza king," made a fortune in silver-mining and real estate. He spent it lavishly as Lieutenant-Governor of Colorado (1879–83), buying a seat in the Senate (1883), building an opera house and otherwise developing Denver. He divorced his first wife to marry a dashing divorcée, secretly in 1882, and publicly with President Arthur as guest of honour in 1883. He became careless in his investments and went bankrupt in 1893. His second wife was found frozen to death in a shack beside the Matchless mine in 1935.

The amazement of the miners when they saw that art and appetite could go hand in hand knew no bounds; when I lit a long cigar they cheered till the silver fell in dust from the roof on our plates; and when I quaffed a cocktail without flinching,[1] they unanimously pronounced me in their grand simple way "a bully boy with no glass eye"—artless and spontaneous praise which touched me more than the pompous panegyrics of literary critics ever did or could. Then I had to open a new vein, or lode, which with a silver drill I brilliantly performed, amidst unanimous applause. The silver drill was presented to me and the lode named "The Oscar." I had hoped that in their simple grand way they would have offered me shares in "The Oscar," but in their artless untutored fashion they did not. Only the silver drill remains as a memory of my night at Leadville.

I have had a delightful time all through California and Colorado and am now returning home, twice as affected as ever, my dear Bernie. Please remember me to dear Dot,[2] to Reggie and all our mutual friends including Monty Morris, who won't write to me or even criticise me. Goodbye. Your sincere friend   OSCAR WILDE

*To Helena Sickert

25 April 1882   *Fremont, Nebraska*

My dear Miss Nellie, Since I wrote to you I have been to wonderful places, to Colorado which is like the Tyrol a little, and has great cañons of red sandstone, and pine trees, and the tops of the mountains all snow-covered, and up a narrow-gauge railway did I rush to the top of a mountain 15,000 feet high, to the great mining city of the west called Leadville, and lectured the miners on the old workers in metal—Cellini and others. All I told them about Cellini and how he cast his Perseus interested them very much, and they were a most courteous audience; typical too—large blonde-bearded, yellow-haired men in red shirts, with the beautiful clear complexions of people who work in silver-mines.

After my lecture I went down a silver-mine, about a mile outside the little settlement, the miners carrying torches before us as it was night. After being dressed in miner's dress I was hurled in a bucket down into the heart of the earth, long galleries of silver-ore, the miners all at work, looking so picturesque in the dim light as they swung the hammers and cleft the

---

[1] Cf. R. L. Stevenson's American experience in 1880: "The playful innocuous American cocktail. I drank it, and lo! veins of living fire ran down my leg; and then a focus of conflagration remained seated in my stomach, not unpleasantly, for a quarter of an hour" (*The Silverado Squatters*, 1883).

[2] The nickname of Dionysius George Boucicault (1859–1929), actor and dramatist. Son of the playwright (see note 4, p. 70), and husband (1901) of the actress Irene Vanbrugh.

stone, beautiful motives for etching everywhere, and for Walter's[1] impressionist sketches. I stayed all night there nearly, the men being most interesting to talk to, and was brought off down the mountain by a special train at 4.30 in the morning.

From there I went to Kansas where I lectured a week. At St Joseph the great desperado of Kansas, Jesse James,[2] had just been killed by one of his followers, and the whole town was mourning over him and buying relics of his house. His door-knocker and dust-bin went for fabulous prices, two speculators absolutely came to pistol-shots as to who was to have his hearth-brush, the unsuccessful one being, however, consoled by being allowed to purchase the water-butt for the income of an English bishop, while his sole work of art, a chromo-lithograph of the most dreadful kind, of course was sold at a price which in Europe only a Mantegna or an undoubted Titian can command!

Last night I lectured at Lincoln, Nebraska, and in the morning gave an address to the undergraduates of the State University there: charming audience—young men and women all together in the same college, attending lectures and the like, and many young admirers and followers among them. They drove me out to see the great prison afterwards! Poor odd types of humanity in hideous striped dresses making bricks in the sun, and all mean-looking, which consoled me, for I should hate to see a criminal with a noble face. Little whitewashed cells, so tragically tidy, but with books in them. In one I found a translation of Dante, and a Shelley. Strange and beautiful it seemed to me that the sorrow of a single Florentine in exile should, hundreds of years afterwards, lighten the sorrow of some common prisoner in a modern gaol,[3] and one murderer with melancholy eyes—to be hung they told me in three weeks—spending that interval in reading novels, a bad preparation for facing either God or Nothing. So every day I see something curious and new, and now think of going to Japan and wish Walter would come or could come with me.

Pray give my love to everybody at home, and believe me your affectionate friend   OSCAR WILDE

To Norman Forbes-Robertson

12 May 1882   [*Windsor Hotel, Montreal*]

My dear Norman, I am so delighted you are coming over. I will see that you have some pleasant houses in Boston to go to. I hope I will be there. You and I will sit and drink "Boy"[4] in our room and watch the large posters of our names. I am now six feet high (my name on the placards), printed it is true in those primary colours against which I pass my life

---

[1] Walter Richard Sickert (1860–1942), the painter.
[2] Jesse James (b. 1847) was murdered by his friend Bob Ford on 3 April.
[3] Wilde himself read the whole of Dante in Reading Gaol.
[4] A slang word for champagne.

protesting, but still it is fame, and anything is better than virtuous obscurity, even one's own name in alternate colours of Albert blue and magenta and six feet high.

This is my view at present from the Windsor Hotel, Montreal. I feel I have not lived in vain. My second lecture at New York was a brilliant success. I lectured at Wallack's Theatre in the afternoon, *not an empty seat,* and I have greatly improved in speaking and in gesture. I am really quite eloquent—at times. I was greatly congratulated.

Tomorrow night I lecture Lorne on dadoes at Ottawa.[1]

A nice friend of yours has just called—Murray Balfour—friend of Miller's. Ever yours   OSCAR

To Mrs George Lewis

3 June [Postmark 1882]   *Boston*

Dear Mrs Lewis, I have sent you a little present of an Indian fan, made by a Canadian tribe I visited in Canada. It is a fanciful thing of feathers, and being yellow will go delightfully with the sunflowers at the top of the long walk at Walton.[2] Please sit there once and fan yourself and entreat that masterly, that trenchant critic of life Katie to honestly acknowledge that she prefers me to the waggonette.

I have just lectured here again, and am now going to New Orleans.

They talk about yellow fever but I think that one who has survived the newspapers is impregnable. After that I don't know where I will go. I

---

[1] The Marquess of Lorne (1845–1914) was Governor-General of Canada 1878–83. In 1871 he married Princess Louise, the fourth daughter of Queen Victoria. He succeeded his father as ninth Duke of Argyll in 1900.

[2] Walton-on-Thames, where the Lewises had a country house called Ashley Cottage. The Indian fan is now in the possession of Mrs Elizabeth Wansbrough.

feel an irresistible desire to wander, and go to Japan, where I will pass my youth, sitting under an almond tree in white blossom, drinking amber tea out of a blue cup, and looking at a landscape without perspective.

I send you a little slip, this morning's interview. The papers are really very nice now and even the *New York Herald* is being converted, while as for Canada it was at my feet.

I often think of you and your charming house where I have passed so many delightful hours, and Phil[1] and Mr Rodd[2] give me little glimpses of you sometimes in their letters.

Pray remember me most kindly to your husband, and believe me most truly yours   OSCAR WILDE

*To James McNeill Whistler

[? *June 1882*]

You dear good-for-nothing old Dry-point! Why do you not write to me? Even an insult would be pleasant, and here am I lecturing on you, see penny rag enclosed, and rousing the rage of all the American artists by so doing. Of course the Salon is a success[3] . . . The little pink lady . . . I remember so well, tell me about them.[4] Also why "a wand," as I see in the *World*; it sounds charming.[5] And the Moon-Lady, the Grey Lady, the beautiful wraith with her beryl eyes, our Lady Archie, how is she?[6] Also when will you come to Japan? Fancy the book, I to write it, you to illustrate it. We would be rich.   OSCAR

[1] Son of Edward Burne-Jones.

[2] James Rennell Rodd (1858–1941), poet and diplomat (later British Ambassador to Italy, 1908–19, and first Lord Rennell of Rodd). He had been a friend of Wilde at Oxford, where he won the Newdigate Prize in 1880. In 1881 he published in London a small book of poems called *Songs of the South*. While in America Wilde went to immense trouble to bring out a new "aesthetic" edition of this book which he retitled *Rose Leaf and Apple Leaf*. He provided a preface and inserted a dedication to himself as Rodd's "Heart's Brother." Not surprisingly, Rodd later complained that the dedication was "too effusive" and asked for it to be removed from unsold copies.

[3] The Paris Salon of 1882, which opened on 1 May, was the first to which Whistler had contributed since 1867. He showed a portrait of Lady Meux entitled *Arrangement in Black and White*.

[4] At the Grosvenor Gallery exhibition of May 1882 Whistler exhibited several works, including another portrait of Lady Meux, called *Harmony in Flesh Colour and Pink*.

[5] According to the *World* of 3 May, "Mr Whistler's wand-like walking stick was one of the most striking objects at the private view of the Grosvenor Gallery. It was longer than himself, and even slimmer, and he balanced it delicately between finger and thumb. He explained that he intended it should become historical, and its appearance doubtless marks a new departure in the fashion of sticks."

[6] Whistler painted several portraits of Lady Archibald Campbell, including one called *The Grey Lady*, which he destroyed unfinished.

To Julia Ward Howe [1]

Augusta, Georgia

My dear Mrs Howe, My present plan is to arrive in New York from Richmond on Wednesday evening, and to leave that night for Newport, being with you Thursday morning and staying, if you will have me, till Saturday. I have an enormous trunk and a valet, but they need not trouble you. I can send them to the hotel. With what incumbrances one travels! It is not in the right harmony of things that I should have a hat-box, a secretary, a dressing-case, a trunk, a portmanteau, and a valet always following me. I daily expect a thunderbolt, but the gods are asleep, though perhaps I had better not talk about them or they will hear me and wake. But what would Thoreau have said to my hat-box! Or Emerson to the size of my trunk, which is Cyclopean! But I can't travel without Balzac and Gautier, and they take up so much room: and as long as I can enjoy talking nonsense to flowers and children I am not afraid of the depraved luxury of a hat-box.

I write to you from the beautiful, passionate, ruined South, the land of magnolias and music, of roses and romance: picturesque too in her failure to keep pace with your keen northern pushing intellect; living chiefly on credit, and on the memory of some crushing defeats. And I have been to Texas, right to the heart of it, and stayed with Jeff Davis at his plantation (how fascinating all failures are!)[2] and seen Savannah, and the Georgia forests, and bathed in the Gulf of Mexico, and engaged in Voodoo rites with the Negroes, and am dreadfully tired and longing for an idle day which we will have at Newport.

Pray remember me to Miss Howe, and believe me very truly yours

OSCAR WILDE

Would you send a line to me at 1267 Broadway[3] to say if it is all right.

---

[1] American author and reformer (1819–1910), author of "The Battle Hymn of the Republic" (1861). Married Samuel Gridley Howe, philanthropist, in 1843. When Wilde was attacked by Colonel Higginson (see p. 35) during his first visit to Boston, Mrs Howe defended him in the press. When he read her letter, Wilde wrote to her: "Your letter is noble and beautiful. I have only just seen it, and shall not forget ever the chivalrous and pure-minded woman who wrote it."

[2] Jefferson Davis (1808–89), American soldier and statesman, was President and Commander-in-Chief of the Confederate States in the Civil War. After the defeat of the South he was imprisoned for two years, then pardoned, and retired to Beauvoir, on the Gulf of Mexico between New Orleans and Mobile, where Wilde visited him.

[3] The headquarters in New York of D'Oyly Carte's American enterprises, including Wilde's tour.

To Mary Anderson[1]

[*Early September 1882*]   *Park Avenue Hotel, New York*

Dear Miss Anderson, Can I see you on Thursday at Long Branch?[2] I will come down in the morning, and sleep at the Elberon so as to have with you a long day. Pray *telegraph* to me here if you will be at home. I cannot write the scenario till I see you and talk to you. All good plays are a combination of the dream of a poet and that practical knowledge of the actor which gives concentration to action, which intensifies situation, and for poetic effect, which is description, substitutes dramatic effect, which is Life. I have much to talk to you about, having thought much since I saw you of what you could do in art and for art. I want you to rank with the great actresses of the earth. I desire your triumph to be for all time and not for the day merely, and having in you a faith which is as flawless as it is fervent I doubt not for a moment that I can and will write for you a play which, created for you, and inspired by you, shall give you the glory of a Rachel,[3] and may yield me the fame of a Hugo.[4] The dream of the sculptor is cold and silent in the marble, the painter's vision immobile on the canvas. I want to see my work return again to life, my lines gain new splendour from your passion, new music from your lips.

If I can do that, and see you in some creation of mine, a living poem yourself, I [*paper torn off at the bottom edge*] of shame and insult, of discourtesy and of dishonour.

I will look out for a *telegram*, if not Thursday, say Friday, but Thursday [*paper torn off*]

---

[1] American actress (1859–1940). After considerable success in England and America she retired from the stage in 1889, married Antonio de Navarro and settled at Broadway in Worcestershire, where she became the "dear enemy" of J. M. Barrie's cricket matches. Wilde agreed to write a play, *The Duchess of Padua*, for her. He completed the play—a blank verse tragedy—in Paris in March 1883 and sent it to her with a long and enthusiastic letter in which he described it as "the masterpiece of all my literary work, the *chef-d'oeuvre* of my youth." She sent a telegram rejecting the play. In 1898 Wilde called it "unfit for publication."

[2] A popular summer resort on the New Jersey coast where Mary Anderson had a country house.

[3] Stage name of French tragic actress Elisa Félix (1821–58).

[4] Victor-Marie Hugo (1802–85), the great French poet, novelist and dramatist.

PART FOUR

LONDON II · 1883-1890

Wilde sailed home from New York on the *Bothnia* on 27 December 1882. After two or three weeks in London he used what was left of his American earnings to spend three months in Paris. There he met Verlaine and Victor Hugo, Mallarmé, Zola, Degas, Edmond de Goncourt and Alphonse Daudet. He had his hair curled in imitation of a bust of Nero in the Louvre and dressed in the height of fashion. "The Oscar of the first period is dead," he said.

To Waldo Story[1]

[*Postmark 31 January 1883*]   *Hôtel Continental, Paris*

I saw a great deal of Jimmy in London *en passant*. He has just finished a second series of Venice Etchings—such water-painting as the gods never beheld. His exhibition opens in a fortnight in a yellow and white room (decorated by the master of course) and with a catalogue which is amazing. He spoke of your art with more enthusiasm than I ever heard him speak of any modern work. For which accept my warm congratulations: praise from him is something.

---

[1] American sculptor (1855–1915), son of William Wetmore Story, the sculptor and poet. Whistler's exhibition, "Arrangement in Yellow and White," had its private view at the Fine Art Society's Rooms on 17 February 1883. The yellow-and-white decoration was carried on to the flowers, pots, chairs, assistants' neckties and Whistler's socks at the private view, which were all yellow. The catalogue mocked the critics, quoting their more ridiculous estimates of Whistler's work and, on its title-page, "Out of their own mouths shall ye judge them."

*To Marie Prescott[1]

[? March–April 1883]   [? Paris]

My dear Miss Prescott, I have received the American papers and thank you for sending them. I think we must remember that no amount of advertising will make a bad play succeed, if it is not a good play well acted. I mean that one might patrol the streets of New York with a procession of vermilion caravans twice a day for six months to announce that *Vera* was a great play, but if on the first night of its production the play was not a strong play, well acted, well mounted, all the advertisements in the world would avail nothing. My name signed to a play will excite some interest in London and America. Your name as the heroine carries great weight with it. What we want to do is to have *all* the real conditions of success in our hands. Success is a science; if you have the conditions, you get the result. Art is the mathematical result of the emotional desire for beauty. If it is not thought out, it is nothing.

As regards dialogue, you can produce tragic effects by introducing comedy. A laugh in an audience does not destroy terror, but, by relieving it, aids it. Never be afraid that by raising a laugh you destroy tragedy. On the contrary, you intensify it. The canons of each art depend on what they appeal to. Painting appeals to the eye, and is founded on the science of optics. Music appeals to the ear and is founded on the science of acoustics. The drama appeals to human nature, and must have as its ultimate basis the science of psychology and physiology. Now, one of the facts of physiology is the desire of any very intensified emotion to be relieved by some emotion that is its opposite. Nature's example of dramatic effect is the laughter of hysteria or the tears of joy. So I cannot cut out my comedy lines. Besides, the essence of good dialogue is interruption. All good dialogue should give the effect of its being made by the reaction of the personages on one another. It should never seem to be ready made by the author, and interruptions have not only their artistic effect but their physical value. They give the actors time to breathe and get new breath power. I remain, dear Miss Prescott, your sincere friend   OSCAR WILDE

To R. H. Sherard[2]

Wednesday [early April 1883]   *Hôtel Voltaire*

My dear Robert, I send you the volume of the true poet, and the false

---

[1] American actress (d. 1923), who had read *Vera* and agreed to play the leading part in it. This letter appeared in the *New York Herald* of 12 August 1883 as a puff for the play. Wilde paid his second and last visit to America to see the production. He sailed from Liverpool on 2 August 1883 in the *Britannic* and reached New York on 11 August. *Vera* opened at the Union Square Theatre on 20 August but ran for only a week. It was described as "a foolish, highly-peppered story of love, intrigue and politics" (*New York Tribune*), "unreal, long-winded and wearisome" (*New York Times*) and "long-drawn dramatic rot" (*New York Herald*). Wilde sailed for home in the *Arizona* on 11 September.

[2] Robert Harborough Sherard (1861–1943), author and journalist, great-grandson

friend:[1] there are some new things in it, "Chartres Cathedral," and the "Viking's Grave," which have much beauty in them, the latter particularly and the "Envoi" I hope you will like. The rhythmical value of prose has never yet been fully tested; I hope to do some more work in that *genre*, as soon as I have sung my Sphinx to sleep, and found a trisyllabic rhyme for catafalque.[2] Ever affectionately yours OSCAR WILDE

To R. H. Sherard

[*Postmark 17 May 1883*]   *8 Mount Street, Grosvenor Square, London*

Dear Robert, Your letter was as loveable as yourself, and this is my first moment after channel-crossings, train-catchings, and my natural rage at the charges for extra luggage from Paris, for sitting down to tell you what pleasure it gave me, and what memories of moonlit meanderings, and sunset strolls, the mere sight of your handwriting brought.

As for the dedication of your poems, I accept it: how could I refuse a gift so musical in its beauty, and fashioned by one whom I love so much as I love you?[3]

To me the mirror of perfect friendship can never be dulled by any treachery, however mean, or disloyalty, however base. Individuals come and go like shadows but the ideal remains untarnished always: the ideal of lives linked together not by affection merely, or the pleasantness of companionship, but by the capacity of being stirred by the same noble things in art and song. For we might bow before the same marble goddess, and with hymns not dissimilar fill the reeds of her flutes: the gold of the night-time, and the silver of the dawn, should pass into perfection for us: and from each string that is touched by the fingers of the player, from each bird that is rapturous in brake or covert, from each hill-flower that blossoms on the hill, we might draw into our hearts the same sense of beauty, and in the House of Beauty meet and join hands.

That is what I think true friendship should be, like that men could make their lives: but friendship is a fire where what is not flawless shrinks into grey ashes, and where what is imperfect is not purified but consumed.

of Wordsworth, first met Wilde in Paris at this time. He spent most of his life in France and Corsica. His father was the Rev. B. Sherard Kennedy, but the son dropped his surname in youth and was thereafter always known as Sherard. Among other books he published biographies of Zola, Daudet and Maupassant (all of whom he had known) and four books and a proliferation of pamphlets about Wilde.

[1] Rennell Rodd (see note 2, p. 45).

[2] It seems certain that Wilde began his long poem *The Sphinx* when he was still at Oxford and finished it now in Paris, though it was not published till 1894. For a rhyme to "catafalque" he had to be content with "Amenalk, the God of Heliopolis."

[3] The dedication to *Whispers, being The Early Poems of Robert Harborough Sherard* (1884) runs: "To Oscar Wilde, Poet and Friend, Affectionately and admiringly Dedicated." Willie Wilde, reviewing the book in *Vanity Fair*, said that it was well named.

There may be much about which we may differ, you and I, more perhaps than we fancy, but in our desire for beauty in all things we are one, and one in our search for that little city of gold where the flute-player never wearies, and the spring never fades, and the oracle is not silent, that little city which is the house of art, and where, with all the music of the spheres, and the laughter of the gods, Art waits for her worshippers. For we at least have not gone out into the desert to seek a reed shaken by the wind, or a dweller in kings' houses, but to a land of sweet waters, and to the well of life; for the nightingale has sung to both of us, and the moon been glad of us, and not to Pallas, or to Hera, have we given the prize, but to her who from the marble of the quarry and the stone of the mine can give us pillared Parthenon and glyptic gem, to her who is the spirit of Beauty, and who has come forth from her hollow hill into the chill evening of this old world, and walks among us visible.

That is, I think, what we are seeking, and that you should seek it with me, you who are yourself so dear to me, gives me faith in our futures, confidence in our love. OSCAR

To Violet Fane[1]

[? *July 1883*]   *9 Charles Street, Grosvenor Square*[2]

Of course I am coming! How could one refuse an invitation from one who is a poem and a poet in one, an exquisite combination of perfection and personality, which are the keynotes of modern art.

It was horrid of me not to answer before, but a nice letter is like a sunbeam and should not be treated as an epistle needing a reply. Besides your invitations are commands.

I look forward to meeting Proteus very much: his sonnets are the cameos of the decadence.[3] Very sincerely yours   OSCAR WILDE

[1] Mary Montgomerie Lamb (1843–1905) married (1) in 1864 Henry Sydenham Singleton (d. 1893); (2) in 1894 the first Lord Currie (1834–1906), H.M. Ambassador in Constantinople 1893–98, in Rome 1898–1902. She wrote under the name Violet Fane, began publishing poems and essays in the 1870's and was the original of one of the characters in *The New Republic* (see note p. 9). Later she published novels and stories.

[2] In the early summer of 1883 Wilde moved into furnished rooms kept by a retired butler and cook at this address. He stayed there until after his marriage in 1884, when he moved to his own house, 16 Tite Street, Chelsea.

[3] Wilfrid Scawen Blunt (1840–1920), poet, anti-Imperialist, champion of lost causes (most of them since won) and breeder of Arab horses. His *The Love Sonnets of Proteus* was first published anonymously, in 1881.

*Telegram: To James McNeill Whistler[1]

[*Circa 10 November 1883*]   *Exeter*

Punch too ridiculous. When you and I are together we never talk about anything except ourselves.[2]   OSCAR WILDE

To Waldo Story

[*Postmark 22 January 1884*]   *Royal Victoria Hotel, Sheffield*

Yes! my dear Waldino, yes! Amazing of course—that was necessary.

Naturally I did not write—the winds carry tidings over the Apennines better than the 2½d post: of course it accounts for the splendid sunsets about which science was so puzzled: Hurrah! *You* had no sunsets when you were engaged—only moonlights.

Well, we are to be married in April, as you were, and then go to Paris, and perhaps to Rome—what do you think? Will Rome be nice in May? I mean, will you and Mrs Waldo be there, and the Pope, and the Peruginos? If so we will arrive.

Her name is Constance,[3] and she is quite young, very grave, and mystical, with wonderful eyes, and dark brown coils of hair: quite perfect, except that she does not think Jimmy the only painter that ever really existed: she would like to bring Titian, or somebody, in by the back door: however, she knows I am the greatest poet, so in literature she is all right: and I have explained to her that you are the greatest sculptor: art instruction cannot go further.

We are of course desperately in love. I have been obliged to be away nearly all the time since our engagement, civilising the provinces by my remarkable lectures, but we telegraph to each other twice a day, and the telegraph clerks have become quite romantic in consequence. I hand in my messages however very sternly, and try to look as if "love" was a crypto-gram for "buy Grand Trunks",[4] and "darling" a cypher for "sell out at par." I am sure it succeeeds.

---

[1] From *Punch* of 10 November 1883:
At the Annual Meeting of the Hogarth Club, "I was standing," says the gentle-man in question, "at the buffet, when I suddenly heard the voice of Mr Oscar Wilde discussing with Mr Whistler and others the attributes of two well-known actresses. The criticism is at least expressive. 'Sarah Bernhardt,' he said, 'is all moonlight and sunlight combined, exceedingly terrible, magnificently glorious. Miss Anderson is pure and fearless as a mountain daisy. Full of change as a river. Tender, fresh, sparkling, brilliant, superb, placid.' "

[2] To this Whistler replied by telegram: "No, no, Oscar, you forget. When you and I are together, we never talk about anything except me."
Both telegrams were published in the *World* of 14 November, and reprinted by Whistler in his book *The Gentle Art of Making Enemies* (1890).

[3] Constance Mary Lloyd (b. 1857) was the daughter of Horace (Horatio) Lloyd, Q.C. (1828–74). She first met Wilde in London in 1881. They became engaged in November 1883 in Dublin where Wilde was lecturing.

[4] Canadian railway shares.

Dear Waldo, I am perfectly happy, and hope that you and Mrs Waldo will be very fond of my wife. I have spoken to her so much about you both that she knows you quite well already, and of course I cannot imagine anyone seeing her and not loving her.

Please give my love to Uncle Sam[1] and the young robust transcendentalist from Boston, Mass, whose novels we all delight in.[2] And remember me most kindly to your wife, and tell her how much I look forward to introducing Constance to her. *Addio*

OSCAR

To Lily Langtry

[*Circa 22 January 1884*]　　　　　　　　　*Royal Victoria Hotel, Sheffield*
My dear Lil, I am really delighted at your immense success; the most brilliant telegrams have appeared in the papers here on your performance in *Peril*.[3] You have done what no other artist of our day has done, invaded America a second time and carried off new victories. But then you are made for victory; it has always flashed in your eyes, and rung in your voice.

And so, I write half to tell you how glad I am at your triumphs—you "Venus Victrix" of our age!—and the other half to tell you that I am going to be married to a beautiful young girl called Constance Lloyd, a grave, slight, violet-eyed little Artemis, with great coils of heavy brown hair which make her flower-like head droop like a flower, and wonderful ivory hands which draw music from the piano so sweet that the birds stop singing to listen to her. We are to be married in April. I hope so much that you will be over then. I am so anxious for you to know and to like her.

I am hard at work lecturing and getting quite rich, though it is horrid being so much away from her, but we telegraph to each other twice a day, and I rush back suddenly from the uttermost parts of the earth to see her for an hour, and do all the foolish things which wise lovers do.

Will you write and wish me happiness, and believe me ever your devoted and affectionate friend　　　　　　　　　OSCAR WILDE

---

[1] Samuel Ward (1814–84), American lobbyist, financier, talker and gastronome. Elder brother of Julia Ward Howe. Described by Lord Rosebery as "the uncle of the human race." He had entertained Wilde lavishly during his 1882 visit to America.

[2] Francis Marion Crawford (1854–1909), nephew of Julia Ward Howe and Uncle Sam, was a prolific novelist who lived in Italy for many years.

[3] An English adaptation of Sardou's *Nos Intimes*, originally produced in London in 1876, which Mrs Langtry first played at Ford's Opera House, Washington, D.C., on 15 December 1883, in the course of her second American tour. She later played in it at the Fifth Avenue Theatre, New York from 7 to 26 January 1884.

To Alfred Milner[1]

[28 May 1884]
My dear Milner, I am going to be married tomorrow—quite privately—but would be so glad to see you at the church and afterwards at 100 Lancaster Gate. Enclosed ticket.[2] Yours   OSCAR WILDE

*To the Editor of the Pall Mall Gazette[3]

[Circa 13 October 1884]
The "Girl Graduate" must of course have precedence, not merely for her sex but for her sanity: her letter is extremely sensible. She makes two points: that high heels are a necessity for any lady who wishes to keep her dress clean from the Stygian mud of our streets, and that without a tight corset "the ordinary number of petticoats and etceteras" cannot be properly or conveniently held up. Now it is quite true that as long as the lower garments are suspended from the hips, a corset is an absolute necessity; the mistake lies in not suspending all apparel from the shoulders. In the latter case a corset becomes useless, the body is left free and unconfined for respiration and motion, there is more health, and consequently more beauty. Indeed all the most ungainly and uncomfortable articles of dress that fashion has ever in her folly prescribed, not the tight corset merely, but the farthingale, the vertugadin, the hoop, the crinoline, and that modern monstrosity the so-called "dress-improver" also, all of them have owed their origin to the same error, the error of not seeing that it is from the shoulders, and from the shoulders only, that all garments should be hung.

And as regards high heels, I quite admit that some additional height to the shoe or boot is necessary if long gowns are to be worn in the street; but what I object to is that the height should be given to the heel only, and not to the sole of the foot also. The modern high-heeled boot is, in fact, merely the clog of the time of Henry VI, with the front prop left out, and its inevitable effect is to throw the body forward, to shorten the steps, and

---

[1] Alfred Milner (1854–1925), afterwards famous as statesman and proconsul, was a friend of Wilde at Oxford, where he was a Balliol undergraduate 1872–76 and a Fellow of New College 1877–81. Created Baron 1901, Viscount 1902.

[2] The printed card reads: "Admit to St James's Church, Sussex Gardens, Thursday, May 29 1884 at 2.30 p.m." The honeymoon was spent in Paris and Dieppe.

[3] Wilde's lecture on "Dress," given at Ealing on 1 October, had been reported in the *Pall Mall Gazette* next day. Mr Wentworth Huyshe's letter appeared on 3 October, and a "Girl Graduate's" on 7 October. Wilde's letter was published on 14 October.

consequently to produce that want of grace which always follows want of freedom.

Why should clogs be despised? Much art has been expended on clogs. They have been made of lovely woods, and delicately inlaid with ivory, and with mother-of-pearl. A clog might be a dream of beauty, and, if not too high or too heavy, most comfortable also. But if there be any who do not like clogs, let them try some adaptation of the trouser of the Turkish lady, which is loose round the limb, and tight at the ankle.

The "Girl Graduate," with a pathos to which I am not insensible, entreats me not to apotheosise "that awful, befringed, beflounced, and bekilted divided skirt." Well, I will acknowledge that the fringes, the flounces, and the kilting do certainly defeat the whole object of the dress, which is that of ease and liberty; but I regard these things as mere wicked superfluities, tragic proofs that the divided skirt is ashamed of its own division. The principle of the dress is good, and, though it is not by any means perfection, it is a step towards it.

Here I leave the "Girl Graduate," with much regret, for Mr Wentworth Huyshe. Mr Huyshe makes the old criticism that Greek dress is unsuited to our climate, and the, to me, somewhat new assertion, that the men's dress of a hundred years ago was preferable to that of the second part of the seventeenth century, which I consider to have been the exquisite period of English costume.

Now, as regards the first of these two statements, I will say, to begin with, that the warmth of apparel does not depend really on the number of garments worn, but on the material of which they are made. One of the chief faults of modern dress is that it is composed of far too many articles of clothing, most of which are of the wrong substance; but over a sub-stratum of pure wool, such as is supplied by Dr Jaeger[1] under the modern German system, some modification of Greek costume is perfectly applic-able to our climate, our country, and our century. This important fact has already been pointed out by Mr E. W. Godwin in his excellent, though too brief, handbook on Dress, contributed to the Health Exhibition.[2] I call it an important fact because it makes almost any form of lovely costume perfectly practicable in our cold climate. Mr Godwin, it is true, points out that the English ladies of the thirteenth century abandoned after some time the flowing garments of the early Renaissance in favour of a tighter mode, such as northern Europe seems to demand. This I quite admit, and its significance; but what I contend, and what I am sure Mr Godwin would agree with me in, is that the principles, the laws of Greek dress may be perfectly realised, even in a moderately tight gown with sleeves: I mean the principle of suspending all apparel from the shoulders, and of relying for beauty of effect, not on the stiff ready-made ornaments of

---

[1] Gustav Jaeger (1832–1917), German naturalist, hygienist and clothing re-former. He advocated a system of sanitary woollen clothing which was popularised by Bernard Shaw.

[2] *Dress, and its relation to health and culture*, one of a series of books published for the International Health Exhibition, 1884. For E. W. Godwin, see note 2, p. 61.

the modern milliner—the bows where there should be no bows, and the flounces where there should be no flounces—but on the exquisite play of light and line that one gets from rich and rippling folds. I am not proposing any antiquarian revival of an ancient costume, but trying merely to point out the right laws of dress, laws which are dictated by art and not by archaeology, by science and not by fashion; and just as the best work of art in our days is that which combines classic grace with absolute reality, so from a continuation of the Greek principles of beauty with the German principles of health will come, I feel certain, the costume of the future.

And now to the question of men's dress, or rather to Mr Huyshe's claim of the superiority, in point of costume, of the last quarter of the eighteenth century over the second quarter of the seventeenth. The broad-brimmed hat of 1640 kept the rain of winter and the glare of summer from the face; the same cannot be said of the hat of one hundred years ago, which, with its comparatively narrow brim and high crown, was the precursor of the modern "chimney-pot:" a wide turned-down collar is a healthier thing than a strangling stock, and a short cloak much more comfortable than a sleeved overcoat, even though the latter may have had "three capes:" a cloak is easier to put on and off, lies lightly on the shoulder in summer, and, wrapped round one in winter, keeps one perfectly warm. A doublet, again, is simpler than a coat and waistcoat; instead of two garments we have one; by not being open, also, it protects the chest better.

Short loose trousers are in every way to be preferred to the tight knee-breeches which often impede the proper circulation of the blood; and, finally, the soft leather boots, which could be worn above or below the knee, are more supple, and give consequently more freedom, than the stiff Hessian which Mr Huyshe so praises. I say nothing about the question of grace and picturesqueness, for I suppose that no one, not even Mr Huyshe, would prefer a macaroni to a cavalier, a Lawrence to a Vandyke, or the third George to the first Charles; but for ease, warmth and comfort this seventeenth-century dress is infinitely superior to anything that came after it, and I do not think it is excelled by any preceding form of costume. I sincerely trust that we may soon see in England some national revival of it.

To Constance Wilde [1]

Tuesday [Postmark 16 December 1884]   *The Balmoral, Edinburgh*[2]

Dear and Beloved, Here am I, and you at the Antipodes. O execrable facts, that keep our lips from kissing, though our souls are one.

---

[1] Except for the brief notes on pp. 129 and 130 this is the only letter from Wilde to his wife which is known to have survived. The rest were almost certainly destroyed by her or her family.

[2] Wilde lectured twice in the Queen Street Hall, Edinburgh, on Saturday, 20 December. At 3 p.m. his subject was "Dress," and at 8 p.m. (when the *Scotsman* reported "a meagre attendance") "The Value of Art in Modern Life."

What can I tell you by letter? Alas! nothing that I would tell you. The messages of the gods to each other travel not by pen and ink and indeed your bodily presence here would not make you more real: for I feel your fingers in my hair, and your cheek brushing mine. The air is full of the music of your voice, my soul and body seem no longer mine, but mingled in some exquisite ecstasy with yours. I feel incomplete without you. Ever and ever yours   OSCAR

Here I stay till Sunday.

*To the Rev. J. Page Hopps[1]

14 January 1885

Dear Mr Hopps, I am very sorry to say that I am confined to the house with a severe cold, caught by lecturing in a Lincolnshire snowstorm, and am not allowed by my doctor to travel. It is with much regret that I find myself unable to join in the meeting tomorrow, as I sympathise most strongly with the object in question. The present style of burying and sorrowing for the dead seems to me to make grief grotesque, and to turn mourning to a mockery. Any reform you can bring about in these customs would be of value quite inestimable. The present ostentation and extravagance of burial rites seems to me to harmonise but ill with the real feeling of those at the doors of whose house the Angel of Death has knocked. The ceremony by which we part from those whom we have loved should not merely be noble in its meaning, but simple in its sincerity. The funeral of Ophelia does not seem to me "a maimed rite" when one thinks of the flowers strewn on her grave. I regret exceedingly that I cannot hear the actual suggestions on the matter which will be made at your meeting. I have always been of opinion that the coffin should be privately conveyed at night-time to the churchyard chapel, and that there the mourners should next day meet. By these means the public procession through the streets would be avoided; and the publicity of funerals is surely the real cause of their expense. As regards dress, I consider that white and violet should be recognised as mourning, and not black merely, particularly in the case of children. The habit of bringing flowers to the grave is now almost universal, and is a custom beautiful in its symbolism; but I cannot help thinking that the elaborate and expensive designs made by the florist are often far less lovely than a few flowers held loose in the hand. There are many other points on which I should have liked to listen, and one point on which I had hoped to have the privilege of speaking. I mean the expression of

[1] John Page Hopps (1834–1911) was first a Baptist and then a Unitarian minister. He was also a religious author and editor. Wilde had been one of the speakers billed to address a meeting "in support of the principles of Funeral and Mourning Reform" in the Temperance Hall, Leicester, on 15 January. At the meeting this letter was read out by Hopps.

sorrow in art. The urns, pyramids and sham sarcophagi—ugly legacies from the eighteenth century to us—are meaningless as long as we do not burn or embalm our dead. If we are to have funeral memorials at all, far better models are to be found in the beautiful crosses of Ireland, such as the cross at Monasterboice, or in the delicate bas-reliefs on Greek tombs. Above all, such art, if we are to have it, should concern itself more with the living than the dead—should be rather a noble symbol for the guiding of life than an idle panegyric on those who are gone. If a man needs an elaborate tombstone in order to remain in the memory of his country, it is clear that his living at all was an act of absolute superfluity. Keats's grave is a hillock of green grass with a plain headstone, and is to me the holiest place in Rome. There is in Westminster Abbey a periwigged admiral in a nightgown hurried off to heaven by two howling cherubs, which is one of the best examples I know of ostentatious obscurity.

Pray offer to the committee of the society my sincere regrets at my inability to be present, and my sincere wishes for the success of your movement. Believe me, sincerely yours   OSCAR WILDE

*To James McNeill Whistler[1]

[*Circa 23 February 1885*]

Dear Butterfly, By the aid of a biographical dictionary I discovered that there were once two painters, called Benjamin West and Paul Delaroche, who recklessly took to lecturing on Art.

[1] On 20 February 1885 Whistler delivered his famous Ten O'Clock lecture on art in the Prince's Hall, London. Next day the *Pall Mall Gazette* published Wilde's account of it (reprinted in *Miscellanies*), in which he praised Whistler's "really marvellous eloquence," described him as "a miniature Mephistopheles, mocking the majority" and the lecture as a masterpiece. Wilde went on:

> That an artist will find beauty in ugliness, *le beau dans l'horrible*, is now a commonplace of the schools, the *argot* of the atelier, but I strongly deny that charming people should be condemned to live with magenta ottomans and Albert blue curtains in their rooms in order that some painter may observe the side lights on the one and the values of the other. Nor do I accept the dictum that only a painter is a judge of painting. I say that only an artist is a judge of art; there is a wide difference. As long as a painter is a painter merely, he should not be allowed to talk of anything but mediums and megilp, and on those subjects should be compelled to hold his tongue; it is only when he becomes an artist that the secret laws of artistic creation are revealed to him. For there are not many arts, but one art merely: poem, picture and Parthenon, sonnet and statue—all are in their essence the same, and he who knows one knows all. But the poet is the supreme artist, for he is the master of colour and of form, and the real musician besides, and is lord over all life and all arts; and so to the poet beyond all others are these mysteries known; to Edgar Allan Poe and to Baudelaire, not to Benjamin West and Paul Delaroche.

Whistler responded with the following letter, dated 21 February, which was printed in the *World* of 25 February:

> I have read your exquisite article in the *Pall Mall*. Nothing is more delicate, in the flattery of "the Poet" to "the Painter," than the *naïveté* of "the Poet," in

As of their works nothing at all remains, I conclude that they explained themselves away. Be warned in time, James; and remain, as I do, incomprehensible: to be great is to be misunderstood.[1] *Tout à vous*   OSCAR

Private

Jimmy! You must *stamp* your letters—they are dear at twopence—and also do send them in proper time. 2.30 on Monday! *Ciel!*

To the Editor of the Pall Mall Gazette[2]

30 March 1885

Sir, I am deeply distressed to hear that tuberose is so called from its being a "lumpy flower." It is not at all lumpy, and, even if it were, no poet should be heartless enough to say so. Henceforth there really must be two derivations for every word, one for the poet and one for the scientist. And in the present case the poet will dwell on the tiny trumpets of ivory into which the white flower breaks, and leave to the man of science horrid

the choice of his Painters—Benjamin West and Paul Delaroche!

You have pointed out that "the Painter's" mission is to find "*le beau dans l'horrible*," and have left to "the Poet" the discovery of "*l'horrible*" *dans* "*le beau*"!

To which Wilde's letter is an answer. It was printed in the *World* of 25 February 1885, and reprinted (with the rest of the controversy) in *The Gentle Art of Making Enemies* (1890).

[1] These seven words are a quotation from Emerson's essay "Self-Reliance."

[2] In the *Pall Mall Gazette* of 27 March Wilde had reviewed four books of verse, including *Tuberose and Meadowsweet* by Mark André Raffalovich. On 30 March this letter appeared under the title THE ROOT OF THE MATTER:

Sir, I am sorry not to be able to accept the graceful etymology of your reviewer who in Friday's *Pall Mall* calls me to task for not knowing how to pronounce the title of my book *Tuberose and Meadowsweet*. I insist, he fancifully says, "on making tuberose a trisyllable always, as if it were a potato blossom and not a flower shaped like a tiny trumpet of ivory." Alas! tuberose is a trisyllable if properly derived from the Latin *tuberosus*, the lumpy flower, having nothing to do with roses or with trumpets of ivory in name any more than in nature. I am reminded by a great living poet that another correctly wrote:

> Or as the moonlight fills the open sky,
> Struggling with darkness, as a tuberose
> Peoples some Indian dell with scents which lie
>
> Like clouds above the flower from which they rose.

In justice to Shelley, whose lines I quote, your readers will admit that I have good authority for making a trisyllable of tuberose. I am, sir, your obedient servant
ANDRÉ RAFFALOVICH

Wilde's letter was printed on 1 April entitled PARNASSUS VERSUS PHILOLOGY. Raffalovich (1864–1934) was a rich Russian who had been educated in France and England. Wilde is reported to have said that he came to London to found a *salon* and only succeeded in founding a saloon. He is believed to have revenged himself by breaking up Wilde's friendship with John Gray (see note p. 155), with whom Raffalovich remained close friends for the rest of his life. During Beardsley's last years he was largely supported by Raffalovich.

allusions to its supposed lumpiness and indiscreet revelations of its private life below ground. In fact, tuber as a derivation is disgraceful. On the roots of verbs Philology may be allowed to speak, but on the roots of flowers she must keep silence. We cannot allow her to dig up Parnassus. And, as regards the word being a trisyllable, I am reminded by a great living poet that another correctly wrote:

> And the jessamine faint, and the sweet tuberose,
> The sweetest flower for scent that blows;
> And all rare blossoms from every clime
> Grew in that garden in perfect prime.[1]

In justice to Shelley, whose lines I quote, your readers will admit that I have good authority for making a dissyllable of tuberose. I am, sir, your obedient servant   THE CRITIC
WHO HAD TO READ FOUR VOLUMES OF MODERN POETRY

To E. W. Godwin[2]

[*April 1885*]   *16 Tite Street*[3]

Dear Godwino, I am glad you are resting.[4] Nature is a foolish place to look for inspiration in, but a charming one in which to forget one ever had any. Of course we miss you, but the white furniture reminds us of you daily, and we find that a rose leaf can be laid on the ivory table without scratching it—at least a white one can. That is something. We look forward to seeing you robust, and full of vigour. My wife sends her best wishes for your health. Ever yours   OSCAR WILDE

---

[1] "The Sensitive Plant." Raffalovich's quotation is from "The Woodman and the Nightingale".

[2] Edward William Godwin, F.S.A., F.R.I.B.A. (1833–86), architect and theatrical designer. At the age of twenty-five he built the Town Hall at Northampton, and later (for his friend Whistler) the White House in Chelsea. (When Whistler was forced by poverty to leave the house, he wrote above the front door: "Except the Lord build the house, they labour in vain that build it. E. W. Godwin, F.S.A., built this one.") Godwin's first wife died young, and in 1868 he set up house in Hertfordshire with the twenty-year-old Ellen Terry, whose child-marriage with the painter G. F. Watts had ended in separation, though not divorce, in 1866. Ellen Terry bore Godwin two children, Gordon and Edith Craig, but after six years of domesticity she returned to the stage. Godwin left her in 1875, and soon afterwards married Beatrix, the schoolgirl daughter of John Birnie Philip, the sculptor responsible for the frieze on the podium of the Albert Memorial. After Godwin's death she married Whistler. Godwin prepared designs for the decoration of Wilde's house in Tite Street and many letters to Godwin complain of difficulties with the builders.

[3] The Wildes moved into Tite Street, Chelsea, on 1 January 1885.

[4] Godwin had begun to suffer from the illness which was to kill him a year later.

To E. W. Godwin

[20 May 1885]

I was in mourning for my uncle, and lo! he speaketh.
                                        Revised Version.[1]

Dear Godwino, I am delighted to know you are somewhere. We thought you were nowhere, and searched for you everywhere, but could not find you anywhere.

Thanks for your praise of my article.[2] The reason I spoke of "Lady Archie's" production was this. I had spoken before of you in *Claudian*, and was afraid that a second mention would look as if you had put me up to praise you. But everyone knows you did it all. The glory is yours entirely.

Do come to town. At Oxford you were mourned with lamentation. The play was charming. See next Saturday's *Dramatic Review* for my account of it. An amazing criticism! with views of archaeology enough to turn Lytton into a pillar of salt.[3]

" My wife has a cold" but in about a month will be over it. I hope it is a boy cold, but will love whatever the gods send.

How about Coombe this year? I must criticise it somewhere.[4] Ever yours   O. W.

---

[1] The complete Revised Version of the Bible (begun 1870) was first published on 19 May 1885. The New Testament had appeared separately in 1881, but this was the first appearance of the Old Testament, and of the complete work.

[2] "Shakespeare and Stage Costume," which appeared in the *Nineteenth Century* for May 1885. It was later reprinted, with some revision, and renamed "The Truth of Masks," in *Intentions* (1891). In it Wilde referred to the scenery and costumes which Godwin had designed for W. G. Wills's play *Claudian* (1883): "Mr E. W. Godwin, one of the most artistic spirits of this century in England, created the marvellous loveliness of the first act of *Claudian*, and showed us the life of Byzantium in the fourth century, not by a dreary lecture and a set of grimy casts, not by a novel which requires a glossary to explain it, but by the visible presentation before us of all the glory of that great town," and much more in the same vein. Apparently Godwin considered he should also have been given full credit for Lady Archibald Campbell's open-air production of the woodland scenes from *As You Like It* in the grounds of Dr McGragh's hydropathic establishment at Coombe Wood, near Kingston-on-Thames in July 1884. Lady Archie (see note 3, p. 36) was a pioneer of the production of pastoral plays.

[3] Wilde's review of *Henry IV, Part I*, the first production of the newly founded Oxford University Dramatic Society at the Town Hall, Oxford, on 15 May, appeared in the *Dramatic Review* of 23 May 1885. In the *Nineteenth Century* of December 1884 in an article on "Mary Anderson's Juliet" Lord Lytton had, in Wilde's words, "laid it down as a dogma of art that archaeology is entirely out of place in the presentation of any of Shakespeare's plays, and the attempt to introduce it one of the stupidest pedantries of an age of prigs."

[4] Wilde published a review of the 1885 revival of Lady Archibald Campbell's production of *As You Like It* in the *Dramatic Review* of 6 June.

To Norman Forbes-Robertson

[*Early June 1885*]   [*16 Tite Street*]

Dear Norman, Thanks for your congratulations.[1] Yes, come tomorrow. The baby is wonderful: it has a bridge to its nose! which the nurse says is a proof of genius! It also has a superb voice, which it freely exercises: its style is essentially Wagnerian.

Constance is doing capitally and is in excellent spirits.

I was delighted to get your telegram. You must get married *at once*! Ever yours   OSCAR

To the Hon. George Curzon[2]

20 July 1885   *16 Tite Street*

Dear Curzon, I want to be one of Her Majesty's Inspectors of Schools! This is ambition—however, I want it, and want it very much, and I hope you will help me. Edward Stanhope[3] has the giving away and, as a contemporary of mine at Oxford, you could give me great help by writing him a letter to say (if you think it) that I am a man of some brains. I won't trouble you with the reasons which make me ask for this post—but I want it and could do the work, I fancy, well.

If you could give me and get me any help you can I will be so much obliged to you, and I know how the party think of you—you brilliant young Coningsby![4]

I hope to get this and to get it with your approval and your good word. I don't know Stanhope personally and am afraid he may take the popular idea of me as a real idler. Would you tell him it is not so? In any case, ever yours   OSCAR WILDE

[1] Wilde's elder son Cyril was born at 16 Tite Street on 5 June 1885.

[2] The Hon. George Nathaniel Curzon (1859–1925), eldest son of the fourth Lord Scarsdale, had been an undergraduate (1878–82) at Balliol College, Oxford, where Wilde met him. He was Conservative M.P. for Southport from 1886 till 1898, when he was created Baron Curzon of Kedleston. Viceroy of India 1898–1905, Foreign Secretary 1919–24, created Marquess 1921.

[3] The Rt Hon. Edward Stanhope (1840–93), second son of the fifth Earl Stanhope. Conservative politician. Vice-President of the Council on Education June 1885. President of the Board of Trade August 1885. Later Secretary of State for the Colonies and for War.

[4] Like the hero of Disraeli's novel (1844) Curzon, newly down from the university, where he had been President of the Union and a Fellow of All Souls, seemed destined to be the bright new star of the Tory Party.

To H. C. Marillier[1]

[*Postmark 12 December 1885*]   *Central Station Hotel, Glasgow*

Dear Harry, I am away in the region of horrible snow and horrible note-paper! Lecturing and wandering—a vagabond with a mission! But your letter has reached me, like a strain of music wind-blown from a far land. You too have the love of things impossible—ἔρως τῶν ἀδυνάτων—*l'amour de l'impossible* (how do men name it?). Some day you will find, even as I have found, that there is no such thing as a romantic experience; there are romantic memories, and there is the desire of romance—that is all. Our most fiery moments of ecstasy are merely shadows of what somewhere else we have felt, or of what we long some day to feel. So at least it seems to me. And, strangely enough, what comes of all this is a curious mixture of ardour and of indifference. I myself would sacrifice everything for a new experience, and I know there is no such thing as a new experience at all. I think I would more readily die for what I do not believe in than for what I hold to be true. I would go to the stake for a sensation and be a sceptic to the last! Only one thing remains infinitely fascinating to me, the mystery of moods. To be master of these moods is exquisite, to be mastered by them more exquisite still. Sometimes I think that the artistic life is a long and lovely suicide, and am not sorry that it is so.

And much of this I fancy you yourself have felt: much also remains for you to feel. There is an unknown land full of strange flowers and subtle perfumes, a land of which it is joy of all joys to dream, a land where all things are perfect and poisonous. I have been reading Walter Scott for the last week: you too should read him, for there is nothing of all this in him.

Write to me at Tite Street, and let me know where you will be. Ever yours   O. W.

---

[1] Henry Currie Marillier (1865–1951) was a Bluecoat Boy (i.e. pupil at Christ's Hospital, then still in London) 1875–84 and lodged at 13 Salisbury Street, Strand, when Wilde was living there (1880–81). Classical scholar of Peterhouse, Cambridge, 1884–87. Became an engineer: for some years partner in W. A. S. Benson's metal works. Took to literary and art journalism. Edited *The Early Work of Aubrey Beardsley* (1899) and published books on various subjects, particularly tapestry, on which he became a great expert. He had recalled himself to Wilde's memory a month earlier and Wilde wrote:

> Of course I remember the blue-coat boy, and am charmed to find he has not forgotten me . . .

> I have a very vivid remembrance of the bright enthusiastic boy who used to bring me my coffee in Salisbury Street, and am delighted to find he is devoted to the muses, but I suppose you don't flirt with all nine ladies at once? Which of them do you really love? Whether or not I can come and see you, you must certainly come and see me when you are in town, and we will talk of the poets and drink Keats's health.

*To the Editor of the Pall Mall Gazette[1]

[*Early February 1886*]

Books, I fancy, may be conveniently divided into three classes:

1. Books to read, such as Cicero's *Letters*, Suetonius, Vasari's *Lives of the Painters*, the *Autobiography of Benvenuto Cellini*, Sir John Mandeville, Marco Polo, St Simon's *Memoirs*, Mommsen, and (till we get a better one) Grote's *History of Greece*.

2. Books to re-read, such as Plato and Keats: in the sphere of poetry, the masters not the minstrels; in the sphere of philosophy, the seers not the *savants*.

3. Books not to read at all, such as Thomson's *Seasons*, Rogers's *Italy*, Paley's *Evidences*, all the Fathers except St Augustine, all John Stuart Mill except the *Essay on Liberty*, all Voltaire's plays without any exception, Butler's *Analogy*, Grant's *Aristotle*, Hume's *England*, Lewes's *History of Philosophy*, all argumentative books and all books that try to prove anything.

The third class is by far the most important. To tell people what to read is, as a rule, either useless or harmful; for the appreciation of literature is a question of temperament not of teaching; to Parnassus there is no primer and nothing that one can learn is ever worth learning. But to tell people what not to read is a very different matter, and I venture to recommend it as a mission to the University Extension Scheme.

Indeed, it is one that is eminently needed in this age of ours, an age that reads so much that it has no time to admire, and writes so much that it has no time to think. Whoever will select out of the chaos of our modern curricula "The Worst Hundred Books," and publish a list of them, will confer on the rising generation a real and lasting benefit.

After expressing these views I suppose I should not offer any suggestions at all with regard to "The Best Hundred Books," but I hope that you will allow me the pleasure of being inconsistent, as I am anxious to put in a claim for a book that has been strangely omitted by most of the excellent judges who have contributed to your columns. I mean the *Greek Anthology*. The beautiful poems contained in this collection seem to me to hold the same position with regard to Greek dramatic literature as do the delicate little figurines of Tanagra to the Pheidian marbles, and to be quite as necessary for the complete understanding of the Greek spirit.

I am also amazed to find that Edgar Allan Poe has been passed over. Surely this marvellous lord of rhythmic expression deserves a place? If, in order to make room for him, it be necessary to elbow out someone else, I should elbow out Southey, and I think that Baudelaire might be most advantageously substituted for Keble. No doubt, both in *The Curse*

---

[1] The *Pall Mall Gazette* had been running a series on "The Best Hundred Books" by "The Best Hundred Judges." This letter appeared on 8 February under the heading TO READ, OR NOT TO READ, with an editorial note: "As we have published so many letters advising what to read, the following advice 'what not to read' from so good an authority as Mr Oscar Wilde may be of service."

of Kehama and in *The Christian Year* there are poetic qualities of a certain kind, but absolute catholicity of taste is not without its dangers. It is only an auctioneer who should admire all schools of art.

To the Editor of the World[1]

[*November 1886*]

Atlas, this is very sad! With our James "vulgarity begins at home," and should be allowed to stay there. *À vous*   OSCAR[2]

To Herbert P. Horne[3]

[*By hand. 7 December 1886*]   *16 Tite Street*

My dear Horne, Of course we will have the tablet. I thought we had fully settled that at Bristol. The little classical façade of the school-house[4] is just the place for it, and it will add historic interest to the building without marring its antiquarian value or eighteenth-century look. I remember your telling me in the train that one of your friends had promised to

[1] On 17 November 1886 Whistler had published in the *World* this letter to the Committee of the National Art Exhibition:

> Gentlemen, I am naturally interested in any effort made among Painters to prove that they are alive, but when I find, thrust in the van of your leaders, the body of my dead 'Arry, I know that putrefaction alone can result. When, following 'Arry, there comes on Oscar, you finish in farce, and bring upon yourselves the scorn and ridicule of your *confrères* in Europe.
> What has Oscar in common with Art? except that he dines at our tables and picks from our platters the plums for the pudding he peddles in the provinces. Oscar—the amiable, irresponsible, esurient Oscar—with no more sense of a picture than of the fit of a coat, has the courage of the opinions—of others! With 'Arry and Oscar you have avenged the Academy.
>   I am, Gentlemen, yours obediently.

According to Whistler's comment in *The Gentle Art of Making Enemies*, he sent Wilde a copy of the letter with the comment: "Oscar, you must really keep outside 'the radius'!" Wilde's reply appeared in the *World* on 24 November. Atlas was the name under which the editor, Edmund Yates, conducted a general editorial column. For 'Arry Quilter, see note p. 37.

[2] On this Whistler commented
"'A poor thing,' Oscar—but, for once, I suppose, 'your own'!"

[3] Architect, writer and connoisseur (1864–1916). Built the Church of the Redeemer, Bayswater Road. From 1886 to 1892 he edited a quarterly magazine called the *Century Guild Hobby Horse*, in which he printed some of his own poems. Before the end of the century he went to live in Florence, where he wrote a biography of Botticelli (1908) and set up the Museo Horne in the Via dei Benci. Rothenstein records Reggie Turner's saying: "Dear Herbert Horne! poring over Botticelli's washing bills—and always a shirt missing!"

[4] Colston's School, Stapleton, Bristol, at which the poet Thomas Chatterton (1752–70) was a pupil. Despite the efforts of Wilde, Horne and others, there is still no memorial to Chatterton in the school.

design one, and I was talking the other day about it to an ardent Chatter-tonian.

Do you think we should have a bas-relief of T. C.? It seems to me that there is really no picture of the poet extant. What do you say to a simple inscription

To the Memory

of

Thomas Chatterton

One of England's greatest poets and sometime pupil at this school.

I prefer the inscription, though a symbolic design might accompany it.

I was very nearly coming to fetch you the night of the fog to come and hear my lecture on Chatterton at the Birkbeck,[1] but did not like to take you out on such a dreadful night. To my amazement I found 800 people there! And they seemed really interested in the marvellous boy.[2]

You must come in for a cigarette some night soon. Sincerely yours

OSCAR WILDE

To Wemyss Reid[3]

[*April 1887*]   *16 Tite Street*

Dear Mr Wemyss Reid, I have read very carefully the numbers of the *Lady's World* you kindly sent me, and would be very happy to join with you in the work of editing and to some extent reconstructing it. It seems to me that at present it is too feminine, and not sufficiently womanly. No one appreciates more fully than I do the value and importance of Dress, in its relation to good taste and good health: indeed the subject is one that I have constantly lectured on before Institutes and Societies of various kinds, but it seems to me that the field of the *mundus muliebris*, the field of mere millinery and trimmings, is to some extent already occupied by such papers as the *Queen* and the *Lady's Pictorial*, and that we should take a

---

[1] Wilde lectured on Chatterton at Birkbeck College, London, on 24 November 1886.

[2] I thought of Chatterton, the marvellous Boy,
     The sleepless Soul that perish'd in its pride.
           Wordsworth: "Resolution and Independence"

[3] Thomas Wemyss Reid (1842–1905), journalist and biographer, was general manager of Cassell's publishing firm 1887–1905. He founded the *Speaker* in 1890 and edited it till 1897. He was knighted in 1894. The *Lady's World*, a shilling monthly, first appeared in November 1886. Wilde made a successful plea that its name be altered to the *Woman's World*, arguing that the original name had "a certain taint of vulgarity about it" and that it was not applicable to a magazine "that aims at being the organ of women of intellect, culture and position." The title was changed in the November 1887 issue, the first under Wilde's editorship. He resigned his editorship after the October 1889 issue, and the paper died a year later.

wider range, as well as a high standpoint, and deal not merely with what women wear, but with what they think, and what they feel. The *Lady's World* should be made the recognised organ for the expression of women's opinions on all subjects of literature, art, and modern life, and yet it should be a magazine that men could read with pleasure, and consider it a privilege to contribute to. We should get if possible the Princess Louise and the Princess Christian to contribute to it: an article from the latter on needlework for instance in connection with the Art School of which she is President would be very interesting. Carmen Sylva and Madame Adam should be got to write: Mrs Julia Ward Howe of Boston should be invited to contribute, as well as some of the other cultured women of America, while our list should include such women as Lady Archibald Campbell, a charming writer, Lady Ardilaun, who might give us some of her Irish experiences, Mrs Jeune, Miss Harrison, Miss Mary Robinson, Miss Olive Schreiner, the author of *South African Farm*; Lady Greville, whose life of Montrose is a very clever monograph, Miss Dorothy Tennant, Lady Verney, Lady Dilke, Lady Dufferin, Lady Constance Howard, Matthew Arnold's daughter, Lady Brassey, Lady Bective, Lady Rosebery, Lady Dorothy Nevill, who could write on the Walpoles, Mrs Singleton (Violet Fane), Lady Diana Huddleston, Lady Catherine Gaskell, Lady Paget, Miss Rosa Mulholland, Hon. Emily Lawless, Lady Harberton, Mrs Charles MacClaren, Lady Pollock, Mrs Fawcett, Miss Pater (sister of the author of *Marius*) and others too numerous to name in a letter.

We should try to get such articles as Mrs Brookfield's on Thackeray's Letters, Miss Stoker's on the Letters of Sheridan, both of which appear this month in two magazines,[1] and though many of our charming women have not had much literary experience they could write for us accounts of great collections of family pictures and the like. Lady Betty Lytton might give us an account of Knebworth (illustrated), or Lady Salisbury a description of Hatfield House: these last have of course written and published, but I don't see why many who have not done so should not make an essay. All women are flattered at being asked to write. Mrs Proctor also would be invaluable if she would give us some of her recollections, and an article by Lady Galway if we could get it would be delightful. But we should not rely exclusively on women, even for signed articles: artists have sex but art has none, and now and then an article by some man of letters would be of service.

Literary criticism I think might be done in the form of paragraphs: that is to say, not from the standpoint of the scholar or the pedant, but from the standpoint of what is pleasant to read: if a book is dull let us say nothing about it, if it is bright let us review it.

From time to time also we must have news from Girton and Newnham Colleges at Cambridge, and from the Oxford colleges for women, and invite articles from the members: Mrs Humphry Ward and Mrs Sidgwick

---

[1] Mrs Brookfield's articles began to appear in *Scribner's* for April 1887, and Matilda Stoker's "Sheridan and Miss Linley" was printed in the *English Illustrated Magazine* for April.

should not be forgotten, and the wife of the young President of Magdalen, Oxford,[1] might write on her own college, or, say, on the attitude of Universities towards women from the earliest times down to the present—a subject never fully treated of.

It seems to me also that just at present there is too much money spent on illustrations, particularly on illustrations of dress. They are also extremely unequal; many are charming, such as that on page 224 of the current number, but many look like advertisements and give an air to the magazine that one wants to avoid, the air of directly puffing some firm or *modiste*. A new cover also would be an improvement: the present one is not satisfactory.

With the new cover we should start our new names, and try and give the magazine a *cachet* at once: let dress have the end of the magazine; literature, art, travel and social studies the beginning. Music in a magazine is somewhat dull, no one wants it; a children's column would be much more popular. A popular serial story is absolutely necessary for the start. It need not be by a woman, and should be exciting but not tragic.

These are the outlines which for the moment suggest themselves to me, and in conclusion let me say that I will be very happy indeed to give any assistance I can in reconstructing the *Lady's World*, and making it the first woman's paper in England. To work for Messrs Cassell is a privilege which I fully recognize, to work with you a pleasure and a privilege that I look forward to. Believe me, dear Mr Reid, truly yours OSCAR WILDE

To Helena Sickert[2]

[*27 May 1887*]   *16 Tite Street*

Dear Miss Nellie, I am going to become an Editor (for my sins or my virtues?) and want you to write me an article. The magazine will try to be representative of the thought and culture of the women of this century, and I am very anxious that those who have had university training, like yourself, should have an organ through which they can express their views on life and things.

As for the subject—a review of the change of Political Economy during the last few years? Or on the value of Political Economy in education? But choose *your own aspect* of the question. About eight pages of printed matter in length, the honorarium a guinea a page, which is the same as the *Nineteenth Century* pays, and more than most of the magazines. I hope

---

[1] Mrs T. Herbert Warren, but Wilde may conceivably have confused her with the wife of the newly appointed President of Trinity, Mrs Margaret L. Woods (1856–1945), whose novel *A Village Tragedy* was published later in 1887, and favourably noticed by Wilde in the *Woman's World*.

[2] Wilde threw himself with immense enthusiasm into the work of remodelling the magazine. He interviewed and wrote a great many letters to potential contributors. This is one example.

you will do this for me, but let me know what subject you like best to write on.[1]

My wife is at home the first and third Thursdays in each month. Do come next Thursday with your mother, and talk over the matter. Believe me, very sincerely yours   OSCAR WILDE

The magazine will be published by *Cassell's*. It is of course a secret just at present.

*To Mrs Bernard Beere

[? *Late October 1887*][2]   *Beaufort Club, 32 Dover Street*

My dear Bernie, I am sure you will be very sorry to hear that I have been in great trouble. Our youngest boy[3] has been so ill that we thought he could never recover, and I was so unhappy over it that all my duties and letters escaped me, otherwise I would have been delighted to have had the chance of seeing you.

I am afraid as it is ten years since I lived in Dublin that all my friends have vanished—all that is who would have appreciated you, and whom you would have liked, but I have no doubt that by this time you are the idol of Hibernia, and all the College boys are in love with you. If they are not, at least they must have lost their old admiration for wit and beauty.

I hope you drive about on outside cars: there are several Dion Boucicaults[4] on the stand opposite the Shelbourne who are delightful creatures.

How nice of the Earthquake to wait till you had left. *Après vous—le tremblement de terre!* Poor Edmund! I hope he had not to run about *en déshabille.*

When do you come back? Why should the cottage be left lonely? Your

---

[1] The only article by Heléna Sickert (H. M. Swanwick) which appeared in the *Woman's World* was on "The Evolution of Economics" in the issue of February 1889.

[2] The only time that Mrs Bernard Beere seems to have acted in Ireland was 24–29 October 1887, when, with much success and "supported by the entire company from the Opera Comique, London," she played the leading parts in *As in a Looking Glass, Masks and Faces* and *Jim the Penman* at the Gaiety Theatre, Dublin. I cannot explain the reference to an earthquake.

[3] Wilde's second son Vyvyan was born on 3 November 1886. His parents usually spelt his name Vivian, but he was christened, and preferred, Vyvyan, which I have used throughout this book.

[4] Dionysius Lardner Boucicault, Irish dramatist and actor (1822–90). Among the best known of his 150 plays and adaptations are *The Corsican Brothers* (1852) and *The Colleen Bawn* (1860). He befriended and defended Wilde during his visit to America.

last dinner was a marvel, one of the pleasantest I was ever at. We have no *lionne* now but Ouida.[1] With best wishes, believe me, ever yours   OSCAR

To Jacomb Hood[2]

[*Early 1888*]   *16 Tite Street*
My dear Hood, Crane's little boy has nothing on, as well as I remember, but your children can be just as you like: perhaps clothes might be advisable.

I forgot one story: the illustration might be of a young Prince kissing the hand of a lovely Princess, who is in a long ermine cloak, with a little cap. She has come from the North Pole to marry him. There are courtiers and *a young page*, looking on.[3] In great haste, yours truly   OSCAR WILDE

To John Ruskin

[*June 1888*]   *16 Tite Street*
Dear Mr Ruskin, I send you my little book, *The Happy Prince and Other Tales*, and need hardly say how gratified I will be if you find in it any charm or beauty.[4]

It was a great pleasure to me to meet you again: the dearest memories of my Oxford days are my walks and talks with you, and from you I learned nothing but what was good.[5] How else could it be? There is in you something of prophet, of priest, and of poet, and to you the gods gave eloquence such as they have given to none other, so that your message might come to us with the fire of passion, and the marvel of music, making the deaf to hear, and the blind to see. I wish I had something better to give you, but, such as it is, take it with my love.   OSCAR WILDE

---

[1] Pen-name of the prolific novelist Maria Louise Ramé or, as she preferred, de la Ramée (1839–1908). Max Beerbohm called her "that unique, flamboyant lady, one of the miracles of modern literature." She contributed four articles to the *Woman's World* between March 1888 and May 1889.

[2] Professional name of George Percy Jacomb-Hood (1857–1929), artist and original member of the New English Art Club. He and Walter Crane (1845–1915) illustrated Wilde's book of fairy stories *The Happy Prince* (1888).

[3] Jacomb Hood faithfully carried out this suggestion in the headpiece-drawing for "The Remarkable Rocket" in *The Happy Prince*.

[4] *The Happy Prince and Other Tales* was published by David Nutt in May 1888. This copy is inscribed "John Ruskin in all love and loyalty from Oscar Wilde, June '88."

[5] Ruskin (1819–1900) was Slade Professor of Art at Oxford 1869–79 & 1883–84.

To Alfred Nutt[1]

Dear Mr Nutt, I will try and arrange with Miss Terry: it certainly would be charming to hear her read "The Happy Prince."

I find I have forgotten the *Century Guild Hobby Horse*. Will you kindly send them a copy for review—at 28 Southampton Street, Strand, W.C. The *Irish Times* I suppose has got its copy? Also, would it not be well to have a *card* for the booksellers to hang up in their shops? It may show Crane's frontispiece as well as the title etc. of the book. And is it not time for a few advertisements? *Punch* and the *World* are capital papers to advertise in—*once*. Mr Pater has written me a wonderful letter about my prose, so I am in high spirits.[2] Yours faithfully   OSCAR WILDE

To the Librarian of Toynbee Hall[3]

[*Postmark 4 July 1888*]   *16 Tite Street*

Dear Sir, I send you by this post a copy of a little book I have just published called *The Happy Prince*, for the library of Toynbee Hall. I hope that it will give pleasure to some of your readers, and remain, yours faithfully   OSCAR WILDE

[1] Alfred Trübner Nutt (1856–1910), head of the publishing business started in 1829 by his father David Nutt (d. 1863). Published the works of W. E. Henley, the Tudor Translations series and other finely produced books. President of the Folk-Lore Society 1897. In the van of the Celtic Revival. Drowned rescuing his invalid son from the Seine.

[2] Pater's letter, written from Brasenose College, Oxford, dated 12 June, reads:

My dear Wilde, I am confined to my room with gout, but have been consoling myself with *The Happy Prince*, and feel it would be ungrateful not to send a line to tell you how delightful I have found him and his companions. I hardly know whether to admire more the wise wit of "The Wonderful [Remarkable] Rocket," or the beauty and tenderness of "The Selfish Giant": the latter certainly is perfect in its kind. Your genuine "little poems in prose," those at the top of pages 10 and 14, for instance, are gems, and the whole, too brief, book abounds with delicate touches and pure English.

I hope to get away in a day or two, and meantime am a debtor in the matter of letters. Ever, very sincerely yours   WALTER PATER

[3] A social settlement in Whitechapel, erected in memory of the social reformer and economist Arnold Toynbee (1852–1883), who had been a contemporary of Wilde at Oxford.

To Thomas Hutchinson [1]

13 July 1888   *16 Tite Street*
My dear Sir, I must thank you for your very charming and graceful letter, but I am afraid that I don't think as much of the young Student as you do. He seems to me a rather shallow young man, and almost as bad as the girl he thinks he loves. The nightingale is the true lover, if there is one. She, at least, is Romance, and the Student and the girl are, like most of us, unworthy of Romance. So, at least, it seems to me, but I like to fancy that there may be many meanings in the tale, for in writing it, and the others, I did not start with an idea and clothe it in form, but began with a form and strove to make it beautiful enough to have many secrets, and many answers.
Truly yours   OSCAR WILDE

To W. E. Henley [2]

[? September 1888]   *16 Tite Street*
My dear Henley, It will give me great pleasure to lunch with you at the Savile on Saturday, though I am afraid that I shall be like a poor lion who has rashly intruded into a den of fierce Daniels. As for proposing me for the Savile, that is of course one of your merry jests. [3]

I am still reading your volume, preparatory to a review which I hope will be ready by the year 1900. I have decided that a great deal of it is poetry, and that, of the rest, part is poesy, and part . . . . [4]

The weather here is rather cloudy this morning, but I hope it will clear up, though I am told that dampness is good for agriculture. Pray remember me to Mrs Henley, and believe me, ever yours   OSCAR WILDE

[1] 1856–1938. Headmaster of Pegswood Voluntary Board School, Northumberland, for more than forty years. Author of *Ballades and other Rhymes of a Country Bookworm* (1888), which contained a parody of one of Wilde's early poems; *Jolts and Jingles: a Book of Poems for Young People* (1889), which was dedicated to Wilde; and *Fireside Flittings: A Book of Homely Essays* (1890). The reference is to Wilde's story "The Nightingale and the Rose" in *The Happy Prince*.

[2] William Ernest Henley (1849–1903), poet, journalist and editor. A courageous but aggressive cripple, who quarrelled with most of his best friends, including R. L. Stevenson. His friendship with Wilde was short-lived.

[3] Wilde was in fact put up for the Savile Club on 13 October 1888. His proposer was the Rev. W. J. Loftie, F.S.A., an old Trinity College, Dublin, man and Assistant Chaplain at the Chapel Royal, Savoy. Thirty-one other members of the Club backed Wilde's candidature, including Henley, Henry James, Edmund Gosse, Rider Haggard, R. A. M. Stevenson, W. H. Pollock, A. G. Ross, Walter Besant, J. K. Stephen, T. H. Warren, George Macmillan and J. W. Mackail, but he was never elected. Candidates for the Savile are not blackballed, but if there is opposition to their election, their names are simply postponed indefinitely.

[4] Wilde's dots. Henley's first collection of poems, *A Book of Verses*, had been published in May 1888. Wilde's review eventually appeared in the December issue of the *Woman's World*.

To Robert Ross[1]

My dear Bobbie, I congratulate you. University life will suit you admirably, though I shall miss you in town. Enclosed is the praise of the Philistines. Are you in College or lodgings? I hope in College; it is much nicer. Do you know Oscar Browning? You will find him everything that is kind and pleasant.

I have been speaking at Stratford about Shakespeare, but in spite of that enjoyed my visit immensely. My reception was semi-royal, and the volunteers played God Save the Queen in my honour.[2] Ever yours

OSCAR WILDE

To W. E. Henley

[? *October 1888*]   *16 Tite Street*

My dear Henley, I am so sorry to hear about your trouble. All poets love their mothers, and as I worship mine I can understand how you feel. I hope there is still some chance.[3] Ever yours affectionately   OSCAR

To Richard Le Gallienne[4]

[*Postmark 25 October 1888*]   *16 Tite Street*

My dear Le Gallienne, The lovely little book has just arrived, and I must

---

[1] Robert Baldwin Ross (1869–1918) was a Canadian. His grandfather Robert Baldwin was the first Prime Minister of Upper Canada; his father John Ross Attorney General. At the age of two, after the death of his father, he was brought to England by his mother to be educated. His schooling is unchronicled, but on 13 October 1888 he went up to King's College, Cambridge, as an undergraduate, to read History. Although he rowed in the college second boat, he was quickly in trouble for publishing in undergraduate periodicals some highly critical remarks about the election of college Fellows, was thrown into the Fountain, contracted pneumonia and left Cambridge abruptly in 1889. He then became a literary journalist and art-critic. He first met Wilde in 1886. For details of his later career and correspondence, see *Robert Ross: Friend of Friends*, edited by Margery Ross (1952).

[2] Wilde had spoken at Stratford on 10 October, proposing the health of his old friend Lord Ronald Gower (see note 2, p. 6) at the unveiling of Gower's statue of Shakespeare and four of his characters in the gardens of the Memorial Theatre.

[3] Henley's mother died on 25 October 1888, aged sixty.

[4] Poet, journalist and littérateur (1866–1947). His father, a Liverpool brewery-manager, had taken him to hear Wilde lecture on "Personal Impressions of America" at Birkenhead on 10 December 1883. He had visited Wilde in London in 1887 and again in June 1888. This manuscript volume of poems contained one commemorating the visit which began:

> With Oscar Wilde, a summer-day
> Passed like a yearning kiss away . . .

send you a line to thank you for so charming a gift. Written by your own hand it has the very quintessence of grace and beauty, and the page on which I find my own name set daintily in dainty music is a real delight to me, for I think often of the young poet who came here so wonderfully and so strangely, and whose memory is always with me.

I hope to see you in London soon. I often think of your visit. Tomorrow I hope to read your book over. It shall be a day of gold and marked with a white pearl. But the singer should be here also. Bother space and time! they spoil life by allowing such a thing as distance. Ever yours

OSCAR WILDE

To W. E. Gladstone[1]

[*2 November 1888*]   *16 Tite Street*

Dear Mr Gladstone, I have to thank you for your very kind letter. I quite understand how difficult, how impossible indeed it is for you to lend your name to memorials of this kind,[2] as many claims must be made upon it, and in the present day, as in olden times, everyone calls upon Achilles.

I can only assure you that though the absence of your name is, I will admit, a disappointment, it does not in the smallest iota alter the deep admiration that I along with my countrymen feel for the one English statesman who has understood us, who has sympathised with us, whom we claim now as our leader, and who, we know well, will lead us to the grandest and justest political victory of this age. I remain, dear Mr Gladstone, most faithfully yours   OSCAR WILDE

*To W. E. Henley

[*November–December 1888*]   *16 Tite Street*

My dear Henley, I am charmed you like my article. I tried to express as nicely as I could my feelings about the Marsyas of the early part of your

---

[1] William Ewart Gladstone (1809–98) had been Liberal Prime Minister three times but in 1888 a Tory Government was in power. Wilde had first written to Gladstone in 1877, and in June 1888 he had sent him a copy of *The Happy Prince*.

[2] In November 1888 the Royal Literary Fund awarded Lady Wilde a grant of £100. Her sponsors included Swinburne and Mahaffy. In May 1890 she was awarded a Civil List Pension of £70 a year. Swinburne was again one of the sponsors.

book, and the Apollo of the latter, to me the lovelier portion.[1] I hope you have read what I say about poor Sharp. I think I have been fair all round—as fair as an Irishman with a temperament ever wants to be. I am dining with Willie Richmond[2] at Hammersmith on Saturday, but if I can come in late will try to do so. I have sent Dunn[3] a wicked little symphony in yellow, suggested by seeing an omnibus (yellow omnibus) crawl across Blackfriars Bridge one foggy day about a week ago. He expresses himself "quite charmed" but says, not unwisely, that he is uncertain about publishing poetry! So I have produced my effect. Ever yours OSCAR

*To W. E. Henley

[? *December 1888*]

Quite right, my dear "Marsyas et Apollo;" to learn how to write English prose I have studied the prose of France. I am charmed that *you* recognise it: that shows I have succeeded. I am also charmed that no one else does: that shows I have succeeded also.

Yes! Flaubert is my master, and when I get on with my translation of the *Tentation* I shall be Flaubert II, *Roi par grâce de Dieu*, and I hope something else beyond.[4]

Where do you think I am not so good? I want very much to know. Of course it is, to me, a new *genre*. Ever yours OSCAR

---

[1] In his long-delayed review of Henley's *A Book of Verses* Wilde had written: "To me there is more of the cry of Marsyas than of the singing of Apollo in the early poems of Mr Henley's volume, 'Rhymes and Rhythms in Hospital' as he calls them. But it is impossible to deny their power." Marsyas was a mortal who challenged Apollo to a musical competition and was flayed alive for his pains. References to this myth recur in most of Wilde's writings. Later in the same article Wilde criticised severely William Sharp's *Romantic Ballads and Poems of Phantasy*. William Sharp (1856–1905) was a Scottish poet, biographer and journalist who wrote Celtic romances under the name Fiona Macleod. On 27 February 1890 W. B. Yeats wrote to Katharine Tynan: "Have you heard Oscar's last good thing? He says that Sharp's motto should be *Acutus descensus averni* (Sharp is the descent into Hell)."

[2] William Blake Richmond (1842–1921), painter. Son of George Richmond R.A. (1809–96), who was a friend of Blake. Slade Professor at Oxford 1878–83, R.A. 1895, knighted 1897. Designed the mosaics in St Paul's.

[3] James Nicol Dunn, Scottish journalist (1856–1919), managing editor of Henley's *Scots Observer*, which first appeared on 24 November. (He was later editor of the *Morning Post*.) The poem Wilde sent him was "Symphony in Yellow," which he declined.

[4] In an undated letter to Alfred Nutt, Wilde wrote: "Do you think (this is private) that a translation of that amazing book of Flaubert's, *La Tentation de St Antoine*, would be a success? I want to do it." See also p. 333.

*To Kate Terry Lewis[1]

[January 1889]   16 Tite Street
My dear Mrs Lewis, Thank you so much for your charming and welcome letter. I am delighted you like the article:[2] underneath the fanciful form it hides some truths, or perhaps some half-truths, about art, which I think require to be put forward, and of which some are, I think, quite new, and none the worse for that. I have blown my trumpet against the gate of dullness, and I hope some shaft has hit *Robert Elsmere* between the joints of his nineteenth edition. It was delightful work writing the article, and it is equally delightful to know that Lady Betty[3] enjoyed it. Ever yours

OSCAR WILDE

*To an Income-tax Inspector

[? April 1889]   [Woman's World, La Belle Sauvage]
Sir, It was arranged last year that I should send in my income-tax return from Chelsea where I reside, as I am resigning my position here and will not be with Messrs Cassell after August. I think it would be better to continue that arrangement. I wish your notices were not so agitating and did not hold out such dreadful threats. A penalty of fifty pounds sounds like a relic of mediæval torture. Your obedient servant   OSCAR WILDE

To W. Graham Robertson[4]

[Postmark 11 May 1889]   16 Tite Street
Do you really live at Sandhills, Witley?[5] Surely not Sandhills! You are

---

[1] Kate Terry (1844–1924), leading actress and elder sister of Ellen Terry, retired from the stage in 1867 on her marriage to Arthur Lewis, a wealthy silk-mercer who had founded the Arts Club in 1863. Grandmother of Sir John Gielgud.

[2] "The Decay of Lying" appeared in the *Nineteenth Century* for January 1889 and was reprinted, revised, in *Intentions* (1891). In it Wilde wrote of Mrs Humphry Ward's best-selling novel (3 vols, February 1888): "*Robert Elsmere* is of course a masterpiece—a masterpiece of the *genre ennuyeux*, the one form of literature that the English people seem to thoroughly enjoy. A thoughtful young friend of ours once told us that it reminded him of the sort of conversation that goes on at a meat tea in the house of a serious Nonconformist family, and we can quite believe it."

[3] Almost certainly Lady Elizabeth Edith (1867–1942), eldest daughter of the first Earl of Lytton. She married (1887) Gerald William Balfour (1853–1945), who succeeded his brother Arthur as second Earl Balfour 1930.

[4] Artist and writer (1866–1948). Painted by Sargent 1894. Formed important collection of Blake drawings. Designed many stage costumes. His successful children's play *Pinkie and the Fairies* was produced by Tree in 1908, though written in the 1890's, for which his autobiography *Time Was* (1931) is a valuable source-book.

[5] In 1888 Graham Robertson and his mother had bought a house in this Surrey hamlet from William Allingham, the poet. They lived there for the rest of their lives. Mrs Robertson died in 1907.

made for olive-groves, and for meadows starred with white narcissi. I am sure this letter will be returned to me by the post office.

I have written to you at Rutland Gate to tell you how sorry I am you have missed Paris, and how much more sorry I am that I did not keep you to your promise. I should have loved to have been with you—Sandhills or no Sandhills.

I send this letter into the air! Will you ever get it? I suppose not. Ever yours
O. W.

To Robert Ross

[*July 1889*]   *16 Tite Street*

Dear Bobbie, Your telegram (of course it was *yours*) has just arrived. So many thanks for it: it was really sweet of you to send it, for indeed the story is half yours, and but for you would not have been written.[1] Are you well again? Terror for Cyril kept me away, but now I may come, may I not?

Write to me a letter. Now that Willie Hughes has been revealed to the world, we must have another secret. Ever yours, dear Bobbie   O. W.

To W. E. Henley

[*July 1889*]   *16 Tite Street*

My dear Henley, To be exiled to Scotland to edit a Tory paper in the wilderness is bad enough, but not to see the wonder and beauty of my discovery of the real Mr W. H. is absolutely dreadful. I sympathise deeply with you, and can only beg you to return to London where you will be able to appreciate a real work of art.

The Philistines in their vilest forms have seized on you. I am so disappointed.[2]

Still, when you return you will be welcome; all is not lost. Ever yours
OSCAR

---

[1] "The Portrait of Mr W. H." appeared in *Blackwood's Magazine* for July 1889 (having been declined by Frank Harris for the *Fortnightly*). In it Wilde sought to identify the dedicatee of Shakespeare's sonnets as a boy-actor called Willie Hughes.

[2] An unsigned notice in the *Scots Observer* of 6 July 1889 had said: "With the exception of one article which is out of place in *Maga*—or, indeed, in any popular magazine—the July number of *Blackwood* is particularly good." *Maga* is slang for *Blackwood's Magazine*.

*To Charles Ricketts[1]

[? *Autumn 1889*]   *16 Tite Street*

My dear Ricketts, It is not a forgery at all; it is an authentic Clouet of the highest authentic value. It is absurd of you and Shannon to try and take me in! As if I did not know the master's touch, or was no judge of frames![2]

Seriously, my dear fellow, it is quite wonderful, and your giving it to me is an act so charming that, in despair of showing you any return, I at once call upon the gods to shower gold and roses on the Vale, or on that part of the Vale where the De Morgans do not live.[3] I am really most grateful (no! that is a horrid word: I am never grateful) I am flattered and fascinated, and I hope we shall always be friends and see each other often.

I must come round and enjoy the company of the Dialists—*par nobile*[4] as they are. Sincerely yours   OSCAR WILDE

*To the Editor of Truth[5]

[*Early January 1890*]   *16 Tite Street*

Sir, I can hardly imagine that the public are in the very smallest degree interested in the shrill shrieks of "Plagiarism" that proceed from time to time out of the lips of silly vanity or incompetent mediocrity.

[1] Charles De Sousy Ricketts (1866–1931), artist, writer, book and stage designer, lived for many years with Charles Hazlewood Shannon (1863–1937), first in a house (which had belonged to Whistler) in a Chelsea cul-de-sac called The Vale. Ricketts was elected R.A. in 1928, Shannon in 1921. Ricketts designed the title-page and binding of *The Picture of Dorian Gray* (1891) and of the limited edition of Wilde's *Poems* (1892), the binding of *Intentions* (1891) and *Lord Arthur Savile's Crime* (1891). Ricketts and Shannon jointly designed and decorated *A House of Pomegranates* (1891). Ricketts designed *The Sphinx* (1894) and the binding for the Collected Edition of 1908. Shannon designed the binding for *Lady Windermere's Fan* (1893), *A Woman of No Importance* (1894), *The Importance of Being Earnest* (1899) and *An Ideal Husband* (1899). Together they ran a privately printed magazine called the *Dial* from 1889 to 1897.

[2] Wilde had asked Ricketts to paint a small Elizabethan picture of Willie Hughes, such as the one in the story which was "quite in Clouet's style," to act as frontispiece to an enlarged edition of "The Portrait of Mr W. H." Ricketts painted it on "a decaying piece of oak and framed it in a fragment of worm-eaten moulding, which my friend Shannon pieced together." The edition did not appear in Wilde's lifetime (but see note p. 122), and at the sale of Wilde's effects on 24 April 1895 the painting was sold for a guinea. François Clouet (d. 1572) was a French painter of miniatures.

[3] William Frend De Morgan (1839–1917), the Pre-Raphaelite artist and potter, had married in 1888 and lived near Ricketts and Shannon in Chelsea. In his late sixties and seventies he achieved considerable success with *Joseph Vance* (1906) and other novels.

[4] Noble pair (Horace, *Satires*, II, iii, 243).

[5] An answer to this letter of Whistler's, which had appeared in *Truth* on 2 January 1890:

  Dear Truth, Among your ruthless exposures of the shams of today, nothing, I confess, have I enjoyed with keener relish than your late tilt at that arch-impostor

79

However, as Mr James Whistler has had the impertinence to attack me with both venom and vulgarity in your columns, I hope you will allow me to state that the assertions contained in his letter are as deliberately untrue as they are deliberately offensive.

The definition of a disciple as one who has the courage of the opinions of his master is really too old even for Mr Whistler to be allowed to claim it, and as for borrowing Mr Whistler's ideas about art, the only thoroughly original ideas I have ever heard him express have had reference to his own superiority over painters greater than himself.

It is a trouble for any gentleman to have to notice the lucubrations of so ill-bred and ignorant a person as Mr Whistler, but your publication of

and pest of the period—the all-pervading plagiarist!

I learn, by the way, that in America he may, under the "Law of '84," as it is called, be criminally prosecuted, incarcerated, and made to pick oakum, as he has hitherto picked brains—and pockets!

How was it that, in your list of culprits, you omitted that fattest of offenders—our own Oscar?

His methods are brought again freshly to my mind, by the indefatigable and tardy Romeike, who sends me newspaper cuttings of "Mr Herbert Vivian's Reminiscences," in which, among other entertaining anecdotes, is told at length the story of Oscar simulating the becoming pride of author, upon a certain evening, in the club of the Academy students, and arrogating to himself the responsibility of the lecture, with which, at his earnest prayer, I had in good fellowship crammed him, that he might not add deplorable failure to foolish appearance, in his anomalous position as art expounder, before his clear-headed audience.

He went forth, on that occasion, as my St John—but, forgetting that humility should be his chief characteristic, and unable to withstand the unaccustomed respect with which his utterances were received, he not only trifled with my shoe, but bolted with the latchet!

Mr Vivian, in his book, tells us, further on, that lately, in an article in the *Nineteenth Century* on "The Decay of Lying," Mr Wilde has deliberately and incautiously incorporated, "without a word of comment," a portion of the well-remembered letter in which, after admitting his rare appreciation and amazing memory, I acknowledge that "Oscar has the courage of the opinions—of others!"

My recognition of this, his latest proof of open admiration, I send him in the following little note, which I fancy you may think *à propos* to publish, as an example to your readers, in similar circumstances, of noble generosity in sweet reproof, tempered, as it should be, to the lamb in his condition:

"Oscar, you have been down the area again, I see!

I had forgotten you, and so allowed your hair to grow over the sore place. And now, while I looked the other way, you have stolen *your own scalp*! and potted it in more of your pudding.

Labby has pointed out that, for the detected plagiarist, there is still one way to self-respect (besides hanging himself, of course), and that is for him boldly to declare, '*Je prends mon bien là où je le trouve.*'

You, Oscar, can go further, and with fresh effrontery, that will bring you the envy of all criminal *confrères*, unblushingly boast, '*Moi, je prends* son *bien là où je le trouve!* '"

Wilde's lecture was given to the Art Students of the Royal Academy on 30 June 1883. This answer of Wilde's appeared in *Truth* on 9 January 1890. Henry Romeike had established his press-cutting agency in London in 1881.

his insolent letter left me no option in the matter. I remain, sir, faithfully yours   OSCAR WILDE[1]

*To the Editor of the Scots Observer[2]

9 July 1890   *16 Tite Street, Chelsea*

Sir, You have published a review of my story, *The Picture of Dorian Gray*.
As this review is grossly unjust to me as an artist, I ask you to allow me to
exercise in your columns my right of reply.

Your reviewer, sir, while admitting that the story in question is "plainly
the work of a man of letters," the work of one who has "brains, and art, and
style," yet suggests, and apparently in all seriousness, that I have written
it in order that it should be read by the most depraved members of the
criminal and illiterate classes. Now, sir, I do not suppose that the criminal
and illiterate classes ever read anything except newspapers. They are
certainly not likely to be able to understand anything of mine. So let them
pass, and on the broad question of why a man of letters writes at all let me
say this. The pleasure that one has in creating a work of art is a purely
personal pleasure, and it is for the sake of this pleasure that one creates.
The artist works with his eye on the object. Nothing else interests him.
What people are likely to say does not even occur to him. He is fascinated
by what he has in hand. He is indifferent to others. I write because it
gives me the greatest possible artistic pleasure to write. If my work pleases
the few, I am gratified. If it does not, it causes me no pain. As for the
mob, I have no desire to be a popular novelist. It is far too easy.

---

[1] Whistler replied with another letter in *Truth* on 16 January, and reprinted all
three letters in *The Gentle Art of Making Enemies* later in the year.

[2] Wilde's only novel, *The Picture of Dorian Gray*, was first published on 20 June
1890, in the July number of *Lippincott's Monthly Magazine*. It was extensively
reviewed. The *Scots Observer*'s anonymous notice on 5 July read:

> Why go grubbing in muck heaps? The world is fair, and the proportion of
> healthy-minded men and honest women to those that are foul, fallen, or unnatural
> is great. Mr Oscar Wilde has again been writing stuff that were better unwritten;
> and while *The Picture of Dorian Gray*, which he contributes to *Lippincott's*, is
> ingenious, interesting, full of cleverness, and plainly the work of a man of letters,
> it is false art—for its interest is medico-legal; it is false to human nature—for its
> hero is a devil; it is false to morality—for it is not made sufficiently clear that the
> writer does not prefer a course of unnatural iniquity to a life of cleanliness, health,
> and sanity. The story—which deals with matters only fitted for the Criminal
> Investigation Department or a hearing *in camerâ*—is discreditable alike to author
> and editor. Mr Wilde has brains, and art, and style; but if he can write for none
> but outlawed noblemen and perverted telegraph-boys, the sooner he takes to
> tailoring (or some other decent trade) the better for his own reputation and the
> public morals.

Although it was for long thought to have been written by W. E. Henley, the paper's
editor, the author was in fact his henchman Charles Whibley (1860–1930). The
outlawed nobleman and perverted telegraph-boys refer to Lord Arthur Somerset
and the Cleveland Street scandal of 1889. This letter of Wilde's appeared on 12
July, under the heading MR WILDE'S REJOINDER.

Your critic then, sir, commits the absolutely unpardonable crime of trying to confuse the artist with his subject-matter. For this, sir, there is no excuse at all. Of one who is the greatest figure in the world's literature since Greek days Keats remarked that he had as much pleasure in conceiving the evil as he had in conceiving the good.[1] Let your reviewer, sir, consider the bearings of Keats's fine criticism, for it is under these conditions that every artist works. One stands remote from one's subject-matter. One creates it, and one contemplates it. The further away the subject-matter is, the more freely can the artist work. Your reviewer suggests that I do not make it sufficiently clear whether I prefer virtue to wickedness or wickedness to virtue. An artist, sir, has no ethical sympathies at all. Virtue and wickedness are to him simply what the colours on his palette are to the painter. They are no more, and they are no less. He sees that by their means a certain artistic effect can be produced, and he produces it. Iago may be morally horrible and Imogen stainlessly pure. Shakespeare, as Keats said, had as much delight in creating the one as he had in creating the other.

It was necessary, sir, for the dramatic development of this story to surround Dorian Gray with an atmosphere of moral corruption. Otherwise the story would have had no meaning and the plot no issue. To keep this atmosphere vague and indeterminate and wonderful was the aim of the artist who wrote the story. I claim, sir, that he has succeeded. Each man sees his own sin in Dorian Gray. What Dorian Gray's sins are no one knows. He who finds them has brought them.

In conclusion, sir, let me say how really deeply I regret that you should have permitted such a notice as the one I feel constrained to write on to have appeared in your paper. That the editor of the *St James's Gazette* should have employed Caliban as his art-critic was possibly natural.[2] The editor of the *Scots Observer* should not have allowed Thersites to make mows in his review. It is unworthy of so distinguished a man of letters. I am, etc.   OSCAR WILDE

---

[1] "The poetical character . . . has as much delight in conceiving an Iago as an Imogen. What shocks the virtuous philosopher delights the cameleon poet." John Keats to Richard Woodhouse, 27 October 1818.

[2] There was a protracted controversy in the columns of the *St James's Gazette* following that newspaper's scurrilous notice on 24 June entitled "A Study in Puppydom." Wilde sent four letters in defence of his novel. His last one on 28 June concluded:

In conclusion, sir, let me ask you not to force on me this continued correspondence, by daily attacks. It is a trouble and a nuisance. As you assailed me first, I have a right to the last word. Let that last word be the present letter, and leave my book, I beg you, to the immortality that it deserves.

To Arthur Fish[1]

[*Postmark 22 July 1890*]   *16 Tite Street*

Dear Arthur Fish, I am very glad to hear you are going to be married, and I need hardly say that I hope you will be very happy. Lord Henry Wotton's views on marriage are quite monstrous, and I highly disapprove of them. I am delighted you like *Dorian Gray*—it has been attacked on ridiculous grounds, but I think will be ultimately recognised as a real work of art with a strong ethical lesson inherent in it. Where are you going for your honeymoon? Believe me, sincerely yours   OSCAR WILDE

To the Editor of the Scots Observer[2]

[? *31*] *July 1890*   *16 Tite Street*

Sir, In a letter dealing with the relations of art to morals recently published in your columns—a letter which I may say seems to me in many respects admirable, especially in its insistence on the right of the artist to select his own subject-matter—Mr Charles Whibley suggests that it must be peculiarly painful for me to find that the ethical import of *Dorian Gray* has been so strongly recognized by the foremost Christian papers of England and America that I have been greeted by more than one of them as a moral reformer!

Allow me, sir, to reassure, on this point, not merely Mr Charles Whibley himself but also your no doubt anxious readers. I have no hesitation in saying that I regard such criticisms as a very gratifying tribute to my story. For if a work of art is rich, and vital, and complete, those who have artistic instincts will see its beauty, and those to whom ethics appeal more strongly than aesthetics will see its moral lesson. It will fill the cowardly with terror, and the unclean will see in it their own shame. It will be to each man what he is himself. It is the spectator, and not life, that art really mirrors.

And so, in the case of *Dorian Gray*, the purely literary critic, as in the *Speaker* and elsewhere, regards it as a "serious and fascinating work of art:" the critic who deals with art in its relation to conduct, as the *Christian Leader* and the *Christian World*, regards it as an ethical parable. *Light*, which I am told is the organ of the English mystics, regards it as "a work of high spiritual import." The *St James's Gazette*, which is seeking apparently to be the organ of the prurient, sees or pretends to see in it all kinds of

---

[1] Journalist (1860–1940). Spent his whole working life as an editor for Messrs Cassell and was Wilde's assistant editor on the *Woman's World*. He was married at Barnet on 19 August 1890.

[2] Since Wilde's last letter the *Scots Observer* had printed on the same subject a letter signed Charles Whibley and citing Maupassant, Dostoievsky, Flaubert, Daudet and Marlowe; another from Whibley in the guise of the original reviewer, signed "Thersites;" and one signed "H" and written by Sir Herbert Stephen (1857–1932), Clerk of Assize for the Northern Circuit. This letter of Wilde's appeared on 2 August under the heading ART AND MORALITY.

dreadful things, and hints at Treasury prosecutions; and your Mr Charles Whibley genially says that he discovers in it "lots of morality." It is quite true that he goes on to say that he detects no art in it. But I do not think that it is fair to expect a critic to be able to see a work of art from every point of view. Even Gautier had his limitations just as much as Diderot had, and in modern England Goethes are rare. I can only assure Mr Charles Whibley that no moral apotheosis to which he has added the most modest contribution could possibly be a source of unhappiness to an artist.

I remain, sir, your obedient servant   OSCAR WILDE

To the Editor of the Scots Observer[1]

13 August 1890   *16 Tite Street*

Sir, I am afraid I cannot enter into any newspaper discussion on the subject of art with Mr Whibley, partly because the writing of letters is always a trouble to me, and partly because I regret to say that I do not know what qualifications Mr Whibley possesses for the discussion of so important a topic. I merely noticed his letter because, I am sure without in any way intending it, he made a suggestion about myself personally that was quite inaccurate. His suggestion was that it must have been painful to me to find that a certain section of the public, as represented by himself and the critics of some religious publications, had insisted on finding what he calls "lots of morality" in my story of *The Picture of Dorian Gray*.

Being naturally desirous of setting your readers right on a question of such vital interest to the historian, I took the opportunity of pointing out in your columns that I regarded all such criticisms as a very gratifying tribute to the ethical beauty of the story, and I added that I was quite ready to recognise that it was not really fair to ask of any ordinary critic that he should be able to appreciate a work of art from every point of view. I still hold this opinion. If a man sees the artistic beauty of a thing, he will probably care very little for its ethical import. If his temperament is more susceptible to ethical than to aesthetic influences, he will be blind to questions of style, treatment, and the like. It takes a Goethe to see a work of art fully, completely, and perfectly, and I thoroughly agree with Mr Whibley when he says that it is a pity that Goethe never had an opportunity of reading *Dorian Gray*. I feel quite certain that he would have been delighted by it, and I only hope that some ghostly publisher is even now distributing shadowy copies in the Elysian fields, and that the cover of Gautier's copy is powdered with gilt asphodels.

You may ask me, sir, why I should care to have the ethical beauty of my

---

[1] The correspondence had now been swollen by two further signed letters from Whibley; and one each from T. E. Brown, the Manx poet-schoolmaster (1830–97), containing much reference to Zola; J. Maclaren Cobban (1849–1903); Vernon Blackburn (1867–1907), the Catholic music-critic; and William Archer, the dramatic critic. Although this letter, which appeared on 16 August under the same heading as its predecessor, was the last Wilde wrote to the *Scots Observer*, the correspondence continued for another three weeks.

story recognised. I answer, simply because it exists, because the thing is there. The chief merit of *Madame Bovary* is not the moral lesson that can be found in it, any more than the chief merit of *Salammbô* is its archaeology; but Flaubert was perfectly right in exposing the ignorance of those who called the one immoral and the other inaccurate; and not merely was he right in the ordinary sense of the word, but he was artistically right, which is everything. The critic has to educate the public; the artist has to educate the critic.

Allow me to make one more correction, sir, and I will have done with Mr Whibley. He ends his letter with the statement that I have been indefatigable in my public appreciation of my own work. I have no doubt that in saying this he means to pay me a compliment, but he really overrates my capacity, as well as my inclination for work. I must frankly confess that, by nature and by choice, I am extremely indolent. Cultivated idleness seems to me to be the proper occupation for man. I dislike newspaper controversies of any kind, and of the two hundred and sixteen criticisms of *Dorian Gray* that have passed from my library table into the waste-paper basket I have taken public notice of only three. One was that which appeared in the *Scots Observer*. I noticed it because it made a suggestion, about the intention of the author in writing the book, which needed correction. The second was an article in the *St James's Gazette*. It was offensively and vulgarly written, and seemed to me to require immediate and caustic censure. The tone of the article was an impertinence to any man of letters. The third was a meek attack in a paper called the *Daily Chronicle*. I think my writing to the *Daily Chronicle* was an act of pure wilfulness. In fact, I feel sure it was. I quite forget what they said.[1] I believe they said that *Dorian Gray* was poisonous, and I thought that, on alliterative grounds, it would be kind to remind them that, however that may be, it is at any rate perfect. That was all. Of the other two hundred and thirteen criticisms I have taken no notice. Indeed, I have not read more than half of them. It is a sad thing, but one wearies even of praise.[2]

---

[1] Part of the review in the *Daily Chronicle* runs: "Dulness and dirt are the chief features of *Lippincott's* this month. The element in it that is unclean, though undeniably amusing, is furnished by Mr Oscar Wilde's story . . . It is a tale spawned from the leprous literature of the French *Décadents*—a poisonous book, the atmosphere of which is heavy with the mephitic odours of moral and spiritual putrefaction."

[2] Some of the most welcome praise came later. Pater's review of *Dorian Gray* did not appear until after publication in book form. In the November 1891 issue of the *Bookman* he wrote:

There is always something of an excellent talker about the writing of Mr Oscar Wilde; and in his hands, as happens so rarely with those who practise it, the form of dialogue is justified by its being really alive.

And in *United Ireland* of 26 September 1891 W. B. Yeats wrote:

Dorian Gray, with all its faults, is a wonderful book. *The Happy Prince* is a volume of as pretty fairy tales as our generation has seen; and *Intentions* hides within its immense paradox some of the most subtle literary criticism we are likely to see for many a long day.

As regards Mr Brown's letter, it is interesting only in so far as it exemplifies the truth of what I have said above on the question of the two obvious schools of critics. Mr Brown says frankly that he considers morality to be the "strong point" of my story. Mr Brown means well, and has got hold of a half-truth, but when he proceeds to deal with the book from the artistic standpoint he, of course, goes sadly astray. To class *Dorian Gray* with M. Zola's *La Terre* is as silly as if one were to class Musset's[1] *Fortunio* with one of the Adelphi melodramas. Mr Brown should be content with ethical appreciation. There he is impregnable.

Mr Cobban opens badly by describing my letter, setting Mr Whibley right on a matter of fact, as an "impudent paradox." The term "impudent" is meaningless, and the word "paradox" is misplaced. I am afraid that writing to newspapers has a deteriorating influence on style. People get violent, and abusive, and lose all sense of proportion, when they enter that curious journalistic arena in which the race is always to the noisiest. "Impudent paradox" is neither violent nor abusive, but it is not an expression that should have been used about my letter. However, Mr Cobban makes full atonement afterwards for what was, no doubt, a mere error of manner, by adopting the impudent paradox in question as his own, and pointing out that, as I had previously said, the artist will always look at the work of art from the standpoint of beauty of style and beauty of treatment, and that those who have not got the sense of beauty, or whose sense of beauty is dominated by ethical considerations, will always turn their attention to the subject-matter and make its moral import the test and touchstone of the poem, or novel, or picture, that is presented to them, while the newspaper critic will sometimes take one side and sometimes the other, according as he is cultured or uncultured. In fact, Mr Cobban converts the impudent paradox into a tedious truism, and, I dare say, in doing so does good service. The English public like tediousness, and like things to be explained to them in a tedious way. Mr Cobban has, I have no doubt, already repented of the unfortunate expression with which he has made his *début*, so I will say no more about it. As far as I am concerned he is quite forgiven.

And finally, sir, in taking leave of the *Scots Observer* I feel bound to make a candid confession to you. It has been suggested to me by a great friend of mine, who is a charming and distinguished man of letters, and not unknown to you personally,[2] that there have been really only two people engaged in this terrible controversy, and that those two people are the editor of the *Scots Observer* and the author of *Dorian Gray*. At dinner this evening, over some excellent Chianti, my friend insisted that under assumed and mysterious names you had simply given dramatic expression to the views of some of the semi-educated classes in our community, and that the letters signed "H" were your own skilful, if somewhat bitter, caricature of the Philistine as drawn by himself. I admit that something

[1] A slip for Gautier, as another correspondent was quick to point out.
[2] According to Stuart Mason, who collected the important reviews and letters about *Dorian Gray* in *Art and Morality* (1912), this was Robert Ross.

of the kind had occurred to me when I read "H's" first letter—the one in which he proposed that the test of art should be the political opinions of the artist, and that if one differed from the artist on the question of the best way of misgoverning Ireland, one should always abuse his work. Still, there are such infinite varieties of Philistines, and North Britain is so renowned for seriousness, that I dismissed the idea as one unworthy of the editor of a Scotch paper. I now fear that I was wrong, and that you have been amusing yourself all the time by inventing little puppets and teaching them how to use big words. Well, sir, if it be so—and my friend is strong upon the point—allow me to congratulate you most sincerely on the cleverness with which you have reproduced that lack of literary style which is, I am told, essential for any dramatic and life-like characterisation. I confess that I was completely taken in; but I bear no malice; and as you have no doubt been laughing at me in your sleeve, let me now join openly in the laugh, though it be a little against myself. A comedy ends when the secret is out. Drop your curtain, and put your dolls to bed. I love Don Quixote, but I do not wish to fight any longer with marionettes, however cunning may be the master-hand that works their wires.[1] Let them go, sir, on the shelf. The shelf is the proper place for them. On some future occasion you can re-label them and bring them out for our amusement. They are an excellent company, and go well through their tricks, and if they are a little unreal, I am not the one to object to unreality in art. The jest was really a good one. The only thing that I cannot understand is why you gave your marionettes such extraordinary and improbable names. I remain, sir, your obedient servant   OSCAR WILDE

[1] In Chapter 26 of the Second Part of the novel, Don Quixote, watching a puppet-show at an inn, gets so carried away by the plot that he draws his sword, intervenes in the play and cuts the puppets to pieces.

PART FIVE

LONDON III · 1891-1895

It was almost certainly in the year 1891 that there entered Wilde's life the man who was to be in some sense his inspiration and in every sense his evil genius. Lord Alfred Bruce Douglas, the third son of the eighth Marquess of Queensberry, had been born in 1870, educated at Winchester, and was now a second-year undergraduate at Magdalen College, Oxford. The poet and critic Lionel Johnson (1867–1902), a Winchester contemporary and Oxford friend, brought him to see Wilde at Tite Street. Douglas says this momentous meeting took place in 1891, and in the vacation, which seems likely. In a letter to More Adey of 7 April 1897 Wilde wrote:

> The friendship began in May 1892 by [Douglas] appealing to me in a very pathetic letter to help him in terrible trouble with people who were blackmailing him. I hardly knew him at the time. I had known him eighteen months, but had only seen him four times in that space.

Eighteen months would put the first meeting back to November 1890, but two months' grace to Wilde's figures would bring it to January 1891, during the Christmas vacation.

There exists a copy of the Large Paper edition of *The Picture of Dorian Gray* (published 1 July 1891) inscribed "Alfred Douglas from his friend who wrote this book. July 91. Oscar," and in an unpublished letter to Frank Harris, dated 20 March 1925, Douglas wrote "the second time he saw me (when he gave me a copy of *Dorian Gray* which I took back with me to Oxford)."

This does not necessarily conflict with the possibility of a first meeting in January, and it is therefore possible that the extra material for the book-edition of *Dorian Gray* was written after the meeting. On the other hand, this material consists mainly of elaboration, and the main characters and episodes in the story were certainly written before Douglas entered Wilde's life.

To George Alexander[1]

[*2 February 1891*]   *16 Tite Street*

My dear Aleck, I am not satisfied with myself or my work. I can't get a grip of the play[2] yet: I can't get my people real. The fact is I worked at it when I was not in the mood for work, and must first forget it, and then go back quite fresh to it. I am very sorry, but artistic work can't be done unless one is in the mood; certainly my work can't. Sometimes I spend months over a thing, and don't do any good; at other times I write a thing in a fortnight.

You will be interested to hear that the *Duchess of Padua* was produced in New York last Wednesday, under the title of *Guido Ferranti*, by Lawrence Barrett.[3] The name of the author was kept a dead secret, and indeed not revealed till yesterday when at Barrett's request I acknowledged the authorship by cable. Barrett wires to me that it was a huge success, and that he is going to run it for his season. He seems to be in great delight over it.

With regard to the cheque for £50 you gave me, shall I return you the money, and end the agreement, or keep it and when the play is written let you have the rights and refusal of it? That will be just as you wish.

I am delighted to hear you had a brilliant opening at the St James's. Ever yours   OSCAR WILDE

To the Editor of the Daily Telegraph[4]

2 February 1891   *London*

Sir, With reference to the interesting article on men's dress and the fashions for next season that appears in today's issue of your paper, will you allow me to point out that the costume worn now by Mr Wyndham[5] in *London Assurance* might be taken as the basis for a new departure, not in the style,

---

[1] Stage name of George Alexander Gibb Samson, English actor and manager (1858–1918). He acted with Irving from 1881 with one brief interval until 1889, when he entered into management on his own. His tenancy of the St James's Theatre began on 31 January 1891 (with *Sunlight and Shadow* by R. C. Carton) and lasted until his death. He was knighted in 1911.

[2] *Lady Windermere's Fan.*

[3] American actor-manager (1838–91). The play seems to have opened on Wednesday, 21 January 1891 (although Wilde clearly thought it was a week later). It ended its run on 14 February. Wilde tried to interest Irving in a London production of it.

[4] This letter was published in the *Daily Telegraph* of 3 February 1891 under the heading FASHIONS IN DRESS. In a covering letter to Edward Lawson Wilde had written: "I don't wish to sign my name, though I am afraid everybody will know who the writer is: one's style is one's signature always." Lawson (1833–1916) was principal proprietor and in practice editor of the *Daily Telegraph*. Born Edward Levy, he assumed the surname of Lawson in 1875, was created a baronet in 1892 and the first Lord Burnham in 1903.   [5] See note 1, p. 126.

but in the colour of modern evening dress.[1] The costume in question belongs to 1840 or 1841, and its charm resides in the fact that the choice of the colour of the coat is left to the taste and fancy and inclination of the wearer. Freedom in such selection of colour is a necessary condition of variety and individualism of costume, and the uniform black that is worn now, though valuable at a dinner-party, where it serves to isolate and separate women's dresses, to frame them as it were, still is dull and tedious and depressing in itself, and makes the aspect of club-life and men's dinners monotonous and uninteresting. The little note of individualism that makes dress delightful can only be attained nowadays by the colour and treatment of the flower one wears. This is a great pity. The colour of the coat should be entirely for the good taste of the wearer to decide. This would give pleasure, and produce charming variety of colour effects in modern life.

Another important point in Mr Wyndham's very graceful and elegant costume is that the decorative value of buttons is recognised. At present we all have more than a dozen useless buttons on our evening coats, and by always keeping them black and of the same colour as the rest of the costume we prevent them being in any way beautiful. Now, when a thing is useless it should be made beautiful, otherwise it has no reason for existing at all. Buttons should be either gilt, as in Mr Wyndham's costume, or of paste, or enamel, or inlaid metal, or any other material that is capable of being artistically treated. The handsome effect produced by servants' liveries is almost entirely due to the buttons they wear.

Nor would these suggested changes be in any way violent, or abrupt, or revolutionary; or calculated to excite terror in the timid, or rage in the dull, or fury in the honest Philistine. For the dress of 1840 is really the same in design and form as ours. Of course, the sleeves are tighter and the cuffs turn each over them, as sleeves should be and as cuffs should do. The trousers, also, are tighter than the present fashion, but the general cut of the dress is the same. It consists, as ours does, of tail-coat, open waistcoat, and trousers.

Two other points may be noticed. The first is that the use of a frill to the shirt prevents the tediousness of a flat polished surface of stiff linen— breaks it up very pleasantly in fact. Modern English evening shirts are too monotonous. In France—or perhaps I should say in Paris—shirts are made much more charming than with us. The second point is the beauty and utility of the cloaks in which Mr Wyndham and Mr Arthur Bourchier make their appearance. They are dark in colour, as, on the whole, cloaks in constant service should be. Their folds are ample, picturesque and comforting. Their bright-coloured linings are delightful, and fanciful and gay. Their capes give warmth and suggest dignity and serve to make the lines of the cloaks richer and more complex. A cloak is an admirable thing. Our nearest approach to it is the Inverness cape, which, when its wings are

[1] Dion Boucicault's comedy *London Assurance* (originally produced in 1841) had been revived at the Criterion Theatre on 27 November 1890, with Charles Wyndham, Arthur Bourchier, Cyril Maude, Mary Moore and Mrs Bernard Beere in the cast.

lined with black satin, is very charming in its way. Still it has, though not sleeves, yet sleeve openings. A cloak can be put on, or thrown off, far more easily. A cloak is also warmer, and can be wrapped round one, if there is a chill wind. We must wear cloaks with lovely linings. Otherwise we shall be very incomplete.

The coat, then, of next season, will be an exquisite colour-note, and have also a great psychological value. It will emphasise the serious and thoughtful side of a man's character. One will be able to discern a man's views of life by the colour he selects. The colour of the coat will be symbolic. It will be part of the wonderful symbolistic movement in modern art. The imagination will concentrate itself on the waistcoat. Waistcoats will show whether a man can admire poetry or not. That will be very valuable. Over the shirt-front Fancy will preside. By a single glance one will be able to detect the tedious. How the change is to be brought about it is not difficult to see. In Paris the Duc de Morny has altered the colour of coats.[1] But the English dislike individualism. Nothing but a resolution on the subject passed solemnly by the House of Commons will do with us. Surely there are some amongst our legislators who are capable of taking a serious interest in serious things? They cannot all be absorbed in the county-court collection of tithes.[2] I sincerely hope that a motion of some kind will be brought forward on the question, and that the First Lord of the Treasury will assign some day for discussion of a topic that is of really national importance. When the motion has been agreed to, servants will, of course, be asked to dress as their masters do now. As a slight compensation to them, their wages should be increased, if not doubled.

Of the moral value and influence of such a charming costume I think I had better say nothing. The fact is that when Mr Wyndham and Mr Arthur Bourchier appear in their delightful dresses they have been behaving very badly. At least Mr Arthur Bourchier has, and Mr Wyndham's conduct seems to me to justify some moral censure at any rate. But if one is to behave badly, it is better to be bad in a becoming dress than in one that is unbecoming, and it is only fair to add that at the end of the play Mr Wyndham accepts his lecture with a dignity and courtesy of manner that can only result from the habit of wearing delightful clothes. I am, sir, your obedient servant   O.

To Stéphane Mallarmé[3]

Mercredi [Postmark 25 February 1891]   *Hôtel de l'Athénée [Paris]*

Cher Maître, Comment dois-je vous remercier pour la gracieuse façon avec laquelle vous m'avez présenté la magnifique symphonie en prose que vous

---

[1] Auguste-Charles-Louis, Duc de Morny (1859–1920), French sportsman and dandy. Son of the famous Duc, who was a bastard half-brother of Napoleon III.

[2] The Tithe Rent-Charge Recovery Bill was then being considered in Committee by the House of Commons.

[3] French symbolist poet (1842–98). He earned his living as a schoolmaster, but

a inspiré les mélodies du génie du grand poète celtique, Edgar Allan Poe.[1]
En Angleterre nous avons de la prose et de la poésie, mais la prose française et la poésie dans les mains d'un maître tel que vous deviennent une et la même chose.

Le privilège de connaître l'auteur de *L'Après-midi d'un Faune* est on ne peut plus flatteur, mais de trouver en lui l'accueil que vous m'avez montré est en vérité inoubliable.

Ainsi, cher maître, veuillez agréer l'assurance de ma haute et très parfaite considération   OSCAR WILDE

*To Cyril Wilde

Tuesday, 3 March [*1891*]   *Hôtel de l'Athénée, 15 Rue Scribe* [*Paris*]

My dearest Cyril, I send you a letter to tell you I am much better. I go every day and drive in a beautiful forest called the Bois de Boulogne, and in the evening I dine with my friend, and sit out afterwards at little tables and see the carriages drive by. Tonight I go to visit a great poet, who has given me a wonderful book about a Raven. I will bring you and Vyvyan back some chocolates when I return.

I hope you are taking great care of dear Mamma. Give her my love and kisses, and also love and kisses to Vyvyan and yourself. Your loving Papa
                                        OSCAR WILDE

To Coulson Kernahan[2]

[*Postmark 7 March 1891*]   *Hôtel de l'Athénée, Rue Scribe, Paris*

My dear Kernahan, Thank you for your charming letter. I have been very ill, and unable to correct my proofs, but have sent them now.

I have changed my mind about correcting the passage about temptation. One can't pull a work of art about without spoiling it. And after all it is merely Luther's *Pecca Fortiter*[3] put dramatically into the lips of a character. Just explain this to Ward & Lock. I am responsible for the book: they are not. If they really feel deeply about it I will try in the revise and invent something else, but don't tell them I said so. It has bothered me terribly, their suggesting changes, etc. One can't do it.

ived only for poetry. His Paris flat in the Rue de Rome became a centre of literary talk and inspiration.
[1] *Le Corbeau*, Mallarmé's prose translation of Poe's poem "The Raven" (1875, second edition 1889).
[2] English author and journalist (1858–1943). He was at this time and for many years literary adviser to Messrs Ward, Lock, who published *The Picture of Dorian Gray* in April 1891. Wilde received £125 on account of a 10 per cent royalty.
[3] "*Esto peccator et pecca fortiter*" (Be a sinner and sin in earnest). Martin Luther, in a letter to Melanchthon (*Lutheri Epistolae*, Jena, 1556, i, 345).

The preface will be as it stands in the *Fortnightly* with a few corrections. I will send it to you tomorrow.[1]

Do you think I should add to the preface the definition of "morbid" and "unhealthy" art I give in the *Fortnightly* for February? The one on morbidity is really good.[2]

Will you also look after my "wills" and "shalls" in proof. I am Celtic in my use of these words, not English.

As soon as I get the revise, and pass it, the book may go to press, but I must pass it first. *This is essential.* Please tell them so.

You are excellent on Rossetti. I read you with delight.[3] Your sincere friend   OSCAR WILDE

To Elizabeth Robins[4]

[*Late March 1891*]   *16 Tite Street*

Dear Miss Robins, I have been very ill—overworked at any rate—and away for rest. But now that I am back I should very much like to have the pleasure of calling on you, and will do so at four o'clock tomorrow.

---

[1] The preface to *The Picture of Dorian Gray* (which consists of twenty-five aphorisms) appeared for the first time (as twenty-three aphorisms) in the March 1891 issue of the *Fortnightly Review*.

[2] In his essay *The Soul of Man Under Socialism* (first published in the February 1891 *Fortnightly*) Wilde gave the following definition of morbidity:

> What is morbidity but a mood of emotion or a mode of thought that one cannot express? The public are all morbid, because the public can never find expression for anything. The artist is never morbid. He expresses everything. He stands outside his subject, and through its medium produces incomparable and artistic effects. To call an artist morbid because he deals with morbidity as his subject-matter is as silly as if one called Shakespeare mad because he wrote *King Lear*.

[3] Kernahan's essay "A Note on Rossetti" first appeared as "Rossetti and the Moralists" in the *Fortnightly Review* for March 1891 and was reprinted in his book *Sorrow and Song* (1894).

[4] American actress and writer (1862–1952). She had acted in America with Edwin Booth, Lawrence Barrett and James O'Neill (father of Eugene O'Neill). In 1885 she married a young American actor called George Richmond Parks, who died in 1887. She came to England in 1888 and recorded the following impression of Wilde in her diary: "His smooth-shaven, rather fat face, rather weak; the frequent smile showed long crowded teeth, a rather interesting presence in spite of certain objectionable points." Many years later, in an appreciation she wrote:

> He was then at the height of his powers and fame and I utterly unknown on this side of the Atlantic. I could do nothing for him; he could and did do everything in his power for me.
>
> He introduced me to Beerbohm Tree and others, encouraged me to cancel an American engagement and try my fortunes here. He warned me against a shady theatre manager, advised me about a reliable agent and solicitor, when I needed their help, and suggested plays for matinée production to introduce the unknown actress to London managers and public.
>
> He was generous, too, in coming to see me act; and in sending or giving afterwards his valuable opinion on play, production and acting.

I should much like to be present at *Hedda Gabler*.¹ Perhaps your acting manager will kindly reserve a stall for me. It is a most interesting play, nor could there be any [better] exponent of its subtlety and tragedy than yourself. Believe me, truly yours   OSCAR WILDE

*To Arthur Conan Doyle²

[? *April 1891*]

Between me and life there is a mist of words always. I throw probability out of the window for the sake of a phrase, and the chance of an epigram makes me desert truth. Still I do aim at making a work of art, and I am really delighted that you think my treatment subtle and artistically good. The newspapers seem to me to be written by the prurient for the Philistine. I cannot understand how they can treat *Dorian Gray* as immoral. My difficulty was to keep the inherent moral subordinate to the artistic and dramatic effect, and it still seems to me that the moral is too obvious.

*To R. Clegg³

[? *April 1891*]   *16 Tite Street*

My dear Sir, Art is useless because its aim is simply to create a mood. It is not meant to instruct, or to influence action in any way. It is superbly

¹ The first production of Ibsen's play in English was at the Vaudeville Theatre on 20 April 1891, with Elizabeth Robins in the title-rôle. Wilde visited the play again on 24 April, sending a telegram in which he referred to her performance as "a real masterpiece of art."

² (1859–1930). When he published this fragment in his *Memories and Adventures* (1924) Conan Doyle introduced it with these words:

Stoddart, the American, proved to be an excellent fellow, and had two others to dinner. They were Gill, a very entertaining Irish M.P., and Oscar Wilde, who was already famous as the champion of aestheticism. It was indeed a golden evening for me. Wilde to my surprise had read *Micah Clarke* and was enthusiastic about it, so that I did not feel a complete outsider.

The result of the evening was that both Wilde and I promised to write books for *Lippincott's Magazine*—Wilde's contribution was *The Picture of Dorian Gray*, a book which is surely upon a high moral plane, while I wrote *The Sign of Four*, in which Holmes made his second appearance.

When his little book came out I wrote to say what I thought of it. His letter is worth reproducing, as showing the true Wilde. I omit the early part in which he comments on my own work in too generous terms.

Joseph Marshall Stoddart (1845–1921) worked for J. B. Lippincott & Co and for a time published under his own name. Wilde met him on his American tour and he published *Rose Leaf and Apple Leaf* at Wilde's prompting (see note 2, p. 45). Thomas Patrick Gill (1858–1931) was an Irish Nationalist M.P. who had American connections in journalism.

³ Unidentified. The last of the aphorisms which form the preface to *The Picture of Dorian Gray* is "All art is quite useless."

sterile, and the note of its pleasure is sterility. If the contemplation of a work of art is followed by activity of any kind, the work is either of a very second-rate order, or the spectator has failed to realise the complete artistic impression.

A work of art is useless as a flower is useless. A flower blossoms for its own joy. We gain a moment of joy by looking at it. That is all that is to be said about our relations to flowers. Of course man may sell the flower, and so make it useful to him, but this has nothing to do with the flower. It is not part of its essence. It is accidental. It is a misuse. All this I fear is very obscure. But the subject is a long one. Truly yours

OSCAR WILDE

*To the Editor of the Pall Mall Gazette[1]

27 August [*1891*]   *Albemarle Chambers, Piccadilly*

Sir, I have read with much astonishment the letter signed "S" that appears in your issue of this evening, and hope that you will allow me to assure the writer of the letter and the public in general that there is no truth whatsoever in the statement made in one of my essays that "Providence and Mr Walter Besant have exhausted the obvious." The public need be under no misapprehension. One has merely to read the ordinary English newspapers and the ordinary English novels of our day to become conscious of the fact that it is only the obvious that occurs, and only the obvious that is written about. Both facts are much to be regretted. I remain, sir, your obedient servant   OSCAR WILDE

*To Pierre Louÿs[2]

28 November 1891   *29 Boulevard des Capucines, Paris*

Cher Monsieur Louÿs, J'accepte avec le plus vif plaisir la gracieuse et charmante invitation que vous et M. Gide[3] ont eu la bonté de m'adresser.

---

[1] An anonymous review of Besant's novel *Armorel of Lyonnesse* in the *Pall Mall Gazette* of 26 August had described the book as "a masterpiece of dull extravagance" and disputed Wilde's epigram in "The Critic as Artist," maintaining that Besant was "all for the far-fetched and unnatural." This provoked a long letter from "S," who defended both Wilde and Besant, remarking that "Mr Wilde . . . was referring to Mr Besant's novels of East-End life . . . In those stories Mr Besant was splendidly obvious." Wilde's letter was published on August 29.

[2] French poet and writer (1870–1925). In 1889 he founded the review *La Conque*, to which Swinburne, Leconte de Lisle, Heredia, Verlaine, Mallarmé, Maeterlinck, André Gide and Moréas were contributors. His first book, *Astarte*, was published in 1892.

[3] André Paul Guillaume Gide (1869–1951), the French writer, appears to have met Wilde for the first time on 27 November, when he wrote to Paul Valéry: *Quelques lignes de quelqu'un d'abruti, qui ne lit plus, qui n'écrit plus, qui ne dort*

Vous m'indiquerez, n'est-ce-pas, l'endroit et l'heure.

Je garde un souvenir délicieux de notre petit déjeuner de l'autre jour, et de l'acceuil sympathique que vous m'avez fait.

J'espère que les jeunes poètes de France m'aimeront un jour, comme moi à ce moment je les aime.

La poésie française a toujours été parmi mes maîtresses les plus adorées, et je serai très content de croire que parmi les poètes de France je trouverai de véritables amis.

Veuillez présenter à M. Gide l'assurance de mes sentiments les plus distingués. Veuillez, cher Monsieur Louÿs, l'agréer   OSCAR WILDE[1]

*To the Editor of the Speaker

[*Early December 1891*]   [*29*] *Boulevard des Capucines, Paris*

Sir, I have just, at a price that for any other English sixpenny paper I would have considered exorbitant, purchased a copy of the *Speaker* at one of the charming kiosks that decorate Paris; institutions, by the way, that I think we should at once introduce into London. The kiosk is a delightful object, and, when illuminated at night from within, as lovely as a fantastic Chinese lantern, especially when the transparent advertisements are from the clever pencil of M. Chéret.[2] In London we have merely the ill-clad newsvendors, whose voice, in spite of the admirable efforts of the Royal College of Music to make England a really musical nation, is always out of tune, and whose rags, badly designed and badly worn, merely emphasise a painful note of uncomely misery, without conveying that impression of picturesqueness which is the only thing that makes the spectacle of the poverty of others at all bearable.

It is not, however, about the establishment of kiosks in London that I wish to write to you, though I am of opinion that it is a thing that the County Council should at once take in hand. The object of my letter is to correct a statement made in a paragraph of your interesting paper.

The writer of the paragraph in question states that the decorative designs

---

plus, ni ne mange, ni ne pense—mais court avec ou sans Louÿs dans les cafés ou les salons serrer des mains et faire des sourires. Heredia, Régnier, Merrill, l'esthète Oscar Wilde, ô admirable, admirable celui-là.

According to his letters he saw Wilde almost every day till 15 December, but the pages in his journal covering those days have been torn out.

[1] Louys's answer is dated 29 November and reads:

Cher Maître, Ce sera, si vous le voulez bien, au café d'Harcourt, place de la Sorbonne, et vers huit heures du soir. Permettez-moi de vous remercier de l'honneur et du plaisir que vous nous faites en acceptant.

Veuillez agréer, cher maître, l'assurance nouvelle de notre affectueux respect.
                                                                PIERRE LOUŸS

[2] Jules Chéret (1836–1932) was a leading French poster-artist. He lived in England 1859–66.

that make lovely my book *A House of Pomegranates*,[1] are by the hand of Mr Shannon, while the delicate dreams that separate and herald each story are by Mr Ricketts. The contrary is the case. Mr Shannon is the drawer of dreams, and Mr Ricketts is the subtle and fantastic decorator. Indeed, it is to Mr Ricketts that the entire decorative design of the book is due, from the selection of the type and the placing of the ornamentation, to the completely beautiful cover that encloses the whole. The writer of the paragraph goes on to state that he does not "like the cover." This is, no doubt, to be regretted, though it is not a matter of much importance, as there are only two people in the world whom it is absolutely necessary that the cover should please. One is Mr Ricketts, who designed it, the other is myself, whose book it binds. We both admire it immensely! The reason, however, that your critic gives for his failure to gain from the cover any impression of beauty seems to me to show a lack of artistic instinct on his part, which I beg you will allow me to try to correct.

He complains that a portion of the design on the left-hand side of the cover reminds him of an Indian club with a house-painter's brush on top of it, while a portion of the design on the right-hand side suggests to him the idea of "a chimney-pot hat with a sponge in it." Now, I do not for a moment dispute that these are the real impressions your critic received. It is the spectator, and the mind of the spectator, as I pointed out in the preface to *The Picture of Dorian Gray*, that art really mirrors. What I want to indicate is this: the artistic beauty of the cover of my book resides in the delicate tracing, arabesques, and massing of many coral-red lines on a ground of white ivory, the colour-effect culminating in certain high gilt notes, and being made still more pleasurable by the overlapping band of moss-green cloth that holds the book together.

What the gilt notes suggest, what imitative parallel may be found to them in that chaos that is termed Nature, is a matter of no importance. They may suggest, as they do sometimes to me, peacocks and pomegranates and splashing fountains of gold water, or, as they do to your critic, sponges and Indian clubs and chimney-pot hats. Such suggestions and evocations have nothing whatsoever to do with the aesthetic quality

---

[1] *A House of Pomegranates*, Wilde's second collection of fairy stories (containing "The Young King," "The Birthday of the Infanta," "The Fisherman and his Soul," and "The Star-child"), dedicated to his wife, was published by Osgood McIlvaine & Co in November 1891. The paragraph in the *Speaker* of November 28 (apparently the book's first notice in the press) reads as follows:

We do not like the outside of the cover of Mr Oscar Wilde's *House of Pomegranates* (Osgood). The Indian club with a house-painter's brush on the top which passes muster for a peacock, and the chimney-pot hat with a sponge in it, which is meant to represent a basket containing a pomegranate, or a fountain, or something of that kind, are grotesque, but not ideally so. The inside of the cover, however, with its olive sheaves of corn falling apart, its fluttering quails, and crawling snails, delights the eye. So do the pictures and the type and the paper. Mr Ricketts has learned the art of drawing dreams and visions, and Mr Shannon can make decorative designs full of charming detail. We can well believe that the book is as delightful as it looks.

Wilde's letter appeared on 5 December.

and value of the design. A thing in Nature becomes much lovelier if it reminds us of a thing in Art, but a thing in Art gains no real beauty through reminding us of a thing in Nature. The primary aesthetic impression of a work of art borrows nothing from recognition or resemblance. These belong to a later and less perfect stage of apprehension. Properly speaking, they are not part of a real aesthetic impression at all, and the constant preoccupation with subject-matter that characterises nearly all our English art-criticism is what makes our art-criticism, especially as regards literature, so sterile, so profitless, so much beside the mark, and of such curiously little account.

I remain, sir, your obedient servant, OSCAR WILDE

*To the Editor of the Pall Mall Gazette

[*Early December 1891*]   *Boulevard des Capucines, Paris*

Sir, I have just had sent to me from London a copy of the *Pall Mall Gazette* containing a review of my book *A House of Pomegranates*.[1] The writer of this review makes a certain suggestion about my book which I beg you will allow me to correct at once.

He starts by asking an extremely silly question, and that is, whether or not I have written this book for the purpose of giving pleasure to the British child. Having expressed grave doubts on this subject, a subject on which I cannot conceive any fairly-educated person having any doubts at all, he proceeds, apparently quite seriously, to make the extremely limited vocabulary at the disposal of the British child the standard by which the prose of an artist is to be judged! Now in building this *House of Pomegranates* I had about as much intention of pleasing the British child as I had of pleasing the British public. Mamilius[2] is as entirely delightful as Caliban is entirely detestable, but neither the standard of Mamilius nor the standard of Caliban is my standard. No artist recognises any standard of beauty but that which is suggested by his own temperament. The artist seeks to realise in a certain material his immaterial idea of beauty, and thus to transform an idea into an ideal. That is the way an artist makes things. That is why an artist makes things. The artist has no other object in making things. Does your reviewer imagine that Mr Shannon, for instance, whose delicate and lovely illustrations he confesses himself quite unable to see, draws for the purpose of giving information to the blind?[3]

I remain, sir, your obedient servant, OSCAR WILDE

[1] This appeared on 30 November 1891, and Wilde's letter on 11 December.
[2] The boy-prince in *A Winter's Tale*.
[3] In fact some of Shannon's illustrations, which were reproduced by a new process that failed, were and are almost invisible.

To Edmond de Goncourt[1]

Cher Monsieur de Goncourt, Quoique la base intellectuelle de mon esthétique soit la Philosophie de l'Irréalité, ou peut-être à cause de cela, je vous prie de me permettre une petite rectification à vos notes sur la conversation où je vous ai parlé de notre cher et noble poète anglais M. Algernon Swinburne et que vous avez insérés dans ces Mémoires qui ont, non seulement pour vos amis, mais pour le public tout entier, une valeur psychologique si haute.

Les soirées qu'on a eu le bonheur de passer avec un grand écrivain comme vous l'êtes sont inoubliables, et voilà pourquoi j'en ai gardé un souvenir très précis. Je suis surpris que vous en ayez reçu une impression assez différente.

Vous proposiez ce matin d'extraire l'hydrogène de l'air pour faire de notre atmosphère une terrible machine de destruction.[2] Ce serait un chef-d'œuvre, sinon de science, au moins d'art. Mais extraire de ma conversation sur M. Swinburne une sensation qui pourrait le blesser, voilà qui m'a causé quelque peine. Sans doute c'était de ma faute. On peut adorer une langue sans bien la parler, comme on peut aimer une femme sans la connaître. Français de sympathie, je suis Irlandais de race, et les Anglais m'ont condamné à parler le langage de Shakespeare.

Vous avez dit que je représentais M. Swinburne comme un fanfaron du vice. Cela étonnerait beaucoup le poète, qui dans sa maison de campagne mène une vie bien austère, entièrement consacrée à l'art et à la littérature.

Voici ce que j'ai voulu dire. Il y a aujourd'hui plus de vingt-cinq ans, M. Swinburne a publié ses *Poèmes et Ballades*, une des œuvres qui ont

---

[1] French diarist, novelist, historian and collector (1822–96). Wilde first met him in Paris in 1883. In 1891 Goncourt's journal was being serialised in the *Echo de Paris*, and on 17 December 1891 there appeared in the entry for 21 April 1883:

> *Le Poète anglais Wilde me disait, ce soir, que le seul Anglais qui avait lu Balzac à l'heure actuelle était Swinburne. Et ce Swinburne, il me le montre comme un fanfaron du vice, qui avait tout fait pour faire croire ses concitoyens à sa pédérastie, à sa bestialité, sans être le moins du monde pédéraste ni bestialitaire.*

Wilde's letter of protest was printed in the *Echo de Paris* of 19 December with these prefatory words:

> *Dans son très intéressant 'Journal,' notre éminent collaborateur et ami, Edmond de Goncourt, avait incidemment relaté une conversation avec le poète anglais Swinburne. Une des plus curieuses personnalités de la littérature anglaise contemporaine, l'esthète Oscar Wilde, qui est en ce moment notre hôte, et le 'great event' des salons littéraires parisiens, lui adresse à ce sujet la très curieuse lettre qui suit. M. O. Wilde s'y excuse de ne point parler suffisamment notre langue, on verra du moins qu'il l'écrit en toute élégance.*

When the 1883 journal was published (as volume vi) in 1892 the whole of the second sentence about Swinburne was omitted, as was Goncourt's description of Wilde (entry of 5 May 1883) as "*cet individu au sexe douteux, au langage de cabotin, aux récits blagueurs.*"

[2] Goncourt referred to this notion in his journal for 25 August 1883.

marqué le plus profondément dans notre littérature une ère nouvelle.
Dans Shakespeare, et dans ses contemporains Webster et Ford, il y a
des cris de nature. Dans l'œuvre de Swinburne, on rencontre pour la
première fois le cri de la chair tourmentée par le désir et le souvenir, la
jouissance et le remords, la fécondité et la stérilité. Le public anglais,
comme d'ordinaire hypocrite, prude et philistin, n'a pas su trouver l'art
dans l'œuvre d'art: il y a cherché l'homme. Comme il confond toujours
l'homme avec ses créations, il pense que pour créer Hamlet il faut être un
peu mélancholique, pour imaginer Lear absolument fou. Ainsi on a fait
autour de M. Swinburne une légende d'ogre et de mangeur d'enfants.
M. Swinburne, aristocrate de race et artiste de tempérament, n'a fait que
rire de ces absurdités. Une telle attitude me semble éloignée de celle
qu'aurait un fanfaron de vice.

Pardonnez-moi cette simple rectification; je suis sûr, puisque vous
aimiez les poètes et que les poètes vous aiment, que vous serez heureux de
la recevoir. J'espère que lorsque j'aurai l'honneur de vous rencontrer de
nouveau, vous trouverez ma manière de m'exprimer en français moins
obscure que le 21 avril 1883.

Veuillez agréer, cher Monsieur de Goncourt, l'assurance de toute mon
admiration.   OSCAR WILDE

To Pierre Louÿs

[*December 1891*]   [*Paris*]

Mon cher ami, Voilà le drame de *Salomé*.[1] Ce n'est pas encore fini ou
même corrigé, mais ça donne l'idée de la *construction*, du motif et du
mouvement dramatique. Ici et là, il y a des lacunes, mais l'idée du drame
est claire.

Je suis encore très enrhumé et je me porte assez mal. Mais je serai tout
à fait bien lundi et je vous attendrai à une heure chez Mignon pour
déjeuner, vous et M. Fort.[2]

Je vous remercie beaucoup, mon cher ami, pour l'intérêt que vous
daignez prendre à mon drame. À toi   OSCAR

[1] Wilde had certainly begun work on *Salome* by 27 October 1891, when Wilfrid
Blunt recorded breakfasting with George Curzon, Wilde and Willy Peel: "Oscar
told us he was writing a play in French to be acted in the Français. He is ambitious
of being a French Academician. We promised to go to the first representation,
George Curzon as Prime Minister." Three manuscripts of *Salome* exist, all in
Wilde's hand and all written in French. The third and apparently final draft
was the one here submitted to Louÿs, and contains his interlinear corrections and
suggested improvements. Where these were on points of grammar Wilde adopted
them, but most of Louÿs's other remarks he deleted or ignored. There may however have been still another intermediate version, since two other French writers,
the Symbolist Adolphe Retté (1863–1910) and Stuart Merrill (see note 2, p. 134),
helped to some extent before Louÿs was brought in. Another French Symbolist
Marcel Schwob (1867–1905), to whom Wilde dedicated *The Sphinx* (1894), read
the proofs and probably made two corrections. Wilde often accented *Salome*, but
not always, and I have omitted the accent except when he was writing in French.
[2] Paul Fort, French poet (1872–1960). Founded the Théâtre d'Art 1890.

To George Alexander[1]

[*Mid-February 1892*]   *Hotel Albemarle*

With regard to the speech of Mrs Erlynne at the end of Act II, you must remember that until Wednesday night Mrs Erlynne rushed off the stage leaving Lord Augustus in a state of bewilderment. Such are the stage directions in the play. When the alteration in the business was made I don't know, but I should have been informed at once. It came on me with the shock of a surprise. I don't in any degree object to it. It is a different effect, that is all. It does not alter the psychological lines of the play. . . . To reproach me on Wednesday for not having written a speech for a situation on which I was not consulted and of which I was quite unaware was, of course, a wrong thing to do. With regard to the new speech written yesterday, personally I think it adequate.[2] I want Mrs Erlynne's whole scene with Lord Augustus to be a "tornado" scene, and the thing to go as quickly as possible. However, I will think over the speech, and talk it over with Miss Terry. Had I been informed of the change I would of course have had more time and when, through illness caused by the worry and anxiety I have gone through at the theatre, I was unable to attend the rehearsals on Monday and Tuesday, I should have been informed by letter.

With regard to your other suggestion about the disclosure of the secret of the play in the second act, had I intended to let out the secret, which is the element of suspense and curiosity, a quality so essentially dramatic, I would have written the play on entirely different lines. I would have made Mrs Erlynne a vulgar horrid woman and struck out the incident of the fan. The audience must not know till the last act that the woman Lady Windermere proposed to strike with her fan was her own mother. The note would be too harsh, too horrible. When they learn it, it is after Lady Windermere has left her husband's house to seek the protection of another man, and their interest is concentrated on Mrs Erlynne, to whom dramatically speaking belongs the last act. Also it would destroy the dramatic wonder excited by the incident of Mrs Erlynne taking the letter and opening it and sacrificing herself in the third act. If they knew Mrs Erlynne was the mother, there would be no surprise in her sacrifice—it would be expected. But in my play the sacrifice is dramatic and unexpected. The cry with which Mrs Erlynne flies into the other room on hearing Lord Augustus's voice, the wild pathetic cry of self-preservation,

[1] *Lady Windermere's Fan* was first produced at the St James's Theatre on 20 February 1892, with Alexander as Lord Windermere, Marion Terry as Mrs Erlynne, H. H. Vincent as Lord Augustus Lorton, and Lily Hanbury as Lady Windermere. It ran until 29 July, was then taken on tour, and returned to the St James's on 31 October. This letter was clearly written during rehearsal.

[2] The text of this letter down to "adequate" is taken from *Sir George Alexander and the St James's Theatre* by A. E. W. Mason (1935), the rest from the original manuscript. There is no proof that these two fragments come from one letter, but it seems probable that they do.

"Then it is I who am lost!" would be repulsive coming from the lips of one known to be the mother by the audience. It seems natural and is very dramatic coming from one who seems to be an adventuress, and who while anxious to save Lady Windermere thinks of her own safety when a crisis comes. Also it would destroy the last act: and the chief merit of my last act is to me the fact that it does not contain, as most plays do, the explanation of what the audience knows already, but that it is the sudden explanation of what the audience desires to know, followed immediately by the revelation of a character as yet untouched by literature.

The question you touch on about the audience misinterpreting the relations of Lord Windermere and Mrs Erlynne depends entirely on the acting. In the first act Windermere must convince the audience of his absolute sincerity in what he says to his wife. The lines show this. He does not say to his wife "there is nothing in this woman's past life that is against her;" he says openly, "Mrs Erlynne years ago sinned. She now wants to get back. Help her to get back." The suggestions his wife makes he doesn't treat trivially and say, "Oh, there is nothing in it. We're merely friends, that is all." He rejects them with horror at the suggestion.

At the ball his manner to her is cold, courteous but somewhat hard— not the manner of a lover. When they think they are alone Windermere uses no word of tenderness or love. He shows that the woman has a hold on him, but one he loathes and almost writhes under.

What is this hold? That is the play.

I have entered at great length into this matter because every suggestion you have made to me I have always carefully and intellectually considered. Otherwise it would have been sufficient to have said, what I am sure you yourself will on reflection recognise, and that is that a work of art wrought out on definite lines, and elaborated from one definite artistic standpoint, cannot be suddenly altered. It would make every line meaningless, and rob each situation of its value. An equally good play could be written in which the audience would know beforehand who Mrs Erlynne really was, but it would require completely different dialogue, and completely different situations. I have built my house on a certain foundation, and this foundation cannot be altered. I can say no more.

With regards to matters personal between us, I trust that tonight will be quite harmonious and peaceful. After the play is produced and before I leave for the South of France where I am obliged to go for my health, it might be wise for us to have at any rate one meeting for the purpose of explanation. Truly yours   OSCAR WILDE

*To Richard Le Gallienne[1]

[*Circa 18 February 1892*]

Dear Poet, Here are two stalls for my play. Come, and bring your poem to sit beside you.

[1] Le Gallienne's "poem" was his wife, Mildred Lee, whom he had married in October 1891. She died in 1894.

*To the Editor of the St James's Gazette

26 February 1892[1]

Sir, Allow me to correct a statement put forward in your issue of this evening, to the effect that I have made a certain alteration in my play in consequence of the criticism of some journalists who write very recklessly and very foolishly in the papers about dramatic art. This statement is entirely untrue, and grossly ridiculous.

The facts are as follows. On last Saturday night, after the play was over, and the author, cigarette in hand, had delivered a delightful and immortal speech, I had the pleasure of entertaining at supper a small number of personal friends: and, as none of them was older than myself, I naturally listened to their artistic views with attention and pleasure. The opinions of the old on matters of Art are, of course, of no value whatsoever. The artistic instincts of the young are invariably fascinating; and I am bound to state that all my friends, without exception, were of opinion that the psychological interest of the second act would be greatly increased by the disclosure of the actual relationship existing between Lady Windermere and Mrs Erlynne—an opinion, I may add, that had previously been strongly held and urged by Mr Alexander. As to those of us who do not look on a play as a mere question of pantomime and clowning, psychological interest is everything, I determined consequently to make a change in the precise moment of revelation. This determination, however, was entered into long before I had the opportunity of studying the culture, courtesy, and critical faculty displayed in such papers as the *Referee, Reynolds,* and the *Sunday Sun.*

When criticism becomes in England a real art, as it should be, and when none but those of artistic instinct and artistic cultivation is allowed to write about works of art, artists will no doubt read criticisms with a certain amount of intellectual interest. As things are at present, the criticisms of ordinary newspapers are of no interest whatsoever, except in so far as they display in its crudest form the extraordinary Bœotianism of a country that has produced some Athenians, and in which other Athenians have come to dwell.

I am, sir, your obedient servant   OSCAR WILDE

To Robert Ross

[? *May-June 1892*]   *Royal Palace Hotel, Kensington*

My dearest Bobbie, Bosie[2] has insisted on stopping here for sandwiches. He is quite like a narcissus—so white and gold. I will come either Wednesday or Thursday night to your rooms. Send me a line. Bosie is so tired:

---

[1] Published on 27 February.

[2] The nickname (a contraction of Boysie) by which Lord Alfred Douglas was known to his family and friends from early childhood.

he lies like a hyacinth on the sofa, and I worship him.
You dear boy. Ever yours   OSCAR

To Will Rothenstein[1]

[*Early July 1892*]   *51 Kaiser-Friedrich's Promenade, Bad-Homburg*[2]
My dear Will, The *Gaulois*, the *Echo de Paris*, and the *Pall Mall* have all
had interviews.[3] I hardly know what new thing there is to say. The
licenser of plays is nominally the Lord Chamberlain, but really a commonplace official—in the present case a Mr Pigott,[4] who panders to the vulgarity and hypocrisy of the English people, by licensing every low farce
and vulgar melodrama. He even allows the stage to be used for the purpose
of the caricaturing of the personalities of artists, and at the same moment
when he prohibited *Salome*, he licensed a burlesque of *Lady Windermere's
Fan* in which an actor dressed up like me and imitated my voice and
manner!!![5]
The curious thing is this: all the arts are free in England, except the
actor's art; it is held by the Censor that the stage degrades and that actors
desecrate fine subjects, so the Censor prohibits not the publication of
Salome but its production. Yet not one single actor has protested against
this insult to the stage—not even Irving, who is always prating about the

[1] English artist (1872–1945). The son of a Bradford wool-merchant, he had
already been a student at the Slade School and was now studying art in Paris. The
first volume of his *Men and Memories* (1931) contains much valuable information
about Wilde and his friends. Rothenstein was knighted 1931.
[2] On 7 July 1892 Constance Wilde wrote to her brother Otho: "Oscar is at Homburg under a régime, getting up at 7.30, going to bed at 10.30, smoking hardly any
cigarettes and being massaged, and of course drinking waters. I only wish I was
there to see it."
[3] About the banning of *Salome*. Rehearsals for its production at the Palace
Theatre, London, with Sarah Bernhardt as Salome, Albert Darmont as Herod, and
costumes by Graham Robertson, were in full swing when the Lord Chamberlain,
towards the end of June, banned the play on the ground that it contained biblical
characters. In at least one of these interviews Wilde was reported as announcing
his departure for France, where it was possible to have works of art produced.
This caused a storm of comment.
[4] Edward F. Smyth Pigott (1826–95) was Examiner of Plays for the Lord
Chamberlain from 1875 to 1895. After his death Bernard Shaw described him as
"a walking compendium of vulgar insular prejudice."
[5] *The Poet and the Puppets*, a musical travesty by Charles Brookfield (1860–1912)
and J. M. Glover (1861–1931), produced at the Comedy Theatre on 19 May 1892,
in which Charles Hawtrey (1858–1923) burlesqued Wilde as "The Poet." Brookfield was the son of Thackeray's friend, and wrote her biography. He also produced
several other books and plays. Although he and Hawtrey were given parts in *An
Ideal Husband*, they are believed to have been the ringleaders in collecting evidence
against Wilde, and they celebrated his conviction by giving a dinner to Lord
Queensberry. Brookfield was made Examiner of Plays 1912.

Art of the Actor. This shows how few actors are artists. All the *dramatic* critics, except Archer of the *World*,[1] agree with the Censor that there should be a censorship over actors and acting! This shows how bad our stage must be, and also shows how Philistine the English journalists are.

I am very ill, dear Will, and can't write any more. Ever yours

OSCAR WILDE

To William Archer

[*Postmark of receipt 22 July 1892*]   *Homburg*

Dear Archer, I am here taking the waters, and have not a copy of *Salome* with me, or would gladly lend it to you, though the refusal of the Licenser to allow the performance of my tragedy was based entirely on his silly vulgar rule about no Biblical *subject* being treated. I don't fancy he ever *read* the play, and if he did, I can hardly fancy even poor Pigott objecting to an artist *treating* his subject in any way he likes. To object to that would be to object to Art entirely—a fine position for a man to adopt, but a little too fine for Pigott, I should imagine.

I want to tell you how gratified I was by your letter in the *P.M.G.*, not merely for its very courteous and generous recognition of my work, but for its strong protest against the contemptible official tyranny that exists in England in reference to the drama. The joy of the ordinary dramatic critic that such tyranny should exist is to me perfectly astounding. I should have thought there would be little pleasure in criticising an art

[1] William Archer, Scottish critic, translator and playwright (1856–1924). Dramatic critic of the *World* (1884–1905). Ibsen's champion and translator in England. His letter of protest against the banning of *Salome*, which was written on 30 June, appeared in the *Pall Mall Gazette* on 1 July 1892, and ran in part:

Sir, Ever since Mr Oscar Wilde told me, a fortnight ago, that his *Salome* had been accepted by Madame Sarah Bernhardt, I have been looking forward, with a certain malign glee, to the inevitable suppression of the play by the Great Irresponsible. Quaint as have been the exploits of that gentleman and his predecessors in the past, the record of the Censorship presents nothing quainter than the present conjuncture. A serious work of art, accepted, studied, and rehearsed by the greatest actress of our time, is peremptorily suppressed, at the very moment when the personality of its author is being held up to ridicule, night after night, on the public stage, with the full sanction and approval of statutory Infallibility. But it is surely unworthy of Mr Wilde's lineage to turn tail and run away from a petty tyranny which lives upon the disunion and apathy of English dramatic authors. Paris does not particularly want Mr Wilde. . . . Here, on the other hand, Mr Wilde's talent is unique. We require it and we appreciate it— those of us, at any rate, who are capable of any sort of artistic appreciation. And especially we require it to aid in the emancipation of art from the stupid meddling of irresponsible officialism. . . .

Before the Select Committee of the House of Commons which sat in 1892 to hear evidence on stage censorship Archer (who was heard on 16 May) was the only witness who advocated the abolition of the censorship. Irving, Clement Scott, Comyns Carr and all the other witnesses spoke strongly in its favour.

where the artist was not free. The whole affair is a great triumph for the Philistine, but only a momentary one. We must abolish the censure. I think we can do it. When I come back I must see you. Ever yours

OSCAR WILDE

*To Lord Alfred Douglas[1]

[? *January 1893*]   [*Babbacombe Cliff*][2]

My Own Boy, Your sonnet[3] is quite lovely, and it is a marvel that those red rose-leaf lips of yours should have been made no less for music of song than for madness of kisses. Your slim gilt soul walks between passion and poetry. I know Hyacinthus, whom Apollo loved so madly, was you in Greek days.

Why are you alone in London, and when do you go to Salisbury?[4] Do go there to cool your hands in the grey twilight of Gothic things, and come here whenever you like. It is a lovely place—it only lacks you; but go to Salisbury first. Always, with undying love, yours   OSCAR

To Lady Mount-Temple[5]

[*8–11 February 1893*]   *Babbacombe Cliff*

Dear Lady Mount-Temple, As I suppose Constance has told you, I have returned to your lovely house in order to be with the children while she is away, and if you still allow me I will gladly and gratefully accept your kind invitation to stay on for a couple of weeks more—till March 1st if it will not inconvenience you, as I find the peace and beauty here so good for troubled nerves, and so suggestive for new work.

Indeed, Babbacombe Cliff has become a kind of college or school, for Cyril studies French in the nursery, and I write my new play in Wonder-

[1] This letter, the exact date of which is conjectural, was later stolen, used as material for attempted blackmail of Wilde, and finally read out in court during the Queensberry and later trials. Wilde stated in evidence that it was written at Babbacombe. A sonnet in French by Pierre Louÿs based on this letter appeared on 4 May 1893 in the *Spirit Lamp*, an Oxford undergraduate periodical edited by Douglas.

[2] Wilde rented Lady Mount-Temple's house near Torquay from mid-November 1892 till February 1893.

[3] "In Sarum Close" (1892). Its third and fourth lines read:

> I thought to cool my burning hands
> In this calm twilight of gray Gothic things.

[4] Where Lady Queensberry had a house called St Ann's Gate in the Close.

[5] Georgina Tollemache (1822–1901), sister of the first Lord Tollemache and widow of William Francis Cowper-Temple, first Lord Mount-Temple (1811–88), politician and heir of both Lord Melbourne and Lord Palmerston. She was a distant cousin of Constance Wilde and was unfailingly kind to her and her children.

land,[1] and in the drawing-room Lord Alfred Douglas—one of Lady Queensberry's sons—studies Plato with his tutor[2] for his degree at Oxford in June. He and his tutor are staying with me for a few days, so I am not lonely in the evenings.

Constance seems very happy in Florence. No doubt you hear from her.

I venture to enclose the formal tribute due to the Lady of The Manor, and with many thanks for your kindness remain most sincerely yours

OSCAR WILDE

To Edmund Gosse[3]

[Date of receipt 23 February 1893] *Babbacombe Cliff*

My dear Gosse, Will you accept a copy of *Salome*,[4] my first venture to use for art that subtle instrument of music, the French tongue. Accept it as a slight tribute of my admiration of your own delicate use of English. Very truly yours OSCAR WILDE

The charming house in which I am staying contains many Burne-Joneses but not one Blue Book! So I send this to your club, along with the play. But I have no fear but that Salome will find her way to that delightful library you have let us know of, and if she be not too Tyrian in her raiment be suffered to abide there for a season. I could desire for her no pleasanter place to live in, and I know that you have a welcome always for things that aim at beauty. Should she try to dance, a stern look from a single tome by an eighteenth-century writer will quell her, for common sense she has none, and reason, a faculty which I am glad to say is rapidly dying out, affrights her terribly.

To Bernard Shaw[5]

[Postmark 23 February 1893] *Babbacombe Cliff*

My dear Shaw, You have written well and wisely and with sound wit on the ridiculous institution of a stage-censorship: your little book on Ibsen-

---

[1] All the rooms at Babbacombe Cliff had names, the bedrooms names of flowers to match the wallpaper. Lady Mount-Temple's boudoir, which had windows on three sides, was called Wonderland. It was hung with works by Rossetti and Burne-Jones.

[2] Campbell Dodgson, who was coaching Douglas for Greats at Oxford.

[3] Civil servant, critic and author (1849–1928). Librarian to the House of Lords 1904–14. Knighted 1925.

[4] The original (French) edition. It was published on 22 February 1893 in Paris by the Librairie de l'Art Indépendant and in London by Elkin Mathews & John Lane.

[5] At this time G. B. S. (1856–1950) was music critic of the *World*. His book *The Quintessence of Ibsenism* had been published in 1891, and his first play, *Widowers' Houses*, performed in December 1892.

ism and Ibsen is such a delight to me that I constantly take it up, and always find it stimulating and refreshing: England is the land of intellectual fogs but you have done much to clear the air: we are both Celtic, and I like to think that we are friends: for these and many other reasons Salome presents herself to you in purple raiment.

Pray accept her with my best wishes, and believe me, very truly yours
OSCAR WILDE[1]

*To Campbell Dodgson[2]

[*Postmark 23 February 1893*]   *Babbacombe Cliff*

My dear Dodgson, We are charmed you like the paper-knife and hope it really brings a pleasant memory to you. For myself, I can only assure you how much I enjoyed your visit. I look forward to seeing you in town, either guarding marvellous Rembrandt etchings, or simply existing beautifully, which is even better, and we must talk of purple things and drink of purple wine.

I am still conducting the establishment on the old lines and really think I have succeeded in combining the advantages of a public school with those of a private lunatic asylum, which, as you know, was my aim. Bosie is very gilt-haired and I have bound *Salome* in purple to suit him. That tragic daughter of passion appeared on Thursday last, and is now dancing for the head of the English public. Should you come across her, tell me how you like her. I want you to like her.

[1] On 28 February Shaw answered from 29 Fitzroy Square: "Salome is still wandering in her purple raiment in search of me, and I expect her to arrive a perfect outcast, branded with inky stamps, bruised by flinging from hard hands into red prison vans, stuffed and contaminated ... I hope soon to send you my play *Widowers' Houses* which you will find tolerably amusing."

[2] Author and iconographer (1867–1948). Scholar of Winchester and New College, where he was a contemporary and friend of Lionel Johnson. Keeper of Prints and Drawings, British Museum 1912–32. For a short period in February 1893 he coached Douglas for Greats at Oxford. In a letter of 8 February to Lionel Johnson, Dodgson describes their visit to Babbacombe Cliff:

Our departure [from Salisbury] was dramatic; Bosie was as usual in a whirl; he had no book, no money, no cigarettes and had omitted to send many telegrams of the first importance. Then, with a minimum of minutes in which to catch our train, we were required to overload a small pony chaise with a vast amount of trunks while I was charged with a fox terrier and a scarlet morocco dispatch-box, a gorgeous and beautiful gift from Oscar. After hurried farewells to the ladies, we started on a wild career, Bosie driving. I expected only to drag my shattered limbs to the Salisbury infirmary, but we arrived whole at the station. ... Our life is lazy and luxurious; our moral principles are lax. We argue for hours in favour of different interpretations of Platonism. Oscar implores me, with outspread arms and tears in his eyes, to let my soul alone and cultivate my body for six weeks. Bosie is beautiful and fascinating, but quite wicked. He is enchanted with Plato's sketch of democratic man, and no arguments of mine will induce him to believe in any absolute standards of ethics or of anything else. We do no logic, no history, but play with pigeons and children and drive by the sea.

All the boys of the school send their best love, and kindest wishes.
Sincerely yours   OSCAR WILDE
                                        Headmaster Babbacombe School.

Babbacombe School

Headmaster—Mr Oscar Wilde
Second Master—Mr Campbell Dodgson
Boys—Lord Alfred Douglas

Rules.

Tea for masters and boys at 9.30 a.m.
Breakfast at 10.30.
Work. 11.30–12.30.
At 12.30 Sherry and biscuits for headmaster and boys (the second master objects to this).
12.40–1.30. Work.
1.30. Lunch.
2.30–4.30. Compulsory hide-and-seek for headmaster.
5. Tea for headmaster and second master, brandy and sodas (not to exceed seven) for boys.
6–7. Work.
7.30. Dinner, with compulsory champagne.
8.30–12. Écarté, limited to five-guinea points.
12–1.30. Compulsory reading in bed. Any boy found disobeying this rule will be immediately woken up.

At the conclusion of the term the headmaster will be presented with a silver inkstand, the second master with a pencil-case, as a token of esteem, by the boys.[1]

*To Pierre Louÿs

[*Postmark 27 February 1893*]   [*Postmark Torquay*]

My dear Pierre, Is the enclosed really all that you have to say to me in return for my choosing you out of all my friends to whom to dedicate *Salome*?[2] I cannot tell you how hurt I am.

Those to whom I merely gave copies have written me charming letters coloured with delicate appreciation of my work. You alone—you whose name I have written in gold on purple—you say nothing, and I don't understand what your telegram means; some trivial jest I suppose; a drop

---

[1] In his manuscript copy of this letter Dodgson added: "As a matter of fact the second master was presented with an enormous paper-weight, with suitable inscriptions, by headmaster and boys."

[2] The original (French) edition of *Salome* was dedicated "*À mon ami Pierre Louÿs.*"

of froth without wine. How you disappoint me! Had you wired "*Je vous remercie*" it would have been enough.

It is new to me to think that friendship is more brittle than love is.

OSCAR WILDE

To Lord Alfred Douglas[1]

[*March 1893*] *Savoy Hotel, London*[2]

Dearest of all Boys, Your letter was delightful, red and yellow wine to me; but I am sad and out of sorts. Bosie, you must not make scenes with me. They kill me, they wreck the loveliness of life. I cannot see you, so Greek and gracious, distorted with passion. I cannot listen to your curved lips saying hideous things to me. I would sooner [be blackmailed by every renter[3] in London] than have you bitter, unjust, hating. I must see you soon. You are the divine thing I want, the thing of grace and beauty; but I don't know how to do it. Shall I come to Salisbury? My bill here is £49 for a week. I have also got a new sitting-room over the Thames. Why are you not here, my dear, my wonderful boy? I fear I must leave; no money, no credit, and a heart of lead. YOUR OWN OSCAR

To J. P. Mahaffy

[? *April 1893*][4] *Haymarket Theatre*

My dear Mahaffy, I am so pleased you like the play,[5] and thank you for your charming letter, all the more flattering to me as it comes not merely from a man of high and distinguished culture, but from one to whom I owe so much personally, from my first and my best teacher, from the scholar who showed me how to love Greek things.

Let me sign myself, in affection and admiration, your old pupil and your old friend OSCAR WILDE

---

[1] This letter was read out in court during the trials. The words in square brackets were apparently thought too shocking or too obscure to be read out. They are supplied from Wilde's later reference to this letter on p. 185.

[2] On his return from Babbacombe, Wilde took rooms at the Savoy, and stayed there for most of the month of March.

[3] A "renter" is a slang term for a man who participates in male homosexual affairs for a reward (originally perhaps for his rent).

[4] It is impossible to date this letter accurately, but it seems more likely to have been written during the run of *A Woman of No Importance* (April–August 1893) than during that of *An Ideal Husband* (January–April 1895).

[5] *A Woman of No Importance* was produced at the Haymarket Theatre on 19 April 1893, with Beerbohm Tree, Mrs Bernard Beere, Fred Terry, Julia Neilson and Mrs Tree in the cast. It ran till 16 August, with a break of three nights in the middle.

To Bernard Shaw

[*Postmark 9 May 1893*] 16 *Tite Street*

My dear Shaw, I must thank you very sincerely for Op. 2 of the great Celtic School.[1] I have read it twice with the keenest interest. I like your superb confidence in the dramatic value of the mere facts of life. I admire the horrible flesh and blood of your creatures, and your preface is a masterpiece—a real masterpiece of trenchant writing and caustic wit and dramatic instinct. I look forward to your Op. 4. As for Op. 5, I am lazy, but am rather itching to be at it. When are you coming to the Haymarket?
Sincerely yours OSCAR WILDE

*To A. Teixeira de Mattos[2]

[? *May 1893*]

My dear Teixeira, There are difficulties about the bust being placed in the Haymarket . . . in the daytime there are the middle classes crowding in, who might break it; in the evening there are the aristocracy crowding out, who might steal it, and I could not sit just now, as I am going to Oxford tomorrow.

Telegram: To Ada Leverson[3]

28 June 1893 *Paddington*

The author of *The Sphinx* will on Wednesday at two eat pomegranates with the Sphinx of Modern Life.

---

[1] Hesketh Pearson brilliantly interpreted the numbers in this letter as follows:

Op. 1 was obviously *Lady Windermere's Fan*; Op. 2 *Widowers' Houses*; Op. 3 *A Woman of No Importance*, then running at the Haymarket Theatre; Op. 4, Shaw's next play, *The Philanderer*; Op. 5, Wilde's next play, *An Ideal Husband*. And so on. Wilde thus paid Shaw the compliment of ranking their works together in the dramatic literature of the age, though he had just scored his second huge success with *A Woman of No Importance*, while Shaw's *Widowers' Houses* had practically been hooted from the stage the previous December. (*G.B.S. A Postscript*, 1951, p. 132.)

This is confirmed by Shaw's copy of *Lady Windermere's Fan*, which is inscribed in Wilde's hand "Op. 1 of the Hibernian School, London '93."

[2] Alexander Louis Teixeira de Mattos (1865–1921) was of Portuguese–Jewish origin, though his father was Dutch and his mother English. He spent most of his life in England, where he worked first as a journalist, and then as one of the most successful translators of his time. In 1900 he married Willie Wilde's widow Lily. His brother Henri Teixeira de Mattos (1856–1908) was a sculptor, and it may have been he who was to make the bust.

[3] Ada Esther Beddington (1862–1933) married Ernest David Leverson, the son of a diamond merchant. She contributed witty pieces to *Punch* and other periodicals, and later published successful novels. She was one of Wilde's closest woman friends and he always called her The Sphinx. They appear to have met in 1892.

To William Wilde

[? *Circa 10 July 1893*]   *The Cottage, Goring-on-Thames*[1]

My dear Willie, This Saturday is, I fear, impossible, as people are staying here, and things are tedious. You and Dan should have come down for the regatta,[2] even in the evening; there were fireworks of surpassing beauty.

I am greatly distressed to hear you and the fascinating Dan are smoking American cigarettes. You really must not do anything so horrid. Charming people should smoke gold-tipped cigarettes or die, so I enclose you a small piece of paper, for which reckless bankers may give you gold, as I don't want you to die. With best love, ever yours   OSCAR

⋆To Lady Queensberry[3]

[*8 November 1893*]   *16 Tite Street*

Dear Lady Queensberry, You have on more than one occasion consulted me about Bosie. Let me write to you now about him.

Bosie seems to me to be in a very bad state of health. He is sleepless, nervous, and rather hysterical. He seems to me quite altered.

He is doing nothing in town. He translated my French play last August.[4] Since then he has really done nothing intellectual. He seems to me to have lost, for the moment only I trust, his interest even in literature. He does absolutely nothing, and is quite astray in life, and may, unless you or Drumlanrig[5] do something, come to grief of some kind. His life seems to me aimless, unhappy and absurd.

All this is a great grief and disappointment to me, but he is very young, and terribly young in temperament. Why not try and make arrangements of some kind for him to go abroad for four or five months, to the Cromers in Egypt if that could be managed, where he would have new surroundings,

---

[1] Wilde took this house from June to October 1893.

[2] Probably Henley Regatta, which in 1893 was held on July 5–7.

[3] Sybil Montgomery (1845–1935), grand-daughter of the first Lord Leconfield, married (1866) John Sholto Douglas, eighth Marquess of Queensberry (1844–1900) and divorced him 1887. Lord Alfred Douglas was her third son. This letter certainly helped to send him abroad for some months (see pp. 155 and 162).

[4] The English translation of *Salome* (1894) was dedicated "To my friend Lord Alfred Bruce Douglas, the translator of my play." It is not known how much Wilde revised the translation before it was published (see pp. 160–162), but, despite the dedication, Douglas's name did not appear on the title-page as translator.

[5] Francis Archibald Douglas, Viscount Drumlanrig (1867–94) was Lady Queensberry's eldest son.

proper friends, and a different atmosphere?[1] I think that if he stays in London he will not come to any good, and may spoil his young life irretrievably, quite irretrievably. Of course it will cost money no doubt, but here is the life of one of your sons—a life that should be brilliant and distinguished and charming—going quite astray, being quite ruined.

I like to think myself his greatest friend—he, at any rate, makes me think so—so I write to you quite frankly to ask you to send him abroad to better surroundings. It would save him, I feel sure. At present his life seems to be tragic and pathetic in its foolish aimlessness.

You will not, I know, let him know *anything about my letter.* I can rely on you, I feel sure. Sincerely yours   OSCAR WILDE

*Telegram: To More Adey[2]

23 November 1893   *St James's Street*
Bosie has influenza and is very pale. The wicked Lane has been routed with slaughter. I have begun a mystery play.   OSCAR

To Lord Alfred Douglas

[? *December 1893*]   10 & 11 *St James's Place,*[3] *S.W.*
My dearest Boy, Thanks for your letter. I am overwhelmed by the wings of vulture creditors, and out of sorts, but I am happy in the knowledge that we are friends again, and that our love has passed through the shadow and the night of estrangement and sorrow and come out rose-crowned as of old. Let us always be infinitely dear to each other, as indeed we have been always.

I hear Bobbie is in town, lame and bearded! Isn't it awful? I have not seen him yet. Lesly Thomson[4] has appeared; he is extremely anxious to devote his entire life to me. Tree[5] has written a long apologetic letter. His

---

[1] Evelyn Baring (1841–1917) was created Lord Cromer 1892, Viscount 1899 and Earl 1901. He was Agent and Consul-General in Egypt 1883–1907.

[2] William More Adey (1858–1942). Published in 1891, under the pseudonym William Wilson, the first English translation of Ibsen's *Brand.* Close friend of Robert Ross, with whom he later ran the Carfax picture gallery. Joint editor of the *Burlington Magazine* 1911–19. For a description of him in later years, see *Siegfried's Journey* by Siegfried Sassoon (1945).

[3] Wilde rented rooms at this address from October 1893 until the end of March 1894, and went there daily to work. Most of *An Ideal Husband* was written there.

[4] English actor (see note 3, p. 126).

[5] Herbert Beerbohm Tree, English actor-manager (1853–1917) and half-brother of Max Beerbohm.

reasons are so reasonable that I cannot understand them: a cheque is the only argument I recognise. Hare[1] returns to town early next week. I am going to make an effort to induce him to see that my new play is a master-piece, but I have grave doubts. This is all the news. How horrid news is. I think of you daily, and am always devotedly yours   OSCAR

To John Lane[2]

[*Circa December 1893*]   *10 & 11 St James's Place*

Dear Mr Lane, The cover of *Salome* is quite dreadful.[3] Don't spoil a lovely book. Have simply a folded vellum wrapper with the design in scarlet—much cheaper, and much better. The texture of the present cover is coarse and common: it is quite impossible and spoils the real beauty of the interior. Use up this horrid Irish stuff for stories, etc: don't inflict it on a work of art like *Salome*. It really will do you a great deal of harm. Every-one will say that it is coarse and inappropriate. I loathe it. So does Beardsley.[4] Truly yours   OSCAR WILDE

*To W. E. Henley

[*Circa 12 February 1894*]   *16 Tite Street*

My dear Henley, I am very sorry indeed to hear of your great loss.[5] I hope you will let me come down quietly to you one evening and over our cigarettes we will talk of the bitter ways of fortune, and the hard ways of life.

But, my dear Henley, to work, to work; that is your duty; that is what remains for natures like ours. Work never seems to me a reality, but a way

[1] John Hare, English actor-manager (1844–1921). He eventually turned down *An Ideal Husband* because he considered the last act unsatisfactory. He had already declined Pinero's *The Second Mrs Tanqueray* as too daring.

[2] English publisher (1854–1925). Born in Devon. Came to London 1868 and worked as a railway clerk at Euston station. In 1887 he joined with Charles Elkin Mathews (1851–1921) in founding the Bodley Head, though his name did not appear in it until 1892. The first book to carry the joint imprint was a new edition of Wilde's *Poems* with designs by Ricketts. Lane and Wilde never liked each other, and Wilde called the manservant in *The Importance of Being Earnest* after him to show his contempt. In 1895 Lane speedily withdrew Wilde's books from circulation.

[3] The English translation of *Salome*, illustrated by Aubrey Beardsley, was pub-lished by Mathews and Lane on 9 February 1894. The ordinary edition was issued in coarse-grained blue canvas, the *édition de luxe* in green silk.

[4] English artist (1872–98). He worked in an insurance office 1889–92, and his drawings were first published in the *Pall Mall Budget* in February 1893. He was later art-editor of the *Yellow Book* (1894–95) and the *Savoy* (1896). His copy of the original edition of *Salome* (1893) is inscribed "March '93. For Aubrey: for the only artist who, besides myself, knows what the dance of the seven veils is, and can see that invisible dance. Oscar."

[5] Henley's daughter Margaret, his only child, died on 11 February 1894, aged six.

of getting rid of reality. You asked me about Degas.[1] Well, he loves to be thought young, so I don't think he would tell his age. He disbelieves in art-education, so I don't think he will name a Master. He despises what he cannot get, so I am sure he will not give any information about prizes or honours. Why say anything about his person? His pastels are himself. Ever yours   OSCAR

To Ralph Payne[2]

[*Postmark 12 February 1894*]   *16 Tite Street*
Dear Mr Payne, The book that poisoned, or made perfect, Dorian Gray does not exist; it is a fancy of mine merely.[3]

I am so glad you like that strange coloured book of mine: it contains much of me in it. Basil Hallward is what I think I am: Lord Henry what the world thinks me: Dorian what I would like to be—in other ages, perhaps.

Will you come and see me?

I am writing a play, and go to St James's Place, number *10*, where I have rooms, every day at 11.30. Come on Tuesday about 12.30, will you? But perhaps you are busy? Still, we can meet, surely, some day. Your hand-writing fascinates me, your praise charms me. Truly yours
OSCAR WILDE

**To Mrs Patrick Campbell*[4]

[*February 1894*]   *Box F.* [*St James's Theatre*]
Dear Mrs Campbell, Mr Aubrey Beardsley, a very brilliant and wonderful young artist, and like all artists a great admirer of the wonder and charm of your art, says that he must once have the honour of being presented to you, if you will allow it. So, with your gracious sanction, I will come round

[1] Presumably Henley wanted to get a statement from Edgar Degas, the French painter (1834–1917), for publication in the *National Observer*.

[2] Unidentified. This letter is addressed to 50 Ennismore Gardens, London.

[3] But in a letter of 15 April 1892 to E. W. Pratt in reply to a similar enquiry Wilde had written: "The book in *Dorian Gray* is one of the many books I have never written, but it is partly suggested by Huysmans's *À Rebours*. . . . It is a fantastic variation on Huysmans's over-realistic study of the artistic temperament in our inartistic age."

[4] Beatrice Stella Tanner, English actress (1865–1940). Married Patrick Campbell 1884. She created the title-role in *The Second Mrs Tanqueray* by A. W. Pinero at the St James's Theatre on 27 May 1893. The play ran until 28 July, went on a provincial tour, and returned to the St James's on 11 November. It was taken off on 21 April 1894. Beardsley's drawing of Mrs Campbell appeared in the first number of the *Yellow Book*.

after Act III with him, and you would gratify and honour him much if you would let him bow his compliments to you. He has just illustrated my play of *Salome* for me, and has a copy of the *édition de luxe* which he wishes to lay at your feet. His drawings are quite wonderful. Very sincerely yours

OSCAR WILDE

To Lord Alfred Douglas

[Circa 16 April 1894]   *16 Tite Street*

My dearest Boy, Your telegram has just arrived; it was a joy to get it, but I miss you so much. The gay, gilt and gracious lad has gone away—and I hate everyone else: they are tedious. Also I am in the purple valleys of despair, and no gold coins are dropping down from heaven to gladden me. London is very dangerous: writters come out at night and writ one, the roaring of creditors towards dawn is frightful, and solicitors are getting rabies and biting people.

How I envy you under Giotto's Tower, or sitting in the loggia looking at that green and gold god of Cellini's. You must write poems like apple blossom.

The *Yellow Book* has appeared. It is dull and loathsome, a great failure. I am so glad.[1]

Always, with much love, yours   OSCAR

To Mrs Bernard Beere

[? April 1894]   *16 Tite Street*

My dear Bernie, Of course: *we* must fly to Australia: I could not let you go alone. I have written to Cartwright—a bald genius who is dear Dot's[2] agent—to ask him if it can be arranged. They have also *Mrs Tanqueray*, in which I long to see you.

---

[1] The first volume of the *Yellow Book* was published on 16 April 1894, and since it seems likely that Wilde saw it immediately, I have suggested the same date for this letter. Douglas, after returning from Egypt, was now paying his first visit to Florence, where, according to his *Autobiography*, he stayed about a month. Wilde joined him there in May, and on 28 May André Gide wrote from there to his mother: "*Qui rencontrai-je ici?—Oscar Wilde!!—Il est vieilli et laid, mais toujours extraordinaire conteur, un peu je pense comme Baudelaire a dû être, mais peut-être moins aigu et plus charmant. Il n'était plus ici que pour un jour, et quittant un appartement qu'il avait loué pour un mois et dont il n'avait profité que quinze jours, il m'en offrait aimablement la succession.*"

[2] See note 2, p. 42. Presumably Mrs Bernard Beere was contemplating a tour in Australia, and wanted to include one of Wilde's plays in her repertory. Dot Boucicault ran the Bijou Theatre in Melbourne 1886–96, and also the Criterion in Sydney. He gave performances of *Lady Windermere's Fan* and *The Importance of Being Earnest*, as well as *The Second Mrs Tanqueray*.

I have also asked Cartwright if Dot is coming over—or I suppose I should say coming *up* from Australia. I believe that absurdly shaped country lies right underneath the floor of one's coal-cellar.

Why rusticate in this reckless way? You are wanted in town. *Once Upon a Time* was dreadful.[1] Since the appearance of Tree in pyjamas there has been the greatest sympathy for Mrs Tree. It throws a lurid light on the difficulties of their married life.

Who is the fortunate mortal who has the honour of entertaining you? I dislike him more than I can tell you. Ever yours   OSCAR

To Lord Alfred Douglas

[*July–August 1894*]   *16 Tite Street*

Dearest Boy, I hope to send you the cigarettes, if Simmonds will let me have them. He has applied for his bill. I am overdrawn £41 at the bank: it really is intolerable the want of money. I have not a penny. I can't stand it any longer, but don't know what to do. I go down to Worthing tomorrow. I hope to do work there. The house, I hear, is very small, and I have no writing room. However, anything is better than London.

Your father is on the rampage again—been to Café Royal to enquire for us, with threats etc. I think now it would have been better for me to have had him bound over to keep the peace, but what a scandal! Still, it is intolerable to be dogged by a maniac.

When you come to Worthing, of course all things will be done for your honour and joy, but I fear you may find the meals, etc, tedious. But you will come, won't you? at any rate for a short time—till you are bored.

Ernesto[2] has written to me begging for money—a very nice letter—but I really have nothing just now.

What purple valleys of despair one goes through! Fortunately there is one person in the world to love. Ever yours   OSCAR

*To George Alexander

[*August 1894*]   *The Haven, 5 Esplanade, Worthing*[3]

Dear Aleck, What do you think of this for a play for you? A man of rank and fashion marries a simple sweet country girl—a lady—but simple and ignorant of fashionable life. They live at his country place and after a time

---

[1] *Once Upon a Time*, a children's play, freely adapted from Ludwig Fulda's *Der Talisman* by Louis N. Parker and H. Beerbohm Tree, was produced at the Haymarket Theatre on 28 March 1894, with Tree, Fred Terry, Julia Neilson and Mrs Tree in the cast. It was withdrawn on 21 April.

[2] Possibly Ernest Scarfe, a valet who was to figure in the trials.

[3] Wilde took rooms for himself and his family at this address for the months of August and September, and there wrote the greater part of *The Importance of Being Earnest*.

he gets bored with her, and invites down a lot of fashionable *fin-de-siècle* women and men. The play opens by his lecturing his wife on how to behave—not to be prudish, etc—and not to mind if anyone flirts with her. He says to her, "I have asked Gerald Lancing who used to admire you so much. Flirt with him as much as you like."

The guests arrive, they are horrid to the wife, they think her dowdy and dull. The husband flirts with Lady X. Gerald is nice and sweet and friendly to the wife.

Act II. The same evening, after dinner. Love scene between the husband and Lady X: they agree to meet in the drawing-room after everyone has retired. The guests bid good-night to the wife. The wife is tired and falls half asleep on a sofa. Enter husband: *he lowers the lamps*: then Lady X arrives: *he locks the door.* Love scene between them: wife hears it all. Suddenly violent beating on the door. Voice of Lady X's husband outside, desiring admittance. Terror of Lady X! Wife rises, turns up the lamp and goes to the door and unlocks it. Lady X's husband enters! Wife says "I am afraid I have kept Lady X up too late; we were trying an absurd experiment in thought reading" (anything will do). Lady X retires with her husband. Wife then left alone with her own husband. He comes towards her. She says "Don't touch me." He retires.

Then enter Gerald, says he has been alarmed by noises, thought there were robbers. Wife tells him everything; he is full of indignation; it is evident he loves the wife. She goes to her room.

Act III. Gerald's rooms. Wife comes to see him: it is clear that they love each other. They settle to go away together. Enter servant with card. The husband has called. The wife is frightened, but Gerald consents to see him. Wife retires into another room.

Husband is rather repentant. He implores Gerald to use his influence with the wife to make her forgive him. (Husband is a gross sentimental materialist.) Gerald promises that he will do so. It is evident that it is a great act of self-sacrifice for him. Exit husband with maudlin expressions of gratitude.

Enter wife: Gerald asks her to go back to her husband. She refuses with scorn. He says "You know what it costs me to ask you to do that. Do you not see that I am really sacrificing myself?" Etc. She considers: "Why should you sacrifice me? I love you. You have made me love you. You have no right to hand my life over to anyone else. All this self-sacrifice is wrong, we are meant to live. That is the meaning of life." Etc. She forces him by her appeals and her beauty and her love to take her away with him.

Three months afterwards: Act IV. Gerald and wife together. She is reading Act IV of *Frou-Frou*.[1] They talk about it. A duel between Gerald and the husband is fixed for the day on which the scene takes place. She is confident he will not be killed. He goes out. Husband enters. Wife proclaims her love for her lover. Nothing would induce her to go back to her husband. Of the two she wishes him to die. "Why?" says husband.

---

[1] In the fourth act of *Frou-Frou* by Meilhac and Halévy (1869) the heroine's husband and lover fight a duel off-stage, in which the lover is mortally wounded.

"Because the father of my child must live." Husband goes out. Pistols are heard. He has killed himself.

Enter Gerald, the husband not having appeared at the duel. "What a coward," says Gerald. "No," she answers, "not at the end. He is dead." "We must love one another devotedly now." Curtain falls with Gerald and the wife clinging to each other as if with a mad desire to make love eternal. *Finis.*

What do you think of this idea?

I think it extremely strong. *I want the sheer passion of love to dominate everything.* No morbid self-sacrifice. No renunciation. A sheer flame of love between a man and a woman. That is what the play is to rise to—from the social chatter of Act I, through the theatrical effectiveness of Act II, up to the psychology with its great *dénouement* in Act III, till love dominates Act IV and accepts the death of the husband as in a way its proper right, leaving love its tragedy, and so making it a still greater passion.

Of course I have only scribbled this off. I only thought of the plot this morning, but I send it to you. I see great things in it, and, if you like it when done, you can have it for America.[1] Ever yours   OSCAR

To Lord Alfred Douglas

[? *August 1894*]   *5 Esplanade, Worthing*

My own dearest Boy, How sweet of you to send me that charming poem.[2] I can't tell you how it touches me, and it is full of that light lyrical grace that you always have—a quality that seems so easy, to those who don't understand how difficult it is to make the white feet of poetry dance lightly among flowers without crushing them, and to those "who know"[3] is so rare and so distinguished. I have been doing nothing here but bathing and playwriting. My play is really very funny: I am quite delighted with it.[4] But it is not shaped yet. It lies in Sibylline leaves about the room, and Arthur[5] has twice made a chaos of it by "tidying up." The result, however, was rather dramatic. I am inclined to think that Chaos is a stronger evidence for an Intelligent Creator than Kosmos is: the view might be expanded.

Percy[6] left the day after you did. He spoke much of you. Alphonso[7] is

---

[1] This scenario was eventually written up by Frank Harris as *Mr and Mrs Daventry.*

[2] Possibly "Jonquil and Fleur-de-Lys" (see note 2, p. 136), which is dated 1894.

[3] Dante, *Inferno*, iv, 131.

[4] *The Importance of Being Earnest.*

[5] The Wildes' butler and factotum.

[6] Not Douglas's brother but an unidentified boy.

[7] Alphonse Conway, a newspaper boy whom Wilde had met on the beach at Worthing. Wilde later took him to Brighton and bought him a new suit. All this was brought up in the Queensberry trial.

still in favour. He is my only companion, along with Stephen. Alphonso always alludes to you as "the Lord," which however gives you, I think, a Biblical Hebraic dignity that gracious Greek boys should *not* have. He also says, from time to time, "Percy was the Lord's favourite," which makes me think of Percy as the infant Samuel—an inaccurate reminiscence, as Percy was Hellenic.

Yesterday (Sunday) Alphonso, Stephen, and I sailed to Littlehampton in the morning, bathing on the way. We took five hours in an awful gale to come back! did not reach the pier till eleven o'clock at night, pitch dark all the way, and a fearful sea. I was drenched, but was Viking-like and daring. It was, however, quite a dangerous adventure. All the fishermen were waiting for us. I flew to the hotel for hot brandy and water, on landing with my companions, and found a letter for you from dear Henry, which I send you: they had forgotten to forward it. As it was past *ten* o'clock on a Sunday night the proprietor could not *sell* us any brandy or spirits of any kind! So he had to *give* it to us. The result was not displeasing, but what laws! A hotel proprietor is not allowed to sell 'necessary harmless' alcohol to three shipwrecked mariners, wet to the skin, because it is Sunday! Both Alphonso and Stephen are now anarchists, I need hardly say.

Your new Sibyl is really wonderful. It is most extraordinary. I must meet her.

Dear, dear boy, you are more to me than any one of them has any idea; you are the atmosphere of beauty through which I see life; you are the incarnation of all lovely things. When we are out of tune, all colour goes from things for me, but we are never really out of tune. I think of you day and night.

Write to me soon, you honey-haired boy! I am always devotedly yours

OSCAR

To W. B. Yeats[1]

[? *August–September 1894*]   *5 Esplanade, Worthing*

Dear Yeats, With pleasure. I don't know that I think "Requiescat"[2] very typical of my work. Still, I am glad you like it.

I have just finished a play, so my handwriting is abominable.

Personally, I would sooner you chose a sonnet: that one on the sale of Keats's love letters: or the one beginning "Not that I love thy children" with which my book opens, but the garden—such as it is—is yours to pluck from. Truly yours   OSCAR WILDE

[1] Yeats was compiling *A Book of Irish Verse*, which was published by Methuen in March 1895. The second sonnet suggested by Wilde is the "Sonnet to Liberty," the opening poem in *Poems* (1881). Yeats, however, adhered to his original choice. In his later anthology, *The Oxford Book of Modern Verse* (1936), Wilde is represented by thirty-nine stanzas of *The Ballad of Reading Gaol*.

[2] This poem, written in memory of Wilde's sister Isola, was first published in *Poems* (1881).

To Elkin Mathews & John Lane[1]

[*Circa 8 September 1894*]   *5 Esplanade, Worthing*

Gentlemen, I have received your letters.

I am informed by Mr Lane that Mr Mathews declines to publish my story on Shakespeare's sonnets "at any price:" and that he himself will not publish it (at any price, I presume) unless he "approves" of it!

Eighteen months ago nearly—at any rate considerably more than a year ago—Mr Lane on behalf of the firm, and using the firm's name, entered into an agreement with me to publish "The Portrait of Mr W. H.": the number of copies to be printed, the royalties to be paid to me, the selection of the artist to whom the style of presentation of the work was to be confided, were all agreed upon : the book was subsequently advertised in the list of the coming publications of the firm: and notices to that effect have appeared in the literary columns of many newspapers. The agreement was stamped in my presence by Mr Lane, and signed by him on behalf of the firm. I do not suggest for a moment that he had not the authority to do so. He acted, I am quite sure, with the full authority of the firm of which he is, or was, a partner. If he did not, it is his affair, not mine.

It is the duty of the firm to publish my book, which they have now advertised for about sixteen months, and which they agreed with me to publish. I have a right to insist upon their doing so: and that right I retain. For the firm to break their agreement with me would be dishonourable, dishonest, and illegal.

Upon the other hand I am quite ready to enter into a compromise. You made an agreement to publish my book on certain terms: you have advertised the book as being about to appear: you have had the rights over the book since last July year. The delay in its publication has been very annoying to me, but I have always behaved towards your firm with perfect courtesy and kindness. Even now, when I am calmly told that one member of the firm refuses, after his stamped agreement nearly eighteen months old, to publish the book "at any price:" and the other calmly tells me that his publication of the book depends on his approval of it: I am not really angry: I am simply amused. However, I am quite ready to let you off your agreement, on condition that you send me a cheque for £25, by return. I think you will agree with me that under the circumstances I am acting with

---

[1] This letter and the next were occasioned by a printed document announcing the termination of the Mathews–Lane partnership on 29 September. The recipient author was asked to say which partner he would like to follow. In the event Lane remained Wilde's publisher, but the longer version of *The Portrait of Mr W. H.* (see note 2, p. 79) never appeared, although at the end of 1893 Mathews & Lane had announced it as "in rapid preparation." The manuscript (105 pages in Wilde's hand, almost twice as long as the original *Blackwood's* version) came to light many years later among the effects of Lane's office manager, Frederic Chapman. The full text was published in a limited edition in New York in 1921 and ten copies of this edition were issued in London. The first regular English edition appeared in 1958, edited by Vyvyan Holland.

great consideration towards your firm. If you do not think so I shall feel that I have been wrong in the estimate I have formed of your desire to act in an honourable and straightforward manner in your business relations with men of letters. Yours faithfully   OSCAR WILDE

To Elkin Mathews & John Lane

[*Circa 22 September 1894*]   *5 Esplanade, Worthing*

Gentlemen, I have received your letter, in which it is stated that Mr Lane will "accept all responsibility assumed by the firm" in the matter of "Mr. W. H." It is always best to write quite plainly in business matters. If this phrase means that Mr Lane is going to publish the book, well and good. *If it means anything else, pray let me know.*

The suggestion that the delay in the production of the book is in any way to be attributed to me can hardly be seriously made. Mr Lane is quite aware that at his urgent solicitation and desire, repeatedly expressed both in London and at Goring, where the agreement was, I believe, finally signed and stamped, the manuscript was handed over by me to Mr Ricketts that he might select the type and form and suitable setting for the book, and convey the manuscript to the printers. The manuscript has been in Mr Ricketts's hands for *more than a year*, during which time I have waited very patiently, as I did not wish to interfere with the production of *The Sphinx*,[1] or to cause any trouble.

Personally, I regret that the firm did not accept my offer for the sum of £25 to be paid over to me for the cancelling of the agreement. It is never pleasant to deal with a publisher who is not really interested in one's work at the moment. That, however, was for the firm to decide. I am pleased to note that in the last letter received by me no absurd statements are made about the members of the firm not having read the work, and so being relieved from any honourable responsibility to publish it. There is no objection to publishers reading the works they produce before publication, but if they enter into an agreement with an author to publish his work, they, if they desire to be considered an honest and honourable firm, cannot plead their own carelessness, or lack of intellectual interest, as an excuse for the non-performance of their agreement. The plea, in the present case, seems intentionally insincere. The firm is under an obligation to me to publish my five-act tragedy, *The Duchess of Padua*, the manuscript of which they have never seen, nor expressed any desire to see. Nor was the manuscript of *Salome* submitted to them beforehand: any desire on the part of Mr Lane to have the manuscript of my French play submitted to him for his approval would I fear have excited considerable amusement in myself and in others.

I note in your letter that you say it has now been arranged that all my

---

[1] *The Sphinx*, with decorations by Ricketts, was published by Mathews & Lane on 11 June 1894.

works are to be handed over to Mr Lane. I think that it should be left to me to decide with which partner I will place my work. I have received the firm's circular on the subject, and am considering the point. There is after all no reason why I should not be treated with the same courtesy that is extended to obscure and humble beginners in the difficult art of Literature.

Personally I am at present in favour of entrusting my plays[1] to Mr Mathews, whose literary enthusiasm about them has much gratified me, and to leave to Mr Lane the incomparable privilege of publishing *The Sphinx*, *Salome*, and my beautiful story on Shakespeare's sonnets.

I would be obliged by a reply to this letter being sent by return. Yours faithfully   OSCAR WILDE

To Arthur L. Humphreys[2]

[? *September 1894*]   *5 Esplanade, Worthing*

Dear Mr Humphreys, Would you kindly send *Cyril*, at 16 Tite Street, a copy of Butcher and Lang's translation of *The Odyssey*—from me. I am very anxious he should read the best book for boys, and those who keep the wonder and joy of boyhood, ever written.

How about *Oscariana*? Let me see some specimen pages, will you? Truly yours   OSCAR WILDE

*To Ada Leverson

[? *23 September 1894*]   [? *Worthing*]

Dear Sphinx, Of course you have been deeply wronged.[3] But there are many bits not unworthy of your brilliant pen: and treachery is inseparable from faith. I often betray myself with a kiss.

Hichens I did not think capable of anything so clever. It is such a bore about journalists, they are so very clever.

[1] Mathews & Lane had published *Lady Windermere's Fan* on 9 November 1893. John Lane published *A Woman of No Importance* on 9 October 1894. Although announced as "in preparation" in 1893, *The Duchess of Padua* was never published by Mathews and Lane.

[2] Bookseller, author and publisher (1865–1946). For many years head of Hatchard's bookshop in Piccadilly. In January 1895 he produced fifty copies of *Oscariana*, a collection of epigrams from Wilde's work chosen by Constance Wilde, and in May a further edition of 200. In May 1895 he issued a privately printed edition (50 copies) of Wilde's *The Soul of Man under Socialism*. He sent Wilde a present of books when he was in prison.

[3] *The Green Carnation*, a witty skit on Wilde and his circle, was first published anonymously by Heinemann on 15 September 1894, and Ada Leverson had been suggested as its author. It was in fact the first book of Robert Smythe Hichens (1864–1950), who later became a prolific novelist, and his name was printed in the fourth impression (1895). He had met Douglas in Cairo.

I suppose you heard about our telegrams.[1]

How sweet of you to have *Intentions* bound for me for your birthday! I simply love that book.

I shall be in town soon, and must come and charm the Sphinx with honey-cakes. The trouble is I left my flute in a railway carriage—and the fauns take so long to cut new reeds. Ever yours   OSCAR

*To the Editor of the Pall Mall Gazette

1 October [*1894*][2]   *Worthing*

Sir, Kindly allow me to contradict, in the most emphatic manner, the suggestion, made in your issue of Thursday last, and since then copied into many other newspapers, that I am the author of *The Green Carnation*.

I invented that magnificent flower. But with the middle-class and mediocre book that usurps its strangely beautiful name I have, I need hardly say, nothing whatsoever to do. The flower is a work of art. The book is not.

I remain, sir, your obedient servant   OSCAR WILDE

*To Ada Leverson

Friday [*5 October 1894*]   *Hotel Metropole, Brighton*

Dear Sphinx, I hope to be in London on the 15th. Will you be there?

Your article in *Punch*[3] I read with joy, and detected you, of course, before you sent it to me.

My friend is not allowed to go out today:[4] I sit by his side and read him passages from his own life. They fill him with surprise. Everyone should keep someone else's diary; I sometimes suspect you of keeping mine.

Is your birthday really the 10th? Mine is the 16th! How tragic: I fear that looks like brother and sister. Perhaps it is better so. Ever yours
                                                                         OSCAR

To George Alexander

[*Circa 25 October 1894*]   *16 Tite Street*

My dear Aleck, I have been ill in bed for a long time, with a sort of

---

[1] In the Introduction to a new edition of *The Green Carnation* (1949) Robert Hichens wrote: "He [Wilde] sent me a bogus telegram about it though it came out anonymously, showing that he had guessed I had written it. Alfred Douglas at the same time sent me a comic telegram, telling me I was discovered, and had better at once flee from the vengeance to come."

[2] Published on 2 October.

[3] Probably "Letters from a Debutante", which appeared anonymously in *Punch* on 6 October 1894. Ada Leverson's last contribution before that was on 4 August.

[4] For Wilde's later account of this illness of Lord Alfred Douglas, see p. 165.

malarial fever, and have not been able to answer your kind letter of invitation. I am quite well now, and, as you wished to see my somewhat farcical comedy, I send you the first copy of it. It is called *Lady Lancing* on the cover: but the real title is *The Importance of Being Earnest*. When you read the play, you will see the punning title's meaning. Of course, the play is not suitable to you at all: you are a romantic actor: the people it wants are actors like Wyndham[1] and Hawtrey. Also, I would be sorry if you altered the definite artistic line of progress you have always followed at the St James's. But, of course, read it, and let me know what you think about it. I have very good offers from America for it.

I read charming accounts of your banquet at Birmingham,[2] and your praise of the English dramatist. I know and admire Pinero's work, but *who is Jones?* Perhaps the name as reported in the London papers was a misprint for something else. I have never heard of Jones. Have you?

Give my kind regards to Mrs Aleck, and believe me, sincerely yours

OSCAR WILDE

To Lord Alfred Douglas

[*Circa 9 November 1894*]   *Albemarle Club*

My dearest Boy, I have been very lonely without you: and worried by money matters. Today is golden enough, but rain has dripped monotonously on all other days.

I went to Haddon Chambers's play:[3] it was not bad, but oh! so badly written! The bows and salutations of the lower orders who thronged the stalls were so cold that I felt it my duty to sit in the Royal Box with the Ribblesdales, the Harry Whites, and the Home Secretary:[4] this exasperated the wretches. How strange to live in a land where the worship of beauty

---

[1] Charles Wyndham (1837–1919), actor-manager. Knighted 1902.

[2] On 24 October Alexander, entertained to lunch by the Birmingham Arts Club, had spoken on "The Future of the Stage." The playwright Henry Arthur Jones (1857–1929) was as well known to Wilde as to everyone else. Jones had scored a number of great successes, and Alexander had produced *The Masqueraders* in April 1894 with Mrs Patrick Campbell as leading lady. They were even now touring with this play and *The Second Mrs Tanqueray*, by Arthur Wing Pinero (1855–1934), which Alexander had produced in May 1893.

[3] *John-a-Dreams* by Haddon Chambers was produced by Tree at the Haymarket Theatre on Thursday 8 November 1894, with Tree himself, Mrs Patrick Campbell, Charles Cartwright, Nutcombe Gould and Lesly Thomson in the cast. It ran until 27 December.

[4] Sir Henry White (1849–1922) was Private Solicitor to the Queen. The fourth Lord Ribblesdale (1854–1925) was Lord-in-Waiting 1880–85 and Master of Buckhounds 1892–95. His portrait by Sargent is in the Tate Gallery. The Home Secretary was Herbert Henry Asquith (1852–1928), who was Liberal Prime Minister 1908–16. Created Earl of Oxford and Asquith 1925. In 1894 he married as his second wife Margot Tennant (1864–1945), to whom Wilde had dedicated "The Star-Child" in *A House of Pomegranates*.

and the passion of love are considered infamous. I hate England: it is only bearable to me because you are here.

Last night I supped at Willis's:[1] there were respectful enquiries after "Lord Douglas." Always yours   OSCAR

Telegram: To Ada Leverson

8 January 1895   *Piccadilly*

Am so pleased, my dear Sphinx. No other voice but yours is musical enough to echo my music. Your article will be worthy of you and of me.[2] Have you a box tomorrow night? If so I will come, as I am still forbidden to go out.   OSCAR

To Ada Leverson

[Circa 14 January 1895]   *Hotel Albemarle*

Dear Sphinx, Oh! how rash of you to trust me with your brilliant article. I had put it into a casket and thrown the key into the waters. But, now I have shattered the casket, I send you the purple papyrus of your perfect panegyric, so full of instinct, of subtlety, of charm—a real model of appreciation. I hope it will be published—in an edition de luxe.

Yes: I fly to Algiers with Bosie tomorrow.[3] I begged him to let me stay to rehearse, but so beautiful is his nature that he declined at once.

Poste Restante *Algiers*

Do write. Ever yours   OSCAR

[1] Willis's Rooms in King Street, St James's, the most famous and fashionable restaurant of the decade. The building later became an auctioneer's saleroom and was destroyed by bombs in 1941.

[2] *An Ideal Husband* was produced at the Haymarket Theatre on 3 January 1895, with Lewis Waller as Sir Robert Chiltern and Charles Hawtrey as Lord Goring. Ada Leverson's short skit appeared anonymously in *Punch* on 12 January 1895, entitled "Overheard Fragment of a Dialogue."

[3] They arrived there on 17 January and ran into André Gide at Blidah on 27 January. Gide spent most of the next few days with Wilde in Algiers, and reported Wilde's leaving there on 31 January, presumably for London. Douglas stayed on at Biskra till 18 February.

To Arthur L. Humphreys

[*Circa 12 February 1895*]   *Hotel Avondale, Piccadilly*

My dear Humphreys, I enclose you a stall for Thursday—the last to be got!
I hope you will enjoy my "trivial" play. It is written by a butterfly for
butterflies.[1] Ever yours   OSCAR WILDE

Telegram: To Ada Leverson

[? *13*] *February 1895*   *Piccadilly*

Thank you dear Sphinx for your two charming and kind letters. The
rehearsals were dreary. The uncultured had caught colds.[2]   OSCAR

To R. V. Shone[3]

[*13 February 1895*]

Dear Mr Shone, Lord Queensberry is at Carter's Hotel, Albemarle Street.
Write to him from Mr Alexander that you regret to find that the seat
given to him was already sold, and return him his money.

This will prevent trouble, I hope. Truly yours   OSCAR WILDE

To Lord Alfred Douglas

[*Circa 17 February 1895*]   *Thos Cook & Son, 33 Piccadilly*

Dearest Boy, Yes: the Scarlet Marquis made a plot to address the audience
on the first night of my play! Algy Bourke[4] revealed it, and he was not

---

[1] *The Importance of Being Earnest* opened at the St James's Theatre on Thursday,
14 February 1895, with Alexander as John Worthing, Allan Aynesworth as Algernon
Moncrieff, Irene Vanbrugh as Gwendolen Fairfax and Rose Leclercq as Lady
Bracknell.

[2] Wilde is quoting from his "The Decay of Lying" where he points out that
people did not see fogs until they were invented by artists:

Now, . . . fogs are carried to excess. They have become the mere mannerism of
a clique, and the exaggerated realism of their method gives dull people bronchitis.
Where the cultured catch an effect, the uncultured catch cold.

[3] Robert V. Shone, business manager of the St James's Theatre. Queensberry
had been planning to create a disturbance during the first night of *The Importance of
Being Earnest*, but when he was unable to get a seat he contented himself with having
a bouquet of vegetables, addressed to Wilde, delivered at the stage door. This
letter is written in pencil.

[4] The Hon. Algernon Henry Bourke (1854–1922), younger son of the sixth Earl
of Mayo.

128

allowed to enter.

He left a grotesque bouquet of vegetables for me! This of course makes his conduct idiotic, robs it of dignity.

He arrived with a prize-fighter!! I had all Scotland Yard—twenty police —to guard the theatre. He prowled about for three hours, then left chattering like a monstrous ape. Percy[1] is on our side.

I feel now that, without your name being mentioned, all will go well.

I had not wished you to know. Percy wired without telling me. I am greatly touched by your rushing over Europe. For my own part I had determined you should know nothing.

I will wire to Calais and Dover, and you will of course stay with me till Saturday. I then return to Tite Street, I think.

Ever, with love, all love in the world, devotedly your   OSCAR

To Constance Wilde

[? *February 1895*][2]   *Hotel Avondale, Piccadilly*

Dear Constance, I think Cyril better *not* come up. I have so telegraphed to Mr Badley.

I am coming to see you at nine o'clock. Please be in—it is important. Ever yours   OSCAR

To Robert Ross

[*28 February 1895*]   *Hotel Avondale, Piccadilly*

Dearest Bobbie, Since I saw you something has happened. Bosie's father has left a card at my club with hideous words on it.[3] I don't see anything now but a criminal prosecution. My whole life seems ruined by this man. The tower of ivory is assailed by the foul thing. On the sand is my life spilt. I don't know what to do. If you could come here at 11.30 please do so tonight. I mar your life by trespassing ever on your love and kindness. I have asked Bosie to come tomorrow. Ever yours   OSCAR[4]

---

[1] Douglas's elder brother Percy Sholto, Lord Douglas of Hawick (1868–1920). He succeeded his father as ninth Marquess of Queensberry in 1900.

[2] It is impossible to date this letter exactly, but Wilde was certainly staying at the Avondale Hotel in February 1895, and may even have written this note on the fatal 28th. It is in pencil, as is the following letter.

[3] Lord Queensberry's card, on which he had written "To Oscar Wilde posing as a somdomite [*sic*]," was left by him with the porter of the Albemarle Club on 18 February. The porter put it in an envelope and handed it to Wilde when he next came to the club, which was on 28 February.

[4] Ross appended this note: "I cannot find Queensberry's original card, but the enclosed was Wilde's letter telling me of it. He sent note by hand, about 6.40, to 24 Hornton Street. I went up that evening at 11.30. Douglas was there. Date Feb 28, 1895."

To Ada Leverson

[*Circa 13 March 1895*]
My dear Friend, A thousand thanks. For a week I go away with Bosie: then return to fight with panthers.[1]   OSCAR
Kind regards to dear Ernest.

To Ernest Leverson

[*March 1895*]   *16 Tite Street*
Dear Ernest, Bosie and I cannot sufficiently thank you for your great kindness to us:[2] we shall never forget it, but shall always cherish in affection and gratitude the friend who at a moment's notice came forward to help us, so gracefully, so kindly, so readily.

In a few days we hope to be free of our monetary obligation; the other obligation of gratitude and *reconnaissance* we would like to always keep.

Our homage to the dear and wonderful Sphinx, and believe me, dear Ernest, your sincere and grateful friend   OSCAR WILDE
Cheque received.

To Constance Wilde

[? *5 April 1895*][3]
Dear Constance, Allow no one to enter my bedroom or sittingroom—except servants—today. See no one but your friends. Ever yours
OSCAR

---

[1] On 1 March Wilde obtained a warrant for the arrest of Queensberry, who on the following day was arrested and charged with criminal libel. Soon after this Wilde and Douglas went to Monte Carlo for a short holiday (see p. 159).

[2] At Wilde's request Leverson had advanced £500 for his legal expenses for the Queensberry trial on the understanding that it would be repaid by Lord Douglas of Hawick and Lady Queensberry.

[3] This letter, which is in an envelope addressed to Mrs Oscar Wilde, 16 Tite Street, was clearly delivered by hand. It cannot be dated with confidence, but the morning of the third and last day of the Queensberry trial, when Wilde knew he could not win, seems a likely time.

*To the Editor of the Evening News

5 April 1895[1]   *Holborn Viaduct Hotel*

It would have been impossible for me to have proved my case without putting Lord Alfred Douglas in the witness-box against his father.

Lord Alfred Douglas was extremely anxious to go into the box, but I would not let him do so.

Rather than put him in so painful a position I determined to retire from the case, and to bear on my own shoulders whatever ignominy and shame might result from my prosecuting Lord Queensberry.[2]   OSCAR WILDE

To Lord Alfred Douglas

[5 April 1895]   *[Cadogan Hotel]*

My dear Bosie, I will be at Bow Street Police Station tonight—no bail possible I am told. Will you ask Percy, and George Alexander, and Waller, at the Haymarket, to attend to give bail.[3]

Would you also wire Humphreys to appear at Bow Street for me.[4] Wire to 41 Norfolk Square, W.

Also, come to see me. Ever yours   OSCAR[5]

---

[1] On the morning of this day the prosecution was forced to withdraw and Queensberry was acquitted.

[2] Douglas maintained to his dying day that, if he had been allowed to give evidence, his revelations of his father's conduct would have discredited Queensberry and won the case for Wilde. But, since the matter at issue was Queensberry's charge against Wilde, no court could possibly have considered Douglas's evidence relevant.

[3] Lewis Waller, English romantic actor (1850–1915), who was producing and acting in *An Ideal Husband,* and Alexander, who was producing and acting in *The Importance of Being Earnest,* both refused to help.

[4] Charles Octavius Humphreys (1828–1902), of the firm of Humphreys, Son & Kershaw, was Wilde's solicitor throughout his trials.

[5] When the police came in the evening to arrest Wilde at the Cadogan Hotel, Douglas had gone to the House of Commons to try and discover from his kinsman George Wyndham whether there was to be a prosecution. When he returned he found Wilde gone and this letter waiting for him.

PART SIX

READING · 1895-1897

On 6 April 1895 Wilde was charged at Bow Street Police Court with offences under Section Eleven of the Criminal Law Amendment Act, 1885. The magistrate, Sir John Bridge, refused bail, and Wilde was imprisoned at Holloway until his first trial began at the Old Bailey on 26 April before Mr Justice Charles. On 1 May the jury disagreed and a new trial was ordered. On 7 May Wilde was released on bail, and on 20 May his second trial began at the Old Bailey before Mr Justice Wills. On 25 May Wilde was found guilty and sentenced to two years' imprisonment with hard labour. The first six months of his sentence were served in Pentonville and Wandsworth prisons, the rest at Reading. For a full account of his trials, see *The Trials of Oscar Wilde*, edited by H. Montgomery Hyde (1948; revised edition 1962).

To Ada and Ernest Leverson

9 April 1895   *H.M. Prison, Holloway*

Dear Sphinx and Ernest, I write to you from prison, where your kind words have reached me and given me comfort, though they have made me cry, in my loneliness. Not that I am really alone. A slim thing, gold-haired like an angel, stands always at my side. His presence overshadows me. He moves in the gloom like a white flower.

With what a crash this fell! Why did the Sibyl[1] say fair things? I thought but to defend him from his father: I thought of nothing else, and now—

I can't write more. How good and kind and sweet you and Ernest are to me.   OSCAR

[1] Mrs Robinson, the fashionable fortune-teller of the time who had prophesied "complete triumph."

To More Adey and Robert Ross

9 April 1895   *H.M. Prison, Holloway*

Dear More and Bobbie, Will you tell the Sphinx, Ernest Leverson, Mrs Bernard Beere (Church Cottage, Marylebone Road) how deeply touched I am by their affection and kindness.

Inform the committee of the New Travellers Club, and also of the Albemarle, that I resign my membership (Piccadilly and Dover Street).

Bosie is so wonderful. I think of nothing else. I saw him yesterday.

They are kind in their way here, but I have no books, nothing to smoke, and sleep very badly. Ever yours   OSCAR

Ask Bobbie to go to Tite Street and get a type-written manuscript, part of my blank-verse tragedy, also a black book containing *La Sainte Courtisane*[1] in bedroom.

To R. H. Sherard

13 April 1895   *H.M. Prison, Holloway*

My dear Robert, I cannot tell you how your letters have cheered and comforted me in this awful, terrible position in which I am placed, and how glad I am that Sarah, and Goncourt, and other artists are sympathising with me. Pray assure Louys, Stuart Merill,[2] Moréas,[3] and all others how touched—touched beyond words—I am. I am sending you a telegram to ask you if you think Sarah would buy *Salome* from me. I am so pressed by my creditors that I don't know where to turn. I would repay her of course, when all comes well, but perhaps if you mentioned to her the need I was in of 10,000 francs (£400) she might do it. Ever, with deepest affection and gratitude   OSCAR

---

[1] When Ross published a fragment of a first draft of this play in the Collected Edition (1908) he wrote: "At the time of Wilde's trial the nearly completed drama was entrusted to Mrs Leverson, who in 1897 [?1898] went to Paris on purpose to restore it to the author. Wilde immediately left the manuscript in a cab. A few days later he laughingly informed me of the loss, and added that a cab was a very proper place for it."

[2] Stuart Fitzrandolph Merrill (1863–1915), American poet who wrote in French and lived in Paris. He had met Wilde in 1890. In November 1895 he drew up a petition to Queen Victoria begging for Wilde's release from prison, but it came to nothing, since scarcely any of the leading French writers agreed to sign it.

[3] Jean Moréas, Graeco-French poet (1856–1910).

To R. H. Sherard

16 April 1895   *H.M. Prison, Holloway*

My dear Robert, You good, daring reckless friend! I was delighted to get your letter, with all its wonderful news. For myself, I am ill—apathetic. Slowly life creeps out of me. Nothing but Alfred Douglas's daily visits quicken me into life, and even him I only see under humiliating and tragic conditions.

Don't fight more than six duels a week! I suppose Sarah is hopeless;[1] but your chivalrous friendship—your fine, chivalrous friendship—is worth more than all the money in the world. Ever yours   OSCAR

To Ada Leverson

23 April 1895   *H.M. Prison, Holloway*

My dear Sphinx, I have just had a charming note from you, and a charming note from Ernest. How good you both are to me!

Willie has been writing me the most monstrous letters. I have had to beg him to stop.[2]

Today Bosie comes early to see me. My counsel seem to wish the case to be tried at once. I don't, nor does Bosie. Bail, or no bail, I think we had better wait.

[*Later*]

I have seen counsel, and Bosie. I don't know what to do. My life seems to have gone from me. I feel caught in a terrible net. I don't know where to turn. I care less when I think that he is thinking of me. I think of nothing else. Ever yours   OSCAR

[1] Sherard described in *Oscar Wilde: The Story of an Unhappy Friendship* (1902) how Sarah Bernhardt received him graciously, wept at the thought of Wilde's plight, and said she could not buy *Salome* but would lend Wilde some money. She made a series of appointments with Sherard, but kept none of them, and sent Wilde nothing.

[2] W. B. Yeats reports Wilde's saying: "My poor brother writes to me that he is defending me all over London; my poor, dear brother, he could compromise a steam-engine."

To Ada Leverson

H.M. Prison, Holloway

My dear Sphinx, I have not had a line today from Fleur-de-Lys.[2] I suppose he is at Rouen. I am so wretched when I don't hear from him, and today I am bored, and sick to the death of imprisonment.

I am reading your books, but I want to be out, and with people I love. The days seem endless.

Your kindness and Ernest's make things better for me. I go on trespassing on it more and more. Oh! I hope all will come well, and that I can go back to Art and Life. Here I sicken in inanition. Ever with great affection yours   OSCAR

Letter from Bosie, at Rouen, just arrived. Please wire my thanks to him. He has cured me of sorrow today.

*Telegram: To Ada Leverson

8 May 1895   *Sloane Square*

Am staying at 146 Oakley Street for a few days.[3] Can I call this evening?
                                                                    OSCAR

To Ada Leverson

[? Early May 1895]   *[? 146 Oakley Street]*

My dear Sweet Kind Friend, I have no words to thank you for all you do for me, but for you and Ernest Bosie and I have deepest love.

I hope to be in better spirits tonight. Your sweetness last night was wonderful. Your flowers are like him—your sending them like yourself. Dear, dear Friend, tonight I see you at 7.45. Ah! you are good and gentle and wonderful. Always devotedly yours   OSCAR

---

[1] The jury at Wilde's first trial had disagreed on 1 May, and on 3 May a judge in Chambers (Baron Pollock) agreed to bail, but Wilde was still awaiting release. Lord Douglas of Hawick and the Rev. Stewart Headlam (see note p. 262) stood surety.

[2] Fleur-de-Lys was one of Wilde's nicknames for Lord Alfred Douglas, who had written a ballad, called "Jonquil and Fleur-de-Lys," about a king's son and a shepherd boy who changed clothes. It was published in his *Poems* (1896). Douglas had left the country on 25 April, the eve of Wilde's first trial. He went unwillingly but at the urgent request of Wilde's lawyers. He stopped in Calais, Rouen and Paris.

[3] When Wilde was released from Holloway on bail on 7 May, he could find no hotel willing to accept him, and was forced to take refuge with his mother in Oakley Street.

*To Lord Alfred Douglas[1]

[20 May 1895]   [? 2 Courtfield Gardens][2]

My child, Today it was asked to have the verdicts rendered separately.
Taylor[3] is probably being judged at this moment, so that I have been able
to come back here. My sweet rose, my delicate flower, my lily of lilies, it
is perhaps in prison that I am going to test the power of love. I am going
to see if I cannot make the bitter waters sweet by the intensity of the love
I bear you. I have had moments when I thought it would be wiser to
separate. Ah! moments of weakness and madness! Now I see that that
would have mutilated my life, ruined my art, broken the musical chords
which make a perfect soul. Even covered with mud I shall praise you,
from the deepest abysses I shall cry to you. In my solitude you will be
with me. I am determined not to revolt but to accept every outrage
through devotion to love, to let my body be dishonoured so long as my soul
may always keep the image of you. From your silken hair to your delicate
feet you are perfection to me. Pleasure hides love from us but pain reveals
it in its essence. O dearest of created things, if someone wounded by
silence and solitude comes to you, dishonoured, a laughing-stock to men,
oh! you can close his wounds by touching them and restore his soul which
unhappiness had for a moment smothered. Nothing will be difficult for
you then, and remember, it is that hope which makes me live, and that
hope alone. What wisdom is to the philosopher, what God is to his saint,
you are to me. To keep you in my soul, such is the goal of this pain which
men call life. O my love, you whom I cherish above all things, white
narcissus in an unmown field, think of the burden which falls to you, a
burden which love alone can make light. But be not saddened by that,

[1] In August 1895, at Sorrento, Douglas wrote an article in passionate defence of
Wilde. It was intended for the *Mercure de France*, but when Wilde heard that it
included some of his letters to Douglas from Holloway Prison, he told Sherard to
prevent its appearance. This he did, and the article was never published (see p. 183
et seq.). Douglas wrote it in English and friends put it into French. A manuscript
of this French translation survives as does one of Stuart Mason's translation back
into English. I have based my text of this letter and of the two others in *Letters* on
Mason's version, but have not hesitated to alter words and phrases, following the
French, into what seems more like Wilde's language, and I have followed the ver-
sions of several sentences given by Douglas in his *Autobiography* (1929). All this
may well have slightly distorted Wilde's words, but their substance need not be
doubted. Douglas says that he later destroyed 150 of Wilde's letters to him, including those from Holloway.
[2] After Wilde had been a few days at Oakley Street, the Leversons took him into
their home at 2 Courtfield Gardens, and he stayed with them until his second trial
opened on 20 May and through it till his conviction on 25 May. Stewart Headlam
recorded that, during the second trial, "each morning I met Mr Wilde and went
with him to the court, and in the evening took him back."
[3] Alfred Waterhouse Somerset Taylor (born *circa* 1862) was well educated and
was said to have run through a fortune of £45,000. His house in Westminster was
used as a meeting-place for male homosexuals. Wilde first met Taylor in 1892.
Although he refused to turn Queen's Evidence against Wilde, and so shared the
same fate, his indictment and trial alongside Wilde certainly prejudiced Wilde's
chances of acquittal. After his release he lived in Canada and the U.S.A.

rather be happy to have filled with an immortal love the soul of a man who now weeps in hell, and yet carries heaven in his heart. I love you, I love you, my heart is a rose which your love has brought to bloom, my life is a desert fanned by the delicious breeze of your breath, and whose cool springs are your eyes; the imprint of your little feet makes valleys of shade for me, the odour of your hair is like myrrh, and wherever you go you exhale the perfumes of the cassia tree.

Love me always, love me always. You have been the supreme, the perfect love of my life; there can be no other.

I decided that it was nobler and more beautiful to stay. We could not have been together. I did not want to be called a coward or a deserter. A false name, a disguise, a hunted life, all that is not for me, to whom you have been revealed on that high hill where beautiful things are transfigured.

O sweetest of all boys, most loved of all loves, my soul clings to your soul, my life is your life, and in all the worlds of pain and pleasure you are my ideal of admiration and joy.   OSCAR

To Robert Ross

10 March 1896   [*H.M. Prison, Reading*][1]

My dear Robbie, I want you to have a letter written at once to Mr Hargrove, the solicitor, stating that as my wife has promised to settle one third

---

[1] Wilde had been moved from Pentonville to Wandsworth on 4 July 1895, and from there to Reading on 20 November. To begin with he was allowed to write only one letter every three months, and the first ones were certainly to his wife and his lawyers. Otho Holland Lloyd (1856–1943), Constance Wilde's only brother, was staying with her at Glion in Switzerland when one of Wilde's prison letters was brought to her by her family solicitor Mr Hargrove. In a letter dated 9 September 1895 to his wife Mary he records what happened:

The first thing Mr Hargrove did was to pull out of his pocket a letter from Oscar; it was for Constance but it had been sent through Mr Hargrove. He, in her interests, had himself read it, and he said that it was one of the most touching and pathetic letters that had ever come under his eye. To cut short a long story it was clear that Mr Hargrove had come prepared to admit the possibility, in view of such a humble, penitent letter, that Constance would give forgiveness to Oscar, a thing which otherwise he would utterly have scouted. . . . So Constance, while saying nothing of my letter, showed him the letter of Mr Sherard, and told him that her mind was already made up not to proceed with the divorce. Of course Mr Hargrove pointed out to her, as he had to do, that in this case she and Oscar must go to the other side of the world with their boys and begin life quite afresh under a new name. But apparently she is ready for that. Myself I believe that in France or Spain they could find a home and friends, while schools could be found for the boys in England, and even that ultimately some ten or fifteen years later Oscar could cautiously make his way back again into England, the more so if works from his pen found readers or an audience in the meantime. All this is supposing him to come through the rest of his term, poor fellow.

And now for Constance's plans. Yesterday she wrote him a few lines to tell him that there was forgiveness for him, and that Cyril never forgets him. By the

on me in the case of her predeceasing me I do not wish any opposition to be made to her purchasing my life-interest.[1] I feel that I have brought such unhappiness on her and such ruin on my children that I have no right to go against her wishes in anything. She was gentle and good to me here, when she came to see me.[2] I have full trust in her. Please have this done *at once*, and thank my friends for their kindness. I feel I am acting rightly in leaving this to my wife.

Please write to Stuart Merrill in Paris, or Robert Sherard, to say how gratified I was at the performance of my play: and have my thanks conveyed to Lugné-Poe;[3] it is something that at a time of disgrace and shame I should be still regarded as an artist. I wish I could feel more pleasure: but I seem dead to all emotions except those of anguish and despair. However, please let Lugné-Poe know that I am sensible of the honour he has done me. He is a poet himself. I fear you will find it difficult to read this, but as I am not allowed writing materials I seem to have forgotten how to write: you must excuse me.

Thank More for exerting himself for books: unluckily I suffer from headaches when I read my Greek and Roman poets, so they have not been of much use, but his kindness was great in getting them sent.[4] Ask him to

same post she wrote to the Governor saying that she would like to be allowed to have an interview with her husband, and she proposes to go over for this purpose to England. . . . I think it will prove that she is acting for the best in taking him back, but only time can show.

[1] Constance Wilde's advisers were anxious for her to buy Wilde's half-share of their marriage settlement from the Official Receiver. Despite Wilde's requests that this should be allowed to happen, his friends had offered the Receiver £50 for Wilde's share.

[2] Lady Wilde had died on 3 February 1896, and Constance travelled specially from Genoa to Reading to break the news to him. Her visit was on 19 February. It was their last meeting. "I went to Reading on Wednesday and saw poor O," she wrote to her brother. "They say he is quite well, but he is an absolute wreck compared with what he was."

[3] Aurélien-Marie Lugné-Poe (1869–1940), the French actor-manager, had produced Wilde's *Salome* at the Théâtre de L'Œuvre in Paris (which he had founded in 1893) on 11 February 1896, with himself as Herod and Lina Munte as Salome. This was the play's first production. Stuart Merrill was the manager of the theatre.

[4] By courtesy of the Home Office I was able to examine the lists of books sent to Wilde in prison. First, through the kindness of R. B. Haldane (1856–1928), Liberal M.P., later Secretary of State for War and twice Lord Chancellor, who visited Wilde in prison, fifteen volumes were sent to Wandsworth in July 1895: the *Confessions* and *De Civitate Dei* (2 vols) of St Augustine, Pascal's *Pensées* and *Provincial Letters*, Pater's *Renaissance*, Mommsen's *History of Rome* (5 vols), and Newman's *Grammar of Assent*, *Apologia*, *Two Essays on Miracles* and *The Idea of a University*. In September 1895 Pater's *Greek Studies*, *Appreciations* and *Imaginary Portraits* were added, and in January 1896 More Adey arranged with the Home Office to send Dante's *Divina Commedia*, Liddell and Scott's Greek Lexicon, Lewis and Short's Latin Dictionary, and the *Corpus Poetarum Latinorum*, followed on 3 February by *Poetae Scenici Graeci*, an Italian dictionary and an Italian grammar.

express also my gratitude to the lady who lives at Wimbledon.[1] Write to me please in answer to this, and tell me about literature—what new books etc: also about Jones's play and Forbes-Robertson's management:[2] about any new tendency in the stage of Paris or London. Also, try and see what Lemaître, Bauër, and Sarcey said of *Salome* and give me a little résumé:[3] please write to Henri Bauër and say I am touched at his writing nicely. Robert knows him. It was sweet of you to come and see me:[4] you must come again next time. Here I have the horror of death with the still greater horror of living: and in silence and misery [*Some lines cut out by prison officials*] but I won't talk more of this. I always remember you with deep affection. Ever your friend   O. W.

I wish Ernest would get from Oakley Street my portmanteau, fur coat, clothes, and the books of *my own writing* I gave my dear mother. Ask Ernest in whose name the burial-ground of my mother was taken. Goodbye.

To Robert Ross

Saturday, [? *23 or 30 May 1896*][5]   [? *H.M. Prison, Reading*]

Dear Robbie, I could not collect my thoughts yesterday, as I did not expect you till today. When you are good enough to come and see me will you always fix the day? Anything sudden upsets me.

You said that Douglas was going to dedicate a volume of poems to me. Will you write at once to him and say he must not do anything of the kind. I could not accept or allow such a dedication. The proposal is revolting and grotesque.[6] Also, he has unfortunately in his possession a number of

---

[1] Adela Schuster (ironically nicknamed Miss Tiny on account of her size), daughter of Leo Schuster, a wealthy Frankfurt banker who had settled in a large villa called Cannizaro at Wimbledon, was a woman of great perception and generosity. While Wilde was out on bail she gave him £1000 for his personal use. Wilde handed the money to Ernest Leverson to hold as trustee, and was later much upset by its use.

[2] *Michael and his Lost Angel* by Henry Arthur Jones had been produced at the Lyceum on 15 January 1896 by Johnston Forbes-Robertson as his first venture in management. It ran for only ten days.

[3] Jules François Elie Lemaître (1854–1914), Henri Bauër (1851–1915) and Francisque Sarcey (1827–99) were three of the leading French dramatic critics. Bauër had reviewed the production of *Salome* favourably in the *Echo de Paris*.

[4] Ross and Leverson had visited Wilde on 25 February 1896.

[5] This letter is difficult to date. The reference to "last Christmas" suggests 1895, but Wilde later placed the dedication incident in May 1896 (see p. 187) and it seems best to follow him. His ignorance of Irving's movements and Stevenson's letters is easily understood. Sherard says that he and Ross visited Wilde on 25 May, but if the Saturday is correct, their visit must have been on the 22nd or the 29th.

[6] When Douglas's *Poems* was published by the *Mercure de France* at the end of 1896 it contained no dedication.

letters of mine. I wish him to at once hand all these without exception over to you; I will ask you to seal them up. In case I die here you will destroy them. In case I survive I will destroy them myself. They must not be in existence. The thought that they are in his hands is horrible to me, and though my unfortunate children will never of course bear my name, still they know whose sons they are and I must try and shield them from the possibility of any further revolting disclosure or scandal.

Also, Douglas has some things I gave him: books and jewellery. I wish these to be also handed over to you—for me. Some of the jewellery I know has passed out of his possession under circumstances unnecessary to detail, but he has still some, such as the gold cigarette-case, pearl chain and enamelled locket I gave him last Christmas. I wish to be certain that he has in his possession nothing that I ever gave him. All these are to be sealed up and left with you. The idea that he is wearing or in possession of anything I gave him is peculiarly repugnant to me. I cannot of course get rid of the revolting memories of the two years I was unlucky enough to have him with me, or of the mode by which he thrust me into the abyss of ruin and disgrace to gratify his hatred of his father and other ignoble passions. But I will not have him in possession of my letters or gifts. Even if I get out of this loathsome place I know that there is nothing before me but a life of a pariah—of disgrace and penury and contempt—but at least I will have nothing to do with him nor allow him to come near me.

So will you write at once to him and get these things: until I know they are in your possession I will be more miserable than usual. It is I know an ungracious thing to ask you to do, and he will perhaps write to you in terms of coarse abuse, as he did to Sherard when he was prevented publishing more of my letters, but I earnestly beg of you not to mind. *As soon* as you have received them please write to me, and make part of your letter just like your other, with all its interesting news of literature and the stage. Let me know why Irving leaves Lyceum etc, what he is playing:[1] what at each theatre: who did Stevenson criticise severely in his letters:[2] anything that will for an hour take my thoughts away from the one revolting subject of my imprisonment.

In writing to Douglas you had better quote my letter fully and frankly, so that he should have no loophole of escape. Indeed he cannot possibly refuse. He has ruined my life—that should content him.

I am deeply touched by the Lady of Wimbledon's kindness. You are very good to come and see me. Kind regards to More, whom I would so like to see.   O. W.

[*Ten words omitted*][3] The Sphinx has some letters of D's to me: they should be returned to him at once, or destroyed.   O. W.

[1] Irving, whose knighthood had been announced on the day of Wilde's conviction, had ended his Lyceum season on 27 July 1895 and then toured America for ten months. He reappeared at the Lyceum in *Cymbeline* on 22 September 1896.

[2] Robert Louis Stevenson had died in Samoa on 3 December 1894, and his *Vailima Letters*, edited by their recipient Sidney Colvin, had been published on 2 November 1895.

[3] A piece of unimportant gossip which might give pain to descendants.

To the Home Secretary [1]

2 July 1896   *H.M. Prison, Reading*

To the Right Honourable Her Majesty's Principal Secretary of State for the Home Department.

The Petition of the above-named prisoner humbly sheweth that he does not desire to attempt to palliate in any way the terrible offences of which he was rightly found guilty, but to point out that such offences are forms of sexual madness and are recognised as such not merely by modern pathological science but by much modern legislation, notably in France, Austria, and Italy, where the laws affecting these misdemeanours have been repealed, on the ground that they are diseases to be cured by a physician, rather than crimes to be punished by a judge. In the works of eminent men of science such as Lombroso and Nordau,[2] to take merely two instances out of many, this is specially insisted on with reference to the intimate connection between madness and the literary and artistic temperament, Professor Nordau in his book on "Degenerescence" published in 1894 having devoted an entire chapter to the petitioner as a specially typical example of this fatal law.

The petitioner is now keenly conscious of the fact that while the three years preceding his arrest were from the intellectual point of view the most brilliant years of his life (four plays from his pen having been produced on the stage with immense success, and played not merely in England, America, and Australia, but in almost every European capital, and many books that excited much interest at home and abroad having been published), still that during the entire time he was suffering from the most horrible form of erotomania, which made him forget his wife and children, his high social position in London and Paris, his European distinction as an artist, the honour of his name and family, his very humanity itself, and left him the helpless prey of the most revolting passions, and of a gang of people who for their own profit ministered to them, and then drove him to

---

[1] This and three other petitions are all written on official forms, on which the opening words as far as "sheweth" are printed. The Home Secretary was Sir Matthew White Ridley, Bart (1842–1904). He was created Viscount 1900. If this appeal seems a little desperate and exaggerated, the reader should remember that Wilde had already been in prison for more than a year, a shattering experience for one of his temperament and circumstances, and had begun to suffer from the painful ear-disease which was to kill him four years later.

[2] Cesare Lombroso (1836–1909) was an Italian criminologist, several of whose books had been translated into English. Max Simon Nordau (1849–1923) was a German author and sociologist. *Degeneration* (1895) was the English translation of the second edition of his book *Entartung* (1893). In Chapter 3 ("Decadents and Aesthetes") of Book Three ("Ego-Mania") Wilde was unfavourably discussed in these contexts, but his trials quickly rendered such judgments obsolete, and in the third German edition of the book (1896) Nordau added a long, up-to-date footnote. Bernard Shaw's attack on the book in the American Anarchist paper *Liberty* in July 1895 was reprinted with revisions as *The Sanity of Art* (1908).

his hideous ruin.

It is under the ceaseless apprehension lest this insanity, that displayed itself in monstrous sexual perversion before, may now extend to the entire nature and intellect, that the petitioner writes this appeal which he earnestly entreats may be at once considered. Horrible as all actual madness is, the terror of madness is no less appalling, and no less ruinous to the soul.

For more than thirteen dreadful months now, the petitioner has been subject to the fearful system of solitary cellular confinement: without human intercourse of any kind; without writing materials whose use might help to distract the mind: without suitable or sufficient books, so essential to any literary man, so vital for the preservation of mental balance: condemned to absolute silence: cut off from all knowledge of the external world and the movements of life: leading an existence composed of bitter degradations and terrible hardships, hideous in its recurring monotony of dreary task and sickening privation: the despair and misery of this lonely and wretched life having been intensified beyond words by the death of his mother, Lady Wilde, to whom he was deeply attached, as well as by the contemplation of the ruin he has brought on his young wife and his two children.

By special permission the petitioner is allowed two books a week to read: but the prison library is extremely small and poor: it hardly contains a score of books suitable for an educated man: the books kindly added at the prisoner's request he has read and re-read till they have become almost meaningless to him: he is practically left without anything to read: the world of ideas, as the actual world, is closed to him: he is deprived of everything that could soothe, distract, or heal a wounded and shaken mind: and horrible as all the physical privations of modern prison life are, they are as nothing compared to the entire privation of literature to one to whom Literature was once the first thing of life, the mode by which perfection could be realised, by which, and by which alone, the intellect could feel itself alive.

It is but natural that living in this silence, this solitude, this isolation from all human and humane influences, this tomb for those who are not yet dead, the petitioner should, day and night in every waking hour, be tortured by the fear of absolute and entire insanity. He is conscious that his mind, shut out artificially from all rational and intellectual interests, does nothing, and can do nothing, but brood on those forms of sexual perversity, those loathsome modes of erotomania, that have brought him from high place and noble distinction to the convict's cell and the common gaol. It is inevitable that it should do so. The mind is forced to think, and when it is deprived of the conditions necessary for healthy intellectual activity, such as books, writing materials, companionship, contact with the living world, and the like, it becomes, in the case of those who are suffering from sensual monomanias, the sure prey of morbid passions, and obscene fancies, and thoughts that defile, desecrate and destroy. Crimes may be forgotten or forgiven, but vices live on: they make their dwelling house in him who by horrible mischance or fate has become their victim: they are embedded in his flesh: they spread over him like a leprosy: they feed on him like a strange disease: at the end they become an essential part of the man: no remorse however poignant can drive them out: no tears however bitter can wash them away: and prison life, by its horrible isolation from all that could save a wretched soul, hands the victim over, like one bound hand and foot, to be possessed and polluted by the thoughts he most loathes and so cannot escape from.

For more than a year the petitioner's mind has borne this. It can bear it no longer. He is quite conscious of the approach of an insanity that will not be confined to one portion of the nature merely, but will extend over all alike, and his desire, his prayer is that his sentence may be remitted now, so that he may be taken abroad by his friends and may put himself under medical care so that the sexual insanity from which he suffers may be cured. He knows only too well that his career as a dramatist and writer is ended, and his name blotted from the scroll of English Literature never to be replaced: that his children cannot bear that name again, and that an obscure life in some remote country is in store for him: he knows that, bankruptcy having come upon him, poverty of a most bitter kind awaits him, and that all the joy and beauty of existence is taken from him for ever: but at least in all his hopelessness he still clings to the hope that he will not have to pass directly from the common gaol to the common lunatic asylum.

Dreadful as are the results of the prison system—a system so terrible that it hardens their hearts whose hearts it does not break, and brutalises those who have to carry it out no less than those who have to submit to it —yet at least amongst its aims is not the desire to wreck the human reason. Though it may not seek to make men better, yet it does not desire to drive them mad, and so, earnestly does the petitioner beg that he may be allowed to go forth while he has still some sanity left: while words have still a meaning, and books a message: while there is still some possibility that, by medical science and humane treatment, balance may be restored to a shaken mind and health given back to a nature that once knew purity: while there is still time to rid the temperament of a revolting madness and to make the soul, even for a brief space, clean.

Most earnestly indeed does the petitioner beg the Home Secretary to take, if he so desires it, the opinion of any recognised medical authorities on what would be the inevitable result of solitary confinement in silence and isolation on one already suffering from sexual monomania of a terrible character.

The petitioner would also point out that while his bodily health is better in many respects here than it was at Wandsworth, where he was for two months in the hospital for absolute physical and mental collapse caused by hunger and insomnia, he has, since he has been in prison, almost entirely lost the hearing of his right ear through an abscess that has caused a perforation of the drum. The medical officer here has stated that he is unable to offer any assistance, and that the hearing must go entirely. The petitioner, however, feels sure that under the care of a specialist abroad his hearing might be preserved to him. He was assured by Sir William Dalby,[1] the great aurist, that with proper care there was no reason at all why he should lose his hearing. But though the abscess has been running now for the entire time of his imprisonment, and the hearing getting worse every week, nothing has been done in the way even of an attempted cure. The ear has been syringed on three occasions with plain water for the purpose of examination, that is all. The petitioner is naturally apprehensive lest, as often happens, the other ear may be attacked in a similar way, and to the misery of a shattered and debilitated mind be added the horrors of complete deafness.

His eyesight, of which like most men of letters he had always been obliged to take great care, has also suffered very much from the enforced living in a whitewashed cell with a flaring gas-jet at night: he is conscious of great weakness and pain in the nerves of the eyes, and objects even at a short distance become blurred. The bright daylight, when taking exercise in the prison-yard, often causes pain and distress to the optic nerve, and during the past four months the consciousness of failing eyesight has been a source of terrible anxiety, and should his imprisonment be continued, blindness and deafness may in all human probability be added to the certainty of increasing insanity and the wreck of the reason.

There are other apprehensions of danger that the limitation of space does not allow the petitioner to enter on: his chief danger is that of madness, his chief terror that of madness, and his prayer that his long imprisonment may be considered with its attendant ruin a sufficient punishment, that the imprisonment may be ended now, and not uselessly or vindictively prolonged till insanity has claimed soul as well as body as its prey, and brought it to the same degradation and the same shame.   OSCAR WILDE[2]

---

[1] William Bartlett Dalby (1840–1918). Knighted 1886.

[2] This petition was forwarded to the Home Office by the Governor of Reading Prison, Major Isaacson, together with a short medical report from the prison doctor, saying that Wilde had put on weight in prison and showed no signs of insanity. Four Prison Visitors were sent to Reading to carry out an enquiry, and on 10 July they reported in much the same terms as the prison doctor. The Home Office then referred the papers to Dr Nicolson, the medical officer at Broadmoor who had examined Wilde at Wandsworth. As a result of Dr Nicolson's recommendations the Home Office on 27 July ordered the Governor to allow Wilde to have writing materials in his cell and a larger supply of books. A list of his requests, written in his own hand, is in the Home Office files. The new Governor, Major J. O. Nelson, deleted some of the titles, and the amended list was approved by the Home Office, with the proviso that the total net cost of the books must not exceed £10, which was the prison's allotment for 1896–97. The list includes a Greek Testament, the works of Chaucer, Marlowe, Spenser, Keats and Tennyson, Percy's *Reliques*, Carlyle's *Sartor Resartus* and *Life of Frederick the Great*, Newman's *Critical and Historical Essays*, Emerson's *Essays*, a prose translation of Dante's *Divine Comedy* and Renan's *Vie de Jésus* and *Les Apôtres* (Wilde explained: "The chaplain sees no objection to these if they are in the original French"). Wilde pointed out that the prison library contained none of Thackeray's or Dickens's novels—"I feel sure that a complete set of their works would be as great a boon to many amongst the other prisoners as it certain would be to myself." A set of Dickens was allowed.

To More Adey

Friday [*25 September 1896*]
[*Postmark 28 September 1896*]   [*H.M. Prison, Reading*]

My dear More, I was greatly delighted to get your letter.[1] I was afraid that Bobbie might have been ill, and that that was the cause of the delay. It was a real pleasure to hear from him at such length, and to see his old wit and pleasant satire running through his budget: I do hope he will be quite well soon. Please thank his mother for her kind messages. I am very glad she has been spared to watch over Bobbie in his illness.

I thank you very much for writing to the Home Secretary.[2] I do hope

---

[1] Part of a draft of Adey's letter of 23 September runs:

Robbie is still at the sea, with his brother and mother, who has taken a house there for him. She sends you kind messages saying she often thinks of you and prays for your welfare. Robbie is going on well, the doctors say, but he suffers a great deal from dyspepsia which affects his spirits very much. You know how much he thinks of and feels for you. He looks very ill still. . . .

Miss Schuster says "Could not Mr Wilde now write down some of the lovely tales he used to tell me? Remind him of one about a nursing-sister who killed the man whom she was nursing. And there was one about the two souls on the banks of the Nile. Were there time I could mention others, but I think the mere reminder of some of his tales may set his mind in that direction and stir the impulse to write. He told me also a beautiful play (just two years ago) that he has not written, about a husband, a wife and her lover, with a plot rather in the style of *Frou-frou*." [see note p. 119] . . .

Acting on advice I have just written to the Home Secretary, undertaking, if are released before May, to accompany you abroad at once, and promising that you will remain there until after the end of May. I hope I did right.

I have also written to your wife saying you are better, as I gave her a very bad account of you after I saw you in July. I think it would be well if you obtained leave to write to her; if you were inclined to consent to her appointing a guardian of whom you approved for your children in case of her death it would be well to tell her so, but I think a letter to her in any case would be a good thing.

If you should hear of anything that I have done on your behalf without your knowledge of which you do not approve, I trust you will repudiate it in as strong terms as you please. If you should have changed your mind about the clothes, let me know when you write, otherwise I will order you a travelling suit from your tailors Doré. I think on the whole my suggestion was the better one, but it really does not matter if you prefer my getting them at Doré's. I shall not go abroad until I am quite certain I cannot be of any use to you here. I hope you do not think I have any feeling against Sherard. I am on perfectly friendly terms with all your friends and get on particularly well with Sherard. I merely object to his frightful indiscretion, which is a positive mania with him and, contrary to his affectionate intentions, does you harm.

[2] Adey's petition to the Home Secretary (which is believed to have been drafted by Bernard Shaw) urging a remission of Wilde's sentence, though printed and ready, was never sent, since almost immediately Adey received a letter from the Home Office saying that "the case of this prisoner has been the subject of careful inquiry and consideration" and that therefore the Home Secretary "has come to the conclusion that no grounds, medical or other, exist which would justify him in advising any mitigation of the sentence."

it will have some effect. But pity seems to beat in vain at the doors of officialism; and power, no less than punishment, kills what else were good and gentle in a man: the man without knowing it loses his natural kindliness, or grows afraid of its exercise. Still, I hope something may be done. I admit that I look forward with horror to the prospect of another winter in prison: there is something terrible in it: one has to get up long before daybreak and in the dark cold cell begin one's work by the flaring gas-jet; through the small barred window only gloom seems to find an entrance: and days often go over without one's being once even in the open air: days on which one stifles: days that are endless in their dull monotony of apathy or despair. If I could be released before the winter comes, it would be everything. On November 19th I will have had eighteen months of this black loathsome life: perhaps then something may be done.[1] I know you will do your best: I have no words for my sense of your great wonderful kindness to me.

With regard to my children, I feel that for their own sake as well as for mine they should not be bred up to look on me with either hatred or contempt: a guardian amongst my wife's relations would be for this reason impossible. Of course I would like Arthur Clifton[2] if he would undertake the charge. And so, would you ask Arthur to be my solicitor now: Humphreys is of course of no use: though paid an enormous fee through Leverson he never once came to see me about my Bankruptcy: so I was allowed to become insolvent when there was no reason.[3] If Arthur will be my solicitor he can on application to the Home Secretary come and see me in the Solicitors' Room here for one hour without the presence of a warder, and with him I could discuss the whole affair, and then write to my wife on the whole subject. I would feel quite safe if Arthur was my children's guardian. And as a solicitor his advice would be of great service. If he

---

[1] On 10 November Wilde sent another petition to the Home Secretary asking to be released on completion of eighteen months' imprisonment. He wrote:

Some alleviations have been granted to the petitioner since the date of his former petition: his ear, that was in danger of total deafness, is now attended to daily: spectacles have been provided for the protection of his eyes: he is allowed a manuscript-book to write in, and out of a list of books, selected by himself and approved of by the Prison Commissioners, a few have been added to the Prison Library: but these alleviations, for which the petitioner is naturally very grateful, count for but little in relieving the terrible mental stress and anguish that the silence and solitude of prison-life intensify daily.

The petition was rejected almost immediately.

[2] Arthur Bellamy Clifton (1862–1932), son of the Professor of Experimental Philosophy at Oxford, was a solicitor who gradually became an art-dealer. In 1898, together with John Fothergill (see note 1, p. 286), he started the Carfax Gallery in Ryder Street and acted as business manager. In 1900 Robert Ross and More Adey joined the gallery, which exhibited early works by Conder, John, Max Beerbohm, Sickert and Rothenstein.

[3] Wilde had been taken from prison for his public examination in the Bankruptcy Court on 24 September 1895. The examination was adjourned until 12 November, when he was again brought up.

could come within the next fortnight it would be a great thing.[1]

I was greatly touched by the extract from the letter of the Lady of Wimbledon. That she should keep a gracious memory of me, and have trust or hope for me in the future, lightens for me many dreadful hours of degradation or despair. I have tried to remember and write down the *Florentine Tragedy*:[2] but only bits of it remain with me, and I find that I cannot invent: the silence, the utter solitude, the isolation from all humane and humanising influences, kill one's brain-power: the brain loses its life: becomes fettered to monotony of suffering. But I take notes of books I read, and copy lines and phrases in poets: the mere handling of pen and ink helps me: the horror of prison is the horror of complete brutalisation: that is the abyss always in front of one, branding itself on one's face daily, and the faces of those one sees. I cling to my notebook: it helps me: before I had it my brain was going in very evil circles.

I am so glad you are friends with Robert Sherard: I have no doubt he is very indiscreet, but he is very true, and saved my letters from being published. I know there was nothing in them but expressions of foolish, misplaced, ill-requited, affection for one of crude and callous nature, of coarse greed, and common appetites, but that is why their publication would have been so shameful. The gibbet on which I swing in history now is high enough. There is no need that he of all men should for his own vanity make it more hideous.

I am so glad Pierre Louÿs has made a great name for himself.[3] He was most cultivated, refined, and gentle. Three years ago he told me I would have to choose between his friendship and my fatal connection with A.D. I need hardly say I chose at once the meaner nature and the baser mind.

---

[1] On 8 October 1896 Arthur Clifton wrote to Carlos Blacker:

I was very much shocked at Oscar's appearance, though scarcely surprised. Fortunately he had his ordinary clothes on: his hair was rather long and he looked dreadfully thin. You can imagine how painful it was to meet him: and he was very much upset and cried a good deal: he seemed quite broken-hearted and kept on describing his punishment as savage. Of course I talked as much as possible about the future, about the friendship of his friends, about his plays and everything I could think of to cheer him up. He was very eager for news and I told him as much as possible of what had happened lately and really I suppose I did most of the talking.

As to business matters, he did not express any decided opinion, but thought he ought to be left something out of the settlement if possible, and I told him what I thought would be a good plan—namely that he should retain about a third of his life-interest: and I told him I would do my best to see that that was arranged.

As I told you, Mrs Wilde, whom I saw immediately after, quite agreed, so there ought to be little difficulty.

He has been reading Pater and Newman lately, one book a week. I do not know what work he does.

He was terribly despondent and said several times that he did not think he would be able to last the punishment out.

[2] *A Florentine Tragedy*, a play in blank verse which Wilde originally intended for Lewis Waller, but never finished.

[3] Louÿs's book *Aphrodite* (1896) was a phenomenal success in France.

148

In what a mire of madness I walked! . . .[1] From your silence I see he still refuses to return my presents and letters . . . It is horrible he should still have the power to wound me and find some curious joy in doing so . . . I won't write about him any more today. He is too evil, and there is a storm outside. . . .

Poor Aubrey: I hope he will get all right.[2] He brought a strangely new personality to English art, and was a master in his way of fantastic grace, and the charm of the unreal. His muse had moods of terrible laughter. Behind his grotesques there seemed to lurk some curious philosophy . . .

As for my clothes, my fur coat is all I need really; the rest I can get abroad. Don't bother yourself. I hope Arthur will come and bring me good news of you and Robbie. Ever yours   OSCAR

To More Adey

8 March 1897   *H.M. Prison, Reading*

My dear More, I am very much obliged to you for your letter, which the Governor has kindly allowed me to have and to answer. My business is I know unpleasant, but then it was not for pleasure that you took its burden on you, so I will write quite frankly to you.

Your news has distressed me a good deal. The claims of my own trustees and my brother-in-law would of course be easily withdrawn, and I thought I could, if the Queensberry debt was paid, as it should have been, by the Queensberry family, have made an effort at any rate to pay off my own personal creditors, who are really very few in number. I see, however, that this cannot be. I will now have to think of how to retain or buy my interest in my books and plays. I do not think they will be valued high. As £150 has been already paid to Humphreys who did nothing to help me (beyond of course forcing me to put in two appearances at the Bankruptcy Court where one would have been sufficient, and engaging their own relative Mr Grain to appear as counsel where no counsel was required) I am reluctant to even write to them.[3] I am very anxious however to know how I can be kept informed of the state of things, so that if my copyrights are to be sold I may have a chance of bidding for them. I am also anxious about my claim to the place in Ireland: it is now in utter rack and ruin, but I am reluctant to see it pass to a stranger: could Mr Holman,[4] already in communication with the Receiver, let you know if anything happens? In the case of my brother's death, without male issue, the Irish property should fetch something: £4000 or £5000 at least.

As regards the Queensberry family, I of course feel very strongly about their allowing me to be made bankrupt by their father for the costs of the

---

[1] All the dots in this letter are Wilde's.

[2] Aubrey Beardsley had already begun to suffer from consumption.

[3] John Peter Grain (1839–1916), barrister brother of Corney Grain, the entertainer, was C. O. Humphreys's brother-in-law. He appeared as counsel for Alfred Taylor in both Wilde's trials, and for Wilde in the Bankruptcy Court.

[4] Martin Holman of the firm of Parker, Garrett & Holman, Adey's solicitors.

trial, and for such an absolutely contemptible sum; less than half, as I told you, of what in three wasted summer months I spent on Bosie at Goring—less than one half! Their idea that it would be a sort of "score" off their father not to pay him his paltry claim showed how utterly blind they were to my feelings. As for Queensberry, I suppose nobody ever had such intense pleasure of a low order at such a low cost as he had. It was in the cheapest of markets that he bought his triumph. Indeed it was the only occasion in his life that he found his pleasures economical. To send a man like myself to prison for £900, and then to take him out and make him an insolvent for £700 more, was a piece of good fortune he never looked for. As regards my own debts, they were hardly anything. Their letting their father triumph a second time over me, rather than pay so petty, so abject a sum as £700, cut me very deeply. And people who live in the world of action don't understand that there is another world in which they who are not free live: a world in which nothing happens but emotions, and in which consequently emotions have a power, a proportion, a permanence that is beyond the possibility of description.

I was told, on Percy's behalf, that he had laid aside the sum of £600 for me, as the equivalent of his father's costs, to be used I suppose in buying back for me the property the Bankruptcy Receiver had seized, and possibly in other ways. I conveyed to him my thanks. I consider Percy a very good-hearted fellow, kind and considerate. I would very much like to see him again sometime. He should of course have paid the costs, and left me then if necessary to settle my other debts. But he, I have no doubt, acted under advice. If he had realised matters a little more he would have seen that he merely doubled his father's delight and exultation by not interfering to prevent my insolvency. It was the only thing Queensberry was afraid of. He need not have been . . .[1] With regard to the whole question the Queensberry family must remember that through them I am in prison, through them a bankrupt, and that they can hardly allow people whom they ruined so completely to go to the workhouse.

I was touched and helped immeasurably by your telling me that some friends of mine have arranged that for eighteen months I am to have enough to live on: that gives me breathing space. But of course I cannot trespass for a lifetime on those on whom I have no more claim than any other of the poor and wretched and homeless people of whom God's world is so full. I couldn't do it. And I may live longer than eighteen months. A heart may be broken and yet fulfil its natural functions. The soul may sit in the shadow of death, and yet the body walk in the ways of life, and breathe and eat and know the sun and rain. I have no organic disease of any kind. I am troubled with insomnia, but I get my four or five hours of sleep every night. Supposing I live on? I should not be at all surprised if I did. I come of a long-lived race. The Queensberry family had better consider the point, the Douglases we will call them, as the other name is loathsome. There are debts of dishonour in a family as well as debts of honour. If the Douglas estates have to be burdened with a prospective claim of some paltry life-

[1] Wilde's dots.

interest, let them be so burdened. A family cannot ruin a man like me, and look on the whole thing merely as a subject for sentiment or reminiscence over the walnuts and the wine. People, as somebody in one of Ibsen's plays says, don't do these things.[1] It is dreadful that it should fall on me to remind them. They should consult their family solicitor, and let him communicate the result to my solicitor. That is all that is necessary.

You say in your letter that Bosie is so anxious to make "some little return" to me for all I "spent on him." Unfortunately, I spent on him my life, my genius, my position, my name in history; for these no little, or big return is possible. But as regards the mere wretched pounds, shillings, and pence side of my ruin—the workhouse aspect—he must seriously consider the whole point. It is his duty to do so. His duty to himself as much, far more indeed, than to me. When people play a tragedy they should play it in the "grand style." All smallness, pettiness, meagreness of mood or gesture is out of place. If the Douglases don't recognise this, let me be informed. But I don't doubt that they will. It is a perfectly obvious matter. And as for me, my life will of course necessarily be one of great retirement, simplicity and economy of living, and many modes of self-denial, imposed and accepted. But a certain small permanence is requisite even for the practice of the virtues of thrift and economy. Bosie must consider the matter. I will be much obliged if you will copy out all that I have written, from the bottom of page one,[2] and send it off to him. It will relieve my own letter to him of a very unpleasing duty, one that a little thought on his part would have spared me.

As regards my children, I sincerely hope I may be recognised by the Court as having some little, I won't say right, but claim to be allowed to see Cyril from time to time: it would be to me a sorrow beyond words if I were not. I do hope the Court will see in me something more than a man with a tragic vice in his life. There is so much more in me, and I always was a good father to both my children. I love them dearly and was dearly loved by them, and Cyril was my friend. And it would be better for them not to be forced to think of me as an outcast, but to know me as a man who has suffered. Pray let everything be done on my behalf that is possible. A little recognition by the Court would help me so much. And it is a terrible responsibility for the Law to say to a father that he is unfit to see his own children: the consciousness of it often makes me unhappy all day long.

As regards my life-interest, should Mr Hargrove make any proposal about it, it of course will be communicated to me by you *at once*. It will require grave consideration. The advances cannot come from me, can they? Should my own solicitor come to see me, pray let it be the last week in this month. I am quite distressed at the idea of his only charging £1. 1 and expenses. I think he should have at least £3. 3. Let the money be got from Leverson, and whatever Mr Stoker[3] is owed be paid to him from the same fund in Leverson's hands.

---

[1] The last line of *Hedda Gabler*.   [2] Here from the bottom of p. 149.
[3] Presumably a partner in Messrs Stoker & Hansell, solicitors.

I fear you see traces of bitterness in my business letters. Yes, that is so. It is very terrible. In the prison in which my body is I am shown much kindness, but in the prison in which my soul is I can show myself none. I hope that neither in your heart nor in Robbie's, nor in the heart of any that have been good to me, will bitterness of any kind ever find a place. It makes one suffer very deeply. Your affectionate friend   OSCAR WILDE

I quite see that I must accept, gratefully indeed, my discharge as a bankrupt, when I get it, and then set to work to try and pay off some of the debts. I suppose it won't be done till I go out of prison? I would like things held over, on account of the sale of copyrights etc. At present I receive no communication at all from the Receiver. That is, I suppose, right.

For the list of books, so many thanks. I am going to ask for a Bible in French: *la Sainte Bible*.

To Lord Alfred Douglas[1]

[*January–March 1897*]   *H.M. Prison, Reading*

Dear Bosie, After long and fruitless waiting I have determined to write to you myself, as much for your sake as for mine, as I would not like to think

---

[1] This long letter was not posted from Reading (see note p. 240), but on the day after Wilde left prison he handed it to Robert Ross (see p. 266), who had two typed copies made. According to Ross he then sent Douglas, not the original manuscript, as Wilde had instructed (see p. 241), but one of the typed copies, which Douglas always denied having received.

In 1905 Ross published extracts, amounting to less than half the letter, under the title *De Profundis* (which was suggested by E. V. Lucas), and a slightly fuller version appeared in the Collected Edition of 1908. Neither of these contained any references to Douglas. In 1909 Ross presented the original manuscript to the British Museum, on condition that no one be allowed to see it for fifty years.

The second typescript, kept by Ross and eventually bequeathed by him to Vyvyan Holland, supplied the text for the "first complete and accurate version" which Mr Holland published, again as *De Profundis*, in 1949. Everyone naturally assumed that typescript and manuscript were identical, and that this edition was indeed complete and accurate, but in fact it was neither. It contained several hundred errors, which can be divided into four main categories:

1. Misreadings of Wilde's hand.
2. Aural misprints, probably caused by Ross's dictating to an ill-educated typist.
3. Ross's "improvement" of Wilde's grammar and syntax.
4. The inexplicable shifting of passages and whole paragraphs from one part of the letter to another.

In addition, Ross removed in all more than a thousand words, almost all of them fiercely critical of Douglas and his father: the description of Lord Queensberry in court (see p. 220) is a striking example. This longest and most important of all Wilde's letters was finally printed exactly as he wrote it, in *Letters*, except that I broke it up into rather more paragraphs than his scanty ration of paper allowed him.

The letter is written on twenty folio sheets (each of four pages) of blue ruled prison paper, with the Royal Arms blind-stamped at the head of each sheet. The sheets are numbered 1 to 18 (including 3A and 5A) in Wilde's hand. On 4 April 1897 the Governor of Reading Gaol, explaining how the letter had been written,

that I had passed through two long years of imprisonment without ever having received a single line from you, or any news or message even, except such as gave me pain.

Our ill-fated and most lamentable friendship has ended in ruin and public infamy for me, yet the memory of our ancient affection is often with me, and the thought that loathing, bitterness and contempt should for ever take that place in my heart once held by love is very sad to me: and you yourself will, I think, feel in your heart that to write to me as I lie in the loneliness of prison-life is better than to publish my letters without my permission or to dedicate poems to me unasked, though the world will know nothing of whatever words of grief or passion, of remorse or indifference you may choose to send as your answer or your appeal.

I have no doubt that in this letter in which I have to write of your life and of mine, of the past and of the future, of sweet things changed to bitterness and of bitter things that may be turned into joy, there will be much that will wound your vanity to the quick. If it prove so, read the letter over and over again till it kills your vanity. If you find in it something of which you feel that you are unjustly accused, remember that one should be thankful that there is any fault of which one can be unjustly accused. If there be in it one single passage that brings tears to your eyes, weep as we weep in prison where the day no less than the night is set apart for tears. It is the only thing that can save you. If you go complaining to your mother, as you did with reference to the scorn of you I displayed in my letter to Robbie, so that she may flatter and soothe you back into self-complacency or conceit, you will be completely lost. If you find one false excuse for yourself, you will soon find a hundred, and be just what you were before. Do you still say, as you said to Robbie in your answer, that I "*attribute unworthy motives*" to you? Ah! you had no motives in life. You had appetites merely. A motive is an intellectual aim. That you were "*very young*" when our friendship began? Your defect was not that you knew so little about life, but that you knew so much. The morning dawn of boyhood with its delicate bloom, its clear pure light, its joy of innocence and expectation you had left far behind. With very swift and running feet you had passed from Romance to Realism. The gutter and the things

wrote to the Prison Commissioners: "Each sheet was carefully numbered before being issued and withdrawn each evening at locking and placed before me in the morning with the usual papers." Careful study of the manuscript makes this statement hard to believe, and I suspect that Major Nelson (see note p. 217) had been much more considerate to Wilde than his official position allowed him to admit to his superiors. My reasons for this belief are:

(a) Sheets 1, 2 and 13 have every appearance of being fair copies. The writing on them is more ordered, neat and compact than anywhere else, and they contain scarcely a correction or second thought, whereas all the other seventeen sheets are heavily corrected.

(b) Only two of the twenty sheets (apart from the last one) finish at the end of a sentence.

(c) In Wilde's covering letter of 1 April 1897 (see p. 241) he quotes from several different sheets at once—"from memory" he says, but his accuracy makes this claim scarcely credible.

that live in it had begun to fascinate you. That was the origin of the trouble in which you sought my aid, and I, so unwisely according to the wisdom of this world, out of pity and kindness gave it to you. You must read this letter right through, though each word may become to you as the fire or knife of the surgeon that makes the delicate flesh burn or bleed. Remember that the fool in the eyes of the gods and the fool in the eyes of man are very different. One who is entirely ignorant of the modes of Art in its revolution or the moods of thought in its progress, of the pomp of the Latin line or the richer music of the vowelled Greek, of Tuscan sculpture or Elizabethan song may yet be full of the very sweetest wisdom. The real fool, such as the gods mock or mar, is he who does not know himself. I was such a one too long. You have been such a one too long. Be so no more. Do not be afraid. The supreme vice is shallowness. Everything that is realised is right. Remember also that whatever is misery to you to read, is still greater misery to me to set down. To you the Unseen Powers have been very good. They have permitted you to see the strange and tragic shapes of Life as one sees shadows in a crystal. The head of Medusa that turns living men to stone, you have been allowed to look at in a mirror merely. You yourself have walked free among the flowers. From me the beautiful world of colour and motion has been taken away.

I will begin by telling you that I blame myself terribly. As I sit here in this dark cell in convict clothes, a disgraced and ruined man, I blame myself. In the perturbed and fitful nights of anguish, in the long monotonous days of pain, it is myself I blame. I blame myself for allowing an unintellectual friendship, a friendship whose primary aim was not the creation and contemplation of beautiful things, to entirely dominate my life. From the very first there was too wide a gap between us. You had been idle at your school, worse than idle at your university. You did not realise that an artist, and especially such an artist as I am,[1] one, that is to say, the quality of whose work depends on the intensification of personality, requires for the development of his art the companionship of ideas, and intellectual atmosphere, quiet, peace, and solitude. You admired my work when it was finished: you enjoyed the brilliant successes of my first nights, and the brilliant banquets that followed them: you were proud, and quite naturally so, of being the intimate friend of an artist so distinguished: but you could not understand the conditions requisite for the production of artistic work. I am not speaking in phrases of rhetorical exaggeration but in terms of absolute truth to actual fact when I remind you that during the whole time we were together I never wrote one single line. Whether at Torquay, Goring, London, Florence or elsewhere, my life, as long as you were by my side, was entirely sterile and uncreative. And with but few intervals you were, I regret to say, by my side always.

I remember, for instance, in September '93, to select merely one instance out of many, taking a set of chambers, purely in order to work undisturbed, as I had broken my contract with John Hare for whom I had promised to write a play, and who was pressing me on the subject. During

[1] Wilde originally wrote "was."

the first week you kept away. We had, not unnaturally indeed, differed on the question of the artistic value of your translation of *Salome*, so you contented yourself with sending me foolish letters on the subject. In that week I wrote and completed in every detail, as it was ultimately performed, the first act of *An Ideal Husband*. The second week you returned and my work practically had to be given up. I arrived at St James's Place every morning at 11.30, in order to have the opportunity of thinking and writing without the interruptions inseparable from my own household, quiet and peaceful as that household was. But the attempt was vain. At twelve o'clock you drove up, and stayed smoking cigarettes and chattering till 1.30, when I had to take you out to luncheon at the Café Royal or the Berkeley. Luncheon with its *liqueurs* lasted usually till 3.30. For an hour you retired to White's. At tea-time you appeared again, and stayed till it was time to dress for dinner. You dined with me either at the Savoy or at Tite Street. We did not separate as a rule till after midnight, as supper at Willis's had to wind up the entrancing day. That was my life for those three months, every single day, except during the four days when you went abroad. I then, of course, had to go over to Calais to fetch you back. For one of my nature and temperament it was a position at once grotesque and tragic.

You surely must realise that now? You must see now that your incapacity of being alone: your nature so exigent in its persistent claim on the attention and time of others: your lack of any power of sustained intellectual concentration: the unfortunate accident—for I like to think it was no more—that you had not yet been able to acquire the "Oxford temper" in intellectual matters, never, I mean, been one who could play gracefully with ideas but had arrived at violence of opinion merely—that all these things, combined with the fact that your desires and interests were in Life not in Art, were as destructive to your own progress in culture as they were to my work as an artist? When I compare my friendship with you to my friendship with such still younger men as John Gray[1] and Pierre Louÿs I feel ashamed. My real life, my higher life was with them and such as they.

Of the appalling results of my friendship with you I don't speak at present. I am thinking merely of its quality while it lasted. It was intellectually degrading to me. You had the rudiments of an artistic temperament in its germ. But I met you either too late or too soon, I don't know which. When you were away I was all right. The moment, in the early December of the year to which I have been alluding, I had succeeded in inducing your mother to send you out of England,[2] I collected again the

[1] John Gray (1866–1934). His book of poems *Silverpoints* (Mathews & Lane, 1893), which was entirely paid for by Wilde, was designed by Ricketts, and in the same year *The Blackmailers*, a play written in collaboration with his close friend André Raffalovich (see note p. 60), was produced at the Prince of Wales Theatre in June. There is no evidence for the persistent suggestion that he was the original of Dorian Gray. In 1904 he edited and published *Last Letters of Aubrey Beardsley*, which were written to Raffalovich. He became a Roman Catholic and at thirty-five was ordained priest. His later years were spent in Edinburgh, where Raffalovich built St Peter's Church for him.   [2] See letter p. 113.

torn and ravelled web of my imagination, got my life back into my own hands, and not merely finished the three remaining acts of *An Ideal Husband*, but conceived and had almost completed two other plays of a completely different type, the *Florentine Tragedy* and *La Sainte Courtisane*, when suddenly, unbidden, unwelcome, and under circumstances fatal to my happiness you returned. The two works left then imperfect I was unable to take up again. The mood that created them I could never recover. You now, having yourself published a volume of verse, will be able to recognise the truth of everything I have said here. Whether you can or not it remains as a hideous truth in the very heart of our friendship. While you were with me you were the absolute ruin of my Art, and in allowing you to stand persistently between Art and myself I give to myself shame and blame in the fullest degree. You couldn't know, you couldn't understand, you couldn't appreciate. I had no right to expect it of you at all. Your interests were merely in your meals and moods. Your desires were simply for amusements, for ordinary or less ordinary pleasures. They were what your temperament needed, or thought it needed for the moment. I should have forbidden you my house and my chambers except when I specially invited you. I blame myself without reserve for my weakness. It was merely weakness. One half-hour with Art was always more to me than a cycle with you. Nothing really at any period of my life was ever of the smallest importance to me compared with Art. But in the case of an artist, weakness is nothing less than a crime, when it is a weakness that paralyses the imagination.

I blame myself again for having allowed you to bring me to utter and discreditable financial ruin. I remember one morning in the early October of '92 sitting in the yellowing woods at Bracknell with your mother. At that time I knew very little of your real nature. I had stayed from a Saturday to Monday with you at Oxford. You had stayed with me at Cromer[1] for ten days and played golf. The conversation turned on you, and your mother began to speak to me about your character. She told me of your two chief faults, your vanity, and your being, as she termed it, *"all wrong about money."* I have a distinct recollection of how I laughed. I had no idea that the first would bring me to prison, and the second to bankruptcy. I thought vanity a sort of graceful flower for a young man to wear; as for extravagance—for I thought she meant no more than extravagance—the virtues of prudence and thrift were not in my own nature or my own race. But before our friendship was one month older I began to see what your mother really meant. Your insistence on a life of reckless profusion: your incessant demands for money: your claim that all your pleasures should be paid for by me whether I was with you or not: brought me after some time into serious monetary difficulties, and what made the extravagances to me at any rate so monotonously uninteresting, as your persistent grasp on my life grew stronger and stronger, was that the money was really spent on little more than the pleasures of eating, drinking, and the like. Now and then it is a joy to have one's table red with wine and roses, but you out-

[1] Wilde rented Grove Farm, Felbrigg, Cromer in August/September 1892 and wrote a great part of *A Woman of No Importance* there.

stripped all taste and temperance. You demanded without grace and received without thanks. You grew to think that you had a sort of right to live at my expense and in a profuse luxury to which you had never been accustomed, and which for that reason made your appetites all the more keen, and at the end if you lost money gambling in some Algiers Casino you simply telegraphed next morning to me in London to lodge the amount of your losses to your account at your bank, and gave the matter no further thought of any kind.

When I tell you that between the autumn of 1892 and the date of my imprisonment I spent with you and on you more than £5000 in actual money, irrespective of the bills I incurred, you will have some idea of the sort of life on which you insisted. Do you think I exaggerate? My ordinary expenses with you for an ordinary day in London—for luncheon, dinner, supper, amusements, hansoms and the rest of it—ranged from £12 to £20, and the week's expenses were naturally in proportion and ranged from £80 to £130. For our three months at Goring my expenses (rent of course included) were £1340. Step by step with the Bankruptcy Receiver I had to go over every item of my life. It was horrible. *"Plain living and high thinking"*[1] was, of course, an ideal you could not at that time have appreciated, but such extravagance was a disgrace to both of us. One of the most delightful dinners I remember ever having had is one Robbie and I had together in a little Soho café, which cost about as many shillings as my dinners to you used to cost pounds. Out of my dinner with Robbie came the first and best of all my dialogues.[2] Idea, title, treatment, mode, everything was struck out at a 3 franc 50 c. *table-d'hôte*. Out of the reckless dinners with you nothing remains but the memory that too much was eaten and too much was drunk. And my yielding to your demands was bad for you. You know that now. It made you grasping often: at times not a little unscrupulous: ungracious always. There was on far too many occasions too little joy or privilege in being your host. You forgot—I will not say the formal courtesy of thanks, for formal courtesies will strain a close friendship—but simply the grace of sweet companionship, the charm of pleasant conversation, that τερπνὸν κακόν[3] as the Greeks called it, and all those gentle humanities that make life lovely, and are an accompaniment to life as music might be, keeping things in tune and filling with melody the harsh or silent places. And though it may seem strange to you that one in the terrible position in which I am situated should find a difference between one disgrace and another, still I frankly admit that the folly of throwing away all this money on you, and letting you squander my fortune to your own hurt as well as to mine, gives to me and in my eyes a note of common profligacy to my Bankruptcy that makes me doubly ashamed of it. I was made for other things.

But most of all I blame myself for the entire ethical degradation I allowed you to bring on me. The basis of character is will-power, and my will-power became absolutely subject to yours. It sounds a grotesque

[1] Wordsworth, "Sonnet written in London, September 1802."
[2] Almost certainly "The Decay of Lying."   [3] Euripides, *Hippolytus*, 384.

thing to say, but it is none the less true. Those incessant scenes that seemed to be almost physically necessary to you, and in which your mind and body grew distorted and you became a thing as terrible to look at as to listen to: that dreadful mania you inherit from your father, the mania for writing revolting and loathsome letters: your entire lack of any control over your emotions as displayed in your long resentful moods of sullen silence, no less than in the sudden fits of almost epileptic rage: all these things in reference to which one of my letters to you, left by you lying about at the Savoy or some other hotel and so produced in Court by your father's Counsel, contained an entreaty not devoid of pathos, had you at that time been able to recognise pathos either in its elements or its expression:[1]—these, I say, were the origin and causes of my fatal yielding to you in your daily increasing demands. You wore one out. It was the triumph of the smaller over the bigger nature. It was the case of that tyranny of the weak over the strong which somewhere in one of my plays I describe as being "the only tyranny that lasts."[2]

And it was inevitable. In every relation of life with others one has to find some *moyen de vivre*. In your case, one had either to give up to you or to give you up. There was no other alternative. Through deep if misplaced affection for you: through great pity for your defects of temper and temperament: through my own proverbial good-nature and Celtic laziness: through an artistic aversion to coarse scenes and ugly words: through that incapacity to bear resentment of any kind which at that time characterised me: through my dislike of seeing life made bitter and uncomely by what to me, with my eyes really fixed on other things, seemed to be mere trifles too petty for more than a moment's thought or interest—through these reasons, simple as they may sound, I gave up to you always. As a natural result, your claims, your efforts at domination, your exactions grew more and more unreasonable. Your meanest motive, your lowest appetite, your most common passion, became to you laws by which the lives of others were to be guided always, and to which, if necessary, they were to be without scruple sacrificed. Knowing that by making a scene you could always have your way, it was but natural that you should proceed, almost unconsciously I have no doubt, to every excess of vulgar violence. At the end you did not know to what goal you were hurrying, or with what aim in view. Having made your own of my genius, my will-power, and my fortune, you required, in the blindness of an inexhaustible greed, my entire existence. You took it. At the one supremely and tragically critical moment of all my life, just before my lamentable step of beginning my absurd action, on the one side there was your father attacking me with hideous cards left at my club, on the other side there was you attacking me with no less loathsome letters. The letter I received from you on the morning of the day I let you take me down to the Police Court to apply for the ridiculous warrant for your father's arrest was one of the worst you ever wrote, and for the most shameful reason. Between you both I lost my head. My judgment forsook me. Terror took its place. I

---

[1] See letter p. iii.   [2] *A Woman of No Importance*, Act III.

saw no possible escape, I may say frankly, from either of you. Blindly I staggered as an ox into the shambles. I had made a gigantic psychological error. I had always thought that my giving up to you in small things meant nothing: that when a great moment arrived I could reassert my will-power in its natural superiority. It was not so. At the great moment my will-power completely failed me. In life there is really no small or great thing. All things are of equal value and of equal size. My habit—due to indifference chiefly at first—of giving up to you in everything had become insensibly a real part of my nature. Without my knowing it, it had stereo-typed my temperament to one permanent and fatal mood. That is why, in the subtle epilogue to the first edition of his essays, Pater says that "Failure is to form habits."[1] When he said it the dull Oxford people thought the phrase a mere wilful inversion of the somewhat wearisome text of Aristot-elian *Ethics*, but there is a wonderful, a terrible truth hidden in it. I had allowed you to sap my strength of character, and to me the formation of a habit had proved to be not Failure merely but Ruin. Ethically you had been even still more destructive to me than you had been artistically.

The warrant once granted, your will of course directed everything. At a time when I should have been in London taking wise counsel, and calmly considering the hideous trap in which I had allowed myself to be caught—the booby-trap as your father calls it to the present day—you insisted on my taking you to Monte Carlo, of all revolting places on God's earth, that all day, and all night as well, you might gamble as long as the Casino remained open. As for me—baccarat having no charms for me—I was left alone outside to myself. You refused to discuss even for five minutes the position to which you and your father had brought me. My business was merely to pay your hotel expenses and your losses. The slightest allusion to the ordeal awaiting me was regarded as a bore. A new brand of champagne that was recommended to us had more interest for you.

On our return to London those of my friends who really desired my welfare implored me to retire abroad, and not to face an impossible trial. You imputed mean motives to them for giving such advice, and cowardice to me for listening to it. You forced me to stay to brazen it out, if possible, in the box by absurd and silly perjuries. At the end, I was of course arrested and your father became the hero of the hour: more indeed than the hero of the hour merely: your family now ranks, strangely enough, with the Immortals: for with that grotesqueness of effect that is as it were a Gothic element in history, and makes Clio the least serious of all the Muses, your father will always live among the kind pure-minded parents of Sunday-school literature, your place is with the Infant Samuel, and in the lowest mire of Malebolge[2] I sit between Gilles de Retz and the Marquis de Sade.[3]

---

[1] In the "Conclusion" to his *Studies in the History of the Renaissance* (1873). The "Conclusion" was omitted from the second edition (1877) but restored in the third (1888), where this sentence is altered to "In a sense it might even be said that our failure is to form habits."

[2] The eighth circle of Dante's *Inferno*.

[3] Gilles de Laval, Sire de Retz or Raiz (1404–40), the comrade-in-arms of Joan

Of course I should have got rid of you. I should have shaken you out of my life as a man shakes from his raiment a thing that has stung him. In the most wonderful of all his plays[1] Æschylus tells us of the great Lord who brings up in his house the lion-cub, the λέοντος ἶνιν, and loves it because it comes bright-eyed to his call and fawns on him for its food: φαιδρωπὸς ποτὶ χεῖρα, σαίνων τε γαστρὸς ἀνάγκαις. And the thing grows up and shows the nature of its race, ἦθος τὸ πρόσθε τοκήων, and destroys the lord and his house and all that he possesses. I feel that I was such a one as he. But my fault was, not that I did not part from you, but that I parted from you far too often. As far as I can make out I ended my friendship with you every three months regularly, and each time that I did so you managed by means of entreaties, telegrams, letters, the interposition of your friends, the interposition of mine, and the like to induce me to allow you back. When at the end of March '93 you left my house at Torquay I had determined never to speak to you again, or to allow you under any circumstances to be with me, so revolting had been the scene you had made the night before your departure. You wrote and telegraphed from Bristol to beg me to forgive you and meet you. Your tutor, who had stayed behind, told me that he thought that at times you were quite irresponsible for what you said and did, and that most, if not all, of the men at Magdalen were of the same opinion. I consented to meet you, and of course I forgave you. On the way up to town you begged me to take you to the Savoy. That was indeed a visit fatal to me.

Three months later, in June, we are at Goring. Some of your Oxford friends come to stay from a Saturday to Monday. The morning of the day they went away you made a scene so dreadful, so distressing that I told you that we must part. I remember quite well, as we stood on the level croquet-ground with the pretty lawn all round us, pointing out to you that we were spoiling each other's lives, that you were absolutely ruining mine and that I evidently was not making you really happy, and that an irrevocable parting, a complete separation was the one wise philosophic thing to do. You went sullenly after luncheon, leaving one of your most offensive letters behind with the butler to be handed to me after your departure. Before three days had elapsed you were telegraphing from London to beg to be forgiven and allowed to return. I had taken the place to please you. I had engaged your own servants at your request. I was always terribly sorry for the hideous temper to which you were really a prey. I was fond of you. So I let you come back and forgave you. Three months later still, in September, new scenes occurred, the occasion of them being my pointing out the schoolboy faults of your attempted translation of *Salome*.[2] You must by this time be a fair enough French scholar to know that the translation was as unworthy of you, as an ordinary

of Arc and a Marshal of France, turned to debauchery, devil-worship and child-murder, for which he was finally executed. The Marquis de Sade (1740–1814), author of *Justine* (1791) and other novels of cruelty which gave rise to the words Sadism and Sadistic, was sentenced to death for various offences but escaped the scaffold and died in a lunatic asylum.

[1] *Agamemnon*. The words quoted occur in lines 717–728.   [2] See note 4, p. 113.

Oxonian, as it was of the work it sought to render. You did not of course know it then, and in one of the violent letters you wrote to me on the point you said that you were under *"no intellectual obligation of any kind"* to me. I remember that when I read that statement, I felt that it was the one really true thing you had written to me in the whole course of our friendship. I saw that a less cultivated nature would really have suited you much better. I am not saying this in bitterness at all, but simply as a fact of companionship. Ultimately the bond of all companionship, whether in marriage or in friendship, is conversation, and conversation must have a common basis, and between two people of widely different culture the only common basis possible is the lowest level. The trivial in thought and action is charming. I had made it the keystone of a very brilliant philosophy expressed in plays and paradoxes. But the froth and folly of our life grew often very wearisome to me: it was only in the mire that we met: and fascinating, terribly fascinating though the one topic round which your talk invariably centred was, still at the end it became quite monotonous to me. I was often bored to death by it, and accepted it as I accepted your passion for going to music-halls, or your mania for absurd extravagances in eating and drinking, or any other of your to me less attractive characteristics, as a thing, that is to say, that one simply had to put up with, a part of the high price one paid for knowing you. When after leaving Goring I went to Dinard for a fortnight you were extremely angry with me for not taking you with me, and, before my departure there, made some very unpleasant scenes on the subject at the Albemarle Hotel, and sent me some equally unpleasant telegrams to a country house I was staying at for a few days. I told you, I remember, that I thought it was your duty to be with your own people for a little, as you had passed the whole season away from them. But in reality, to be perfectly frank with you, I could not under any circumstances have let you be with me. We had been together for nearly twelve weeks. I required rest and freedom from the terrible strain of your companionship. It was necessary for me to be a little by myself. It was intellectually necessary. And so I confess I saw in your letter, from which I have quoted, a very good opportunity for ending the fatal friendship that had sprung up between us, and ending it without bitterness, as I had indeed tried to do on that bright June morning at Goring, three months before. It was however represented to me—I am bound to say candidly by one of my own friends[1] to whom you had gone in your difficulty—that you would be much hurt, perhaps almost humiliated at having your work sent back to you like a schoolboy's exercise; that I was expecting far too much intellectually from you; and that, no matter what you wrote or did, you were absolutely and entirely devoted to me. I did not want to be the first to check or discourage you in your beginnings in literature: I knew quite well that no translation, unless one done by a poet, could render the colour and cadence of my work in any adequate measure: devotion seemed to me, seems to me still, a wonderful thing, not to be lightly thrown away: so I

[1] Wilde originally wrote "Robbie."

took the translation and you back. Exactly three months later, after a series of scenes culminating in one more than usually revolting, when you came one Monday evening to my rooms accompanied by two of your friends, I found myself actually flying abroad next morning to escape from you, giving my family[1] some absurd reason for my sudden departure, and leaving a false address with my servant for fear you might follow me by the next train. And I remember that afternoon, as I was in the railway-carriage whirling up to Paris, thinking what an impossible, terrible, utterly wrong state my life had got into, when I, a man of world-wide reputation, was actually forced to run away from England, in order to try and get rid of a friendship that was entirely destructive of everything fine in me either from the intellectual or ethical point of view: the person from whom I was flying being no terrible creature sprung from sewer or mire into modern life with whom I had entangled my days, but you yourself, a young man of my own social rank and position, who had been at my own college at Oxford, and was an incessant guest at my house. The usual telegrams of entreaty and remorse followed: I disregarded them. Finally you threatened that unless I consented to meet you, you would under no circumstances consent to proceed to Egypt. I had myself, with your know-ledge and concurrence, begged your mother to send you to Egypt away from England, as you were wrecking your life in London. I knew that if you did not go it would be a terrible disappointment to her, and for her sake I did meet you, and under the influence of great emotion, which even you cannot have forgotten, I forgave the past; though I said nothing at all about the future.

On my return to London next day I remember sitting in my room and sadly and seriously trying to make up my mind whether or not you really were what you seemed to me to be, so full of terrible defects, so utterly ruinous both to yourself and to others, so fatal a one to know even or to be with. For a whole week I thought about it, and wondered if after all I was not unjust and mistaken in my estimate of you. At the end of the week a letter from your mother is handed in. It expressed to the full every feeling I myself had about you. In it she spoke of your blind exaggerated vanity which made you despise your home, and treat your elder brother —that *candidissima anima*—"as a Philistine:" of your temper which made her afraid to speak to you about your life, the life she felt, she knew, you were leading: about your conduct in money matters, so distressing to her in more ways than one: of the degeneration and change that had taken place in you. She saw, of course, that heredity had burdened you with a terrible legacy, and frankly admitted it, admitted it with terror: he is "the one of my children who has inherited the fatal Douglas temperament," she wrote of you. At the end she stated that she felt bound to declare that your friendship with me, in her opinion, had so intensified your vanity that it had become the source of all your faults, and earnestly begged me not to meet you abroad. I wrote to her at once, in reply, and told her that I agreed entirely with every word she had said. I added much more. I

[1] Wilde originally wrote "wife."

went as far as I could possibly go. I told her that the origin of our friendship was you in your undergraduate days at Oxford coming to beg me to help you in very serious trouble of a very particular character. I told her that your life had been continually in the same manner troubled. The reason of your going to Belgium you had placed to the fault of your companion in that journey, and your mother had reproached me with having introduced you to him. I replaced the fault on the right shoulders, on yours. I assured her at the end that I had not the smallest intention of meeting you abroad, and begged her to try to keep you there, either as an honorary *attaché*, if that were possible, or to learn modern languages, if it were not; or for any reason she chose, at least during two or three years, and for your sake as well as for mine.

In the meantime you are writing to me by every post from Egypt. I took not the smallest notice of any of your communications. I read them, and tore them up. I had quite settled to have no more to do with you. My mind was made up, and I gladly devoted myself to the Art whose progress I had allowed you to interrupt. At the end of three months, your mother, with that unfortunate weakness of will that characterises her, and that in the tragedy of my life has been an element no less fatal than your father's violence, actually writes to me herself—I have no doubt, of course, at your instigation—tells me that you are extremely anxious to hear from me, and in order that I should have no excuse for not communicating with you, sends me your address in Athens, which, of course, I knew perfectly well. I confess I was absolutely astounded at her letter. I could not understand how, after what she had written to me in December, and what I in answer had written to her, she could in any way try to repair or to renew my unfortunate friendship with you. I acknowledged her letter, of course, and again urged her to try and get you connected with some Embassy abroad,[1] so as to prevent your returning to England, but I did not write to you, or take any more notice of your telegrams than I did before your mother had written to me. Finally you actually telegraphed to my wife begging her to use her influence with me to get me to write to you. Our friendship had always been a source of distress to her: not merely because she had never liked you personally, but because she saw how your continual companionship altered me, and not for the better: still, just as she had always been most gracious and hospitable to you, so she could not bear the idea of my being in any way unkind—for so it seemed to her—to any of my friends. She thought, knew indeed, that it was a thing alien to my character. At her request I did communicate with you. I remember the wording of my telegram quite well. I said that time healed every wound but that for many months to come I would neither write to you nor see you. You started without delay for Paris, sending me passionate telegrams on the road to beg me to see you once, at any rate. I declined. You arrived in Paris late on a Saturday night, and found a brief

---

[1] When Douglas left Egypt in March 1894 he was appointed Honorary Attaché to Lord Currie, the Ambassador at Constantinople, but did not take up the appointment.

letter from me waiting for you at your hotel stating that I would not see you. Next morning I received in Tite Street a telegram of some ten or eleven pages in length from you. You stated in it that no matter what you had done to me you could not believe that I would absolutely decline to see you: you reminded me that for the sake of seeing me even for one hour you had travelled six days and nights across Europe without stopping once on the way: you made what I must admit was a most pathetic appeal, and ended with what seemed to me a threat of suicide, and one not thinly veiled. You had yourself often told me how many of your race there had been who had stained their hands in their own blood; your uncle certainly, your grandfather possibly; many others in the mad, bad line from which you come.[1] Pity, my old affection for you, regard for your mother to whom your death under such dreadful circumstances would have been a blow almost too great for her to bear, the horror of the idea that so young a life, and one that amidst all its ugly faults had still promise of beauty in it, should come to so revolting an end, mere humanity itself—all these, if excuses be necessary, must serve as my excuse for consenting to accord you one last interview. When I arrived in Paris, your tears, breaking out again and again all through the evening, and falling over your cheeks like rain as we sat, at dinner first at Voisin's, at supper at Paillard's afterwards: the unfeigned joy you evinced at seeing me, holding my hand whenever you could, as though you were a gentle and penitent child: your contrition, so simple and sincere, at the moment: made me consent to renew our friendship. Two days after we had returned to London, your father saw you having luncheon with me at the Café Royal, joined my table, drank of my wine, and that afternoon, through a letter addressed to you, began his first attack on me.[2]

It may be strange, but I had once again, I will not say the chance, but the duty of separating from you forced on me. I need hardly remind you that I refer to your conduct to me at Brighton from October 10th to 13th, 1894. Three years ago is a long time for you to go back. But we who live in prison, and in whose lives there is no event but sorrow, have to measure time by throbs of pain, and the record of bitter moments. We have nothing else to think of. Suffering—curious as it may sound to you—is the means by which we exist, because it is the only means by which we become conscious of existing; and the remembrance of suffering in the past is necessary to us as the warrant, the evidence, of our continued identity. Between myself and the memory of joy lies a gulf no less deep than that between myself and joy in its actuality. Had our life together been as the world fancied it to be, one simply of pleasure, profligacy and laughter, I would not be able to recall a single passage in it. It is because it was full of moments and days tragic, bitter, sinister in their warnings, dull or dreadful in their monotonous scenes and unseemly violences, that I can see or hear each separate incident in its detail, can indeed see or hear little else. So

---

[1] The seventh Marquess of Queensberry (1818–58) died in a shooting accident. His youngest son, Lord James Edward Sholto Douglas (1855–91), cut his own throat in the Euston Hotel. [2] *Circa* 1 April 1894.

much in this place do men live by pain that my friendship with you, in the way through which I am forced to remember it, appears to me always as a prelude consonant with those varying modes of anguish which each day I have to realise; nay more, to necessitate them even; as though my life, whatever it had seemed to myself and to others, had all the while been a real Symphony of Sorrow, passing through its rhythmically-linked movements to its certain resolution, with that inevitableness that in Art characterises the treatment of every great theme.

I spoke of your conduct to me on three successive days, three years ago, did I not? I was trying to finish my last play at Worthing by myself. The two visits you had paid to me had ended. You suddenly appeared a third time bringing with you a companion whom you actually proposed should stay in my house. I (you must admit now quite properly) absolutely declined. I entertained you, of course; I had no option in the matter: but elsewhere, and not in my own home. The next day, a Monday, your companion returned to the duties of his profession, and you stayed with me. Bored with Worthing, and still more, I have no doubt, with my fruitless efforts to concentrate my attention on my play, the only thing that really interested me at the moment, you insist on being taken to the Grand Hotel at Brighton. The night we arrive you fall ill with that dreadful low fever that is foolishly called the influenza, your second, if not third attack.[1] I need not remind you how I waited on you, and tended you, not merely with every luxury of fruit, flowers, presents, books, and the like that money can procure, but with that affection, tenderness and love that, whatever you may think, is not to be procured for money. Except for an hour's walk in the morning, an hour's drive in the afternoon, I never left the hotel. I got special grapes from London for you, as you did not care for those the hotel supplied, invented things to please you, remained either with you or in the room next to yours, sat with you every evening to quiet or amuse you.

After four or five days you recover, and I take lodgings in order to try and finish my play. You, of course, accompany me. The morning after the day on which we were installed I feel extremely ill. You have to go to London on business, but promise to return in the afternoon. In London you meet a friend, and do not come back to Brighton till late the next day, by which time I am in a terrible fever, and the doctor finds I have caught the influenza from you. Nothing could have been more uncomfortable for anyone ill than the lodgings turn out to be. My sitting-room is on the first floor, my bedroom on the third. There is no manservant to wait on one, not even anyone to send out on a message, or to get what the doctor orders. But you are there. I feel no alarm. The next two days you leave me entirely alone without care, without attendance, without anything. It was not a question of grapes, flowers, and charming gifts: it was a question of mere necessaries: I could not even get the milk the doctor had ordered for me: lemonade was pronounced an impossibility: and when I begged you to procure me a book at the bookseller's, or if they had not got whatever I had fixed on to choose something else, you never even take

[1] See p. 125.

the trouble to go there. And when I was left all day without anything to read in consequence, you calmly tell me that you bought me the book and that they promised to send it down, a statement which I found out by chance afterwards to have been entirely untrue from beginning to end. All the while you are of course living at my expense, driving about, dining at the Grand Hotel, and indeed only appearing in my room for money. On the Saturday night, you having left me completely unattended and alone since the morning, I asked you to come back after dinner, and sit with me for a little. With irritable voice and ungracious manner you promise to do so. I wait till eleven o'clock and you never appear. I then left a note for you in your room just reminding you of the promise you had made me, and how you had kept it. At three in the morning, unable to sleep, and tortured with thirst, I made my way, in the dark and cold, down to the sitting-room in the hopes of finding some water there. I found *you*. You fell on me with every hideous word an intemperate mood, an undisciplined and untutored nature could suggest. By the terrible alchemy of egotism you converted your remorse into rage. You accused me of selfishness in expecting you to be with me when I was ill; of standing between you and your amusements; of trying to deprive you of your pleasures. You told me, and I know it was quite true, that you had come back at midnight simply in order to change your dress-clothes, and go out again to where you hoped new pleasures were waiting for you, but that by leaving for you a letter in which I had reminded you that you had neglected me the whole day and the whole evening, I had really robbed you of your desire for more enjoyments, and diminished your actual capacity for fresh delights. I went back upstairs in disgust, and remained sleepless till dawn, nor till long after dawn was I able to get anything to quench the thirst of the fever that was on me. At eleven o'clock you came into my room. In the previous scene I could not help observing that by my letter I had, at any rate, checked you in a night of more than usual excess. In the morning you were quite yourself. I waited naturally to hear what excuses you had to make, and in what way you were going to ask for the forgiveness that you knew in your heart was invariably waiting for you, no matter what you did; your absolute trust that I would always forgive you being the thing in you that I always really liked the best, perhaps the best thing in you to like. So far from doing that, you began to repeat the same scene with renewed emphasis and more violent assertion. I told you at length to leave the room: you pretended to do so, but when I lifted up my head from the pillow in which I had buried it, you were still there, and with brutality of laughter and hysteria of rage you moved suddenly towards me. A sense of horror came over me, for what exact reason I could not make out; but I got out of my bed at once, and bare-footed and just as I was, made my way down the two flights of stairs to the sitting-room, which I did not leave till the owner of the lodgings— whom I had rung for—had assured me that you had left my bedroom, and promised to remain within call, in case of necessity. After an interval of an hour, during which time the doctor had come and found me, of course, in a state of absolute nervous prostration, as well as in a worse condition of fever than I had been at the outset, you returned silently, for money: took what you could find on the dressing-table and mantelpiece, and left the house with your luggage. Need I tell you what I thought of you during the two wretched lonely days of illness that followed? Is it necessary for me to state that I saw clearly that it would be a dishonour to myself to continue even an acquaintance with such a one as you had showed yourself to be? That I recognised that the ultimate moment had come, and recognised it as being really a great relief? And that I knew that for the future my Art and Life would be freer and better and more beautiful in every possible way? Ill as I was, I felt at ease. The fact that the separation was irrevocable gave me peace. By Tuesday the fever had left me, and for the first time I dined downstairs. Wednesday was my birthday.[1] Amongst the telegrams and communications on my table was a letter in your handwriting. I opened it with a sense of sadness over me. I knew that the time had gone by when a pretty phrase, an expression of affection, a word of sorrow would make me take you back. But I was entirely deceived. I had underrated you. The letter you sent to me on my birthday was an elaborate repetition of the two scenes, set cunningly and carefully down in black and white! You mocked me with common jests. Your one satisfaction in the whole affair was, you said, that you retired to the Grand Hotel, and entered your luncheon to my account before you left for town. You congratulated me on my prudence in leaving my sickbed, on my sudden flight downstairs. *"It was an ugly moment for you,"* you said, *"uglier than you imagine."* Ah! I felt it but too well. What it had really meant I did not know: whether you had with you the pistol you had bought to try and frighten your father with, and that, thinking it to be unloaded, you had once fired off in a public restaurant in my company:[2] whether your hand was moving towards a common dinner-knife that by chance was lying on the table between us: whether, forgetting in your rage your low stature and inferior strength, you had thought of some specially personal insult, or attack even, as I lay ill there: I could not tell. I do not know to the present moment. All I know is that a feeling of utter horror had come over me, and that I had felt that unless I left the room at once, and got away, you would have done, or tried to do, something that would have been, even to you, a source of lifelong shame. Only once before in my life had I experienced such a feeling of horror at any human being. It was when in my library at Tite Street, waving his small hands in the air in epileptic fury, your father, with his bully, or his friend, between us, had stood uttering every foul word his foul mind could think of, and screaming the loathsome threats he afterwards with such cunning carried out. In the latter case he, of course, was the one who had to leave the room first. I drove him out. In your case I went. It was not the first time I had been obliged to save you from yourself.

You concluded your letter by saying: *"When you are not on your pedestal*

---

[1] In 1894 Wilde's birthday (16 October) was a Tuesday, and Ross changed this sentence accordingly.

[2] The Berkeley, in Piccadilly.

you are not interesting. The next time you are ill I will go away at once."
Ah! what coarseness of fibre does that reveal! What an entire lack of
imagination! How callous, how common had the temperament by that
time become! *"When you are not on your pedestal you are not interesting.
The next time you are ill I will go away at once."* How often have those
words come back to me in the wretched solitary cell of the various prisons
I have been sent to. I have said them to myself over and over again, and
seen in them, I hope unjustly, some of the secret of your strange silence.
For you to write thus to me, when the very illness and fever from which I
was suffering I had caught from tending you, was of course revolting in its
coarseness and crudity; but for any human being in the whole world to
write thus to another would be a sin for which there is no pardon, were
there any sin for which there is none.

I confess that when I had finished your letter I felt almost polluted, as if
by associating with one of such a nature I had soiled and shamed my life
irretrievably. I had, it is true, done so, but I was not to learn how fully
till just six months later on in life. I settled with myself to go back to
London on the Friday,[1] and see Sir George Lewis personally and request
him to write to your father to state that I had determined never under any
circumstances to allow you to enter my house, to sit at my board, to talk to
me, walk with me, or anywhere and at any time to be my companion at all.
This done I would have written to you just to inform you of the course of
action I had adopted; the reasons you would inevitably have realised for
yourself. I had everything arranged on Thursday night, when on Friday
morning, as I was sitting at breakfast before starting, I happened to open
the newspaper and saw in it a telegram stating that your elder brother, the
real head of the family, the heir to the title, the pillar of the house, had been
found dead in a ditch with his gun lying discharged beside him.[2] The
horror of the circumstances of the tragedy, now known to have been an
accident, but then stained with a darker suggestion; the pathos of the
sudden death of one so loved by all who knew him, and almost on the eve,
as it were, of his marriage; my idea of what your own sorrow would, or
should be; my consciousness of the misery awaiting your mother at the
loss of the one to whom she clung for comfort and joy in life, and who, as
she told me once herself, had from the very day of his birth never caused
her to shed a single tear; my consciousness of your own isolation, both
your other brothers being out of Europe, and you consequently the only
one to whom your mother and sister could look, not merely for companionship in their sorrow, but also for those dreary responsibilities of dreadful
detail that Death always brings with it; the mere sense of the *lacrimae
rerum*, of the tears of which the world is made, and of the sadness of all
human things—out of the confluence of these thoughts and emotions
crowding into my brain came infinite pity for you and your family. My
own griefs and bitternesses against you I forgot. What you had been to me
in my sickness, I could not be to you in your bereavement. I telegraphed

[1] 19 October 1894.
[2] Lord Drumlanrig was killed by the explosion of his gun on 18 October 1894.

168

at once to you my deepest sympathy, and in the letter that followed invited you to come to my house as soon as you were able. I felt that to abandon you at that particular moment, and formally through a solicitor, would have been too terrible for you.

On your return to town from the actual scene of the tragedy to which you had been summoned, you came at once to me very sweetly and very simply, in your suit of woe, and with your eyes dim with tears. You sought consolation and help, as a child might seek it. I opened to you my house, my home, my heart. I made your sorrow mine also, that you might have help in bearing it. Never, even by one word, did I allude to your conduct towards me, to the revolting scenes, and the revolting letter. Your grief, which was real, seemed to me to bring you nearer to me than you had ever been. The flowers you took from me to put on your brother's grave were to be a symbol not merely of the beauty of his life, but of the beauty that in all lives lies dormant and may be brought to light.

The gods are strange. It is not of our vices only they make instruments to scourge us.[1] They bring us to ruin through what in us is good, gentle, humane, loving. But for my pity and affection for you and yours, I would not now be weeping in this terrible place.

Of course I discern in all our relations, not Destiny merely, but Doom: Doom that walks always swiftly, because she goes to the shedding of blood. Through your father you come of a race, marriage with whom is horrible, friendship fatal, and that lays violent hands either on its own life or on the lives of others. In every little circumstance in which the ways of our lives met; in every point of great, or seemingly trivial import in which you came to me for pleasure or for help; in the small chances, the slight accidents that look, in their relation to life, to be no more than the dust that dances in a beam, or the leaf that flutters from a tree, Ruin followed, like the echo of a bitter cry, or the shadow that hunts with the beast of prey. Our friendship really begins with your begging me in a most pathetic and charming letter to assist you in a position appalling to anyone, doubly so to a young man at Oxford: I do so, and ultimately through your using my name as your friend with Sir George Lewis, I begin to lose his esteem and friendship, a friendship of fifteen years' standing. When I was deprived of his advice and help and regard I was deprived of the one great safeguard of my life.

You send me a very nice poem, of the undergraduate school of verse, for my approval: I reply by a letter of fantastic literary conceits:[2] I compare you to Hylas, or Hyacinth, Jonquil or Narcisse, or someone whom the great god of Poetry favoured, and honoured with his love. The letter is like a passage from one of Shakespeare's sonnets, transposed to a minor key. It can only be understood by those who have read the *Symposium* of Plato, or caught the spirit of a certain grave mood made beautiful for us in Greek marbles. It was, let me say frankly, the sort of letter I would, in a happy if wilful moment, have written to any graceful young man of either University who had sent me a poem of his own making, certain that he

---

[1] *King Lear*, Act V, scene iii.   [2] See letter p. 107.

would have sufficient wit or culture to interpret rightly its fantastic phrases. Look at the history of that letter! It passes from you into the hands of a loathsome companion: from him to a gang of blackmailers: copies of it are sent about London to my friends, and to the manager of the theatre where my work is being performed:[1] every construction but the right one is put on it: Society is thrilled with the absurd rumours that I have had to pay a huge sum of money for having written an infamous letter to you: this forms the basis of your father's worst attack: I produce the original letter myself in Court to show what it really is: it is denounced by your father's Counsel as a revolting and insidious attempt to corrupt Innocence: ultimately it forms part of a criminal charge: the Crown takes it up: the Judge sums up on it with little learning and much morality: I go to prison for it at last. That is the result of writing you a charming letter.

While I am staying with you at Salisbury you are terribly alarmed at a threatening communication from a former companion of yours: you beg me to see the writer and help you: I do so: the result is Ruin to me. I am forced to take everything you have done on my own shoulders and answer for it. When, having failed to take your degree, you have to go down from Oxford, you telegraph to me in London to beg me to come to you. I do so at once: you ask me to take you to Goring, as you did not like, under the circumstances, to go home: at Goring you see a house that charms you: I take it for you: the result from every point of view is Ruin to me. One day you come to me and ask me, as a personal favour to you, to write something for an Oxford undergraduate magazine, about to be started by some friend of yours, whom I had never heard of in all my life, and knew nothing at all about. To please you—what did I not do always to please you?—I sent him a page of paradoxes destined originally for the *Saturday Review*.[2] A few months later I find myself standing in the dock of the Old Bailey on account of the character of the magazine. It forms part of the Crown charge against me. I am called upon to defend your friend's prose and your own verse. The former I cannot palliate; the latter I, loyal to the bitter extreme, to your youthful literature as to your youthful life, do very strongly defend, and will not hear of your being a writer of indecencies. But I go to prison, all the same, for your friend's undergraduate magazine, and "the Love that dares not tell its name."[3] At Christmas I give you a "very pretty present," as you described it in your letter of thanks, on which

[1] Beerbohm Tree.

[2] Thirty-five aphorisms of Wilde's were published as "Phrases and Philosophies for the Use of the Young" in the first (and only) issue of the *Chameleon*, an Oxford undergraduate magazine issued in December 1894. Much play was made with them at Wilde's trial, and also with two other items in the magazine—a poem of Douglas's called "Two Loves" and an anonymous story called "The Priest and the Acolyte," which was attributed to Wilde but was in fact written by the magazine's editor, John Francis Bloxam, an undergraduate of Exeter College.

[3] The last lines of "Two Loves" run:

" I am true Love, I fill
The hearts of boy and girl with mutual flame."
Then sighing said the other, "Have thy will,
I am the Love that dare not speak its name."

I knew you had set your heart, worth some £40 or £50 at most. When the crash of my life comes, and I am ruined, the bailiff who seizes my library, and has it sold, does so to pay for the "very pretty present." It was for that the execution was put into my house. At the ultimate and terrible moment when I am taunted, and spurred-on by your taunts, to take an action against your father and have him arrested, the last straw to which I clutch in my wretched efforts to escape is the terrible expense. I tell the solicitor in your presence that I have no funds, that I cannot possibly afford the appalling costs, that I have no money at my disposal. What I said was, as you know, perfectly true. On that fatal Friday[1] instead of being in Humphreys's office weakly consenting to my own ruin, I would have been happy and free in France, away from you and your father, unconscious of his loathsome card, and indifferent to your letters, if I had been able to leave the Avondale Hotel. But the hotel people absolutely refused to allow me to go. You had been staying with me for ten days: indeed you had ultimately, to my great and, you will admit, rightful indignation, brought a companion of yours to stay with me also: my bill for the ten days was nearly £140. The proprietor said he could not allow my luggage to be removed from the hotel till I had paid the account in full. That is what kept me in London. Had it not been for the hotel bill I would have gone to Paris on Thursday morning.

When I told the solicitor I had no money to face the gigantic expense, you interposed at once. You said that your own family would be only too delighted to pay all the necessary costs: that your father had been an incubus to them all: that they had often discussed the possibility of getting him put into a lunatic asylum so as to keep him out of the way: that he was a daily source of annoyance and distress to your mother and to everyone else: that if I would only come forward to have him shut up I would be regarded by the family as their champion and their benefactor: and that your mother's rich relations themselves would look on it as a real delight to be allowed to pay all costs and expenses that might be incurred in any such effort. The solicitor closed at once, and I was hurried to the Police Court. I had no excuse left for not going. I was forced into it. Of course your family don't pay the costs, and, when I am made bankrupt, it is by your father, and *for* the costs—the meagre balance of them—some £700.[2] At the present moment my wife, estranged from me over the important question of whether I should have £3 or £3. 10 a week to live on, is preparing a divorce suit, for which, of course, entirely new evidence and an entirely new trial, to be followed perhaps by more serious proceedings, will be necessary. I, naturally, know nothing of the details. I merely know the name of the witness on whose evidence my wife's solicitors rely. It is your own Oxford servant, whom at your special request I took into my service for our summer at Goring.

[1] 1 March 1895.
[2] This (or rather £677) was the amount of Queensberry's taxed costs in Wilde's unsuccessful action against him. The total of Wilde's debts was £6000, but Queensberry was the petitioning creditor whose action made Wilde a bankrupt.

But, indeed, I need not go on further with more instances of the strange Doom you seem to have brought on me in all things big or little. It makes me feel sometimes as if you yourself had been merely a puppet worked by some secret and unseen hand to bring terrible events to a terrible issue. But puppets themselves have passions. They will bring a new plot into what they are presenting, and twist the ordered issue of vicissitude to suit some whim or appetite of their own. To be entirely free, and at the same time entirely dominated by law, is the eternal paradox of human life that we realise at every moment; and this, I often think, is the only explanation possible of your nature, if indeed for the profound and terrible mysteries of a human soul there is any explanation at all, except one that makes the mystery more marvellous still.

Of course you had your illusions, lived in them indeed, and through their shifting mists and coloured veils saw all things changed. You thought, I remember quite well, that your devoting yourself to me, to the entire exclusion of your family and family life, was a proof of your wonderful appreciation of me, and your great affection. No doubt to you it seemed so. But recollect that with me was luxury, high living, unlimited pleasure, money without stint. Your family life bored you. The "cold cheap wine of Salisbury," to use a phrase of your own making, was distasteful to you. On my side, and along with my intellectual attractions, were the fleshpots of Egypt. When you could not find me to be with, the companions whom you chose as substitutes were not flattering.

You thought again that in sending a lawyer's letter to your father to say that, rather than sever your eternal friendship with me, you would give up the allowance of £250 a year which, with I believe deductions for your Oxford debts, he was then making you, you were realising the very chivalry of friendship, touching the noblest note of self-denial. But your surrender of your little allowance did not mean that you were ready to give up even one of your most superfluous luxuries, or most unnecessary extravagances. On the contrary. Your appetite for luxurious living was never so keen. My expenses for eight days in Paris for myself, you, and your Italian servant were nearly £150: Paillard alone absorbing £85. At the rate at which you wished to live, your entire income for a whole year, if you had taken your meals alone, and been especially economical in your selection of the cheaper form of pleasures, would hardly have lasted you for three weeks. The fact that in what was merely a pretence of bravado you had surrendered your allowance, such as it was, gave you at last a plausible reason for your claim to live at my expense, or what you thought a plausible reason: and on many occasions you seriously availed yourself of it, and gave the very fullest expression to it: and the continued drain, principally of course on me, but also to a certain extent, I know, on your mother, was never so distressing, because in my case at any rate, never so completely unaccompanied by the smallest word of thanks, or sense of limit.

You thought again that in attacking your own father with dreadful letters, abusive telegrams, and insulting postcards you were really fighting your mother's battles, coming forward as her champion, and avenging the no doubt terrible wrongs and sufferings of her married life. It was quite an illusion on your part; one of your worst indeed. The way for you to have avenged your mother's wrongs on your father, if you considered it part of a son's duty to do so, was by being a better son to your mother than you had been: by not making her afraid to speak to you on serious things: by not signing bills the payment of which devolved on her: by being gentler to her, and not bringing sorrow into her days. Your brother Francis[1] made great amends to her for what she had suffered, by his sweetness and goodness to her through the brief years of his flower-like life. You should have taken him as your model. You were wrong even in fancying that it would have been an absolute delight and joy to your mother if you *had* managed through me to get your father put into prison. I feel sure you were wrong. And if you want to know what a woman really feels when her husband, and the father of her children, is in prison dress, in a prison cell, write to my wife and ask her. She will tell you.

I also had my illusions. I thought life was going to be a brilliant comedy, and that you were to be one of many graceful figures in it. I found it to be a revolting and repellent tragedy, and that the sinister occasion of the great catastrophe, sinister in its concentration of aim and intensity of narrowed will-power, was yourself, stripped of that mask of joy and pleasure by which you, no less than I, had been deceived and led astray.

You can now understand—can you not?—a little of what I am suffering. Some paper, the *Pall Mall Gazette* I think, describing the dress-rehearsal of one of my plays, spoke of you as following me about like my shadow: the memory of our friendship is the shadow that walks with me here: that seems never to leave me: that wakes me up at night to tell me the same story over and over till its wearisome iteration makes all sleep abandon me till dawn: at dawn it begins again: it follows me into the prison-yard and makes me talk to myself as I tramp round: each detail that accompanied each dreadful moment I am forced to recall: there is nothing that happened in those ill-starred years that I cannot recreate in that chamber of the brain which is set apart for grief or for despair: every strained note of your voice, every twitch and gesture of your nervous hands, every bitter word, every poisonous phrase comes back to me: I remember the street or river down which we passed, the wall or woodland that surrounded us, at what figure on the dial stood the hands of the clock, which way went the wings of the wind, the shape and colour of the moon.

There is, I know, one answer to all that I have said to you, and that is that you loved me: that all through those two and a half years during which the Fates were weaving into one scarlet pattern the threads of our divided lives you really loved me. Yes: I know you did. No matter what your conduct to me was I always felt that at heart you really did love me. Though I saw quite clearly that my position in the world of Art, the interest my personality had always excited, my money, the luxury in which I lived, the thousand and one things that went to make up a life so charmingly, so wonderfully improbable as mine was, were, each and all of them,

---

[1] Drumlanrig.

elements that fascinated you and made you cling to me: yet besides all this there was something more, some strange attraction for you: you loved me far better than you loved anybody else. But you, like myself, have had a terrible tragedy in your life, though one of an entirely opposite character to mine. Do you want to learn what it was? It was this. In you Hate was always stronger than Love. Your hatred of your father was of such stature that it entirely outstripped, o'erthrew, and overshadowed your love of me. There was no struggle between them at all, or but little; of such dimensions was your Hatred and of such monstrous growth. You did not realise that there is no room for both passions in the same soul. They cannot live together in that fair carven house. Love is fed by the imagination, by which we become wiser than we know, better than we feel, nobler than we are: by which we can see Life as a whole: by which, and by which alone, we can understand others in their real as in their ideal relations. Only what is fine, and finely conceived, can feed Love. But anything will feed Hate. There was not a glass of champagne you drank, not a rich dish you ate of in all those years, that did not feed your Hate and make it fat. So to gratify it, you gambled with my life, as you gambled with my money, carelessly, recklessly, indifferent to the consequence. If you lost, the loss would not, you fancied, be yours. If you won, yours, you knew, would be the exultation, and the advantages of victory.

Hate blinds people. You were not aware of that. Love can read the writing on the remotest star, but Hate so blinded you that you could see no further than the narrow, walled-in, and already lust-withered garden of your common desires. Your terrible lack of imagination, the one really fatal defect of your character, was entirely the result of the Hate that lived in you. Subtly, silently, and in secret, Hate gnawed at your nature, as the lichen bites at the root of some sallow plant, till you grew to see nothing but the most meagre interests and the most petty aims. That faculty in you which Love would have fostered, Hate poisoned and paralysed. When your father first began to attack me it was as your private friend, and in a private letter to you. As soon as I had read the letter, with its obscene threats and coarse violences, I saw at once that a terrible danger was looming on the horizon of my troubled days: I told you I would not be the catspaw between you both in your ancient hatred of each other: that I in London was naturally much bigger game for him than a Secretary for Foreign Affairs at Homburg:[1] that it would be unfair to me to place me even for a moment in such a position: and that I had something better to do with my life than to have scenes with a man drunken, *déclassé*, and half-witted as he was. You could not be made to see this. Hate blinded you. You insisted that the quarrel had really nothing to do with me: that you would not

[1] In 1893 Queensberry's eldest son, Drumlanrig, who was then private secretary to Lord Rosebery (Foreign Secretary in Gladstone's last Government), was created Baron Kelhead in the Union peerage (all Queensberry's titles being Scottish). Queensberry approved this action and wrote to thank Gladstone, but within a month he was sending abusive letters to the Queen, Gladstone, Rosebery, and his own son. He followed Rosebery to Homburg, threatening to horsewhip him, and was only persuaded to desist by the Prince of Wales.

allow your father to dictate to you in your private friendships: that it would be most unfair of me to interfere. You had already, before you saw me on the subject, sent your father a foolish and vulgar telegram, as your answer.[1] That of course committed you to a foolish and vulgar course of action to follow. The fatal errors of life are not due to man's being unreasonable: an unreasonable moment may be one's finest moment. They are due to man's being logical. There is a wide difference. That telegram conditioned the whole of your subsequent relations with your father, and consequently the whole of my life. And the grotesque thing about it is that it was a telegram of which the commonest street-boy would have been ashamed. From pert telegrams to priggish lawyers' letters was a natural progress, and the result of your lawyer's letters to your father was, of course, to urge him on still further. You left him no option but to go on. You forced it on him as a point of honour, or of dishonour rather, that your appeal should have the more effect. So the next time he attacks me, no longer in a private letter and as your private friend, but in public and as a public man. I have to expel him from my house. He goes from restaurant to restaurant looking for me, in order to insult me before the whole world, and in such a manner that if I retaliated I would be ruined, and if I did not retaliate I would be ruined also. *Then* surely was the time when *you* should have come forward, and said that you would not expose me to such hideous attacks, such infamous persecution, on your account, but would, readily and at once, resign any claim you had to my friendship? You feel that now, I suppose. But it never even occurred to you then. Hate blinded you. All you could think of (besides of course writing to him insulting letters and telegrams) was to buy a ridiculous pistol that goes off in the Berkeley under circumstances that create a worse scandal than ever came to *your* ears. Indeed the idea of your being the object of a terrible quarrel between your father and a man of my position seemed to delight you. It, I suppose very naturally, pleased your vanity, and flattered your self-importance. That your father might have had your body, which did not interest me, and left me your soul, which did not interest him, would have been to you a distressing solution of the question. You scented the chance of a public scandal and flew to it. The prospect of a battle in which you would be safe delighted you. I never remember you in higher spirits than you were for the rest of that season. Your only disappointment seemed to be that nothing actually happened, and that no further meeting or fracas had taken place between us. You consoled yourself by sending him telegrams of such a character that at last the wretched man wrote to you and said that he had given orders to his servants that no telegram was to be brought to him under any pretence whatsoever. That did not daunt you. You saw the immense opportunities afforded by the open postcard, and availed yourself of them to the full. You hounded him on in the chase still more. I do not suppose he would ever really have given it up. Family instincts were strong in him. His hatred of you was just as persistent as

[1] This telegram (which was dated 2 April 1894) read: "WHAT A FUNNY LITTLE MAN YOU ARE."

your hatred of him, and I was the stalking-horse for both of you, and a mode of attack as well as a mode of shelter. His very passion for notoriety was not merely individual but racial. Still, if his interest had flagged for a moment your letters and postcards would soon have quickened it to its ancient flame. They did so. And he naturally went on further still. Having assailed me as a private gentleman and in private, as a public man and in public, he ultimately determines to make his final and great attack on me as an artist, and in the place where my Art is being represented. He secures by fraud a seat for the first night of one of my plays, and contrives a plot to interrupt the performance, to make a foul speech about me to the audience, to insult my actors, to throw offensive or indecent missiles at me when I am called before the curtain at the close, utterly in some hideous way to ruin me through my work. By the merest chance, in the brief and accidental sincerity of a more than usually intoxicated mood, he boasts of his intention before others. Information is given to the police, and he is kept out of the theatre. You had your chance then. Then was your opportunity. Don't you realise now that you should have seen it, and come forward and said that you would not have my Art, at any rate, ruined for your sake? You knew what my Art was to me, the great primal note by which I had revealed, first myself to myself, and then myself to the world; the real passion of my life; the love to which all other loves were as marsh-water to red wine, or the glow-worm of the marsh to the magic mirror of the moon. Don't you understand now that your lack of imagination was the one really fatal defect of your character? What you had to do was quite simple, and quite clear before you, but Hate had blinded you, and you could see nothing. I could not apologise to your father for his having insulted me and persecuted me in the most loathsome manner for nearly nine months. I could not get rid of you out of my life. I had tried it again and again. I had gone so far as actually leaving England and going abroad in the hope of escaping from you. It had all been of no use. You were the only person who could have done anything. The key of the situation rested entirely with yourself. It was the one great opportunity you had of making some slight return to me for all the love and affection and kindness and generosity and care I had shown you. Had you appreciated me even at a tenth of my value as an artist you would have done so. But Hate blinded you. The faculty "by which, and by which alone, we can understand others in their real as in their ideal relations"[1] was dead in you. You thought simply of how to get your father into prison. To see him "in the dock," as you used to say: that was your one idea. The phrase became one of the many *scies* of your daily conversation. One heard it at every meal. Well, you had your desire gratified. Hate granted you every single thing you wished for. It was an indulgent Master to you. It is so, indeed, to all who serve it. For two days you sat on a high seat with the Sheriffs, and feasted your eyes with the spectacle of your father standing in the dock of the Central Criminal Court. And on the third day I took his place. What had occurred? In your hideous game of hate together, you

[1] Cf. p. 174, line 13.

176

had both thrown dice for my soul, and you happened to have lost. That was all.

You see that I have to write your life to you, and you have to realise it. We have known each other now for more than four years. Half of the time we have been together: the other half I have had to spend in prison as the result of our friendship. Where you will receive this letter, if indeed it ever reaches you, I don't know. Rome, Naples, Paris, Venice, some beautiful city on sea or river, I have no doubt, holds you. You are surrounded, if not with all the useless luxury you had with me, at any rate with everything that is pleasurable to eye, ear, and taste. Life is quite lovely to you. And yet, if you are wise, and wish to find Life much lovelier still, and in a different manner, you will let the reading of this terrible letter—for such I know it is—prove to you as important a crisis and turning-point of your life as the writing of it is to me. Your pale face used to flush easily with wine or pleasure. If, as you read what is here written, it from time to time becomes scorched, as though by a furnace-blast, with shame, it will be all the better for you. The supreme vice is shallowness. Whatever is realised is right.

I have now got as far as the House of Detention, have I not? After a night passed in the Police Cells I am sent there in the van. You were most attentive and kind. Almost every afternoon, if not actually every afternoon till you go abroad, you took the trouble to drive up to Holloway to see me. You also wrote very sweet and nice letters. But that it was not your father but you who had put me into prison, that from beginning to end you were the responsible person, that it was through you, for you, and by you that I was there, never for one instant dawned upon you. Even the spectacle of me behind the bars of a wooden cage could not quicken that dead unimaginative nature. You had the sympathy and the sentimentality of the spectator of a rather pathetic play. That you were the true author of the hideous tragedy did not occur to you. I saw that you realised nothing of what you had done. I did not desire to be the one to tell you what your own heart should have told you, what it indeed would have told you if you had not let Hate harden it and make it insensate. Everything must come to one out of one's own nature. There is no use in telling a person a thing that they don't feel and can't understand. If I write to you now as I do it is because your own silence and conduct during my long imprisonment have made it necessary. Besides, as things had turned out, the blow had fallen upon me alone. That was a source of pleasure to me. I was content for many reasons to suffer, though there was always to my eyes, as I watched you, something not a little contemptible in your complete and wilful blindness. I remember your producing with absolute pride a letter you had published in one of the halfpenny newspapers about me.[1] It was a very

[1] In April 1895, when Wilde was in Holloway awaiting trial, the *Star* ran a lengthy correspondence about his case. On 15 April Robert Buchanan (author and dramatist, 1841–1901) wrote:

Is it not high time that a little charity, Christian or anti-Christian, were imported into this land of Christian shibboleths and formulas? . . . I for one, at any rate, wish to put on record my protest against the cowardice and cruelty of English-

prudent, temperate, indeed commonplace production. You appealed to the *"English sense of fair play,"* or something very dreary of that kind, on behalf of *"a man who was down."* It was the sort of letter you might have written had a painful charge been brought against some respectable person with whom personally you had been quite unacquainted. But you thought it a wonderful letter. You looked on it as a proof of almost quixotic chivalry. I am aware that you wrote other letters to other newspapers that they did not publish.[1] But then they were simply to say that you hated your father. Nobody cared if you did or not. Hate, you have yet to learn, is, intellectually considered, the Eternal Negation. Considered from the point of view of the emotions it is a form of Atrophy, and kills everything but itself. To write to the papers to say that one hates someone else is as if one

men towards one who was, until recently, recognised as a legitimate contributor to our amusement, and who is, when all is said and done, a scholar and a man of letters ... Let us ask ourselves, moreover, who are casting these stones, and whether they are those "without sin amongst us" or those who are themselves notoriously corrupt.

On 18 April Lord Queensberry took up Buchanan's last sentence as a possible accusation against himself and countered by asking "Is Mr Buchanan himself without sin?"

On 20 April a long letter from Douglas was printed. It included the following:

When the great British public has made up its great British mind to crush any particular unfortunate whom it holds in its power, it generally succeeds in gaining its object, and it is not fond of those who dare to question its power, or its right to do as it wishes. I feel, therefore, that I am taking my life in my hands in daring to raise my voice against the chorus of the pack of those who are now hounding Mr Oscar Wilde to his ruin ... I am simply the *vox in solitudine clamantis* raising my feeble protest; not in the expectation of making head against the wave of popular or newspaper clamour, but rather dimly hoping to catch the ear and the sympathy of one or two of those strong and fearless men and women who have before now defied the shrieks of the mob. To such as these I appeal to interfere and stay the hand of "Judge Lynch." And I submit that Mr Oscar Wilde has been tried by the newspapers before he has been tried by a jury, that his case has been almost hopelessly prejudiced in the eyes of the public from whom the jury who must try his case will be drawn, and that he is practically being delivered over bound to the fury of a cowardly and brutal mob. ...

The correspondence continued, with further letters from Buchanan and Douglas, until 25 April (the day before Wilde's first trial opened), when Queensberry wrote:

Were I the authority that had to mete out to him his punishment, I would treat him with all possible consideration as a sexual pervert of utterly diseased mind, not as a sane criminal. If this is sympathy Mr Wilde has it from me to this extent.

[1] On 13 June 1895 Labouchere's *Truth*, which had been violently anti-Wilde during and after his trials, printed the following from Douglas:

I stayed for three weeks after Mr Wilde's arrest, and visited him every day, and I did everything my mind could devise to help him, and I left on the day before his trial at his own most urgent request, and at the equally urgent request of his legal advisers, who assured me that my presence in the country could only do him harm, and that if I were called as a witness I should infallibly destroy what small chance he had of acquittal. Mr Wilde's own counsel absolutely declined to call me as a witness, fearing the harm I might do him in cross-examination, so that had I been called as a witness at all, it would have only been under a subpœna from the prosecution. Now, sir, you must give the devil his due, and granting, for the sake of argument, that I am an excep-

were to write to the papers to say that one had some secret and shameful malady: the fact that the man you hated was your own father, and that the feeling was thoroughly reciprocated, did not make your Hate noble or fine in any way. If it showed anything it was simply that it was an hereditary disease.

I remember again, when an execution was put into my house, and my books and furniture were seized and advertised to be sold,[1] and Bankruptcy was impending, I naturally wrote to tell you about it. I did not mention that it was to pay for some gifts of mine to you that the bailiffs had entered the home where you had so often dined. I thought, rightly or wrongly, that such news might pain you a little. I merely told you the bare facts. I thought it proper that you should know them. You wrote back from Boulogne in a strain of almost lyrical exultation. You said that you knew your father was "hard up for money," and had been obliged to raise £1500 for the expenses of the trial, and that my going bankrupt was really a "splendid score" off him, as he would not then be able to get any of his costs out of me! Do you realise now what Hate blinding a person is? Do you recognise now that when I described it as an Atrophy destructive of everything but itself, I was scientifically describing a real psychological fact? That all my charming things were to be sold: my Burne-Jones drawings: my Whistler drawings: my Monticelli: my Simeon Solomons: my china: my Library with its collection of presentation volumes from almost every poet of my time, from Hugo to Whitman, from Swinburne to Mallarmé, from Morris to Verlaine; with its beautifully bound editions of my father's and mother's works; its wonderful array of college and school prizes, its éditions de luxe, and the like; was absolutely nothing to you. You said it was a great bore: that was all. What you really saw in it was the possibility that your father might ultimately lose a few hundred pounds, and that paltry consideration filled you with ecstatic joy. As for the costs of the trial, you may be interested to know that your father openly said in the Orleans Club that if it had cost him £20,000 he would have considered the money thoroughly well spent, he had extracted such enjoyment, and delight, and triumph out of it all. The fact that he was able not merely to put me into prison for two years, but to take me out for an afternoon and make me a public bankrupt was an extra-refinement of pleasure that he had not expected. It was the crowning-point of my humiliation, and of his complete and perfect victory. Had your father had no claim for his costs

---

tional young scoundrel, you have no right to call me a coward. Perhaps you will pause to consider whether or not it is consistent with cowardice to do what I did—remain for three weeks in London with the daily and momentary expectation of being arrested and consigned to a fate like Mr Wilde's, receiving every day letters of warning, implored by all my friends and relations to go and save myself, and held up to execration by every catchpenny rag in England. On 28 June Douglas also wrote a long letter to W. T. Stead, editor of the *Review of Reviews*, and on 1 June 1896 published an article on *L'affaire Wilde* in the *Revue Blanche*.
[1] The contents of 16 Tite Street, including all Wilde's books and papers, were forcibly sold on 24 April 1895, at the insistence of his creditors.

on me, you, I know perfectly well, would, as far as words go, at any rate have been most sympathetic about the entire loss of my library, a loss irreparable to a man of letters, the one of all my material losses the most distressing to me. You might even, remembering the sums of money I had lavishly spent on you and how you had lived on me for years, have taken the trouble to buy in some of my books for me. The best all went for less than £150: about as much as I would spend on you in an ordinary week. But the mean small pleasure of thinking that your father was going to be a few pence out of pocket made you forget all about trying to make me a little return, so slight, so easy, so inexpensive, so obvious, and so enormously welcome to me, had you brought it about. Am I right in saying that Hate blinds people? Do you see it now? If you don't, try to see it.

How clearly I saw it then, as now, I need not tell you. But I said to myself: "*At all costs I must keep Love in my heart. If I go into prison without Love what will become of my Soul?*" The letters I wrote to you at that time from Holloway were my efforts to keep Love as the dominant note of my own nature. I could if I had chosen have torn you to pieces with bitter reproaches. I could have rent you with maledictions. I could have held up a mirror to you, and shown you such an image of yourself that you would not have recognised it as your own till you found it mimicking back your gestures of horror, and then you would have known whose shape it was, and hated it and yourself for ever. More than that indeed. The sins of another were being placed to my account. Had I so chosen, I could on either trial have saved myself at his expense, not from shame indeed but from imprisonment. Had I cared to show that the Crown witnesses—the three most important—had been carefully coached by your father and his solicitors, not in reticences merely, but in assertions, in the absolute transference, deliberate, plotted, and rehearsed, of the actions and doings of someone else on to me, I could have had each one of them dismissed from the box by the Judge, more summarily than even wretched perjured Atkins was.[1] I could have walked out of Court with my tongue in my cheek, and my hands in my pockets, a free man. The strongest pressure was put upon me to do so. I was earnestly advised, begged, entreated to do so by people whose sole interest was my welfare, and the welfare of my house. But I refused. I did not choose to do so. I have never regretted my decision for a single moment, even in the most bitter periods of my imprisonment. Such a course of action would have been beneath me. Sins of the flesh are nothing. They are maladies for physicians to cure, if they should be cured. Sins of the soul alone are shameful. To have secured my acquittal by such means would have been a life-long torture to me. But do you really think that you were worthy of the love I was showing you then, or that for a single moment I thought you were? Do you really think that at any

[1] Frederick Atkins was at times a billiard-marker and a bookmaker's clerk. When he gave evidence for the Crown at Wilde's first trial, he perjured himself so flagrantly that the judge described him in his summing up as "a most reckless, unreliable, unscrupulous, and untruthful witness." Wilde, who admitted having taken Atkins with him on a trip to Paris, was acquitted of the charges brought in respect of this witness.

period in our friendship you were worthy of the love I showed you, or that for a single moment I thought you were? I knew you were not. But Love does not traffic in a marketplace, nor use a huckster's scales. Its joy, like the joy of the intellect, is to feel itself alive. The aim of Love is to love: no more, and no less. You were my enemy: such an enemy as no man ever had. I had given you my life, and to gratify the lowest and most contemptible of all human passions, Hatred and Vanity and Greed, you had thrown it away. In less than three years you had entirely ruined me from every point of view. For my own sake there was nothing for me to do but to love you. I knew, if I allowed myself to hate you, that in the dry desert of existence over which I had to travel, and am travelling still, every rock would lose its shadow, every palm tree be withered, every well or water prove poisoned at its source. Are you beginning now to understand a little? Is your imagination wakening from the long lethargy in which it has lain? You know already what Hate is. Is it beginning to dawn on you what Love is, and what is the nature of Love? It is not too late for you to learn, though to teach it to you I may have had to go to a convict's cell.

After my terrible sentence, when the prison-dress was on me, and the prison-house closed, I sat amidst the ruins of my wonderful life, crushed by anguish, bewildered with terror, dazed through pain. But I would not hate you. Every day I said to myself, "*I must keep Love in my heart today, else how shall I live through the day.*" I reminded myself that you meant no evil, to me at any rate: I set myself to think that you had but drawn a bow at a venture, and that the arrow had pierced a King between the joints of the harness.[1] To have weighed you against the smallest of my sorrows, the meanest of my losses, would have been, I felt, unfair. I determined I would regard you as one suffering too. I forced myself to believe that at last the scales had fallen from your long-blinded eyes. I used to fancy, and with pain, what your horror must have been when you contemplated your terrible handiwork. There were times, even in those dark days, the darkest of all my life, when I actually longed to console you. So sure was I that at last you had realised what you had done.

It did not occur to me then that you could have the supreme vice, shallowness. Indeed, it was a real grief to me when I had to let you know that I was obliged to reserve for family business my first opportunity of receiving a letter: but my brother-in-law had written to me to say that if I would only write once to my wife she would, for my own sake and for our children's sake, take no action for divorce. I felt my duty was to do so. Setting aside other reasons, I could not bear the idea of being separated from Cyril, that beautiful, loving, loveable child of mine, my friend of all friends, my companion beyond all companions, one single hair of whose little golden head should have been dearer and of more value to me than, I will not merely say you from top to toe, but the entire chrysolite of the whole world:[2] was so indeed to me always, though I failed to understand it till too late.

Two weeks after your application, I get news of you. Robert Sherard,

<hr />

[1] *Kings*, xxii, 34.   [2] Cf. *Othello*, Act II, scene i.

that bravest and most chivalrous of all brilliant beings, comes to see me, and amongst other things tells me that in that ridiculous *Mercure de France*, with its absurd affectation of being the true centre of literary corruption, you are about to publish an article on me with specimens of my letters. He asks me if it really was by my wish. I was greatly taken aback, and much annoyed, and gave orders that the thing was to be stopped at once.[1] You had left my letters lying about for blackmailing companions to steal, for hotel servants to pilfer, for housemaids to sell. That was simply your careless want of appreciation of what I had written to you. But that you should seriously propose to publish selections from the balance was almost incredible to me. And which of my letters were they? I could get no information. That was my first news of you. It displeased me.

The second piece of news followed shortly afterwards. Your father's solicitors had appeared in the prison, and served me personally with a Bankruptcy notice, for a paltry £700, the amount of their taxed costs. I was adjudged a public insolvent, and ordered to be produced in Court. I felt most strongly, and feel still, and will revert to the subject again, that these costs should have been paid by your family. You had taken personally on yourself the responsibility of stating that your family would do so. It was that which had made the solicitor take up the case in the way he did. You were absolutely responsible. Even irrespective of your engagement on your family's behalf you should have felt that as you had brought the whole ruin on me, the least that could have been done was to spare me the additional ignominy of bankruptcy for an absolutely contemptible sum of money, less than half of what I spent on you in three brief summer months at Goring. Of that, however, no more here. I did through the solicitor's clerk, I fully admit, receive a message from you on the subject, or at any rate in connection with the occasion. The day he came to receive my depositions and statements, he leant across the table—the prison warder being present—and having consulted a piece of paper which he pulled from his pocket, said to me in a low voice: "Prince Fleur-de-Lys[2] wishes to be remembered to you." I stared at him. He repeated the message again. I did not know what he meant. "The gentleman is abroad at present," he added mysteriously. It all flashed across me, and I remember that, for the first and last time in my entire prison-life, I laughed. In that laugh was all the scorn of all the world. Prince Fleur-de-Lys! I saw— and subsequent events showed me that I rightly saw—that nothing that had happened had made you realise a single thing. You were in your own eyes still the graceful prince of a trivial comedy, not the sombre figure of a tragic show. All that had occurred was but as a feather for the cap that gilds a narrow head, a flower to pink the doublet that hides a heart that Hate, and Hate alone, can warm, that Love, and Love alone, finds cold. Prince Fleur-de-Lys! You were, no doubt, quite right to communicate with me under an assumed name. I myself, at that time, had no name at all. In the great prison where I was then incarcerated I was merely the figure and letter of a little cell in a long gallery, one of a thousand lifeless numbers,

---

[1] See note p. 137.   [2] See note 2, p. 136.

as of a thousand lifeless lives. But surely there were many real names in real history which would have suited you much better, and by which I would have had no difficulty at all in recognising you at once? I did not look for you behind the spangles of a tinsel vizard only suitable for an amusing masquerade. Ah! had your soul been, as for its own perfection even it should have been, wounded with sorrow, bowed with remorse, and humble with grief, such was not the disguise it would have chosen beneath whose shadow to seek entrance to the House of Pain! The great things of life are what they seem to be, and for that reason, strange as it may sound to you, are often difficult to interpret. But the little things of life are symbols. We receive our bitter lessons most easily through them. Your seemingly casual choice of a feigned name was, and will remain, symbolic. It reveals you.

Six weeks later a third piece of news arrives. I am called out of the Hospital Ward, where I was lying wretchedly ill, to receive a special message from you through the Governor of the Prison. He reads me out a letter you had addressed to him in which you stated that you proposed to publish an article "on the case of Mr Oscar Wilde," in the *Mercure de France* ("a magazine," you added for some extraordinary reason, "corresponding to our English *Fortnightly Review*") and were anxious to obtain my permission to publish extracts and selections from—what letters? The letters I had written to you from Holloway Prison! The letters that should have been to you things sacred and secret beyond anything in the whole world! These actually were the letters you proposed to publish for the jaded *décadent* to wonder at, for the greedy *feuilletoniste* to chronicle, for the little lions of the *Quartier Latin* to gape and mouth at! Had there been nothing in your own heart to cry out against so vulgar a sacrilege you might at least have remembered the sonnet he wrote who saw with such sorrow and scorn the letters of John Keats sold by public auction in London and have understood at last the real meaning of my lines

> I think they love not Art
> Who break the crystal of a poet's heart
> That small and sickly eyes may glare or gloat.[1]

For what was your article to show? That I had been too fond of you? The Paris *gamin* was quite aware of the fact. They all read the newspapers, and most of them write for them. That I was a man of genius? The French understood that, and the peculiar quality of my genius, much better than you did, or could have been expected to do. That along with genius goes often a curious perversity of passion and desire? Admirable: but the subject belongs to Lombroso rather than to you. Besides, the pathological phenomenon in question is also found amongst those who have not genius. That in your war of hate with your father I was at once shield and weapon to each of you? Nay more, that in that hideous hunt for my life, that took place when the war was over, he never could have

---

[1] The closing lines of the octave of Wilde's sonnet "On the Sale by Auction of Keats's Love Letters".

reached me had not your nets been already about my feet? Quite true: but I am told that Henri Bauër had already done it extremely well.[1] Besides, to corroborate his view, had such been your intention, you did not require to publish my letters; at any rate those written from Holloway Prison.

Will you say, in answer to my questions, that in one of my Holloway letters I had myself asked you to try, as far as you were able, to set me a little right with some small portion of the world? Certainly, I did so. Remember how and why I am here, at this very moment. Do you think I am here on account of my relations with the witnesses on my trial? My relations, real or supposed, with people of that kind were matters of no interest to either the Government or Society. They knew nothing of them, and cared less. I am here for having tried to put your father into prison. My attempt failed of course. My own Counsel threw up their briefs. Your father completely turned the tables on me, and had *me* in prison, has me there still. That is why there is contempt felt for me. That is why people despise me. That is why I have to serve out every day, every hour, every minute of my dreadful imprisonment. That is why my petitions have been refused.

You were the only person who, and without in any way exposing your-self to scorn or danger or blame, could have given another colour to the whole affair: have put the matter in a different light: have shown to a certain degree how things really stood. I would not of course have expected, nor indeed wished you to have stated how and for what purpose you had sought my assistance in your trouble at Oxford: or how, and for what purpose, if you had a purpose at all, you had practically never left my side for nearly three years. My incessant attempts to break off a friendship that was so ruinous to me as an artist, as a man of position, as a member of society even, need not have been chronicled with the accuracy with which they have been set down here. Nor would I have desired you to have described the scenes you used to make with such almost monoton-ous recurrence: nor to have reprinted your wonderful series of telegrams to me with their strange mixture of romance and finance; nor to have quoted from your letters the more revolting or heartless passages, as I have been forced to do. Still, I thought it would have been good, as well for you as for me, if you had made some protest against your father's version of our friendship, one no less grotesque than venomous, and as absurd in its reference to you as it was dishonouring in its reference to me. That version has now actually passed into serious history: it is quoted, believed, and chronicled: the preacher has taken it for his text, and the moralist for his barren theme: and I who appealed to all the ages have had to accept my verdict from one who is an ape and a buffoon. I have said, and with some bitterness, I admit, in this letter that such was the irony of things

[1] On 3 June 1895 Bauër published a powerful article in the *Echo de Paris*, attack-ing the barbarity of Wilde's sentence, the stupidity of punishing homosexuals, and the hypocrisy of the English. Queensberry he described as "*type de brute sportive malfaisante, mauvais mari, méchant père*," typical of England and her reputation for "*pudibonderie menteuse.*"

that your father would live to be the hero of a Sunday-school tract: that you would rank with the infant Samuel: and that my place would be between Gilles de Retz and the Marquis de Sade. I dare say it is best so. I have no desire to complain. One of the many lessons that one learns in prison is that things are what they are, and will be what they will be. Nor have I any doubt but that the leper of mediævalism, and the author of *Justine*, will prove better company than *Sandford and Merton*.[1]

But at the time I wrote to you I felt that for both our sakes it would be a good thing, a proper thing, a right thing *not* to accept the account your father had put forward through his Counsel for the edification of a Philistine world, and that is why I asked you to think out and write something that would be nearer the truth. It would at least have been better for you than scribbling to the French papers about the domestic life of your parents. What did the French care whether or not your parents had led a happy domestic life? One cannot conceive a subject more entirely uninteresting to them. What did interest them was how an artist of my distinction, one who by the school and movement of which he was the incarnation had exercised a marked influence on the direction of French thought, could, having led such a life, have brought such an action. Had you proposed for your article to publish the letters, endless I fear in number, in which I had spoken to you of the ruin you were bringing on my life, of the madness of moods of rage that you were allowing to master you to your own hurt as well as to mine, and of my desire, nay, my determination to end a friendship so fatal to me in every way, I could have understood it, though I would not have allowed such letters to be published: when your father's Counsel desiring to catch me in a contradiction suddenly produced in Court a letter of mine, written to you in March '93,[2] in which I stated that, rather than endure a repetition of the hideous scenes you seemed to take such a terrible pleasure in making, I would readily consent to be "blackmailed by every renter in London,"[3] it was a very real grief to me that that side of my friendship with you should incidentally be revealed to the common gaze: but that you should have been so slow to see, so lacking in all sensitiveness, and so dull in apprehension of what is rare, delicate and beautiful, as to propose yourself to publish the letters in which, and through which, I was trying to keep alive the very spirit and soul of Love, that it might dwell in my body through the long years of that body's humiliation—this was, and still is to me, a source of the very deepest pain, the most poignant disappointment. Why you did so, I fear I know but too well. If Hate blinded your eyes, Vanity sewed your eyelids together with threads of iron. The faculty "by which, and by which alone, one can understand others in their real as in their ideal relations,"[4] your narrow egotism had blunted, and long disuse had made of no avail. The imagination was as much in prison as I was. Vanity had barred up the windows, and the name of the warder was Hate.

[1] *The History of Sandford and Merton*, an improving and immensely popular book for children by Thomas Day (1748–89), was originally published 1783–89.
[2] See letter p. 111.   [3] Cf. note 1, p. 111.   [4] Cf. p. 174.

All this took place in the early part of November of the year before last. A great river of life flows between you and a date so distant. Hardly, if at all, can you see across so wide a waste. But to me it seems to have occurred, I will not say yesterday, but today. Suffering is one long moment. We cannot divide it by seasons. We can only record its moods, and chronicle their return. With us time itself does not progress. It revolves. It seems to circle round one centre of pain. The paralysing immobility of a life, every circumstance of which is regulated after an unchangeable pattern, so that we eat and drink and walk and lie down and pray, or kneel at least for prayer, according to the inflexible laws of an iron formula: this immobile quality, that makes each dreadful day in the very minutest detail like its brother, seems to communicate itself to those external forces the very essence of whose existence is ceaseless change. Of seed-time or harvest, of the reapers bending over the corn, or the grape-gatherers threading through the vines, of the grass in the orchard made white with broken blossoms, or strewn with fallen fruit, we know nothing, and can know nothing. For us there is only one season, the season of Sorrow. The very sun and moon seem taken from us. Outside, the day may be blue and gold, but the light that creeps down through the thickly-muffled glass of the small iron-barred window beneath which one sits is grey and niggard. It is always twilight in one's cell, as it is always midnight in one's heart. And in the sphere of thought, no less than in the sphere of time, motion is no more. The thing that you personally have long ago forgotten, or can easily forget, is happening to me now, and will happen to me again to-morrow. Remember this, and you will be able to understand a little of why I am writing to you, and in this manner writing.

A week later,[1] I am transferred here. Three more months go over and my mother dies. You knew, none better, how deeply I loved and honoured her. Her death was so terrible to me that I, once a lord of language, have no words in which to express my anguish and my shame. Never, even in the most perfect days of my development as an artist, could I have had words fit to bear so august a burden, or to move with sufficient stateliness of music through the purple pageant of my incommunicable woe. She and my father had bequeathed me a name they had made noble and honoured not merely in Literature, Art, Archæology and Science, but in the public history of my own country in its evolution as a nation. I had disgraced that name eternally. I had made it a low byword among low people. I had dragged it through the very mire. I had given it to brutes that they might make it brutal, and to fools that they might turn it into a synonym for folly. What I suffered then, and still suffer, is not for pen to write or paper to record. My wife, at that time kind and gentle to me, rather than that I should hear the news from indifferent or alien lips, travelled, ill as she was, all the way from Genoa to England to break to me herself the tidings of so irreparable, so irredeemable a loss. Messages of sympathy reached me from all who had still affection for me. Even people who had not known me personally, hearing what a new sorrow had come into my broken life,

[1] Wilde originally wrote "On the 13th of November."

wrote to ask that some expression of their condolence should be conveyed to me. You alone stood aloof, sent me no message, and wrote me no letter. Of such actions, it is best to say what Virgil says to Dante of those whose lives have been barren in noble impulse and shallow of intention: "*Non ragioniam di lor, ma guarda, e passa.*"[1]

Three more months go over. The calendar of my daily conduct and labour that hangs on the outside of my cell-door, with my name and sentence written upon it, tells me that it is Maytime. My friends come to see me again. I enquire, as I always do, after you. I am told that you are in your villa at Naples, and are bringing out a volume of poems. At the close of the interview it is mentioned casually that you are dedicating them to me. The tidings seemed to give me a sort of nausea of life. I said nothing, but silently went back to my cell with contempt and scorn in my heart. How could you dream of dedicating a volume of poems to me without first asking my permission? Dream, do I say? How could you dare to do such a thing? Will you give as your answer that in the days of my greatness and fame I had consented to receive the dedication of your early work? Certainly, I did so; just as I would have accepted the homage of any other young man beginning the difficult and beautiful art of literature. All homage is delightful to an artist, and doubly sweet when youth brings it. Laurel and bay leaf wither when aged hands pluck them. Only youth has a right to crown an artist. That is the real privilege of being young, if youth only knew it. But the days of abasement and infamy are different from those of greatness and of fame. You have yet to learn that Prosperity, Pleasure and Success may be rough of grain and common in fibre, but that Sorrow is the most sensitive of all created things. There is nothing that stirs in the whole world of thought or motion to which Sorrow does not vibrate in terrible if exquisite pulsation. The thin beaten-out leaf of tremulous gold that chronicles the direction of forces that the eye cannot see is in comparison coarse.[2] It is a wound that bleeds when any hand but that of Love touches it and even then must bleed again, though not for pain.

You could write to the Governor of Wandsworth Prison to ask my permission to publish my letters in the *Mercure de France*, "*corresponding to our* English *Fortnightly Review.*" Why not have written to the Governor of the Prison at Reading to ask my permission to dedicate your poems to me, whatever fantastic description you may have chosen to give of them? Was it because in the one case the magazine in question had been prohibited by me from publishing letters, the legal copyright of which, as you are of course perfectly well aware, was and is vested entirely in me, and in the other you thought that you could enjoy the wilfulness of your own way without my knowing anything about it till it was too late to interfere? The mere fact that I was a man disgraced, ruined, and in prison should have made you, if you desired to write my name on the fore-page of your work, beg it of me as a favour, an honour, a privilege. That is the way in which

---

[1] "Let us not speak of them, but look, and pass on." (*Inferno,* iii, 51.)
[2] Perhaps a reference to the Gold-Leaf Electroscope, invented in 1787, to detect charges of static electricity, though "direction" makes no sense.

one should approach those who are in distress and sit in shame.

Where there is Sorrow there is holy ground. Some day you will realise what that means. You will know nothing of life till you do. Robbie, and natures like his, can realise it. When I was brought down from my prison to the Court of Bankruptcy between two policemen, Robbie waited in the long dreary corridor, that before the whole crowd, whom an action so sweet and simple hushed into silence, he might gravely raise his hat to me, as handcuffed and with bowed head I passed him by. Men have gone to heaven for smaller things than that. It was in this spirit, and with this mode of love that the saints knelt down to wash the feet of the poor, or stooped to kiss the leper on the cheek. I have never said one single word to him about what he did. I do not know to the present moment whether he is aware that I was even conscious of his action. It is not a thing for which one can render formal thanks in formal words. I store it in the treasury-house of my heart. I keep it there as a secret debt that I am glad to think I can never possibly repay. It is embalmed and kept sweet by the myrrh and cassia of many tears. When Wisdom has been profitless to me, and Philosophy barren, and the proverbs and phrases of those who have sought to give me consolation as dust and ashes in my mouth, the memory of that little lowly silent act of Love has unsealed for me all the wells of pity, made the desert blossom like a rose, and brought me out of the bitterness of lonely exile into harmony with the wounded, broken and great heart of the world. When you are able to understand, not merely how beautiful Robbie's action was, but why it meant so much to me, and always will mean so much, then, perhaps, you will realise how and in what spirit you should have approached me for permission to dedicate to me your verses.

It is only right to state that in any case I would not have accepted the dedication. Though, possibly, it would under other circumstances have pleased me to have been asked, I would have refused the request for *your* sake, irrespective of any feelings of my own. The first volume of poems that in the very springtime of his manhood a young man sends forth to the world should be like a blossom or flower of spring, like the white thorn in the meadow at Magdalen, or the cowslips in the Cumnor fields. It should not be burdened by the weight of a terrible, a revolting tragedy, a terrible, a revolting scandal. If I had allowed my name to serve as herald to the book it would have been a grave artistic error. It would have brought a wrong atmosphere round the whole work, and in modern art atmosphere counts for so much. Modern life is complex and relative. Those are its two distinguishing notes. To render the first we require atmosphere with its subtlety of *nuances*, of suggestion, of strange perspectives: as for the second we require background. That is why Sculpture has ceased to be a representative art; and why Music *is* a representative art; and why Literature is, and has been, and always will remain the supreme representative art.

Your little book should have brought with it Sicilian and Arcadian airs, not the pestilent foulness of the criminal dock or the close breath of the convict cell. Nor would such a dedication as you proposed have been merely an error of taste in Art; it would from other points of view have been entirely unseemly. It would have looked like a continuance of your conduct before and after my arrest. It would have given people the impression of being an attempt at foolish bravado: an example of that kind of courage that is sold cheap and bought cheap in the streets of shame. As far as our friendship is concerned Nemesis has crushed us both like flies. The dedication of verses to me when I was in prison would have seemed a sort of silly effort at smart repartee, an accomplishment on which in your old days of dreadful letter-writing—days never, I sincerely hope for your sake, to return—you used openly to pride yourself and about which it was your joy to boast. It would not have produced the serious, the beautiful effect which I trust—I believe indeed—you had intended. Had you consulted me, I would have advised you to delay the publication of your verses for a little; or, if that proved displeasing to you, to publish anonymously at first, and then when you had won lovers by your song—the only sort of lovers really worth the winning—you might have turned round and said to the world "These flowers that you admire are of my sowing, and now I offer them to one whom you regard as a pariah and an outcast, as my tribute to what I love and reverence and admire in him." But you chose the wrong method and the wrong moment. There is a tact in love, and a tact in literature: you were not sensitive to either.

I have spoken to you at length on this point in order that you should grasp its full bearings, and understand why I wrote at once to Robbie in terms of such scorn and contempt of you,[1] and absolutely prohibited the dedication, and desired that the words I had written of you should be copied out carefully and sent to you. I felt that at last the time had come when you should be made to see, to recognise, to realise a little of what you had done. Blindness may be carried so far that it becomes grotesque, and an unimaginative nature, if something be not done to rouse it, will become petrified into absolute insensibility, so that while the body may eat, and drink, and have its pleasures, the soul, whose house it is, may, like the soul of Branca d'Oria in Dante, be dead absolutely.[2] My letter seems to have arrived not a moment too soon. It fell on you, as far as I can judge, like a thunderbolt. You describe yourself, in your answer to Robbie, as being "deprived of all power of thought and expression." Indeed, apparently, you can think of nothing better than to write to your mother to complain. Of course, she, with that blindness to your real good that has been her ill-starred fortune and yours, gives you every comfort she can think of, and lulls you back, I suppose, into your former unhappy, unworthy condition; while as far as I am concerned, she lets my friends know that she is "very much annoyed" at the severity of my remarks about you. Indeed it is not merely to my friends that she conveys her sentiments of annoyance, but also to those—a very much larger number, I need hardly remind you—who are not my friends: and I am informed now, and through channels very kindly-disposed to you and yours, that in consequence of this a great deal of the sympathy that, by reason of my distinguished genius and terrible

[1] See pp. 140–141.   [2] *Inferno*, xxxiii, 135–147.

sufferings, had been gradually but surely growing up for me, has been entirely taken away. People say "Ah! he first tried to get the kind father put into prison and failed: now he turns round and blames the innocent son for his failure. How right we were to despise him! How worthy of contempt he is!" It seems to me that, when my name is mentioned in your mother's presence, if she has no word of sorrow or regret for her share—no slight one—in the ruin of my house, it would be more seemly if she remained silent. And as for you—don't you think now that, instead of writing to *her* to complain, it would have been better for you, in every way, to have written to *me* directly, and to have had the courage to say to me whatever you had or fancied you had to say? It is nearly a year ago now since I wrote that letter. You cannot have remained during that entire time "deprived of all power of thought and expression." Why did you not write to me? You saw by my letter how deeply wounded, how outraged I was by your whole conduct. More than that; you saw your entire friendship with me set before you, at last, in its true light, and by a mode not to be mistaken. Often in old days I had told you that you were ruining my life. You had always laughed. When Edwin Levy[1] at the very beginning of our friendship, seeing your manner of putting me forward to bear the brunt, and annoyance, and expense even of that unfortunate Oxford mishap of yours, if we must so term it, in reference to which his advice and help had been sought, warned me for the space of a whole hour against knowing you, you laughed, as at Bracknell I described to you my long and impressive interview with him. When I told you how even that unfortunate young man who ultimately stood beside me in the Dock had warned me more than once that you would prove far more fatal in bringing me to utter destruction than any even of the common lads whom I was foolish enough to know, you laughed, though not with such sense of amusement. When my more prudent or less well-disposed friends either warned me or left me, on account of my friendship with you, you laughed with scorn. You laughed immoderately when, on the occasion of your father writing his first abusive letter to you about me, I told you that I knew I would be the mere cats-paw of your dreadful quarrel and come to some evil between you. But every single thing had happened as I had said it would happen, as far as the result goes. You had no excuse for not seeing how all things had come to pass. Why did you not write to me? Was it cowardice? Was it callousness? What was it? The fact that I was outraged with you, and had expressed my sense of the outrage, was all the more reason for writing. If you thought my letter just, you should have written. If you thought it in the smallest point unjust, you should have written. I waited for a letter. I felt sure that at last you would see that, if old affection, much-protested love, the thousand acts of ill-requited kindness I had showered on you, the thousand unpaid debts of gratitude you owed me—that if all these were nothing to you, mere duty itself, most barren of all bonds between man and man, should

[1] Possibly some kind of money-lender or private inquiry agent and conceivably the Edwin Levy (died 1895) who was one of the proprietors of J. Lyons & Co. and was described in an obituary as the "confidential agent" of Napoleon III.

have made you write. You cannot say that you seriously thought I was obliged to receive none but business communications from members of my family. You knew perfectly well that every twelve weeks Robbie was writing to me a little budget of literary news. Nothing can be more charming than his letters, in their wit, their clever concentrated criticism, their light touch: they are real letters: they are like a person talking to one: they have the quality of a French *causerie intime*: and in his delicate modes of deference to me, appealing at one time to my judgment, at another to my sense of humour, at another to my instinct for beauty or to my culture, and reminding me in a hundred subtle ways that once I was to many an arbiter of style in Art, the supreme arbiter to some, he shows how he has the tact of love as well as the tact of literature. His letters have been the little messengers between me and that beautiful unreal world of Art where once I was King, and would have remained King, indeed, had I not let myself be lured into the imperfect world of coarse uncompleted passions, of appetite without distinction, desire without limit, and formless greed. Yet, when all is said, surely you might have been able to understand, or conceive, at any rate, in your own mind, that, even on the ordinary grounds of mere psychological curiosity, it would have been more interesting to me to hear from *you* than to learn that Alfred Austin was trying to bring out a volume of poems,[1] or that Street was writing dramatic criticisms for the *Daily Chronicle*,[2] or that by one who cannot speak a panegyric without stammering Mrs Meynell had been pronounced to be the new Sibyl of Style.[3]

Ah! had *you* been in prison—I will not say through any fault of mine, for that would be a thought too terrible for me to bear—but through fault of your own, error of your own, faith in some unworthy friend, slip in sensual mire, trust misapplied, or love ill-bestowed, or none, or all of these —do you think that I would have allowed you to eat your heart away in darkness and solitude without trying in some way, however slight, to help you to bear the bitter burden of your disgrace? Do you think that I would not have let you know that if you suffered, I was suffering too: that if you wept, there were tears in my eyes also: and that if you lay in the house of bondage and were despised of men, I out of my very griefs had built a house in which to dwell until your coming, a treasury in which all that men had denied to you would be laid up for your healing, one hundredfold in increase? If bitter necessity, or prudence, to *me* more bitter still, had prevented my being near you, and robbed me of the joy of your presence,

<hr>

[1] Alfred Austin (1835–1913) eventually succeeded Tennyson as Poet Laureate in 1896, after a four-year interregnum. In 1887 Wilde had written in the *Pall Mall Gazette*: "Mr Austin is neither an Olympian nor a Titan, and all the puffing in Paternoster Row cannot set him on Parnassus." In 1895, when asked who he thought should be the next Laureate, Wilde wrote (in the *Idler* for April): "Mr Swinburne is already the Poet Laureate of England. The fact that his appointment to this high post has not been degraded by official confirmation renders his position all the more unassailable. He whom all poets love is the Poet Laureate always."

[2] George Slythe Street (1867–1936), journalist and author of *The Autobiography of a Boy* (1894) and other books.

[3] In December 1895 Coventry Patmore (1823–96) had written to the *Saturday Review*, advocating the claims of Alice Meynell (1847–1922) to the Laureateship.

though seen through prison-bars and in a shape of shame, I would have written to you in season and out of season in the hope that some mere phrase, some single word, some broken echo even of Love might reach you. If you had refused to receive my letters, I would have written none the less, so that you should have known that at any rate there were always letters waiting for you. Many have done so to me. Every three months people write to me, or propose to write to me. Their letters and communications are kept. They will be handed to me when I go out of prison. I know that they are there. I know the names of the people who have written them. I know that they are full of sympathy, and affection, and kindness. That is sufficient for me. I need to know no more. Your silence has been horrible. Nor has it been a silence of weeks and months merely, but of years; of years even as they have to count them who, like yourself, live swiftly in happiness, and can hardly catch the gilt feet of the days as they dance by, and are out of breath in the chase after pleasure. It is a silence without excuse; a silence without palliation. I knew you had feet of clay. Who knew it better? When I wrote, among my aphorisms, that it was simply the feet of clay that made the gold of the image precious,[1] it was of you I was thinking. But it is no gold image with clay feet that you have made of yourself. Out of the very dust of the common highway that the hooves of horned things pash into mire you have moulded your perfect semblance for me to look at, so that, whatever my secret desire might have been, it would be impossible for me now to have for you any feeling other than that of contempt and scorn, for myself any feeling other than that of contempt and scorn either. And setting aside all other reasons, your indifference, your worldly wisdom, your callousness, your prudence, whatever you may choose to call it, has been made doubly bitter to me by the peculiar circumstances that either accompanied or followed my fall.

Other miserable men, when they are thrown into prison, if they are robbed of the beauty of the world, are at least safe, in some measure, from the world's most deadly slings, most awful arrows. They can hide in the darkness of their cells, and of their very disgrace make a mode of sanctuary. The world, having had its will, goes its way, and they are left to suffer undisturbed. With me it has been different. Sorrow after sorrow has come beating at the prison doors in search of me. They have opened the gates wide and let them in. Hardly, if at all, have my friends been suffered to see me. But my enemies have had full access to me always. Twice in my public appearances at the Bankruptcy Court, twice again in my public transferences from one prison to another, have I been shown under conditions of unspeakable humiliation to the gaze and mockery of men. The messenger of Death has brought me his tidings and gone his way, and in entire solitude, and isolated from all that could give me comfort, or suggest relief, I have had to bear the intolerable burden of misery and remorse that the memory of my mother placed upon me, and places on me

---

[1] *The Picture of Dorian Gray*, ch. xv. This chapter first appeared in the book-edition of April 1891.

still. Hardly has that wound been dulled, not healed, by time, when violent and bitter and harsh letters come to me from my wife through her solicitor. I am, at once, taunted and threatened with poverty. That I can bear. I can school myself to worse than that. But my two children are taken from me by legal procedure.[1] That is and always will remain to me a source of infinite distress, of infinite pain, of grief without end or limit. That the law should decide, and take upon itself to decide, that I am one unfit to be with my own children is something quite horrible to me. The disgrace of prison is as nothing compared to it. I envy the other men who tread the yard along with me. I am sure that their children wait for them, look for their coming, will be sweet to them.

The poor are wiser, more charitable, more kind, more sensitive than we are. In their eyes prison is a tragedy in a man's life, a misfortune, a casualty, something that calls for sympathy in others. They speak of one who is in prison as of one who is "*in trouble*" simply. It is the phrase they always use, and the expression has the perfect wisdom of Love in it. With people of our rank it is different. With us prison makes a man a pariah. I, and such as I am, have hardly any right to air and sun. Our presence taints the pleasures of others. We are unwelcome when we reappear. To revisit the glimpses of the moon[2] is not for us. Our very children are taken away. Those lovely links with humanity are broken. We are doomed to be solitary, while our sons still live. We are denied the one thing that might heal us and help us, that might bring balm to the bruised heart, and peace to the soul in pain.

And to all this has been added the hard, small fact that by your actions and by your silence, by what you have done and by what you have left undone, you have made every day of my long imprisonment still more difficult for me to live through. The very bread and water of prison fare you have by your conduct changed. You have rendered the one bitter and the other brackish to me. The sorrow you should have shared you have doubled, the pain you should have sought to lighten you have quickened to anguish. I have no doubt that you did not mean to do so. I know that you did not mean to do so. It was simply that "one really fatal defect of your character, your entire lack of imagination."

And the end of it all is that I have got to forgive you. I must do so. I don't write this letter to put bitterness into your heart, but to pluck it out of mine. For my own sake I must forgive you. One cannot always keep an adder in one's breast to feed on one, nor rise up every night to sow thorns in the garden of one's soul. It will not be difficult at all for me to do so, if you help me a little. Whatever you did to me in old days I always readily forgave. It did you no good then. Only one whose life is without stain of any kind can forgive sins. But now when I sit in humiliation and disgrace it is different. My forgiveness should mean a great deal to you now.

---

[1] Constance Wilde's summons had been heard by Mr Justice Kekewich in the Chancery Division on 12 February 1897. The resulting order gave Constance custody of the children, with herself and Adrian Hope (see note p. 227) as their guardians.

[2] *Hamlet*, Act I, scene iv.

Some day you will realise it. Whether you do so early or late, soon or not at all, my way is clear before me. I cannot allow you to go through life bearing in your heart the burden of having ruined a man like me. The thought might make you callously indifferent, or morbidly sad. I must take the burden from you and put it on my own shoulders.

I must say to myself that neither you nor your father, multiplied a thousand times over, could possibly have ruined a man like me: that I ruined myself: and that nobody, great or small, can be ruined except by his own hand. I am quite ready to do so. I am trying to do so, though you may not think it at the present moment. If I have brought this pitiless indictment against you, think what an indictment I bring without pity against myself. Terrible as what you did to me was, what I did to myself was far more terrible still.

I was a man who stood in symbolic relations to the art and culture of my age. I had realised this for myself at the very dawn of my manhood, and had forced my age to realise it afterwards. Few men hold such a position in their own lifetime and have it so acknowledged. It is usually discerned, if discerned at all, by the historian, or the critic, long after both the man and his age have passed away. With me it was different. I felt it myself, and made others feel it. Byron was a symbolic figure, but his relations were to the passion of his age and its weariness of passion. Mine were to something more noble, more permanent, of more vital issue, of larger scope.

The gods had given me almost everything. I had genius, a distinguished name, high social position, brilliancy, intellectual daring: I made art a philosophy, and philosophy an art: I altered the minds of men and the colours of things: there was nothing I said or did that did not make people wonder: I took the drama, the most objective form known to art, and made it as personal a mode of expression as the lyric or the sonnet, at the same time that I widened its range and enriched its characterisation: drama, novel, poem in rhyme, poem in prose, subtle or fantastic dialogue, whatever I touched I made beautiful in a new mode of beauty: to truth itself I gave what is false no less than what is true as its rightful province, and showed that the false and the true are merely forms of intellectual existence. I treated Art as the supreme reality, and life as a mere mode of fiction: I awoke the imagination of my century so that it created myth and legend around me: I summed up all systems in a phrase, and all existence in an epigram.

Along with these things, I had things that were different. I let myself be lured into long spells of senseless and sensual ease. I amused myself with being a *flâneur*, a dandy, a man of fashion. I surrounded myself with the smaller natures and the meaner minds. I became the spend-thrift of my own genius, and to waste an eternal youth gave me a curious joy. Tired of being on the heights I deliberately went to the depths in the search for new sensations. What the paradox was to me in the sphere of thought, perversity became to me in the sphere of passion. Desire, at the end, was a malady, or a madness, or both. I grew careless of the lives of others. I took pleasure where it pleased me and passed on.

I forgot that every little action of the common day makes or unmakes character, and that therefore what one has done in the secret chamber one has some day to cry aloud on the housetops. I ceased to be Lord over myself. I was no longer the Captain of my Soul, and did not know it. I allowed you to dominate me, and your father to frighten me. I ended in horrible disgrace. There is only one thing for me now, absolute Humility: just as there is only one thing for you, absolute Humility also. You had better come down into the dust and learn it beside me.

I have lain in prison for nearly two years. Out of my nature has come wild despair; an abandonment to grief that was piteous even to look at: terrible and impotent rage: bitterness and scorn: anguish that wept aloud: misery that could find no voice: sorrow that was dumb. I have passed through every possible mood of suffering. Better than Wordsworth himself I know what Wordsworth meant when he said:

> Suffering is permanent, obscure, and dark
> And has the nature of Infinity.[1]

But while there were times when I rejoiced in the idea that my sufferings were to be endless, I could not bear them to be without meaning. Now I find hidden away in my nature something that tells me that nothing in the whole world is meaningless, and suffering least of all. That something hidden away in my nature, like a treasure in a field, is Humility.

It is the last thing left in me, and the best: the ultimate discovery at which I have arrived: the starting-point for a fresh development. It has come to me right out of myself, so I know that it has come at the proper time. It could not have come before, nor later. Had anyone told me of it, I would have rejected it. Had it been brought to me, I would have refused it. As I found it, I want to keep it. I must do so. It is the one thing that has in it the elements of life, of a new life, a *Vita Nuova* for me. Of all things it is the strangest. One cannot give it away, and another may not give it to one. One cannot acquire it, except by surrendering everything that one has. It is only when one has lost all things, that one knows that one possesses it.

Now that I realise that it is in me, I see quite clearly what I have got to do, what, in fact, I must do. And when I use such a phrase as that, I need not tell you that I am not alluding to any external sanction or command. I admit none. I am far more of an individualist than I ever was. Nothing seems to me of the smallest value except what one gets out of oneself. My nature is seeking a fresh mode of self-realisation. That is all I am concerned with. And the first thing that I have got to do is to free myself from any possible bitterness of feeling against you.

I am completely penniless, and absolutely homeless. Yet there are worse things in the world than that. I am quite candid when I tell you that rather than go out from this prison with bitterness in my heart against you or against the world I would gladly and readily beg my bread from door to door. If I got nothing at the house of the rich, I would get something at

---

[1] *The Borderers*, Act III; "has" should be "shares."

the house of the poor. Those who have much are often greedy. Those who have little always share. I would not a bit mind sleeping in the cool grass in summer, and when winter came on sheltering myself by the warm close-thatched rick, or under the penthouse of a great barn, provided I had love in my heart. The external things of life seem to me now of no importance at all. You can see to what intensity of individualism I have arrived, or am arriving rather, for the journey is long, and "where I walk there are thorns."[1]

Of course I know that to ask for alms on the highway is not to be my lot, and that if ever I lie in the cool grass at night-time it will be to write sonnets to the Moon. When I go out of prison, Robbie will be waiting for me on the other side of the big iron-studded gate, and he is the symbol not merely of his own affection, but of the affection of many others besides. I believe I am to have enough to live on for about eighteen months at any rate, so that, if I may not write beautiful books, I may at least read beautiful books, and what joy can be greater? After that, I hope to be able to re-create my creative faculty. But were things different: had I not a friend left in the world: were there not a single house open to me even in pity: had I to accept the wallet and ragged cloak of sheer penury: still as long as I remained free from all resentment, hardness, and scorn, I would be able to face life with much more calm and confidence than I would were my body in purple and fine linen, and the soul within it sick with hate. And I shall really have no difficulty in forgiving you. But to make it a pleasure for me you must feel that you want it. When you really want it you will find it waiting for you.

I need not say that my task does not end there. It would be comparatively easy if it did. There is much more before me. I have hills far steeper to climb, valleys much darker to pass through. And I have to get it all out of myself. Neither Religion, Morality, nor Reason can help me at all.

Morality does not help me. I am a born antinomian. I am one of those who are made for exceptions, not for laws. But while I see that there is nothing wrong in what one does, I see that there is something wrong in what one becomes. It is well to have learned that.

Religion does not help me. The faith that others give to what is unseen, I give to what one can touch, and look at. My Gods dwell in temples made with hands, and within the circle of actual experience is my creed made perfect and complete: too complete it may be, for like many or all of those who have placed their Heaven in this earth, I have found in it not merely the beauty of Heaven, but the horror of Hell also. When I think about Religion at all, I feel as if I would like to found an order for those who cannot believe: the Confraternity of the Fatherless one might call it, where on an altar, on which no taper burned, a priest, in whose heart peace had no dwelling, might celebrate with unblessed bread and a chalice empty of wine. Everything to be true must become a religion. And agnosticism should have its ritual no less than faith. It has sown its martyrs, it should

[1] *A Woman of No Importance*, Act IV.

reap its saints, and praise God daily for having hidden Himself from man. But whether it be faith or agnosticism, it must be nothing external to me. Its symbols must be of my own creating. Only that is spiritual which makes its own form. If I may not find its secret within myself, I shall never find it. If I have not got it already, it will never come to me.

Reason does not help me. It tells me that the laws under which I am convicted are wrong and unjust laws, and the system under which I have suffered a wrong and unjust system. But, somehow, I have got to make both of these things just and right to me. And exactly as in Art one is only concerned with what a particular thing is at a particular moment to oneself, so it is also in the ethical evolution of one's character. I have got to make everything that has happened to me good for me. The plank-bed, the loathsome food, the hard ropes shredded into oakum till one's finger-tips grow dull with pain, the menial offices with which each day begins and finishes, the harsh orders that routine seems to necessitate, the dreadful dress that makes sorrow grotesque to look at, the silence, the solitude, the shame—each and all of these things I have to transform into a spiritual experience. There is not a single degradation of the body which I must not try and make into a spiritualising of the soul.

I want to get to the point when I shall be able to say, quite simply and without affectation, that the two great turning-points of my life were when my father sent me to Oxford, and when society sent me to prison. I will not say that it is the best thing that could have happened to me, for that phrase would savour of too great bitterness towards myself. I would sooner say, or hear it said of me, that I was so typical a child of my age that in my perversity, and for that perversity's sake, I turned the good things of my life to evil, and the evil things of my life to good. What is said, however, by myself or by others matters little. The important thing, the thing that lies before me, the thing that I have to do, or be for the brief remainder of my days one maimed, marred, and incomplete, is to absorb into my nature all that has been done to me, to make it part of me, to accept it without complaint, fear, or reluctance. The supreme vice is shallowness. Whatever is realised is right.

When first I was put into prison some people advised me to try and forget who I was. It was ruinous advice. It is only by realising what I am that I have found comfort of any kind. Now I am advised by others to try on my release to forget that I have ever been in a prison at all. I know that would be equally fatal. It would mean that I would be always haunted by an intolerable sense of disgrace, and that those things that are meant as much for me as for anyone else—the beauty of the sun and the moon, the pageant of the seasons, the music of daybreak and the silence of great nights, the rain falling through the leaves, or the dew creeping over the grass and making it silver—would all be tainted for me, and lose their healing power and their power of communicating joy. To reject one's own experiences is to arrest one's own development. To deny one's own experiences is to put a lie into the lips of one's own life. It is no less than a denial of the Soul. For just as the body absorbs things of all kinds, things common and unclean no less than those that the priest or a vision has cleansed, and converts them into swiftness or strength, into the play of beautiful muscles and the moulding of fair flesh, into the curves and colours of the hair, the lips, the eye: so the Soul, in its turn, has its nutritive functions also, and can transform into noble moods of thought, and passions of high import, what in itself is base, cruel, and degrading: nay more, may find in these its most august modes of assertion, and can often reveal itself most perfectly through what was intended to desecrate or destroy.

The fact of my having been the common prisoner of a common gaol I must frankly accept, and, curious as it may seem to you, one of the things I shall have to teach myself is not to be ashamed of it. I must accept it as a punishment, and if one is ashamed of having been punished, one might just as well never have been punished at all. Of course there are many things of which I was convicted that I had not done, but then there are many things of which I was convicted that I had done, and a still greater number of things in my life for which I never was indicted at all. And as for what I have said in this letter, that the gods are strange, and punish us for what is good and humane in us as much as for what is evil and perverse, I must accept the fact that one is punished for the good as well as for the evil that one does. I have no doubt that it is quite right one should be. It helps one, or should help one, to realise both, and not to be too conceited about either. And if I then am not ashamed of my punishment, as I hope not to be, I shall be able to think, and walk, and live with freedom.

Many men on their release carry their prison along with them into the air, hide it as a secret disgrace in their hearts, and at length like poor poisoned things creep into some hole and die. It is wretched that they should have to do so, and it is wrong, terribly wrong, of Society that it should force them to do so. Society takes upon itself the right to inflict appalling punishments on the individual, but it also has the supreme vice of shallowness, and fails to realise what it has done. When the man's punishment is over, it leaves him to himself: that is to say it abandons him at the very moment when its highest duty towards him begins. It is really ashamed of its own actions, and shuns those whom it has punished, as people shun a creditor whose debt they cannot pay, or one on whom they have inflicted an irreparable, an irredeemable wrong. I claim on my side that if I realise what I have suffered, Society should realise what it has inflicted on me: and that there should be no bitterness or hate on either side.

Of course I know that from one point of view things will be made more difficult for me than for others; must indeed, by the very nature of the case, be made so. The poor thieves and outcasts who are imprisoned here with me are in many respects more fortunate than I am. The little way in grey city or green field that saw their sin is small: to find those who know nothing of what they have done they need go no further than a bird might fly between the twilight before dawn and dawn itself: but for me "the world is shrivelled to a handsbreadth,"[1] and everywhere I turn my name is

---

[1] *A Woman of No Importance*, Act IV.

written on the rocks in lead. For I have come, not from obscurity into the momentary notoriety of crime, but from a sort of eternity of fame to a sort of eternity of infamy, and sometimes seem to myself to have shown, if indeed it required showing, that between the famous and the infamous there is but one step, if so much as one.

Still, in the very fact that people will recognise me wherever I go, and know all about my life, as far as its follies go, I can discern something good for me. It will force on me the necessity of again asserting myself as an artist, and as soon as I possibly can. If I can produce even one more beautiful work of art I shall be able to rob malice of its venom, and coward-ice of its sneer, and to pluck out the tongue of scorn by the roots. And if life be, as it surely is, a problem to me, I am no less a problem to Life. People must adopt some attitude towards me, and so pass judgment both on themselves and me. I need not say I am not talking of particular individuals. The only people I would care to be with now are artists and people who have suffered: those who know what Beauty is, and those who know what Sorrow is: nobody else interests me. Nor am I making any demands on Life. In all that I have said I am simply concerned with my own mental attitude towards life as a whole: and I feel that not to be ashamed of having been punished is one of the first points I must attain to, for the sake of my own perfection, and because I am so imperfect.

Then I must learn how to be happy. Once I knew it, or thought I knew it, by instinct. It was always springtime once in my heart. My tempera-ment was akin to joy. I filled my life to the very brim with pleasure, as one might fill a cup to the very brim with wine. Now I am approaching life from a completely new standpoint, and even to conceive happiness is often extremely difficult for me. I remember during my first term at Oxford reading in Pater's *Renaissance*[1]—that book which has had such a strange influence over my life—how Dante places low in the Inferno those who wilfully live in sadness, and going to the College Library and turning to the passage in the *Divine Comedy* where beneath the dreary marsh lie those who were "sullen in the sweet air," saying for ever through their sighs:

Tristi fummo
nell' aer dolce che dal sol s'allegra.[2]

I knew the Church condemned *accidia*, but the whole idea seemed to me quite fantastic, just the sort of sin, I fancied, a priest who knew nothing about real life would invent. Nor could I understand how Dante, who says that "sorrow remarries us to God,"[3] could have been so harsh to those who were enamoured of melancholy, if any such there really were. I had no idea that some day this would become to me one of the greatest temptations of my life.

[1] In the essay on "The Poetry of Michelangelo."
[2] Sad once were we,
In the sweet air made gladsome by the sun.
(*Inferno*, vii, 121–22, H. F. Cary's translation.)
[3] *Purgatorio*, xxiii, 81.

While I was in Wandsworth Prison I longed to die. It was my one desire. When after two months in the Infirmary I was transferred here, and found myself growing gradually better in physical health, I was filled with rage. I determined to commit suicide on the very day on which I left prison. After a time that evil mood passed away, and I made up my mind to live, but to wear gloom as a King wears purple: never to smile again: to turn whatever house I entered into a house of mourning: to make my friends walk slowly in sadness with me: to teach them that melancholy is the true secret of life: to maim them with an alien sorrow: to mar them with my own pain. Now I feel quite differently. I see it would be both ungrateful and unkind of me to pull so long a face that when my friends came to see me they would have to make their faces still longer in order to show their sympathy, or, if I desired to entertain them, to invite them to sit down silently to bitter herbs and funeral baked meats. I must learn how to be cheerful and happy.

The last two occasions on which I was allowed to see my friends here I tried to be as cheerful as possible, and to show my cheerfulness in order to make them some slight return for their trouble in coming all the way from town to visit me. It is only a slight return, I know, but it is the one, I feel certain, that pleases them most. I saw Robbie for an hour on Saturday week, and I tried to give the fullest possible expression to the delight I really felt at our meeting.[1] And that, in the views and ideas I am here shaping for myself, I am quite right is shown to me by the fact that now for the first time since my imprisonment I have a real desire to live.

There is before me so much to do that I would regard it as a terrible tragedy if I died before I was allowed to complete at any rate a little of it. I see new developments in Art and Life, each one of which is a fresh mode of perfection. I long to live so that I can explore what is no less than a new world to me. Do you want to know what this new world is? I think you can guess what it is. It is the world in which I have been living.

Sorrow, then, and all that it teaches one, is my new world. I used to live entirely for pleasure. I shunned sorrow and suffering of every kind. I hated both. I resolved to ignore them as far as possible, to treat them, that is to say, as modes of imperfection. They were not part of my scheme of life. They had no place in my philosophy. My mother, who knew life as a whole, used often to quote to me Goethe's lines—written by Carlyle in a book he had given her years ago—and translated, I fancy, by him also:

> Who never ate his bread in sorrow,
>   Who never spent the midnight hours
> Weeping and waiting for the morrow,
>   He knows you not, ye Heavenly Powers.[2]

[1] This probably refers to Saturday, 27 February 1897, when Ross and Adey paid Wilde a visit.

[2] Carlyle's translation of Goethe's *Wilhelm Meister's Apprenticeship*, Bk. ii, ch. 13, where "midnight" is "darksome," "waiting" is "watching," and "Heavenly" is "gloomy."

They were the lines that noble Queen of Prussia, whom Napoleon treated with such coarse brutality, used to quote in her humiliation and exile:[1] they were lines my mother often quoted in the troubles of her later life: I absolutely declined to accept or admit the enormous truth hidden in them. I could not understand it. I remember quite well how I used to tell her that I did not want to eat my bread in sorrow, or to pass any night weeping and watching for a more bitter dawn. I had no idea that it was one of the special things that the Fates had in store for me; that for a whole year of my life, indeed, I was to do little else. But so has my portion been meted out to me; and during the last few months I have, after terrible struggles and difficulties, been able to comprehend some of the lessons hidden in the heart of pain. Clergymen, and people who use phrases without wisdom, sometimes talk of suffering as a mystery. It is really a revelation. One discerns things that one never discerned before. One approaches the whole of history from a different standpoint. What one had felt dimly through instinct, about Art, is intellectually and emotionally realised with perfect clearness of vision and absolute intensity of apprehension.

I now see that sorrow, being the supreme emotion of which man is capable, is at once the type and test of all great Art. What the artist is always looking for is that mode of existence in which soul and body are one and indivisible: in which the outward is expressive of the inward: in which Form reveals. Of such modes of existence there are not a few: youth and the arts preoccupied with youth may serve as a model for us at one moment: at another, we may like to think that, in its subtlety and sensitiveness of impression, its suggestion of a spirit dwelling in external things and making its raiment of earth and air, of mist and city alike, and in the morbid sympathy of its moods, and tones and colours, modern landscape art is realising for us pictorially what was realised in such plastic perfection by the Greeks. Music, in which all subject is absorbed in expression and cannot be separated from it, is a complex example, and a flower or a child a simple example of what I mean: but Sorrow is the ultimate type both in life and Art.

Behind Joy and Laughter there may be a temperament, coarse, hard and callous. But behind Sorrow there is always Sorrow. Pain, unlike Pleasure, wears no mask. Truth in Art is not any correspondence between the essential idea and the accidental existence; it is not the resemblance of shape to shadow, or of the form mirrored in the crystal to the form itself: it is no Echo coming from a hollow hill, any more than it is the well of silver water in the valley that shows the Moon to the Moon and Narcissus to Narcissus. Truth in Art is the unity of a thing with itself: the outward rendered expressive of the inward: the soul made incarnate: the body instinct with spirit. For this reason there is no truth comparable to Sorrow. There are times when Sorrow seems to me to be the only truth. Other

[1] Louisa (1776–1810), wife of King Frederick William III. She is said to have copied these lines when she and her husband were in flight after the Battle of Jena (1806). After the total defeat of Prussia in 1807 she went to Tilsit to plead unavailingly for generous terms from Napoleon, who had consistently but vainly tried to blacken her character.

things may be illusions of the eye or the appetite, made to blind the one and cloy the other, but out of Sorrow have the worlds been built, and at the birth of a child or a star there is pain.

More than this, there is about Sorrow an intense, an extraordinary reality. I have said of myself that I was one who stood in symbolic relations to the art and culture of my age. There is not a single wretched man in this wretched place along with me who does not stand in symbolic relations to the very secret of life. For the secret of life is suffering. It is what is hidden behind everything. When we begin to live, what is sweet is so sweet to us, and what is bitter so bitter, that we inevitably direct all our desires towards pleasure, and seek not merely for "a month or twain to feed on honeycomb,"[1] but for all our years to taste no other food, ignorant the while that we may be really starving the soul.

I remember talking once on this subject to one of the most beautiful personalities I have ever known:[2] a woman, whose sympathy and noble kindness to me both before and since the tragedy of my imprisonment have been beyond power and description: one who has really assisted me, though she does not know it, to bear the burden of my troubles more than anyone else in the whole world has: and all through the mere fact of her existence: through her being what she is, partly an ideal and partly an influence, a suggestion of what one might become, as well as a real help towards becoming it, a soul that renders the common air sweet, and makes what is spiritual seem as simple and natural as sunlight or the sea, one for whom Beauty and Sorrow walk hand in hand and have the same message. On the occasion of which I am thinking I recall distinctly how I said to her that there was enough suffering in one narrow London lane to show that God did not love man, and that wherever there was any sorrow, though but that of a child in some little garden weeping over a fault that it had or had not committed, the whole face of creation was completely marred. I was entirely wrong. She told me so, but I could not believe her. I was not in the sphere in which such belief was to be attained to. Now it seems to me that Love of some kind is the only possible explanation of the extraordinary amount of suffering that there is in the world. I cannot conceive any other explanation. I am convinced that there is no other, and that if the worlds have indeed, as I have said, been built out of Sorrow, it has been by the hands of Love, because in no other way could the Soul of man for whom the worlds are made reach the full stature of its perfection. Pleasure for the beautiful body, but Pain for the beautiful Soul.

When I say that I am convinced of these things I speak with too much pride. Far off, like a perfect pearl, one can see the city of God. It is so wonderful that it seems as if a child could reach it in a summer's day. And so a child could. But with me and such as I am it is different. One can realise a thing in a single moment, but one loses it in the long hours that follow with leaden feet. It is so difficult to keep "heights that the soul is competent to gain."[3] We think in Eternity, but we move slowly through

[1] Swinburne: "Before Parting" (*Poems and Ballads*, 1866): "feed" should be "live." [2] Adela Schuster.
[3] Wordsworth: *The Excursion*, iv, 139.

Time: and how slowly time goes with us who lie in prison I need not speak again, nor of the weariness and despair that creep back into one's cell, and into the cell of one's heart, with such strange insistence that one has, as it were, to garnish and sweep one's house for their coming, as for an unwelcome guest, or a bitter master, or a slave whose slave it is one's chance or choice to be. And, though at present you may find it a thing hard to believe, it is true none the less that for you, living in freedom and idleness and comfort, it is more easy to learn the lessons of Humility than it is for me, who begin the day by going down on my knees and washing the floor of my cell. For prison-life, with its endless privations and restrictions, makes one rebellious. The most terrible thing about it is not that it breaks one's heart—hearts are made to be broken—but that it turns one's heart to stone. One sometimes feels that it is only with a front of brass and a lip of scorn that one can get through the day at all. And he who is in a state of rebellion cannot receive grace, to use the phrase of which the Church is so fond—so rightly fond, I dare say—for in life, as in Art, the mood of rebellion closes up the channels of the soul, and shuts out the airs of heaven. Yet I must learn these lessons here, if I am to learn them anywhere, and must be filled with joy if my feet are on the right road, and my face set towards the "gate which is called Beautiful,"[1] though I may fall many times in the mire, and often in the mist go astray.

This new life, as through my love of Dante I like sometimes to call it, is, of course, no new life at all, but simply the continuance, by means of development, and evolution, of my former life. I remember when I was at Oxford saying to one of my friends—as we were strolling round Magdalen's narrow bird-haunted walks one morning in the June before I took my degree—that I wanted to eat of the fruit of all the trees in the garden of the world, and that I was going out into the world with that passion in my soul. And so, indeed, I went out, and so I lived. My only mistake was that I confined myself so exclusively to the trees of what seemed to me the sun-gilt side of the garden, and shunned the other side for its shadow and its gloom. Failure, disgrace, poverty, sorrow, despair, suffering, tears even, the broken words that come from the lips of pain, remorse that makes one walk in thorns, conscience that condemns, self-abasement that punishes, the misery that puts ashes on its head, the anguish that chooses sackcloth for its raiment and into its own drink puts gall—all these were things of which I was afraid. And as I had determined to know nothing of them, I was forced to taste each one of them in turn, to feed on them, to have for a season, indeed, no other food at all. I don't regret for a single moment having lived for pleasure. I did it to the full, as one should do everything that one does to the full. There was no pleasure I did not experience. I threw the pearl of my soul into a cup of wine. I went down the primrose path to the sound of flutes. I lived on honeycomb. But to have continued the same life would have been wrong because it would have been limiting. I had to pass on. The other half of the garden had its secrets for me also. Of course all this is foreshadowed and prefigured in my art. Some of it is

---

[1] *Acts*, iii, 2.

in "The Happy Prince:" some of it in "The Young King," notably in the passage where the Bishop says to the kneeling boy, "Is not He who made misery wiser than thou art?" a phrase which when I wrote it seemed to me little more than a phrase: a great deal of it is hidden away in the note of Doom that like a purple thread runs through the gold cloth of *Dorian Gray*: in "The Critic as Artist" it is set forth in many colours: in *The Soul of Man* it is written down simply and in letters too easy to read: it is one of the refrains whose recurring *motifs* make *Salome* so like a piece of music and bind it together as a ballad: in the prose-poem of the man who from the bronze of the image of the "Pleasure that liveth for a Moment" has to make the image of the "Sorrow that abideth for Ever" it is incarnate.[1] It could not have been otherwise. At every single moment of one's life one is what one is going to be no less than what one has been. Art is a symbol, because man is a symbol.

It is, if I can fully attain to it, the ultimate realisation of the artistic life. For the artistic life is simple self-development. Humility in the artist is his frank acceptance of all experiences, just as Love in the artist is simply that sense of Beauty that reveals to the world its body and its soul. In *Marius the Epicurean* Pater seeks to reconcile the artistic life with the life of religion in the deep, sweet and austere sense of the word. But Marius is little more than a spectator: an ideal spectator indeed, and one to whom it is given "to contemplate the spectacle of life with appropriate emotions," which Wordsworth defines as the poet's true aim:[2] yet a spectator merely, and perhaps a little too much occupied with the comeliness of the vessels of the Sanctuary to notice that it is the Sanctuary of Sorrow that he is gazing at.

I see a far more intimate and immediate connection between the true life of Christ and the true life of the artist, and I take a keen pleasure in the reflection that long before Sorrow had made my days her own and bound me to her wheel I had written in *The Soul of Man* that he who would lead a Christ-like life must be entirely and absolutely himself, and had taken as my types not merely the shepherd on the hillside and the prisoner in his cell but also the painter to whom the world is a pageant and the poet for whom the world is a song. I remember saying once to André Gide, as we sat together in some Paris café, that while Metaphysics had but little real interest for me, and Morality absolutely none, there was nothing that either Plato or Christ had said that could not be transferred immediately into the sphere of Art, and there find its complete fulfilment. It was a generalisation as profound as it was novel.

Nor is it merely that we can discern in Christ that close union of personality with perfection which forms the real distinction between classi-

---

[1] A slight misquotation of Wilde's prose poem "The Artist," which first appeared in the *Fortnightly Review* for July 1894.

[2] Wilde must have been thinking of Pater's essay on Wordsworth in *Appreciations* (1889). After quoting Wordsworth on "the operations of the elements and the appearances of the visible universe, on storm and sunshine, on the revolutions of the seasons, on cold and heat, on loss of friends and kindred, on injuries and resentments, on gratitude and hope, on fear and sorrow," Pater comments: "To witness this spectacle with appropriate emotions is the aim of all culture."

cal and romantic Art and makes Christ the true precursor of the romantic movement in life, but the very basis of his nature was the same as that of the nature of the artist, an intense and flamelike imagination. He realised in the entire sphere of human relations that imaginative sympathy which in the sphere of Art is the sole secret of creation. He understood the leprosy of the leper, the darkness of the blind, the fierce misery of those who live for pleasure, the strange poverty of the rich. You can see now—can you not?—that when you wrote to me in my trouble, "When you are not on your pedestal you are not interesting. The next time you are ill I will go away at once," you were as remote from the true temper of the artist as you were from what Matthew Arnold calls "the secret of Jesus."[1] Either would have taught you that whatever happens to another happens to oneself, and if you want an inscription to read at dawn and at night-time and for pleasure or for pain, write up on the wall of your house in letters for the sun to gild and the moon to silver "*Whatever happens to another happens to oneself,*" and should anyone ask you what such an inscription can possibly mean you can answer that it means "Lord Christ's heart and Shakespeare's brain."

Christ's place indeed is with the poets. His whole conception of Humanity sprang right out of the imagination and can only be realised by it. What God was to the Pantheist, man was to him. He was the first to conceive the divided races as a unity. Before his time there had been gods and men. He alone saw that on the hills of life there were but God and Man, and, feeling through the mysticism of sympathy that in himself each had been made incarnate, he calls himself the Son of the One or the son of the other, according to his mood. More than anyone else in history he wakes in us that temper of wonder to which Romance always appeals. There is still something to me almost incredible in the idea of a young Galilean peasant imagining that he could bear on his own shoulders the burden of the entire world: all that had been already done and suffered, and all that was yet to be done and suffered: the sins of Nero, of Cæsar Borgia, of Alexander VI., and of him who was Emperor of Rome and Priest of the Sun:[2] the sufferings of those whose name is Legion and whose dwelling is among the tombs,[3] oppressed nationalities, factory children, thieves, people in prison, outcasts, those who are dumb under oppression and whose silence is heard only of God: and not merely imagining this but actually achieving it, so that at the present moment all who come in contact with his personality, even though they may neither bow to his altar nor kneel before his priest, yet somehow find that the ugliness of their sins is taken away and the beauty of their sorrow revealed to them.

I have said of him that he ranks with the poets. That is true. Shelley and Sophocles are of his company. But his entire life also is the most wonderful of poems. For "pity and terror"[4] there is nothing in the entire

---

[1] "But there remains the question what righteousness really is. The method and secret and sweet reasonableness of Jesus." (*Literature and Dogma*, ch. xii.)

[2] The Emperor Heliogabalus.   [3] *Mark*, v, 5 and 9.

[4] Aristotle, *Poetics*, ch. xiii.

cycle of Greek Tragedy to touch it. The absolute purity of the protagonist raises the entire scheme to a height of romantic art from which the sufferings of "Thebes and Pelops' line"[1] are by their very horror excluded, and shows how wrong Aristotle was when he said in his treatise on the Drama that it would be impossible to bear the spectacle of one blameless in pain.[2] Nor in Æschylus or Dante, those stern masters of tenderness, in Shakespeare, the most purely human of all the great artists, in the whole of Celtic myth and legend where the loveliness of the world is shown through a mist of tears, and the life of a man is no more than the life of a flower, is there anything that for sheer simplicity of pathos wedded and made one with sublimity of tragic effect can be said to equal or approach even the last act of Christ's Passion. The little supper with his companions, one of whom had already sold him for a price: the anguish in the quiet moonlit olive-garden: the false friend coming close to him so as to betray him with a kiss: the friend who still believed in him and on whom as on a rock he had hoped to build a House of Refuge for Man denying him as the bird cried to the dawn: his own utter loneliness, his submission, his acceptance of everything: and along with it all such scenes as the high priest of Orthodoxy rending his raiment in wrath, and the Magistrate of Civil Justice calling for water in the vain hope of cleansing himself of that stain of innocent blood that makes him the scarlet figure of History: the coronation-ceremony of Sorrow, one of the most wonderful things in the whole of recorded time: the crucifixion of the Innocent One before the eyes of his mother and of the disciple whom he loved: the soldiers gambling and throwing dice for his clothes: the terrible death by which he gave the world its most eternal symbol: and his final burial in the tomb of the rich man, his body swathed in Egyptian linen with costly spices and perfumes as though he had been a King's son—when one contemplates all this from the point of view of Art alone one cannot but be grateful that the supreme office of the Church should be the playing of the tragedy without the shedding of blood, the mystical presentation by means of dialogue and costume and gesture even of the Passion of her Lord, and it is always a source of pleasure and awe to me to remember that the ultimate survival of the Greek Chorus, lost elsewhere to art, is to be found in the servitor answering the priest at Mass.

Yet the whole life of Christ—so entirely may Sorrow and Beauty be made one in their meaning and manifestation—is really an idyll, though it ends with the veil of the temple being rent, and the darkness coming over the face of the earth, and the stone rolled to the door of the sepulchre. One always thinks of him as a young bridegroom with his companions, as indeed he somewhere describes himself, or as a shepherd straying through a valley with his sheep in search of green meadow or cool stream, or as a singer trying to build out of music the walls of the city of God, or as a lover for whose love the whole world was too small. His miracles seem to

---

[1] Milton: *Il Penseroso.* "and" should be "or." [2] *Poetics,* ch. xiii.

me as exquisite as the coming of Spring, and quite as natural. I see no difficulty at all in believing that such was the charm of his personality that his mere presence could bring peace to souls in anguish, and that those who touched his garments or his hands forgot their pain: or that as he passed by on the highway of life people who had seen nothing of life's mysteries saw them clearly, and others who had been deaf to every voice but that of Pleasure heard for the first time the voice of Love and found it as "musical as is Apollo's lute:" [1] or that evil passions fled at his approach, and men whose dull unimaginative lives had been but a mode of death rose as it were from the grave when he called them: or that when he taught on the hillside the multitude forgot their hunger and thirst and the cares of this world, and that to his friends who listened to him as he sat at meat the coarse food seemed delicate, and the water had the taste of good wine, and the whole house became full of the odour and sweetness of nard.

Renan in his *Vie de Jésus*—that gracious Fifth Gospel, the Gospel according to St Thomas one might call it—says somewhere that Christ's great achievement was that he made himself as much loved after his death as he had been during his lifetime. [2] And certainly, if his place is among the poets, he is the leader of all the lovers. He saw that love was that lost secret of the world for which the wise men had been looking, and that it was only through love that one could approach either the heart of the leper or the feet of God.

And, above all, Christ is the most supreme of Individualists. Humility, like the artistic acceptance of all experiences, is merely a mode of manifestation. It is man's soul that Christ is always looking for. He calls it "God's Kingdom"—ἡ βασιλεία τοῦ θεοῦ—and finds it in everyone. He compares it to little things, to a tiny seed, to a handful of leaven, to a pearl. That is because one only realises one's soul by getting rid of all alien passions, all acquired culture, and all external possessions be they good or evil.

I bore up against everything with some stubbornness of will and much rebellion of nature till I had absolutely nothing left in the world but Cyril. I had lost my name, my position, my happiness, my freedom, my wealth. I was a prisoner and a pauper. But I had still one beautiful thing left, my own eldest son. Suddenly he was taken away from me by the law. It was a blow so appalling that I did not know what to do, so I flung myself on my knees, and bowed my head, and wept and said "The body of a child is as the body of the Lord: I am not worthy of either." That moment seemed to save me. I saw then that the only thing for me was to accept everything. Since then—curious as it will no doubt sound to you—I have been happier.

It was of course my soul in its ultimate essence that I had reached. In many ways I had been its enemy, but I found it waiting for me as a friend. When one comes in contact with the soul it makes one simple as a child, as Christ said one should be. It is tragic how few people ever "possess their

---

[1] Milton: *Comus*, 478.

[2] "*S'être fait aimer, 'à ce point qu'après sa mort on ne cessa pas de l'aimer,' voilà le chef-d'œuvre de Jésus et ce qui frappa le plus ses contemporains.*" (Ch. xxviii).

souls" before they die.[1] "Nothing is more rare in any man," says Emerson, "than an act of his own."[2] It is quite true. Most people are other people. Their thoughts are someone else's opinions, their life a mimicry, their passions a quotation. Christ was not merely the supreme Individualist, but he was the first in History. People have tried to make him out an ordinary Philanthropist, like the dreadful philanthropists of the nineteenth century, or ranked him as an Altruist with the unscientific and sentimental. But he was really neither one nor the other. Pity he has, of course, for the poor, for those who are shut up in prisons, for the lowly, for the wretched, but he has far more pity for the rich, for the hard Hedonists, for those who waste their freedom in becoming slaves to things, for those who wear soft raiment and live in Kings' houses. Riches and Pleasure seemed to him to be really greater tragedies than Poverty and Sorrow. And as for Altruism, who knew better than he that it is vocation not volition that determines us, and that one cannot gather grapes off thorns or figs from thistles?

To live for others as a definite self-conscious aim was not his creed. It was not the basis of his creed. When he says "Forgive your enemies," it is not for the sake of the enemy but for one's own sake that he says so, and because Love is more beautiful than Hate. In his entreaty to the young man whom when he looked on he loved, "Sell all that thou hast and give it to the poor," it is not of the state of the poor that he is thinking but of the soul of the young man, the lovely soul that wealth was marring. In his view of life he is one with the artist who knows that by the inevitable law of self-perfection the poet must sing, and the sculptor think in bronze, and the painter make the world a mirror for his moods, as surely and as certainly as the hawthorn must blossom in Spring, and the corn burn to gold at harvest-time, and the Moon in her ordered wanderings change from shield to sickle, and from sickle to shield.

But while Christ did not say to men, "Live for others," he pointed out that there was no difference at all between the lives of others and one's own life. By this means he gave to man an extended, a Titan personality. Since his coming the history of each separate individual is, or can be made, the history of the world. Of course Culture has intensified the personality of man. Art has made us myriad-minded. Those who have the artistic temperament go into exile with Dante and learn how salt is the bread of others and how steep their stairs:[3] they catch for a moment the serenity and calm of Goethe, and yet know but too well why Baudelaire cried to God:

[1] And see all sights from pole to pole,
   And glance, and nod, and bustle by—
   And never once possess our soul
   Before we die.
                    Matthew Arnold, "A Southern Night."
[2] In his lecture "The Preacher," published posthumously in *Lectures and Biographical Sketches* (1883).
[3] See note p. 3.

O Seigneur, donnez-moi la force et le courage
De contempler mon corps et mon cœur sans dégout.[1]

Out of Shakespeare's sonnets they draw, to their own hurt it may be, the secret of his love and make it their own: they look with new eyes on modern life because they have listened to one of Chopin's nocturnes, or handled Greek things, or read the story of the passion of some dead man for some dead woman whose hair was like threads of fine gold and whose mouth was as a pomegranate. But the sympathy of the artistic temperament is necessarily with what has found expression. In words or in colour, in music or in marble, behind the painted masks of an Æschylean play or through some Sicilian shepherd's pierced and jointed reeds the man and his message must have been revealed.

To the artist, expression is the only mode under which he can conceive life at all. To him what is dumb is dead. But to Christ it was not so. With a width and wonder of imagination, that fills one almost with awe, he took the entire world of the inarticulate, the voiceless world of pain, as his kingdom, and made of himself its eternal mouthpiece. Those of whom I have spoken, who are dumb under oppression and "whose silence is heard only of God," he chose as his brothers. He sought to become eyes to the blind, ears to the deaf, and a cry on the lips of those whose tongue had been tied. His desire was to be to the myriads who had found no utterance a very trumpet through which they might call to Heaven. And feeling, with the artistic nature of one to whom Sorrow and Suffering were modes through which he could realise his conception of the Beautiful, that an idea is of no value till it becomes incarnate and is made an image, he makes of himself the image of the Man of Sorrows, and as such has fascinated and dominated Art as no Greek god ever succeeded in doing.

For the Greek gods, in spite of the white and red of their fair fleet limbs, were not really what they appeared to be. The curved brow of Apollo was like the sun's disk crescent over a hill at dawn, and his feet were as the wings of the morning, but he himself had been cruel to Marsyas and had made Niobe childless: in the steel shields of the eyes of Pallas there had been no pity for Arachne: the pomp and peacocks of Hera were all that was really noble about her: and the Father of the Gods himself had been too fond of the daughters of men. The two deep suggestive figures of Greek mythology were, for religion, Demeter, an earth-goddess, not one of the Olympians, and, for art, Dionysus, the son of a mortal woman to whom the moment of his birth had proved the moment of her death also.

But Life itself from its lowliest and most humble sphere produced one far more marvellous than the mother of Proserpina or the son of Semele. Out of the carpenter's shop at Nazareth had come a personality infinitely greater than any made by myth or legend, and one, strangely enough, destined to reveal to the world the mystical meaning of wine and the real beauty of the lilies of the field as none, either on Cithaeron or at Enna,

---

[1] From "*Un Voyage à Cythère*" in *Les Fleurs du Mal* (1857).

had ever done it.[1]

The song of Isaiah, "*He is despised and rejected of men, a man of sorrows and acquainted with grief: and we hid as it were our faces from him,*"[2] had seemed to him to be a prefiguring of himself, and in him the prophecy was fulfilled. We must not be afraid of such a phrase. Every single work of art is the fulfilment of a prophecy. For every work of art is the conversion of an idea into an image. Every single human being should be the fulfilment of a prophecy. For every human being should be the realisation of some ideal, either in the mind of God or in the mind of man. Christ found the type, and fixed it, and the dream of a Virgilian poet, either at Jerusalem or at Babylon, became in the long progress of the centuries incarnate in him for whom the world was waiting.[3] "*His visage was marred more than any man's, and his form more than the sons of men,*"[4] are among the signs noted by Isaiah as distinguishing the new ideal, and as soon as Art understood what was meant it opened like a flower at the presence of one in whom truth in Art was set forth as it had never been before. For is not truth in Art, as I have said, "that in which the outward is expressive of the inward; in which the soul is made flesh, and the body instinct with spirit: in which Form reveals"?[5]

To me one of the things in history the most to be regretted is that the Christ's own renaissance which had produced the Cathedral of Chartres, the Arthurian cycle of legends, the life of St Francis of Assisi, the art of Giotto, and Dante's *Divine Comedy*, was not allowed to develop on its own lines but was interrupted and spoiled by the dreary classical Renaissance that gave us Petrarch, and Raphael's frescoes, and Palladian architecture, and formal French tragedy, and St Paul's Cathedral, and Pope's poetry, and everything that is made from without and by dead rules, and does not spring from within through some spirit informing it. But wherever there is a romantic movement in Art, there somehow, and under some form, is Christ, or the soul of Christ. He is in *Romeo and Juliet*, in the *Winter's Tale*, in Provençal poetry, in "The Ancient Mariner," in "La Belle Dame sans Merci," and in Chatterton's "Ballad of Charity."

We owe to him the most diverse things and people. Hugo's *Les Misérables*, Baudelaire's *Fleurs du Mal*, the note of pity in Russian novels, the stained glass and tapestries and quattrocento work of Burne-Jones and Morris, Verlaine and Verlaine's poems, belong to him no less than the Tower of Giotto, Lancelot and Guinevere, Tannhäuser, the troubled romantic marbles of Michael Angelo, pointed architecture, and the love of children and flowers—for both of whom, indeed, in classical art there was but little place, hardly enough for them to grow or play in, but who from the twelfth century down to our own day have been continually making their appearance in art, under various modes and at various times, coming fitfully and wilfully as children and flowers are apt to do, Spring always

---

[1] Mount Cithaeron was the scene of the Bacchic orgies in honour of Dionysus, son of Semele. It was from the flower-filled meadows of Enna that Proserpina was seized by Pluto and carried off to the underworld.   [2] *Isaiah*, liii, 3.

[3] Cf. Virgil's fourth Eclogue: "*Jam redit et virgo.*"

[4] *Isaiah*, lii, 14.   [5] Cf. p. 201.

seeming to one as if the flowers had been hiding, and only came out into the sun because they were afraid that grown-up people would grow tired of looking for them and give up the search, and the life of a child being no more than an April day on which there is both rain and sun for the narcissus.

And it is the imaginative quality of Christ's own nature that makes him this palpitating centre of romance. The strange figures of poetic drama and ballad are made by the imagination of others, but out of his own imagination entirely did Jesus of Nazareth create himself. The cry of Isaiah had really no more to do with his coming than the song of the nightingale has to do with the rising of the moon—no more, though perhaps no less. He was the denial as well as the affirmation of prophecy. For every expectation that he fulfilled, there was another that he destroyed. In all beauty, says Bacon, there is "some strangeness of proportion,"[1] and of those who are born of the spirit, of those, that is to say, who like himself are dynamic forces, Christ says that they are like the wind that "bloweth where it listeth and no man can tell whence it cometh or whither it goeth."[2] That is why he is so fascinating to artists. He has all the colour-elements of life: mystery, strangeness, pathos, suggestion, ecstasy, love. He appeals to the temper of wonder, and creates that mood by which alone he can be understood.

And it is to me a joy to remember that if he is "of imagination all compact,"[3] the world itself is of the same substance. I said in *Dorian Gray*[4] that the great sins of the world take place in the brain, but it is in the brain that everything takes place. We know now that we do not see with the eye or hear with the ear. They are merely channels for the transmission, adequate or inadequate, of sense-impressions. It is in the brain that the poppy is red, that the apple is odorous, that the skylark sings.

Of late I have been studying the four prose-poems about Christ with some diligence. At Christmas I managed to get hold of a Greek Testament, and every morning, after I have cleaned my cell and polished my tins, I read a little of the Gospels, a dozen verses taken by chance anywhere. It is a delightful way of opening the day. To you, in your turbulent, ill-disciplined life, it would be a capital thing if you would do the same. It would do you no end of good, and the Greek is quite simple. Endless repetition, in and out of season, has spoiled for us the *naïveté*, the freshness, the simple romantic charm of the Gospels. We hear them read far too often, and far too badly, and all repetition is anti-spiritual. When one returns to the Greek it is like going into a garden of lilies out of some narrow and dark house.

And to me the pleasure is doubled by the reflection that it is extremely probable that we have the actual terms, the *ipsissima verba*, used by Christ. It was always supposed that Christ talked in Aramaic. Even Renan thought so. But now we know that the Galilean peasants, like the Irish peasants of our own day, were bilingual, and that Greek was the ordinary language

[1] "Of Beauty."   [2] *John*, iii, 8.
[3] *A Midsummer Night's Dream*, Act V, scene i.   [4] Chapter 2.

of intercourse all over Palestine, as indeed all over the Eastern world. I never liked the idea that we only knew of Christ's own words through a translation of a translation. It is a delight to me to think that as far as his conversation was concerned, Charmides[1] might have listened to him, and Socrates reasoned with him, and Plato understood him: that he really said ἐγώ εἰμι ὁ ποιμὴν ὁ καλός:[2] that when he thought of the lilies of the field, and how they neither toil nor spin, his absolute expression was καταμάθετε τὰ κρίνα τοῦ ἀγροῦ πῶς αὐξάνει· οὐ κοπιᾷ οὐδὲ νήθει,[3] and that his last word when he cried out "My life has been completed, has reached its fulfilment, has been perfected," was exactly as St John tells us it was: τετέλεσται:[4] no more.

And while in reading the Gospels—particularly that of St John himself, or whatever early Gnostic took his name and mantle—I see this continual assertion of the imagination as the basis of all spiritual and material life, I see also that to Christ imagination was simply a form of Love, and that to him Love was Lord in the fullest meaning of the phrase. Some six weeks ago I was allowed by the Doctor to have white bread to eat instead of the coarse black or brown bread of ordinary prison fare. It is a great delicacy. To you it will sound strange that dry bread could possibly be a delicacy to anyone. I assure you that to me it is so much so that at the close of each meal I carefully eat whatever crumbs may be left on my tin plate, or have fallen on the rough towel that one uses as a cloth so as not to soil one's table: and do so not from hunger—I get now quite sufficient food—but simply in order that nothing should be wasted of what is given to me. So one should look on love.

Christ, like all fascinating personalities, had the power not merely of saying beautiful things himself, but of making other people say beautiful things to him; and I love the story St Mark tells us about the Greek woman —the γυνὴ Ἑλληνίς—who, when as a trial of her faith he said to her that he could not give her the bread of the children of Israel, answered him that the little dogs—κυνάρια, "little dogs" it should be rendered—who are under the table eat of the crumbs that the children let fall.[5] Most people live *for* love and admiration. But it is *by* love and admiration that we should live.[6] If any love is shown us we should recognise that we are quite unworthy of it. Nobody is worthy to be loved. The fact that God loves man shows that in the divine order of ideal things it is written that eternal love is to be given to what is eternally unworthy. Or if that phrase seems to you a bitter one to hear, let us say that everyone is worthy of love, except he who thinks that he is. Love is a sacrament that should be taken kneeling, and *Domine*,

---

[1] The central character of Plato's dialogue *Charmides*, where he appears as a beautiful young man typifying the central theme of σωφροσύνη or moderation. Wilde's long poem of the same name is about an imaginary character.

[2] "I am the Good Shepherd" (*John*, x, 11 and 14).

[3] "Consider the lilies of the field, how they grow; they toil not, neither do they spin" (*Matthew*, vi, 28).

[4] "It is finished" (*John*, xix, 30).   [5] *Mark*, vii, 26–30.

[6] Cf. "We live by admiration, hope and love" (Wordsworth, *The Excursion*, iv, 763).

non sum dignus should be on the lips and in the hearts of those who receive it. I wish you would sometimes think of that. You need it so much.

If I ever write again, in the sense of producing artistic work, there are just two subjects on which and through which I desire to express myself: one is "Christ, as the precursor of the Romantic movement in life:" the other is "the Artistic life considered in its relation to Conduct." The first is, of course, intensely fascinating, for I see in Christ not merely the essentials of the supreme romantic type, but all the accidents, the wilfulnesses even, of the romantic temperament also. He was the first person who ever said to people that they should live "flower-like" lives. He fixed the phrase. He took children as the type of what people should try to become. He held them up as examples to their elders, which I myself have always thought the chief use of children, if what is perfect should have a use. Dante describes the soul of man as coming from the hand of God "weeping and laughing like a little child," and Christ also saw that the soul of each one should be "*a guisa di fanciulla, che piangendo e ridendo pargoleggia.*"[1] He felt that life was changeful, fluid, active, and that to allow it to be stereotyped into any form was death. He said that people should not be too serious over material, common interests: that to be un-practical was a great thing: that one should not bother too much over affairs. "The birds didn't, why should man?" He is charming when he says, "Take no thought for the morrow. Is not the *soul* more than meat? Is not the *body* more than raiment?"[2] A Greek might have said the latter phrase. It is full of Greek feeling. But only Christ could have said both, and so summed up life perfectly for us.

His morality is all sympathy, just what morality should be. If the only thing he had ever said had been "Her sins are forgiven her because she loved much," it would have been worth while dying to have said it. His justice is all poetical justice, exactly what justice should be. The beggar goes to heaven because he had been unhappy. I can't conceive a better reason for his being sent there. The people who work for an hour in the vineyard in the cool of the evening receive just as much reward as those who had toiled there all day long in the hot sun. Why shouldn't they? Probably no one deserved anything. Or perhaps they were a different kind of people. Christ had no patience with the dull lifeless mechanical systems that treat people as if they were things, and so treat everybody alike: as if anybody, or anything for that matter, was like aught else in the world. For him there were no laws: there were exceptions merely.

That which is the very keynote of romantic art was to him the proper basis of actual life. He saw no other basis. And when they brought him one taken in the very act of sin and showed him her sentence written in the law and asked him what was to be done, he wrote with his finger on the ground as though he did not hear them, and finally, when they pressed him again and again, looked up and said "Let him of you who has never sinned be the first to throw the stone at her." It was worth while living to have said that.

[1] *Purgatorio*, xvi, 86–87.   [2] *Matthew*, vi, 34 and 25.

Like all poetical natures, he loved ignorant people. He knew that in the soul of one who is ignorant there is always room for a great idea. But he could not stand stupid people, especially those who are made stupid by education—people who are full of opinions not one of which they can understand, a peculiarly modern type, and one summed up by Christ when he describes it as the type of one who has the key of knowledge, can't use it himself, and won't allow other people to use it, though it may be made to open the gate of God's Kingdom. His chief war was against the Philistines. That is the war every child of light has to wage. Philistinism was the note of the age and community in which he lived. In their heavy inaccessibility to ideas, their dull respectability, their tedious orthodoxy, their worship of vulgar success, their entire preoccupation with the gross materialistic side of life, and their ridiculous estimate of themselves and their importance, the Jew of Jerusalem in Christ's day was the exact counterpart of the British Philistine of our own. Christ mocked at the "whited sepulchres" of respectability, and fixed that phrase for ever. He treated worldly success as a thing to be absolutely despised. He saw nothing in it at all. He looked on wealth as an encumbrance to a man. He would not hear of life being sacrificed to any system of thought or morals. He pointed out that forms and ceremonies were made for man, not man for forms and ceremonies. He took Sabbatarianism as a type of the things that should be set at nought. The cold philanthropies, the ostentatious public charities, the tedious formalisms so dear to the middle-class mind, he exposed with utter and relentless scorn. To us, what is termed Orthodoxy is merely a facile un-intelligent acquiescence, but to them, and in their hands, it was a terrible and paralysing tyranny. Christ swept it aside. He showed that the spirit alone was of value. He took a keen pleasure in pointing out to them that though they were always reading the Law and the Prophets they had not really the smallest idea of what either of them meant. In opposition to their tithing of each separate day into its fixed routine of prescribed duties, as they tithed mint and rue, he preached the enormous importance of living completely for the moment.

Those whom he saved from their sins are saved simply for beautiful moments in their lives. Mary Magdalen, when she sees Christ, breaks the rich vase of alabaster that one of her seven lovers had given her and spills the odorous spices over his tired, dusty feet, and for that one moment's sake sits for ever with Ruth and Beatrice in the tresses of the snow-white Rose of Paradise.[1] All that Christ says to us by way of a little warning is that *every* moment should be beautiful, that the soul should *always* be ready for the coming of the Bridegroom, *always* waiting for the voice of the Lover. Philistinism being simply that side of man's nature that is not illuminated by the imagination, he sees all the lovely influences of life as modes of Light: the imagination itself is the world-light, τὸ φῶς τοῦ κοσμοῦ: the world is made by it, and yet the world cannot understand it: that is because the imagination is simply a manifestation of Love, and it is love, and the capacity for it, that distinguishes one human being from another.

[1] Cf. Dante, *Paradiso*, xxx–xxxii.

But it is when he deals with the Sinner that he is most romantic, in the sense of most real. The world had always loved the Saint as being the nearest possible approach to the perfection of God. Christ, through some divine instinct in him, seems to have always loved the sinner as being the nearest possible approach to the perfection of man. His primary desire was not to reform people, any more than his primary desire was to relieve suffering. To turn an interesting thief into a tedious honest man was not his aim. He would have thought little of the Prisoners' Aid Society and other modern movements of the kind. The conversion of a Publican into a Pharisee would not have seemed to him a great achievement by any means. But in a manner not yet understood of the world he regarded sin and suffering as being in themselves beautiful, holy things, and modes of perfection. It *sounds* a very dangerous idea. It is so. All great ideas *are* dangerous. That it was Christ's creed admits of no doubt. That it is the true creed I don't doubt myself.

Of course the sinner must repent. But why? Simply because otherwise he would be unable to realise what he had done. The moment of repentance is the moment of initiation. More than that. It is the means by which one alters one's past. The Greeks thought that impossible. They often say in their gnomic aphorisms "Even the Gods cannot alter the past."[1] Christ showed that the commonest sinner could do it. That it was the one thing he could do. Christ, had he been asked, would have said—I feel quite certain about it—that the moment the prodigal son fell on his knees and wept he really made his having wasted his substance with harlots, and then kept swine and hungered for the husks they ate, beautiful and holy incidents in his life. It is difficult for most people to grasp the idea. I dare say one has to go to prison to understand it. If so, it may be worth while going to prison.

There is something so unique about Christ. Of course, just as there are false dawns before the dawn itself, and winter-days so full of sudden sunlight that they will cheat the wise crocus into squandering its gold before its time, and make some foolish bird call to its mate to build on barren boughs, so there were Christians before Christ. For that we should be grateful. The unfortunate thing is that there have been none since. I make one exception, St Francis of Assisi. But then God had given him at his birth the soul of a poet, and he himself when quite young had in mystical marriage taken Poverty as his bride; and with the soul of a poet and the body of a beggar he found the way to perfection not difficult. He understood Christ, and so he became like him. We do not require the *Liber Conformitatum*[2] to teach us that the life of St Francis was the true *Imitatio Christi*: a poem compared to which the book that bears that name is merely prose. Indeed, that is the charm about Christ, when all is said. He is just like a work of art himself. He does not really teach one anything, but by being brought into his presence one becomes something. And everybody is

[1] Cf. Aristotle, *Ethics*, vi, 2 and Pindar, *Olympia*, ii, 17.
[2] A massive compilation illustrating the similarities in the lives of Christ and St Francis, written by Fr. Bartholomaeus de Pisa in the fourteenth century and first printed in 1510.

predestined to his presence. Once at least in his life each man walks with Christ to Emmaus.

As regards the other subject, the relation of the artistic life to conduct, it will no doubt seem strange to you that I should select it. People point to Reading Gaol, and say "There is where the artistic life leads a man." Well, it might lead one to worse places. The more mechanical people, to whom life is a shrewd speculation dependent on a careful calculation of ways and means, always know where they are going, and go there. They start with the desire of being the Parish Beadle, and, in whatever sphere they are placed, they succeed in being the Parish Beadle and no more. A man whose desire is to be something separate from himself, to be a Member of Parliament, or a successful grocer, or a prominent solicitor, or a judge, or something equally tedious, invariably succeeds in being what he wants to be. That is his punishment. Those who want a mask have to wear it.

But with the dynamic forces of life, and those in whom those dynamic forces become incarnate, it is different. People whose desire is solely for self-realisation never know where they are going. They can't know. In one sense of the word it is, of course, necessary, as the Greek oracle said, to know oneself.[1] That is the first achievement of knowledge. But to recognise that the soul of a man is unknowable is the ultimate achievement of Wisdom. The final mystery is oneself. When one has weighed the sun in a balance, and measured the steps of the moon, and mapped out the seven heavens star by star, there still remains oneself. Who can calculate the orbit of his own soul? When the son of Kish went out to look for his father's asses, he did not know that a man of God was waiting for him with the very chrism of coronation, and that his own soul was already the Soul of a King.

I hope to live long enough, and to produce work of such a character, that I shall be able at the end of my days to say, "Yes: this is just where the artistic life leads a man." Two of the most perfect lives I have come across in my own experience are the lives of Verlaine and of Prince Kropotkin: both of them men who passed years in prison: the first, the one Christian poet since Dante, the other a man with the soul of that beautiful white Christ that seems coming out of Russia.[2] And for the last seven or eight months, in spite of a succession of great troubles reaching me from the outside world almost without intermission, I have been placed in direct contact with a new spirit working in this prison through men and things, that has helped me beyond any possibility of expression in words; so that while for the first year of my imprisonment I did nothing else, and can remember doing nothing else, but wring my hands in impotent despair, and say "What an ending! What an appalling ending!" now I try to say to myself, and sometimes when I am not torturing myself

---

[1] γνῶθι σεαυτόν (know thyself) was inscribed over the entrance to the temple of Apollo at Delphi.

[2] Paul Marie Verlaine (1844–96) was imprisoned for wounding Rimbaud with a revolver shot. Prince Peter Alexeievitch Kropotkin, Russian author, geographer and anarchist (1842–1921) was imprisoned for his political views and actions.

do really and sincerely say, "What a beginning! What a wonderful beginning!" It may really be so. It may become so. If it does, I shall owe much to this new personality that has altered every man's life in this place.[1]

Things in themselves are of little importance, have indeed—let us for once thank Metaphysics for something that she has taught us—no real existence. The spirit alone is of importance. Punishment may be inflicted in such a way that it will heal, not make a wound, just as alms may be given in such a manner that the bread changes to a stone in the hands of the giver. What a change there is—not in the regulations, for they are fixed by iron rule, but in the spirit that uses them as its expression—you can realise when I tell you that had I been released last May, as I tried to be, I would have left this place loathing it and every official in it with a bitterness of hatred that would have poisoned my life. I have had a year longer of imprisonment, but Humanity has been in the prison along with us all, and now when I go out I shall always remember great kindnesses that I have received here from almost everybody, and on the day of my release will give my thanks to many people and ask to be remembered by them in turn.

The prison-system is absolutely and entirely wrong. I would give anything to be able to alter it when I go out. I intend to try. But there is nothing in the world so wrong but that the spirit of Humanity, which is the spirit of Love, the spirit of the Christ who is not in Churches, may make it, if not right, at least possible to be borne without too much bitterness of heart.

I know also that much is waiting for me outside that is very delightful, from what St Francis of Assisi calls "*my brother the wind*" and "*my sister the rain*," lovely things both of them, down to the shop-windows and sunsets of great cities. If I made a list of all that still remains to me, I don't know where I should stop: for, indeed, God made the world just as much for me as for anyone else. Perhaps I may go out with something I had not got before. I need not tell you that to me Reformations in Morals are as meaningless and vulgar as Reformations in Theology. But while to propose to be a better man is a piece of unscientific cant, to have become a *deeper* man is the privilege of those who have suffered. And such I think I have become. You can judge for yourself.

If after I go out a friend of mine gave a feast, and did not invite me to it, I shouldn't mind a bit. I can be perfectly happy by myself. With freedom, books, flowers, and the moon, who could not be happy? Besides, feasts are not for me any more. I have given too many to care about them. That side of life is over for me, very fortunately I dare say. But if, after I go out, a friend of mine had a sorrow, and refused to allow me to share it, I should feel it most bitterly. If he shut the doors of the house of mourning against me I would come back again and again and beg to be admitted, so that I might share in what I was entitled to share in. If he thought me unworthy, unfit to weep with him, I should feel it as the most poignant humiliation, as the most terrible mode in which disgrace could be inflicted on me. But

[1] Major James Osmond Nelson, who had taken over the Governorship of Reading Prison in July 1896.

that could not be. I have a right to share in Sorrow, and he who can look at the loveliness of the world, and share its sorrow, and realise something of the wonder of both, is in immediate contact with divine things, and has got as near to God's secret as anyone can get.

Perhaps there may come into my art also, no less than into my life, a still deeper note, one of greater unity of passion, and directness of impulse. Not width but intensity is the true aim of modern Art. We are no longer in Art concerned with the type. It is with the exception we have to do. I cannot put my sufferings into any form they took, I need hardly say. Art only begins where Imitation ends. But something must come into my work, of fuller harmony of words perhaps, of richer cadences, of more curious colour-effects, of simpler architectural-order, of some æsthetic quality at any rate.

When Marsyas was "torn from the scabbard of his limbs"—*dalla vagina delle membre sue,*[1] to use one of Dante's most terrible, most Tacitean phrases —he had no more song, the Greeks said. Apollo had been victor. The lyre had vanquished the reed. But perhaps the Greeks were mistaken. I hear in much modern Art the cry of Marsyas.[2] It is bitter in Baudelaire, sweet and plaintive in Lamartine, mystic in Verlaine. It is in the deferred resolutions of Chopin's music. It is in the discontent that haunts the recurrent faces of Burne-Jones's women. Even Matthew Arnold, whose song of Callicles tells of "the triumph of the sweet persuasive lyre," and the "famous final victory," in such a clear note of lyrical beauty—even he, in the troubled undertone of doubt and distress that haunts his verse, has not a little of it.[3] Neither Goethe nor Wordsworth could heal him, though he followed each in turn, and when he seeks to mourn for "Thyrsis" or to sing of "the Scholar Gipsy," it is the reed that he has to take for the rendering of his strain. But whether or not the Phrygian Faun[4] was silent, I cannot be. Expression is as necessary to me as leaf and blossom are to the black branches of the trees that show themselves above the prison wall and are so restless in the wind. Between my art and the world there is now a wide gulf, but between Art and myself there is none. I hope at least that there is none.

To each of us different fates have been meted out. Freedom, pleasure, amusements, a life of ease have been your lot, and you are not worthy of it. My lot has been one of public infamy, of long imprisonment, of misery, of ruin, of disgrace, and I am not worthy of it either—not yet, at any rate. I remember I used to say that I thought I could bear a real tragedy if it came to me with purple pall and a mask of noble sorrow,[5] but that the dreadful thing about modernity was that it put Tragedy into the raiment of

[1] Dante, *Paradiso*, i, 20.   [2] Cf. note 1, p. 76.
[3] Oh, that Fate had let me see
   That triumph of the sweet persuasive lyre,
   That famous, final victory,
   When jealous Pan with Marsyas did conspire.
                              (*Empedocles on Etna.*)
[4] "Marsyas, that unhappy Faun" (*Empedocles on Etna*).
[5] "Some noble grief that we think will lend the purple dignity of tragedy to our days" ("The Critic as Artist," Part II, in *Intentions*).

Comedy, so that the great realities seemed commonplace or grotesque or lacking in style. It is quite true about modernity. It has probably always been true about actual life. It is said that all martyrdoms seemed mean to the looker-on.[1] The nineteenth century is no exception to the general rule.

Everything about my tragedy has been hideous, mean, repellent, lacking in style. Our very dress makes us grotesques. We are the zanies of sorrow. We are clowns whose hearts are broken. We are specially designed to appeal to the sense of humour. On November 13th 1895 I was brought down here from London.[2] From two o'clock till half-past two on that day I had to stand on the centre platform of Clapham Junction in convict dress and handcuffed, for the world to look at. I had been taken out of the Hospital Ward without a moment's notice being given to me. Of all possible objects I was the most grotesque. When people saw me they laughed. Each train as it came up swelled the audience. Nothing could exceed their amusement. That was of course before they knew who I was. As soon as they had been informed, they laughed still more. For half an hour I stood there in the grey November rain surrounded by a jeering mob. For a year after that was done to me I wept every day at the same hour and for the same space of time. That is not such a tragic thing as possibly it sounds to you. To those who are in prison, tears are a part of every day's experience. A day in prison on which one does not weep is a day on which one's heart is hard, not a day on which one's heart is happy.

Well, now I am really beginning to feel more regret for the people who laughed than for myself. Of course when they saw me I was not on my pedestal. I was in the pillory. But it is a very unimaginative nature that only cares for people on their pedestals. A pedestal may be a very unreal thing. A pillory is a terrific reality. They should have known also how to interpret sorrow better. I have said that behind Sorrow there is always Sorrow. It were still wiser to say that behind sorrow there is always a soul. And to mock at a soul in pain is a dreadful thing. Unbeautiful are their lives who do it. In the strangely simple economy of the world people only get what they give, and to those who have not enough imagination to penetrate the mere outward of things and feel pity, what pity can be given save that of scorn?

I have told you this account of the mode of my being conveyed here simply that you should realise how hard it has been for me to get anything out of my punishment but bitterness and despair. I have however to do it, and now and then I have moments of submission and acceptance. All the spring may be hidden in a single bud, and the low ground-nest of the lark may hold the joy that is to herald the feet of many rose-red dawns, and so perhaps whatever beauty of life still remains to me is contained in some moment of surrender, abasement and humiliation. I can, at any rate, merely proceed on the lines of my own development, and by accepting all that has happened to me make myself worthy of it.

People used to say of me that I was too individualistic. I must be far more of an individualist than I ever was. I must get far more out of myself

---

[1] Emerson: "Essay on Experience."   [2] Actually 20 November.

than I ever got, and ask far less of the world than I ever asked. Indeed my ruin came, not from too great individualism of life, but from too little. The one disgraceful, unpardonable, and to all time contemptible action of my life was my allowing myself to be forced into appealing to Society for help and protection against your father. To have made such an appeal against anyone would have been from the individualist point of view bad enough, but what excuse can there ever be put forward for having made it against one of such nature and aspect?

Of course once I had put into motion the forces of Society, Society turned on me and said, "Have you been living all this time in defiance of my laws, and do you now appeal to those laws for protection? You shall have those laws exercised to the full. You shall abide by what you have appealed to." The result is I am in gaol. And I used to feel bitterly the irony and ignominy of my position when in the course of my three trials, beginning at the Police Court, I used to see your father bustling in and out in the hopes of attracting public attention, as if anyone could fail to note or remember the stableman's gait and dress, the bowed legs, the twitching hands, the hanging lower lip, the bestial and half-witted grin. Even when he was not there, or was out of sight, I used to feel conscious of his presence, and the blank dreary walls of the great Court-room, the very air itself, seemed to me at times to be hung with multitudinous masks of that apelike face. Certainly no man ever fell so ignobly, and by such ignoble instruments, as I did. I say, in *Dorian Gray* somewhere,[1] that "a man cannot be too careful in the choice of his enemies." I little thought that it was by a pariah that I was to be made a pariah myself.

This urging me, forcing me to appeal to Society for help, is one of the things that make me despise you so much, that make me despise myself so much for having yielded to you. Your not appreciating me as an artist was quite excusable. It was temperamental. You couldn't help it. But you might have appreciated me as an Individualist. For that no culture was required. But you didn't, and so you brought the element of Philistinism into a life that had been a complete protest against it, and from some points of view a complete annihilation of it. The Philistine element in life is not the failure to understand Art. Charming people such as fishermen, shepherds, ploughboys, peasants and the like know nothing about Art, and are the very salt of the earth. He is the Philistine who upholds and aids the heavy, cumbrous, blind mechanical forces of Society, and who does not recognise the dynamic force when he meets it either in a man or a movement.

People thought it dreadful of me to have entertained at dinner the evil things of life, and to have found pleasure in their company. But they, from the point of view through which I, as an artist in life, approached them, were delightfully suggestive and stimulating. It was like feasting with panthers. The danger was half the excitement. I used to feel as the snake-charmer must feel when he lures the cobra to stir from the painted cloth or reed-basket that holds it, and makes it spread its hood at his bidding, and

---

[1] Chapter I.

sway to and fro in the air as a plant sways restfully in a stream. They were
to me the brightest of gilded snakes. Their poison was part of their perfection. I did not know that when they were to strike at me it was to be at
your piping and for your father's pay. I don't feel at all ashamed of having
known them. They were intensely interesting. What I do feel ashamed of
is the horrible Philistine atmosphere into which you brought me. My
business as an artist was with Ariel. You set me to wrestle with Caliban.
Instead of making beautiful coloured, musical things such as *Salome*,
and the *Florentine Tragedy*, and *La Sainte Courtisane*, I found myself forced
to send long lawyer's letters to your father and constrained to appeal to the
very things against which I had always protested. Clibborn and Atkins
were wonderful in their infamous war against life.[1] To entertain them was
an astounding adventure. Dumas *père*, Cellini, Goya, Edgar Allan Poe, or
Baudelaire, would have done just the same. What is loathsome to me is the
memory of interminable visits paid by me to the solicitor Humphreys in
your company, when in the ghastly glare of a bleak room you and I would
sit with serious faces telling serious lies to a bald man, till I really groaned
and yawned with *ennui*. *There* is where I found myself after two years'
friendship with you, right in the centre of Philistia, away from everything
that was beautiful, or brilliant, or wonderful, or daring. At the end I had
to come forward, on your behalf, as the champion of Respectability in
conduct, of Puritanism in life, and of Morality in Art. *Voilà où mènent les
mauvais chemins!*[2]

And the curious thing to me is that you should have tried to imitate your
father in his chief characteristics. I cannot understand why he was to you
an exemplar, where he should have been a warning, except that whenever
there is hatred between two people there is bond or brotherhood of some
kind. I suppose that, by some strange law of the antipathy of similars,
you loathed each other, not because in so many points you were so different, but because in some you were so like. In June 1893 when you left
Oxford, without a degree and with debts, petty in themselves, but considerable to a man of your father's income, your father wrote you a very
vulgar, violent and abusive letter. The letter you sent him in reply was in
every way worse, and of course far less excusable, and consequently you
were extremely proud of it. I remember quite well your saying to me with
your most conceited air that you could beat your father "at his own trade."

[1] Clibborn, referred to in the Queensberry trial as Cliburn, was a professional
blackmailer who failed to extort any money from Wilde in respect of the letter to
Lord Alfred Douglas (printed on p. 107), which had been stolen from Douglas by
an agent of the blackmailing gang. Clibborn was later sentenced to seven years'
penal servitude for blackmailing offences.

Atkins (for whom see note p. 180) is here probably a slip for Allen, a blackmailing
associate of Clibborn's.

[2] The last five words are the title of the third part of Balzac's *Splendeurs et
Misères des Courtisanes*, in which the misguided life of Lucien de Rubempré comes
to its pitiful and tragic end. O'Sullivan records Wilde's saying: "When I was a boy
my two favourite characters were Lucien de Rubempré and Julien Sorel [in
Stendhal's *Le Rouge et le Noir*]. Lucien hanged himself, Julien died on the scaffold,
and I died in prison."

Quite true. But what a trade! What a competition! You used to laugh and sneer at your father for retiring from your cousin's house where he was living in order to write filthy letters to him from a neighbouring hotel. You used to do just the same to me. You constantly lunched with me at some public restaurant, sulked or made a scene during luncheon, and then retired to White's Club and wrote me a letter of the very foulest character. The only difference between you and your father was that after you had dispatched your letter to me by special messenger, you would arrive yourself at my rooms some hours later, not to apologise, but to know if I had ordered dinner at the Savoy, and if not, why not. Sometimes you would actually arrive before the offensive letter had been read. I remember on one occasion you had asked me to invite to luncheon at the Café Royal two of your friends, one of whom I had never seen in my life. I did so, and at your special request ordered beforehand a specially luxurious luncheon to be prepared. The *chef*, I remember, was sent for, and particular instructions given about the wines. Instead of coming to luncheon you sent me at the Café an abusive letter, timed so as to reach me after we had been waiting half an hour for you. I read the first line, and saw what it was, and putting the letter in my pocket, explained to your friends that you were suddenly taken ill, and that the rest of the letter referred to your symptoms. In point of fact I did not read the letter till I was dressing for dinner at Tite Street that evening. As I was in the middle of its mire, wondering with infinite sadness how you could write letters that were really like the froth and foam on the lips of an epileptic, my servant came in to tell me that you were in the hall and were very anxious to see me for five minutes. I at once sent down and asked you to come up. You arrived, looking I admit very frightened and pale, to beg my advice and assistance, as you had been told that a man from Lumley, the solicitor, had been enquiring for you at Cadogan Place, and you were afraid that your Oxford trouble or some new danger was threatening you. I consoled you, told you, what proved to be the case, that it was merely a tradesman's bill probably, and let you stay to dinner, and pass your evening with me. You never mentioned a single word about your hideous letter, nor did I. I treated it as simply an unhappy symptom of an unhappy temperament. The subject was never alluded to. To write to me a loathsome letter at 2.30, and fly to me for help and sympathy at 7.15 the same afternoon, was a perfectly ordinary occurrence in your life. You went quite beyond your father in such habits, as you did in others. When his revolting letters to you were read in open Court he naturally felt ashamed and pretended to weep. Had your letters to him been read by his own Counsel still more horror and repugnance would have been felt by everyone. Nor was it merely in style that you "beat him at his own trade," but in mode of attack you distanced him completely. You availed yourself of the public telegram, and the open postcard. I think you might have left such modes of annoyance to people like Alfred Wood whose sole source of income it is.[1] Don't you? What was a profession to him and his class was a pleasure to you, and a very evil one.

[1] A blackmailer who gave evidence at Wilde's trials.

Nor have you given up your horrible habit of writing offensive letters, after all that has happened to me through them and for them. You still regard it as one of your accomplishments, and you exercise it on my friends, on those who have been kind to me in prison like Robert Sherard and others. That is disgraceful of you. When Robert Sherard heard from me that I did not wish you to publish any article on me in the *Mercure de France*, with or without letters, you should have been grateful to him for having ascertained my wishes on the point, and for having saved you from, without intending it, inflicting more pain on me than you had done already. You must remember that a patronising and Philistine letter about "fair play" for a "man who is down" is all right for an English newspaper. It carries on the old traditions of English journalism in regard to their attitude towards artists. But in France such a tone would have exposed me to ridicule and you to contempt. I could not have allowed any article till I had known its aim, temper, mode of approach and the like. In art good intentions are not of the smallest value. All bad art is the result of good intentions.

Nor is Robert Sherard the only one of my friends to whom you have addressed acrimonious and bitter letters because they sought that my wishes and my feelings should be consulted in matters concerning myself, the publication of articles on me, the dedication of your verses, the surrender of my letters and presents, and such like. You have annoyed or sought to annoy others also.

Does it ever occur to you what an awful position I would have been in if for the last two years, during my appalling sentence, I had been dependent on you as a friend? Do you ever think of that? Do you ever feel any gratitude to those who by kindness without stint, devotion without limit, cheerfulness and joy in giving, have lightened my black burden for me, have visited me again and again, have written to me beautiful and sympathetic letters, have managed my affairs for me, have arranged my future life for me, have stood by me in the teeth of obloquy, taunt, open sneer or insult even? I thank God every day that he gave me friends other than you. I owe everything to them. The very books in my cell are paid for by Robbie out of his pocket-money. From the same source are to come clothes for me, when I am released. I am not ashamed of taking a thing that is given by love and affection. I am proud of it. But do you ever think of what my friends such as More Adey, Robbie, Robert Sherard, Frank Harris,[1] and Arthur Clifton, have been to me in giving me comfort, help, affection, sympathy and the like? I suppose that has never dawned on you. And yet

---

[1] James Thomas (Frank) Harris (1856–1931), author, editor and adventurer. Having spent much of his youth in America he returned to England and in 1883 became editor of the *Evening News*. He edited the *Fortnightly Review* from 1886 to 1894 and became editor of the *Saturday Review* in 1894. He was in many ways a scoundrel, and his gifts as an imaginative romancer are now more apparent in his biographies and autobiography than in his fiction. Nevertheless his *Oscar Wilde, His Life and Confessions* (1916), though factually unreliable, has considerable impressionistic merit, and the nicest thing about him was his almost unfailing kindness and generosity to Wilde.

—if you had any imagination in you—you would know that there is not a single person who has been kind to me in my prison-life, down to the warder who may give me a good-morning or a good-night that is not one of his prescribed duties—down to the common policemen who in their homely rough way strove to comfort me on my journeys to and fro from the Bankruptcy Court under conditions of terrible mental distress—down to the poor thief who, recognising me as we tramped round the yard at Wandsworth, whispered to me in the hoarse prison-voice men get from long and compulsory silence: *"I am sorry for you: it is harder for the likes of you than it is for the likes of us"*—not one of them all, I say, the very mire from whose shoes you should not be proud to be allowed to kneel down and clean.

Have you imagination enough to see what a fearful tragedy it was for me to have come across your family? What a tragedy it would have been for anyone at all, who had a great position, a great name, anything of importance to lose? There is hardly one of the elders of your family—with the exception of Percy, who is really a good fellow—who did not in some way contribute to my ruin.

I have spoken of your mother to you with some bitterness, and I strongly advise you to let her see this letter, for your own sake chiefly. If it is painful to her to read such an indictment against one of her sons, let her remember that *my* mother, who intellectually ranks with Elizabeth Barrett Browning, and historically with Madame Roland,[1] died broken-hearted because the son of whose genius and art she had been so proud, and whom she had regarded always as a worthy continuer of a distinguished name, had been condemned to the treadmill for two years. You will ask me in what way your mother contributed to my destruction. I will tell you. Just as you strove to shift on to me all your immoral responsibilities, so your mother strove to shift on to me all her moral responsibilities with regard to you. Instead of speaking directly to you about your life, as a mother should, she always wrote privately to me with earnest, frightened entreaties not to let you know that she was writing to me. You see the position in which I was placed between you and your mother. It was one as false, as absurd, and as tragic as the one in which I was placed between you and your father. In August 1892, and on the 8th of November in the same year, I had two long interviews with your mother about you. On both occasions I asked her why she did not speak directly to you yourself. On both occasions she gave the same answer: *"I am afraid to: he gets so angry when he is spoken to."* The first time, I knew you so slightly that I did not understand what she meant. The second time, I knew you so well that I understood perfectly. (During the interval you had had an attack of jaundice and been ordered by the doctor to go for a week to Bournemouth, and had induced me to accompany you as you hated being alone.) But the

[1] Manon Jeanne Phlipon, bluestocking and hostess (1754–93), married (1781) Jean Marie Roland (1734–93), who later held office in the Revolutionary Government. Eventually they fell foul of Marat, Madame Roland was arrested, wrote her *Mémoires* in the Conciergerie, and was guillotined, after exclaiming "O Liberty! What crimes are committed in thy name!" Her husband killed himself two days later.

first duty of a mother is not to be afraid of speaking seriously to her son. Had your mother spoken seriously to you about the trouble she saw you were in in July 1892 and made you confide in her it would have been much better, and much happier ultimately for both of you. All the underhand and secret communications with me were wrong. What was the use of your mother sending me endless little notes, marked "Private" on the envelope, begging me not to ask you so often to dinner, and not to give you any money, each note ending with an earnest postscript *"On no account let Alfred know that I have written to you"*? What good could come of such a correspondence? Did you ever wait to be asked to dinner? Never. You took all your meals as a matter of course with me. If I remonstrated, you always had one observation: *"If I don't dine with you, where am I to dine? You don't suppose that I am going to dine at home?"* It was unanswerable. And if I absolutely refused to let you dine with me, you always threatened that you would do something foolish, and always did it. What possible result could there be from letters such as your mother used to send me, except that which did occur, a foolish and fatal shifting of the moral responsibility on to my shoulders? Of the various details in which your mother's weakness and lack of courage proved so ruinous to herself, to you, and to me, I don't want to speak any more, but surely, when she heard of your father coming down to my house to make a loathsome scene and create a public scandal, she might then have seen that a serious crisis was impending, and taken some serious steps to try and avoid it? But all she could think of doing was to send down plausible George Wyndham[1] with his pliant tongue to propose to me—what? That I should "gradually drop you"!

As if it had been possible for me to gradually drop you! I had tried to end our friendship in every possible way, going so far as actually to leave England and give a false address abroad in the hopes of breaking at one blow a bond that had become irksome, hateful, and ruinous to me. Do you think that I *could* have "gradually dropped" you? Do you think that would have satisfied your father? You know it would not. What your father wanted, indeed, was not the cessation of our friendship, but a public scandal. That is what he was striving for. His name had not been in the papers for years. He saw the opportunity of appearing before the British public in an entirely new character, that of the affectionate father. His sense of humour was roused. Had I severed my friendship with you it would have been a terrible disappointment to him, and the small notoriety of a second divorce suit, however revolting its details and origin, would have proved but little consolation to him.[2] For what he was aiming at was

---

[1] The Rt Hon. George Wyndham (1863-1913), son of the Hon. Percy Scawen Wyndham and grandson of the first Lord Leconfield. He had been M.P. for Dover since 1889, and private secretary to Mr Balfour 1887-92. He later reached the Cabinet. He wrote a number of books on literary subjects and was a kinsman of Lord Alfred Douglas.

[2] Queensberry, having been divorced by his first wife in 1887, remarried in 1893 a Miss Ethel Weeden, who obtained a decree of nullity against him on 24 October 1894.

popularity, and to pose as a champion of purity, as it is termed, is, in the present condition of the British public, the surest mode of becoming for the nonce a heroic figure. Of this public I have said in one of my plays that if it is Caliban for one half of the year, it is Tartuffe for the other,[1] and your father, in whom both characters may be said to have become incarnate, was in this way marked out as the proper representative of Puritanism in its aggressive and most characteristic form. No gradual dropping of you would have been of any avail, even had it been practicable. Don't you feel now that the only thing for your mother to have done was to have asked me to come to see her, and had you and your brother present, and said definitely that the friendship must absolutely cease? She would have found in me her warmest seconder, and with Drumlanrig and myself in the room she need not have been afraid of speaking to you. She did not do so. She was afraid of her responsibilities, and tried to shift them on to me. One letter she did certainly write to me. It was a brief one, to ask me not to send the lawyer's letter to your father warning him to desist. She was quite right. It was ridiculous my consulting lawyers and seeking their protection. But she nullified any effect her letter might have produced by her usual postscript: "*On no account let Alfred know that I have written to you.*"

You were entranced at the idea of my sending lawyers' letters to your father, as well as yourself. It was your suggestion. I could not tell you that your mother was strongly against the idea, for she had bound me with the most solemn promises never to tell you about her letters to me, and I foolishly kept my promise to her. Don't you see that it was wrong of her not to speak directly to you? That all the backstairs-interviews with me, and the area-gate correspondence were wrong? Nobody can shift their responsibilities on anyone else. They always return ultimately to the proper owner. Your one idea of life, your one philosophy, if you are to be credited with a philosophy, was that whatever you did was to be paid for by someone else: I don't mean merely in the financial sense—that was simply the practical application of your philosophy to everyday life—but in the broadest, fullest sense of transferred responsibility. You made that your creed. It was very successful as far as it went. You forced me into taking the action because you knew that your father would not attack your life or yourself in any way, and that I would defend both to the utmost, and take on my own shoulders whatever would be thrust on me. You were quite right. Your father and I, each from different motives of course, did exactly as you counted on our doing. But somehow, in spite of everything, you have not really escaped. The "infant Samuel theory," as for brevity's sake one may term it, is all very well as far as the general world goes. It may be a good deal scorned in London, and a little sneered at in Oxford, but that is merely because there are a few people who know you in each place, and because in each place you left traces of your passage. Outside of a small set in those two cities, the world looks on you as the good young

[1] This remark does not occur in any of Wilde's published plays, but was part of a long speech at the beginning of Act III of *A Woman of No Importance* which Tree persuaded Wilde to omit. See *Beerbohm Tree* by Hesketh Pearson (1956), p. 69.

man who was very nearly tempted into wrong-doing by the wicked and immoral artist, but was rescued just in time by his kind and loving father. It sounds all right. And yet, you know you have not escaped. I am not referring to a silly question asked by a silly juryman, which was of course treated with contempt by the Crown and by the Judge.[1] No one cared about that. I am referring perhaps principally to yourself. In your own eyes, and some day you will have to think of your conduct, you are not, cannot be quite satisfied at the way in which things have turned out. Secretly you must think of yourself with a good deal of shame. A brazen face is a capital thing to show the world, but now and then when you are alone, and have no audience, you have, I suppose, to take the mask off for mere breathing purposes. Else, indeed, you would be stifled.

And in the same manner your mother must at times regret that she tried to shift her grave responsibilities on someone else, who already had enough of a burden to carry. She occupied the position of both parents to you. Did she really fulfil the duties of either? If I bore with your bad temper and your rudeness and your scenes, she might have borne with them too. When last I saw my wife—fourteen months ago now—I told her that she would have to be to Cyril a father as well as a mother. I told her everything about your mother's mode of dealing with you in every detail as I have set it down in this letter, only of course far more fully. I told her the reason of the endless notes with "Private" on the envelope that used to come to Tite Street from your mother, so constantly that my wife used to laugh and say that we must be collaborating in a society novel or something of that kind. I implored her not to be to Cyril what your mother was to you. I told her that she should bring him up so that if he shed innocent blood he would come and tell her, that she might cleanse his hands for him first, and then teach him how by penance or expiation to cleanse his soul afterwards. I told her that if she was frightened of facing the responsibility of the life of another, though her own child, she should get a guardian to help her. That she has, I am glad to say, done. She has chosen Adrian Hope, a man of high birth and culture and fine character, her own cousin, whom you met once at Tite Street, and with him Cyril and Vyvyan have a good chance of a beautiful future.[2] Your mother, if

---

[1] On 25 May 1895, the sixth and last day of Wilde's final trial, during the Judge's summing-up, the following dialogue took place:

The Foreman of the Jury In view of the intimacy between Lord Alfred Douglas and Wilde, was a warrant ever issued for the apprehension of Lord Alfred Douglas?
Mr Justice Wills I should think not. We have not heard of it.
The Foreman of the Jury Was it ever contemplated?
Mr Justice Wills Not to my knowledge. A warrant would in any case not be issued without evidence of some fact, of something more than intimacy. I cannot tell, nor need we discuss that, because Lord Alfred Douglas may yet have to answer a charge. He was not called. There may be a thousand considerations of which we may know nothing that might prevent his appearance in the witness-box. I think you should deal with the matter upon the evidence before you.
[2] Adrian Charles Francis Hope (1858–1904) remained the official guardian of the children after Wilde and his wife were dead. He was a connection by marriage of

227

she was afraid of talking seriously to you, should have chosen someone amongst her own relatives to whom you might have listened. But she should not have been afraid. She should have had it out with you and faced it. At any rate, look at the result. Is she satisfied and pleased?

I know she puts the blame on me. I hear of it, not from people who know you, but from people who do not know you, and do not desire to know you. I hear of it often. She talks of the influence of an elder over a younger man, for instance. It is one of her favourite attitudes towards the question, and it is always a successful appeal to popular prejudice and ignorance. I need not ask you what influence I had over you. You know I had none. It was one of your frequent boasts that I had none, and the only one indeed that was well-founded. What was there, as a mere matter of fact, in you that I could influence? Your brain? It was undeveloped. Your imagination? It was dead. Your heart? It was not yet born. Of all the people who have ever crossed my life you were the one, and the only one, I was unable in any way to influence in any direction. When I lay ill and helpless in a fever caught from tending on you, I had not sufficient influence over you to induce you to get me even a cup of milk to drink, or to see that I had the ordinary necessaries of a sickroom, or to take the trouble to drive a couple of hundred yards to a bookseller's to get me a book at my own expense. When I was actually engaged in writing, and penning comedies that were to beat Congreve for brilliancy, and Dumas *fils* for philosophy, and I suppose everybody else for every other quality, I had not sufficient influence with you to get you to leave me undisturbed as an artist should be left. Wherever my writing room was, it was to you an ordinary lounge, a place to smoke and drink hock-and-seltzer in, and chatter about absurdities. The "influence of an elder over a younger man" is an excellent theory till it comes to my ears. Then it becomes grotesque. When it comes to your ears, I suppose you smile—to yourself. You are certainly entitled to do so. I hear also much of what she says about money. She states, and with perfect justice, that she was ceaseless in her entreaties to me not to supply you with money. I admit it. Her letters were endless, and the postscript *"Pray do not let Alfred know that I have written to you"* appears in them all. But it was no pleasure to me to have to pay every single thing for you from your morning shave to your midnight hansom. It was a horrible bore. I used to complain to you again and again about it. I used to tell you—you remember, don't you?—how I loathed your regarding me as a *"useful"* person, how no artist wishes to be so regarded or so treated; artists, like art itself, being of their very essence quite useless. You used to get very angry when I said it to you. The truth always made you angry. Truth, indeed, is a thing that is most painful to listen to and most painful to utter. But it did not make you alter your views or your mode of life. Every day I had to pay for every single thing you did all day long. Only a person of absurd good nature or of indescribable folly would have done so. I unfortunately was a complete com-

Constance Wilde, and was Secretary to the Hospital for Sick Children, Great Ormond Street, from 1888.

bination of both. When I used to suggest that your mother should supply you with the money you wanted, you always had a very pretty and graceful answer. You said that the income allowed her by your father—some £1500 a year I believe—was quite inadequate to the wants of a lady of her position, and that you could not go to her for more money than you were getting already. You were quite right about her income being one absolutely unsuitable to a lady of her position and tastes, but you should not have made that an excuse for living in luxury on me: it should on the contrary have been a suggestion to you for economy in your own life. The fact is that you were, and are I suppose still, a typical sentimentalist. For a sentimentalist is simply one who desires to have the luxury of an emotion without paying for it. To propose to spare your mother's pocket was beautiful. To do so at my expense was ugly. You think that one can have one's emotions for nothing. One cannot. Even the finest and the most self-sacrificing emotions have to be paid for. Strangely enough, that is what makes them fine. The intellectual and emotional life of ordinary people is a very contemptible affair. Just as they borrow their ideas from a sort of circulating library of thought—the *Zeitgeist* of an age that has no soul— and send them back soiled at the end of each week, so they always try to get their emotions on credit, and refuse to pay the bill when it comes in. You should pass out of that conception of life. As soon as you have to pay for an emotion you will know its quality, and be the better for such knowledge. And remember that the sentimentalist is always a cynic at heart. Indeed sentimentality is merely the bank holiday of cynicism. And delightful as cynicism is from its intellectual side, now that it has left the Tub for the Club, it never can be more than the perfect philosophy for a man who has no soul.[1] It has its social value, and to an artist all modes of expression are interesting, but in itself it is a poor affair, for to the true cynic nothing is ever revealed.

I think that if you look back now to your attitude towards your mother's income, and your attitude towards my income, you will not feel proud of yourself, and perhaps you may some day, if you don't show your mother this letter, explain to her that your living on me was a matter in which my wishes were not consulted for a moment. It was simply a peculiar, and to me personally most distressing, form that your devotion to me took. To make yourself dependent on me for the smallest as well as the largest sums lent you in your own eyes all the charm of childhood, and in the insisting on my paying for every one of your pleasures you thought that you had found the secret of eternal youth. I confess that it pains me when I hear of your mother's remarks about me, and I am sure that on reflection you will agree with me that if she has no word of regret or sorrow for the ruin your race has brought on mine it would be better if she remained silent. Of course there is no reason she should see any portion of this letter that refers to any mental development I have been going through, or to any point of departure I hope to attain to. It would not be interesting to her.

---

[1] Diogenes, the Cynic philosopher (419–324 B.C.), lived in a tub.

But the parts concerned purely with your life I should show her if I were you.

If I were you, in fact, I would not care about being loved on false pretences. There is no reason why a man should show his life to the world. The world does not understand things. But with people whose affection one desires to have it is different. A great friend of mine—a friend of ten years' standing[1]—came to see me some time ago and told me that he did not believe a single word of what was said against me, and wished me to know that he considered me quite innocent, and the victim of a hideous plot concocted by your father. I burst into tears at what he said, and told him that while there was much amongst your father's definite charges that was quite untrue and transferred to me by revolting malice, still that my life had been full of perverse pleasures and strange passions, and that unless he accepted that fact as a fact about me and realised it to the full, I could not possibly be friends with him any more, or ever be in his company. It was a terrible shock to him, but we are friends, and I have not got his friendship on false pretences. I have said to you that to speak the truth is a painful thing. To be forced to tell lies is much worse.

I remember as I was sitting in the dock on the occasion of my last trial listening to Lockwood's[2] appalling denunciation of me—like a thing out of Tacitus, like a passage in Dante, like one of Savonarola's indictments of the Popes at Rome—and being sickened with horror at what I heard. Suddenly it occurred to me, *"How splendid it would be, if I was saying all this about myself!"* I saw then at once that what is said of a man is nothing. The point is, who says it. A man's very highest moment is, I have no doubt at all, when he kneels in the dust, and beats his breast, and tells all the sins of his life. So with you. You would be much happier if you let your mother know a little at any rate of your life from yourself. I told her a good deal about it in December 1893, but of course I was forced into reticences and generalities. It did not seem to give her any more courage in her relations with you. On the contrary. She avoided looking at the truth more persistently than ever. If you told her yourself it would be different. My words may perhaps be often too bitter to you. But the facts you cannot deny. Things were as I have said they were, and if you have read this letter as carefully as you should have done you have met yourself face to face.

I have now written, and at great length, to you in order that you should realise what you were to me before my imprisonment, during those three years' fatal friendship: what you have been to me during my imprisonment, already within two moons of its completion almost: and what I hope to be to myself and to others when my imprisonment is over. I cannot reconstruct my letter, or rewrite it. You must take it as it stands, blotted in many places with tears, in some with the signs of passion or pain, and make

---

[1] Frank Harris, according to himself, but more likely Sherard, who records a similar confession.

[2] The Solicitor-General, Sir Frank Lockwood (1847–97), who led for the prosecution in Wilde's second trial.

it out as best you can, blots, corrections and all. As for the corrections and *errata*, I have made them in order that my words should be an absolute expression of my thoughts, and err neither through surplusage nor through being inadequate. Language requires to be tuned, like a violin: and just as too many or too few vibrations in the voice of the singer or the trembling of the string will make the note false, so too much or too little in words will spoil the message. As it stands, at any rate, my letter has its definite meaning behind every phrase. There is in it nothing of rhetoric. Wherever there is erasion or substitution, however slight, however elaborate, it is because I am seeking to render my real impression, to find for my mood its exact equivalent. Whatever is first in feeling comes always last in form.

I will admit that it is a severe letter. I have not spared you. Indeed you may say that, after admitting that to weigh you against the smallest of my sorrows, the meanest of my losses, would be really unfair to you, I have actually done so, and made scruple by scruple the most careful assay of your nature. That is true. But you must remember that you put yourself into the scales.

You must remember that, if when matched with one mere moment of my imprisonment the balance in which you lie kicks the beam, Vanity made you choose the balance, and Vanity made you cling to it. *There* was the one great psychological error of our friendship, its entire want of proportion. You forced your way into a life too large for you, one whose orbit transcended your power of vision no less than your power of cyclic motion, one whose thoughts, passions and actions were of intense import, of wide interest, and fraught, too heavily indeed, with wonderful or awful consequence. Your little life of little whims and moods was admirable in its own little sphere. It was admirable at Oxford, where the worst that could happen to you was a reprimand from the Dean or a lecture from the President, and where the highest excitement was Magdalen becoming head of the river, and the lighting of a bonfire in the quad as a celebration of the august event. It should have continued in its own sphere after you left Oxford. In yourself, you were all right. You were a very complete specimen of a very modern type. It was simply in reference to me that you were wrong. Your reckless extravagance was not a crime. Youth is always extravagant. It was your forcing me to pay for your extravagances that was disgraceful. Your desire to have a friend with whom you could pass your time from morning to night was charming. It was almost idyllic. But the friend you fastened on should not have been a man of letters, an artist, one to whom your continual presence was as utterly destructive of all beautiful work as it was actually paralysing to the creative faculty. There was no harm in your seriously considering that the most perfect way of passing an evening was to have a champagne dinner at the Savoy, a box at a Music-Hall to follow, and a champagne supper at Willis's as a *bonne-bouche* for the end. Heaps of delightful young men in London are of the same opinion. It is not even an eccentricity. It is the qualification for becoming a member of White's. But you had no right to require of me that I should become the purveyor of such pleasures for you. It showed your lack of any real appreciation of my genius. Your quarrel with your father, again, whatever one may think about its character, should obviously have remained a question entirely between the two of you. It should have been carried on in a backyard. Such quarrels, I believe, usually are. Your mistake was in insisting on its being played as a tragi-comedy on a high stage in History, with the whole world as the audience, and myself as the prize for the victor in the contemptible contest. The fact that your father loathed you, and that you loathed your father, was not a matter of any interest to the English public. Such feelings are very common in English domestic life, and should be confined to the place they characterise: the home. Away from the home-circle they are quite out of place. To translate them is an offence. Family-life is not to be treated as a red flag to be flaunted in the streets, or a horn to be blown hoarsely on the housetops. You took Domesticity out of its proper sphere, just as you took yourself out of your proper sphere.

And those who quit their proper sphere change their surroundings merely, not their natures. They do not acquire the thoughts or passions appropriate to the sphere they enter. It is not in their power to do so. Emotional forces, as I say somewhere in *Intentions*, are as limited in extent and duration as the forces of physical energy.[1] The little cup that is made to hold so much can hold so much and no more, though all the purple vats of Burgundy be filled with wine to the brim, and the treaders stand knee-deep in the gathered grapes of the stony vineyards of Spain. There is no error more common than that of thinking that those who are the causes or occasions of great tragedies share in the feelings suitable to the tragic mood: no error more fatal than expecting it of them. The martyr in his "shirt of flame"[2] may be looking on the face of God, but to him who is piling the faggots or loosening the logs for the blast the whole scene is no more than the slaying of an ox is to the butcher, or the felling of a tree to the charcoal-burner in the forest, or the fall of a flower to one who is mowing down the grass with a scythe. Great passions are for the great of soul, and great events can be seen only by those who are on a level with them.

I know of nothing in all Drama more incomparable from the point of view of Art, or more suggestive in its subtlety of observation, than Shakespeare's drawing of Rosencrantz and Guildenstern. They are Hamlet's college friends. They have been his companions. They bring with them memories of pleasant days together. At the moment when they come across him in the play he is staggering under the weight of a burden intolerable to one of his temperament. The dead have come armed out of the grave to impose on him a mission at once too great and too mean for him. He is a dreamer, and he is called upon to act. He has the nature of the poet and he is asked to grapple with the common complexities of cause and effect, with life in its practical realisation, of which he knows nothing, not with life in its ideal essence, of which he knows much. He has no

---

[1] "The Critic as Artist," Part II.
[2] "Like a pale martyr in his shirt of fire" (Alexander Smith: *A Life-Drama*, scene ii).

conception of what to do, and his folly is to feign folly. Brutus used madness as a cloak to conceal the sword of his purpose, the dagger of his will,[1] but to Hamlet madness is a mere mask for the hiding of weakness. In the making of mows and jests he sees a chance of delay. He keeps playing with action, as an artist plays with a theory. He makes himself the spy of his proper actions, and listening to his own words knows them to be but "words, words, words." Instead of trying to be the hero of his own history, he seeks to be the spectator of his own tragedy. He disbelieves in everything, including himself, and yet his doubt helps him not, as it comes not from scepticism but from a divided will.

Of all this, Guildenstern and Rosencrantz realise nothing. They bow and smirk and smile, and what the one says the other echoes with sicklier iteration. When at last, by means of the play within the play and the puppets in their dalliance, Hamlet "catches the conscience" of the King, and drives the wretched man in terror from his throne, Guildenstern and Rosencrantz see no more in his conduct than a rather painful breach of court-etiquette. That is as far as they can attain to in "the contemplation of the spectacle of life with appropriate emotions."[2] They are close to his very secret and know nothing of it. Nor would there be any use in telling them. They are the little cups that can hold so much and no more. Towards the close it is suggested that, caught in a cunning springe set for another, they have met, or may meet with a violent and sudden death. But a tragic ending of this kind, though touched by Hamlet's humour with something of the surprise and justice of comedy, is really not for such as they. They never die. Horatio who, in order to "report Hamlet and his cause aright to the unsatisfied,"

> Absents him from felicity a while
> And in this harsh world draws his breath in pain,

dies, though not before an audience, and leaves no brother. But Guildenstern and Rosencrantz are as immortal as Angelo and Tartuffe, and should rank with them. They are what modern life has contributed to the antique ideal of friendship. He who writes a new *De Amicitia* must find a niche for them and praise them in Tusculan prose. They are types fixed for all time. To censure them would show a lack of appreciation. They are merely out of their sphere: that is all. In sublimity of soul there is no contagion. High thoughts and high emotions are by their very existence isolated. What Ophelia herself could not understand was not to be realised by "Guildenstern and gentle Rosencrantz," by "Rosencrantz and gentle Guildenstern." Of course I do not propose to compare you. There is a wide difference between you. What with them was chance, with you was choice. Deliberately and by me uninvited you thrust yourself into my sphere, usurped there a place for which you had neither right nor qualifications, and having by curious persistence, and by the rendering of your very

---

[1] Not the Brutus of Shakespeare's *Julius Caesar*, but Junius Brutus who expelled Tarquin, the last King of Rome.
[2] See note p. 204.

presence a part of each separate day, succeeded in absorbing my entire life, could do no better with that life than break it in pieces. Strange as it may sound to you, it was but natural that you should do so. If one gives to a child a toy too wonderful for its little mind, or too beautiful for its but half-awakened eyes, it breaks the toy, if it is wilful; if it is listless it lets it fall and goes its way to its own companions. So it was with you. Having got hold of my life, you did not know what to do with it. You couldn't have known. It was too wonderful a thing to be in your grasp. You should have let it slip from your hands and gone back to your own companions at their play. But unfortunately you were wilful, and so you broke it. That, when everything is said, is perhaps the ultimate secret of all that has happened. For secrets are always smaller than their manifestations. By the displacement of an atom a world may be shaken. And that I may not spare myself any more than you I will add this: that dangerous to me as my meeting with you was, it was rendered fatal to me by the particular moment in which we met. For you were at that time of life when all that one does is no more than the sowing of the seed, and I was at that time of life when all that one does is no less than the reaping of the harvest.

There are some few things more about which I must write to you. The first is about my Bankruptcy. I heard some days ago, with great disappointment I admit, that it is too late now for your family to pay your father off, that it would be illegal, and that I must remain in my present painful position for some considerable time to come. It is bitter to me because I am assured on legal authority that I cannot even publish a book without the permission of the Receiver to whom all the accounts must be submitted. I cannot enter into a contract with the manager of a theatre, or produce a play without the receipts passing to your father and my few other creditors. I think that even you will admit now that the scheme of "scoring off" your father by allowing him to make me a bankrupt has not really been the brilliant all-round success you imagined it was going to turn out. It has not been so to me at any rate, and my feelings of pain and humiliation at my pauperism should have been consulted rather than your own sense of humour, however caustic or unexpected. In point of actual fact, in permitting my Bankruptcy, as in urging me on to the original trial, you really were playing right into your father's hands, and doing just what he wanted. Alone, and unassisted, he would from the very outset have been powerless. In you—though you did not mean to hold such a horrible office —he has always found his chief ally.

I am told by More Adey in his letter that last summer you really did express on more than one occasion your desire to repay me "a little of what I spent" on you. As I said to him in my answer, unfortunately I spent on you my art, my life, my name, my place in history, and if your family had all the marvellous things in the world at their command, or what the world holds as marvellous, genius, beauty, wealth, high position and the like, and laid them all at my feet, it would not repay me for one tithe of the smallest things that have been taken from me, or one tear of the least tears that I have shed. However, of course everything one does has to be paid for. Even to the Bankrupt it is so. You seem to be under the impression that Bankruptcy is a convenient means by which a man can avoid paying his debts, a "score off his creditors" in fact. It is quite the other way. It is the method by which a man's creditors "score off" him, if we are to continue your favourite phrase, and by which the Law by the confiscation of all his property forces him to pay every one of his debts, and if he fails to do so leaves him as penniless as the commonest mendicant who stands in an archway, or creeps down a road, holding out his hand for the alms for which, in England at any rate, he is afraid to ask. The Law has taken from me not merely all that I have, my books, furniture, pictures, my copyright in my published works, my copyright in my plays, everything in fact from *The Happy Prince* and *Lady Windermere's Fan* down to the stair-carpets and door-scraper of my house, but also all that I am ever going to have. My interest in my marriage-settlement, for instance, was sold. Fortunately I was able to buy it in through my friends. Otherwise, in case my wife died, my two children during my lifetime would be as penniless as myself. My interest in our Irish estate, entailed on me by my own father, will I suppose have to go next. I feel very bitterly about its being sold, but I must submit.

Your father's seven hundred pence—or pounds is it?—stand in the way, and must be refunded. Even when I am stripped of all I have, and am ever to have, and am granted a discharge as a hopeless Insolvent, I have still got to pay my debts. The Savoy dinners—the clear turtle-soup, the luscious ortolans wrapped in their crinkled Sicilian vine-leaves, the heavy amber-coloured, indeed almost amber-scented champagne—Dagonet 1880, I think, was your favourite wine?—all have still to be paid for. The suppers at Willis's, the special *cuvée* of Perrier-Jouet reserved always for us, the wonderful *pâtés* procured directly from Strasburg, the marvellous *fine champagne* served always at the bottom of great bell-shaped glasses that its bouquet might be the better savoured by the true epicures of what was really exquisite in life—these cannot be left unpaid, as bad debts of a dishonest *client*. Even the dainty sleeve-links—four heart-shaped moon-stones of silver mist, girdled by alternate ruby and diamond for their setting—that I designed, and had made at Henry Lewis's as a special little present to you, to celebrate the success of my second comedy—these even—though I believe you sold them for a song a few months afterwards —have to be paid for. I cannot leave the jeweller out of pocket for the presents I gave you, no matter what you did with them. So, even if I get my discharge, you see I have still my debts to pay.

And what is true of a bankrupt is true of everyone else in life. For every single thing that is done someone has to pay. Even you yourself—with all your desire for absolute freedom from all duties, your insistence on having everything supplied to you by others, your attempts to reject any claim on your affection, or regard, or gratitude—even you will have some day to reflect seriously on what you have done, and try, however unavailingly, to make some attempt at atonement. The fact that you will not be able really to do so will be part of your punishment. You can't wash your hands of all responsibility, and propose with a shrug or a smile to pass on to a new friend and a freshly spread feast. You can't treat all that you have brought upon me as a sentimental reminiscence to be served up occasionally with the cigarettes and *liqueurs*, a picturesque background to a modern life of pleasure like an old tapestry hung in a common inn. It may for the moment have the charm of a new sauce or a fresh vintage, but the scraps of a banquet grow stale, and the dregs of a bottle are bitter. Either today, or tomorrow, or some day you have got to realise it. Otherwise you may die without having done so, and then what a mean, starved, unimaginative life you would have had. In my letter to More I have suggested one point of view from which you had better approach the subject as soon as possible. He will tell you what it is. To understand it you will have to cultivate your imagination. Remember that imagination is the quality that enables one to see things and people in their real as in their ideal relations. If you cannot realise it by yourself, talk to others on the subject. I have had to look at my past face to face. Look at your past face to face. Sit down quietly and consider it. The supreme vice is shallowness. Whatever is realised is right. Talk to your brother about it. Indeed the proper person to talk to *is* Percy. Let him read this letter, and know all the circumstances of our friendship. When things are clearly put before him, no judgment is better. Had we told him the truth, what a lot would have been saved to me of suffering and disgrace! You remember I proposed to do so, the night you arrived in London from Algiers. You absolutely refused. So when he came in after dinner we had to play the comedy of your father being an insane man subject to absurd and unaccountable delusions. It was a capital comedy while it lasted, none the less so because Percy took it all quite seriously. Unfortunately it ended in a very revolting manner. The subject on which I write now is one of its results, and if it be a trouble to you, pray do not forget that it is the deepest of my humiliations, and one I must go through. I have no option. You have none either.

The second thing about which I have to speak to you is with regard to the conditions, circumstances, and place of our meeting when my term of imprisonment is over. From extracts from your letter to Robbie written in the early summer of last year I understand that you have sealed up in two packages my letters and my presents to you—such at least as remain of either—and are anxious to hand them personally to me. It is, of course, necessary that they should be given up. You did not understand why I wrote beautiful letters to you, any more than you understood why I gave you beautiful presents. You failed to see that the former were not meant to be published, any more than the latter were meant to be pawned. Besides, they belong to a side of life that is long over, to a friendship that somehow you were unable to appreciate at its proper value. You must look back with wonder now to the days when you had my entire life in your hands. I too look back to them with wonder, and with other, with far different, emotions.

I am to be released, if all goes well with me, towards the end of May, and hope to go at once to some little seaside village abroad with Robbie and More Adey. The sea, as Euripides says in one of his plays about Iphigenia, washes away the stains and wounds of the world. Θάλασσα κλύζει πάντα τ᾽ανθρώπων κακά.[1]

I hope to be at least a month with my friends, and to gain, in their healthful and affectionate company, peace, and balance, and a less troubled heart, and a sweeter mood. I have a strange longing for the great simple primeval things, such as the Sea, to me no less of a mother than the Earth. It seems to me that we all look at Nature too much, and live with her too little. I discern great sanity in the Greek attitude. They never chattered about sunsets, or discussed whether the shadows on the grass were really mauve or not. But they saw that the sea was for the swimmer, and the sand for the feet of the runner. They loved the trees for the shadow that they cast, and the forest for its silence at noon. The vineyard-dresser wreathed his hair with ivy that he might keep off the rays of the sun as he stooped over the young shoots, and for the artist and the athlete, the two types that Greece gave us, they plaited into garlands the leaves of the bitter laurel and of the wild parsley which else had been of no service to man.

We call ourselves a utilitarian age, and we do not know the uses of any single thing. We have forgotten that Water can cleanse, and Fire purify, and that the Earth is mother to us all. As a consequence our Art is of the Moon and plays with shadows, while Greek art is of the Sun and deals directly with things. I feel sure that in elemental forces there is purification, and I want to go back to them and live in their presence. Of course, to one so modern as I am, *enfant de mon siècle*, merely to look at the world will be always lovely. I tremble with pleasure when I think that on the very day of my leaving prison both the laburnum and the lilac will be blooming in the gardens, and that I shall see the wind stir into restless beauty the swaying gold of the one, and make the other toss the pale purple of its plumes so that all the air shall be Arabia for me. Linnæus fell on his knees and wept for joy when he saw for the first time the long heath of some English upland made yellow with the tawny aromatic blossoms of the common furze, and I know that for me, to whom flowers are part of desire, there are tears waiting in the petals of some rose. It has always been so with me from my boyhood. There is not a single colour hidden away in the chalice of a flower, or the curve of a shell, to which, by some subtle sympathy with the very soul of things, my nature does not answer. Like Gautier I have always been one of those *pour qui le monde visible existe*.[2]

Still, I am conscious now that behind all this Beauty, satisfying though it be, there is some Spirit hidden of which the painted forms and shapes are but modes of manifestation, and it is with this Spirit that I desire to become in harmony. I have grown tired of the articulate utterances of men and things. The Mystical in Art, the Mystical in Life, the Mystical in

[1] *Iphigenia in Tauris*, 1193.
[2] "*Critiques et louanges me louent et m'abiment sans comprendre un mot de ce que je suis. Toute ma valeur, ils n'ont jamais parlé de cela, c'est que je suis un homme pour qui le monde visible existe*" (Gautier, as reported in the Goncourt Journal for 1 May 1857.) Wilde used the phrase in Chapter ix of *Dorian Gray*, describing Dorian.

Nature—this is what I am looking for, and in the great symphonies of Music, in the initiation of Sorrow, in the depths of the Sea I may find it. It is absolutely necessary for me to find it somewhere.

All trials are trials for one's life, just as all sentences are sentences of death, and three times have I been tried. The first time I left the box to be arrested, the second time to be led back to the House of Detention, the third time to pass into a prison for two years. Society, as we have constituted it, will have no place for me, has none to offer; but Nature, whose sweet rains fall on unjust and just alike, will have clefts in the rocks where I may hide, and secret valleys in whose silence I may weep undisturbed. She will hang the night with stars so that I may walk abroad in the darkness without stumbling, and send the wind over my footprints so that none may track me to my hurt: she will cleanse me in great waters, and with bitter herbs make me whole.

At the end of a month, when the June roses are in all their wanton opulence, I will, if I feel able, arrange through Robbie to meet you in some quiet foreign town like Bruges, whose grey houses and green canals and cool still ways had a charm for me, years ago. For the moment you will have to change your name. The little title of which you were so vain—and indeed it made your name sound like the name of a flower—you will have to surrender, if you wish to see *me*; just as *my* name, once so musical in the mouth of Fame, will have to be abandoned by me, in turn. How narrow, and mean, and inadequate to its burdens is this century of ours! It can give to Success its palace of porphyry, but for Sorrow and Shame it does not keep even a wattled house in which they may dwell: all it can do for *me* is to bid me alter my name into some other name, where even mediaevalism would have given me the cowl of the monk or the face-cloth of the leper behind which I might be at peace.

I hope that our meeting will be what a meeting between you and me should be, after everything that has occurred. In old days there was always a wide chasm between us, the chasm of achieved Art and acquired culture: there is a still wider chasm between us now, the chasm of Sorrow: but to Humility there is nothing that is impossible, and to Love all things are easy.

As regards your letter to me in answer to this, it may be as long or as short as you choose. Address the envelope to "The Governor, H.M. Prison, Reading." Inside, in another, and an open envelope, place your own letter to me: if your paper is very thin do not write on both sides, as it makes it hard for others to read. I have written to you with perfect freedom. You can write to me with the same. What I must know from you is why you have never made any attempt to write to me, since the August of the year before last, more especially after, in the May of last year, eleven months ago now, you knew, and admitted to others that you knew, how you had made me suffer, and how I realised it. I waited month after month to hear from you. Even if I had not been waiting but had shut the doors against you, you should have remembered that no one can possibly shut the doors against Love for ever. The unjust judge in the Gospels rises up at length to give a just decision because Justice comes knocking daily at his door; and at night-time the friend, in whose heart there is no real friendship, yields at length to his friend "because of his importunity."[1] There is no prison in any world into which Love cannot force an entrance. If you did not understand that, you did not understand anything about Love at all. Then, let me know all about your article on me for the *Mercure de France*. I know something of it. You had better quote from it. It is set up in type. Also, let me know the exact terms of your Dedication of your poems. If it is in prose, quote the prose; if in verse, quote the verse. I have no doubt that there will be beauty in it. Write to me with full frankness about yourself: about your life: your friends: your occupations: your books. Tell me about your volume and its reception. Whatever you have to say for yourself, say it without fear. Don't write what you don't mean: that is all. If anything in your letter is false or counterfeit I shall detect it by the ring at once. It is not for nothing, or to no purpose, that in my lifelong cult of literature I have made myself

> Miser of sound and syllable, no less
> Than Midas of his coinage.[2]

Remember also that I have yet to know you. Perhaps we have yet to know each other.

For yourself, I have but this last thing to say. Do not be afraid of the past. If people tell you that it is irrevocable, do not believe them. The past, the present and the future are but one moment in the sight of God, in whose sight we should try to live. Time and space, succession and extension, are merely accidental conditions of Thought. The Imagination can transcend them, and move in a free sphere of ideal existences. Things, also, are in their essence what we choose to make them. A thing *is*, according to the mode in which one looks at it. "Where others," says Blake, "see but the Dawn coming over the hill, I see the sons of God shouting for joy."[3] What seemed to the world and to myself my future I lost irretrievably when I let myself be taunted into taking the action against your father: had, I dare say, lost it really long before that. What lies before me is my past. I have got to make myself look on that with different eyes, to make the world look on it with different eyes, to make God look on it with different eyes. This I cannot do by ignoring it, or slighting it, or praising it, or denying it. It is only to be done by fully accepting it as an inevitable part of the evolution of my life and character: by bowing my head to everything that I have suffered. How far I am away from the true temper of soul, this letter in its changing, uncertain moods, its scorn and bitterness, its aspirations and its failure to realise those aspirations, shows you quite clearly. But do not forget in what a terrible school I am sitting at my task. And incomplete, imperfect, as I am, yet from me you may have

---

[1] *Luke*, xi, 5–8.   [2] Keats: "Sonnet on the Sonnet."
[3] "What," it will be Questioned, "When the Sun rises, do you not see a round disk of fire somewhat like a Guinea?" O no, no, I see an Innumerable company of the Heavenly host crying, "Holy, Holy, Holy is the Lord God Almighty" ("A Vision of the Last Judgment"). See also *Job*, xxxviii, 7.

still much to gain. You came to me to learn the Pleasure of Life and the Pleasure of Art. Perhaps I am chosen to teach you something much more wonderful, the meaning of Sorrow, and its beauty. Your affectionate friend   OSCAR WILDE

To Robert Ross

1 April 1897   *H.M. Prison, Reading*

My dear Robbie, I send you, in a roll separate from this, my letter to Alfred Douglas, which I hope will arrive safe.[1] As soon as you, and of course More Adey whom I always include with you, have read it, I want you to have it carefully copied for me. There are many reasons why I wish this to be done. One will suffice. I want you to be my literary executor in case of my death, and to have complete control over my plays, books and papers. As soon as I find I have a legal right to make a will I will do so. My wife does not understand my art, nor could be expected to have any interest in it, and Cyril is only a child. So I turn naturally to you, as indeed I do for everything, and would like you to have all my works. The deficit that their sale will produce may be lodged to the credit of Cyril and Vyvyan.

Well, if you are my literary executor, you must be in possession of the only document that really gives any explanation of my extraordinary behaviour with regard to Queensberry and Alfred Douglas. When you have read the letter you will see the psychological explanation of a course of conduct that from the outside seems a combination of absolute idiocy with vulgar bravado. Some day the truth will have to be known: not necessarily in my lifetime or in Douglas's: but I am not prepared to sit in the grotesque pillory they put me into, for all time: for the simple reason that I inherited from my father and my mother a name of high distinction in literature and art, and I cannot, for eternity, allow that name to be the shield and catspaw of the Queensberrys. I don't defend my conduct. I explain it.

Also there are in the letter certain passages which deal with my mental development in prison, and the inevitable evolution of character and intellectual attitude towards life that has taken place: and I want you, and others who still stand by me and have affection for me, to know exactly in what mood and manner I hope to face the world. Of course from one point of view I know that on the day of my release I shall be merely passing from one prison into another, and there are times when the whole world

[1] On 2 April the Governor wrote to the Prison Commission to ask whether the preceding letter, "written during the last three or four months," might be sent out. On 6 April the Commission wrote to say this was impossible, but the letter could be kept and handed to the prisoner on his release. This was done on 18 May and Wilde handed it to Ross at Dieppe when he landed there on 20 May.

seems to me no larger than my cell, and as full of terror for me. Still I believe that at the beginning God made a world for each separate man, and in that world which is within us one should seek to live. At any rate, you will read those parts of my letter with less pain than the others. Of course I need not remind *you* how fluid a thing thought is with me—with us all— and of what an evanescent substance are our emotions made. Still, I do see a sort of possible goal towards which, through art, I may progress. It is not unlikely that you may help me.

As regards the mode of copying: of course it is too long for any amanuensis to attempt: and your own handwriting, dear Robbie, in your last letter seems specially designed to remind me that the task is not to be yours. I may wrong you, and hope I do, but it really looks as if you were engaged in writing a three-volume novel on the dangerous prevalence of communistic opinions among the rich, or some dreadful subject of vital interest, or in some other way wasting a youth that I cannot help saying has always been, and will always remain, quite full of promise. I think that the only thing to do is to be thoroughly modern, and to have it type-written. Of course the manuscript should not pass out of your control, but could you not get Mrs Marshall to send down one of her type-writing girls—women are the most reliable, as they have no memory for the important—to Hornton Street or Phillimore Gardens to do it under your supervision?[1] I assure you that the type-writing machine, when played with expression, is not more annoying than the piano when played by a sister or near relation. Indeed many, among those most devoted to domesticity, prefer it.

I wish the copy to be done not on tissue paper but on good paper such as is used for plays, and a wide rubricated margin should be left for corrections. The copy done and verified from the manuscript, the original should be despatched to A.D. by More, and another copy done by the typewriter so that *you* should have a copy as well as myself.[2] Also I would wish two typewritten copies to be made from the fourth page of sheet 9 to the last page of sheet 14: from "and the end of it ... I must forgive you" down to "Between art and myself there is none" (I quote from memory). Also on page 3 of sheet 18 from "I am to be released if all goes well" to "bitter herbs ... whole" on page 4.[3] These welded together with anything else you may extract that is good and nice in intention, such as first page of sheet 15, I wish sent, one copy to the Lady of Wimbledon—whom I have spoken of, without mentioning her name—the other to Frankie Forbes-Robertson.[4] I know both these sweet women will be interested to know something of what is happening to my soul—not in the theological sense, but merely in the sense of the spiritual consciousness that is separate from the actual occupations of the body. It is a sort of message or letter I send them—the only one, of course, I dare send. If Frankie wishes she can

[1] More Adey lived at 24 Hornton Street, Kensington, and Robert Ross nearby at 11 Upper Phillimore Gardens.

[2] See note p. 152.

[3] Most of these two passages were included in *De Profundis* (1905).

[4] Frances Forbes-Robertson (1866–1956). Novelist, sister of Johnston, Norman, Eric and Ian.

show it to her brother Eric, of whom I was always fond, but of course it is a strict secret from the general world. The Lady of Wimbledon will know that too.

If the copying is done at Hornton Street the lady type-writer might be fed through a lattice in the door like the Cardinals when they elect a Pope, till she comes out on the balcony and can say to the world "*Habet Mundus Epistolam;*" for indeed it is an Encyclical Letter, and as the Bulls of the Holy Father are named from their opening words, it may be spoken of as the *Epistola: In Carcere et Vinculis.*

There is no need to tell A. D. that a copy has been taken, unless he should write and complain of injustice in the letter or misrepresentation: then he should be told that a copy has been taken. I earnestly hope the letter will do him good. It is the first time anyone has ever told him the truth about himself. If he is allowed to think that the letter is merely the result of the influence of a plank-bed on style, and that my views are distorted by the privations of prison-life, no good will follow. I hope someone will let him know that the letter is one he thoroughly deserves, and that if it is unjust, he thoroughly deserves injustice. Who indeed deserves it more than he who was always so unjust to others?

In point of fact, Robbie, prison-life makes one see people and things as they really are. That is why it turns one to stone. It is the people outside who are deceived by the illusion of a life in constant motion. They revolve with life and contribute to its unreality. We who are immobile both see and know. Whether or not the letter does good to his narrow nature and hectic brain, to me it has done great good. I have "cleansed my bosom of much perilous stuff,"[1] to borrow a phrase from the poet whom you and I once thought of rescuing from the Philistines.[2] I need not remind you that mere expression is to an artist the supreme and only mode of life. It is by utterance that we live. Of the many, many things for which I have to thank the Governor there is none for which I am more grateful than for his permission to write fully to A. D. and at as great length as I desired. For nearly two years I had within me a growing burden of bitterness, much of which I have now got rid of. On the other side of the prison-wall there are some poor black soot-smirched trees that are just breaking out into buds of an almost shrill green. I know quite well what they are going through. They are finding expression.

There is another very serious thing about which I have to write to you, and I address myself to you because I have got to blame you, and I am far too fond of you to blame you to anyone else. On the 20th March 1896,[3] more than a year ago now, I wrote to you in the very strongest terms telling you that I could not bear the idea of any discord being made between

---

[1] *Macbeth*, Act V, scene iii.

[2] Dr Max Meyerfield in the notes to his German translation says that this refers to Ross's joking suggestion of founding an Anti-Shakespeare Society to combat exaggerated Bardolatry, and that Douglas's sonnet "To Shakespeare" (published in *The City of the Soul*, 1899) was written in anger at the suggestion.

[3] Actually 10 March. See p. 138.

myself and my wife on such a subject as money, after her sweetness in coming here from Italy to break to me the news of my mother's death, and that I desired my friends to withdraw their proposal to purchase my life-interest against her wishes. You should have seen that my wishes were carried out. You were very wrong not to do so. I was quite helpless in prison and I relied on you. You thought that the thing to do was the clever thing, the smart thing, the ingenious thing. You were under a mistake. Life is not complex. We are complex. Life is simple, and the simple thing is the right thing. Look at the result! Are you pleased with it?

Again, a complete error was made in the estimate formed of Mr Hargrove. He was regarded as a solicitor of the Humphreys class, one who would threaten to gain an end, bluster, extort, and the like. Quite the contrary. He is a man of very high character, and extremely good social position. Whatever he said he meant. The idea of putting me—a wretched prisoner and pauper—up to fight Mr Hargrove and Sir George Lewis was grotesque. The idea of bidding against them absurd. Mr Hargrove—the family solicitor of the Lloyds for thirty years—would advance my wife £10,000 if she wanted it, and not feel it. I asked Mr Holman whether in case of a divorce a settlement was not *ipso facto* broken. I received no answer. I find that it is as I suspected.

Again, how silly the long serious letters advising me "not to surrender my rights over my children," a phrase that occurs seven times in the correspondence. My rights! I had none. A claim that a formal appeal to a Judge in Chambers can quash in ten minutes is not a right. I am quite astounded at the position I have been placed in. How much better if you had done as I asked you, as at that time my wife was kind and ready to let me see my two children and be with them occasionally.[1] A. D. put me into a false position with regard to his father, forced me into it, and held me there. More Adey, with the best intentions, forced me into a false position with regard to my wife. Even had I any legal rights—and I have none—how much more charming to have privileges given to me by affection than to extort them by threats. My wife was very sweet to me, and now she, very naturally, goes right against me. Of her character also a wrong estimate was made. She warned me that if I let my friends bid against her she would proceed to a certain course, and she will do so.

---

[1] On 26 March Constance Wilde had written from Italy to her brother:

I have again had pressure put upon me to persuade me to go back to Oscar, but I am sure you will agree that it is impossible. I am told that I would save a human soul, but I have no influence over Oscar. I have had none, and though I think he is affectionate I see no reason for believing that I should be able now to perform miracles, and I must look after my boys and not risk their future. What do you think I should do? The Ranee [of Sarawak, Lady Brooke, with whom she was staying] thinks that he has fallen and cannot rise. That is rather like Humpty Dumpty, but then I think his fate is rather like Humpty Dumpty's, quite as tragic and quite as impossible to put right.

Again, Swinburne says to Marie Stuart in one of his poems,

> But surely you were something better
> Than innocent![1]

and really my friends must face the fact that (setting aside such details in my indictment as belonged to my bosom-friend, three in number) I am not in prison as an innocent man. On the contrary, my record of perversities of passion and distorted romances would fill many scarlet volumes. I think it right to mention this—however surprising, and no doubt shocking, it will sound to many—because More Adey in his letter tells me that the opposite side will be obliged to furnish strict details of the dates and places and exact circumstances of the terrible charges to be brought against me. Does he seriously imagine that if I submitted to more cross-examination I would be believed? Does he propose I should do so, and repeat the Queensberry fiasco? It is the case that the charges are not true. But that is a mere detail. If a man gets drunk, whether he does so on white wine or red is of no importance. If a man has perverse passions, their particular mode of manifestation is of no importance either.

I said from the first that I relied entirely on my wife's condonation. I now learn that no condonation is of any value where more than one offence may be charged. My wife has simply to say that she condoned X, but knew nothing of Y, and would not hear of condoning Z. There is a little shilling book—ninepence for cash—called *Every Man his own Lawyer*. If my friends had only sent it to me, or even read it themselves, all this trouble, expense, and worry would have been saved. However, while I blame you *ab initio*, I am now in a mood of mind that makes me think that everything that happens is for the best, and that the world is not a mere chaos in which chance and cleverness clash. What I have to do is simply this. I have got to submit to my divorce. I don't think that the Government could possibly prosecute me again. Even for a British Government it would be too brutal a procedure. I have also, before that, to restore to my wife my interest in the settlement-money before it is taken from me. I have thirdly to state that I will accept nothing from her at all in the way of income or allowance. This seems to be the simple, straightforward, and gentlemanly thing to do. It is a great blow to me. I feel the legal deprivation of my children poignantly.

My friendship with A. D. brought me first to the dock of the Criminal Court, then to the dock of the Bankruptcy Court, and now to the dock of the Divorce Court. As far as I can make out (not having the shilling primer on the subject) there are no more docks into which he can bring me. If so, I can draw a breath of relief. But I want you to seriously consider my proposal, to ask More to do so, and his lawyer, and to write to me, and to get More to write to me, as soon as possible about it. I think my wife will have no objection to refunding the £75 paid for the *damnosa hæreditas* of my life-interest. She is quite just on money matters. But personally I

[1] From "Adieux à Marie Stuart," published in *Tristram of Lyonesse and other Poems* (1882).

hope there will be no bargaining. A grave mistake has been made. Submission has to follow. I propose that my life-interest should be restored to my wife, its rightful owner, as a parting gift from me. It will render my exit from marriage less ignominious than to wait for its being done by legal coercion. Whether I am married or not is a matter that does not concern me. For years I disregarded the tie. But I really think that it is hard on my wife to be tied to me. I always thought so. And, though it may surprise some of my friends, I am really very fond of my wife and very sorry for her. I sincerely hope she may have a happy marriage, if she marries again. She could not understand me, and I was bored to death with the married life. But she had some sweet points in her character, and was wonderfully loyal to me. On this point of my surrendering everything, pray let More and yourself write at once, after you have considered the point.

Also, I would take it as a great favour if More would write to the people who pawned or sold my fur coat since my imprisonment, and ask them from me whether they would be kind enough to state where it was sold or pawned as I am anxious to trace it, and if possible get it back. I have had it for twelve years, it was all over America with me, it was at all my first nights, it knows me perfectly, and I really want it. The letter should be quite courteous, addressed first to the man: if he doesn't answer, to the woman. As it was the wife who pressed me to leave it in her charge, it might be mentioned that I am surprised and distressed, particularly as I paid out of my own pocket *since my imprisonment* all the expenses of her confinement, to the extent of £50 conveyed through Leverson. This might be stated as a reason for my being distressed. Their letters must be kept. I have a most particular reason for wishing it to be done—in fact, one vitally important. And the letter being one of civil request, with the reasons set forth, cannot involve argument or denial. I just require documentary evidence for my protection.

I hope to see Frank Harris on Saturday week, or soon. The news of the copying of my letter will be welcome, when I hear from you about my divorce. If Arthur Clifton would like to see the copy show it to him, or your brother Aleck.[1] Ever yours   OSCAR WILDE

To Robert Ross [2]

6 April [*1897*]   *H.M. Prison, Reading*
My dear Robbie, I am going to delay for a short time my letter to Alfred

---

[1] Alexander Galt Ross (1860–1927), elder brother of Robert Ross. A founder and secretary of the Society of Authors. Accompanied Rider Haggard to Iceland in 1888. After a brief period of literary work he became a partner in a bill-broking firm.

[2] This letter repeats much of the previous one (which may well have been withheld by the prison authorities). I have therefore here omitted the long discussion of financial matters.

Douglas for certain reasons, some of which, though not all, are suggested in a letter I am sending to More Adey at the same time as this.

I write to you now, partly for the pleasure of writing to you and getting from you in return one of your delightful literary letters, and partly because I have to blame you, and I cannot bear the idea of doing that indirectly, or in a letter addressed to another.

[*passage omitted. See p. x*]

Now to other points.

I have never had the chance of thanking you for the books. They were most welcome. Not being allowed the magazines was a blow, but Meredith's novel charmed me.[1] What a sane artist in temper! He is quite right in his assertion of sanity as the essential in romance. Still, up to the present only the abnormal have found expression in life and literature.

Rossetti's letters are dreadful. Obviously forgeries by his brother.[2] I was interested however to see how my grand-uncle's *Melmoth*[3] and my mother's *Sidonia* had been two of the books that fascinated his youth. As regards the conspiracy against him in later years I believe it really existed, and that the funds for it came out of Hake's bank. The conduct of a thrush in Cheyne Walk seems to me most suspicious, though William Rossetti says, "I could discern nothing in the thrush's song at all out of the common."[4]

Stevenson letters most disappointing also.[5] I see that romantic surroundings are the worst surroundings possible for a romantic writer. In Gower Street Stevenson could have written a new *Trois Mousquetaires*. In Samoa he wrote letters to *The Times* about Germans. I see also the traces of a terrible *strain* to lead a natural life. To chop wood with any advantage to oneself, or profit to others, one should not be able to describe the process. In point of fact the natural life is the unconscious life. Stevenson merely extended the sphere of the artificial by taking to digging. The

---

[1] *The Amazing Marriage* (1895).

[2] *Dante Gabriel Rossetti, his Family-Letters, with a Memoir by William Michael Rossetti* (2 vols, 1895).

[3] See note 2, p. 266.

[4] This incident in fact took place at Broadlands in Hampshire. W. M. Rossetti wrote:

> I remember there was once a thrush hard by, which, to my hearing, simply trilled its own lay on and off. My brother discerned a different note, and conceived that the thrush had been trained to ejaculate something insulting to him. Such is perverted fantasy—or I may rather infer such is an outcome of chloral-dosing.

The poet Dr Thomas Gordon Hake (1809–95) was one of D. G. Rossetti's closest friends. His son Alfred Egmont Hake, author of *Free Trade in Capital* (1891) and other books, invented a new system of banking which had amused Wilde.

[5] *Vailima Letters* (1895). See note 2, p. 141.

whole dreary book has given me a lesson. If I spend my future life reading Baudelaire in a *café* I shall be leading a more natural life than if I take to hedger's work or plant cacao in mud-swamps.

En Route is most over-rated.[1] It is sheer journalism. It never makes one hear a note of the music it describes. The subject is delightful, but the style is of course worthless, slipshod, flaccid. It is worse French than Ohnet's.[2] Ohnet tries to be commonplace and succeeds. Huysmans tries not to be, and is . . .[3] Hardy's novel[4] is pleasant, and Frederic's very interesting in matter. . . .[5] Later on, there being hardly any novels in the prison library for the poor imprisoned fellows I live with, I think of presenting the library with about a dozen good novels: Stevenson's (none here but *The Black Arrow*!), some of Thackeray's (none here). Jane Austen (none here), and some good *Dumas-père-like* books, by Stanley Weyman for instance, and any modern young man.[6] You mentioned Henley had a *protégé*?[7] Also the "Antony Hope" man.[8] After Easter, you might make out a list of about fourteen, and apply to let me have them. They would please the few who do not care about Goncourt's journal. Don't forget. I would pay myself for them.

I have a horror myself of going out into a world without a single book of my own. I wonder would there be any of my friends who would give me a few books, such as Cosmo Lennox,[9] Reggie Turner,[10] Gilbert Burgess,[11] Max,[12] and the like? You know the sort of books I want: Flaubert, Steven-

---

[1] This novel by Joris-Karl Huysmans (1848–1907) was first published in 1895.

[2] Georges Ohnet, prolific and popular French novelist (1848–1918).

[3] All dots in this letter are Wilde's.

[4] *The Well-Beloved* (published 16 March 1897).

[5] *Illumination* by the American novelist Harold Frederic (1856–98).

[6] Stanley John Weyman (1855–1928) had already published nine historical novels, including *Under the Red Robe* (1894) and *Memoirs of a Minister of France* (1895).

[7] Probably H. G. Wells, whose first novel, *The Time Machine* (1895), had been serialised by Henley in the *New Review*.

[8] Pen-name of Anthony Hope Hawkins (1863–1933), author of many books. In 1894 he had scored a double success with *The Dolly Dialogues* and *The Prisoner of Zenda*.

[9] Cosmo Charles Gordon-Lennox (1869–1921), wealthy grandson of the fifth Duke of Richmond. Actor (as Cosmo Stuart), playwright and successful adaptor of French plays. Played the part of the Vicomte de Nanjac in the original production of *An Ideal Husband*.

[10] 1869–1938. Illegitimate son of Lionel Lawson, who was an uncle of the first Lord Burnham (see note 4, p. 90). Journalist and wit. Lived mostly abroad. Published a number of novels. Oxford and lifelong friend of Max Beerbohm.

[11] English author and journalist (1868–1911). On 9 January 1895, six days after the first night of *An Ideal Husband*, he published in the *Sketch* a long interview with Wilde. This ends with Wilde's saying:

"I am sure that you must have a great future in literature before you."
"*What makes you think so?*" I asked, as I flushed with pleasure at the prediction.
"Because you seem to be such a very bad interviewer. I feel sure that you must write poetry. I certainly like the colour of your necktie very much. Good-bye."

[12] Max Beerbohm (1872–1956) responded to this appeal and sent four books, including his own *Works* and *The Happy Hypocrite* (1896). See p. 276.

son, Baudelaire, Maeterlinck, Dumas *père*, Keats, Marlowe, Chatterton, Coleridge, Anatole France, Gautier, Dante and all Dante literature; Goethe and ditto: and so on. I would feel it a great compliment to have books waiting for me, and perhaps there may be some friends who would like to be kind to me. One is really very grateful, though I fear I often seem not to be. But then remember I have had incessant worries besides prison-life.

In answer to this you can send me a long letter all about plays and books. Your handwriting, in your last, was so dreadful that it looked as if you were writing a three-volume novel on the terrible spread of communistic ideas among the rich, or in some other way wasting a youth that always has been, and always will remain, quite full of promise. If I wrong you in ascribing it to such a cause you must make allowances for the morbidity produced by long imprisonment. But do write clearly. Otherwise it looks as if you had nothing to conceal.

There is much that is horrid, I suppose, in this letter. But I had to blame you to yourself, not to others. Read my letter to More. F. Harris comes to see me on Saturday, I hope. Remember me to Arthur Clifton and his wife, who, I find, is so like Rossetti's wife—the same lovely hair—but of course a sweeter nature, though Miss Siddal is fascinating, and her poem A1.[1] Ever yours   OSCAR

P.S. The names of the mystical books in *En Route* fascinate me. Try and get some of them for me when I go out. Also, try and get me a good life of St Francis of Assisi.

To Thomas Martin[2]

[*Circa April 1897*]

My dear friend, What have I to write about except that if you had been an officer in Reading Prison a year ago my life would have been much happier. Everyone tells me I am looking better—and happier.

That is because I have a good friend who gives me the *Chronicle*, and *promises* me ginger biscuits![3]   O. W.

. . . .

You must get me his address some day—he is such a good fellow. Of course I would not for worlds get such a friend as you are into *any danger*.

[1] This poem, "A Year and a Day" by Rossetti's wife Elizabeth Siddal, is printed in the Rossetti letters referred to earlier.

[2] Thomas Martin, a native of Belfast, came to Reading as a warder some seven weeks before Wilde's release. He was always kind to Wilde and constantly broke the regulations to bring him extra food, as well as the *Daily Chronicle* and other papers. He contributed a chapter to Sherard's *Life of Oscar Wilde* (1906). These are examples of the surreptitious notes, written on odd scraps of paper, which Wilde passed to him in prison.

[3] At the bottom of this note Martin wrote in pencil: "Your ungrateful I done more than promise."

I quite understand your feelings.

The *Chronicle* is capital today. You must get A S/2 to come out and clean on Saturday morning and I will give him my note then myself.

.   .   .   .   .

I hope to write about prison life and to try and change it for others, but it is too terrible and ugly to make a work of art of. I have suffered too much in it to write plays about it.

.   .   .   .   .

So sorry you have no key. Would like a long talk with you. Any more news?

To More Adey

6 May 1897   *H.M. Prison, Reading*

My dear More, Many thanks for your letter. Hansell[1] has written at last and forwarded a draft of the agreement to be drawn up between my wife and myself. It is couched in legal language, and of course quite unintelligible to me. The only thing I can make out is the close, where it is laid down that I am to be deprived of my £150 if I know any "disreputable" people. As good people, as they are grotesquely termed, *will* not know me, and I am not to be *allowed* to know wicked people, my future life, as far as I can see at present, will be passed in comparative solitude. I have written to Hansell that artists and the criminal classes are the only people who will know me, and that the conditions would place him, if seriously insisted on, in an absurd position: but what I want now is a legal condonation from my wife of the past, so as not to have it raked up again and again. For the rest, to have been divorced would have been horrible of course, but now that the children are publicly taken from me by a Judge's order, and it is decided that I am unfit to be with Cyril, I am very disheartened: all I want is peace: all I ever wanted was peace: I loathe legal worries.

I don't know when you are coming: it had better be soon: I hope you have written to the *Commissioners* for permission to have the private room and a visit of an hour in duration: in the case of a special visit the Governor has no authority to grant these privileges himself, otherwise he would have gladly done so.

As to Ricketts, I see his presence troubles you: well, I thought, as he had applied so often, it was not for me to refuse a kindly offer from an artist of whom I am very fond, but I think that after half-an-hour I will ask Ricketts to leave us together to talk business: he will quite understand that I have lots of tedious and uninteresting things to settle. So then you and I and Robbie will have half-an-hour for everything.

[1] Arthur D. Hansell, of the firm of Stoker & Hansell, solicitors, whom Wilde had engaged to protect his interests in connection with his marriage settlement.

As regards clothes etc: Robbie kindly said he would get me a blue-serge suit from Doré and an ulster: this I suppose he has done. Frank Harris also offered me some kindnesses of the same kind, so I have already written to him to say what I want in the way of other clothes, *and boots*, and to ask for the things to be sent to you, not later than Thursday 13th. Hats I ought to have a lot of, but I suppose they have disappeared: Heath, Albert Gate, was my hatter, and understands my needs: I would like a brown hat, and a grey hat, soft felt, seaside things. Would you, if there is time, get me *eighteen* collars made after the pattern you have, or say two dozen. Also, order me two dozen white handkerchiefs, and a dozen with coloured borders. Also some neckties: some dark blue with white spots and diapers, and some of whatever is being worn for summer wear. I also want eight pair of socks, coloured summer things; my size in gloves is $8\frac{1}{4}$, as my hand is so broad, but my socks need only be for an 8 glove in proportion. Also, I want two or three sets of plain mother-of-pearl (by the way I want to make "nacred" an English word) studs—nacred studs: you know how difficult they are to get abroad. Also, some nice French soap, Houbigant's if you can get it: Pritchard of King Street, St James's, used to have it for me: either "Peau d'Espagne" or "Sac de Laitue" would do: a case of three. Also, some scent; Canterbury Wood Violet I would like, and some "Eau de Lubin" for the toilet, a large bottle. Also some of Pritchard's tooth-powder, and a medium toothbrush. My hair has become very grey: I am under the impression that it is quite white, but I believe that is an exaggeration: there is a wonderful thing called Koko Marikopas, to be got at 233 Regent Street, which is a wonderful hair-tonic: the name alone seems worth the money, so please get a large bottle. I want, for psychological reasons, to feel entirely physically cleansed of the stain and soil of prison life, so these things are all—trivial as they may sound—really of great importance. I don't know if there are any night-shirts? If not, please order me half a dozen; the size of my collar will show how wide the neck should be, also, the sleeve of my shirt for length of arm: the actual length—well, I am six feet, and I like long shirts. I like them made with a turn-down collar, and a breast-pocket for a handkerchief: coloured border to collar and cuffs. If "the dreadful people" don't give up my two rugs, will you buy me one—a travelling Scotch rug, with a good fringe: *not* a tartan, of course: nor a shepherd's-plaid pattern: but the sort of fleecy striped thing. I feel I here convey no idea. All these, if possible, out of the wonderful £25: pray keep envelope of the latter, that I may try to guess from whose generous hand it has come.[1]

As for Reggie Turner, please tell him from me how charmed and touched I am by his delightful present:[2] it is most sweet and generous of him, and I accept his gift with gratitude and delight: in fact I must thank him in person, if he will let me: I hope he will come to see me between the date of my leaving here, and my starting with Frank Harris. My plans

[1] The donor was Adey himself.
[2] A dressing-case.

250

are as follows. I have had no reply from the Home Secretary,[1] I need hardly say; and as Hansell proposes to come on Saturday the 15th with the deeds for my signature, it makes it very troublesome. I must alter Hansell's date, I suppose. In any case my idea is this. If I am kept, as I suppose I shall be, till the 19th, I wish a carriage to be here at six o'clock: by 6.15 I will be ready. The carriage, by the Governor's permission, is to drive into the prison: it is to be a closed one. In this I go to *Twyford*, six miles off: there breakfast and change, and make my way to Folkestone, Twyford being on main line. Cross over by night-boat to Boulogne, and sleep there. Stay either at Boulogne, or in the immediate vicinity by the sea, for four or five days to recruit. Then join Frank Harris and go to the Pyrenees.[2] So you see Reggie Turner could come to Boulogne, on the Thursday. Ask him to. Of course he is to keep all this a dead secret. Also, on no account is Alfred Douglas to be told. I will see him after my voyage with Frank Harris and receive from him my letters and what is left of my presents. But not before. For him to appear at Boulogne would be horrible. I could not stand it.

Bobbie wrote to me that Leverson would hand over the money all right: it should be about £450. If you or Bobbie would keep it for me I would be much obliged. Out of his original loan of £500 Leverson has already had £250: he must wait a little for the balance. I hope you will have received the money from him by the time I see you.

As regards Humphreys, I am under the impression that I left there my dressing bag containing my silver brushes and a suit of clothes and things: would you find out? and if so, the brushes and razors I would like. Razors and shaving things, by the way, are a necessity to be procured in England. If the bag with the silver brushes is not at Humphreys, it must be with the people who sold my furs, and they should be asked for it. They also have a dark ulster of mine.

I wish you would see if you could get me a travelling basket with strap for books: one that could go under the seat of a railway carriage: Lady Brownlow[3] gave me one, of green wicker that was charming, but I don't know where it is now. In Bond Street, or at the Stores, I fancy you could get one. They are most useful. I will let Robbie know when he comes what English books I would like.

On the strength of Percy's promise to pay £500, Humphreys claims from me £150 for the expenses of Bankruptcy. I don't know if Leverson has paid this. Percy said he would pay half. It has to be paid, so if Percy does not pay half, I must pay it all through Leverson. Leverson will of course keep back what is necessary for Humphreys's bill.

I am still anxious to know if my bags with letters have been removed from Humphreys. I would like them to be at Hornton Street.

---

[1] Wilde had petitioned the Home Secretary on 22 April asking to be released on Saturday, 15 May, in order to "avoid the notoriety and annoyance of newspaper interviews" if released on the due date of 19 May.

[2] Frank Harris had invited Wilde to join him on a driving tour in the Pyrenees.

[3] Adelaide (1844–1917), daughter of the eighteenth Earl of Shrewsbury and Talbot, married (1868) the third Earl Brownlow (1844–1921).

I am very sorry to hear Robbie has not been well. When I wrote to him about people giving me books, I meant that many literary people had sent messages through him, and I would have been touched by their giving me one of their books on my release: Stuart Merrill, Lugné-Poe, and the like. It was a whim I had. I don't know if Reggie ever hears from Charlie Hickey?[1] If he does I wish he would ask Charlie to write to me (under cover to Reggie) and tell me how he is, and where. I have pleasant memories of him.

If the Twyford scheme is all right, perhaps this would be a good programme. Breakfast at Twyford: luncheon at Richmond with Frank Harris: dinner at Folkestone: supper at Boulogne. I would like to see Frank before my going to the Pyrenees. I wonder am I to see you on Saturday? I still suspect you of wishing to incarcerate me in a Trappist monastery, and will tax you with it in Robbie's presence. With thousand thanks, Ever yours

OSCAR WILDE

Friday [*7 May*]

The answer has just come from the Home Secretary. It is the customary refusal.

O. W.

To Robert Ross

13 May[2] [*1897*]   *H.M. Prison, Reading*

My dear Robbie, I am sorry that the last visit was such a painful and unsatisfactory one. To begin with I was wrong to have Ricketts present: he meant to be cheering, but I thought him trivial: everything he said, including his remark that he supposed time went very fast in prison (a singularly unimaginative opinion, and one showing an entirely inartistic lack of sympathetic instinct), annoyed me extremely. Then your letter of Sunday had of course greatly distressed me. You and More had both assured me that there was enough money waiting for me to enable me to live comfortably and at ease for "eighteen months or two years." I now find that there is exactly £50 for that purpose, and that out of this have to come the costs of two solicitors who have already had long interviews with Mr Hargrove and incurred much expense! The balance is for me!

My dear Robbie, if the £50 covers the law-costs I shall be only too pleased. If there is any balance remaining I don't want to know anything about it. Pray don't offer it to me. Even in acts of charity there should

---

[1] He was in France with Douglas in 1895 and is described by Douglas in his *Autobiography* (1929), as "a charming boy about a couple of years younger than myself and well known to Oscar, a son of Colonel Hickey."

[2] Because of his mental agitation Wilde wrote "April" by mistake. It also seems likely that the date should be 15 May since the letter to Adey to which he refers is thus dated.

be some sense of humour. You have caused me the greatest pain and disappointment by foolishly telling me a complete untruth. How much better for me had you said to me, "Yes, you will be poor, and there are worse things than poverty. You have got to learn how to face poverty;" simply, directly, and straightforwardly. But when a wretched man is in prison, the people who are outside either treat him as if he was dead, and dispose of his effects, or treat him as if he was a lunatic, and pretend to carry out his wishes and don't, or regard him as an idiot, to be humoured, and tell him silly and unnecessary lies, or look on him as a thing so low, so degraded, as to have no feelings at all, a thing whose entire life, in its most intimate relations with wife and child, and with all that wife and child represent to a ruined man, is to be bandied about like a common shuttle-cock in a vulgar game, in which victory or failure are of really little interest, as it is not the life of the players that is at stake, but only someone else's life.

I am afraid that you don't realise what my wife's character and conduct have been towards me. You don't seem to understand her. From the very first she forgave me, and was sweet beyond words to me. After my seeing her here when we had arranged everything between us, and I was to have £200 a year during her life, and *one third* if I survived her, and our arrangements about the children and their transference to her guardianship had been made, so far as her expressing her desire to have nothing done in a public court but to have everything done privately between us was concerned, I wrote to you to say that all opposition to my wife's purchase of my life-interest was to be withdrawn, as she had been very sweet to me and I was quite satisfied with her offer, and I expressly stated that I begged that my friends would do nothing of any kind that would imperil the reconciliation and affection between myself and my wife.

You wrote at once to say that my wishes would be carried out, and that my friends would never dream of doing anything that would endanger my friendly relation with my wife. I believed you, and trusted you. You did not tell me the truth, you and my friends did not carry out my directions, and what is the result? Instead of £200 a year I have £150. Instead of one third of the interest, which on the death of my wife's mother will amount to about £1500 a year, I have no more than a bare £150 to the end of my days. My children will have £600 or £700 a year *apiece*. Their father will remain a pauper.

But that is not all. That is merely the common money side. My children are taken from me by an order of the court. I am legally no longer their father. I have no right to speak to them. If I try to communicate with them I can be put into prison for contempt of court. My wife also is of course wounded with me for what she considers a breach of faith on my part. On Monday I sign here a deed of separation of the most painfully stringent kind and of the most humiliating conditions. If I try to communicate with my wife against her will, or without her leave, I lose my wretched £150 a year at once. My life is to be ruled after a pattern of respectability. My friends are to be such as a respectable solicitor would approve of. *I owe this, Robbie, to your not telling me the truth, and not carrying out my instructions. I merely wanted my friends not to interfere.* I did not ask them to do anything. I begged them to do nothing.

More tells me that every single thing he did, he did with the sanction and advice of your brother Aleck, whom he describes as a "sober business-like" person. Was Aleck aware that I distinctly forbade my friends to bid against my wife for my life-interest? That it was against my directions? Was it by his advice that you wrote me the letter containing the fatal untruth that has caused all this annoyance, loss, and misery? "*I have acted throughout under the advice of Aleck*" are More's words.

And the grotesque thing about it all is that I now discover, when it is too late to do anything, that the entire proceedings have been done at *my* expense, that *I* have had to pay for Holman, whose advice and opinions have been worthless and pernicious, and that the whole cost has fallen upon *me*: so that out of £150 given to More Adey "*for my use*" and aid nothing now remains at all but I suppose about £1. 10. 6.

Don't you see what a wonderful thing it would have been for me had you been able to hand me the £150 on my going out on Wednesday? How welcome such a sum would have been! Of what incalculable value! Now the whole thing, without my permission being asked, is spent in a stupid and ill-advised attempt to arrange my relations with my wife against my wife's wishes, in making discord, in promoting estrangement. My soul and the soul of my wife met in the valley of the shadow of death: she kissed me: she comforted me: she behaved as no woman in history, except my own mother perhaps, could have behaved. You and my other friends have so little imagination, so little sympathy, so little power of appreciating what was beautiful, noble, lovely and of good report that you can think of nothing better—you, More Adey and, I am told, your brother Aleck—than to rush in between us with an entirely ignorant solicitor and part us first and then make mischief between us.

And all this you do with my own money without telling me. You pose as the generous friends. When I asked More Adey where the money was to come from for all the expense, he smiled very sweetly and mysteriously and said "Don't trouble, dear Oscar, it will all be right. You have good friends." I now find that it was *my* money paying for everything. Let us be quite frank. Do you think, Robbie, that if More Adey had candidly told me that he had been given (by strangers to him and to me, he says) this £150 "*for my use*," that I would have *allowed* him to spend it in going to law with my wife? I should have told him to keep it for me when I went out. More says, or will say, that the money was to be spent at his "discretion:" quite so: but for *my* use, and I, and not More Adey, am the proper judge of what is for my use. The money was spent stupidly, wrongly, unjustly, and to my irreparable injury. As a result of More Adey's use of my money I find myself with a seriously diminished income, with my children taken away by the law, and separated from my wife on harsh and unseemly terms. And not till the whole sum has been expended am I informed that the money was mine.

I have written bitterly about Frank Harris, because he came down to make gorgeous offers of his cheque-book to any extent I required and then sent a verbal message to say he had changed his mind,[1] but what shall I say of More Adey, you, and Aleck, who expend £150 of my own money, money given for my use, in a litigation against which I protested from the beginning, begun against my orders, and with difficulty ended at my entreaties? I see no excuse at all for More Adey and you all spending my money in this way, or in any way without consulting me. I would like to know if Aleck approved of this behaviour towards me.

I asked in one of my letters if Alfred Douglas had been directing these operations. I am sorry I did so. It was unjust. It was unjust to unfortunate Alfred Douglas. He once played dice with his father for my life, and lost. I don't think he would again do so. In the whole of this law-business my life has been gambled for and staked on the board with utter recklessness. In the centre of it all has been a man whom I don't know, but who I now understand has secretly been my solicitor for more than a year, a man of the name of Holman. Flaubert once made *la Bêtise Humaine* incarnate in two retired solicitors or solicitors' clerks called *Bouvard et Pécuchet*.[2] The opinions of this man Holman, my secret solicitor, if collected as *Holmaniana* would prove a serious rival to Flaubert's grotesques. For sheer crass stupidity, they, if correctly reported, are perfectly astounding. The reckless gambling with my life has had, if a tragedy to me, at least its comic choragus in Holman, the leader of the Dunces.

Just recall events. The result of my directions about my wife being allowed to purchase my life-interest being disobeyed was, as you remember, that I received a letter from Mr Hargrove saying that in consequence of the opposition to my wife it had been determined to reduce my allowance to £150 a year for life. That this sum itself was conditional on my friends at once withdrawing their opposition. Failing this Mr Hargrove said he would be obliged to deprive me of my children, my wife, and my income.

---

[1] In a letter to Adey dated 12 May Wilde described a visit by Frank Harris on 7 April. Wilde had been deeply moved by Harris's promise to send him a cheque for £500 on his release. The letter continues:

> I now learn that he has sent a verbal message through you to say he is very sorry but cannot do it. Of course nothing would induce me to go on this driving-tour with him after that. I hardly suppose he expects it. Would you kindly write to him that you gave me his message and that I was a good deal distressed, as I had unfortunately received similar messages from everyone else who had been kind enough to promise me money, and that I found myself in such a painful and parlous state as regards my finances that I could not think of any pleasant pleasure excursion such as he had proposed till I had in some way settled my affairs and seen a possible future. This will end the driving-tour, and there is nothing in the message that could hurt his feelings, so pray give it in my own words. In fact Frank Harris has no feelings. It is the secret of his success. Just as the fact that he thinks that other people have none either is the secret of the failure that lies in wait for him somewhere on the way of Life.

[2] Gustave Flaubert (1821–80) spent the last nine years of his life writing his satirical novel *Bouvard et Pécuchet*, but he never finished it, and it was published as a considerable fragment in 1881.

The tidings fell on me like a thunderbolt. I was aghast. I had been under the impression that my wife had bought the interest, or that at any rate everything had been arranged for her so doing, in the preceding March. I am told that everything has been done by friends in my real interest, and that if I will only trust in them everything will be right. I am forced by them into the fatal false position that proved my ruin. "We all," writes More Adey, "beg you not to surrender your legal rights over your wife and your children." What absurd nonsense. I had *no* rights over my wife and my children. That is not a right which a formal application by a solicitor's clerk can deprive one of in twenty minutes. You should read Carlyle. A right is an articulated might.

Mr Holman, I was told, was specially strong on the subject of my not surrendering my "legal rights over my wife and children." Mr Hargrove warns me, warns More Adey, warns Holman. I am told that Holman considers that "Mr Hargrove is merely trying to frighten you by threats. That he has no intention of carrying them out." Poor Holman! His psychological estimate of Mr Hargrove was sadly to seek. My friends, reckless, as it was with my life and my money they were gambling, procure from the Receiver my life-interest at the cost of £75. To achieve this, they think of two *clever* lies, as they fancy them to be. Holman tells Mr Hargrove that a large sum of money is at my disposal, and that I am in no want of money at all. It is supposed—*O sancta simplicitas!*—that this will overawe Mr Hargrove and prevent him bidding against you! The sole result is that Mr Hargrove tells my wife that he has it on the authority of Holman that I am going to be in no want of money, so that there is not the smallest necessity for increasing the £150. So my wife writes to me at Christmas and advises me to invest the money in an annuity, so as to increase my income! She naturally supposed that it was about £3,000: something that one could buy an annuity with. So did I. I find that the entire sum was £150, of which everything except about thirty-five shillings has to go in law-expenses.

The other clever lie is to pretend to Mr Hargrove that you are not my agents but quite independent people, while assuring the Registrar of Bankruptcy that you are really my agents. As for me, you tell me that you are acting independently, but I find it is with my money. More Adey really expected Mr Hargrove to believe in the ridiculous comedy. So did Holman. I need hardly say that Mr Hargrove was not taken in for a single moment. He directed all his attacks on me. That is why More Adey and Holman and you were so brave. Nothing could exceed the heroism with which you exposed me to danger.

Of course there was always the peril in your eyes that my wife and I might come to a private agreement together, as we wished to do. So I am earnestly begged to promise to sign no private agreement of any kind. One of the best Holmaniana I have is that "any such agreement would be illegal and not binding." Can one conceive such a stupid opinion! It is however urged on me from every side. Finally I am induced to solemnly promise that I will not sign any private agreement without warning Holman first.

It may seem odd to you but my one desire was to have all my arrangements with my wife quite private, the terms to be arranged between ourselves. But for your interference this would have been accomplished.

Finally the fight began. More writes a triumphant letter. He has secured the life-interest, and demanded at the point of the bayonet "£200 during your wife's life, and one third after her death should you survive her." There was a slight want of imagination in the terms, as they were exactly what my wife had offered and I had accepted in March. My friends, thinking to extort more, had disobeyed my instructions. Consequently my terms are reduced. Then my friends come down to the original offer. Mr Hargrove takes no notice at all of the purchase of the life-interest. He had warned Holman and More Adey. They had disregarded his warnings. Why did he take no notice?

He took no notice because he had in his pocket Inderwick's[1] clear statement that on my divorce my marriage-settlement would be broken. I had written on this point to Holman. No notice was taken at all. The point was considered of no importance. Yet it was the pivot of the whole thing. My interest depended on my wife's good will. If she divorced me it returned to her. Mr Hargrove proceeded to have it returned to her, poor Holman and More Adey not having the smallest idea of what he was aiming at, or understanding one little iota of the whole situation. Their entire incapacity to realise the position is utterly astonishing, and incredible.

Mr Hargrove, there being no necessity to take the smallest notice of anyone who has bought my life-interest, suddenly deprives me of my children. This and the death of my mother are the two terrible things of my prison-life, of all my life. Holman didn't care, they were not his children. More was not interested. Even you, who were fond of them, of whom they were fond, who knew my idolatrous love of Cyril, even you took no notice. You never wrote me a line to say you were sorry at such a tragedy coming on me. You were absolutely indifferent. To me it was a blow appalling. I shall never get over it. That a Court of Law should decide that I am unfit to be with my own children is so terrible that to expunge it from the scroll of History and of Life I would gladly remain in this lonely cell for two more years—oh! for ten years if needs be. I don't care to live if I am so degraded that I am unfit to be with my own child.

What does Holman say? Well, I have received a message from More Adey to say "Holman declares himself very well satisfied so far." Can one conceive such nonsense! But he gives Holman's sapient reasons.

(1) "No costs were given against me." As regards this, the costs could not have been more than £3. 10. and no one gives costs against a bankrupt. I have no estate.

(2) "An account is to be furnished of the progress of the education of my children twice a year to me." As to this, it is quite untrue. The Court naturally requires an account to be handed in by the guardians for the Court's information. I get no account. I can employ a Queen's Counsel

[1] Frederic Andrew Inderwick, Q.C. (1836–1904).

257

and make an application to know if Cyril is learning to cipher, or if Vyvyan's spelling is improved. That is all.

(3) "I have liberty to make an application if I like." Certainly, but only on points of common ordinary law: viz. if I heard that the children were badly fed, or insufficiently clothed. What a privilege! Do you think they are likely to be?

(4) "Mr Holman is of opinion that this action shows that Mr Hargrove will *not* apply for a divorce." This is a typical specimen of Holmaniana. If he knew anything about law or equity this ignorant and absurd solicitor would know that it was absolutely necessary for my wife to apply for and gain a divorce once she had charge of the children. Why? Because she had to make an affidavit that she could adequately provide for the suitable education of my children before the Court would even listen to an application to remove them from me. She was pledged to secure the life-interest. By buying it you had forced her to do so. Step by step More Adey forced my wife to bring the divorce suit. She had no option. She struggled for two years not to do it. It was reserved for my friends to force it on her. Try and realise that, my dear Robbie, and you will understand my feelings. But, you and More Adey say now, "You are *not* deprived of access to your children." This is solemnly written down in the statement left here on Tuesday last. It is true that through a technical error it is not specified that I am to have no access, but perhaps you would like to hear a letter from Hansell on the subject, dated *April 10th*. He writes as follows: "The Court does not expressly forbid access. But it is understood that should you try to make any attempt to communicate with them an order would be issued expressly restraining you." Note the words: "*any attempt to communicate with them.*" Are you satisfied now?

But, you said with triumphant emphasis on Tuesday, Holman says that the order of the Court does not restrain you abroad! This is an excellent bit of Holmaniana. Of course it does not. The bye-laws of the Reading Vestry are not binding on the green water-streets of Venice. The laws passed by the English Parliament do not bind the inhabitants of France. But who ever said they did? If I try to see the children two things happen.

(1) I lose my entire income, as the children being in charge of my wife it comes under the head of "molestation or annoyance."

(2) She at once is forced to deprive the boys of the advantage of a foreign education, to remove them to England to the jurisdiction of the Court. In England, if I try to write to them even, I can be put in prison for contempt of court. Do you understand all this? Is it dawning on you what More Adey and you and my friends have done?

The most shameful conduct on More Adey's part and the part of my friends was when my wife proceeded to the divorce. You were utterly regardless of me and my safety and position. You simply were gambling with my life. My father used to have a story about an English landlord who wrote from the Carlton to his Irish agent and said "Don't let the tenants imagine that by shooting you they will at all intimidate me."

More Adey and you took up exactly the same position with regard to me. You did not care what happened.

Do you think I am writing mere rhetoric? Let me quote to you your friend More Adey's letter conveying to me the news that George Lewis was going to divorce me on appalling charges of a new and more infamous character. "*We*," he says, "your friends" that is—"we will have nothing whatever to do with your relations to your wife and we will not be *influenced by threats of a divorce, a matter in which we have no concern.*"! . . .¹

There are your friend's words: that is the attitude of you, More Adey, and your brother Aleck, apparently. You were all keen to repeat the Queensberry scandal and affair. First a civil trial, with me cross-examined by Carson. Then a report by the judge to the Treasury. I am divorced, and re-tried and sent to prison! That is what you were working for. Oh! but, says More Adey, when we advised you to resist and meet the "tainted" evidence we didn't mean it. We meant that you might "have time to get abroad." So the great scheme was that I should be divorced on hideous grounds, and should live in exile. As my divorce would annul my settlement I would of course have had no income at all. And when I was skulking abroad More Adey would have written to me and said, "We have succeeded in all we aimed at: you have now no longer (1) any wife (2) any children (3) any income (4) any possibility of ever coming to London to produce a play. Mr Holman says he is very well satisfied on the whole."

My dear Robbie, if that had happened, how would you have compared yourself, as a friend of mine, with wretched Alfred Douglas? I can only tell you that he would have shown up very well beside you. And really now that I reflect on your conduct and More Adey's to me in this matter I feel I have been unjust to that unfortunate young man.

In point of fact, Robbie, you had better realise that of all the incompetent people on the face of God's earth in any matter requiring wisdom, common sense, straightforwardness, ordinary intelligence, More Adey is undoubtedly the chief. I have written to him a letter about himself which I beg you will at once go and study. He is cultivated. He is sympathetic. He is kind. He is patient. He is gentle. He is affectionate. He is full of charming emotional qualities. He is modest—too much so—about his intellectual attainments. I value his opinion of a work of art far more than he does himself. I think he should have made, and still can make, a mark in literature. But in matters of business he is the most solemn donkey that ever stepped. He has neither memory, nor understanding, nor capacity to realise a situation, or appreciate a point. His gravity of manner makes his entire folly mask as wisdom. Every one is taken in. He is so serious in manner that one believes he can form an intellectual opinion. He can't. He is *extremely dense* in all matters requiring lucidity or imagination or instinct. In business matters he is *stupid*. The harm he has done me is irreparable, and he is as pleased as possible with himself. Now I have realised this, I feel it right, Robbie, that you should know it. If you have

¹ Wilde's dots.

259

ever thought him sensible, give up the idea. He is incapable, as I have written to him, of managing the domestic affairs of a tom-tit in a hedge for a single afternoon. He is a *stupid man*, in practical concerns.[1]

You are a dear affectionate, nice, loving fellow: but of course in all matters requiring business faculty utterly foolish. I didn't expect advice from you. I would have as soon expected it from Cyril. I merely expected the truth. I was quite disappointed. You have behaved very wrongly.

More gets my letter when you get this. He is to go to Leverson's *at once*. His accepting a *post-dated* cheque is really too idiotic. My plans he will tell you. Come when you like to this place near Havre. You shall be as welcome as a flower, and attacked till you know yourself. You have a heavy *atonement* before you. Kindly show Aleck this letter. Ever yours

O. W.

Of course it is understood that Alfred Douglas is not to be at Havre. You must write to him and say that I will receive any letter from him through you, but that he is not to attempt to see me, till I allow him. I believe he desires to return my letters and presents personally. He can do so, later on, in a month.

To Thomas Martin

[*17 May 1897*]   [*H.M. Prison, Reading*]

Please find out for me the name of A.2.11. Also: the names of the children who are in for the rabbits, and the amount of the fine.[2] Can I pay

---

[1] In the letter of 15 May to More Adey Wilde wrote:

The entire correspondence of you and Robbie with me should be published. The best title would be *Letters from two Idiots to a Lunatic*, I should fancy.

My dear More, the time is come when you should recognise one thing: that is that in all business matters even of the simplest kind your judgment is utterly incompetent, your opinion either foolish or perverted, and your capacity to understand the most ordinary circumstances of actual life absolutely *nil*. You are a man of singular culture: of grave and castigated taste in style: you can discern the intellectual architecture of work that seems to others flamboyant or fantastic by an immediate sympathy of recognition: to discern the classical element in contemporary work is your function, one that you should more fully recognise than you do. You have not in literature ever tried to do yourself justice. In your nature you are most sympathetic. You would love to help others. You are patient to excess. Your forbearance is beautiful. But you have not got enough common sense to manage the affairs of a tom-tit in a hedge. Everything that you do is wrong and done in the wrong manner. Robbie is better as a guide, for if he is quite irrational he has the advantage of being always illogical, so he occasionally comes to a right conclusion. But you not merely are equally irrational, but are absolutely logical: you start always from the wrong premises, and arrive logically at the wrong conclusion. As soon as I see in your letter, 1, 2, 3, I know you have been doing something utterly foolish and are giving utterly foolish reasons.

[2] A.2.11. was a half-witted soldier called Prince (see pp. 273–275). By paying their fines Wilde secured the release of these three children, who had been convicted of snaring rabbits. Warder Martin gave a biscuit to one of the children who was crying, and was dismissed from the service in consequence (see pp. 269–271).

this, and get them out? If so I will get them out tomorrow. Please, dear friend, do this for me. I must get them out. Think what a thing for me it would be to be able to help three little children. I would be delighted beyond words. If I can do this by paying the fine, tell the children that they are to be released tomorrow by a friend, and ask them to be happy, and not to tell anyone.

To More Adey

[*Postmark 17 May 1897*]   *H.M. Prison, Reading*

Dear More, It is right to tell you that the Home Secretary against my earnest entreaties is to send me to London, the one place I wished to avoid. I am to be transferred to Pentonville tomorrow, the day announced in the papers for my transference to Wormwood Scrubs. The transference is to be conducted with humanity. I am to wear my own clothes, and not to be handcuffed. My clothes are so dreadful that I wish I had thought of having clothes here, but it will have to stand as it is.

I have written to Reggie[1] to ask him to meet me and go abroad with me. I am so hurt with you and Robbie—not so much for what you have done, but for your failing to realise what you have done, your lack of imagination, which shows lack of sympathy, your blindness to your astounding conduct in spending money without my consent that would have been of priceless service to me—that if you came abroad with me it would only distress us both: I could talk to you of nothing but of the mode in which you very nearly repeated down to the smallest detail the whole of the Queensberry episode: forcing me into a civil trial, into a loathsome divorce, to be followed either by my arrest, in case I followed your advice and resisted the "tainted evidence," or by my eternal exile, in case I followed your other advice and got "safe abroad:" in both cases being condemned to sheer pauperism, as the marriage settlement being broken *ipso facto* on my divorce, my prospective interest in it after my wife's death should I

---

[1] Wilde wrote two letters to Turner on 17 May (one of which was smuggled out of the prison). In them he again went over his complaints against Ross and Adey and said that Turner was the only friend he wanted to go away with him. Turner replied that he would be unable to meet Wilde out of prison since it might mean the loss of his allowance. He continued:

And now, dear Oscar, you must allow me to say something to you about More and Bobbie, as you have written to me about them. The most beautiful thing I have ever known is Bobbie's devotion to you. He has never had any other thought than of you; never once, for one minute, has he forgotten you; he has only looked forward to one thing, the time when he would be able to talk to you freely and affectionately again. It is very rare to find such complete devotion, and I fear, dear Oscar, that you have gone very near to breaking his heart. He and I are going to Dieppe together tonight and we shall see you tomorrow, and I feel certain that then all differences and bitterness will be forgotten, but I am certain that when you come to talk over what has been done for you, you will see that all has been in the best way when one remembers the terribly difficult position.

survive her would be absolutely *nil*. An order of the Court would have been obtained at once.

This, my dear More, is what you were preparing for me. If after a week you care to come to Havre and give me some explanation, I shall be delighted to see you. I hope Robbie will come with you.

5 o'clock

I have seen Hansell and signed the deed of separation. I do not really like going to Stewart Headlam's,[1] as I don't care much about it. I know him but slightly, and a hotel would be better.

I have written to Reggie Turner to ask him to go and stay at a hotel so that I could go to his rooms and change: I mean a quiet hotel somewhere near Euston Road. Of course if it is impossible, it is impossible. But if Reggie engages rooms I can go there and change and breakfast. Only Reggie will have to sleep at the hotel.

Of course I really will be glad to see you the morning of my release, and I know you have taken a great deal of trouble about it. So come either to the prison with Reggie or to his rooms if that is more convenient. But we must not talk about business.

Receiving no telegram about Leverson is terrible. I am utterly upset.

I think you will agree with me that I have fully carried out your advice about Leverson and been most patient with him. It seems the wrong way to treat him. I feel sure that a man of that kind should be strongly dealt with. Your method at any rate has been a terrible failure.[2]

I hear now that Dieppe has been fixed on. I am so well known there that I dislike it, and the air is relaxing, but I suppose one can move on. I am told Robbie is to be there. Very well, but you yourself would find little pleasure in my society. I feel so bitterly about so many things, that I forget many other acts of simple kindness that did me good not harm. I admit you have had endless trouble, but then you must remember I asked you through Robbie to leave my wife and myself alone: we were on terms of affection, and I was grateful to her. The rushing in to try to get more money for me was wrong. It has resulted in less money, and in a separation and the deprivation of my children, the last quite appalling.

[1] The Rev. Stewart Duckworth Headlam (1847–1924), educated at Eton and Cambridge, had been for many years a vicar in the East End of London, but his Socialism and religious unorthodoxy cost him his position in the Church. He founded the Guild of St Matthew, and the Church and Stage Guild, and was for a dozen years editor of and chief contributor to the *Church Reformer*. He was now living at 31 Upper Bedford Place, Bloomsbury. He had private means, and, although he scarcely knew Wilde, had gone bail for him in 1895 because he thought the case was being prejudged and now offered his house as temporary asylum.

[2] Wilde's accusations about Leverson's handling of his financial affairs were baseless and Wilde's turning against his friend and benefactor was simply a manifestation of the distorted obsession about money which overcame him at this time (see his own words on page 281). Leverson was not a rich man. It was not he but his wife who was Wilde's close friend, and there is no doubt that throughout he treated Wilde with the utmost fairness and generosity.

Your intentions were always good and kind: your heart was always ready to vibrate in true sympathy: but your judgment was wrong: and the worse the results the worse your advice got. It was a miracle I escaped the divorce, the exile, the entire abandonment.

However, for your real heart-actions, your unwearying good nature, and desire to help me, I thank you very deeply. In a week I hope to be in a sweeter mood and to have lost some of my present bitterness. Then let us meet and talk about literature, in which your instinct is always right, your judgment castigated and serene, your sympathies intellectual. I hope you will hand all money to Reggie. As soon as Leverson has paid let me know. I of course cannot leave England without the money, and I don't want to have to go to his house for it. Ever yours   OSCAR

PART SEVEN

BERNEVAL · 1897

Wilde left Reading on the evening of 18 May 1897. Before he left the Governor handed him the manuscript of his long letter to Douglas. Only two reporters were at the gates to see him go. Dressed in plain clothes and accompanied by two prison officers, he was driven in a cab to Twyford station, where they took the London train. They left it at Westbourne Park and travelled on by cab to Pentonville prison, where Wilde spent the night.

At 6.15 next morning he was fetched in a cab by More Adey and Stewart Headlam. They managed to avoid the press, and drove straight to Headlam's house, 31 Upper Bedford Place, Bloomsbury, where Wilde changed and breakfasted. Soon afterwards he was visited by Ernest and Ada Leverson, who recorded the scene[1]:

> He came in, and at once he put us at our ease. He came in with the dignity of a king returning from exile. He came in talking, laughing, smoking a cigarette, with waved hair and a flower in his buttonhole, and he looked markedly better, slighter, and younger than he had two years previously. His first words were, "Sphinx, how marvellous of you to know exactly the right hat to wear at seven o'clock in the morning to meet a friend who has been away! You can't have got up, you must have sat up." He talked on lightly for some time, then wrote a letter, and sent it in a cab to a Roman Catholic Retreat, asking if he might retire there for six months. . . .
>
> "Do you know one of the punishments that happen to people who have been 'away'? They are not allowed to read *The Daily Chronicle*! Coming along I begged to be allowed to read it in the train. 'No!' Then I suggested I might be allowed to read it upside down. This they consented to allow, and I read all the way *The Daily Chronicle* upside

---

[1] *Letters to the Sphinx from Oscar Wilde, with Reminiscences of the Author* by Ada Leverson (1930).

down, and never enjoyed it so much. It's really the only way to read newspapers."

The man returned with the letter. We all looked away while Oscar read it. They replied that they could not accept him in the Retreat at his impulse of the moment. It must be thought over for at least a year. In fact they refused him.

Then he broke down and sobbed bitterly.

The rest of Wilde's journey to freedom has been described by Ross:[1]

According to the arrangements he was to come over by the morning boat to Dieppe where Reggie Turner and myself had got rooms for him at the Hôtel Sandwich. Wilde talked so much and insisted on seeing so many people that he missed the train, so in the afternoon went down with Adey to Newhaven, waited till late afternoon and crossed by the night boat.

We met them at half past four in the morning, a magnificent spring morning such as Wilde anticipated in the closing words of *De Profundis*. As the steamer glided into the harbour Wilde's tall figure, dominating the other passengers, was easily recognised from the great crucifix on the jetty where we stood. That striking beacon was full of significance for us. Then we began running to the landing stage and Wilde recognised us and waved his hand and his lips curled into a smile. His face had lost all its coarseness and he looked as he must have looked at Oxford in the early days before I knew him and as he only looked again after death. A good many people, even friends, thought his appearance almost repulsive, but the upper part of his face was extraordinarily fine and intellectual.

There was the usual irritating delay and then Wilde with that odd elephantine gait which I have never seen in anyone else stalked off the boat. He was holding in his hand a large sealed envelope. "This, my dear Bobbie, is the great manuscript about which you know. More has behaved very badly about my luggage and was anxious to deprive me of the blessed bag which Reggie gave me." Then he broke into great Rabelaisian sort of laughter. The manuscript was of course *De Profundis*.

All Wilde's luggage was new and marked S.M. as he had decided to adopt the name of Sebastian Melmoth:[2] it was Turner's gift to him. He used to chaff a great deal about it and for the next few days in arguments with Turner always said "I can never forget that you gave me a bag." This does not sound very amusing and I only mention the incident as illustrating the childish spirits in which Wilde was at the moment. . . .

---

[1] In the unfinished preface to his projected collection of Wilde's letters to him, published for the first time in *Letters*.

[2] From the "Wandering Jew" hero of *Melmoth the Wanderer* (1820) by the Irish writer Charles Robert Maturin (1782–1824), who was Wilde's great-uncle. Robert Ross and More Adey had collaborated in an anonymous biographical introduction to a new edition of the novel in 1892, and Ross suggested this alias to Wilde. The Christian name Sebastian was probably in memory of the martyred saint.

During that day and for many days afterwards he talked of nothing but Reading Prison and it had already become for him a sort of enchanted castle of which Major Nelson was the presiding fairy. The hideous machicolated turrets were already turned into minarets, the very warders into benevolent Mamelukes and we ourselves into Paladins welcoming Cœur de Lion after his captivity. . . .

Telegram: To Robert Ross

19 *May 1897*   *Newhaven*

Arriving by night boat. Am so delighted at prospect of seeing you and Reggie. You must not mind the foolish unkind letters. More has been such a good friend to me and I am so grateful to you all I cannot find words to express my feelings. You must not dream of waiting up for us. In the morning we will meet. Please engage rooms for us at your hotel. When I see you I shall be quite happy, indeed I am happy now to think I have such wonderful friendship shown to me.   SEBASTIAN MELMOTH

To Ada Leverson

[20 *May 1897*]   *Hôtel Sandwich, Dieppe*

Dear Sphinx, I was so charmed with seeing you yesterday morning that I must write a line to tell you how sweet and good it was of you to be of the very first to greet me. When I think that Sphinxes are minions of the moon, and that you got up early before dawn, I am filled with wonder and joy.

I often thought of you in the long black days and nights of my prison-life, and to find you just as wonderful and dear as ever was no surprise. The beautiful are always beautiful.

This is my first day of real liberty, so I try to send you a line, and with kind regards to dear Ernest whom I was pleased to see again, ever affectionately yours   OSCAR WILDE

I am staying here as Sebastian Melmoth—not Esquire but Monsieur Sebastien Melmoth.[1] I have thought it better that Robbie should stay here under the name of Reginald Turner, and Reggie under the name of R. B. Ross. It is better that they should not have their own names.

---

[1] Wilde occasionally wrote Sebastien, but more often Sebastian.

To Frank Harris

[*Circa 20 May 1897*]   *Hôtel Sandwich, Dieppe*

My dear Frank, Just a line to thank you for your great kindness to me, for the lovely clothes, and for the generous cheque.

You have been a real good friend to me, and I shall never forget your kindness: to remember such a debt as mine to you—a debt of kind fellowship—is a pleasure.

About our tour, later on let us think about it. My friends have been so kind to me here that I am feeling happy already. Ever yours

OSCAR WILDE

If you write to me please do so under cover to R. B. Ross, who is here with me.

To Mrs Bernard Beere

[*Circa 22 May 1897*]   *Hôtel Sandwich, Dieppe*

My dear good beautiful Friend, Your letter has given me so much pleasure. I knew you would always be sweet and good to me—far more now, if that were possible, than ever, for now I need sympathy, and know its value: a kind word to me now is as lovely to me as a flower is, and love can heal all wounds.

I cannot write much for I am nervous—dazed with the wonder of the wonderful world: I feel as if I had been raised from the dead. The sun and the sea seem strange to me.

But, dear Bernie, although my life looks ruined to the outer world, to me it is not so. I know you will like to hear that somehow I feel that out of it all—out of the silence, the solitary life, the hunger, the darkness, the pain, the abandonment, the disgrace—out of these things I may get some good. I was living a life unworthy of an artist. It was wrong of me. Worse things might have happened to your old friend, dear, than two years' hard labour—terrible though they were. At least I hope to grow to feel so. Suffering is a terrible fire; it either purifies or destroys: perhaps I may be a better fellow after it all. Do write to me here—Monsieur Sebastian Melmoth is my name now to the world. With love and gratitude, ever yours

OSCAR

*To A. M. Lugné-Poe

de la part de M. Sebastien Melmoth[1]

Lundi, le 24 Mai 1897   *Hôtel Sandwich, Dieppe*

L'auteur de *Salomé* prie le Tétrarque de Judée de lui faire l'honneur de déjeuner avec lui demain matin à midi.[2]

---

[1] Many of the letters from Dieppe and Berneval (and later) are thus headed, but to save space I have not repeated the words.

[2] Lugné-Poe had played the part of Herod, Tetrarch of Judaea, in the first production of *Salome* (see note 3, p. 139).

*To the Editor of the Daily Chronicle

27 May [1897][1]   [*Dieppe*]

Sir, I learn with great regret, through the columns of your paper, that the warder Martin, of Reading Prison, has been dismissed by the Prison Commissioners for having given some sweet biscuits to a little hungry child. I saw the three children myself on the Monday preceding my release. They had just been convicted, and were standing in a row in the central hall in their prison dress, carrying their sheets under their arms previous to their being sent to the cells allotted to them. I happened to be passing along one of the galleries on my way to the reception room, where I was to have an interview with a friend. They were quite small children, the youngest—the one to whom the warder gave the biscuits—being a tiny little chap, for whom they had evidently been unable to find clothes small enough to fit. I had, of course, seen many children in prison during the two years during which I was myself confined. Wandsworth Prison especially contained always a large number of children. But the little child I saw on the afternoon of Monday the 17th, at Reading, was tinier than any one of them. I need not say how utterly distressed I was to see these children at Reading, for I knew the treatment in store for them. The cruelty that is practised by day and night on children in English prisons is incredible, except to those that have witnessed it and are aware of the brutality of the system.

People nowadays do not understand what cruelty is. They regard it as a sort of terrible mediæval passion, and connect it with the race of men like Eccelino da Romano,[2] and others, to whom the deliberate infliction of pain gave a real madness of pleasure. But men of the stamp of Eccelino are merely abnormal types of perverted individualism. Ordinary cruelty is simply stupidity. It is the entire want of imagination. It is the result in our days of stereotyped systems of hard-and-fast rules, and of stupidity. Wherever there is centralisation there is stupidity. What is inhuman in modern life is officialism. Authority is as destructive to those who exercise it as it is to those on whom it is exercised. It is the Prison Board, and the system that it carries out, that is the primary source of the cruelty that is exercised on a child in prison. The people who uphold the system have excellent intentions. Those who carry it out are humane in intention also.

---

[1] This letter was thus dated when it appeared in the *Daily Chronicle*, under the heading THE CASE OF WARDER MARTIN, SOME CRUELTIES OF PRISON LIFE, on 28 May, but it was presumably begun on or soon after the 24th, when the *Daily Chronicle* printed a letter from Warder Martin recounting the circumstances of his dismissal (see note p. 260) and added an editorial comment: "We are, of course, unable to verify our correspondent's statement, but we print his letter."

On the 28th Wilde's letter was backed up by two leading articles, and another letter from Martin, discussing the Home Secretary's denial (in reply to a question from Michael Davitt) that the facts were as Martin had stated them.

[2] Ghibelline leader (1194-1259). His cruelties earned him a place in Dante's *Inferno*.

Responsibility is shifted on to the disciplinary regulations. It is supposed that because a thing is the rule it is right.

The present treatment of children is terrible, primarily from people not understanding the peculiar psychology of a child's nature. A child can understand a punishment inflicted by an individual, such as a parent or guardian, and bear it with a certain amount of acquiescence. What it cannot understand is a punishment inflicted by society. It cannot realise what society is. With grown people it is, of course, the reverse. Those of us who are either in prison or have been sent there, can understand, and do understand, what that collective force called society means, and whatever we may think of its methods or claims, we can force ourselves to accept it. Punishment inflicted on us by an individual, on the other hand, is a thing that no grown person endures, or is expected to endure.

The child consequently, being taken away from its parents by people whom it has never seen, and of whom it knows nothing, and finding itself in a lonely and unfamiliar cell, waited on by strange faces, and ordered about and punished by the representatives of a system that it cannot understand, becomes an immediate prey to the first and most prominent emotion produced by modern prison life—the emotion of terror. The terror of a child in prison is quite limitless. I remember once in Reading, as I was going out to exercise, seeing in the dimly lit cell right opposite my own a small boy. Two warders—not unkindly men—were talking to him, with some sternness apparently, or perhaps giving him some useful advice about his conduct. One was in the cell with him, the other was standing outside. The child's face was like a white wedge of sheer terror. There was in his eyes the terror of a hunted animal. The next morning I heard him at breakfast-time crying, and calling to be let out. His cry was for his parents. From time to time I could hear the deep voice of the warder on duty telling him to keep quiet. Yet he was not even convicted of whatever little offence he had been charged with. He was simply on remand. That I knew by his wearing his own clothes, which seemed neat enough. He was, however, wearing prison socks and shoes. This showed that he was a very poor boy, whose own shoes, if he had any, were in a bad state. Justices and magistrates, an entirely ignorant class as a rule, often remand children for a week, and then perhaps remit whatever sentence they are entitled to pass. They call this "not sending a child to prison." It is, of course, a stupid view on their part. To a little child, whether he is in prison on remand or after conviction is not a subtlety of social position he can comprehend. To him the horrible thing is to be there at all. In the eyes of humanity it should be a horrible thing for him to be there at all.

This terror that seizes and dominates the child, as it seizes the grown man also, is of course intensified beyond power of expression by the solitary cellular system of our prisons. Every child is confined to its cell for twenty-three hours out of the twenty-four. This is the appalling thing. To shut up a child in a dimly lit cell, for twenty-three hours out of the twenty-four, is an example of the cruelty of stupidity. If an individual, parent or guardian, did this to a child, he would be severely punished. The Society for the Prevention of Cruelty to Children would take the matter up at once. There would be on all hands the utmost detestation of whomsoever had been guilty of such cruelty. A heavy sentence would, undoubtedly, follow conviction. But our own actual society does worse itself, and to the child to be so treated by a strange abstract force, of whose claims it has no cognisance, is much worse than it would be to receive the same treatment from its father or mother, or someone it knew. The inhuman treatment of a child is always inhuman, by whomsoever it is inflicted. But inhuman treatment by society is to the child the more terrible because there is no appeal. A parent or guardian can be moved, and let out a child from the dark lonely room in which it is confined. But a warder cannot. Most warders are very fond of children. But the system prohibits them from rendering the child any assistance. Should they do so, as Warder Martin did, they are dismissed.

The second thing from which a child suffers in prison is hunger. The food that is given to it consists of a piece of usually badly-baked prison bread and a tin of water for breakfast at half-past seven. At twelve o'clock it gets dinner, composed of a tin of coarse Indian meal stirabout, and at half-past five it gets a piece of dry bread and a tin of water for its supper. This diet in the case of a strong grown man is always productive of illness of some kind, chiefly, of course, diarrhœa, with its attendant weakness. In fact in a big prison astringent medicines are served out regularly by the warders as a matter of course. In the case of a child, the child is, as a rule, incapable of eating the food at all. Anyone who knows anything about children knows how easily a child's digestion is upset by a fit of crying, or trouble and mental distress of any kind. A child who has been crying all day long, and perhaps half the night, in a lonely dimly-lit cell, and is preyed upon by terror, simply cannot eat food of this coarse, horrible kind. In the case of the little child to whom Warder Martin gave the biscuits, the child was crying with hunger on Tuesday morning, and utterly unable to eat the bread and water served to it for its breakfast. Martin went out after the breakfasts had been served, and bought the few sweet biscuits for the child rather than see it starving. It was a beautiful action on his part, and was so recognised by the child, who, utterly unconscious of the regulation of the Prison Board, told one of the senior warders how kind this junior warder had been to him. The result was, of course, a report and a dismissal.

I know Martin extremely well, and I was under his charge for the last seven weeks of my imprisonment. On his appointment at Reading he had charge of Gallery C, in which I was confined, so I saw him constantly. I was struck by the singular kindness and humanity of the way in which he spoke to me and to the other prisoners. Kind words are much in prison, and a pleasant "Good-morning" or "Good-evening" will make one as happy as one can be in prison. He was always gentle and considerate. I happen to know another case in which he showed great kindness to one of the prisoners, and I have no hesitation in mentioning it. One of the most horrible things in prison is the badness of the sanitary arrangements. No prisoner is allowed under any circumstances to leave his cell after half-past five p.m. If, consequently, he is suffering from diarrhœa, he has to use his cell as a latrine, and pass the night in a most fetid and unwholesome atmosphere. Some days before my release Martin was going the rounds at half-past seven with one of the senior warders for the purpose of collecting the oakum and tools of the prisoners. A man just convicted, and suffering from violent diarrhœa in consequence of the food, as is always the case, asked the senior warder to allow him to empty the slops in his cell on account of the horrible odour of the cell and the possibility of illness again in the night. The senior warder refused absolutely; it was against the rules. The man had to pass the night in this dreadful condition. Martin, however, rather than see this wretched man in such a loathsome predicament, said he would empty the man's slops himself, and did so. A warder emptying a prisoner's slops is, of course, against the rules, but Martin did this act of kindness to the man out of the simple humanity of his nature, and the man was naturally most grateful.

As regards the children, a great deal has been talked and written lately about the contaminating influence of prison on young children. What is said is quite true. A child is utterly contaminated by prison life. But the contaminating influence is not that of the prisoners. It is that of the whole prison system—of the governor, the chaplain, the warders, the lonely cell, the isolation, the revolting food, the rules of the Prison Commissioners, the mode of discipline, as it is termed, of the life. Every care is taken to isolate a child from the sight even of all prisoners over sixteen years of age. Children sit behind a curtain in chapel, and are sent to take exercise in small sunless yards—sometimes a stone-yard, sometimes a yard at the back of the mills—rather than that they should see the elder prisoners at exercise. But the only really humanising influence in prison is the influence of the prisoners. Their cheerfulness under terrible circumstances, their sympathy for each other, their humility, their gentleness, their pleasant smiles of greeting when they meet each other, their complete acquiescence in their punishments, are all quite wonderful, and I myself learned many sound lessons from them. I am not proposing that the children should not sit behind a curtain in chapel, or that they should take exercise in a corner of the common yard. I am merely pointing out that the bad influence on children is not, and could never be, that of the prisoners, but is, and will always remain, that of the prison system itself. There is not a single man in Reading Gaol that would not gladly have done the three children's punishment for them. When I saw them last it was on the Tuesday following their conviction. I was taking exercise at half-past eleven with about twelve other men, as the three children passed near us, in charge of a warder, from the damp, dreary stone-yard in which they had been at their exercise. I saw the greatest pity and sympathy in the eyes of my companions as they looked at them. Prisoners are, as a class, extremely kind and sympathetic to each other. Suffering and the community of suffering makes people kind, and day after day as I tramped the yard I used to feel with pleasure and comfort what Carlyle calls somewhere "the silent rhythmic charm of human companionship."[1] In this, as in all other things, philanthropists and people of that kind are astray. It is not the prisoners who need reformation. It is the prisons.

Of course no child under fourteen years of age should be sent to prison at all. It is an absurdity, and, like many absurdities, of absolutely tragic results. If, however, they are to be sent to prison, during the daytime they should be in a workshop or schoolroom with a warder. At night they should sleep in a dormitory, with a night-warder to look after them. They should be allowed exercise for at least three hours a day. The dark, badly ventilated, ill-smelling prison cells are dreadful for a child, dreadful indeed for anyone. One is always breathing bad air in prison. The food given to children should consist of tea and bread-and-butter and soup. Prison soup is very good and wholesome. A resolution of the House of Commons could settle the treatment of children in half an hour. I hope you will use your influence to have this done. The way that children are treated at present is really an outrage on humanity and common sense. It comes from stupidity.

Let me draw attention now to another terrible thing that goes on in English prisons, indeed in prisons all over the world where the system of silence and cellular confinement is practised. I refer to the large number of men who become insane or weak-minded in prison. In convict prisons this is, of course, quite common; but in ordinary gaols also, such as that I was confined in, it is to be found.

About three months ago I noticed amongst the prisoners who took exercise with me a young man who seemed to me to be silly or half-witted. Every prison, of course, has its half-witted clients, who return again and again, and may be said to live in the prison. But this young man struck me as being more than usually half-witted on account of his silly grin and idiotic laughter to himself, and the peculiar restlessness of his eternally twitching hands. He was noticed by all the other prisoners on account of the strangeness of his conduct. From time to time he did not appear at exercise, which showed me that he was being punished by confinement to his cell. Finally, I discovered that he was under observation, and being watched night and day by warders. When he did appear at exercise he always seemed hysterical, and used to walk round crying or laughing. At chapel he had to sit right under the observation of two warders, who carefully watched him all the time. Sometimes he would bury his head in his hands, an offence against the chapel regulations, and his head would be immediately struck by a warder so that he should keep his eyes fixed permanently in the direction of the Communion-table. Sometimes he would cry—not making any disturbance—but with tears streaming down his face and an hysterical throbbing in the throat. Sometimes he would grin idiot-like to himself and make faces. He was on more than one occasion sent out of chapel to his cell, and of course he was continually punished. As the bench on which I used to sit in chapel was directly behind the bench at the end of which this unfortunate man was placed I had full

---

[1] "Shooting Niagara: and After?" (1867), Section IX.

opportunity of observing him. I also saw him, of course, at exercise continually, and I saw that he was becoming insane, and was being treated as if he was shamming.

On Saturday week last I was in my cell at about one o'clock occupied in cleaning and polishing the tins I had been using for dinner. Suddenly I was startled by the prison silence being broken by the most horrible and revolting shrieks, or rather howls, for at first I thought some animal like a bull or a cow was being unskilfully slaughtered outside the prison walls. I soon realised, however, that the howls proceeded from the basement of the prison, and I knew that some wretched man was being flogged. I need not say how hideous and terrible it was for me, and I began to wonder who it was who was being punished in this revolting manner. Suddenly it dawned upon me that they might be flogging this unfortunate lunatic. My feelings on the subject need not be chronicled; they have nothing to do with the question.

The next day, Sunday 16th, I saw the poor fellow at exercise, his weak, ugly, wretched face bloated by tears and hysteria almost beyond recognition. He walked in the centre ring along with the old men, the beggars, and the lame people, so that I was able to observe him the whole time. It was my last Sunday in prison, a perfectly lovely day, the finest day we had had the whole year, and there, in the beautiful sunlight, walked this poor creature—made once in the image of God—grinning like an ape, and making with his hands the most fantastic gestures, as though he was playing in the air on some invisible stringed instrument, or arranging and dealing counters in some curious game. All the while these hysterical tears, without which none of us ever saw him, were making soiled runnels on his white swollen face. The hideous and deliberate grace of his gestures made him like an antic. He was a living grotesque. The other prisoners all watched him, and not one of them smiled. Everybody knew what had happened to him, and that he was being driven insane—was insane already. After half an hour he was ordered in by the warder, and I suppose punished. At least he was not at exercise on Monday, though I think I caught sight of him at the corner of the stone-yard, walking in charge of a warder.

On the Tuesday—my last day in prison—I saw him at exercise. He was worse than before, and again was sent in. Since then I know nothing of him, but I found out from one of the prisoners who walked with me at exercise that he had had twenty-four lashes in the cookhouse on Saturday afternoon, by order of the visiting justices on the report of the doctor. The howls that had horrified us all were his.

This man is undoubtedly becoming insane. Prison doctors have no knowledge of mental disease of any kind. They are as a class ignorant men. The pathology of the mind is unknown to them. When a man grows insane, they treat him as shamming. They have him punished again and again. Naturally the man becomes worse. When ordinary punishments are exhausted, the doctor reports the case to the justices. The result is flogging. Of course the flogging is not done with a cat-of-nine-tails. It is what is called birching. The instrument is a rod; but the result on the wretched half-witted man may be imagined.

His number is, or was, A.2.11. I also managed to find out his name. It is Prince. Something should be done at once for him. He is a soldier, and his sentence is one of court-martial. The term is six months. Three have yet to run. May I ask you to use your influence to have this case examined into, and to see that the lunatic prisoner is properly treated?[1]

No report of the Medical Commissioners is of any avail. It is not to be trusted. The medical inspectors do not seem to understand the difference between idiocy and lunacy—between the entire absence of a function or organ and the diseases of a function or organ. This man A.2.11 will, I have no doubt, be able to tell his name, the nature of his offence, the day of the month, the date of the beginning and expiration of his sentence, and answer any ordinary simple question; but that his mind is diseased admits of no doubt. At present it is a horrible duel between himself and the doctor. The doctor is fighting for a theory. The man is fighting for his life. I am anxious that the man should win. But let the whole case be examined into by experts who understand brain-disease, and by people of humane feelings who have still some common sense and some pity. There is no reason that the sentimentalist should be asked to interfere. He always does harm.

The case is a special instance of the cruelty inseparable from a stupid system, for the present Governor of Reading is a man of gentle and humane character, greatly liked and respected by all the prisoners. He was appointed in July last, and though he cannot alter the rules of the prison system he has altered the spirit in which they used to be carried out under his predecessor. He is very popular with the prisoners and with the warders. Indeed he has quite altered the whole tone of the prison life. Upon the other hand, the system is of course beyond his reach so far as altering its rules is concerned. I have no doubt that he sees daily much of what he knows to be unjust, stupid, and cruel. But his hands are tied. Of course I have no knowledge of his real views of the case of A.2.11, nor, indeed, of his views on our present system. I merely judge him by the complete change he brought about in Reading Prison. Under his predecessor the system was carried out with the greatest harshness and stupidity.

I remain, sir, your obedient servant   OSCAR WILDE

To Reginald Turner

[*Postmark 27 May 1897*]   *Hôtel de la Plage, Berneval-sur-Mer,*
Dieppe

My dear Reggie, Thank you so much for the charming books: the poems are wonderfully fresh and buoyant: the guide-book to Berkshire is very lax in style, and it is difficult to realise that it is constructed on any metrical

---

[1] For earlier reference to Prince, see note p. 260.

system. The matter, however, is interesting, and the whole book no doubt symbolic.

This is my first day here. Robbie and I arrived last night. The dinner was excellent,and we tried to eat enough for eight as we occupy so many rooms. However we soon got tired. Only the imagination of man is limitless. The appetite seems curiously bounded. This is one of the many lessons I have learnt.

I have just read Max's *Happy Hypocrite*,[1] beginning at the end, as one should always do. It is quite wonderful, and to one who was once the author of *Dorian Gray*, full of no vulgar surprises of style or incident.

The population came at dawn to look at my dressing-case. I showed it to them, piece of silver by piece of silver. Some of the old men wept for joy. Robbie detected me at Dieppe in the market place of the sellers of perfumes, spending all my money on orris-root and the tears of the narcissus and the dust of red roses. He was very stern and led me away. I have already spent my entire income for two years. I see now that this lovely dressing-case with its silver vials thirsty for distilled odours will gradually lead me to the perfection of poverty. But it seemed to me to be cruel not to fill with rose-petals the little caskets shaped so cunningly in the form of a rose.

Dear Reggie, it was a great delight seeing you, and I shall never forget your kindness or the beauty of your friendship. I hope before the summer ends to see you again. Do write to me from time to time, and remember me to the Sphinx, and all those who do not know her secret. I know it of course. The open secret of the Sphinx is Ernest. Ever yours

OSCAR WILDE

To Max Beerbohm

[*Circa 28 May 1897*]   *Hôtel de la Plage, Berneval-sur-Mer*

My dear Max, I cannot tell you what a real pleasure it was to me to find your delightful present waiting for me on my release from prison, and to receive the charming and sweet messages you sent me. I used to think gratitude a heavy burden for one to carry. Now I know that it is something that makes the heart lighter. The ungrateful man seems to me to be one who walks with feet and heart of lead. But when one has learnt, however inadequately, what a lovely thing gratitude is, one's feet go lightly over sand or sea, and one finds a strange joy revealed to one, the joy of counting up, not what one possesses, but what one owes. I hoard my debts now in the treasury of my heart, and, piece of gold by piece of gold, I range them in order at dawn and at evening. So you must not mind my saying that I am grateful to you. It is simply one of certain new pleasures that I have discovered.

The Happy Hypocrite is a wonderful and beautiful story, though I do not like the cynical directness of the name. The name one gives to one's work,

[1] First published by John Lane in 1896. See note 2, p. 247.

poem or picture—and all works of art are either poems or pictures, and the best both at once—is the last survival of the Greek Chorus. It is the only part of one's work in which the artist speaks directly in his own person, and I don't like you wilfully taking the name given by the common spectators, though I know what a joy there is in picking up a brickbat and wearing it as a buttonhole. It is the origin of the name of all schools of art. Not to like anything you have done is such a new experience to me that, not even for a silver dressing-case full of objects of exquisite inutility such as dear Reggie in his practical thoughtfulness provided for me on my release, shall I surrender my views. But in years to come, when you are a very young man, you will remember what I have said, and recognise its truth, and, in the final edition of the work, leave the title unchanged. Of that I feel certain. The gift of prophecy is given to all who do not know what is going to happen to themselves.

The implied and accepted recognition of *Dorian Gray* in the story cheers me. I had always been disappointed that my story had suggested no other work of art in others. For whenever a beautiful flower grows in a meadow or lawn, some other flower, so like it that it is differently beautiful, is sure to grow up beside it, all flowers and all works of art having a curious sympathy for each other. I feel also on reading your surprising and to me quite novel story how useless it is for gaolers to deprive an artist of pen and ink. One's work goes on just the same, with entrancing variations.

In case you should feel anxious about me, let me assure you frankly that the difference in colour between the two sheets of paper that compose this letter is the result not of poverty, but of extravagance. Do send me a line, to my new name. Sincerely yours   OSCAR WILDE

To Robert Ross

[*28 May 1897*]   *Hôtel de la Plage, Berneval-sur-Mer*

My dear Robbie, This is my first day alone, and of course a very unhappy one. I begin to realise my terrible position of isolation, and I have been rebellious and bitter of heart all day. Is it not sad? I thought I was accepting everything so well and so simply, and I have had moods of rage passing over my nature, like gusts of bitter wind or storm spoiling the sweet corn, or blasting the young shoots. I found a little chapel, full of the most fantastic saints, so ugly and Gothic, and painted quite gaudily—some of them with smiles carved to a *rictus* almost, like primitive things—but they all seemed to me to be idols. I laughed with amusement when I saw them. Fortunately there was a lovely crucifix in a side-chapel—not a Jansenist one, but with wide-stretched arms of gold. I was pleased at that, and wandered then by the cliffs where I fell asleep on the warm coarse brown sea-grass. I had hardly any sleep last night. Bosie's revolting letter was in the room, and foolishly I had read it again and left it by my bedside. My dream was that my mother was speaking to me with some sternness,

277

and that she was in trouble. I quite see that whenever I am in danger she will in some way warn me. I have a real terror now of that unfortunate ungrateful young man with his unimaginative selfishness and his entire lack of all sensitiveness to what in others is good or kind or trying to be so. I feel him as an evil influence, poor fellow. To be with him would be to return to the hell from which I do think I have been released. I hope never to see him again.

For yourself, dear sweet Robbie, I am haunted by the idea that many of those who love you will and do think it selfish of me to allow you and wish you to be with me from time to time. But still they might see the difference between your going about with me in my days of gilded infamy—my Neronian hours, rich, profligate, cynical, materialistic—and your coming to comfort me, a lonely dishonoured man, in disgrace and obscurity and poverty. How lacking in imagination they are! If I were rich again and sought to repeat my former life I don't think you would care very much to be with me. I think you would regret what I was doing, but now, dear boy, you come with the heart of Christ, and you help me intellectually as no one else can or ever could do. You are helping me to save my soul alive, not in the theological sense, but in the plain meaning of the words, for my soul was really dead in the slough of coarse pleasures, my life was unworthy of an artist: you can heal me and help me. No other friend have I now in this beautiful world. I want no other. Yet I am distressed to think that I will be looked on as careless of your own welfare, and indifferent of your good. You are made to help me. I weep with sorrow when I think how much I need help, but I weep with joy when I think I have you to give it to me.

I do hope to do some work in these six weeks, that when you come I shall be able to read you something. I know you love me, but I want to have your respect, your sincere admiration, or rather, for that is a word of ill-omen, your sincere appreciation of my effort to recreate my artistic life. But if I have to think that I am harming you, all pleasure in your society will be tainted for me. With you at any rate I want to be free of any sense of guilt, the sense of spoiling another's life. Dear boy, I couldn't spoil your life by accepting the sweet companionship you offer me from time to time. It is not for nothing that I named you in prison St Robert of Phillimore.[1] Love can canonise people. The saints are those who have been most loved.

[1] In *Letters to the Sphinx* Ada Leverson recorded Wilde's improvisation of this fable:
Saint Robert of Phillimore
There was a certain Saint, who was called Saint Robert of Phillimore. Every night, while the sky was yet black, he would rise from his bed and, falling on his knees, pray to God that He, of His great bounty, would cause the sun to rise and make bright the earth. And always, when the sun rose, Saint Robert knelt again and thanked God that this miracle had been vouchsafed. Now, one night, Saint Robert, wearied by the vast number of more than usually good deeds that he had done that day, slept so soundly that when he awoke the sun had already risen, and the earth was already bright. For a few moments Saint Robert looked grave and troubled, but presently he fell down on his knees and thanked God that, despite

I only made one mistake in prison in things that I wrote of you or to you in my book. My poem should have run, "When I came out of prison *you* met me with garments, with spices, with wise counsel. You met me with love."[1] Not others did it, but you. I really laugh when I think how true in detail the lines are.

8.30. I have just received your telegram.[2] A man bearded, no doubt for purposes of disguise, dashed up on a bicycle, brandishing a blue telegram. I knew it was from you. Well, I am really pleased, and look forward to the paper. I do think it will help. I now think I shall write my prison article for the *Chronicle*. It is interested in prison-reform, and the thing would not look an advertisement.

Let me know your opinion. I intend to write to Massingham.[3] Reading between the lines of your telegram I seem to discern that you are pleased. The telegram was much needed. They had offered me serpent for dinner! A serpent cut up, in an umber-green sauce! I explained that I was not a *mangeur de serpents*[4] and have converted the *patron*. No serpent is now to be served to any guest. He grew quite hot over it. What a good thing it is that I am an experienced ichthyologist!

I enclose a lot of letters. Please put money orders in them and send them off. Put those addressed to the prison in a larger envelope, each of them, addressed by yourself, if possible legibly. They are my debts of honour, and I must pay them. Of course you must read the letters. Explain to Miss Meredith[5] that letters addressed C.3.3,[6] 24 Hornton Street are for you. The money is as follows. Of course it is a great deal but I thought I would have lots:

Jackson	£1.		
Fleet	£1. 10.		
Ford	£2. 10		
Stone	£3.		
× Eaton	£2.	The letters must go *at once*.	
× Cruttenden	£2.	At least those marked ×	
Bushell	£2. 10.		

the neglectfulness of His servant, He had yet caused the sun to rise and make bright the earth.

[1] Wilde's words ran:
> When I came out of prison some met me with garments
> and spices and others with wise counsel.
> You met me with love.

They were later intended as a second dedication to *The Ballad of Reading Gaol*, but were removed at the proof stage (see note 3, p. 317).

[2] Announcing the *Daily Chronicle* publication of Wilde's letter of 27 May.

[3] Henry William Massingham (1860–1924) was editor of the *Daily Chronicle* (1895–99) and of the *Nation* (1907–23).

[4] Like the lesser breeds without the city walls of Carthage in Flaubert's *Salammbô*, ch. iv.

[5] More Adey's housekeeper at 24 Hornton Street.

[6] Wilde's number in Reading Gaol, indicating the third cell on the third floor of Block C.

× Millward	£2	10.
Groves[1]	£3.	10.
	£20.	10.
W. Smith	£2.	

How it mounts up! But now I have merely Jim Cuthbert December 2, Jim Huggins October 9, and Harry Elvin November 6. They can keep. On second thoughts I have sent only one to the prison. Please be careful not to mix the letters. They are all *nuanced*.

I want some pens, and some red ties. The latter for literary purposes of course.

I wrote to Courtenay Thorpe[2] this morning: also to Mrs Stannard and sent her flowers.[3]

More forwards me a poem from Bosie—a love-lyric! It is absurd.

Tardieu[4] has written mysteriously warning me of dangerous friends in Paris. I hate mystery: it is so obvious.

Keep Romeike on the war-trail.

The *Figaro* announced me bicycling at Dieppe! They always confuse you and me. It really is delightful. I will make no protest. You are the best half of me.

I am very tired, and the rain is coming down. You will be glad to hear that I have not been planting *cacao* in plantain swamps, and that "Lloyd" is not now sitting on the verandah, nor is "Fanny" looking after the "labour-boys," and that of "Belle" I know nothing.[5] So now, dear Colvin (what an awful pen!) I mean dear Robbie, good night.

With all love and affection, yours   OSCAR

*To an Unidentified Correspondent

[*Circa 28 May 1897*]   c/o *Stoker and Hansell, 14 Gray's Inn Square,*
                                                        [*Berneval-sur-Mer*]

My dear Friend, I send you a line to show you that I haven't forgotten

---

[1] A warder at Reading.

[2] English actor (1854–1927). Played much Ibsen.

[3] Henrietta Eliza Vaughan Palmer (1856–1911) married Arthur Stannard in 1884. She was a prolific and popular novelist under the pseudonym John Strange Winter. Her novel *Bootle's Baby* (1885) sold in enormous numbers. Ruskin referred to her as "the author to whom we owe the most finished and faithful rendering ever yet given of the character of the British soldier." She was first President of the Writers Club (1892) and gave as her recreations "the study of hair and skin culture." At this time she and her husband were living in Dieppe.

[4] Eugène Tardieu (1851–1920) was responsible for the French translation of *The Picture of Dorian Gray* (1895), and also for prose translations of Lord Alfred Douglas's poems in Douglas's first book *Poems* (1896).

[5] A parody of Robert Louis Stevenson's *Vailima Letters* to Sidney Colvin. (See also pp. 246 and 285). The references are to Stevenson's step-son, wife and step-daughter.

you. We were old friends in gallery C.3, were we not? I hope you are getting on well and in employment.

Don't, like a good little chap, get into trouble again. You would get a terrible sentence. I send you £2 just for luck. I am quite poor myself now, but I know you will accept it just as a remembrance. There is also 10/- which I wish you would give to a little dark-eyed chap who had a month in, I think, C.4.14. He was in from February 6th to March 6th— a little chap from Wantage, I think, and a jolly little fellow. We were great friends. If you know him give it to him from C.3.3.

I am in France by the sea, and I suppose I am getting happy again. I hope so. It was a bad time for me, but there were many good fellows in Reading. Send me a line c/o my solicitors to my own name. Your friend

C.3.3

To Major J. O. Nelson [1]

[28 May 1897]   Hôtel de la Plage, Berneval-sur-Mer

Dear Major Nelson, I had of course intended to write to you as soon as I had safely reached French soil, to express, however inadequately, my real feelings of what you must let me term, not merely sincere, but *affectionate* gratitude to you for your kindness and gentleness to me in prison, and for the real care that you took of me at the end, when I was mentally upset and in a state of very terrible nervous excitement. You must not mind my using the word "gratitude." I used to think gratitude a burden to carry. Now I know that it is something that makes the heart lighter. The un-grateful man is one who walks slowly with feet and heart of lead. But when one knows the strange joy of gratitude to God and man the earth becomes lovelier to one, and it is a pleasure to count up, not one's wealth but one's debts, not the little that one possesses, but the much that one owes.

I abstained from writing, however, because I was haunted by the memory of the little children, and the wretched half-witted lad who was flogged by the doctor's orders. I could not have kept them out of my letter, and to have mentioned them to you might have put *you* in a difficult position. In your reply you *might* have expressed sympathy with my views —I think you would have—and then on the appearance of my public letter you might have felt as if I had, in some almost ungenerous or thought-less way, procured your private opinion on official things, for use as corroboration.

I longed to speak to you about these things on the evening of my depar-ture, but I felt that in my position as a prisoner it would have been wrong of me to do so, and that it would or might have put you in a difficult position afterwards, as well as at the time. I only hear of my letter being published by a telegram from Mr Ross, but I hope they have printed it in

---

[1] The Governor of Reading Prison. See note p. 217.

full, as I tried to express in it my appreciation and admiration of your own humane spirit and affectionate interest in *all* the prisoners under your charge. I did not wish people to think that any exception had been specially made for me. Such exceptional treatment as I received was by order of the Commissioners. You gave me the same kindness as you gave to everyone. Of course I made more demands, but then I think I had really more needs than others, and I lacked often their cheerful acquiescence.

Of course I side with the prisoners: I was one, and I belong to their class now. I am not a scrap ashamed of having been in prison. I am horribly ashamed of the materialism of the life that brought me there. It was quite unworthy of an artist.

Of Martin, and the subjects of my letter, I of course say nothing at all, except that the **man** who could change the system—if any one man can do so—is yourself. At present I write to ask you to allow me to sign myself, once at any rate in life, your sincere and grateful friend

OSCAR WILDE

To Robert Ross

[*29-30 May 1897*] *Hôtel de la Plage, Berneval-sur-Mer*

My dear Robbie, Your letter is quite admirable, but, dear boy, don't you see how right *I* was to write to the *Chronicle*? All good impulses are right. Had I listened to some of my friends I would never have written.

I am sending a postscript to Massingham—of some importance: if he publishes it, send it to me.

I have also asked him if he wishes my prison experiences, and if he would share in a syndicate. I think now, as the length of my letter is so great, that I could do *three* articles on Prison Life. Of course much will be psychological and introspective: and one will be on Christ as the Precursor of the Romantic Movement in Life, that lovely subject which was revealed to me when I found myself in the company of the same sort of people Christ liked, outcasts and beggars.[1]

I am terrified about Bosie. More writes to me that he has been practically interviewed about me! It is awful. More, desiring to spare me pain, I suppose, did not send me the paper, so I have had a wretched night.

Bosie can almost ruin me. I earnestly beg that some entreaty be made to him not to do so a second time. His letters to me are infamous.

I have heard from my wife. She sends me photographs of the boys— such lovely little fellows in Eton collars—but makes no promise to allow me to see them: she says *she* will see me, twice a year, but I want my boys.[2]

[1] The only further prose writing of Wilde's about his prison experiences was a second letter to the *Daily Chronicle* in March 1898 (see p. 334).

[2] On 24 May Constance Wilde wrote from Italy to her brother: "O has written me a letter full of penitence and I have answered it," and on 5 August: "Oscar wanted me to bring the boys to Dieppe, and then wanted to come to me, but I think Mr Blacker has persuaded him to wait and come to me at Nervi when I am settled." For Carlos Blacker see note 1, p. 302.

It is a terrible punishment, dear Robbie, and oh! how well I deserve it. But it makes me feel disgraced and evil, and I don't want to feel that. Let me have the *Chronicle* regularly. Also write often. It is very good for me to be alone. I am working. Dear Robbie, ever yours   OSCAR

To Robert Ross

Monday Night, 31 May [1897]   [*Hôtel de la Plage, Berneval-sur-Mer*]

My dearest Robbie, I have decided that the only way in which to get boots properly is to go to France to receive them. The *douane* charged three francs! How could you frighten me as you did? The next time you order boots please come to Dieppe to get them sent to you. It is the only way, and it will be an excuse for seeing me.

I am going tomorrow on a pilgrimage. I always wanted to be a pilgrim, and I have decided to start early tomorrow to the shrine of Notre Dame de Liesse. Do you know what Liesse is? It is an old word for joy. I suppose the same as Letizia, *laetitia*. I just heard of the shrine, or chapel, tonight, *by chance*, as you would say, from the sweet woman of the *auberge*, a perfect dear, who wants me to live always at Berneval! She says Notre Dame de Liesse is wonderful, and helps everyone to the secret of joy. I do not know how long it will take me to get to the shrine, as I must walk. But, from what she tells me, it will take at least six or seven minutes to get there, and as many to come back. In fact the chapel of Notre Dame de Liesse is just fifty yards from the hotel! Isn't it extraordinary? I intend to start after I have had my coffee, and then to bathe. Need I say that this is a miracle? I wanted to go on a pilgrimage, and I find the little grey stone chapel of Our Lady of Joy is brought to me. It has probably been waiting for me all these purple years of pleasure, and now it comes to meet me with Liesse as its message. I simply don't know what to say. I wish you were not so hard to poor heretics,[1] and would admit that even for the sheep who has no shepherd there is a Stella Maris to guide it home. But you and More, especially More, treat me as a Dissenter. It is very painful, and quite unjust.

Yesterday I attended Mass at ten o'clock and afterwards bathed. So I went into the water without being a Pagan. The consequence was that I was *not* tempted by either Sirens, or Mermaidens, or any of the green-haired following of Glaucus. I really think that this is a remarkable thing. In my pagan days the sea was always full of tritons blowing conches, and other unpleasant things. Now it is quite different. And yet you treat me as the President of Mansfield College: and after I had canonised you, too![2]

Dear boy, I wish you would tell me if your religion makes you happy. You conceal your religion from me in a monstrous way. You treat it like

---

[1] Ross and Adey were both Roman Catholics.

[2] Mansfield is a Congregationalist college at Oxford, established in 1889. For the canonisation of Ross, see note p. 278.

writing in the *Saturday Review* for Pollock,[1] or dining in Wardour Street off the fascinating dish that is served with tomatoes and makes men mad. I know it is useless asking you. So don't tell me.

I felt an outcast in chapel yesterday—not really, but a little in exile. I met a dear farmer in a cornfield, and he gave me a seat in his *banc* in church: so I was quite comfortable. He now visits me twice a day, and as he has no children, and is rich, I have made him promise to adopt *three*— two boys and a girl. I told him that if he wanted them, he would find them. He said he was afraid that they would turn out badly. I told him everyone did that. He really has promised to adopt three orphans! He is now filled with enthusiasm at the idea. He is to go to the *curé* and talk to him. He told me that his own father had fallen down in a fit one day as they were talking together, and that he had caught him in his arms, and put him to bed, where he died, and that he himself had often thought how dreadful it was that if he had a fit there was no one to catch him in his arms. It is quite clear that he must adopt orphans, is it not?

I feel that Berneval is to be my home. I really do. Notre Dame de Liesse will be sweet to me, if I go on my knees to her, and she will advise me. It is extraordinary being brought here by a white horse that was a native of the place, and knew the road, and wanted to see its parents, now of advanced years. It is also extraordinary that I knew Berneval existed, and was arranged for me.

M. Bonnet wants to build me a chalet![2] 1,000 metres of ground (I don't know how much that is, but I suppose about 100 miles) and a chalet with a studio, a balcony, a *salle-à-manger*, a huge kitchen, and three bedrooms, a view of the sea, and trees—all for 12,000 francs, £480. If I can write a play I am going to have it begun. Fancy one's own lovely house and grounds in France for £480! No rent of any kind. Pray consider this, and approve, if you think right. Of course not till I have done my play.

An old gentleman lives here in the hotel. He dines alone in his rooms, and then sits in the sun. He came here for two days, and has stayed two years. His sole sorrow is that there is no theatre. Monsieur Bonnet is a little heartless about this, and says that as the old gentleman goes to bed at eight o'clock, a theatre would be of no use to him. The old gentleman says he only goes to bed at eight o'clock because there is no theatre. They argued the point yesterday for an hour. I side with the old gentleman, but Logic sides with Monsieur Bonnet, I believe.

I had a sweet letter from the Sphinx. She gives me a delightful account of Ernest subscribing to Romeike while his divorce suit was running, and not being pleased with some of the notices.[3] Considering the growing appreciation of Ibsen I must say that I am surprised the notices were not

[1] Walter Herries Pollock (1850–1928), poet, author and journalist, was editor of the *Saturday Review* 1883–94.

[2] O. J. Bonnet was the *patron* of the Hôtel de la Plage, and also the local estate agent.

[3] Ernest Leverson had recently been cited as co-respondent in a divorce case. On the evening of the trial Ada Leverson, to show her loyalty, sat with him in the front of a box at a fashionable theatre.

better, but nowadays everybody is jealous of everyone else, except, of course, husband and wife. I think I shall keep this last remark of mine for my play.

Have you got back my silver spoon from Reggie?[1] You got my silver brushes out of Humphreys, who is bald, so you might easily get my spoon out of Reggie, who has so many, or used to have. You know my crest is on it. It is a bit of Irish silver, and I don't want to lose it. There is an excellent substitute called Britannia metal, very much liked at the Adelphi and elsewhere. Wilson Barrett writes, "I prefer it to silver." It would suit dear Reggie admirably. Walter Besant[2] writes, "I use none other." Mr Beerbohm Tree also writes, "Since I have tried it I am a different actor. My friends hardly recognise me." So there is obviously a demand for it.

I am going to write a Political Economy in my heavier moments. The first law I lay down is "Wherever there exists a demand, there is *no* supply." This is the only law that explains the extraordinary contrast between the soul of man, and man's surroundings. Civilizations continue because people hate them. A modern city is the exact opposite of what everyone wants. Nineteenth-century dress is the result of our horror of the style. The tall hat will last as long as people dislike it.

Dear Robbie, I wish you would be a little more considerate, and not keep me up so late talking to you. It is very flattering to me and all that, but you should remember that I need rest. Goodnight. You will find some cigarettes and some flowers by your bedside. Coffee is served *below* at eight o'clock. Do you mind? If it is too early for you, I don't at all mind lying in bed an extra hour. I hope you will sleep well. You should, as Lloyd is *not* on the verandah.[3]

Tuesday morning [1 June 1897]. 9.30.

The sea and sky one opal, no horrid drawing-master's line between them, just one fishing boat, going slowly, and drawing the wind after it. I am going to bathe.

Six o'clock

Bathed and have seen a chalet here, which I wish to take for the season —quite charming: a splendid view: a large writing-room; a dining-room, and three lovely bedrooms, besides servant's room, also a huge balcony.

I don't know the *scale* of my drawing. But the rooms are *larger* than the plan is.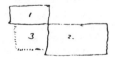

---

[1] Turner had told Ross the following two lines of dialogue he had invented: "He was born with a silver spoon in his mouth." "Yes! but there was someone else's crest on it." Ross had passed them on to Wilde who said he would like to use them in his next play.

[2] Popular novelist (1836–1901).

[3] See note 5, p. 280.

1. *Salle-à-manger*	All on ground floor, with steps
2. *Salon*	from balcony to ground.
3. Balcony	

The rent for the season or year is what do you think—*£32*. Of course I must have it: I will take my meals here, separate and reserved table: it is within two minutes' walk. Do tell me to take it: when you come again your room will be waiting for you. All I need is a *domestique*. The people here are most kind.

I made my pilgrimage. The interior of the chapel is of course a modern horror, but there is a black image of Notre Dame de Liesse. The chapel is as tiny as an undergraduate's room at Oxford. I hope to get the *curé* to celebrate Mass in it soon. As a rule the service is only held there in July–August: but I want to see a Mass quite close.

There is also another thing I must write to you about.

I adore this place. The whole country is lovely, and full of forest and deep meadow. It is simple and healthy. If I live in Paris I may be doomed to things I don't desire. I am afraid of big towns. Here I get up at 7.30. I am happy all day. I go to bed at ten o'clock. I am frightened of Paris. I want to live here.

I have seen the terrain. It is the best here, and the only one left. I must build a house. If I could build a chalet for 12,000 francs—*£500*, and live in a home of my own, how happy I would be. I must raise the money somehow. It would give me a home, quiet, retired, healthy, and near England. If I lived in Egypt I know what my life would be. If I lived in the South of Italy I know I should be idle, and worse. I want to live here. Do think over this, and send me over the architect.[1] Monsieur Bonnet is excellent, and is ready to carry out my ideas. I want a little chalet of wood and plastered walls, the wooden beams showing, and the white squares of plaster diapering the framework, like, I regret to say, Shakespeare's house: like old English sixteenth-century farmers' houses. So your architect has me waiting for him, as he is waiting for me.

Do you think this idea absurd?

I got the *Chronicle*: many thanks. I see the writer on Prince—A.2.11— does not mention my name; foolish of her; it is a woman.[2]

I, as you, the poem of my days, are away, am forced to write poetry. I have begun something that I think will be very good.[3]

I breakfast tomorrow with the Stannards: what a great passionate

[1] John Rowland Fothergill (1876–1957) had studied at the Slade and was a friend of Ross, Rothenstein and other artists. At this time he was a student at the London School of Architecture, and his copy of *The Ballad of Reading Gaol* is inscribed "To Rowland Fothergill, the Architect of the Moon, with the compliments of the author O.W." He later spent twelve years as an archaeologist, helping his American friend Edward Perry Warren (1864–1928) to form the collection of classical antiquities in the Boston Museum of Fine Arts, and finally achieved fame as an innkeeper in England.

[2] On 31 May the *Daily Chronicle* printed a letter on Prince by E. Livingston Prescott, the pen-name of Edith Katharine Spicer-Jay, novelist (d. 1901).

[3] *The Ballad of Reading Gaol.*

splendid writer John Strange Winter is! How little people understand her work! *Bootle's Baby* is *une œuvre symboliste*: it is really only the style and the subject that are wrong. Pray never speak lightly of *Bootle's Baby*—indeed, pray never speak of it at all; I never do. Ever yours

OSCAR

Please send a *Chronicle* to my wife, Mrs C. M. Holland, Maison Benguerel, Bevaix, près de Neuchâtel, just marking it, and if my second letter appears, mark that. Also one to Mrs Arthur Stannard, 28 Rue de la Halle-au-Blé, Dieppe. Also, cut out the letter and enclose it in an envelope to Mr Arthur Cruttenden, Poste Restante, G.P.O. Reading, with just these lines:

> Dear Friend, The enclosed will interest you. There is also another letter waiting in the Post Office for you from me, with a little money. Ask for it, if you have not got it. Yours sincerely   C.3.3

I have no one but you, dear Robbie, to do anything. Of course the letter to Reading must go *at once*, as my friends come out on *Wednesday* morning early.

To Lord Alfred Douglas

[? *2 June 1897*]   *Hôtel de la Plage, Berneval-sur-Mer*

My dear Boy, If you *will* send me back beautiful letters, with bitter ones of your own, of course you will never remember my address. It is as above.

Of Lugné-Poe, of course, I know nothing except that he is singularly handsome, and seems to me to have the personality of a good actor, for personality does not require intellect to help it: it is a dynamic force of its own, and is often as superbly unintelligent as the great forces of nature, like the lightning that shook at sudden moments last night over the sea that slept before my window.

The production of *Salome* was the thing that turned the scale in my favour, as far as my treatment in prison by the Government was concerned, and I am deeply grateful to all concerned in it. Upon the other hand I could not give my next play for nothing, as I simply do not know how I shall live after the summer is over unless I at once make money. I am in a terrible and dangerous position, for money that I had been assured was set aside for me was not forthcoming when I wanted it. It was a horrible disappointment: for I have of course begun to live as a man of letters should live—that is with a private sitting-room and books and the like. I can see no other way of living, if I am to write, though I can see many others, if I am not.

If then Lugné-Poe can give me no money, of course I shall not consider myself bound to him. But the play in question—being religious in surroundings and treatment of subject[1]—is not a play for a *run*, at all. Three performances are the most I think I could expect. All I want is to have

[1] Perhaps *Ahab and Isabel* or *Pharaoh*, plays discussed at this period but never written.

my artistic reappearance, and my own rehabilitation through art, in *Paris*, not in London. It is a homage and a debt I owe to that great city of art.

If anyone else with money would take the play, and let Lugné-Poe play the part, I would be more than content. In any case I am not bound, and, what is of more import, the play is not written! I am still trying to finish my necessary correspondence, and to express suitably my deep gratitude to all who have been kind to me.

As regards *Le Journal*, I would be charmed to write for it, and will try and get it regularly. I do not like to *abonner* myself at the office as I am anxious that my address should not be known. I think I had better do it at Dieppe, from where I get the *Echo de Paris*.

I hear the *Jour* has had a sort of interview—a false one—with you.[1] This is very distressing: as much, I don't doubt, to you as to me. I hope however that it is not the cause of the duel you hint at. Once you get to fight duels in France, you have to be *always* doing it, and it is a nuisance. I do hope that you will always shelter yourself under the accepted right of any English gentleman to decline a duel, unless of course some personal fracas or public insult takes place. Of course you will never dream of fighting a duel for *me*: that would be awful, and create the worst and most odious impression.

Always write to me about your art and the art of others. It is better to meet on the double peak of Parnassus than elsewhere. I have read your poems with great pleasure and interest:[2] but on the whole your best work is to me still the work you did two years and a half ago—the ballads, and bits of the play. Of course your own personality has had for many reasons to express itself *directly* since then, but I hope you will go on to forms more remote from actual events and passions. One can really, as I say in *Intentions*, be far more subjective in an *objective* form than in any other way.[3] If I were asked of myself as a dramatist, I would say that my unique position was that I had taken the Drama, the most objective form known to art, and made it as personal a mode of expression as the Lyric or the Sonnet, while enriching the characterisation of the stage, and enlarging— at any rate in the case of *Salome*—its artistic horizon. You have real sympathy with the Ballad. Pray again return to it. The Ballad is the true origin of the romantic Drama, and the true predecessors of Shakespeare are not the tragic writers of the Greek or Latin stage, from Aeschylus to Seneca, but the ballad-writers of the Border. In such a ballad as *Gilderoy* one has the prefiguring note of the romance of *Romeo and Juliet*, different though the plots are. The recurring phrases of *Salome*, that bind it to-

---

[1] This interview, signed Adolphe Possien, appeared on 28 May on the front page of *Le Jour*. In it Douglas described Wilde's sufferings in prison and blamed English hypocrisy. The editorial comment was hostile, declaring that in Paris the name of Oscar Wilde was synonymous with *"pathologie passionnelle."*

[2] Presumably the published *Poems* of 1896.

[3] "The Critic as Artist," Part II.

288

gether like a piece of music with recurring *motifs*, are, and were to me, the artistic equivalent of the refrains of old ballads. All this is to beg you to write ballads.

I do not know whether I have to thank you or More for the books from Paris, probably both. As I have divided the books, so you must divide the thanks.

I am greatly fascinated by the *Napoléon* of La Jeunesse.[1] He must be most interesting. André Gide's book fails to fascinate me.[2] The egoistic note is, of course, and always has been to me, the primal and ultimate note of modern art, but *to be an Egoist one must have an Ego*. It is not everyone who says "I, I" who can enter into the Kingdom of Art. But I love André personally very deeply, and often thought of him in prison, as I often did of dear Reggie Cholmondeley, with his large faun's eyes and honey-sweet smile. Give him my fondest love.[3] Ever yours   OSCAR

Kindly forward enclosed card to Reggie, with my address. Tell him to keep *both* a secret.

To Robert Ross

Thursday 3 June
2.45 p.m. (Berneval time)
Latitude and Longitude not marked on the sea
A.D. *1897*

Dear Robbie, The entirely business-like tone of your letter just received makes me nervous that you are a prey of terrible emotions, and that it is merely a form of the calm that hides a storm. Your remark also that my letter is "undated," while as a reproach it wounds me, also seems to denote a change in your friendship towards me. I have now put the date and other facts at the head of my letter.

I get no cuttings from Paris, which makes me irritable when I hear of things appearing. Not knowing the day of the false interview with Bosie I ordered, fortunately, copies of the paper for *three successive days*: they have just arrived, and I see an impertinent *démenti* of Bosie's denial.

---

[1] *L'Imitation de Notre-Maître Napoléon* by Ernest Horry Cohen La Jeunesse (1874–1917) appeared in 1897. He had already published in 1896 "*un livre irrespectueux et bizarre*" called *Les Nuits, les Ennuis et les Ames de nos plus notoires Contemporains*, in which he parodied Daudet, Bourget, Anatole France (whose secretary he had been), Loti, Coppée and Huysmans. His biographer wrote: "*Sa vie s'écoula dans les cafés et sur le boulevard ou il promenait l'étrange silhouette, popularisée par les caricaturistes, d'un bohème négligé, aux doigts chargés de bagues, assidu des absinthes sacramentelles, noctambule gaspillant dans des brilliantes causeries avec Alphonse Allais, Alfred Jarry, Jean de Mitty, Oscar Wilde, un abondant savoir, un esprit mordant, une faconde extraordinaire.*"

[2] *Les Nourritures Terrestres* (1897).

[3] Thomas Tatton Reginald Cholmondeley (1865–1902), fourth son of the Hon. Thomas Grenville Cholmondeley and grandson of the first Lord Delamere. He lived mostly in Paris.

Bosie has also written to me to say he is on the eve of a duel! I suppose about this. They said his costume was *ridicule*. I have written to him to beg him *never* to fight duels, as once one does it one has to go on. And though it is not dangerous, like our English cricket or football is, still it is a tedious game to be always playing.

Besides, to fight with the common interviewer is to fight with the dead, a thing either farcical or tragic.

Ernest Dowson,[1] Conder,[2] and Dal Young[3] come out here this afternoon to dine and sleep—at least I know they dine, but I believe they never sleep.

I think the *Chronicle* are nervous. They have not answered yet or anything. Of course with them I am all right, if they take my work. *Who is my Receiver?* I want his name and address. Ever yours   OSCAR

To Lord Alfred Douglas

Friday, 4 June [1897] 2.30   [*Hôtel de la Plage, Berneval-sur-Mer*]

My dear Boy, I have just got your letter, but Ernest Dowson, Dal Young, and Conder are here, so I cannot read it, except the last three lines. I love the last words of anything: the end in art is the beginning. Don't think I don't love you. Of course I love you more than anyone else. But our lives are irreparably severed, as far as meeting goes. What is left to us is the knowledge that we love each other, and every day I think of you, and I know you are a poet, and that makes you doubly dear and wonderful. My friends here have been most sweet to me, and I like them all very much. Young is the best of fellows, and Ernest has a most interesting nature. He is to send me some of his work.

We all stayed up till three o'clock; very bad for me, but it was a delightful experience. Today is a day of sea-fog, and rain—my first. Tomorrow I go with fishers to fish, but I will write to you tonight.

Ever, dear boy, with fondest love   OSCAR

[1] English poet (1867–1900). He had met Wilde in 1890, and with Robert Sherard visited him at Oakley Street in the dark days between his trials.

[2] Charles Conder (1868–1909), English artist, who had lived in Australia. He became famous for his designs for fans and for his delicate water-colours painted on silk. Wilde much admired his work, and Rothenstein records his saying: "Dear Conder! With what exquisite subtlety he goes about persuading someone to give him a hundred francs for a fan, for which he was fully prepared to pay three hundred!"

[3] Dalhousie Young (1866–1921) was an English composer and pianist. A pupil of Leschetizky and Paderewski, he made his debut in Rome 1893, and in London 1895. Very soon after Wilde's conviction Young, then a stranger, had the courage to publish a pamphlet entitled *Apologia pro Oscar Wilde*. Later in 1897 there was a plan for Wilde to write for Young the libretto of an opera to be called *Daphnis and Chloe*. Nothing came of this although Young made Wilde an advance payment of £100.

To Ernest Dowson

[? *5 June 1897*]   *Hôtel de la Plage, Berneval-sur-Mer*

Cher Monsieur le Poète, It was most kind of you coming to see me, and I thank you very sincerely and gratefully for your pleasant companionship and the many gentle ways by which you recalled to me that, once at any rate, I was a Lord of Language, and had myself the soul of a poet. Of course I am lonely after the departure of my three good friends—le Poète, le Philosophe, and le Peintre—but I have no mourning-suit, so all I can do is to wear my red tie "with a difference"![1]

I am breakfasting with the Stannards at Dieppe on Wednesday, and will be at the Café Suisse at *3.15*. If you happen to be there it would be kind of you to introduce me to Jean who has the boats or knows about them. I have a wild desire for the sea. I feel that water purifies, and that in nature there is, for me at any rate, healing power.

Of course don't put yourself out to come in from your forest—but if you happen to be in Dieppe, I would like to be introduced to Jean.

There is a sea-mist today, and my fishermen have not come up the chalk ravine to search for me. I long to get your poems. The sea's "restless chime"[2] makes me hungry for poetry. Sincerely yours   OSCAR WILDE

To Robert Ross

Saturday, *5 June* [*1897*]   [*Hôtel de la Plage, Berneval-sur-Mer*]

My dear Robbie, I propose to *live* at Berneval. I will *not* live in Paris, nor in Algiers, nor in southern Italy. Surely a house for a year, if I choose to continue there, at £32 is absurdly cheap! I could not live cheaper at a hotel. You are penny foolish and pound foolish—a dreadful state for any financier to be in. I told M. Bonnet that my banker was *M. Ross et Cie, Banquiers célèbres de Londres*: and now you suddenly show me that you have really no place among the great financial people, and are afraid of any investment over £31. 10. It is merely the extra 10/- that baffles you. As regards people living on me in the extra bedrooms: dear boy, there is no one who would stay with me but you, and you will pay your own bill at the hotel for meals, and as for your room the charge will be nominally 2 fr. 50 a night, but there will be *lots* of extras, such as *bougie, bain,* and hot water: all cigarettes smoked in the bedrooms are charged extra: washing is extra: and if any one does not take the extras, of course he is charged more. *Bain 25 c. Pas de bain 50 c. Cigarette dans la chambre-à-coucher, 10 c. pour chaque cigarette. Pas de cigarettes dans la chambre-à-coucher, 20 c. chaque cigarette.* This is the *système* in all good hotels. If Reggie comes, of course he will pay a little more. I cannot forget that he gave me a dressing-case.

---

[1] *Hamlet*, Act IV, scene 5.   [2] See note 1, p. 293.

Sphinxes pay a hundred per cent more than anyone else. They always did in ancient Egypt. Architects, on the other hand, are taken at a reduction. I have special terms for architects.[1]

But seriously, Robbie, if anyone stayed with me, of course they would pay their *pension* at the hotel. They would have to: except architects. A modern architect, like modern architecture, doesn't pay. But then I only know one architect, and you are hiding him somewhere from me. I am beginning to believe that he is as extinct as the Dado, of which now only fossil remains are found, chiefly in the vicinity of Brompton, where they are sometimes discovered by workmen excavating. They are usually embedded in the old Lincrusta-Walton strata, and are rare consequently.[2]

I visited *M. le Curé* today: he has a charming house in a *jardin potager*: he showed me over the church: tomorrow I sit in the choir by his special invitation. He showed me all his vestments: tomorrow he really will be charming in his red. He knows I am a heretic, and believes that Pusey is still alive. He says that God will convert England on account of England's kindness to the *prêtres exilés* at the time of the Revolution. It is to be the reward of that sea-lashed island. Stained-glass windows are wanted in the church: he only has six: fourteen more are needed. He gets them at 300 francs (£12) a window in Paris! I was nearly offering half a dozen, but remembered you, and so only gave him something *pour ses pauvres*. You had a narrow escape, Robbie. You should be thankful.

I hope the £40 is on its way, and that the £60 will follow. I am going to hire a boat. It will save walking, and so be an economy in the end. Dear Robbie, I must start well. If the life of St Francis awaits me I shall not be angry. Worse things might happen. Ever yours   OSCAR

To Lord Alfred Douglas

Sunday night, 6 June [*1897*]   [*Hôtel de la Plage, Berneval-sur-Mer*]

My dearest Boy, I must give up this *absurd* habit of writing to you every day. It comes of course from the strange new joy of talking to you daily. But next week I must make a resolution to write to you only every *seven* days, and then on the question of the relations of the sonnet to modern life, and the importance of your writing romantic ballads, and the strange beauty of that lovely line of Rossetti's, suppressed till lately by his brother,

---

[1] John Fothergill.

[2] In 1877 Frederick Walton invented a raised-surface wall-covering which became very popular and is still manufactured. The name Lincrusta is a compound of the Latin *linum* (flax) and *crusta* (relief), and its chief ingredient is solidified linseed oil. In *Son of Oscar Wilde* Vyvyan Holland records that in the smoking-room at 16 Tite Street "the walls were covered with the peculiar wallpaper of that era known as Lincrusta-Walton and had a William Morris pattern of dark red and dull gold; when you poked it with your finger, it popped and split, and your finger might even go through, so this was not much encouraged."

where he says that "the sea ends in a sad blueness beyond rhyme."[1] Don't you think it lovely? "In a sad *blueness* beyond rhyme." *Voilà "l'influence du bleu dans les arts*," with a vengeance!

I am so glad you went to bed at seven o'clock. Modern life is terrible to vibrating delicate frames like yours: a rose-leaf in a storm of hard hail is not so fragile. With us who are modern it is the *scabbard* that wears out the sword.

Will you do this for me? Get *Le Courier de la Presse* to procure a copy of *Le Soir*, the *Brussels* paper, somewhere between the 26th and the 31st of May last, which has an article on my letter to the *Chronicle*, a translation of it, I believe, and notices. It is of vital importance for me to have it as soon as possible. My *Chronicle* letter is to be published as a pamphlet with a postscript, and I need the *Soir*.[2] I don't want to write myself for it, for obvious reasons. Dear boy, I hope you are still sweetly asleep: you are so absurdly sweet when you are asleep. I have been to Mass at ten o'clock and to Vespers at three o'clock. I was a little bored by a sermon in the morning, but Benediction was delightful. I am seated in the Choir! I suppose sinners should have the high places near Christ's altar? I know at any rate that Christ would not turn me out.

Remember, after a few days, only *one letter a week*. I *must* school myself to it.

En attendant, yours with all love   OSCAR,
                                                                     Poète-forçat

To Reginald Turner

[? *7 June 1897*]   *Hôtel de la Plage, Berneval-sur-Mer*
My dear Reggie, It is all very well giving me a lovely silver dressing-case, and meeting me at Dieppe, and behaving like an angel: but what is the result? Simply that I come to you to ask you to do something more. I can't help it. Why do you insist on behaving like an angel, if you object to my treating you as one?

Read *first* enclosed letter, before you go any further. It is necessary that you should do so. This is vital. Also it is Act I.

[1] On 28 September 1849 D. G. Rossetti included in a letter from abroad to his brother William a short poem called "At Boulogne. Upon the Cliffs: Noon," which begins:

> The sea is in its listless chime,
> Like Time's lapse rendered audible;
> The murmur of the earth's large shell.
> In a sad blueness beyond rhyme
> It ends.

W. M. Rossetti omitted the poem from the *Collected Works* of 1886, but printed it in the *Family-Letters* of 1895.

[2] Wilde's *Daily Chronicle* letter of 28 May was reprinted by Murdoch & Co as a pamphlet called *Children in Prison and Other Cruelties of Prison Life*, and prefaced by a brief publisher's note dated February 1898.

Have you read it?
(Interval of five minutes. No band: only a cigarette.)

If so, what do you say to such a nice simple sweet letter from *Jim Cuthbert's pal* who came out on June the 2nd, and found a little £2, *no more*, waiting for him at the Post Office from me? You see what a good chap he is: he was one of my great friends in Reading; he and Jim Cuthbert and Harry Elvin were *my* pals: hearts of gold.

Now I have asked him to come and stay a week here with me, so that he may have a holiday after eighteen months' hard labour.

His offence, I told you. He was a soldier, dined too well, or perhaps too badly, and "made hay" in the harness room of the regimental stables: the sort of thing one was "gated" for at Oxford, or fined £5 for by the Proctor. He has never taken anything by fraud or by violence. He is a good chap, and has a nice sweet nature.

I had better say candidly that he is not "a beautiful boy." He is twenty-nine years of age, but looks a little older, as he inherits hair that catches silver lines early: he has also a slight, but still *real*, moustache. I am thankful and happy to be able to say that I have no feeling for him, nor could have, other than affection and friendship. He is simply a manly simple fellow, with the nicest smile and the pleasantest eyes, and I have no doubt a confirmed "*mulierast*," to use Robbie's immortal phrase.

So you see my feelings towards him. It is sad to have to explain them, but it is only fair to you.

Now Robbie has whatever little money I possess, but he is very severe on me for having sent some money to four chaps released last week. He says I can't afford it. But, dear Reggie, I must look after my prison-friends, if my good friends, like you, look after me.

I have a cheque for £40, but it will take a week to cash it, as I cannot go to Dieppe till Wednesday, and of course, as the bank does not know me, the cheque will have to be cleared in London before I touch the money here. So Monday is the earliest I can realise.

I want you then to lend me £6. *10*. till next week, if you possibly can.

Arthur Cruttenden requires clothes—a blue-serge suit, a pair of brown leather boots, some shirts, and a hat. This will cost money, and his ticket here will cost something.

So I have written to him to tell him that a good friend of mine—a Jim Cuthbert of the name of R. Turner—will send him from me £6. *10*., so that he can get clothes, and be here on Saturday afternoon next, for a week. I hope in the meantime to get him a place, when his holidays with me end.[1]

---

[1] Turner provided the money and Cruttenden duly spent a week at Berneval. In a letter dated 21 June Wilde wrote:

Of course all you said to me, dear Reggie, was quite true: but you must understand that I have the deepest desire to try and be of a little help to other fellows who were in trouble with me. I used to be utterly reckless of young lives: I used to take up a boy, love him "passionately," and then grow bored with him, and often take no notice of him. That is what I regret in my past life. Now I feel

Of course if you would not mind being good to a friend of mine, it would be very sweet of you if you would let him come to see you on Friday morning. He will show you, by my orders, my letter to him, and you can tell him some good place in the Strand to go to, for clothes etc., and also clear up any mysteries about any details of dress and apparel. If you can do this, *just send him £1 to come up with*, and let him have the £5. 10 when he arrives. Tell him that it, the £5. 10, is waiting for him, and that he must bring up whatever he has already in the way of clothes.

He is not English: he is American: but has no accent at all. He always wrapped up well at night in his native land.

You don't know, Reggie, what a pleasure it is to me to think I shall have the chance of being kind to a chap who has been in trouble with me. I look forward to it with tears of joy and gratitude.

Of course if you can't see him, simply send him the money: but I would like you to see him, and to say some kind words to him. We all come out of prison as sensitive as children.

Next week you shall have the £6. 10. I simply dare not tell Robbie to give it, because he scolds me, and I hate giving him pain. I know he is right, but still I have £200 left, and £3 a week, and in a few months I shall be making money, I hope.

Send me a line at once to say if you can do all this: and if Cruttenden can go on Saturday, see that he learns about trains, and send me a wire to inform me, so that I may meet him all right at Dieppe.

If you will do this, I will give you back the dressing-case: at least I will keep it for you always: it is the same thing.

I anxiously await a letter from you. I know that, *if you can*, you will let A. C. call on you on Friday morning. It would so please him, and so fascinate me. Ever yours   OSCAR

P.S. Of course send me back Arthur Cruttenden's letter. I wouldn't part with it for many £6. 10.: nor indeed show it to anyone but you, *and Robbie* if he wouldn't lecture me about giving away among *four* fellow-prisoners and *four* warders (*including* £5 to Martin) the sum of £20! Huge I know for me, but still it is little for kindness shown. I may not have the chance again. I only know five chaps now in Reading Gaol. By the end of the year—on December 2 in fact—all my friends, thank God, will be free men, as I am. So unless I do a little *now*, I shall lose my chance.

Dear Reggie, if you will manage all this for me and A. C. you will, in some other way than the mere repayment of the £6. 10 next week, reap a harvest of deep gold in the heart of the great world. I know it. I have been taught it in cell C.3.3.

that if I can really help others it will be a little attempt, however small, at expiation. To be of real assistance to even one of them would give me joy beyond what I can express to you.

Postcard: To Robert Ross

Tuesday evening, 8 June [1897]   Berneval-sur-Mer

Dear Robbie, I am greatly distressed to learn from your letter that you received *three* letters from me on *one* morning. How awful! Of course it is the result of the "English Sunday." I will no longer write to you in the temporal vicinity of that day. I will simply send you twice a week my *Berneval, Day by Day.* (If the *Daily Chronicle* cares, you might arrange for simultaneous publication in their columns.) Will Rothenstein is organising a Pilgrimage to the Sinner this week. He brings, as his offering, silent songs on stone.[1]   S. M.

To Will Rothenstein

Wednesday [Postmark 9 June 1897]   Hôtel de la Plage, Berneval-sur-Mer

My dear good Friend, I cannot tell you how pleased I was to get your kind and affectionate letter yesterday, and I look forward with real delight to the prospect of seeing you, though it be only for a day. I am going into Dieppe to breakfast with the Stannards, who have been most kind to me, and I will send you a telegram from there. I do hope you can come to-morrow by the day boat, so that you and your friend can dine and sleep here. There is no one in this little inn but myself, but it is most comfortable, and the chef—there is a real chef—is an artist of great distinction; he walks in the evening by the sea to get ideas for the next day. Is it not sweet of him? I have taken a chalet for the whole season for £32, so I shall be able I hope to work again, and write plays or something.

I know, dear Will, you will be pleased to know that I have not come out of prison an embittered or disappointed man. On the contrary: in many ways I have gained much. I am not really ashamed of having been in prison: I often was in more shameful places: but I *am* really ashamed of having led a life unworthy of an artist. I don't say that Messalina is a better companion than Sporus,[2] or that the one is all right and the other all wrong: I know simply that a life of definite and studied materialism, and a philosophy of appetite and cynicism, and a cult of sensual and senseless ease, are bad things for an artist: they narrow the imagination, and dull the more delicate sensibilities. I was all wrong, my dear boy, in my life. I was not getting the best out of me. *Now* I think that with good health and the friendship of a few good simple nice fellows like yourself, and a quiet mode of living, with isolation for thought, and freedom from the endless hunger for pleasures that wreck the body and imprison the soul—well, I

---

[1] Whistler's definition of lithographs.

[2] Messalina was the faithless and depraved wife of the Emperor Claudius, and Sporus the effeminate favourite of the Emperor Nero, with whom, according to Suetonius, he went through a form of marriage.

think I may do things yet that you all may like. Of course I have lost much, but still, my dear Will, when I reckon up all that is *left* to me, the sun and the sea of this beautiful world; its dawns dim with gold and its nights hung with silver; many books, and all flowers, and a few good friends; and a brain and body to which health and power are not denied—really I am *rich* when I count up what I still have: and as for money, my money did me horrible harm. It wrecked me. I hope just to have enough to enable me to live simply and write well.

So remember that you will find me in many respects very happy, and of course, by your sweetness in coming to see me, you will bring me happiness along with you.

As for the silent songs on stone, I am charmed at the prospect of having something of yours. It is awfully good of you to think of it. I have had many sweet presents, but none I shall value more than yours.

You ask me if you can bring me anything from London. Well, the salt soft air kills my cigarettes, and I have no box in which to keep them. If you are in a millionaire condition and could bring me a box for keeping cigarettes in, it would be a great boon. At Dieppe there is nothing between a trunk and a *bonbonnière*. I do hope to see you tomorrow (Thursday) for dinner and sleep. If not, well Friday morning. I am up now at eight o'clock regularly!

I hope you never forget that *but for me* you would not be *Will* Rothenstein: *Artist*. You would simply be *William* Rothenstein, *R.A.* It is one of the most important facts in the history of art.

I look forward greatly to knowing Strangman.[1] His translating *Lady Windermere* is delightful. Your sincere and grateful friend

OSCAR WILDE

Postcard: To Robert Ross

Sunday, 13 June [1897]   [*Hôtel de la Plage, Berneval-sur-Mer*]

Dear Robbie, Thank you so much for red ties and scarlet sonnets. I move in to my chalet on Wednesday.

I observed a slight tendency to Mrs Daubeny's ailments:[2] but you are all right now. Have just seen a *première communion*, very sweet, and flowerlike with children. The *curé's* hopes are at their highest. *Sed non sum dignus.*   S. M.

---

[1] Edward Strangman. Irish. Born 1866. Educated at Pembroke College, Oxford. Called to the Bar (Inner Temple) 1898. Friend of Rothenstein and Conder. Employee of Smithers.

[2] The wife of Archdeacon Daubeny in *A Woman of No Importance* never appears, but is described at different times as suffering from headaches, deafness, gout, defective memory and an inability to eat solid food.

Postcard: To Robert Ross

Tuesday, 15 June [1897]   [*Berneval-sur-Mer*]

Dear Robbie, You have never told me anything about the type-writer, or my letter: pray let there be no further conspiracies. I feel apprehensive. It is only by people writing to me the worst that I can know the best.

Also, could all the remainder of my money be transferred to Dieppe? I thought *you* had it all. But you say not.

The *New Review* portrait of the Queen is wonderful.[1] I am going to hang it on the walls of the chalet. Every poet should gaze at the portrait of his Queen, all day long.   S. M.

To Lord Alfred Douglas

Thursday, 17 June [1897] 2 o'clock p.m.   *Café Suisse, Dieppe*

My dearest Boy, I have been obliged to ask my friends to leave me, as I am so upset and distressed in nerve by my solicitor's letter, and the apprehension of serious danger, that simply I must be alone. I find that any worry utterly destroys my health, and makes me horrid and irritable and unkind, though I hate to be so.

Of course at present it is impossible for us to meet.[2] I have to find out what grounds my solicitor has for his sudden action, and of course if your father—or rather Q, as I only know him and think of him—if Q came over and made a scene and scandal it would utterly destroy my possible future and alienate all my friends from me. I owe to my friends everything, including the clothes I wear, and I would be wretched if I did anything that would separate them from me.

So simply we must write to each other: about the things we love, about poetry and the coloured arts of our age, and that passage of ideas into images that is the intellectual history of art. I think of you always, and love you always, but chasms of moonless night divide us. We cannot cross it without hideous and nameless peril.

Later on, when the alarm in England is over, when secrecy is possible, and silence forms part of the world's attitude, we may meet, but at present you see it is impossible. I would be harassed, agitated, nervous. It would be no joy for me to let you see me as I am now.

You must go to some place where you can play golf and get back your lily and rose. Don't, like a good boy, telegraph to me unless on a matter of vital import: the telegraph office is seven miles off, and I have to pay the

---

[1] A reproduction of William Nicholson's famous woodcut of Queen Victoria with her dog was issued with the June 1897 issue of the *New Review*. André Gide remembered it pinned to the wall in the chalet.

[2] Arrangements had been completed for Douglas to visit Berneval that week.

facteur, and also reply, and yesterday with three separate *facteurs,* and three separate replies, I was *sans le sou,* and also mentally upset in nerve. Say please to Percy that I will accept a bicycle with many thanks for his kindness: I want to get it here, where there is a great champion who teaches everyone, and has English machines: it will cost £15. If Percy will send me £15 to enclosed name and address in a cheque, it will make me very happy. Send him my card.

Ever yours (rather maimed and mutilated)   OSCAR

Postcard: To Robert Ross

Monday, 21 June [*1897*]   [*Berneval-sur-Mer*]

Dear Robbie, Just a line to wish you a very happy Jubilee, and many of them.[1] I fear I cannot hope to live long enough to see more than five or six more myself, but with you it is different. I don't know the exact route of the procession, but I suppose the dear Queen passes by Upper Phillimore Gardens and will look up and see you waving the flags of no nations. Of course we are having "Queen's weather" here. It began today. Yesterday nothing but the prayers at *Vêpres* prevented it from snowing.   S. M.

To Lord Alfred Douglas

Wednesday, 23 June [*1897*]   *Café Suisse, Dieppe*

My darling Boy, Thanks for your letter received this morning. My *fête* was a huge success: fifteen *gamins* were entertained on strawberries and cream, apricots, chocolates, cakes, and *sirop de grenadine.* I had a huge iced cake with *Jubilé de la Reine Victoria* in pink sugar just rosetted with green, and a great wreath of red roses round it all. Every child was asked beforehand to choose his present: they all chose instruments of music!!!

> 6 *accordions*
> 5 *trompettes*
> 4 *clairons.*

They sang the Marseillaise and other songs, and danced a *ronde,* and also played "God save the Queen:" they said it was "God save the Queen," and I did not like to differ from them. They also all had flags which I gave them. They were most gay and sweet. I gave the health of *La Reine d'Angleterre,* and they cried "*Vive la Reine d'Angleterre*"!!!! Then I gave "*La France, mère de tous les artistes,*" and finally I gave *Le Président de la République*: I thought I had better do so. They cried out with one accord "*Vivent le Président de la République et Monsieur Melmoth*"!!! So I found my name

---

[1] Queen Victoria's Diamond Jubilee was celebrated on 22 June 1897.

coupled with that of the President. It was an amusing experience as I am hardly more than a month out of gaol.

They stayed from 4.30 to seven o'clock and played games: on leaving I gave them each a basket with a jubilee cake frosted pink and inscribed, and *bonbons*.

They seem to have made a great demonstration in Berneval-le-Grand, and to have gone to the house of the Mayor and cried "*Vive Monsieur le Maire! Vive la Reine d'Angleterre. Vive Monsieur Melmoth!*" I tremble at my position.

Today I have come in with Ernest Dowson to dine with the painter Thaulow,[1] a giant with the temperament of Corot. I sleep here and go back tomorrow.

I will write tomorrow on things. Ever, dearest boy, yours   OSCAR

To Robert Ross

20 July [*1897*]   *Chalet Bourgeat, Berneval-sur-Mer*

My dearest Robbie, Your excuse of "domesticity" is of course most treacherous: I have missed your letters very much. Pray write at least twice a day, and write at length. You now only write about Dixon. As regards him, tell him that the expense of bringing him to London is too heavy. I don't think I would like the type-written manuscript[2] sent to him. It might be dangerous. Better to have it done in London, scratching out Bosie's name, mine at the close, and the address. Mrs Marshall can be relied on.

The pictures, as I said, insure for £50.

As regards Bosie, I feel you have been, as usual, forbearing and sweet, and too good-tempered. What he must be made to feel is that his vulgar and ridiculous assumption of social superiority must be retracted and apologised for. I have written to him to tell him that *quand on est gentilhomme on est gentilhomme*, and that for him to try and pose as your social superior because he is the third son of a Scotch marquis and you the third son of a commoner is offensively stupid. There is no difference between gentlemen. Questions of titles are matters of heraldry—no more. I wish you would be strong on this point; the thing should be thrashed out of him. As for his coarse ingratitude in abusing you, to whom, as I have told him, I owe any possibility I have of a new and artistic career, and indeed of life at all, I have no words in which to express my contempt for his lack of imaginative insight, and his dullness of sensitive nature. It makes me quite furious. So pray write, when next you do so, quite calmly, and say that you will not allow any nonsense of social superiority and that if he cannot understand that gentlemen are gentlemen and no more, you have no desire to hear again from him.

[1] Fritz Thaulow (1847–1906), a Norwegian landscape-artist and designer.
[2] Of the letter known as *De Profundis*.

I expect you on August the First: also, the architect.

The poem is nearly finished. Some of the verses are awfully good.

Wyndham comes here tomorrow to see me: for the adaptation of Scribe's *Le Verre d'Eau*: which of course you have to do. Bring *Esmond* with you, and any Queen Anne chairs you have: just for the style.[1]

I am so glad More is better.

The sketch of Frank Harris in *John Johns* is superb. Who wrote the book? It is a wonderful indictment.[2] Ever yours OSCAR

Postcard: To Reginald Turner

20 July [*1897*]   [*Berneval-sur-Mer*]

Mr Sebastian Melmoth would like to hear from Mr Turner on any important or unimportant matter, as soon as possible.

To Reginald Turner

Saturday [*Postmark 31 July 1897*]   *Berneval-sur-Mer*

My dear Reggie, The most lovely clock has arrived, and I hear it is from you. It is most sweet of you to give it to me, and you will be pleased, and perhaps astonished, to hear that though it is quite beautiful, and has a lovely face and wonderful slim restless hands, yet it is strangely punctual in all its habits, business-like in its methods, of ceaseless industry, and knows all that the sun is doing. I hope you will come here and see it. It has been greatly admired by all the inhabitants. Come any time you like. I am not responsible for the architecture of the chalet: all that I am responsible for at Berneval are the sunsets and the sea.

I don't know if you are with Bosie, but send this to his care.[3] Affectionately yours OSCAR

---

[1] *Le Verre d'Eau* (1840), a comedy by Eugène Scribe (1791–1861), is set at the Court of Queen Anne in London. Wilde's plan to translate and adapt it for Charles Wyndham came to nothing.

[2] *The Adventures of John Johns*, a novel by Frederic Carrel (1869–1928), published in February 1897. The central character was clearly based on Frank Harris.

[3] This letter is addressed to Reginald Turner, c/o Lord Alfred Douglas, Villa Myosotis, Villeville-sur-Mer, Calvados.

To Carlos Blacker[1]

Café Suisse, Dieppe

My dear Friend, I am simply heart-broken at what you tell me. I don't mind my life being wrecked—that is as it should be—but when I think of poor Constance I simply want to kill myself.[2] But I suppose I must live through it all. I don't care. Nemesis has caught me in her net: to struggle is foolish. Why is it that one runs to one's ruin? Why has destruction such a fascination? Why, when one stands on a pinnacle, must one throw oneself down? No one knows, but things are so.

Of course I think it would be much better for Constance to see me,[3] but you think not. Well, you are wiser. My life is spilt on the sand—red wine on the sand—and the sand drinks it because it is thirsty, for no other reason.

I wish I could see you. Where I shall be in September I don't know. I don't care. I fear we shall never see each other again. But all is right: the gods hold the world on their knees. I was made for destruction. My cradle was rocked by the Fates. Only in the mire can I know peace. Ever yours   OSCAR

To Reginald Turner

Tuesday 10 August [*1897*] [*Dieppe*]

My dear Reggie, Will you come over here on Saturday next, by the afternoon boat? Robbie is here, and we want you so much. It is quite quiet and the weather is charming. Also last night acrobats arrived. Smithers,[4] the

---

[1] Carlos Blacker (1859–1928) was an Englishman of independent means who lived mostly abroad, especially in Paris, where he took a passionate interest in the Dreyfus case. He was an excellent talker, friend, correspondent and linguist, learning a new language every two years. In his old age he learned Hebrew, so that if he went to Heaven he could talk to God in His own language. He appears to have had some financial interest in the original production of *Lady Windermere's Fan*.

[2] Constance Wilde was already suffering from the creeping spinal paralysis which was soon to kill her.

[3] Constance Wilde was staying with Blacker and his wife, and Wilde had suggested visiting her.

[4] Leonard Charles Smithers (1861–1907) was born in Sheffield and in 1888 while working there as a solicitor had written Wilde a letter of appreciation about "The Happy Prince." In 1891 he abandoned Sheffield and the law and set up in London as bookseller and publisher. Although he was known to trade in pornography, and was reported as saying "I'll publish anything that the others are afraid of," he published, besides Wilde's last three books, the poems of Ernest Dowson and Arthur Symons, the *Savoy*, much of Aubrey Beardsley's work, and the first collected drawings of Max Beerbohm, who long afterwards described him as "a strange and rather depressing person, a north-countryman, known to have been engaged in the sale of disreputable books." Robert Ross considered him "the most delightful and irresponsible publisher I ever met." His private life was uncontrolled, and he is believed to have died of drink and drugs.

publisher and owner of Aubrey, comes over on Sunday and we all dine with him: then we go to Berneval.

I do not know if you know Smithers: he is usually in a large straw hat, has a blue tie delicately fastened with a diamond brooch of the impurest water—or perhaps wine, as he never touches water: it goes to his head at once. His face, clean-shaven as befits a priest who serves at the altar whose God is Literature, is wasted and pale—not with poetry, but with poets, who, he says, have wrecked his life by insisting on publishing with him. He loves first editions, especially of women: little girls are his passion. He is the most learned erotomaniac in Europe. He is also a delightful companion, and a dear fellow, very kind to me.

You will on arrival proceed without delay to the *Café Suisse*, where Robbie and I will be waiting for you.

If you don't come I shall be quite wretched. I long to see you again. Ever yours   OSCAR

Postcard: To Reginald Turner

Wednesday, 11 August [1897]   [*Postmark Dieppe*]

Dear Reggie, I hope you got my letter all right, and that we shall see you on Saturday. By my elaborate description of Smithers you are certain not to recognise him. Bring over your play, and let me hear it. Ever yours
                                                                    O. W.

To Will Rothenstein

14 August 1897   *Berneval-sur-Mer*

My dear Will, I don't know if the enclosed will suit. If so, pray use it.[1] Also don't forget to come and see me as soon as possible. I simply long for your delightful companionship. Robbie Ross and Sherard are here at present: the latter goes away today. We all go to Dieppe to dine with Smithers. Ever yours   O. W.

He founded a school, and has survived all his disciples. He has always thought too much about himself, which is wise; and written too much about others, which is foolish. His prose is the beautiful prose of a poet, and his poetry the beautiful poetry of a prose-writer. His personality is insistent. To converse with him is a physical no less than an intellectual recreation. He is never forgotten by his enemies, and often forgiven by his friends. He has added several new words to the language, and his style is

---

[1] Rothenstein's book *English Portraits* (1898) consisted of twenty-four lithographed drawings, with a brief note on each sitter. These were anonymous and by different hands; Wilde had been asked to describe W. E. Henley.

an open secret. He has fought a good fight, and has had to face every difficulty except popularity.

!!! !!!

To Will Rothenstein

24 August 1897   *Berneval-sur-Mer*

My dear Will, Of course I only did it to oblige you.[1] My name was not to be appended, nor was there to be any honorarium of any kind. It was to oblige you I did it, but with me, as with you, as with all artists, one's work *est à prendre ou à laisser*. I couldn't go into the details of coarse and notorious facts. I know Henley edited the *National Observer*, and was a very bitter and in some respects a cowardly journalist in his conduct. I get the *National Review*[2] regularly, and its dullness and stupidity are beyond words. I am only concerned with the essence of the man, not with his accidents, miry or other.

When I said of W. E. H. that his prose was the prose of a poet, I paid him an undeserved compliment. His prose is jerky, spasmodic, and he is incapable of the beautiful architecture of a long sentence, which is the fine flower of prose-writing, but I praised him for the sake of antithesis: "his poetry is the beautiful poetry of a prose-writer:" that refers to Henley's finest work: the Hospital Poems, which are in *vers libres*, and *vers libres* are prose. The author by dividing the lines shows you the rhythm he wishes you to follow. But all that one is concerned with is *literature*. Poetry is not finer than prose, nor prose finer than poetry. When one uses the words poetry and prose, one is merely referring to certain technical modes of word-music, melody and harmony one might say, though they are not exclusive terms, and though I praised Henley too much, too extravagantly, when I said his prose was the beautiful prose of a poet, the latter part of the sentence is a subtle aesthetic appreciation of his *vers libres*, which W. E. H., if he has any critical faculty left, would be the first to appreciate! You seem to me to have misunderstood the sentence. Mallarmé would understand it. But the matter is of no importance. Everybody is greedy of common panegyrics, and W. E. H. would much sooner have a long list of his literary failures chronicled with dates.

I am still here, though the wind blows terribly. Your lovely lithographs are on my walls, and you will be pleased to hear that I do not propose to ask you to alter them, though I am *not* the editor of a "paying publication."

I am delighted to hear the Monticelli is sold, though Obach does not say for how much.[3] Dal Young is coming out here tomorrow and I will tell

---

[1] The note on W. E. Henley was eventually written by Max Beerbohm.

[2] A slip for the *New Review*, which Henley edited from 1895 to 1898.

[3] A picture by the French painter Adolphe Joseph Thomas Monticelli (1824–86), which had belonged to Wilde. At the Tite Street sale (see note p. 179) Rothenstein bought it for £8, and now sold it for Wilde's benefit. Obach was a picturedealer in Cockspur Street, London. His business, founded in 1855, was in 1911 merged with that of Messrs Colnaghi.

him. He seems to be under the impression that he bought it. Of course I know nothing about the facts of the case.

Robbie Ross had to go back to England on Thursday last, and I fear will not be able to come again this year.

I don't know where I shall go myself. I am not in the mood to do the work I want, and I fear I shall never be. The intense energy of creation has been kicked out of me. I don't care now to struggle to get back what, when I had it, gave me little pleasure. Ever yours   O. W.

To Robert Ross

Tuesday, 24 August [*1897*]   *Berneval-sur-Mer*

My dearest Robbie, Thanks for the cheque. I have sent it to the Dieppe bank.

My poem is still unfinished, but I have made up my mind to finish it this afternoon, and send it to be type-written.[1] Once I see it, even type-written, I shall be able to correct it: *now* I am tired of the manuscript.

Do you think this verse good? I fear it is out of harmony, but wish you were here to talk about it. I miss you dreadfully, dear boy.

> The Governor was strong upon
> The Regulation Act:
> The Doctor said that Death was but
> A scientific fact;
> And twice a day the Chaplain called
> And left a little Tract.

It is, of course, about the condemned man's life before his execution. I have got in "latrine:" it looks beautiful.

Since Bosie wrote that he could not afford forty francs to come to Rouen to see me, he has never written. Nor have I. I am greatly hurt by his meanness and lack of imagination. Ever yours   OSCAR

To Lord Alfred Douglas

Tuesday, 7.30 [? *31 August 1897*]   *Café Suisse, Dieppe*

My own Darling Boy, I got your telegram half an hour ago, and just send you a line to say that I feel that my only hope of again doing beautiful work in art is being with you. It was not so in old days, but now it is different, and you can really recreate in me that energy and sense of joyous power on which art depends. Everyone is furious with me for going back to you, but they don't understand us. I feel that it is only with you that I

---

[1] On the same day Wilde sent *The Ballad of Reading Gaol* to Smithers to be type-written—"It is not yet finished, but I want to see it type-written. I am sick of my manuscript."

can do anything at all. Do remake my ruined life for me, and then our friendship and love will have a different meaning to the world.

I wish that when we met at Rouen we had not parted at all.[1] There are such wide abysses now of space and land between us. But we love each other. Goodnight, dear. Ever yours   OSCAR

To Carlos Blacker

Monday [*Postmark 6 September 1897*]   *Grand Hôtel de France, Rouen*

My dear Carlos, The weather has been so dreadful at Berneval that I have come here, where the weather is much worse. I cannot stay in the North of Europe; the climate kills me. I don't mind being alone when there is sunlight, and a *joie de vivre* all about me, but my last fortnight at Berneval has been black and dreadful, and quite suicidal. I have never been so unhappy. I am trying to get some money to go to Italy, and hope to be able to find my way to Sicily, but the expenses of travelling are frightening. I don't suppose I shall see you before I go, as I think you said you could not come to France before the end of September, and the journey from Basle is, I suppose, very long and tedious.

I am greatly disappointed that Constance has not asked me to come and see the children. I don't suppose now I shall ever see them. Ever yours
                                                                         OSCAR

Write to me at Berneval-sur-Mer.

---

[1] This fateful meeting seems to have taken place on August 28–29. In his *Autobiography* Douglas wrote: "Poor Oscar cried when I met him at the station. We walked about all day arm in arm, or hand in hand, and were perfectly happy."

PART EIGHT

NAPLES · 1897-1898

The only record of Wilde's journey from Berneval to Naples is that given by Vincent O'Sullivan.[1] In his *Aspects of Wilde* (1936), he tells how he met Wilde in Paris in response to a letter. Over lunch Wilde explained that he wanted to go to Italy:

> He talked of all this for some time, giving details, some of which it was hard for me to follow from lack of knowledge of the elements of the matter. So far as I remember, the main difficulty was that his wife's friends and relations wanted to keep him from rejoining Lord Alfred Douglas, who was at Naples. Then he added: "I am not telling all this to you because I want advice. I have thought it all out and I would not take advice from anyone." I assured him that nothing was farther from my thoughts than to offer him advice. That indeed was so, both because I should have thought it presumptuous to offer advice to a man so much beyond me both in years and achievement, and also because it was utterly indifferent to me what he did or where he went.
>
> Finally he declared: "I shall go to Italy tonight. Or rather, I would go, but I am in an absurd position. I have no money."
>
> Upon leaving the restaurant we drove to the Banque de Paris et des Pays-Bas in the rue d'Antin where I had an account. He stayed in the cab and I brought him out the sum he wanted. It is one of the few things I look back on with satisfaction. It is not every day that one has the chance of relieving the anxiety of a genius and a hero. I think he left Paris the same evening; certainly very soon.

[1] Irish-American poet and novelist (1868–1940). He spent most of his life in France. His *Aspects of Wilde* (1936) is one of the most perceptive and reliable books on the subject.

307

To Robert Ross

Tuesday, 21 September 1897　　　　*Hôtel Royal des Étrangers, Naples*

My dearest Robbie, Your letter has reached me here.

My going back to Bosie was psychologically inevitable: and, setting aside the interior life of the soul with its passion for self-realisation at all costs, the world forced it on me.

I cannot live without the atmosphere of Love: I must love and be loved, whatever price I pay for it. I could have lived all my life with you, but you have other claims on you—claims you are too sweet a fellow to disregard—and all you could give me was a week of companionship. Reggie gave me three days, and Rowland[1] a sextette of suns, but for the last month at Berneval I was so lonely that I was on the brink of killing myself. The world shuts its gateway against me, and the door of Love lies open.

When people speak against me for going back to Bosie, tell them that he offered me love, and that in my loneliness and disgrace I, after three months' struggle against a hideous Philistine world, turned naturally to him. Of course I shall often be unhappy, but still I love him: the mere fact that he wrecked my life makes me love him. "*Je t'aime parce que tu m'as perdu*" is the phrase that ends one of the stories[2] in *Le Puits de Sainte Claire*—Anatole France's book—and it is a terrible symbolic truth.

We hope to get a little villa or apartments somewhere, and I hope to do work with him. I think I shall be able to do so. I think he will be kind to me; I only ask that. So do let people know that my only hope of life or literary activity was in going back to the young man whom I loved before with such tragic issue to my name.

No more today. Ever yours　　　　　　　　　　　　　　　　OSCAR

To Carlos Blacker

Thursday, 23 September [1897]　　　　*Hôtel Royal des Étrangers, Naples*

My dear Carlos, Your letter was forwarded to me here from Paris. I will go and see Constance in October.

I know that all you have written to me about my coming here comes from the sympathy and loyalty of your great generous heart, and I am sorry that my being here gives you pain. It gives pain to most of my friends: but I cannot help it: I must remake my maimed life on my own lines. Had Constance allowed me to see my boys, my life would, I think, have been quite different. But this she would not do. I don't in any way venture to blame her for her action, but every action has its consequence.

I waited three months. At the expiration of that long, lonely time, I had to take my life into my own hands.

---

[1] John Rowland Fothergill.
[2] "*L'Humaine Tragédie.*" The book was published in 1895.

I intend to winter here. Perhaps live here. Much depends of course on my ability to write again.

You must not, dear Carlos, pass harsh judgments on me, whatever you may hear. It is not for pleasure that I come here, though pleasure, I am glad to say, walks all round. I come here to try to realise the perfection of my temperament and my soul. We have all to choose our own methods. I have chosen mine. My friends in England are greatly distressed. Still, they are good friends to me: and will remain so, most of them at any rate. You must remain so too. Ever yours   OSCAR

To Reginald Turner

[*Postmark 23 September 1897*]   *Hôtel Royal des Étrangers, Naples*

My dear Reggie, Bosie and I came here on Monday: we met at Aix: and spent a day at Genoa.

Much that you say in your letter is right, but still you leave out of consideration the great love I have for Bosie. I love him, and have always loved him. He ruined my life, and for that very reason I seem forced to love him more: and I think that now I shall do lovely work. Bosie is himself a poet, far the first of all the young poets of England, an exquisite artist in lyric and ballad. It is to a poet that I am going back. So when people say how dreadful of me to return to Bosie, do say *no*—say that I love him, that he is a poet, and that, after all, whatever my life may have been ethically, it has always been *romantic*, and Bosie is my romance. My romance is a tragedy of course, but it is none the less a romance, and he loves me very dearly, more than he loves or can love anyone else, and without him my life was dreary.

So stick up for us, Reggie, and be nice.

I had a charming letter from Eugene, for which thank him. Ever yours
OSCAR

To Robert Ross

Friday [*1 October 1897*]   *Villa Giudice, Posilippo, Naples*

Dearest Robbie, I have not answered your letters, because they distressed me and angered me, and I did not wish to write to *you* of all people in the world in an angry mood. You have been such a good friend to me. Your love, your generosity, your care of me in prison and out of prison are the most lovely things in my life. Without you what would I have done? As you remade my life for me you have a perfect right to say what you choose to me, but I have no right to say anything to you except to tell you how grateful I am to you, and what a pleasure it is to feel gratitude and love at the same time for the same person.

I daresay that what I have done is fatal, but it had to be done. It was

309

necessary that Bosie and I should come together again; I saw no other life for myself. For himself he saw no other: all we want now is to be let alone, but the Neapolitan papers are tedious and wish to interview me, etc. They write nicely of me, but I don't want to be written about. I want peace—that is all. Perhaps I shall find it.

Now to literature. Of course I want you to help me.

I have sent Smithers my poem with directions for a type-written copy to be sent at once to *you*: please send me any suggestions and criticisms that occur to you.

Also, see Smithers, and *Pinker*:[1] Pinker lives at Effingham House. I must have £300 at least—more, if possible. The poem is to be published simultaneously in the *New York Journal* and by *Smithers*. I think bits of the poem very good now, but I will never again out-Kipling Henley.

Bosie has written three lovely sonnets, which I have called "The Triad of the Moon"—they are quite wonderful.[2] He has sent them to Henley. I have also got him to send his sonnet on Mozart to the *Musician*.[3]

Tomorrow I begin the *Florentine Tragedy*. After that I must tackle *Pharaoh*.

We have a lovely villa over the sea; and a nice piano. I take lessons in Italian conversation from Rocco three times a week.

My handwriting is now dreadful, as bad as yours. Ever yours   OSCAR

To Leonard Smithers

Friday [*?1 October 1897*]   *Villa Giudice, Posilippo*
[*Postmark of receipt 11 October 1897*]

Dear Smithers, Your letter has just arrived, and as the enclosure seems to have slipped out I wired at once to you to ask you to *telegraph* the £20 through Cook's office. I do hope you will do so. The crisis is of a grave and usual character—were it unique I would not feel so agitated.

I have decided long ago that I would not send my poem to the *Chronicle*, as it is far too long for a paper. It is now 600 lines almost, so Symons need not prophesy—he is unnecessary.[4]

I am going to ask £300 for my poem from America! It is well worth it. Do at once send me specimen type.

---

[1] James Brand Pinker (1863–1922), one of the first of the literary agents.

[2] They were included in Douglas's second volume of poems, *The City of the Soul* (1899), which was published anonymously.

[3] A weekly magazine which ran only from 12 May to 17 November 1897. No poem by Douglas appeared in it.

[4] The cause of Wilde's jokingly contemptuous attitude towards the poet and critic Arthur Symons (1865–1945) at this period is unknown, but it persisted at any rate until Symons's favourable review of *The Ballad of Reading Gaol* in the *Saturday Review* of 12 March 1898.

Also have you good initial letters? Let me see them. By spacing the intervals of the poem well I think it will be almost a book. Wherever a space occurs one should have a fresh page—begin a fresh page.

One can always fall back on vegetable parchment for a cover; it is rather nice really, and is very good for jam and poetry.

How *can* you keep on asking is Lord Alfred Douglas in Naples? You know quite well he is—we are together. He understands me and my art, and loves both. I hope never to be separated from him. He is a most delicate and exquisite poet, besides—far the finest of all the young poets in England. You have got to publish his next volume; it is full of lovely lyrics, flute-music and moon-music, and sonnets in ivory and gold. He is witty, graceful, lovely to look at, loveable to be with. He has also ruined my life, so I can't help loving him—it is the only thing to do.

My wife's letter came too late. I had waited four months in vain, and it was only when the children had gone back to school that she asked me to come to her—whereas what I want is the love of my children. It is now irretrievable, of course. But in questions of the emotions and their romantic qualities, unpunctuality is fatal.

I dare say I may have more misfortunes yet. Still, I can write as well, I think, as I used to write. Half as well would satisfy me.

With regard to the postal arrangements in France, I am still of opinion that one *can*. The bet holds good, for the third time now. Ever yours

OSCAR WILDE

To Robert Ross

Friday [8 October 1897]   *Villa Giudice, Posilippo*

My dear Robbie, Thanks so much for your letter. Smithers took my letter a little too seriously. It was unfair of him, as I certainly did not take his advice seriously, though he gave me a great deal of it, with reference to my wife, through the medium of his type-writer. He is a very good fellow, and most kind to me.

With much of your criticism I agree. The poem suffers under the difficulty of a divided aim in style. Some is realistic, some is romantic: some poetry, some propaganda. I feel it keenly, but as a whole I think the production interesting: that it is interesting from more points of view than one is artistically to be regretted.

With regard to the adjectives, I admit there are far too many "dreadfuls" and "fearfuls." The difficulty is that the objects in prison have no shape or form. To take an example: the shed in which people are hanged is a little shed with a glass roof, like a photographer's studio on the sands at Margate. For eighteen months I thought it *was* the studio for photographing prisoners. There is no adjective to describe it. I call it "hideous" because it became so to me after I knew its use. In itself it is a wooden, oblong, narrow shed with a glass roof.

A cell again may be described *psychologically*, with reference to its effect on the soul: in itself it can only be described as "whitewashed" or "dimly-lit." It has no shape, no contents. It does not exist from the point of view of form or colour.

In point of fact, describing a prison is as difficult artistically as describing a water-closet would be. If one had to describe the latter in literature, prose or verse, one could merely say it was well, or badly, papered: or clean or the reverse: the horror of prison is that everything is so simple and commonplace in itself, and so degrading, and hideous, and revolting in its effect.

The *Musician* expressed a great desire to publish the poem: I refused then: now I think I would accept *any* English paper. If the *Musician* would offer £50, it would be a great thing. But, of course, I would prefer the *Sunday Sun*, or *Reynolds*. If the *Saturday* will take it, well and good. I can't offer it myself, but Smithers might.

It is very annoying that I cannot get a copy of the poem. I sent it exactly two weeks ago, and until I get it I cannot pull it together. I write daily on the subject to Smithers. He takes no notice. I am not reproaching him for this: I am merely stating a fact.

I am going to retain the opening of Part IV, but to cut out three stanzas at opening of Part III.

As regards the spirits, I think the *grotesqueness* of the scene to a certain degree makes their speech possible, but Bosie agrees with you: though we do not hold your views on the Ghost in *Hamlet*: there is so little parallel between lyrical and dramatic poetry or method.

I have had no money at all for three days, so cannot buy note-paper. This is *your* foolscap. Ever yours   OSCAR

To Leonard Smithers

Saturday, 16 October [1897]   *Posilippo [Postmark Capri]*

My dear Smithers, It is a pleasing reflection for me to think that I have one duty left in life—that of writing to you daily—and that I perform it duly and cheerfully.

I suppose that Sherard was in his cups at the Authors' Club.[1] He was

---

[1] Sherard's account of this incident (*Oscar Wilde: The Story of an Unhappy Friendship*, 1902) runs:

A few days later it became known that Oscar Wilde had resumed the friendship which had brought disaster and ruin upon him.

I heard of it in London, one afternoon when I was in the smoking-room of a literary club. With no other purpose than to distress me, two men [Smithers and Vincent O'Sullivan], who were both the worse for liquor, called on me there and triumphantly announced that Oscar Wilde had gone to the Villa G[iudice], and had there taken up his permanent abode.

I said it was a great and an unfortunate mistake on his part; that his action would everywhere be misconstrued; that his traducers and enemies would be

in his grenadine all the time he was at Berneval with me. I have written to him, without of course mentioning your name, simply to ask him when he takes upon himself to censure my life not to talk so loud that I can hear him at Naples. It is inartistic to play Tartuffe as if it was Termagant.

I am delighted to hear O'Sullivan is coming to Naples, and hope he will come soon. I had a charming breakfast with him in Paris.

The reason you should publish Lord Alfred Douglas's poems is that it will ensure you a niche in the History of English Literature. To be the herald of such music would be fame. I am pained to think that you might throw away such a wonderful chance in life.

I am anxious about Pinker. Of course *he* does not give the money—he only asks for it—and takes ten per cent. Robbie Ross has promised to wire to me how the negotiations promise.

Your £10 has made a great difference in my simple household, and this morning the servants are singing like larks. Ever yours   OSCAR WILDE

To Leonard Smithers

Tuesday, 19 October 1897   *Hôtel Royal des Étrangers, Naples*

Dear Smithers, As an edition of 500—of which 100 will go to press, author, etc. practically—will only just pay expenses, and leave me £20 in your debt, I now think that it would be better after all to publish the poem in a paper. It is too long for the *Chronicle*, and Frank Harris has been so offensive to me and about me that I don't think negotiations possible with him.

My idea is *Reynolds*. It has, for some odd reason, always been nice to me, and used to publish my poems when I was in prison, and write nicely about me.[1] Also, it circulates widely amongst the criminal classes, to which I now belong, so I shall be read by my peers—a new experience for me. I have written to Robbie Ross about the matter.

There are, I think, still 400 people left amongst the lovers of poetry to buy our edition up.

I have had a letter from Ernest Dowson to say he gave you £10 of his debt to me to send to me. This seems improbable, as I have heard nothing of it from you, but I have no doubt he "means well."

I am eagerly waiting for the type-written copies. Truly yours
OSCAR WILDE

justified in the eyes of the world, and many sympathies would be alienated.

A lying account of my words was immediately transmitted to Naples, and some days later I received from my friend a letter which distressed me greatly, for it showed me in what an unhappy state of mind he was.

[1] *Reynolds* and the *Daily Chronicle* were the only papers that reported Wilde's trials impartially.

*To Leonard Smithers

In the desert of my life you raised up the lovely mirage of the great sum of
£20. You said that its conversion into a reality was a matter of days. On
the faith of this I took a lovely villa on the Bay of Naples which I cannot
inhabit as I have to take all my meals at the hotel. This is the simple
truth . . .

Your letter received today is dated *Monday* last—and Dowson wrote to
me that he had given you £10 for me on Saturday. What does this mean?
Will you write to him and ask an explanation? It seems a disgraceful thing
for him to have said. I will write to him about it myself.[1]

To Robert Ross

Thursday [28 October 1897]   *Villa Giudice, Posilippo*

Dear Robbie, I have sent Smithers the corrected copy.[2] I don't think I
can do much more with the poem. All your suggestions were very interesting, but, of course, I have not taken them all: "black dock's dreadful
pen" for instance is my own impression of the place in which I stood: it is
burned into my memory.

As regards page 13, "goes for ever through the land with the red feet
of Cain," I have altered that, not on account of Hood,[3] but because I use
Cain later on, and he is too big to be used twice with effect.

But do you think that in the corrected version I should have for the last
line "And binds it with a chain"? Otherwise it is too like the end of *The
Sphinx*.[4]

I fear I have built air-castles of false gold on my dreams of America.
My hope now is in Miss Marbury,[5] who is on the spot. But I should like
Murphy,[6] if he has authority, to see the poem. He represents the greatest
paper in America. You will consider the point. Ever yours   OSCAR

---

[1] The £10 had been sent but had been delayed in the post.

[2] The typed fair copy of *The Ballad* on which Wilde had made corrections.

[3]   He told how murderers walk the earth
      Beneath the curse of Cain.
        ("The Dream of Eugene Aram")

[4] The last line of *The Sphinx* runs:

    And weeps for every soul that dies, and weeps for every soul in vain.

and the revised stanza of *The Ballad* ends:

    And makes it bleed great gouts of blood,
    And makes it bleed in vain!

[5] Elisabeth Marbury (1856–1933) was a leading play-agent in New York. She
first met Wilde during his lecture-tour in 1882, and handled all his plays in
America. In her autobiography, *My Crystal Ball* (1923), she gives a short, sympathetic and largely inaccurate record of Wilde.

[6] Unidentified, except that he seems to have been the London representative of
the *New York Journal*.

To Leonard Smithers

My dear Smithers, Your letter announcing proofs just received. I expect the latter this afternoon.

With regard to the description of a prison doctor: the passage in which it occurs does not refer to a particular execution, but to executions in general. I was not present at the Reading execution, nor do I know anything about it. I am describing a general scene with general types. The Governor of Reading for instance was a "mulberry-faced Dictator:"[1] a great red-faced, bloated Jew who always looked as if he drank, and did so: his name was Isaacson; he did not, could not have had a "*yellow* face" of Doom or anything else. Brandy was the flaming message of his pulpy face. By "Caiaphas" I do not mean the present Chaplain of Reading: he is a good-natured fool, one of the silliest of God's silly sheep: a typical clergyman in fact. I mean any priest of God who assists at the unjust and cruel punishments of man.

I will change *one* word so as to avoid being misunderstood. I will put "while *some* coarse-mouthed doctor" etc. That simply describes the *type* of prison-doctor in England. As a class they are brutes, and excessively cruel.

The Chiswick Press is idiotic.[2]

I hope you sent Miss Marbury the poem. Otherwise she cannot get offers. If you have not, perhaps better wait till the proofs arrive. But I suppose America is a foolish dream as far as buying my poem goes.

I still go to Cook's every day to enquire if there is a telegram of £10 for me. For four days I have had no cigarettes, no money to buy them, or notepaper. I wish you would make an effort. Ever yours   o. w.

To Leonard Smithers

My dear Smithers, Your telegram has just arrived: and I am very much obliged to you for your kindness, as in the midst of my hideous worries the lack of any money at all was paralysing. Now, I can really think about my position, and form some judgment as to whether it is worth while fighting on against the hideous forces of the world. Personally I don't think it is, but Vanity, that great impulse, still drives me to think of a possible future of self-assertion. It seems absurd to be beaten by the want of money. And

[1] Tennyson: "Lucretius," referring to Sulla, the Roman dictator, whose face was said to resemble a mulberry sprinkled with meal.

[2] The Chiswick Press, the printers of *The Ballad of Reading Gaol*, were clearly nervous of being involved in a libel action by the Reading doctor. Their name did not appear in *The Ballad* until the seventh edition.

yet I feel that every problem in life must be solved on its own conditions. And Financial Problems can be solved only by Finance. Genius, Art, Romance, Passion, and the like are useless when the point at issue is one of figures. A solution for an algebraic problem is not to be found in the sense of Beauty, however developed.

The proofs also have arrived:[1] in old days of power and personality I always insisted that my proofs should be sent to me on the paper to be ultimately used. Otherwise I would not have been able to judge of the look of a page. Of course the paper of these proofs is awful, and the whole thing looks to me mean in consequence. The type is good: though I think the ?'s lacking in style, and the stops, especially the full-stops, characterless. But setting this aside, the whole thing looks too meagre for a 3/6 book. When one remembers what thick cloth-bound volumes the public buys nowadays for 3/6 or 2/6, it seems to me that they will think twice before they pay 3/6 for what looks like a thin sixpenny pamphlet, lacking in all suggestion of permanence of form. The public is largely influenced by the *look* of a book. So are we all. It is the only artistic thing about the public.

I had intended that wherever there was a break (marked by a leaf) in my poem, a *new* page should begin. This would give the book thickness and an air of responsibility. Whether it would really look well, I cannot say: you are, of course, the better judge. Failing this, it really would be better to print on alternate leaves, as you suggested. As it stands, it is not adequate to 3/6.

The drawback of beginning a new page at every break is that it makes the poem look piecemeal, and robs it of the impression of continuous unity of development. The advantage is the increase of the number of pages. I really think that printing on alternate pages is the best. You say this will necessitate a cloth binding. Well, let us have one. A plain olive-green, or cinnamon cloth, with a white back gold-lettered.[2] The colours, nowadays, in cloths are lovely.

The title-page is not good. (I hope, by the way, you have a double proof?) The "By C.3.3." is far too small. Also, as a general rule in art, I think that the less the type is changed on a page the better. Too many types spoil the looking. Nor do I care for, or indeed stand, the placing of the "By C.3.3."

Why not   The

Ballad of Reading Gaol

    | By
    | C.3.3.

Indeed place "By C.3.3." quite at the side, so as to draw down the type-design to the publisher's lines and fill the page. As a rule in English books the publisher's name looks a sudden intrusion into a page more candid without it, whereas it should be part of it all.

---

[1] The first printed proofs.   [2] This suggestion was carried out.

I would suggest the same type for the full title and the suggestion of the author. The publisher's name and address, of course, smaller.

The type for the Dedication is *revolting*. It is like a bad brass by Gilbert Scott.[1] There need be no suggestion of a Pugin tombstone about it.[2] Joy and Assertion are its notes.

At the close of each Canto a leaf is out of place. It marks transition, not finality.

The "In Memoriam" page is an example of what I mean by the in-artistic effect of changing type: it looks like a page of specimen-types for a printer's apprentice. It should be quite simple, and no tombstone Gothic about the words "In Memoriam." On the whole I think now that the combination of Latin and English is wrong. What do you say to this? (not in tombstone-type)

In Memory

of

R. J. M.

late of H.M. Dragoon Guards.

Died in H.M. Prison, Reading

July 13

1896.[3]

Or, shall we put "Her Majesty's" in full? Perhaps not, as it would go badly with Gaol or Prison: though the official address on prison note-paper (paper of a loathsome blue colour) is *H.M. Prison*. Perhaps "Died in Reading Gaol, Berkshire" would suit the title better. It would not suggest that there was any sneer in the title.

---

[1] George Gilbert Scott (1811–78), English architect and "restorer" of churches. He was knighted for designing the Albert Memorial in Kensington Gardens.

[2] Augustus Welby Northmore Pugin (1812–52), an English architect of French extraction, was one of the leaders of the neo-Gothic movement. He helped Sir Charles Barry to design the new Houses of Parliament 1837–43.

[3] Apparently Wilde's original plan was to disguise the identity and circumstances of the man he was commemorating, but he changed his mind, and the final dedication read:

In Memoriam

C. T. W.

Sometime Trooper of the Royal Horse Guards.

Obiit H.M. Prison, Reading, Berkshire,

July 7th, 1896.

Charles Thomas Wooldridge, aged 30, was hanged in Reading Gaol on 7 July 1896 for the murder of his wife.

The additional dedication (see note 1, p. 279) was now removed. On 16 November Ross had written to Smithers:

> I want to write to you about the dedication. Please do not tell Oscar my views or quote my views to him as it will merely irritate him and at all events while the poem is in progress he must be kept in good humour . . . I think the dedication with or without initials is ROT and at all events quite unsuitable to a poem of that sort . . . I am convinced that dear Oscar meant to tell me and Douglas and two or three other people that each was intended. That only amuses me.

Do you think "Hanged in Reading Gaol" would either be too like G. R. Sims,[1] or give away the plot of the poem?

Or do you think that the words "In Memory of R. J. M." would be enough? I now, sometimes, think so. It would excite interest, without giving away the plot. It is a difficult point. Please consult with Robbie. Alfred Douglas thinks that if I don't put that R. J. M. died in Reading Prison people might think that it was all imaginary. This is a sound objection.

As regards the doctor, I have written to you today. To sacrifice the stanza on the dung-heap of the Chiswick Press would be absurd. Would you kindly say that the description is generic, and that the Reading doctor is a thin sallow man with an aquiline nose, and that the description is imaginary, just like the yellow face of the Governor, or the Caiaphas-chaplain. It does not occur in any description of Reading Gaol. It is abstract. The only people I have libelled in the poem are the Reading warders. They were—most of them—as good as possible to me. But to poetry all must be sacrificed, even warders.

Robbie has written me a very acrimonious letter to assure me that he never showed you any letters of mine, except passages on business. But you wrote to me "Is it *kind* or *just* of you to write to Ross that I dictated to my type-writer advice about your wife and your conduct to her?" So Robbie must have thought my remarks on the subject of a business-character. They really were not. But Robbie is on horseback at present. He can ride everything, except Pegasus.

I hope to send you the proofs tomorrow. Do you think that copy-righting *portions* of the poem will prevent the piracy of quotation in the papers? I don't. I think the only chance is to go for a big thing and to publish the poem in America at one dollar. This of course would rank as general expenses. So you would have half the profits in America, and they *may be* great. But the moment you publish in England, the American papers, under pretence of criticism, will publish the whole affair. That is certain.

I now think that we must wait till after Christmas. If we are to secure America we must. And the 1st of January would not be a bad date. Consider the point.

You suggest "gray" instead of "grey" in one passage. But I have "grey" everywhere else. Is there any rule about it? I only know that Dorian *Gray* is a classic, and deservedly. Excuse this brief letter.[2] I am in a hurry to buy cigarettes—the first for four days. Sincerely yours

OSCAR WILDE

---

[1] George Robert Sims (1847–1922) was a prolific and very successful playwright, journalist and versifier, particularly as Dagonet in the *Referee*. His melodramas *The Lights of London* (1881) and *Harbour Lights* (1885) had long runs, and his ballad beginning "It is Christmas Day in the Workhouse" was a great favourite.

[2] The original covers eight quarto pages.

To More Adey

Sunday [*Postmark 21 November 1897*]　　　　*Villa Giudice, Posilippo*

My dear More, I cannot tell you the utter astonishment with which I read your letter.

You tell me that you, and Bobbie, on being asked whether Bosie was "a disreputable person" felt bound at once to say yes: and that you declared that my wife was acting "strictly within her legal rights according to the agreement" in depriving me of my allowance, because I have the pleasure of Bosie's companionship, the only companionship in the world open to me.

In what way, my dear More, is Bosie more disreputable than either you or Robbie?

When you came to see me at Reading in November 1895, my wife, on being informed of this by my sister-in-law, wrote to me a most violent letter, in which she said—I quote from her letter now before me—"I hear with horror that Mr More Adey has been to see you. Is this your promise to lead a new life? What am I to think of you if you still have intercourse with your old infamous companions? I require you to assure me that you will never see him again, or any people of that kind" etc. etc.

That is my wife's view of you, based on the information supplied to her by George Lewis about you, and Robbie, and other friends of mine. My wife also knows what Robbie's life is and has been.

May I ask, if you had come to give me the pleasure of your companionship in my lonely life, whether Robbie would have at once agreed that you were a "disreputable person" and that I had forfeited all claim to my allowance in consequence?

If Robbie had lived with me, would you have taken the same course?

I simply don't know how to describe my feelings of utter amazement and indignation.

As for Hansell, he calmly writes to me that he considers "*any member* of the Queensberry family" is "a disreputable person." Conceive such ignorance, such impertinence. If Lord Douglas of Hawick offered me the shelter of his roof I was to be left a pauper!

Hansell is bound to decide according to the legal agreement: it is his duty to do so. I say nothing about his failing in his duty to me as a client. That would only give him pleasure. But simply as an arbitrator, in a question of life and death practically, he utterly ignores the wording of the agreement, and gives a decision entirely illegal, entirely unjust, in order, I suppose, to curry favour with Mr Hargrove, or to experience for the first time in his life the priggish pleasure of what he ignorantly thinks is a moral attitude.

When he tells me in black and white that if Percy came and stayed with me he would regard me as living with a disreputable person, he shows his entire disregard of the legal agreement of whose clauses he was stupidly made arbitrator.

As for you and Robbie calmly acquiescing in this monstrous injustice,

I do not know what to think about either of you. I simply cannot comprehend it, nor can I write, today, any more about it. Ever yours   OSCAR[1]

To More Adey

Saturday [Postmark 27 November 1897]   *Villa Giudice, Posilippo*

My dear More, I have not yet heard anything from you in answer to my letter. But Hansell has written to me stating that his decision is irrevocable.

I now want to know if there cannot be a compromise made. I am quite ready to agree not to live in the same house with Bosie again. Of course to promise to cut him, or not to speak to him, or not to associate with him, would be absurd. He is the only friend with whom I can be in contact, and to live without some companion is impossible. I had silence and solitude for two years: to condemn me now to silence and solitude would be barbarous.

It is not a matter of much importance, but I never wrote to my wife that I was going "to keep house with Alfred Douglas." I thought "keep house" was only a servant-girl's expression.

My wife wrote me a very violent letter on September 29 last saying: "I *forbid* you to see Lord Alfred Douglas. I forbid you to return to your filthy, insane life. I forbid you to live at Naples. I will not allow you to come to Genoa." I quote her words.[2]

I wrote to her to say that I would never dream of coming to see her against her will, that the only reason that would induce me to come to see her was the prospect of a greeting of sympathy with me in my misfortunes,

---

[1] When the atmosphere was calmer, Adey wrote a long letter to Wilde on 6 January 1898, in which he defended himself:

> You interpreted a sentence of mine about Mrs Wilde's having acted strictly within her legal rights, to mean that I had somehow admitted that Bosie was a disreputable character. I made no admissions about Bosie of any kind. His character did not enter into the question at all. The question was merely one of fact—whether you and he were living together or not. This question had been laid before the arbitrator, without my knowledge, before my interview with Holman took place. I had nothing to do with it. . . . Mrs Wilde did act strictly within her legal rights by appealing to the arbitrator according to the agreement; your friends, as the other parties to it, had therefore nothing to do but submit to his decision. There was no ground on which to oppose Mrs Wilde; it would have been a purely vexatious opposition, worse than useless to you, and we had no money to pay solicitors for carrying on a fruitless correspondence merely to gain time.

[2] Constance's letter has perished, but on 26 September 1897 she wrote to Carlos Blacker:

> I have today written a note to Oscar saying that I required an immediate answer to my question whether he had been to Capri or whether he had met anywhere that appalling individual. I also said that he evidently did not care much for his boys since he neither acknowledged their photos which I sent him nor the remembrances that *they* sent him. I hope it was not too hard of me to write this, but it was quite necessary.

and affection, and pity. That for the rest, I only desired peace, and to live my own life as best I could. That I could not live in London, or, as yet, in Paris, and that I certainly hoped to winter at Naples. To this I received no answer.

I do think that, if we engage not to live together, I might be still left the wretched £3 a week—so little, but still something. How on earth am I to live?

Do, if possible, try to arrange something. I know you all think I am wilful, but it is the result of the nemesis of character, and the bitterness of life. I was a problem for which there was no solution. Ever yours

OSCAR

To Leonard Smithers

Sunday [? *28 November 1897*]   *Posilippo*

Dear Smithers, Do try and make the Chiswick Press less mad and less maddening. I now have "While *some* coarse-mouthed doctor straddles by, with *a* flattened bulldog nose, fingering *the* watch" etc. If they ask you is there no offence in it, say it is simply miching mallecho, but to say it with style wear sables.[1] However, if they kick, I cannot sacrifice the lines about the watch, so I enclose a feeble substitute, but I shall be outraged and perhaps outrageous if it is used.[2]

I wish you would start a Society for the Defence of Oppressed Personalities: at present there is a gross European concert headed by brutes and solicitors against us. It is really ridiculous that after my entire life has been wrecked by Society, people should still propose to exercise social tyranny over me, and try to force me to live in solitude—the one thing I can't stand. I lived in silence and solitude for two years in prison. I did not think that on my release my wife, my trustees, the guardians of my children, my few friends, such as they are, and my myriad enemies would combine to force me by starvation to live in silence and solitude again. After all in prison we had food of some kind: it was revolting, and made as loathsome as possible on purpose, and quite inadequate to sustain life in health. Still, there *was* food of some kind. The scheme now is that I am to live in silence and solitude and have no food at all. Really, the want of imagination in people is appalling. This scheme is put forward on moral grounds! It is proposed to leave me to die of starvation, or to blow my brains out in a Naples urinal. I never came across anyone in whom the moral sense was dominant who was not heartless, cruel, vindictive, log-

[1] Cf. *Hamlet*, Act III, scene 2.
[2] This stanza finally read:

> He does not rise in piteous haste
>   To put on convict-clothes,
> While some coarse-mouthed Doctor gloats, and notes
>   Each new and nerve-twitched pose,
> Fingering a watch whose little ticks
>   Are like horrible hammer-blows.

stupid, and entirely lacking in the smallest sense of humanity. Moral people, as they are termed, are simple beasts. I would sooner have fifty unnatural vices than one unnatural virtue. It is unnatural virtue that makes the world, for those who suffer, such a premature Hell.

All this has, of course, direct reference to my poem: and indeed is the usual way in which poets write to publishers.

I have decided to put back the opening of Canto *Three*, because it is dramatically necessary for the telling of the story. The reader wants to know where the condemned man was, and what he was doing. I wish it were better, but it *isn't* and can't be. I think it aids the narrative immensely. So stick it in. For the rest I think I have corrected enough. The popularity of the poem will be largely increased by the author's painful death by starvation. The public love poets to die in that way. It seems to them dramatically right. Perhaps it is. Ever yours   o. w.

To Robert Ross

Monday [*6 December 1897*]   *Villa Giudice* [*Posilippo*]

My dear Robbie, I know that it would have been impossible for you to have prevented Hansell's decision: what hurt me was that no effort was made, and I still hold that More was wrong in saying that my wife was "acting strictly within her rights according to the legal agreement." Hansell is of the same opinion. He writes to me that he gave his decision, not on the grounds of the written agreement, but on the understanding that existed that I was not to live with Bosie.

He told me at *Reading* that he would decide so. At that time I did not want ever to see Bosie again, so I didn't mind. Afterwards was a different thing. I then had a right to claim that the strictest *legal* interpretation should be put on the wording of a very elaborate agreement. Bosie is of course a gilded pillar of infamy in this century, but whether he is *legally* disreputable is another question.

I knew that I was running a fearful risk of losing my income by being with Bosie. I was warned on all sides: my eyes were not blinded: still I was a good deal staggered by the blow: one may go to a dentist of one's own free will, but the moment of tooth-extraction is painful: and More's acquiescence in Mr Hargrove's refusal to pay Mr Holman wounded me, and I shot poisoned arrows back. Arthur Clifton is trying to arrange some terms with Adrian Hope, and I of course engage never to live in the same house as Bosie again. I hope Arthur will do this, but Adrian Hope has never answered my letter to him. I have not much hope, however. Things have come to a crash of a terrible character. You have done wonderful things for me, but the Nemesis of circumstances, the Nemesis of character, have been too strong for me—and as I said to More I think I was a problem for which there was no solution. Money alone could have helped me, not to solve, but to avoid solving the difficulty.

As for your letter to Smithers, I don't think you should have taken up

322

such an attitude about me in consequence of some phrase in a letter of someone else's, with which I had nothing to do. You wrote to Smithers "I *hope* you will *refuse* to publish Oscar Wilde's poem if he insists on publishing first in a paper." The question of Smithers's publishing in book-form something that had appeared in a periodical was a question for him. What you meant of course was that you hoped Smithers would induce me to consent not to publish in a periodical: in point of fact Smithers wrote to me seven weeks ago that he did not care twopence whether I published previously or not. He did this in an answer to a letter of mine in which I told him that I had refused an offer from the *Musician*, on the ground that it would spoil Smithers's book. Bosie did not, and does not, see why, if I got £25 or £50 from a paper for the poem, you should try to induce Smithers to refuse to publish in book-form. Such things are constantly done. In any case it was a matter for Smithers to decide, and he had previously assured me that he did not care a scrap. This was the meaning of Bosie's no doubt too vivacious expression, and there is no offence in its substance, while, as for the form, I don't think that in the correspondence of either of you Form has been the predominant note, or the sense of Beauty the indwelling spirit. In any case it has nothing to do with me. I hope Smithers will show you all my letters to him in which you are mentioned. I am greatly and rightly pained at your writing to him that our intimate friendship is over, and that you find you have no longer my confidence in business matters. The former is a question at any rate for yourself: the latter statement is unjust, unwarranted, and unkind.

And on the whole I do think you make wonderfully little allowance for a man like myself, now ruined, broken-hearted, and thoroughly unhappy. You stab me with a thousand phrases: if one phrase of mine shrills through the air near you, you cry out that you are wounded to death. Ever yours

OSCAR[1]

To Leonard Smithers

Saturday [*11 December 1897*]   *Villa Giudice* [*Posilippo*]
[*Postmark 12 December 1897*]

My dear Smithers, A holograph letter from you is indeed a curiosity of literature, and I treasure it for its manner no less than for its matter.

As for dear Robbie, if he will kindly send me out a pair of his oldest boots I will blacken them with pleasure, and send them back to him with a sonnet. I have loved Robbie all my life, and have not the smallest intention of giving up loving him. Of all my old friends he is the one who has the

---

[1] On the same day, Wilde wrote to Smithers:

I am quite broken-hearted about Bobbie's attitude towards me, and the way he has written of me to Alfred Douglas. But nothing can ever spoil the memory of his wonderful devotion to me, or rob me of the pleasure of being deeply grateful to him for the love he showed me. Alfred Douglas is on his way to Paris.

most beautiful nature; had my other friends been like him, I would not be the pariah-dog of the nineteenth century. But natures like his are not found twice in a life-time.

When dear Robbie heavily bombarded me (an unfair thing, as unfortified places are usually respected in civilised war) I bore it with patriarchal patience. I admit, however, that when he seemed to me slightly casual about someone else, I sent up a rocket of several colours. I am sorry I did so. But what is there in my life for which I am not sorry? And how useless it all is! My life cannot be patched up. There is a doom on it. Neither to myself, nor others, am I any longer a joy. I am now simply an ordinary pauper of a rather low order: the fact that I am also a pathological problem in the eyes of German scientists is only interesting to German scientists: and even in their works I am tabulated, and come under the law of *averages*! *Quantum mutatus*![1]

Now to the title-page, which I enclose. The *C.3.3* is not good. It is too thin. It should be as black and thick as the title. There may be some difficulty about the numerals, but the *C* seems to me much thinner than the *G* in "Gaol."

Also, your name is too large. I am not discussing the relative values of publisher and poet, as the poet's name is not mentioned. But the title of the poem is the foremost thing. By printing your name in the same type, or near it, the printers have spoiled the page. There is no balance, and it looks as if the poem was by Leonard Smithers.

It was much better in the second proof. You have marked on that that your name is to be "one size larger type." They seem to have made it three sizes larger. Personally, I think that there should be simply *two* types —one for the title and pseudonym, the other for publisher and address and date. If you wish a third type, take the one of L.S. in the title-page of O'Sullivan's book.[2] Also, surely the spacing of the full title should be equalised. There seems to me too much white between

Gaol

→

By

→

3.

I do think it would look better together, made more of a block of. In any case your name is evidently out of all proportion—I speak typographically.

I think that you had better send me no more proofs of the poem. I have the *maladie de perfection* and keep on correcting. I know I have got it now to a fairly high standard, but I don't want to polish for ever. So *after you get* the proofs, I think you yourself could see that all my corrections were carried out, and let me have merely the title-page and "In Memoriam"

---

[1] *Quantum mutatus ab illo* (How changed). Virgil, *Aeneid*, II, 274.

[2] Smithers had just sent Wilde a copy of Vincent O'Sullivan's poems—*The Houses of Sin*—which he had published.

page. This is out of regard for your time and pocket. I would also like to see the cover.[1]

I think that if you try and get in your name and address on the back, where the lettering is to be, it will be too crowded. I propose simply "The Ballad of Reading Gaol." But you will see yourself. However, I see your name is all right on O'Sullivan's back.

Robbie has just sent me the *Weekly Sun*. I do not know if this is a sign of forgiveness or the reverse. Ever yours   OSCAR WILDE

---

[1] When Wilde eventually saw the final version he wrote to Smithers on 7 February 1898:

I am really charmed with the book . . . The title-page is a masterpiece—one of the best I have ever seen. I am really so cheerfully grateful to you, my dear fellow, for the care and trouble you have taken.

PART NINE

PARIS · 1898-1900

After he and Douglas had parted (see p. 330), Wilde paid a short visit to Taormina in Sicily in December 1897. In January he was back in Naples and he returned to Paris in February. The exact date is not known, but he may well have reached Paris on Sunday 13 February, the day on which Smithers published *The Ballad of Reading Gaol*.

To Robert Ross

[? *18 February 1898*]   *Hôtel de Nice, Rue des Beaux-Arts, Paris*
My dearest Robbie, Thanks so much for the cuttings.

Smithers is absurd, only printing 400 copies, to begin with,[1] and not advertising. I fear he has missed a popular "rush." He is so fond of "suppressed" books that he suppresses his own. Don't tell him this from me. I have written to him.

It is very unfair of people being horrid to me about Bosie and Naples. A patriot put in prison for loving his country loves his country, and a poet in prison for loving boys loves boys. To have altered my life would have been to have admitted that Uranian[2] love is ignoble. I hold it to be noble— more noble than other forms. Ever yours   OSCAR

---

[1] Smithers had eventually capitulated and printed another 400, so that the first edition of *The Ballad* consisted of 800 copies at 2/6, plus thirty numbered copies printed on Japanese vellum at 21/-.

[2] i.e. homosexual. The word was apparently first used in this sense by the Austrian writer Karl Heinrich Ulrichs (1825–95). It was derived from the Greek Uranos (Heaven) in the belief that such love was of a higher order than ordinary love, and referred to Plato's *Symposium* (181 C). In 1896 André Raffalovich published a book in French called *Uranisme et Unisexualité*, containing a chapter on Wilde which had been separately published in 1895.

To Will Rothenstein

My dear Will, I cannot tell you how touched I am by your letter, and by all you say of my poem. Why on earth don't you write literary criticisms for papers? I wish *The Ballad* had fallen into your hands. No one has said things so *sympathiques*, so full of delicate insight, so large, from the point of view of art, as you. Your letter has given me more pleasure, more pride, than anything has done since the poem appeared.

Yes: it is something to have made a "sonnet out of skilly" (Cunninghame Graham will explain to you what skilly is.[1] You must never know by personal experience). And I *do* think the whole affair "realised," and that is triumph.

I hope you will be in Paris some time this spring, and come and see me.

I see by the papers that you are still making mortals immortal, and I wish you were working for a Paris newspaper, that I could see your work making *kiosques* lovely. Ever yours   OSCAR

To Frank Harris

My dear Frank, I cannot express to you how deeply touched I am by your letter: it is *une vraie poignée de main*. I simply long to see you, and to come again in contact with your strong, sane, wonderful personality.

I cannot understand about the poem. My publisher tells me that, as I had begged him to do, he sent the two *first* copies to the *Saturday* and the *Chronicle*, and he also tells me that Arthur Symons told him he had written specially to you to ask you to allow him to do a *signed* article. I suppose publishers are untrustworthy. They certainly always look it. I hope *some* notice will appear, as your paper, or rather yourself, is a great force in London, and when you speak men listen. I, of course, feel that the poem is too autobiographical and that *real* experiences are alien things that should never influence one, but it was wrung out of me, a cry of pain, the cry of Marsyas, not the song of Apollo. Still, there are some good things in it. I feel as if I had made a sonnet out of skilly! And that is something.

When you return from Monte Carlo please let me know. I long to dine with you.

As regards a comedy, my dear Frank, I have lost the mainspring of life

---

[1] Robert Bontine Cunninghame Graham (1852–1936), the most picturesque Scot of his time, traveller, poet, horseman, scholar, Scottish Nationalist, laird and Socialist, author of many volumes of stories, essays and sketches. He wrote Wilde a letter in praise of *The Ballad* and he himself had been imprisoned for six weeks at Pentonville for his part in the Trafalgar Square riots of 1887. Skilly was a kind of thin gruel given to prisoners.

and art, *la joie de vivre*; it is dreadful. I have pleasures, and passions, but the joy of life is gone. I am going under: the morgue yawns for me. I go and look at my zinc-bed there. After all, I had a wonderful life, which is, I fear, over. But I must dine once with you first. Ever yours   o. w.

To Leonard Smithers

[*Postmark 25 February 1898*]   *Hôtel de Nice*

My dear Smithers, We have waited for you for hours. Surely you have not left Paris? It seems impossible, as the city wears its wonted air of joy. Please see about the leaflet, and the Author's Edition with a cover by Ricketts—a new colour and a *remarque* in gold.[1] The *D.T.*, by the influence of Reggie Turner, has been forced to notice the book, but grudgingly and badly.[2] Do send me all the papers that have notices tomorrow. I have hopes of the *Academy*.

Will you kindly send me *six* copies of the Second Edition.[3] It was a great delight seeing you, and I must thank you for all your kindness to me. Maurice[4] sends his kindest regards. We met by chance this morning, and I hope to see him again this evening. Ever yours   o. w.

To Robert Ross

Wednesday [? *2 March 1898*]   [*Paris*]

My dear Robbie, A thousand thanks for all the trouble you are taking for me. You, although a dreadful *low-Church* Catholic, as a little Christian sit in the snow-white rose.[5] Christ did not die to save people, but to teach people how to save each other. This is, I have no doubt, a grave heresy, but it is also a fact.

I have *not* read your letter to Constance. I would sooner leave it to you.

---

[1] The third edition of *The Ballad* (March 1898) consisted of 99 copies signed by the author and was bound in purple and white linen, with a leaf-design by Ricketts stamped in gold.

[2] The *Daily Telegraph*, for which Turner was now working, reviewed *The Ballad* briefly on 23 February.

[3] The second edition (of 1000 copies) contained a number of verbal corrections. It was printed on 24 February and issued before the end of the month.

[4] Maurice Gilbert, one of Wilde's closest and most devoted friends during these last years. Except that his father was English and his mother French, I have failed to discover anything about him.

[5] See note p. 214.

You have the tact of affection and kindness, and I would sooner return it unread.[1]

The facts of Naples are very bald and brief.

Bosie, for four months, by endless letters, offered me a "*home*." He offered me love, affection, and care, and promised that I should never want for anything. After four months I accepted his offer, but when we met at *Aix* on our way to Naples I found that he had no money, no plans, and had forgotten all his promises. His one idea was that I should raise money for us both. I did so, to the extent of £*120*. On this Bosie lived, quite happy. When it came to his having, of course, to repay his own *share*, he became terrible, unkind, mean, and penurious, except where his own pleasures were concerned, and when my allowance ceased, he left.

With regard to the £*500*, which he said was "a debt of honour" etc. he has written to me to say that he admits that it is a debt of honour, but that "lots of gentlemen don't pay their debts of honour," that it is "quite a common thing," and that no one thinks anything the worse of them.

I don't know what you said to Constance, but the bald fact is that I accepted the offer of a "*home*," and found that I was expected to provide the money, and that when I could no longer do so, I was left to my own devices.

It is, of course, the most bitter experience of a bitter life; it is a blow quite awful and paralysing, but it had to come, and I know it is better that I should never see him again. I don't want to. He fills me with horror.

Ever yours   O. W.

To Leonard Smithers

Monday [*Postmark 7 March 1898*]   [*Postmark Paris*]

My dear Smithers, I am very glad you went to Margate, which, I believe, is the *nom-de-plume* of Ramsgate. It is a quiet nice spot not vulgarised by crowds of literary people. I hope it has done you and your companions good.

I sent off the sheets yesterday.[2] Maurice sent them off; he was most kind and wrote nearly all the signatures, as I, I don't know why, was rather tired. He writes much better than I do, so his copies should fetch 30/- at least.

I have read *Henley*—it is very coarse and vulgar, and entirely lacking in literary or gentlemanly instinct.[3] He is so proud of having written *vers*

---

[1] On 21 February Wilde had written to Ross:

I am going to write to Constance to say that really now my income, such as it is, must be restored. Bosie and I are irrevocably parted—we can never be together again—and it is absurd to leave me to starve. Will you suggest this to her, if you write?

[2] The unbound copies or "sheets" of the signed (third) edition of *The Ballad*.

[3] Henley's unsympathetic review of *The Ballad* appeared anonymously in the *Outlook* of 5 March.

libres on his scrofula that he is quite jealous if a poet writes a lyric on his prison.

Will you kindly send Henry Davray,[1] 33 Avenue d'Orléans, Paris, a copy of the second edition *at once*: and also another to *me*. I want to see the corrections, and Davray must have for his translation the (so far) ultimate form of the great work.

It is to appear in the *Mercure de France* for the First of April, a day on which all poems should be published.

But, if it would not cost much, I think a small (300) edition, with a French version, might sell well here. I will speak to Vallette tomorrow about it.[2]

I suppose Symons will be in *next* week's *Saturday*.

The *Academy* arrived all right; it is a heavy judicial charge.[3] People don't understand that criticism is prejudice, because to understand one must love, and to love one must have passion. It is only the unimaginative who are ever fair. But I am glad they noticed it.

Would you have copies sent to: Rev. Page Hopps,[4] Leicester; the Baron von Gleoden,[5] Taormina, Sicily; Illustrio Signor Alberto Stopford,[6] Taormina, Sicily; Laurence Housman Esq.,[7] c/o Grant Richards, Publisher; all with the printed slip of "author's compliments."

Do you think the religious papers would review it? I think it would be worth while trying. Ever yours   o. w.

---

[1] French author, journalist, anglophile and translator from the English (1873–1944). For many years he was in charge of foreign literature in the *Mercure de France*. His translation, *La Ballade de la Geôle de Reading*, appeared in the May issue of the magazine and the proposed volume publication took place in the autumn. Davray's *Oscar Wilde: La Tragédie Finale* was published in 1928.

[2] Alfred Vallette (1858–1935) founded the *Mercure de France* 1889–90 and edited it until his death. He married the novelist Rachilde.

[3] A long, pompous and patronising review of *The Ballad* had appeared in the *Academy* of 26 February. The anonymous critic complained that Wilde was "not as whole-souled a battler for truth as he should be," and compared the poem to Thomas Hood's "Dream of Eugene Aram:" "Hood's work is, we think, the finer of the two: it has more concentration, its author had more nervous strength, was a more dexterous master of words, was superior to morbidity and hysteria."

[4] See p. 58.

[5] A German who settled at Taormina in the nineties and died there in 1931. He acquired some reputation for his photographs of Sicilian youths posed "noble and nude and antique" in the guise of Theocritan goatherds or shepherds.

[6] Albert Henry Stopford (b. 1860), great-grandson of the third Earl of Courtown, was prominent in London society until he moved to the Continent.

[7] English author (1867–1959). Wilde, in a letter dated 9 August 1897 which has recently come to light, thanked him for sending one of his books (probably *All Fellows*) and also mentioned A. E. Housman's *A Shropshire Lad*: "I have lately been reading your brother's lovely lyrical poems, so you see you have both of you given me that rare thing happiness." In his *Echo de Paris* (1923) Laurence Housman recorded an impression of Wilde's conversation in Paris during his last years.

To Carlos Blacker

[*Postmark 9 March 1898*]   *Hôtel de Nice*

My dear Carlos, I cannot express to you how thrilled and touched by emotion I was when I saw your handwriting last night. Please come and see me tomorrow (Thursday) at five o'clock if you possibly can: if not, pray make some other appointment: I want particularly to see you, and long to shake you by the hand again, and to thank you for all the sweet and wonderful kindness you and your wife have shown to Constance and the boys.[1]

---

[1] On 4 March Constance Wilde had written to Blacker:

Oscar is or at least was at the Hôtel de Nice, Rue des Beaux-Arts. Would it be at all possible for you to go and see him there, or is it asking too much of you? He has, as you know, behaved exceedingly badly both to myself and my children and all possibility of our living together has come to an end, but I am interested in him, as is my way with anyone that I have once known. Have you seen his new poem, and would you like a copy, as if so I will send you one? His publisher lately sent me a copy which I conclude came from him. Can you find this out for me, and if you do see him tell him that I think *The Ballad* exquisite, and I hope that the great success it has had in London at all events will urge him on to write more. I hear that he does nothing now but drink and I heard that he had left Lord A. and had received £200 from Lady Q. on condition that he did not see him again, but of course this may be untrue. Is Lord A. in Paris? Do what seems right to you.

When Wilde and Douglas had separated in Naples, Lady Queensberry paid Wilde £200, through More Adey on her son's behalf. In a letter of 17 March 1898 Wilde told Ross that this was part of "a debt of honour" of £500 Douglas owed him. He denied it was paid on condition he did not live with Douglas—"I know that Bosie made terms with his mother, but that is not my concern."

On 10 March Constance Wilde wrote again to Blacker:

The result of your writing to O. is that he has written to me more or less demanding money as of right. Fortunately for him, hearing that he was in great straits, I had yesterday, or rather the day before, sent him £40 through Robbie Ross. He says that I owe him £78 and hopes that I will send it. I know that he is in great poverty, but I don't care to be written to as though it were my fault. He says that he loved too much and that that is better than hate! This is true abstractedly, but his was an unnatural love, a madness that I think is worse than hate. I have no hatred for him, but I confess that I am afraid of him.

When Wilde tried to involve Blacker in his arguments over money she wrote to him on 20 March:

Oscar is so pathetic and such a born actor, and I am hardened when I am away from him. No words will describe my horror of that BEAST, for I will call him nothing else, A. D. Fancy Robbie receiving abusive letters from him, and you know perfectly well that they are sent with Oscar's knowledge and consent. I do not wish him dead, but considering how he used to go on about Willie's extravagance and about his cruelty in forcing his mother to give him money, I think that he might leave his wife and children alone. I beg that you will not let him know that you have seen these letters [from Ross], only I wish you to realize that he knew perfectly well that he was forfeiting his income, small as it was, in going back to Lord A., and that it is absurd of him to say now that I acted without his knowledge. He owes, I am certain, more than £60 in Paris, and if I pay money now he will think that he can write to me at any time for more. I have absolutely no-one to fall back upon, and I will not get into debt for anyone. The boys' expenses

I am living here quite alone: in one room, I need hardly say, but there is an armchair for you. I have not seen Alfred Douglas for three months: he is I believe on the Riviera. I don't think it probable that we shall ever see each other again. The fact is that if he is ever with me again he loses £10 a month of his allowance, and as he has only £400 a year he has adopted the wise and prudent course of conduct.

I am so glad my poem has had a success in England. I have had for some weeks a copy for you—of the first edition—by me, which I long to present to you.

It appears with a French translation in the *Mercure de France* for April, and I hope to have it published in book form also, in a limited edition of course, but it is my *chant de cygne*, and I am sorry to leave with a cry of pain—a song of Marsyas, not a song of Apollo; but Life, that I have loved so much—too much—has torn me like a tiger, so when you come and see me, you will see the ruin and wreck of what once was wonderful and brilliant, and terribly improbable. But the French men of letters and artists are kind to me, so I spend my evenings reading the *Tentation* by Flaubert. I don't think I shall ever write again: *la joie de vivre* is gone, and that, with will-power, is the basis of art.

When you come ask for Monsieur Melmoth. Ever yours   OSCAR

To Robert Ross

Friday [? *18 March 1898*]   [*Paris*]

My dear Robbie, Many thanks for the cheque, which I received this morning. The absurd money-changer, blind to his own interests, declared that he did not know your name! So I have to wait till Monday to touch the gold, but I have borrowed twenty francs from the concierge, so am all right.

I wish you could come over—for three days at any rate.

Bosie is, I believe, going to Venice, but I have not heard from him for ages. What do you think of his going back to London? He tells me he returns there with his mother in May. I think it is premature. I mean of course from the point of view of "social recognition" which he desires so much, and, *I* fear, so much in vain. It is not his past, but his future, that people so much object to, I am afraid.

will go on increasing until they are grown up and settled, and I *will* educate them and give them what they reasonably require. As Oscar will not bargain or be anything but exceedingly extravagant, why should *I* do with my money what is utterly foreign to my nature? If I were living on someone else's money, it would be a different thing and pride would make me do even what I hate. But Oscar has no pride. When he had this disastrous law-suit, he borrowed £50 from me, £50 from my cousin, and £100 from my aunt. The £50 I repaid my cousin, the £100 never has been, and I suppose never will be, repaid. I was left penniless, and borrowed £150 from Burne-Jones, and I have never borrowed a penny since. I still owe money in London which I am trying to pay, but all these things are nothing to Oscar as long as someone supports him! . . .

I suppose you know that he made his mother leave the hotel at Mentone because the proprietor refused to publish his name among the fashionable arrivals. They have rooms now, I believe.

The reviews you sent me are excellent, and really the Press has behaved very well, and Henley's hysterical personalities have done no harm, but rather the contrary. I am quite obliged to him for playing the rôle of the *Advocatus Diaboli* so well. Without it my beatification as a saint would have been impossible, but I shall now live as the Infamous St Oscar of Oxford, Poet and Martyr. My niche is just below that of the Blessed St Robert of Phillimore, Lover and Martyr—a saint known in *Hagiographia* for his extraordinary power, not in resisting, but in supplying temptations to others. This he did in the solitude of great cities, to which he retired at the comparatively early age of eight.[1] Ever yours   O. W.

To George Ives[2]

[*Postmark 21 March 1898*]   *Hôtel de Nice*

My dear George, Thanks so much for your letter. Your charming friend came to see me one morning at the hotel, and was most delightful. I hope to see him again in a few days. He seems quite fascinated by Paris.

Thanks so much for ordering my book: it is now in its fifth edition. Smithers has put a flaming advertisement into the *Athenaeum*, headed

"3000 copies sold in three weeks."

When I read it I feel like Lipton's tea!

Yes: I have no doubt we shall win, but the road is long, and red with monstrous martyrdoms. Nothing but the repeal of the Criminal Law Amendment Act would do any good. That is the essential. It is not so much public opinion as public officials that need educating. Ever yours
                                                                OSCAR

To the Editor of the Daily Chronicle[3]

23 *March* [*1898*]   [*Paris*]

Sir, I understand that the Home Secretary's Prison Reform Bill is to be read this week for the first or second time, and as your journal has been the one paper in England that has taken a real and vital interest in this important question, I hope that you will allow me, as one who has had

---

[1] See note p. 278.

[2] Author and criminologist (1867–1950).

[3] This letter appeared in the *Daily Chronicle*, under the heading DON'T READ THIS IF YOU WANT TO BE HAPPY TODAY, on 24 March, when the House of Commons began the debate on the second reading of the Prison Bill. This, which introduced some of the improvements suggested by Wilde, became law in August as the Prison Act.

long personal experience of life in an English gaol, to point out what reforms in our present stupid and barbarous system are urgently necessary.

From a leading article that appeared in your columns about a week ago, I learn that the chief reform proposed is an increase in the number of inspectors and official visitors, that are to have access to our English prisons.

Such a reform as this is entirely useless. The reason is extremely simple. The inspectors and justices of the peace that visit prisons come there for the purpose of seeing that the prison regulations are duly carried out. They come for no other purpose, nor have they any power, even if they had the desire, to alter a single clause in the regulations. No prisoner has ever had the smallest relief, or attention, or care from any of the official visitors. The visitors arrive not to help the prisoners, but to see that the rules are carried out. Their object in coming is to ensure the enforcement of a foolish and inhuman code. And, as they must have some occupation, they take very good care to do it. A prisoner who has been allowed the smallest privilege dreads the arrival of the inspectors. And on the day of any prison inspection the prison officials are more than usually brutal to the prisoners. Their object is, of course, to show the splendid discipline they maintain.

The necessary reforms are very simple. They concern the needs of the body and the needs of the mind of each unfortunate prisoner. With regard to the first, there are three permanent punishments authorised by law in English prisons:

1. Hunger.
2. Insomnia.
3. Disease.

The food supplied to prisoners is entirely inadequate. Most of it is revolting in character. All of it is insufficient. Every prisoner suffers day and night from hunger. A certain amount of food is carefully weighed out ounce by ounce for each prisoner. It is just enough to sustain, not life exactly, but existence. But one is always racked by the pain and sickness of hunger.

The result of the food—which in most cases consists of weak gruel, badly-baked bread, suet, and water—is disease in the form of incessant diarrhœa. This malady, which ultimately with most prisoners becomes a permanent disease, is a recognised institution in every prison. At Wandsworth Prison, for instance—where I was confined for two months, till I had to be carried into hospital, where I remained for another two months—the warders go round twice or three times a day with astringent medicines, which they serve out to the prisoners as a matter of course. After about a week of such treatment it is unnecessary to say the medicine produces no effect at all. The wretched prisoner is then left a prey to the most weakening, depressing, and humiliating malady that can be conceived; and if, as often happens, he fails, from physical weakness, to complete his required revolutions at the crank or the mill he is reported for idleness, and punished with the greatest severity and brutality. Nor is this all.

Nothing can be worse than the sanitary arrangements of English prisons. In old days each cell was provided with a form of latrine. These latrines have now been suppressed. They exist no longer. A small tin vessel is supplied to each prisoner instead. Three times a day a prisoner is allowed to empty his slops. But he is not allowed to have access to the prison lavatories, except during the one hour when he is at exercise. And after five o'clock in the evening he is not allowed to leave his cell under any pretence, or for any reason. A man suffering from diarrhœa is consequently placed in a position so loathsome that it is unnecessary to dwell on it, that it would be unseemly to dwell on it. The misery and tortures that prisoners go through in consequence of the revolting sanitary arrangements are quite indescribable. And the foul air of the prison cells, increased by a system of ventilation that is utterly ineffective, is so sickening and unwholesome that it is no uncommon thing for warders, when they come in the morning out of the fresh air and open and inspect each cell, to be violently sick. I have seen this myself on more than three occasions, and several of the warders have mentioned it to me as one of the disgusting things that their office entails on them.

The food supplied to prisoners should be adequate and wholesome. It should not be of such a character as to produce the incessant diarrhœa that, at first a malady, becomes a permanent disease.

The sanitary arrangements in English prisons should be entirely altered. Every prisoner should be allowed to have access to the lavatories when necessary, and to empty his slops when necessary. The present system of ventilation in each cell is utterly useless. The air comes through choked-up gratings, and through a small ventilator in the tiny barred window, which is far too small, and too badly constructed, to admit any adequate amount of fresh air. One is only allowed out of one's cell for one hour out of the twenty-four that compose the long day, and so for twenty-three hours one is breathing the foulest possible air.

With regard to the punishment of insomnia, it only exists in Chinese and English prisons. In China it is inflicted by placing the prisoner in a small bamboo cage; in England by means of the plank bed. The object of the plank bed is to produce insomnia. There is no other object in it, and it invariably succeeds. And even when one is subsequently allowed a hard mattress, as happens in the course of imprisonment, one still suffers from insomnia. For sleep, like all wholesome things, is a habit. Every prisoner who has been on a plank bed suffers from insomnia. It is a revolting and ignorant punishment.

With regard to the needs of the mind, I beg that you will allow me to say something.

The present prison system seems almost to have for its aim the wrecking and the destruction of the mental faculties. The production of insanity is, if not its object, certainly its result. That is a well ascertained fact. Its causes are obvious. Deprived of books, of all human intercourse, isolated from every humane and humanising influence, condemned to eternal silence, robbed of all intercourse with the external world, treated like an unintelligent animal, brutalised below the level of any of the brute-creation, the wretched man who is confined in an English prison can hardly escape becoming insane. I do not wish to dwell on these horrors; still less to excite any momentary sentimental interest in these matters. So I will merely, with your permission, point out what should be done.

Every prisoner should have an adequate supply of good books. At present, during the first three months of imprisonment, one is allowed no books at all, except a Bible, prayer-book, and hymn-book. After that, one is allowed one book a week. That is not merely inadequate, but the books that compose an ordinary prison library are perfectly useless. They consist chiefly of third-rate, badly-written, religious books, so-called, written apparently for children, and utterly unsuitable for children or for anyone else. Prisoners should be encouraged to read, and should have whatever books they want, and the books should be well chosen. At present the selection of books is made by the prison chaplain.

Under the present system a prisoner is only allowed to see his friends four times a year, for twenty minutes each time. This is quite wrong. A prisoner should be allowed to see his friends once a month, and for a reasonable time. The mode at present in vogue of exhibiting a prisoner to his friends should be altered. Under the present system the prisoner is either locked up in a large iron cage or in a large wooden box, with a small aperture, covered with wire netting, through which he is allowed to peer. His friends are placed in a similar cage, some three or four feet distant, and two warders stand between, to listen to, and, if they wish, stop or interrupt the conversation such as it may be. I propose that a prisoner should be allowed to see his relatives or friends in a room. The present regulations are inexpressibly revolting and harassing. A visit from our relatives or friends is to every prisoner an intensification of humiliation and mental distress. Many prisoners, rather than support such an ordeal, refuse to see their friends at all. And I cannot say I am surprised. When one sees one's solicitor, one sees him in a room with a glass door, on the other side of which stands the warder. When a man sees his wife and children, or his parents, or his friends, he should be allowed the same privilege. To be exhibited, like an ape in a cage, to people who are fond of one, and of whom one is fond, is a needless and horrible degradation.

Every prisoner should be allowed to write and receive a letter at least once a month. At present one is allowed to write only four times a year. This is quite inadequate. One of the tragedies of prison life is that it turns a man's heart to stone. The feelings of natural affection, like all other feelings, require to be fed. They die easily of inanition. A brief letter, four times a year, is not enough to keep alive the gentler and more humane affections by which ultimately the nature is kept sensitive to any fine or beautiful influences that may heal a wrecked and ruined life.

The habit of mutilating and expurgating prisoners' letters should be stopped. At present, if a prisoner in a letter makes any complaint of the prison system, that portion of his letter is cut out with a pair of scissors. If, upon the other hand, he makes any complaint when he speaks to his friends through the bars of the cage, or the aperture of the wooden box, he is brutalised by the warders, and reported for punishment every week till his next visit comes round, by which time he is expected to have learned, not wisdom, but cunning, and one always learns that. It is one of the few things that one does learn in prison. Fortunately, the other things are, in some instances, of higher import.

If I may trespass on your space for a little longer, may I say this? You suggested in your leading article that no prison chaplain should be allowed to have any care or employment outside the prison itself. But this is a matter of no moment. The prison chaplains are entirely useless. They are, as a class, well-meaning, but foolish, indeed silly, men. They are of no help to any prisoner. Once every six weeks or so a key turns in the lock of one's cell door, and the chaplain enters. One stands, of course, at attention. He asks one whether one has been reading the Bible. One answers "Yes" or "No," as the case may be. He then quotes a few texts, and goes out and locks the door. Sometimes he leaves a tract.

The officials who should not be allowed to hold any employment outside the prison, or to have any private practice, are the prison doctors. At present the prison doctors have usually, if not always, a large private practice, and hold appointments in other institutions. The consequence is that the health of the prisoners is entirely neglected, and the sanitary condition of the prison entirely overlooked. As a class I regard, and have always from my earliest youth regarded, doctors as by far the most humane profession in the community. But I must make an exception for prison doctors. They are, as far as I came across them, and from what I saw of them in hospital and elsewhere, brutal in manner, coarse in temperament, and utterly indifferent to the health of the prisoners or their comfort. If prison doctors were prohibited from private practice they would be compelled to take some interest in the health and sanitary condition of the people under their charge.

I have tried to indicate in my letter a few of the reforms necessary to our English prison system. They are simple, practical, and humane. They are, of course, only a beginning. But it is time that a beginning should be made, and it can only be started by a strong pressure of public opinion formularised in your powerful paper, and fostered by it.

But to make even these reforms effectual, much has to be done. And the first, and perhaps the most difficult task is to humanise the governors of prisons, to civilise the warders and to Christianise the chaplains. Yours, etc.　　THE AUTHOR OF "THE BALLAD OF READING GAOL"

Telegram: To Robert Ross

[*Postmark 12 April 1898*]　　　　　　　　　　　　　　　　　*Paris*

Constance is dead.[1] Please come tomorrow and stay at my hotel. Am in great grief.　　　　　　　　　　　　　　　　　OSCAR

[1] Constance Wilde died at Genoa on 7 April 1898, aged forty, and was buried in the Protestant cemetery there.

To Carlos Blacker

[*12 or 13 April 1898*]   [*Paris*]

My dear Carlos, It is really awful. I don't know what to do. If we had only met once, and kissed each other.

It is too late. How awful life is. How good you were to come at once. I have gone out as I don't dare to be by myself. Ever yours   OSCAR

*To Leonard Smithers

2 May 1898   *Paris*

Do you think that a shilling edition (on grey paper but not in blunt type) would sell?—of *The Ballad*. I think so. I suppose the type still stands, so the expense is small. The cover should be grey with red letters—vermilion—and at the end we might have a good selection of press notices. If someone like Davitt[1] would write a preface it would add to it very much. Could you get an estimate of 1000 copies at 1/-? The poem should still be on one side only of the paper, I think, unless the paper is too bad to bear the test of a blank surface. I sent Robbie the *Revue Blanche* for you to look at: a capital series.

Would you kindly let me have eight copies of *The Ballad*, and a copy of *Dorian Gray* also, as soon as possible. Did you send Stead[2] a copy?

To Leonard Smithers

[*Circa 4 May 1898*]   [*Paris*]

My dear Smithers, I am delighted to see that you *don't* know your "Browning". I hope you never will. But, to avoid any discussion on printing, let me remind you of the lines

"Or some scrofulous French novel
On grey paper with blunt type,

---

[1] Michael Davitt, Irish writer and Socialist politician (1846–1906). Suffered frequent imprisonment for Fenian, Land League and similar activities. Several times elected to Parliament. His published works include *Leaves from a Prison Diary* (1885). He asked two questions in the House of Commons about the dismissal of Warder Martin. Wilde had written to him a year before about the treatment of the prisoner Prince: "No one knows better than yourself how terrible life in an English prison is and what cruelties result from the stupidity of officialism, and the immobile ignorance of centralisation."

[2] William Thomas Stead (1849–1912), editor of the *Pall Mall Gazette* 1883–89. In 1885 he organised a campaign against the white slave traffic and organised vice, in a series of articles called "Maiden Tribute of Modern Babylon." In 1890 he started the *Review of Reviews*, which was surprisingly generous about Wilde in 1895. Stead later became an ardent spiritualist. He was drowned in the *Titanic*.

Once you glance in it, you grovel
Neck and crop in Satan's gripe."

It is out of a poem called, I think, "A Spanish Cloister," and I quote the last two lines inaccurately, I am glad to say.[1]

I am quite prepared for sixpence a copy, but please get estimates, so as to be sure that there will be a margin. Your estimate of 10,000 copies is flattering, but is it safe? I would like the cover to be grey, not black.[2]

I don't know what you mean by talking of Ricketts's "design," and the advisability of using it. A badly-drawn leaf flung casually on a cover is not a design at all. It is a mistake—nothing more.

I don't know who would be the right man for a preface, perhaps T. P. O'Connor.[3] It should be largely on prison-reform. Perhaps John Burns[4]

Let us have good paper, not what Robbie calls "*home-made* paper"! but something decent.

With regard to the press-notices, I merely want the assertion of the poem's reception. You remember the doubt there was about it, and how when you printed only 400 copies of the first edition the cocks in the Arcade crew thirty-three times.[5]

The accounts of the two editions should be *separate*: they are different affairs.

Could you send a paragraph to the papers to say that *The Ballad* has been translated into French by M. Henry Davray and appears in the current number of the *Mercure de France*: and that it will shortly appear in book-form in Paris, the English on one side, the French on the other.

Have you a copy of Aubrey's drawing of Mlle de Maupin?[6] There is a young Russian here, who is a great amateur of Aubrey's art, who would love to have one. He is a great collector, and rich. So you might send him a copy and name a price, and also deal with him for drawings by Aubrey. His name is Serge de Diaghilew, Hôtel St James, Rue St Honoré, Paris.[7]

If you don't feel up to charging much for the Mlle de Maupin, which I suppose is inexpensive, you might send it to him for nothing, and propose

[1] See stanza viii of Browning's *Soliloquy of the Spanish Cloister*.

[2] This plan for a shilling or sixpenny edition of *The Ballad* came to nothing.

[3] Thomas Power O'Connor (1848–1929), journalist and politician, was Nationalist M.P. for the Scotland Division of Liverpool 1885–1929. Founded and was first editor of the *Star*, the *Sun*, the *Sunday* (later the *Weekly*) *Sun*, *M.A.P.* and *T.P.'s Weekly*. Made a Privy Councillor 1924.

[4] Labour politician (1858–1943). He was arrested and imprisoned with Cunninghame Graham in 1887 (see note p. 328). President of the Board of Trade 1914. He resigned from the Cabinet on the outbreak of war.

[5] Smithers's publishing office was then in the Royal Arcade, Old Bond Street.

[6] Beardsley had begun to illustrate Gautier's *Mademoiselle de Maupin* for Smithers, but completed only six drawings (which Smithers reproduced by photogravure and sold in a portfolio). These included a water-colour drawing of the heroine, intended as a frontispiece, of which Smithers sold coloured photogravure reproductions, 100 copies at a guinea, and a further 30 at higher prices.

[7] This remarkable man (1872–1929), who was to change the art of ballet throughout the world, was at this time simply a member of the Russian intelligentsia, dabbling in painting and a new artistic review. He had met Beardsley at Dieppe.

a deal. I said to him I would get you to send him one, but do what you think is in your own interest. If you want a guinea—and what gentleman does not?—and the price is a guinea, by all means enclose your account. In any case he wants it, and can pay.

Your delay in coming over is painful. Also, you must make friends with Conder: it is absurd not to know the unknowable. Ever yours   O. W.

Type-write Alexander's copy and send it to me. This will save great expense in printing etc.[1]

To Robert Ross

My dear Robbie, Something must be done. Friday and Saturday I had not a penny, and had to stay in my room, and as they only give breakfast at the hotel, *not* dinner, I was dinnerless.[2] My quarter is really due the 18th May: it began the 18th May and was always paid in advance. The November allowance was suppressed, but the February was paid by my wife, and the May is due on the 18th.

In any case, as I would like it always paid through you, could *you* get someone to advance the money, so as to be paid now, and when it *is* paid you simply hand over the cheque.

I enclose what seems a legal document. I judge solely from its want of style. Armed with this, surely, dear Robbie, you could get me £30 at least, if not £38. 10. I am quite off my balance with want and worries, and have also had to have an operation on my throat, unpaid for yet, except in pain.[3]
Ever yours   OSCAR

*To Leonard Smithers

You are so accustomed to. bringing out books limited to an edition of three copies, one for the author, one for yourself, and one for the Police, that I really feel you are sinking beneath your standard in producing a six-penny edition of anything. Perhaps, as I want the poem to reach the

---

[1] Presumably the only available copy of *The Importance of Being Earnest*, from which Smithers could print, was George Alexander's prompt copy.

[2] Wilde had moved to the Hôtel d'Alsace, Rue des Beaux Arts, at the end of March.

[3] On receipt of this letter Ross wrote to Smithers:

I had a fearful letter from poor Oscar who seems in a dreadful state of poverty even allowing for slight exaggeration. He says he had no dinner on Friday or Saturday. If you could sell the 'Réjane' for me at once send Oscar £5 as soon as possible . . . Tell Oscar that a 'friend' is sending the money. There is no need to mention my name.

poorer classes, we might give away a cake of Maypole soap with each copy: I hear it dyes people the most lovely colours, and is also cleansing.[1]

To Robert Ross

[Circa 28 May 1898]   [Paris]

My dear Robbie, A thousand thanks for the cheque. May I ask *when* the June £10 comes due? Of course the 1st of the month; otherwise I will never be able to keep my accounts straight.

Of course nothing can be done about rooms till you decide, and have the collection for the sweet sinner of England in hand, but I still suspect you of having a flat of some kind concealed about your person. My instinct in such points is unerring.

I wish you would write and tell me how much you love Maurice. He is a great dear, and loves us all, a born Catholic in romance; he is always talking of you and Reggie.

Yesterday he and I and Bosie went to the Salon. As modern art had a chastening effect on Maurice, and he seemed sad, we went afterwards to the *Foire aux Invalides*, where Maurice won a knife, by foolishly throwing a ring over something.

Robert Sherard is here. On Wednesday he created a horrible scene in Campbell's Bar[2] by bawling out "*À bas les juifs*," and insulting and assaulting someone whom he said was a Jew. The fight continued in the street, and Robert tried to create an Anti-Semite, Anti-Dreyfusard demonstration. He succeeded, and was ultimately felled to the ground by the Jew!

Bosie and I met him at Campbell's by chance on the next day. Campbell told him that the only reason he would consent to serve him was that Bosie and I had shaken hands with him! This rather amused me, when I remember Robert's monstrous moralising about us, and how nobody should know us. Robert looked quite dreadful, all covered with cigar-ash, stains of spilt whiskey, and mud. He was unshaven, and his face in a dreadful state. He had no money, and borrowed a franc from Bosie.

Yesterday he turned up again, and had to receive a rather insolent lecture from Campbell, who told him he preferred Jews to drunkards in his bar. He was much depressed, so of course I gave him drinks and cigarettes and all he wanted. To show his gratitude he insisted on reciting *The Ballad of Reading Gaol*, at the top of his voice, and assuring me that I was "*le plus grand maître de la littérature moderne, et le plus grand homme du monde.*" At the end he got very tedious, and lest I might love my poem less than I

---

[1] A contemporary advertisement runs:

MAYPOLE SOAP
FOR HOME DYEING
DYES ANY COLOUR
WON'T WASH OUT OR FADE.

[2] In the Rue St. Honoré.

wish to, I went away. Poor Robert, he really is quite insane, and unbearable, except to very old friends who bear much. He begged me to lunch with him and to bring Maurice, but I declined, feigning temporary good health as my excuse! His asking me to bring Maurice was astounding, as when he was last in Paris he refused to call on me because M. was staying with me, and generally was offensive about a lovely and loveable friendship. He has gone to the country today; I hope he will get better. Years ago he was a very good and dear fellow.

I dined last night with Robert d'Humières, a very charming young Frenchman, whom I first met, years ago, at Frank Schuster's.[1] He had asked a poet to meet me, and I believe I was rather wonderful.

I liked the review you sent me immensely. Do you know the writer? It is a very good appreciation.

This letter seems not at all business-like, but Maurice's account of you has somewhat disturbed the severe Spartan Ideal I had formed of you lately. Ever yours   OSCAR

To Robert Ross

1 June 1898   [*Paris*]

My dear Robbie, People who repent in sackcloth are dreary, but those who repent in a suit by Doré, and intend this suit for another, are worthy of Paradise. It is most sweet of you, and the colour I would like is *blue*, like the suit I had last year.

A rather painful fact, apparent to all, must now be disclosed. Pray mention it to no one but Doré, and break it to him gently. I am distinctly stouter than I was when the last suit was made. I should say a good inch and a half. I *can* still button the old Doré suit, but it is tight, and the two lower buttons drag. I would like the same stuff, if possible; it is such good stuff, and has lasted so well.

Bosie is now inseparable from Maurice; they have gone again to Nogent. I made Maurice put a postscript into a rather silly letter, inspired by Bosie, which he sent off to you today. I think letters of that kind quite stupid and witless, but Bosie has no real enjoyment of a joke unless he thinks there is a good chance of the other person being pained or annoyed. It is an entirely English trait, the English type and symbol of a joke being the jug on the half-opened door, or the distribution of orange-peel on the pavement of a crowded thoroughfare.

I hope that the beautiful blue suit will be brought over by either you or Reggie. If not, let Smithers be told that the duty is his. I hear that the Custom House is exorbitant, and sends you papers on which they have thrown sand.

[1] (1840–1928). Brother of Adela. Wealthy music-lover and social figure. Vicomte Robert d'Humières (1869–1915, killed in action) helped Louis Fabulet with his translations of Kipling, who wrote a preface to the English edition (1905) of d'Humières's *L'Ile et L'Empire de Grande Bretagne* (1904).

I find I have written the beginning of a letter to a French poet on the other side of this, so cannot write more. Fabulet is the author of *La Crise*, an attempt at an anarchical poem, a dull thing at best.[1] Ever yours

OSCAR

To Robert Ross

[*August 1898*]   *Hôtel d'Alsace, Rue des Beaux-Arts*

Dear Robbie, Where are you? I received the cheque all right, but there was no pen or ink in the *département* in which I was (Seine-et-Oise) so could not acknowledge it.

I have been with Rothenstein and Conder. They have both been very nice to me. The Seine is lovely, and there are wonderful backwaters, with willows and poplars, with water-lilies and turquoise kingfishers. I bathed twice a day, and spent most of my time in rowing about. Nichol,[2] the son of the Glasgow professor, was there also—a nice fellow, but insane. He cannot think or talk, so he quotes Swinburne's *Poems and Ballads* always, instead of conversation—a capital idea, after all.

Will you let me dedicate *The Importance of Being Earnest* to you? I would so much like to write your name on the dedication-page, or, at any rate, your initials. The evening papers might disclose your identity if properly approached. Ever yours   OSCAR

To Robert Ross

[*Circa 23 November 1898*]   *Grand Café, 14 Boulevard des Capucines, Paris*

My dear Robbie, The clothes are quite charming—suitable to my advanced age. The trousers are too tight round the waist. That is the result of my rarely having good dinners: nothing fattens so much as a dinner at 1 fr. 50, but the blue waistcoat is a dream. Smithers I received in the same parcel. He was quite wonderful, and depraved, went with monsters to the sound of music, but we had a good time, and he was very nice.

Would it bother you if I asked you to let me have my allowance for December now? A wretched inn-keeper at Nogent to whom I owe 100 francs, out of a bill of 300, threatens to sell Reggie's dressing-case, my overcoat, and two suits, if I don't pay him by Saturday. He has been detaining the things, and now threatens a sale. It is less than a week, so perhaps you might manage it without too much worry to yourself.

---

[1] Louis Fabulet (1862–1933), apart from *La Crise* (1896), was chiefly noted for his translations of Kipling and other English and American writers. The abortive letter to him on the back of this sheet runs: "*Cher Monsieur Fabulet, Je vous remercie bien de votre charmante lettre, et de . . .*"

[2] John Pringle Nichol. His father John Nichol (1833–94) had been Professor of English Literature at Glasgow 1861–89, and was a lifelong friend of Swinburne.

Sir John[1] was astonishing, went through a romance with an absurd Boulevard boy, who, of course, cheated him, and treated him badly. The reason was that Sir John had given him a suit of clothes—an admirable reason. To undress is romance, to dress, philanthropy. You are quite philanthropic to me, but you are also romantic—the sole instance of the lack of philosophy in clothes. Do let me have a cheque: if you can, by return. Ever yours OSCAR

To Robert Ross

Friday [*25 November 1898*]   *Paris*

My dear Robbie, I am so sorry about my excuse. I had forgotten I had used Nogent before. It shows the utter collapse of my imagination, and rather distresses me.

Do let me know about Bosie. I suppose that London takes no notice at all: that is the supreme punishment.[2]

I have corrected two-thirds of my proofs,[3] and await the last act. I don't want to make threats, but remember that the dedication is not yet written, and I may write

To
R. B. Ross
in recognition of his good advice.

That would be terrible, so do not lecture till *after Dec. 7th.*[4]

I see a great deal of La Jeunesse, who is more intolerable than ever, and I dined with Strong,[5] who has reduced Maurice to a state of silent frightened idiocy. Dogma without Literature is bad for boys. Ever yours OSCAR

To H. C. Pollitt[6]

[*Postmark 26 November 1898*]   *Hotel d'Alsace*

Dear Mr Pollitt, I should like a photograph of you, of all things. Pray let me have one. There is no duty (Custom-House) except on purely British products, and I am sure you do not come under that category. So the post will safely convey me your profile.

My "trivial comedy for serious people" comes out in a few weeks, if Shannon will do as he did for my other plays—strew three gilt petals on a

[1] The nickname of I. D. W. Ashton, whom Wilde had met at Naples. I have failed to identify him further.

[2] Douglas was paying his first visit to London since 1895.

[3] Of *The Importance of Being Earnest.*

[4] The dedication finally read: TO ROBERT BALDWIN ROSS/IN APPRECIATION/IN AFFECTION.

[5] Rowland Strong (1865–1924). Paris correspondent of the *New York Times, Observer* and *Morning Post.* Said to have been a fervent anti-Semite. Author of successful book, *Where and How to Dine in Paris* (1900).

[6] Herbert Charles Pollitt (1871–1942), a native of Kendal in Westmorland, had been an undergraduate at Trinity College, Cambridge, 1889–92, and made a name there as an amateur ballet-dancer. He preferred Jerome to his own Christian names and signed himself so in his letters to Wilde.

345

purple field, but I don't know if he will be idle enough. I hear rumours of industry in the Richmond vale.

You ask me what I am writing: very little: I am always worried by that mosquito, money; bothered about little things, such as hotel-bills, and the lack of cigarettes and little silver *francs*. Peace is as requisite to the artist as to the saint: my soul is made mean by sordid anxieties. It is a poor ending, but I had been accustomed to purple and gold.

I like your Christian name so much: I suppose you are your own lion?[1]
Sincerely yours   OSCAR WILDE

To Louis Wilkinson[2]

[*Postmark 14 December 1898*]   *Hôtel d'Alsace*

Dear Mr Wilkinson, Certainly: you can dramatise my play, but please tell me if the version is yours, and how the play is constructed.

Who acts Dorian Gray? He should be beautiful.

My work is so far in your hands that I rely on your artistic instinct that the play shall have some quality of beauty and style.

You can have four performances, and if there should be any notices of the play in papers, pray let me see them.

Your letter of last summer gave me great pleasure. Pray let me know all about yourself. Who are you? What are you doing or going to do? Send me your photograph.

Write to me at the above address, and direct the envelope to *Sebastian Melmoth*, a fantastic name that I shall explain to you some day. Sincerely yours   OSCAR WILDE

To Robert Ross

Wednesday [*14 December 1898*]
                    Taverne F. Pousset, 14 Boulevard des Italiens, Paris

My dear Robbie, Just a line to say that I leave with Frank Harris for Napoule, near Cannes, tomorrow night.[3] Frank has been most kind, and nice, and, of course, we have dined and lunched together every day at Durand's. At least I lunch at one o'clock, and dine at eight o'clock. Frank arrives at 2.30 and 9.15. It is rather a bore, and no one should make unpunctuality a formal rule, and degrade it to a virtue, but I have admirable,

---

[1] St Jerome, the translator of the Vulgate, is usually portrayed reading or writing with a lion seated beside him.

[2] Louis Umfreville Wilkinson (1881–1966) was at this time a Radley schoolboy. He subsequently published many novels and other books under the name Louis Marlow. In his *Seven Friends* (1953) he quotes many of Wilde's letters to him, and confesses that he invented an "Ipswich Dramatic Society" and its wish to dramatise *The Picture of Dorian Gray*, so as to get into correspondence with Wilde, whom he never met.

[3] In the event Wilde went without Harris, who joined him later. Harris helped pay Wilde's debts in Paris before leaving and paid most of his expenses in Napoule.

though lonely, meals. Frank insists on my being always at high intellectual pressure; it is most exhausting; but when we arrive at Napoule I am going to break the news to him—now an open secret—that I have softening of the brain, and cannot always be a genius. I shall send you my address to-morrow.

Ashton is with me; he is more penniless than ever, poor dear fellow; and Walter, that snub-nosed little horror, has just gone back to England, so Sir John is sad and sentimental. Ever yours   OSCAR

To Mrs Leonard Smithers

28 December [*1898*]   *Hôtel des Bains, Napoule, Cannes*

Dear Mrs Smithers, Thank you so much for your charming card: I wish I could come to your party, but I am a wretched walker and would probably not arrive till midsummer.

I wish there was some chance of your coming out here: the weather is lovely—blue and gold weather—and the warm sun broods on the sea. Leonard must be quite exhausted with neglecting his business, and the rest would do him good.

I often think of your delightful visits to Berneval: if you will only come to luncheon at Napoule I promise you acrobats! And good cooking. The *chef* here is a much purer poet than John Davidson is.

I see I have made a dreadful blot on this page. It looks like a Conder fan, in its early stages, so pray excuse it; and believe me, with many thanks, sincerely yours   OSCAR WILDE

To Robert Ross

2 February 1899   *Napoule*

My dear Robbie, Thank you for the cheque, duly received. Your account of Henry James has much amused Frank Harris: it is a delightful story for your memorabilia.

Today, for the first time, rain—quite an Irish day. Yesterday was lovely. I went to Cannes to see the *Bataille des Fleurs*. The loveliest carriage—all yellow roses, the horses with traces and harness of violets—was occupied by an evil-looking old man, English: on the box, beside the coachman, sat his valet, a very handsome boy, all wreathed with flowers. I murmured "Imperial, Neronian Rome."

I have signed the copies of the play for Smithers, a "Japanese" for you. Smithers will show you my list: if I have forgotten anyone, let me know. Of course dear More Adey has a "large-paper:" and also Reggie.

Harold Mellor[1] will be in London at the end of the month. He is going

---

[1] Harold Mellor (1868–1925) was the neurotic son of a Bolton cotton-spinner. His father died in 1893, leaving him wealthy, and he spent most of the rest of his life abroad, finally committing suicide in his villa at Cannes.

there to get me some neckties. I have asked him to write and let you know. He is a charming fellow, very cultivated, though he finds that Literature is an inadequate expression of Life. That is quite true: but a work of Art is an adequate expression of Art; that is its aim. Only that. Life is merely the *motif* of a pattern. I hope all things are well with you. Frank Harris is upstairs, thinking about Shakespeare at the top of his voice.[1] I am earnestly idling. Ever yours   OSCAR

To Reginald Turner

[*Postmark 3 February 1899*]   *Hôtel des Bains, Napoule*

My dear Reggie, I hope you are in better spirits. Poor dear Sir John was always in the best spirits (and water): the most good-hearted of the alcoholic. Life goes on very pleasantly here. Frank Harris is of course exhausting. After our literary talk in the evening I stagger to my room, bathed in perspiration. I believe he talks the Rugby game.

Max's caricature in the *Chronicle* is a masterpiece—as far as George Moore goes: it is a most brilliant and bitter rendering of that vague formless obscene face. The Archer is *manqué*—not at all like. I showed the drawing to Frank, who was in ecstasies over the Moore, and would like to have a replica of it by Max.[2]

I am sending you, of course, a copy of my book. It was extraordinary reading the play over. How I used to toy with that tiger Life! I hope you will find a place for me amongst your nicest books, not near anything by Hichens or George Moore. I should like it to be within speaking distance of *Dorian Gray*. You will also get a copy addressed to Charlie Hickey. How is that dear boy? I wish you would import him.

There is a *Carnaval* at Nice on Sunday. I hope to run over: on Sundays there are no confetti, which is a blessing. Ever yours   OSCAR

To Robert Ross

[*Circa 1 March 1899*]   *Gland, Canton Vaud, Switzerland*

My dear Robbie, Thanks for your charming letter, which I found waiting for me here on my arrival from Genoa yesterday.

It was a great pleasure writing your name on the page of dedication.

---

[1] Instalments of "The True Shakespeare—an Essay in Realistic Criticism" by Frank Harris had appeared in the *Saturday Review* from March to December 1898. This essay formed the basis of Harris's book *The Man Shakespeare* (1909).

[2] Max Beerbohm's caricature appeared in the *Daily Chronicle* on 30 January 1899, illustrating a long letter from W. B. Yeats on "Mr Moore, Mr Archer and the Literary Theatre." It represents George Moore as a tipsy Irish peasant with a trailed coat in one hand and a shillelagh in the other. William Archer, dressed in kilt and glengarry, has one foot on Moore's coat, at which he is pointing in an admonitory way.

I only wish it was a more wonderful work of art—of higher seriousness of intent—but it has some amusing things in it, and I think the tone and temper of the whole thing bright and happy.[1]

I went to Genoa to see Constance's grave. It is very pretty—a marble cross with dark ivy-leaves inlaid in a good pattern. The cemetery is a garden at the foot of the lovely hills that climb into the mountains that girdle Genoa. It was very tragic seeing her name carved on a tomb—her surname, my name, not mentioned of course—just "Constance Mary, daughter of Horace Lloyd, Q.C." and a verse from *Revelations*. I brought some flowers. I was deeply affected—with a sense, also, of the uselessness of all regrets. Nothing could have been otherwise, and Life is a very terrible thing.

This is a pretty house on the Lake. We look over to the snows and hills of Savoy. Geneva is half an hour by rail. You are to come whenever you like. April is lovely here, I believe, and flaunts in flowers.

There is an Italian cook, also the lad Eolo, who waits at table. His father told Mellor at Spezia that he was christened Eolo because he was born on a night on which there was a dreadful wind! I think it is rather nice to have thought of such a name. An English peasant would probably have said "We called him John, sir, because we were getting in the hay at the time."[2]

There is no truth at all in Sedger's advertisement, and I am very angry about it.[3] It is quite monstrous. My only chance is a play produced anonymously. Otherwise the First Night would be a horror, and people would find meanings in every phrase.

I am going to try a bicycle. I have never forgotten the lesson you so kindly gave me: even my leg remembers it.

Do write again soon. Have I forgotten anyone to whom I should send a copy? Ever yours   OSCAR

To Frank Harris

[*Circa 19 March 1899*]   *Gland, Switzerland*

My dear Frank, I am, as you see from above, in Switzerland with Mellor: a rather dreadful combination. The villa is pretty, and on the borders of the Lake with pretty pines about: on the other side are the mountains of Savoy and Mont Blanc: we are an hour, by a slow train, from Geneva. But

[1] The inscription in Ross's copy of *The Importance of Being Earnest* reads: "To the Mirror of Perfect Friendship: Robbie: whose name I have written on the portal of this little play. Oscar. February '99."

[2] Cf. *The Duchess of Padua*, Act II:

Duke: "Why were you called Dominick?"

First Citizen (scratching his head): "Marry, because I was born on Saint George's day."

[3] Horace Sedger (1853–1917), English theatrical manager. Wilde had sold him an option on the play which eventually appeared as *Mr and Mrs Daventry* (see note p. 362).

349

Mellor is tedious, and lacks conversation: also he gives me Swiss wine to drink: it is horrid: he occupies himself with small economies, and mean domestic interests. So I suffer very much. *Ennui* is the enemy.

I want to know if you will allow me to dedicate to you my next play, *An Ideal Husband*, which Smithers is bringing out for me in the same form as the other, of which I hope you received your copy. I should so much like to write your name and a few words on the dedicatory page.[1]

I look back with joy and regret to the lovely sunlight of the Riviera, and the charming winter you so generously and kindly gave me: it was most good of you: nor can it ever be forgotten by me.

Next week a petroleum launch is to arrive here, so that will console me a little, as I love to be on water: and the Savoy side is starred with pretty villages and green valleys.

Of course we won our bet. The phrase on Shelley is in Arnold's preface to Byron: but Mellor won't pay me![2] He suffers agony over a franc. It is very annoying as I have had no money since my arrival here. However I regard the place as a Swiss *pension*, where there is no weekly bill.

My kindest regards to your wife.[3] Ever yours   OSCAR

To Robert Ross

Tuesday [6 June 1899]   *Hôtel Marsollier, Rue Marsollier, Paris*[4]

My dear Robbie, Thanks for your letter. Smithers has not yet sent the cheque. He says in his letter that he will do so when he sees you.

Paris is awfully hot: quite dreadful. I long to be away.

I saw Ada Rehan[5] and Augustin Daly[6] the other night at the Café de la Paix, where Bosie had invited me to dine. They were most charming:

---

[1] The dedication to *An Ideal Husband*, published in July 1899, reads: TO FRANK HARRIS / A SLIGHT TRIBUTE TO / HIS POWER AND DISTINCTION / AS AN ARTIST / HIS CHIVALRY AND NOBILITY / AS A FRIEND.

[2] "Shelley, beautiful and ineffectual angel, beating in the void his luminous wings in vain." From the preface to *Poetry of Byron*, chosen and arranged by Matthew Arnold (1881). Reprinted in *Essays in Criticism, Second Series* (1888).

[3] The year before Harris had eloped with an Irish beauty called Helen (Nellie) O'Hara, to whom he remained married for the rest of his life.

[4] Wilde left Gland on 1 April and went to Santa Margherita. Ross rescued him and took him back to Paris in April or May.

[5] American actress (1860–1916), who became a great favourite in London and New York. All her best work was done under Daly's management, and her failure after his death inspired the belief that she had depended on him as Trilby on Svengali.

[6] American dramatist and manager (1839–99). He first brought his company to London in 1884, with Ada Rehan and John Drew heading the cast. He eventually had his own theatre, named after him, in both London and New York. He had made Wilde an offer for a play in 1897.

her hair has turned quite white. I accused her at once of dyeing her hair white. She was delighted.

They also want me to write something for them.[1]

I have made friends with a charming American youth, expelled from Harvard for immoral conduct! He is very amusing and good-looking.

Ever yours   OSCAR

To Frances Forbes-Robertson

[*June 1899*]   *Hôtel Marsollier*

My dear, sweet, beautiful Friend, Eric has just sent me your charming letter, and I am delighted to have a chance of sending you my congratulations on your marriage, and all the good wishes of one who has always loved and admired you.[2] I met Eric by chance, and he told me he had been over to the marriage. He was as picturesque and sweet as usual, but more than usually vague. I was quite furious with him. He could not quite remember who it was you had married, or whether he was fair or dark, young or old, tall or small. He could not remember where you were married, or what you wore, or whether you looked more than usually beautiful. He said there were a great many people at the wedding, but could not remember their names. He remembered, however, Johnston being present. He spoke of the whole thing as a sort of landscape in a morning mist. Your husband's name he could not for the moment recall: but said he thought he had it written down at home. He went dreamily away down the Boulevard followed by violent reproaches from me, but they were no more to him than the sound of flutes: he wore the sweet smile of those who are always looking for the moon at mid-day.

So, dear Frankie, you are married, and your husband is a "king of men"!

[1] Graham Robertson in his *Time Was* described Ada Rehan's account of this incident:

She and the Dalys had been dining at a restaurant and, looking up, she had seen Oscar Wilde sitting with some men at a neighbouring table and looking at her tentatively . . . "I didn't know what to do," she told me. "Mr and Mrs Daly were with me and I could not tell how they would feel about it. You never *do* know with men when they are going to feel very proper and when they are not."

"And *was* Mr Daly feeling proper?"I enquired.

"No," said poor Ada, "he wasn't. It was such a relief: if I could not have bowed I should have cried. So Mr Wilde came over and sat with us and talked so charmingly—it was just like old times—we had a lovely evening. And then, only a few days later, Mr Daly died. Arrangements had to be made and Mrs Daly was not equal to taking them in hand. I seemed to be all alone, and so confused and frightened. And then Oscar Wilde came to me and was more good and helpful than I can tell you—just like a very kind brother. I shall always think of him as he was to me through those few dreadful days."

Augustin Daly died in Paris on 7 June 1899.

[2] Frances Forbes-Robertson married Henry Dawes Harrod in London on 10 April 1899. For the first three years of their married life they lived in Anglesey.

That is as it should be: those who wed the daughters of the gods are kings, or become so.

I have nothing to offer you but one of my books, that absurd comedy *The Importance of being Earnest*, but I send it to you, in the hopes it may live on one of your bookshelves and be allowed to look at you from time to time. Its dress is pretty: it wears Japanese vellum, and belongs to a limited family of *nine*, it is not on speaking terms with the popular edition: it refuses to recognise the poor relations whose value is only seven and sixpence. Such is the pride of birth. It is a lesson.[1]

Ah! how delightful it would be to be with you and your husband in your own home! But my dear child, how could I get to you? Miles of sea, miles of land, the purple of mountains and the silver of rivers divide us: you don't know how poor I am: I have no money at all: I live, or am supposed to live, on a few francs a day: a bare remnant saved from shipwreck. Like dear St Francis of Assisi I am wedded to Poverty: but in my case the marriage is not a success: I hate the Bride that has been given to me: I see no beauty in her hunger and her rags: I have not the soul of St Francis: my thirst is for the beauty of life: my desire for its joy. But it was dear of you to ask me, and do tell the "king of men" how touched and grateful I am by the invitation you and he have sent me.

And, also, sometimes send me a line to tell me of the beauty you have found in life. I live now on echoes, as I have little music of my own. Your old friend   OSCAR

To Louis Wilkinson

[*Postmark 4 January 1900*]   *Hôtel d'Alsace*

My dear Boy, I am very glad you have met my Australian friend: he is a charming fellow. Remember me to him.

So you are coming abroad. I think it is an admirable idea. Radley had nothing left to teach you, though you could have taught it much: did so, I doubt not.

I fear you would not like my hotel. I live there because I have no money ever. It is an absurd place: it is not a background: the only thing really nice in the whole hotel is your own photograph: but one cannot, or one should not, play Narcissus to a photograph: even water is horribly treacherous: the eyes of one who loves one are the only mirror.

You asked me about "Melmoth:" of course I have not changed my name: in Paris I am as well known as in London: it would be childish. But to prevent postmen having fits I sometimes have my letters inscribed with the name of a curious novel by my grand-uncle, Maturin: a novel that was part of the romantic revival of the early century, and though

---

[1] This copy on Japanese vellum is inscribed: "To Frankie on her happy marriage from her old friend and comrade the Author.   June '99."

imperfect, a pioneer: it is still read in France and Germany: Bentley republished it some years ago. I laugh at it, but it thrilled Europe, and is played as a play in modern Spain. Write soon. Ever your friend OSCAR

To Leonard Smithers

[Circa 24 February 1900]   *[Paris]*

My dear Smithers, I am greatly distressed to hear of Ernest's death: how sudden it must have been![1] Poor wounded wonderful fellow that he was, a tragic reproduction of all tragic poetry, like a symbol, or a scene. I hope bay-leaves will be laid on his tomb, and rue, and myrtle too, for he knew what love is.

He was a sweet singer, with a note all the lovelier because it reminds us of how thrushes sang in Shakespeare's day. If he is not yet laid to rest or unrest, do put some flowers for me on his grave.

I have been very ill, in bed since Monday, some disease with a hybrid-Greek name: it attacks the throat and the soul.

How is Althea?[2] Has she still the green wand? Ever yours

OSCAR WILDE

To Robert Ross

Wednesday [? 28 February 1900][3]   *Hôtel d'Alsace*

My dear Robbie, How could I have written to you during the last three months considering that I have been in bed since last Monday. I am very ill and the doctor is making all kinds of experiments. My throat is a lime kiln, my brain a furnace and my nerves a coil of angry adders. I am apparently in much the same state as yourself.

Maurice—you remember Maurice?—has kindly come to see me and I've shared all my medicines with him, shown him what little hospitality I can. We are both horrified to hear that Bosie's suspicions of you are quite justified. That and your being a Protestant make you terribly *unique* (I have told Maurice how to spell the last word as I was afraid that he might have used a word which often occurs in the Protestant bible).[4]

[1] Ernest Dowson died in Robert Sherard's house at Catford on 23 February 1900. He was buried in the Roman Catholic part of Lewisham Cemetery on 27 February.
[2] Althea Gyles, English artist (1868–1949). She illustrated an edition of Wilde's poem "The Harlot's House," which Smithers (masquerading as the Mathurin Press) published in 1904.
[3] For many years this was accepted as Wilde's last surviving letter, but the references to having been in bed since Monday with a bad throat tally exactly with the preceding letter, and the references to mussel-poisoning and Rome prove that it was written before Wilde's visit to Rome. It is in another hand (clearly Maurice Gilbert's) except for the last eighteen words, which are in Wilde's.
[4] Presumably eunuch.

Aleck[1] lunched with Bosie and me one day and I lunched alone with him another. He was most friendly and pleasant and gave me a depressing account of you. I see that you, like myself, have become a *neurasthenic*. I have been so for four months, quite unable to get out of bed till the afternoon, quite unable to write letters of any kind. My doctor has been trying to cure me with arsenic and strychnine but without much success, as I became poisoned through eating mussels, so you see what an exacting and tragic life I have been leading. Poisoning by mussels is very painful and when one has one's bath one looks like a leopard. Pray never eat mussels.

As soon as I get well I'll write you a long letter, though your letter asking me to stay with you in Rome never reached me.

Thanks so much for the cheque, but your letter was really too horrid. With love, ever yours   OSCAR

To Robert Ross

Thursday [*Late March 1900*]   *Grand Café, 14 Boulevard des Capucines,*
Paris

Dear Robbie, I am so annoyed at your not writing to me every day that I must come and talk to you.

Mellor, with whom I am now friends (below zero of course) has invited me to go to Italy to the extent of £50! When that gives out I shall have to walk home, but as I want to see you, I have consented to go, and hope to be in Rome in about ten days. It will be delightful to be together again, and this time I really must become a Catholic, though I fear that if I went before the Holy Father with a blossoming rod it would turn at once into an umbrella or something dreadful of that kind. It is absurd to say that the age of miracles is past. It has not yet begun.

Your story of dear Rowland is charming. How dangerous it is to be called "John" is the moral. Anything may happen to a person called John.[1]

You have not yet broken to me the impression I produced on Aleck. I suppose it was painful. All went well till an unlucky thing occurred.

Only an hour after I, with "waving hands" like Tennyson's Vivien,[2] had evolved a new evangel of morals, dear Aleck passed before the little *café* behind the Madeleine, and saw me with a beautiful boy in grey velvet

---

[1] Aleck Ross.
[2] For Merlin, overtalk'd and overworn,
    Had yielded, told her all the charm, and slept.

    Then, in one moment, she put forth the charm
    Of woven paces and of waving hands,
    And in the hollow oak he lay as dead,
    And lost to life and use and name and fame.

                                        (*Idylls of the King*)

—half rough, all Hylas. Alas, the eye he turned on me was not the sightless one.[1] His smile was terrible. It was like one of Besant's novels.

I really felt it very much. At luncheon I had been singularly ethical. I am always ethical at the Café de la Paix.

Wire, or write at once to me, chez Mellor, Gland, Vaud, and tell me a good hotel. Also bed out some Narcissi. It is their season.

With best love, dear horrid irritating Robbie, yours   OSCAR

To Robert Ross

16 April [*1900*]   *c/o Cook & Son, Piazza di Spagna, Rome*

My dear Robbie, I simply cannot write. It is too horrid, not *of* me, but *to* me. It is a mode of paralysis—a *cacoethes tacendi*[2]—the one form that malady takes in me.

Well, all passed over very successfully. Palermo, where we stayed eight days, was lovely. The most beautifully situated town in the world, it dreams away its life in the Conca d'Oro, the exquisite valley that lies between two seas. The lemon-groves and the orange-gardens were so entirely perfect that I became again a Pre-Raphaelite, and loathed the ordinary Impressionists, whose muddy souls and blurred intelligences would have rendered but by mud and blur those "golden lamps hung in a green night"[3] that filled me with such joy. The elaborate and exquisite detail of the true Pre-Raphaelites is the compensation they offer us for the absence of motion; Literature and Music being the only arts that are not immobile.

Then nowhere, not even at Ravenna, have I seen such mosaics. In the Cappella Palatina, which from pavement to domed ceilings is all gold, one really feels as if one was sitting in the heart of a great honeycomb *looking* at angels singing; and looking at angels, or indeed at people singing, is much nicer than listening to them. For this reason the great artists always give to their angels lutes without strings, pipes without vent-holes, and reeds through which no wind can wander or make whistlings.

Monreale you have heard of, with its cloisters and cathedral. We often drove there, the *cocchieri* most dainty finely-carved boys. In them, not in the Sicilian horses, is race seen. The most favoured were Manuele, Francesco, and Salvatore. I loved them all, but only remember Manuele.

I also made great friends with a young Seminarist who lived *in* the Cathedral of Palermo, he and eleven others in little rooms beneath the roof, like birds.

---

[1] Aleck Ross had lost the sight of one eye in early youth.

[2] Craving for silence. Cf. the *scribendi cacoethes* (itch for writing) of Juvenal, Satire VII, 52.

[3] He hangs in shades the Orange bright
Like golden Lamps in a green Night.
(Andrew Marvell: "Bermudas")

Every day he showed me all over the Cathedral, and I really knelt before the huge porphyry sarcophagus in which Frederick the Second lies. It is a sublime bare monstrous thing, blood-coloured, and held up by lions, who have caught some of the rage of the great Emperor's restless soul. At first, my young friend, Giuseppe Loverde by name, gave *me* information: but on the third day I gave information to him, and re-wrote History as usual, and told him all about the Supreme King and his Court of Poets, and the terrible book that he never wrote.[1] Giuseppe was fifteen, and most sweet. His reason for entering the Church was singularly mediaeval. I asked him why he thought of becoming a *clerico*: and how.

He answered "My father is a cook, and most poor, and we are many at home, so it seemed to me a good thing that there should be in so small a house as ours one mouth less to feed, for, though I am slim, I eat much: too much, alas! I fear."

I told him to be comforted, because God used poverty often as a means of bringing people to Him, and used riches never, or but rarely. So Giuseppe was comforted, and I gave him a little book of devotion, very pretty, and with far more pictures than prayers in it; so of great service to Giuseppe, whose eyes are beautiful. I also gave him many *lire*, and prophesied for him a Cardinal's hat, if he remained very good, and never forgot me. He said he never would: and indeed I don't think he will, for every day I kissed him behind the high altar.

At Naples we stopped three days. Most of my friends are, as you know, in prison, but I met some of nice memory, and fell in love with a Sea-God, who for some extraordinary reason is at the Regia Marina School, instead of being with Triton.

We came to Rome on Holy Thursday. H. M. left on Saturday for Gland, and yesterday,[2] to the terror of Grissell[3] and all the Papal Court, I appeared in the front rank of the pilgrims in the Vatican, and got the blessing of the Holy Father[4]—a blessing they would have denied me.

He was wonderful as he was carried past me on his throne, not of flesh and blood, but a white soul robed in white, and an artist as well as a saint —the only instance in History, if the newspapers are to be believed.

I have seen nothing like the extraordinary grace of his gesture, as he rose, from moment to moment, to bless—possibly the pilgrims, but certainly me. Tree should see him. It is his only chance.

I was deeply impressed, and my walking-stick showed signs of budding; would have budded indeed, only at the door of the chapel it was taken

---

[1] Frederick II (1194–1250), Roman Emperor, King of Sicily and Jerusalem, popularly known as *Stupor Mundi*. Italian poetry, according to Dante, was born at his court, and he was suspected by the Papal party of writing a book called *De Tribus Impostoribus* (the three impostors—Moses, Jesus and Mahomet).

[2] Easter Day 1900 was on 15 April.

[3] Hartwell de la Garde Grissell (1839–1907) had been a Chamberlain of Honour to the Pope since 1869. Wilde had met him on his visit to Rome in 1877.

[4] Leo XIII (1810–1903), Pope from 1878.

from me by the Knave of Spades. This strange prohibition is, of course, in honour of Tannhäuser.[1]

How did I get the ticket? By a miracle, of course. I thought it was hopeless, and made no effort of any kind. On Saturday afternoon at five o'clock Harold and I went to have tea at the Hôtel de l'Europe. Suddenly, as I was eating buttered toast, a man, or what seemed to be one, dressed like a hotel porter, entered and asked me would I like to see the Pope on Easter Day. I bowed my head humbly and said *"Non sum dignus,"* or words to that effect. He at once produced a ticket!

When I tell you that his countenance was of supernatural ugliness, and that the price of the ticket was thirty pieces of silver, I need say no more.

An equally curious thing is that whenever I pass the hotel, which I do constantly, I see the same man. Scientists call that phenomenon an obsession of the visual nerve. You and I know better.

On the afternoon of Easter Day I heard vespers at the Lateran: music quite lovely: at the close a Bishop in red, and with red gloves—such as Pater talks of in *Gaston de Latour*—came out on the balcony and showed us the relics.[2] He was swarthy, and wore a yellow mitre. A sinister mediaeval man, but superbly Gothic, just like the Bishops carved on stalls or on portals. And when one thinks that once people mocked at stained-glass attitudes! They are the only attitudes for the clothed. The sight of this Bishop, whom I watched with fascination, filled me with the sense of the great realism of Gothic art. Neither in Greek nor in Gothic art is there any pose. Posing was invented by bad portrait-painters, and the first person who ever posed was a stockbroker, and he has gone on ever since.

Homer talks much—a little too much—of you. He slightly suspects you of treachery, and your immediate return seems to him problematical. Your allusion to his conduct on a postcard was mysterious. How was the "revision" painful?

I have added one Pietro Branca-d'Oro to the group. He is dark, and gloomy, and I love him very much.

I send you a photograph I took on Palm Sunday at Palermo. Do send me some of yours, and love me always, and try to read this letter. It is a labour of a week to read it.

Kindest regards to your dear mother. Always   OSCAR

---

[1] Wilde several times referred to Tannhäuser's pilgrimage as a penitent to Rome, and the blossoming of the Pope's staff (see Act III of Wagner's opera). Cf. *The Ballad of Reading Gaol*, section IV:

> Since the barren staff the pilgrim bore
> Bloomed in the great Pope's sight.

[2] There is a bishop in *Gaston de Latour*, but the colour of his gloves is not mentioned. Wilde was probably confusing him with the Bishop of Auxerre in Pater's "Denys L'Auxerrois" (in *Imaginary Portraits*, 1887), who, "in vestments of deep red in honour of the relics, blessed the new shrine . . . At last from a little narrow chest, into which the remains [of the saint] had been almost crushed together, the bishop's red-gloved hands drew the dwindled body."

To Robert Ross

My dear Robbie, A thousand thanks for all your trouble. The cheque arrived safely this morning.

Of course I got your telegram, from Milan, and wrote to you at the Hôtel Cavour—a long, interesting, and of course seriously compromising letter. Should it fall into the hands of the authorities you will be immortal.

I have not seen the Holy Father since Thursday, but am bearing up wonderfully well. I am sorry to say he has approved of a dreadful handkerchief, with a portrait of himself in the middle, and basilicas at the corners. It is very curious the connection between Faith and bad art: I feel it myself. Where I see the Pope I admire Bernini: but Bernini had a certain dash and life and assertion—theatrical life, but life for all that: the handkerchief is a dead thing.[1]

By the way, did I tell you that on Easter Sunday I was completely cured of my mussel-poisoning? It is true, and I always knew I would be. Five months under a Jewish physician at Paris not merely did not heal me, but made me worse: the blessing of the Vicar of Christ made me whole. Armand Point, the French painter,[2] a bad Botticelli-Jones artist, is here, and has promised to do me a *tabella votiva*. The only difficulty is the treatment of the mussels. They are not decorative, except the shells, and I didn't eat the shells.

I have been three times to see the great Velasquez of the Pamfili Pope: it is quite the grandest portrait in the world. The entire man is there.[3] I also go to look at that beautiful voluptuous marble boy I went to worship with you at the Museo Nazionale. What a lovely thing it is!

I have given up Armando, a very smart elegant young Roman Sporus. He was beautiful, but his requests for raiment and neckties were incessant: he really bayed for boots, as a dog moonwards. I now like Arnaldo: he was Armando's greatest friend, but the friendship is over. Armando is *un invidioso*[4] apparently, and is suspected of having stolen a lovely covert-coat in which he patrols the Corso. The coat is so delightful, and he looks so handsome in it, that, although the coat wasn't mine, I have forgiven him the theft.

Omero has never received your letter. I need not say I have not given him your London address—at least not your real one: he now believes that your real name is Edmondo Gosse, and that your address is the Savile. I also added that some of your more intimate friends prefer to write to you

---

[1] Giovanni Lorenzo Bernini (1598–1680), Italian painter, sculptor and architect, designed the palace of Pope Urban VIII and the great colonnade of St Peter's.

[2] (1861–1949).

[3] This portrait of Pope Innocent X (1574–1655) hangs in the Doria Palace in Rome.

[4] Jealous.

Reginaldo Turner
                          Avvocato
                    The Reform Club:
but that I, from old associations, prefer to address you as
                       Sir Wemyss Reid,
so I fancy there will be many interesting letters arriving in London.

Yesterday a painful thing happened. You know the terrible, the awe-inspiring effect that Royalty has on me: well, I was outside the Caffè Nazionale taking iced coffee with *gelato*—a most delightful drink—when the King drove past. I at once stood up, and made him a low bow, with hat doffed—to the admiration of some Italian officers at the next table. It was only when the King had passed that I remembered I was *Papista* and *Nerissimo*![1] I was greatly upset: however I hope the Vatican won't hear about it.

I enclose you a little cutting that appeared in Palermo while I was there. My incognito vanished in three hours, and the students used to come to the café to talk—or rather to listen. To their great delight I always denied my identity. On being asked my name, I said every man has only one name. They asked me what name that was. "Io"[2] was my answer. This was regarded as a wonderful reply, containing in it all philosophy.

Rome is burning with heat: really terrible: but at 4.30 I am going to the Borghese, to look at daisies, and drink milk: the Borghese milk is as wonderful as the Borghese daisies. I also intend to photograph Arnaldo. By the way, can you photograph cows well? I did one of cows in the Borghese so marvellous that I destroyed it: I was afraid of being called the modern Paul Potter.[3] Cows are very fond of being photographed, and, unlike architecture, don't move.

I propose to go to Orvieto tomorrow: I have never seen it, and I must revisit Tivoli. How long I shall stay here I don't know—a fortnight perhaps.

Write always to Cook's. Love to More and Reggie. Ever yours OSCAR

To Robert Ross

Thursday [*May 1900*]   *Rome*

Dearest Robbie, Your telegram just arrived: its deciphering was most fascinating work: we all felt like the archaeologists over the stone at the Lapis Niger: which stone I believe to be an early example of Roman humour: Fescennine licence it was called later on.[4]

[1] Very black. A term in use amongst the Roman nobility, meaning ultra-Catholic. There was at this time a great antipathy between regal and Papal circles, and the Pope was known as the Prisoner in the Vatican.
[2] Italian for I.   [3] Dutch animal painter (1625–54).
[4] The Lapis Niger is the legendary sepulchre of Romulus in the Comitium adjoining the Forum. In 1899 a black pavement was excavated nearby.

I wrote to you yesterday, to the Cavour. Today is wet and stormy, but I have again seen the Holy Father. Each time he dresses differently; it is most delightful. Today over his white and purple a velvet cape edged with ermine, and a huge scarlet and gold stole. I was deeply moved as usual.

I gave a ticket to a new friend, *Dario*. I like his name so much: it was the first time he had ever seen the Pope: and he transferred to me his adoration of the successor of Peter: would I fear have kissed me on leaving the Bronze Gateway had I not sternly repelled him. I have become very cruel to boys, and no longer let them kiss me in public.

The pilgrims arrive in great black swarms: I am sure that Pharaoh was punished by a plague of them: some of them, however, go mad. Three cases yesterday. They are much envied by their more sane brethren.

I wish you would write to me about Venice: it is really absurd: is it due to Symonds? Renters in gondolas are grotesque.

How is dear More? He was missed as usual at the Vatican. Carlyle Stebbing does not suit St Peter's; its astounding proportions *increase* his size: it is most curious.[1] Write soon. Ever yours   OSCAR

To Robert Ross

[*May-June 1900*]   *Hôtel d'Alsace, Paris*

Dearest Robbie, I have at last arrived. I stayed ten days with Harold Mellor at Gland: the automobile was delightful, but, of course, it broke down: they, like all machines, are more wilful than animals—nervous, irritable, strange things: I am going to write an article on "nerves in the inorganic world."

Frank Harris is here, also Bosie. I asked Bosie what you suggested—without naming any sum at all—after dinner. He had just won £400 at the races, and £800 a few days before, so he was in high spirits. When I spoke to him he went into paroxysms of rage, followed by satirical laughter, and said it was the most monstrous suggestion he had ever heard, that he would do nothing of the kind, that he was astounded at my suggesting such a thing, that he did not recognise I had any claim of any kind on him. He was really revolting: I was quite disgusted. I told Frank Harris about it, and he was greatly surprised: but made the wise observation "One should never ask for anything: it is always a mistake." He said I should have got someone to sound Bosie, and ask him for me. I had also the same idea, but you did not seem to like the prospect of a correspondence with Bosie where money was concerned, and I am not surprised.

It is a most horrible and really heart-breaking affair. When I remember his letters at Dieppe, his assurances of eternal devotion, his entreaties that I should always live with him, his incessant offers of all his life and belong-

---

[1] Wilde is clearly referring to Carlisle James Scott Spedding (1852–1915), who in 1894 was appointed Private Chamberlain of the Sword and Cloak to Pope Leo XIII. Spedding is said to have been one of the greatest bores of his time.

ings, his desire to atone in some way for the ruin he and his family brought on me—well, it sickens me, it gives me nausea.

The affair occurred in the Café de la Paix, so, of course, I made no scene. I said that if he did not recognise my claim there was nothing more to be said.[1]

We dined last night with Frank Harris at Maire's. I was quite as usual, but he[2] really is, now that he has money, become mean, and narrow, and greedy. He always accused you of having the bourgeois commercial view of money, instead of the generous, chivalrous, aristocratic view, but he really has out-Heroded Herod this time. "I can't afford to spend anything except on myself" was one of his observations. I thought of you, and dear More, and all your generosity and chivalry and sacrifice for me. It is an ugly thing; it taints life.

Send me my cheque, like a good boy. Ever yours   OSCAR

I am horrified about Smithers. It really is too bad.[3]

To George Alexander

[? *July 1900*]   *Hôtel d'Alsace*

My dear Aleck, It was really a great pleasure to see you again, and to receive your friendly grasp of the hand after so many years. Nor shall I forget your dear wife's charming and affectionate greeting of me. I know now how to value things like that.

With regard to your proposal to spread the payment for the plays over a certain time, I know it was dictated by sheer kindness and the thoughtfulness of an old friend.[4]

If you would send Robert Ross £20 on the first of every month for me it would be a great boon. He would send it on to me, as he looks after all my affairs. His address is R. B. Ross, 24 Hornton Street, Kensington W. I would then have before me a year free from worry, and perhaps may do something you would like. Could you do this for me?

I was delighted to see you so well, and so unchanged.

Kindest wishes to your wife. Sincerely yours   OSCAR WILDE

---

[1] In a later letter to Ross Wilde wrote:

Frank Harris is very wonderful and really very good and *sympathique*. He always comes two hours late for meals, but in spite of that is delightful. He keeps Bosie in order: the age of miracles is clearly not over.

[2] i.e. Douglas.

[3] Smithers's financial collapse had begun, though he was not officially adjudged bankrupt until 18 September.

[4] At the time of Wilde's bankruptcy Alexander had bought the acting rights of *Lady Windermere's Fan* and *The Importance of Being Earnest*. He made some voluntary payments to Wilde and bequeathed the rights to Wilde's son.

To Robert Ross

Saturday, 1 September [*1900*]   [*Paris*]

My dear Robbie, Thanks for the cheque. Your letter is very maddening: nothing about yourself: no details, and yet you know I love middle-class tragedies, and the little squabbles that build up family life in England. I have had delightful letters from you quite in the style of Jane Austen. You, I know, are the Cinderella of your family, and lead them all a dreadful life, like your *Märchen*-prototype. You turned your dear mother's carriage into a pumpkin, and won't let your sisters wear your slippers, and always have the comfortable ingle-nook by the fire, except in summer, when you make poor Aleck sit there.

The "Mellor cure" was dull, but I got better. He is now in Paris with his slave Eolo, who like all slaves is most tyrannical. He and I, however, are great friends. I think Harold is on the verge of acute melancholia. At present he has almost arrived at total abstinence—drinks and talks mineral waters. I like people who talk wine.

So Bosie is in London: where is he staying? Do you think he has really spent all his money? It is a great pity if he has. How is dear More? And Reggie? Paris is full of second-rate tourists. German and American are the only languages one hears. It is dreadful. Ever yours   OSCAR

To Frank Harris[1]

20 November 1900   *Hôtel d'Alsace*

Dear Frank, I have now been in bed for nearly ten weeks[2] and am still extremely ill, having had a relapse a fortnight ago. I must, however, for many reasons write to you at once on the question of the money you owe me. The expenses of my illness amount to close on £200 and I must beg

---

[1] Except for the last two lines, this letter, apparently the last Wilde wrote, is in the hand of Maurice Gilbert. It is one of a number written at this period to Frank Harris on the subject of the play *Mr and Mrs Daventry*, which opened at the Royalty Theatre on 25 October with Mrs Patrick Campbell and Fred Kerr in the title-rôles. The original idea was entirely Wilde's, as written to Alexander in 1894 (see p. 118), but the final play was written by Harris alone. Before and during the negotiations with Harris, Wilde had sold some sort of options on the play to the American actress Mrs Brown-Potter (1859–1936), Horace Sedger, Ada Rehan, the theatrical manager Louis Nethersole (1865–1936), and Smithers. As soon as Harris announced the production of the play he was compelled to buy off some or all of these people and naturally withheld the £150 he had promised to pay Wilde. Harris had many faults, but lack of generosity to Wilde was not one of them. The play was first published in 1956, with a full introduction by H. Montgomery Hyde, discussing this whole perplexed matter.

[2] Wilde had had an operation on 10 October.

that you pay me immediately the sum for which you are still indebted to me. On September 26th, nearly two months ago, you drew up an agreement in your own handwriting promising to pay me within a week from that date the sum of £175 besides one-fourth of all profits. You explained to me that you had left your cheque-book in London, but that you would send me a cheque on your return, which was fixed for the following day. You gave me £25 on account, and I naturally accepted the word of one of my oldest friends, backed up by an agreement drawn out by yourself, not actually signed, but I gave you a receipt for the entire sum. I no more doubted that you would pay me in the course of a week than I doubted of the shining of sun or moon. A week passed over without my hearing a line from you, and finally the surgeon felt it his duty to inform me that unless I was operated on immediately it would be too late, and that the consequences of the delay would probably be fatal. With great difficulty I managed to raise amongst my friends, or rather the sum was raised for me by them, the 1500 francs which was the surgeon's fee, and was duly operated on under chloroform. I then telegraphed to you to ask you to send the money you owed me at once. All I received from you in return was £25. You then took no further notice of the matter but left me for a whole month in the most terrible position I have ever been in. I do not wish to criticise your conduct towards me, I merely state the plain facts. You owe at present, on your agreement of two months ago, the sum of £125. You also owe me £25 additional, my share of the £100 paid over in advance by Mrs Campbell. You told me at Durand's that this sum was not in advance of fees. I should like to know whether this is the case or not. The play has now been running for, I believe, three weeks and I have received no account of the receipts or royalties. A statement of the receipts and my proportion of author's fees should, of course, be sent to me every week. I must ask you to at once settle up accounts, as I cannot possibly go on living in the present manner, with two doctors and attendants, a medical nurse and all the terrible expenses incident on a long and dangerous illness.

With regard to Smithers, I am, I need hardly say, astounded that you should have allowed yourself to be blackmailed by him, but your proposal to recoup yourself out of the money you owe me and to sequestrate my small share of the profits, is of course out of the question. I could not allow it for a moment. Smithers had an agreement with me some years ago to write him a play within a certain given time. I was unable to carry out my side of the agreement, and Smithers formally relinquished to me in Paris any claim he had on me for the broken agreement. It is true I did not get Smithers's pronunciation in writing, but Smithers was at that time a great friend of mine, and in his case, as later on in yours, I considered the word of a friend adequate. I promised him in return to give him the publishing rights of two of my plays,[1] as well as the copyright of a poem for which illustrations were at that time being made by an artist of great ability.[2] Since that time Smithers, as you know, has become bankrupt, and

---

[1] *An Ideal Husband* and *The Importance of Being Earnest*.
[2] Althea Gyles (see note 2, p. 353).

I am one of his creditors. Had Smithers considered that his agreement with me was still valid he would naturally have entered it as an asset against me, but he did not do so, showing clearly that the agreement in his opinion had lapsed in reality as it had lapsed in time. His coming to you and attempting to extort money from you is really an act of blackmailing, for if my lapsed agreement with him has the value of five shillings, it belongs of course to the Official Receiver, and Smithers has no more right to deal with it or treat it as his property than the man in the street. It is unnecessary to tell you, I presume, that what Smithers has done is a most serious offence against the bankruptcy laws, and if it came to the knowledge of the Official Receiver, Smithers would find himself in a very painful, possibly criminal position. If you will put these facts before your lawyer he will tell you that I am perfectly right. And I should fancy that unless Smithers has spent the £100 he extorted from you in whiskeys and sodas, your solicitor will be able to recover the money for you. However that is your business, not mine, but as Smithers is having a very bad time with the Official Receiver, I should not fancy that he would care to risk imprisonment.

When the man Nethersole intruded here almost daily during the worst crisis of my illness and tried to blackmail me on the ground that he had managed to secure a copy of the scenario, and that a play belonged to any man who had a copy of the scenario, if under these circumstances I had been foolish enough to hand him £200, I think you would have been rather amused if I had written subsequently to you to claim the £200 from your pocket. But, without adducing parallels, your lawyer will tell you that Smithers's action is entirely illegal, and that you were very foolish to yield to it for a moment.

As for me, I regret what has occurred for your sake, but I cannot recoup you, nor should you for a moment expect me to do so. The important thing, however, is to settle up our accounts and I must beg you to send me by return the £150 you owe me, as well as any royalties that may be due.

I need not say how distressed I am that things should have turned out in this manner between us, but you must remember that the fault is in no sense mine. Had you kept your word to me, fulfilled the agreement and sent me the money that was due to me and for which I gave you a receipt which you still hold, all would have been well; and indeed I myself would have perfectly recovered two weeks ago, had it not been for the state of mental anxiety which your conduct kept me in all day long, with its accompanying sleeplessness at night, a sleeplessness over which none of the opiates the doctors dared to order me seemed to have any effect. Today is Tuesday the 20th. I rely on receiving from you the £150 you owe me. Sincerely yours   OSCAR WILDE

EPILOGUE

*Robert Ross to More Adey[1]

14 December 1900

On Tuesday, October 9th, I wrote to Oscar, from whom I had not heard for some time, that I would be in Paris on Thursday, October the 18th for a few days, when I hoped to see him. On Thursday, October 11th, I got a telegram from him as follows: "Operated on yesterday—come over as soon as possible." I wired that I would endeavour to do so. A wire came in response, "Terribly weak—please come." I started on the evening of Tuesday, October 16th. On Wednesday morning I went to see him about 10.30. He was in very good spirits; and though he assured me his sufferings were dreadful, at the same time he shouted with laughter and told many stories against the doctors and himself. I stayed until 12.30 and returned about 4.30, when Oscar recounted his grievances about the Harris play. Oscar, of course, had deceived Harris about the whole matter—as far as I could make out the story. Harris wrote the play under the impression that only Sedger had to be bought off at £100, which Oscar had received in advance for the commission; whereas Kyrle Bellew,[2] Louis Nethersole, Ada Rehan, and even Smithers, had all given Oscar £100 on different occasions, and all threatened Harris with proceedings. Harris, therefore, only gave Oscar £50 on account, as he was obliged to square these people first—hence Oscar's grievance. When I pointed out to him that he was in a much better position than formerly, because Harris, at any rate, would eventually pay off the people who had advanced money and that Oscar would eventually get something himself, he replied in the characteristic way, "Frank has deprived me of my only source of income by taking a play on which I could always have raised £100."

I continued to see Oscar every day until I left Paris. Reggie and myself sometimes dined or lunched in his bedroom, when he was always very talkative, although he looked very ill. On October 25th my brother Aleck

---

[1] Text from Frank Harris: *Oscar Wilde, His Life and Confessions* (New York, 1918).

[2] English actor (1855–1911) who was for a long time associated with Mrs Brown-Potter.

came to see him, when Oscar was in particularly good form. His sister-in-law, Mrs Willie, and her husband, Teixeira, were then passing through Paris on their honeymoon, and came at the same time. On this occasion he said he was "dying above his means" . . . he would never outlive the century . . . the English people would not stand him—he was responsible for the failure of the Exhibition, the English having gone away when they saw him there so well-dressed and happy . . . all the French people knew this, too, and would not stand him any more.

On October the 29th Oscar got up for the first time at mid-day, and after dinner in the evening insisted on going out—he assured me that the doctor had said he might do so and would not listen to any protest.

I had urged him to get up some days before as the doctor said he might do so, but he had hitherto refused. We went to a small café in the Latin Quarter, where he insisted on drinking absinthe. He walked there and back with some difficulty, but seemed fairly well. Only I thought he had suddenly aged in face, and remarked to Reggie next day how different he looked when up and dressed. He appeared *comparatively* well in bed. (I noticed for the first time that his hair was slightly tinged with grey. I had always remarked that his hair had never altered its colour while he was in Reading; it retained its soft brown tone. You must remember the jests he used to make about it, he always amused the warders by saying that his hair was perfectly white.)

Next day I was not surprised to find Oscar suffering with a cold and great pain in his ear; however, Dr Tucker[1] said he might go out again, and the following afternoon, a very mild day, we drove in the Bois. Oscar was much better, but complained of giddiness; we returned about 4.30. On Saturday morning, November 3rd, I met the *Panseur*[2] Hennion (Reggie always called him the *Libre Panseur*); he came every day to dress Oscar's wounds. He asked me if I was a great friend or knew Oscar's relatives. He assured me that Oscar's general condition was very serious—that he could not live more than three or four months unless he altered his way of life—that I ought to speak to Dr Tucker, who did not realise Oscar's serious state—that the ear trouble was not of much importance in itself, but a grave symptom.

On Sunday morning I saw Dr Tucker—he is a silly, kind, excellent man; he said Oscar ought to write more, that he was much better, and that his condition would only become serious when he got up and went about in the usual way. I begged him to be frank. He promised to ask Oscar if he might talk to me openly on the subject of Oscar's health. I saw him on the Tuesday following by appointment; he was very vague; and though he endorsed Hennion's view to some extent, said that Oscar was getting well now, though he could not live long unless he stopped drinking. On going to see Oscar later in the day I found him very agitated. He said he did not want to know what the doctor had told me. He said he did not care if he

---

[1] The British Embassy doctor, Dr Maurice Edmund A'Court Tucker, of 3 Faubourg St Honoré.

[2] Dresser or male nurse.

had only a short time to live, and then went off on to the subject of his debts, which I gather amounted to something over more than £400. He asked me to see that at all events some of them were paid if I was in a position to do so after he was dead; he suffered remorse about some of his creditors. Reggie came in shortly afterwards much to my relief. Oscar told us that he had had a horrible dream the previous night—"that he had been supping with the dead." Reggie made a very typical response, "My dear Oscar, you were probably the life and soul of the party." This delighted Oscar, who became high-spirited again, almost hysterical. I left feeling rather anxious. That night I wrote to Douglas saying that I was compelled to leave Paris, that the doctor thought Oscar very ill, that ——[1] ought to pay some of his bills as they worried him very much, and the matter was retarding his recovery—a great point made by Dr Tucker. On November 2nd, All Souls' Day, I had gone to Père Lachaise with ——.[1] Oscar was much interested and asked me if I had chosen a place for his tomb. He discussed epitaphs in a perfectly light-hearted way, and I never dreamt he was so near death.

On Monday, November 12th, I went to the Hôtel d'Alsace with Reggie to say good-bye, as I was leaving for the Riviera next day. It was late in the evening after dinner. Oscar went all over his financial troubles. He had just had a letter from Harris about the Smithers claim, and was much upset; his speech seemed to me a little thick, but he had been given morphia the previous night, and he always drank too much champagne during the day. He knew I was coming to say good-bye, but paid little attention when I entered the room, which at the time I thought rather strange; he addressed all his observations to Reggie. While we were talking, the post arrived with a very nice letter from Alfred Douglas, enclosing a cheque.[2] It was partly in response to my letter I think. Oscar wept a little but soon recovered himself. Then we all had a friendly discussion, during which Oscar walked around the room and declaimed in rather an excited way. About 10.30 I got up to go. Suddenly Oscar asked Reggie and the nurse to leave the room for a minute, as he wanted to say good-bye. He rambled at first about his debts in Paris: and then he implored me not to go away, because he felt that a great change had come over him during the last few days. I adopted a rather stern attitude, as I really thought that Oscar was simply hysterical, though I knew that he was genuinely upset at my departure. Suddenly he broke into a violent sobbing, and said he would never see me again because he felt that everything was at an end. This very painful incident lasted about three-quarters of an hour.

He talked about various things which I can scarcely repeat here. Though it was very harrowing, I really did not attach any importance to my farewell, and I did not respond to poor Oscar's emotion as I ought to have done, especially as he said, when I was going out of the room, "Look out for some little cup in the hills near Nice where I can go when I am

---

[1] Name omitted by Harris.
[2] According to Douglas (*Autobiography*, p. 323) this was for £10.

better, and where you can come and see me often." Those were the last articulate words he ever spoke to me.

I left for Nice the following evening, November 13th.

During my absence Reggie went every day to see Oscar, and wrote me short bulletins every other day. Oscar went out several times with him driving, and seemed much better. On Tuesday, November 27th, I received the first of Reggie's letters, which I enclose (the others came after I had started), and I started back for Paris; I send them because they will give you a very good idea of how things stood. I had decided that when I had moved my mother to Mentone on the following Friday, I would go to Paris on Saturday, but on the Wednesday evening, at five-thirty, I got a telegram from Reggie saying, "Almost hopeless." I just caught the express and arrived in Paris at 10.20 in the morning. Dr Tucker and Dr Klein, a specialist called in by Reggie, were there. They informed me that Oscar could not live for more than two days. His appearance was very painful, he had become quite thin, the flesh was livid, his breathing heavy. He was trying to speak. He was conscious that people were in the room, and raised his hand when I asked him whether he understood. He pressed our hands. I then went in search of a priest, and after great difficulty found Father Cuthbert Dunne,[1] of the Passionists, who came with me at once and administered Baptism and Extreme Unction—Oscar could not take the Eucharist. You know I had always promised to bring a priest to Oscar when he was dying, and I felt rather guilty that I had so often dissuaded him from becoming a Catholic, but you know my reasons for doing so. I then sent wires to Frank Harris, to Holman (for communicating with Adrian Hope) and to Douglas. Tucker called again later and said that Oscar might linger a few days. A *garde malade* was requisitioned as the nurse had been rather overworked.

Terrible offices had to be carried out into which I need not enter. Reggie was a perfect wreck.

He and I slept at the Hotel d'Alsace that night in a room upstairs. We were called twice by the nurse, who thought Oscar was actually dying. About 5.30 in the morning a complete change came over him, the lines of the face altered, and I believe what is called the death rattle began, but I had never heard anything like it before; it sounded like the horrible turning of a crank, and it never ceased until the end. His eyes did not respond to the light test any longer. Foam and blood came from his mouth, and had to be wiped away by someone standing by him all the time. At 12 o'clock I went out to get some food, Reggie mounting guard. He went out at 12.30. From 1 o'clock we did not leave the room; the painful noise from the throat became louder and louder. Reggie and myself destroyed letters to keep ourselves from breaking down. The two nurses were out, and the proprietor of the hotel had come up to take their place; at 1.45 the time of his breathing altered. I went to the bedside and held his hand, his pulse began to flutter. He heaved a deep sigh, the only natural one I had heard

<hr>

[1] Father Cuthbert Dunne C.P. (1869–1950), a native of Dublin, was at this time attached to the Passionist Church, St Joseph's, in the Avenue Hoche, Paris.

since I arrived, the limbs seemed to stretch involuntarily, the breathing came fainter; he passed at 10 minutes to 2 p.m. exactly.[1]

After washing and winding the body, and removing the appalling *débris* which had to be burnt, Reggie and myself and the proprietor started for the Mairie to make the official declaration. There is no use recounting the tedious experiences which only make me angry to think about. The excellent Dupoirier lost his head and complicated matters by making a mystery over Oscar's name, though there was a difficulty, as Oscar was registered under the name of Melmoth at the hotel, and it is contrary to the French law to be under an assumed name in your hotel. From 3.30 till 5 p.m. we hung about the Mairie and the Commissaire de Police offices. I then got angry and insisted on going to Gesling, the undertaker to the English Embassy, to whom Father Cuthbert had recommended me. After settling matters with him I went off to find some nuns to watch the body. I thought that in Paris of all places this would be quite easy, but it was only after incredible difficulties I got two Franciscan sisters.

Gesling was most intelligent and promised to call at the Hôtel d'Alsace at 8 o'clock next morning. While Reggie stayed at the hotel interviewing journalists and clamorous creditors, I started with Gesling to see officials. We did not part till 1.30, so you can imagine the formalities and oaths and exclamations and signing of papers. Dying in Paris is really a very difficult and expensive luxury for a foreigner.

It was in the afternoon the District Doctor called and asked if Oscar had committed suicide or was murdered. He would not look at the signed certificates of Klein and Tucker. Gesling had warned me the previous evening that owing to the assumed name and Oscar's identity, the authorities might insist on his body being taken to the Morgue. Of course I was appalled at the prospect; it really seemed the final touch of horror. After examining the body, and, indeed, everybody in the hotel, and after a series of drinks and unseasonable jests, and a liberal fee, the District Doctor consented to sign the permission for burial. Then arrived some other revolting official; he asked how many collars Oscar had, and the value of his umbrella. (This is quite true, and not a mere exaggeration of mine.) Then various poets and literary people called, Raymond de la Tailhade, Tardieu, Charles Sibleigh, Jehan Rictus, Robert d'Humières, George Sinclair, and various English people, who gave assumed names, together with two veiled women. They were all allowed to see the body when they signed their names. . . .[2]

I am glad to say dear Oscar looked calm and dignified, just as he did when he came out of prison, and there was nothing at all horrible about the body after it had been washed. Around his neck was the blessed rosary

[1] On Friday, 30 November 1900. The latest medical opinion is that he died of an intercranial complication of suppurative *otitis media*, or middle-ear disease, of which his illness in prison (see p. 145) was an earlier symptom. See "The Last Illness of Oscar Wilde" by Terence Cawthorne, F.R.C.S., in the *Proceedings of the Royal Society of Medicine*, February 1959.
[2] Presumably Harris's dots.

which you gave me, and on the breast a Franciscan medal given me by one of the nuns, a few flowers placed there by myself and an anonymous friend who had brought some on behalf of the children, though I do not suppose the children know that their father is dead. Of course there was the usual crucifix, candles and holy water.

Gesling had advised me to have the remains placed in the coffin at once, as decomposition would begin very rapidly, and at 8.30 in the evening the men came to screw it down. An unsuccessful photograph of Oscar was taken by Maurice Gilbert at my request, the flashlight did not work properly. Henry Davray came just before they had put on the lid. He was very kind and nice. On Sunday, the next day, Alfred Douglas arrived, and various people whom I do not know called. I expect most of them were journalists. On Monday morning[1] at 9 o'clock, the funeral started from the hotel—we all walked to the Church of St Germain des Prés behind the hearse—Alfred Douglas, Reggie Turner and myself, Dupoirier, the proprietor of the hotel, Henri the nurse, and Jules, the servant of the hotel, Dr Hennion and Maurice Gilbert, together with two strangers whom I did not know. After a low mass, said by one of his *vicaires* at the altar behind the sanctuary, part of the burial office was read by Father Cuthbert. The *Suisse* told me that there were fifty-six people present—there were five ladies in deep mourning—I had ordered three coaches only, as I had sent out no official notices, being anxious to keep the funeral quiet. The first coach contained Father Cuthbert and the acolyte; the second Alfred Douglas, Turner, the proprietor of the hotel, and myself; the third contained Madame Stuart Merrill, Paul Fort, Henry Davray and Sarluis;[2] a cab followed containing strangers unknown to me. The drive took one hour and a half; the grave is at Bagneux, in a temporary concession hired in my name—when I am able I shall purchase ground elsewhere, at Père la Chaise for choice. I have not yet decided what to do, or the nature of the monument. There were altogether twenty-four wreaths of flowers; some were sent anonymously. The proprietor of the hotel supplied a pathetic bead trophy, inscribed, "*À mon locataire*," and there was another of the same kind from the "*service de l'hôtel*," the remaining twenty-two were, of course, of real flowers. Wreaths came from, or at the request of, the following: Alfred Douglas, More Adey, Reginald Turner, Miss Schuster, Arthur Clifton, the *Mercure de France*, Louis Wilkinson, Harold Mellor, Mr and Mrs Teixeira de Mattos, Maurice Gilbert, and Dr Tucker. At the head of the coffin I placed a wreath of laurels inscribed, "A tribute to his literary achievements and distinction." I tied inside the wreath the following names of those who had shown kindness to him during or after his imprisonment, "Arthur Humphreys, Max Beerbohm, Arthur Clifton, Ricketts, Shannon, Conder, Rothenstein, Dal Young, Mrs Leverson, More Adey, Alfred Douglas, Reginald Turner, Frank Harris, Louis Wilkinson,

---

[1] December 3.
[2] Léonard Sarluis (1874–1949) was a Dutch-Jewish painter and book-illustrator who came to Paris in 1894 and was later naturalised.

Mellor, Miss Schuster, Rowland Strong," and by special request a friend who wished to be known as "C.B."[1]

I can scarcely speak in moderation of the magnanimity, humanity and charity of Dupoirier, the proprietor of the Hôtel d'Alsace. Just before I left Paris Oscar told me he owed him over £190. From the day Oscar was laid up he never said anything about it. He never mentioned the subject to me until after Oscar's death, and then I started the subject. He was present at Oscar's operation, and attended to him personally every morning. He paid himself for luxuries and necessities ordered by the doctor or by Oscar out of his own pocket. I hope that —— or ——[2] will at any rate pay him the money still owing. Dr Tucker is also owed a large sum of money. He was most kind and attentive, although I think he entirely misunderstood Oscar's case.

Reggie Turner had the worst time of all in many ways—he experienced all the horrible uncertainty and the appalling responsibility of which he did not know the extent. It will always be a source of satisfaction to those who were fond of Oscar, that he had someone like Reggie near him during his last days while he was articulate and sensible of kindness and attention.

———————

A plain tombstone was later set above the grave at Bagneux, bearing these words from the twenty-ninth chapter of the Book of Job: *Verbis meis addere nihil audebant et super illos stillabat eloquium meum.*[3]

In 1909 Wilde's body was moved to the cemetery of Père Lachaise in Paris, where it rests under Epstein's monument and Wilde's own words:

> And alien tears will fill for him
> Pity's long-broken urn
> For his mourners will be outcast men,
> And outcasts always mourn.

---

[1] Presumably Carlos Blacker.
[2] Names omitted by Harris. Probably Douglas and Harris.
[3] "To my words they durst add nothing, and my speech dropped upon them." (Douai version.)

INDEX OF RECIPIENTS

GENERAL INDEX

Where there is a footnote giving a person's main biographical particulars it will be found on the first page mentioned after the person's name.

Archer, William
only critic to oppose censorship of *Salome*, 106; and *Dorian Gray*, 84 n; Max's caricature of, 348
Architect (of the Moon), *see* Fothergill
Ariel
W's business as artist with, 221
Aristotle
his *Ethics* wearisome, 159; quoted and refuted by W, 205–206; quoted by W, 215
Armando (boy)
W gives up, 358
Arnaldo (boy)
preferred to Armando, 358
Arnold, Matthew
W sends Helena Sickert poems of, 23; W sends *Poems* to, 28; quoted by W, 205, 208, 218; W wins bet about quotation from, 350
Art and Morality
and *Dorian Gray*, 86 n
Arthur (factotum)
causes chaos by tidying up, 120
"Artist, The" (prose-poem)
the note of doom in, 204
Ashton, I. D. W. ("Sir John")
cheated by boy, 345; more penniless than ever, 347; always in the best spirits (and water), 348
Asquith, H. H.
W sits in Royal Box with, 126
Athenaeum, The
Smithers advertises *Ballad* in, 334
Athens
W visits, 14; Douglas stays at, 163
Atkins, Frederick
wretched and perjured, 180; Allen probably mistaken for, 221
Augustine, St
works of sent to W in prison, 139 n
Aurora Leigh
much the greatest work in our literature, 9; sent to Ward, 9; simply "*intense*", 10
Austen, Jane
lack of books by in Reading Gaol, 247; Ross's letters in style of, 362
Austin, Alfred
his new volume, 191; W on, 191 n
Auteri-Manzocchi, Salvatore
crowned in Milan, 4
Authors' Club
Sherard censures W at, 312 n
Avondale Hotel
W stays at, 128–129; W unable to

leave, 171
Aynesworth, Allan
in *Importance*, 128 n

Babbacombe Cliff
W stays at, 107–110; names of rooms at, 108 n; "school" at, 107–108, 110; W's stay at uncreative, 154
Bacon, Francis
quoted by W, 211
Bagneux
W buried at, in temporary concession, 370; text on W's grave at, 371
Balcombe, Florence
more lovely than ever, 15; W writes to from Bournemouth, 19; W sends crown of flowers to, 28
Balfour, Murray
calls on W at Montreal, 44
Ballad of Reading Gaol, The
stanzas chosen by Yeats, 121 n; second dedication to, 279 n, 317; begun at Berneval, 286; nearly finished, 301; not yet finished, 305; to be typed, 305; new stanza sent to Ross, 305; corrected typescript sent to Smithers, 31p; Symons's review of, 310 n; too long for *Chronicle*, 310, 313; suffers from divided aim, 311; W without copy of, 312; W awaiting typed fair copies of, 313; returned to Smithers corrected, 314; W cannot do much more to, 314; unplaceable in America, 315; printed by Chiswick Press, 315; fears of libel in, 315; proofs arrive, 316; looks like sixpenny pamphlet, 316; binding discussed, 316; suggested title-page, 316; dedication discussed, 317–318; possibility of piracy of in U.S., 318; stanza quoted, 321 n; W has corrected enough, 322; its popularity to be increased by author's death from starvation, 322; title-page discussed, 324; publication date, 327; details of second and third editions, 329 n; praised by Rothenstein, 328; too autobiographical, 328; Author's (signed) Edition of, 329; Henley reviews, 330 n; French translation of, 331, 333; *Academy* reviews, 331; W's *chant de cygne*, 333; 1/- or 6d. edition suggested, 339–340, 341; W asks for eight copies of, 339; Sherard insists on reciting, 343; quoted, 357 n; quoted on W's tomb, 371

Balzac, Honoré de
W can't travel without, 46; W quotes
221; Lucien de Rubempré one of W's
favourite characters in youth, 221 n
Bankruptcy
Humphreys fails to see W about, 147;
W's public examination in, 147 n;
Grain acts for W in, 149; a note of
profligacy in W's, 157; details of W's,
171 n; Queensberry's pleasure at W's,
179; W served with notice of, 182;
Ross's noble action in Court of, 188;
W's two appearances in Court of, 192;
policemen's kindness to W in Court
of, 224; W's prolonged, 234
Barrett, Lawrence
produces *Duchess of Padua* as *Guido
Ferranti*, 90
Barrett, Wilson
and Britannia metal, 285
Baudelaire, Charles
preferred to Keble, 65; Gide compares W to, 117 n; quoted by W, 208–
209; Christ and *Fleurs du Mal*, 210;
the bitter cry of Marsyas in, 218;
would have entertained Clibborn and
Allen, 221; natural to W to read in
café, 247; W wants poems of, 248
Bauër, Henri
reviews *Salome* favourably, 140 n; his
powerful article in *Echo de Paris*, 184
Beardsley, Aubrey
dislikes binding of *Salome*, 115; supported by Raffalovich, 60 n and John
Gray, 60 n; *Salome* inscribed to,
115 n; W presents to Mrs Campbell,
116–117; W's estimate of, 149; Diaghilew's appreciation of, 340; his drawings for *Mademoiselle de Maupin*, 340n
Beerbohm, Max
suggested as possible donor of books,
247; his response, 247 n; W writes to
from Berneval, 276; W on *Happy
Hypocrite*, 276; writes note on Henley, 304 n; his *Chronicle* caricature
discussed, 348; named on laurel
wreath, 370
Beere, Mrs Bernard
W describes Mormons and Leadville
to, 40–42; her visit to Dublin, 70; in
Woman of No Importance, 111 n;
plans to visit Australia, 117–118; W
deeply touched by kindness and
affection of, 134
Berkeley Hotel
Douglas taken to lunch at, 153;
Douglas fires gun in, 167, 175

Berneval-sur-Mer
W stays at, 275–305; W feels will be
his home, 284; lack of theatre at, 284;
W happy all day at, 286; W proposes
to live at, 291; W's *Berneval, Day by
Day* recommended for *Chronicle*, 296;
Douglas's visit to cancelled, 298; W
responsible for sunsets at sea at, 301;
W cannot stand, 306; W's final loneliness at, 308; Sherard in his grenadine
at, 313
Bernhardt, Sarah
W would have married with pleasure,
25 n; W more lionised than, 32; re-
hearses *Salome*, 105; sympathises
with W, 134; asked to buy *Salome*,
134; hopeless, 135
Bernini
W admires when he sees Pope, 358
Besant, Walter
and Britannia metal, 285; backs W
for Savile Club, 73 n; and the obvious, 96; Aleck Ross's terrible smile
like a novel by, 355
Bible, The
Revised Version parodied, 62; no
dramatic presentation of allowed, 106;
W in prison asks for French version,
152; *Kings* quoted, 180; *Acts* quoted,
203; *Mark* quoted, 205, 212; *Isaiah*
quoted, 210; W reads the Gospels,
211 *et seq*; *John* quoted, 212; *Matthew*
quoted, 212, 213; verse from *Revelations* on Constance's grave, 349; verse
from *Job* on W's grave at Bagneux,
371
Bingham, Notts
W stays at, 6
Blacker, Carlos
Constance stays with, 302 n; Clifton's
letter to, 148 n; persuades W to post-
pone seeing Constance, 282 n; W
details plans to, 306; W explains his
actions to, 308; Constance's letters to,
320 n, 332 n; invited to Hôtel de
Nice, 332; W's gratitude to, 339;
named on laurel wreath, 371
Blackwood's Magazine
"Mr W.H." published in, 78 n
Blake, William
quoted by W, 239
Blidah
Gide meets W and Douglas at, 127 n
Blunt, Wilfrid Scawen
his diary quoted on *Salome*,
Bobbie, *see* Ross, Robert

Bonnet, O. J.
wants W to build chalet, 284; argues about lack of theatre, 284; and W's plans, 286; Ross described as banker to, 291

Bootle's Baby
by Mrs Stannard, 280; *une œuvre symboliste*, 287

Borghese Gardens
its milk as wonderful as its daisies, 359

Bosie, *see* Douglas, Lord Alfred

Boston
W lectures at, 33

Botticelli
taken for new drink in Leadville, 41

Boucicault, D. G. (Dot)
W sends love to, 42; his activities in Australia, 117

Boucicault, Dionysius L. (Dion)
Dublin cabmen likened to, 70; costumes in his *London Assurance*, 91

Bouncer, *see* Ward, William

Bourchier, Arthur
In *London Assurance*, 91, 92

Bourget, Paul
La Jeunesse's parody of, 289 n

Bourke, Hon. Algernon
reveals Queensberry's plot, 128

Bow Street Police Station
W taken to, 131; W charged at, 133

Boy, *see* Champagne

Bracknell
W's conversation with Lady Queensberry at, 156; W tells Douglas of Levy's warning at, 190

Bramley, Rev. H. R.
W writes to from Corfu, 14

Branca-d'Oro, Pietro (boy)
W loves very much, 357

Brighton
Douglas ill at, 125, 165; W ill at, 165–166, 228

Brooke, Lady (Ranee of Sarawak)
on W's fall, 243

Brookfield, Charles
collaborates in *Poet and Puppets*, 105 n; collects evidence for Queensberry, 105

Brookfield, Mrs
her articles on Thackeray's letters, 68

Brown, T. E.
and *Dorian Gray*, 84 n, 86

Browning, Elizabeth Barrett
and *Aurora Leigh*, 9, 10; Lady Wilde compared to, 224

Browning, Oscar
W stays with, 24; W asks for testimonial from, 24

Browning, Robert
W sends *Poems* to, 28 n; quoted by W, 339–340

Brownlow, Countess of
her gift of travelling basket to W, 251

Brown-Potter, Cora
her rights in *Mr and Mrs Daventry*, 362 n

Brutus, Junius
his madness compared to Hamlet's, 233

Buchanan, Robert,
pleads for charity towards W, 177 n, 178 n

Burgess, Gilbert
suggested as possible donor of books, 247; his interview with W, 247 n

Burne-Jones, Edward
W sends messages to family of, 32, 38; his works at Babbacombe, 108 n; W's drawings by sold, 179; Christ and, 210; the cry of Marsyas in women of, 218; Constance borrows £150 from, 333

Burne-Jones, Philip
sends W news to America, 45

Burns, John
possible introducer of shilling or sixpenny edition of *Ballad*, 340

Bushell (prisoner)
sent money by W, 279; letter possibly to, 280

Byron, Lord
W compares himself with, 194; W wins bet about phrase in Arnold's introduction to, 350

C.3.3
W'a number in Reading Gaol, 279; W signs letter as, 281, 287; on title-page of *Ballad*, 316, 324

Cadogan Hotel
W writes from, 131; W arrested at, 131 n

Café de la Paix, Paris
W meets Daly and Ada Rehan at, 350; W always ethical at, 355; Douglas makes scene in, 360-361

Café Royal, London
Queensberry threatens at, 118; Douglas taken to lunch at, 155; Queensberry sees W and Douglas at, 164; Douglas's behaviour at, 222

Calais
W fetches Douglas back from, 155

Caliban
as art-critic, 82; entirely detestable, 99; W set to wrestle with, 221; British public is for half the year, 226

Campbell, Lady Archie
sends W telegram with Whistler, 36;
the Moon-Lady, 45; her pastoral
plays, 62 n; and *Woman's World*,
68
Campbell, Mrs Patrick
W takes Beardsley to see, 116–117; in
The Masqueraders, 126 n; in *John-a-
Dreams*, 126 n; pays Harris £100,
363; in *Mr and Mrs Daventry*,
362 n
Campbell's Bar, Paris
Sherard creates scene in, 343
Canada
W lectures in, 43–44
Cannes
W sees *Bataille des Fleurs* at, 347
Carlyle, Thomas
W asks in prison for books by, 145 n;
his translation of Goethe quoted, 200;
quoted by W, 272
Carrel, Frederic
portrays Harris in *Adventures of John
Johns*, 301
Carson, Edward
W imagines himself re-examined by,
209
Carte, Richard D'Oyly
promotes W's American tour, 31
Cartwright, Charles
a bald genius, 117
Cassell, Messrs
and *Woman's World*, 69; and Arthur
Fish, 83 n
Cellini, Benvenuto
W lectures on in Leadville, 42; would
have entertained Clibborn and Allen,
221
Censorship
and *Salome*, 105–106, Archer on, 106–
107; Irving, Scott and Carr in favour
of, 106 n; must be abolished, 107;
Shaw praised for opposing, 108
Century Guild Hobby Horse, The
Horne edits, 66 n; *Happy Prince* sent
to, 72
Chambers, C. Haddon
his *John-a-Dreams* badly written, 126
Champagne
in America, 43, offered to Norman
Forbes-Robertson, 43; a new brand
for Douglas, 159; Dagonet 1880
Douglas's favourite, 235; W drinks
too much, 367
Chance, H. F.
Oxford friend of W, 12
Charles, Mr Justice,
judge at first trial, 133

Charles Street, Mayfair
W stays at No 9, 52
Chatterton, Thomas
W plans memorial to, 66–67; W lec-
tures on, 67; his "Ballad of Charity,"
210; W wants works of, 248
Chaucer
W in prison asks for poems of, 145 n
Chéret, Jules
his posters praised, 97
Chiswick Press
print *Ballad* and fear libel, 315, 318,
321
Cholmondeley, Reginald
remembered by W in prison, 289
Chopin
effect of his nocturnes, 209; the cry of
Marsyas in music of, 218
Christ, *see* Jesus
Christian Leader, The
praises *Dorian Gray*, 83
Christian World, The
praises *Dorian Gray*, 83
Clapham Junction
W's terrible experience at, 219
Cleveland Street
scandal of 1889, 81 n
Clibborn
his infamous war against life, 221
Clifton, Arthur
W would like as guardian of his chil-
dren, 147; his account of W in prison,
148 n; W hopes to see, 149; his comfort and help to W, 223; W's letter to
be shown to, 245; his wife's resemblance to Mrs Rossetti, 248; tries to
arrange terms with Hope, 322; sends
wreath to W's funeral, 370; named on
laurel wreath, 370
Clio
least serious of Muses, 159
Clouet, François
Ricketts's picture of Mr W.H. declared worthy of, 79
Cobban, J. Maclaren
and *Dorian Gray*, 83 n, 86
Coleridge, S. T.
W wants books by, 248
Colvin, Sidney
W accused of talking like, 36; W's dislike of, 37 n; repudiated by W, 37;
and Griggsville, 103; Indians very
like, 37, 38; edits *Vailima Letters*,
246 n; W parodies letters to, 280, 285
Conder, Charles
visits W at Berneval, 290; unknowable, but Smithers to make friends
with, 341; at La Roche-Guyon, 344;

Davidson, John
Napoule chef a purer poet than, 347

Davis, Jefferson
W visits, 46

Davitt, Michael
suitable introducer for shilling or six-penny edition of *Ballad*, 339; W writes to about Prince and prison life, 339 n; asks question in House about Warder Martin, 269 n

Davray, Henry D.
to translate *Ballad*, 331; calls after W's death, 370; attends W's funeral, 370

De Amicitia (Cicero)
a new one should include Rosen-crantz and Guildenstern, 233

"Decay of Lying, The"
a trumpet against the gate of dullness 77; *Robert Elsmere* mocked in, 77 n; suggestion of plagiarism in, 80; quoted by W, 128 n

Degas, Edgar
W meets in Paris, 49; W describes, 116

Delaroche, Paul
explained away, 59–60

De Mitty, Jean
and La Jeunesse, 289 n

De Morgan, William
no gold or roses for, 79

De Profundis
here printed in full, 152–240; history of MS and publication of, 152 n; MS handed to Ross, 240 n, 266; W's suggested title for, 242; delayed at Reading, 245–246; W asks about typing of, 300

d'Humières, Robert
W dines with in Paris, 343; calls after W's death, 369

Diaghilew, Serge de
W meets in Paris, 340; his interest in Beardsley, 340

Diary
everyone should keep someone else's, 125

Dickens, Charles
W rivals as lecturer, 31; W in prison asks for works of, 145 n

Diderot, Denis
his limitations, 84

Dieppe
W spends part of honeymoon at, 55 n; MS of *De Profundis* handed to Ross at, 152 n, 266; Ross and Turner to go ahead to, 261 n; finally decided on, 262; W arrives at, 266; Ross stern

with W at, 276; W announced as bicycling at, 280; boots best bought at, 283; W anxious to see sons at, 282 n; W to breakfast with Stannards at, 286, 291; plans to meet Dowson at, 291; no cigarette-boxes at, 297; Diaghilew meets Beardsley at, 340 n; Douglas's letters to remembered, 360

Dinard
W spends fortnight at, 161

Diogenes
referred to by W, 289

Dixon
a possible typist for *De Profundis*, 300

Doctors
brutal in prisons, 338

Dodgson, Campbell
presented with paper-weight, 109, 110 n; "second master" at Babba-combe, 108; tutors Douglas, 110

Dolores (opera)
performed at Milan, 4

Don Quixote
quoted by W, 87

Doré (tailor)
Adey promises to order W suit from, 146 n; Ross promises clothes from, 250; W asks for blue suit from, 343; secret to be disclosed to, 343

Dostoievsky
cited by Whibley, 83 n

Dot, *see* Boucicault, D. G.

Douglas, Lord Alfred (Bosie)
introduced to W by Johnson, 89; copy of *Dorian Gray* inscribed to, 89; unreliable in matters of fact, xii; "quite like a narcisus," 105; "I worship him," 106; sends W sonnet, 107; at Salisbury, 107; W's letter to used for blackmail, 107 n; studies Plato at Babbacombe, 108; *Salome* bound in purple to suit gilt hair of, 109; and "Babbacombe School," 110; makes scenes, 111; W's letter to read in court, 111 n; English *Salome* dedicated to, 113 n; his translation of *Salome*, 113 n, 161; his future discussed with his mother, 113–114; W's greatest friend, 114; envied in Florence, 117, joined there by W, 117 n; asked to Worthing, 118; would be bored there, 118; sends poem to W, 120; W reports to from Worthing, 120–121; and *The Green Carnation* 124; his illness at Brighton, 125; enquired after at Willis's, 127; his peom "Two loves" partly quoted, 170 n;

Douglas of Hawick, Lord—*cont.*
really good fellow, 224; his refusal or inability to pay, 251; W accepts bicycle from, 298; considered disreputable by Hansell, 319

Dowson, Ernest
visits W at Berneval, 290; W plans to meet in Dieppe, 291; W to dine with 300; asked to repay debt, 313, 314; W's distress at death of, 353; his gifts analysed, 353

Doyle, Arthur Conan
and *Dorian Gray*, 95; on Stoddart and *Sign of Four*, 95 n

Drawings by Wilde in text
of Auteri-Manzocchi, 4; of Henry Irving, 27; of cambric ruff, 34; of Mormons, 40; of his name on poster, 44; of ground-plan of chalet, 285

Dress Reform
W advocates, 55-57; W on men's, 90-92

Drumlanrig, Viscount
possible good influence on Douglas, 113; his death, 168; Lady Queensberry's grief for, 168; Douglas puts flowers on grave of, 169; his goodness to his mother, 173; created Baron Kelhead, 174 n; would have protected his mother, 226

Duchess of Padua, The
W and Mary Anderson, 47; produced in N.Y. as *Guido Ferranti*, 90; Mathews & Lane under obligation to publish, 123; quoted, 349 n

Dumas, Alexandre, *père*
would have entertained Clibborn and Allen, 221; lack of books like his in Reading Gaol, 247; W wants books by, 248

Dumas, Alexandre, *fils*
surpassed by W, 228

Dunlop, A. C.
W talks sentimental religion to, 12

Dunn, Father Cuthbert
called by Ross, 368; receives W into Church of Rome, 368; recommends undertaker, 369; conducts W's funeral service and burial, 370

Dunn, James Nicol
W sends poem to, 76

Dunskie, *see* Hunter-Blair, David

Dupoirier, Edouard
at W's deathbed, 368; loses his head, 369; follows W's coffin, 370; his touching wreath, 370; his magnanimity, humanity and charity, 371; money owed to, 371

Ear trouble
W's in prison, 145; W dies of, 369

Eccelino da Romano
cited as monster of cruelty, 269

Echo de Paris
interview on banning of *Salome*, 105; Bauër's pro-W article in, 184; obtained by W at Dieppe, 288

Edinburgh
W writes from, 57

Egoist
must have an Ego, 289; Gide as, 289

Elsmere, Robert
hit between joints of nineteenth edition, 77; a masterpiece of the *genre ennuyeux*, 77 n

Elvin, Harry (prisoner)
W plans to help, 280; heart of gold, 294

Emerson, R. W.
and W's trunk, 46; quoted by W, 60, 208, 219; W in prison asks for essays of, 145 n

Eolo (boy)
waits at table at Gland, 349; origin of name of, 349; most tyrannical with Mellor, 362

Ernesto, *see* Scarfe, Ernest

Eugene (friend of Turner)
W hears from, 309

Euripides
quoted by W, 157, 237

Evening News, The
W writes to after Queensberry trial, 131

Every Man his own Lawyer
recommended to W's friends, 244

Fabulet, Louis
W's abortive letter to, 344; his translations of Kipling, 343 n

Fane, Violet
a poem and a poet in one, 52; possible contributor to *Woman's World*, 68

Felbrigg, Norfolk
Douglas stays with W at, 156

Fescennine licence
in Rome, 359

Figaro, Le
announces W bicycling at Dieppe, 280

Fish Arthur
his forthcoming marriage, 83

Flaubert, Gustave
Holman a serious rival to *Bouvard et Pécuchet* of, 255; "my master," 76; W's wish to translate, 76 n; cited by

Flaubert, Gustave—*cont.*
Whibley, 83 n; artistically right, 85;
W wants books by, 247; *Salammbô*
quoted by W, 279; reads *Tentation* by,
333
Fleur-de-Lys, *see* Douglas, Lord Alfred
Florentine Tragedy, A
W tries to remember in prison, 148;
almost completed, 156; a beautiful
coloured, musical thing, 221; to be
begun tomorrow, 310
Forbes, Archibald
his dispute with W, 32–33; sends
lying telegrams, 37, 40
Forbes-Robertson, Eric
parts of *De Profundis* to be shown to,
241; picturesque and sweet as usual,
351
Forbes-Robertson, Frances (Frankie)
parts of *De Profundis* to be sent to,
241; W writes and sends wedding
present to, 351; her marriage, 351 n;
her inscription in *Importance*, 352 n
Forbes-Robertson, Ian
W visits in America, 39
Forbes-Robertson, Johnston
W sends love to, 40; W asks about
management of, 141; at Frankie's
wedding, 351
Forbes-Robertson, Norman
thanked for defending W, 39; plans
to visit U.S., 43; encouraged to get
married, 63
Ford (prisoner)
sent money by W, 279; letter possibly
to, 280
Fort, Paul
invited to lunch, 101; attends W's
funeral, 370
Fortnightly Review, The
publishes *Soul of Man*, 94 n; publishes preface to *Dorian Gray*, 94;
Douglas compares *Mercure de France*
to, 183, 187; "The Artist" published
in, 204 n
Fothergill, John Rowland
the Architect of the Moon, 286;
wanted at Berneval, 286; special
terms for in chalet, 292; invited to
Berneval, 301; gave W a sextette of
suns, 308
France, Anatole
W wants books by, 248; La Jeunesse's
parody of, 289 n; quoted by W, 308
Francis of Assisi, St
and Christ, 210; the only Christian
since Christ, 215; quoted by W, 217;

W asks for good life of, 248; W would
not dislike living like, 292; W wedded
to Poverty like, 352
Frankie, *see* Forbes-Robertson, Frances
Frederic, Harold
Illumination very interesting in mat-
ter, 247
Frederick II, Emperor
W visits tomb of, 356
Frou-Frou
heroine of W's plot reads, 119; W's
scenario compared to, 146 n
Funeral reform
W's letter in favour of, 58

Gaulois, Le
interview on banning of *Salome*, 105
Gautier, Théophile
W can't travel without, 46; his limita-
tions, 84; imagined reading *Dorian
Gray* in Elysian fields, 84; *Fortunio*
misattributed, 86; W compares him-
self to, 237; W wants poems of, 248;
Beardsley's illustrations for *Mademoi-
selle de Maupin*, 340 n
Genoa
Constance Wilde travels from to
Reading to break news of Lady
Wilde's death, 139 n, 186; W and
Douglas spend day at, 309; Con-
stance forbids W to come to, 320;
Constance dies at, 338; W visits
Constance's grave at, 349
Gesling (undertaker)
and W's funeral, 369, 370
Gide, André
W meets in Paris, 96; reports W's
saying, ix; contributes to *La Conque*,
96 n; his account of W in Paris, 97 n;
describes meeting W in Florence,
117 n; meets W and Douglas at
Blidah, 127 n; W's remark to, 204;
an Egoist without an Ego, 289;
remembers Nicholson woodcut in
Chalet, 298
Gilbert, Maurice
sends regards to Smithers, 329; signs
copies for W, 330; Ross asked if he
loves, 342; chastened by modern art
but wins knife at fair, 342; Sherard's
change of heart towards, 343; Douglas
inseparable from, 343; Strong's bad
effect on, 345; W shares medicines
with, 353; W dictates letter to, 353,
362 n; photographs W after death,
370; follows W's coffin, 370; sends
wreath to W's funeral, 370

Gilbert, W. S.
his Bunthorne taken for W, 31
Gilderoy
prefigures *Romeo and Juliet*, 288
Giotto
Douglas envied under Tower of, 117;
Christ and, 210
Gladstone, W. E.
W sends *Poems* to, 28 n; *Happy
Prince* sent to, 75 n; refuses to back
Lady Wilde's claim, 75 n; Queens-
berry writes abusively to, 174 n
Gland, Switzerland
W stays with Mellor at, 348–349; a
further ten days at, 360; W's last visit
to, 362
Gloeden, Baron von
Ballad sent to, 331
Glover, J. M.
collaborates in *Poet and Puppets*, 105 n
Godwin, E. W.
and Whistler's house, 61 n; and 16
Tite Street, 61; his handbook on
dress, 56; mourned at Oxford, 62
Goethe
rare in Modern England, 84; would
have been delighted by *Dorian Gray*,
84; Carlyle's translation of quatrain
quoted, 200; the serenity and calm of,
208; Arnold not healed by, 218; W
wants works and literature of, 248
Goncourt, Edmond de
W meets in Paris, 49; W challenges
passage in *Journal* of, 100–101; *Journal* quoted, 100 n, 237; forecasts
hydrogen bomb, 100; sympathises
with W, 134; *Journal* not appreciated
by all prisoners, 247
Gordon-Lennox, Cosmo (Cosmo
Stuart)
suggested as possible donor of books,
247; in *Ideal Husband*, 247 n
Goring-on-Thames
W stays at, 113; three wasted summer
months at, 150; W's stay at uncreative, 154, and expensive, 157; Douglas's behaviour at, 160, 161, 170, 182
Gosse, Edmund
Salome sent to, 108; backs W for
Savile Club, 73 n; W takes his name
in vain, 358
Goulding, ?William Joshua
with W in Italy, 5 n; with W in
Greece, 15 n
Gower, Lord Ronald
describes W at Oxford, 6 n; W pro-
poses health of, 74

Goya
would have entertained Clibborn and
Allen, 221
Grain, J. P.
acts for Taylor, and in Bankruptcy
Court for W, 149
Gray, John
compared favourably with Douglas,
155; his friendship with Raffalovich,
60 n; *Silverpoints* paid for by W,
155 n; not original of Dorian Gray,
155 n
Greece
W visits, 14–15
Greek Anthology, The
W praises, 65
Green Carnation, The
Ada Leverson wrongly suspected
author of, 124; W denies authorship
of, 125
Grissell, H. de la G.
W blessed by Pope to terror of, 356
Grosvenor Gallery
Pater's praise of W's article on, 19
Groves, George (warder)
sent money by W, 280
Guido Ferranti, see *Duchess of Padua,
The*
Gyles, Althea
W asks after, 353; illustrates "Harlot's
House," 353 n; an artist of great
ability, 363

Haggard, Rider
backs W for Savile Club, 73 n
Hake, A. E.
and Rossetti, 246
Haldane, R. B.
his kindness to W in prison, 139 n
Hanbury, Lily
in *Lady Windermere*, 102 n
Hansell, A. D.
W's correspondence with, 249; proposes to visit W at Reading, 251; W's
letter from, 258; W sees at Reading,
262; his attitude outrageous, 319;
bound to follow legal agreement, 319;
his decision irrevocable, 320, 322
Happy Hypocrite, The
W on, 276–277
"Happy Prince, The"
possibility of Ellen Terry reading, 72;
the note of doom in, 204
Happy Prince and other Tales, The
illustrated by Hood and Crane, 71;
sent to Ruskin, 71; its publication,
71 n; sent to Gladstone, 75 n; Pater's

Holland, Vyvyan—*cont.*
ised chocolates, 93; W's love for, 151; and *De Profundis*, 152 n; Adrian Hope guardian of, 193, 227; his photograph sent to W, 282; W anxious to see at Dieppe, 282 n; on Lincrusta-Walton, 292 n; W realises he will never see, 306

Holloway Prison
W imprisoned in, 133–136; Douglas's visits to W in, 177

Holman, Martin
Adey's solicitor, 149; in communication with Official Receiver, 149 n; and W's possible divorce, 243; his advice worthless, 254; a serious rival to Flaubert's grotesques, 255; the leader of the Dunces, 255; Holmaniana, 255, 256, 257–258; well satisfied, 259

Holmes, Oliver Wendell
W meets in Boston, and sends *Poems* to, 33

Homburg
W takes cure at, 105–106; Queensberry pursues Lord Rosebery to, 174

Home Secretary
W's petitions to, 142–145, 147 n; Adey's petition to, 146 n; refusal received from, 252; sends W to Pentonville for release, 261

Homer (boy)
talks much of Ross, 357; W gives false names and addresses to, 358–359

Hood, Jacomb
illustrates W stories, 71

Hood, Thomas
alteration in *Ballad* not on account of, 314; *Ballad* compared to "Eugene Aram" of, 331 n

Hope, Adrian
made guardian of W's children, 227, 193 n; Clifton tries to arrange terms with, 322 n

Hope, Anthony
lack of books by in Reading Gaol, 247

Hopps, Rev. J. Page
and funeral reform, 58; *Ballad* sent to, 331

Horace
quoted by W, 79

Horne, Herbert P.
and a Chatterton memorial, 66, 67

Hornton Street
De Profundis to be typed in, 241; W's bags to be taken to, 251; W's letters addressed to, 279

Hôtel d'Alsace, Paris
W moves to, 341; breakfast only meal provided at, 341; Ross and Turner visit W at, 365; Ross and Turner sleep at, 368; W dies at, 369

Hôtel de Nice, Paris
W stays at, 327–334

Hôtel Marsollier, Paris
W stays at, 350–351

Houghton, Lord
W appeals to about Keats tablet, 16

House of Pomegranates, A
reviewed by *Speaker*, 97–99; publishing details of, 98 n; reviewed by *P.M.G.*, 99; not written for British child, 99

Housman, A. E.
sends *Shropshire Lad* to W, 331 n

Housman, Laurence
Ballad sent to, 331; thanked for kindness and letter, 331

Howe, Julia Ward
W writes to from Deep South, 46; defends W against Higginson, 46 n; possible contributor to *Woman's World*, 68

Hughes, Willie
W's choice for Shakespeare's W.H., 78; Ricketts's picture of, 250

Hugo, Victor
Duchess of Padua may give W fame of, 47; W meets in Paris, 49; W loses inscribed books by, 179; Christ and *Les Misérables*, 210

Humphreys, Arthur L.
publishes *Oscariana*, 124; publishes *Soul of Man*, 124 n; *Odyssey* ordered from, 124; sent stall for *Importance*, 128; named on laurel wreath, 370

Humphreys, C. O.
to appear at Bow Street for W, 131; fails to see W about Bankruptcy, 147; W in office of, 171; W tells serious lies to, 221; Hargrove wrongly classed with, 243; W's things left with, 251; claims £150, 251; silver brushes recovered from, 285

Humpty Dumpty
W likened to, 243 n

Hunt, Violet
W sends poem to, 26

Hunter-Blair, David (Dunskie)
in Rome with Ward, 13; W sends message to, 16; at Keats's grave with W, 18

Huyshe, Wentworth
opposed by W on dress reform, 56–57

Johnson, Lionel—*cont.*
son friend of, 109; Dodgson's letter to, 109
Jones, Henry Arthur
W's pretended ignorance of, 126; W asks about play of, 140
Jonquil, *see* Douglas, Lord Alfred
Jour, Le
prints interview with Douglas, 288, 289
Journal, Le
W charmed to write for, 288

Keats House, Chelsea
possible origin of name, 26 n; W lives at, 26–29
Keats, John
his memorial tablet in Rome, 16; W's sonnet on his grave sent to Lord Houghton and quoted, 16–17; W at grave of, 16; W's sonnet on his grave, 17; W sent MS poem by, 38; his grave the holiest place in Rome, 59; to be re-read, 65; quoted on Shakespeare, 82; W's sonnet on the sale of his letters recommended to Yeats, 121; W's sonnet on the sale of his letters quoted, 183; W in prison asks for poems of, 145 n; Christ and, 210; quoted by W, 239; W wants works of, 248
Keble, John
his poems inferior to Baudelaire's, 65
Kekewich, Mr Justice
Constance Wilde's summons heard by, 193 n
Kempis, St Thomas à
as bedtime reading, 9; his *Imitatio Christi* and St Francis, 215
Kernahan, Coulson
and proofs of *Dorian Gray*, 93–94; excellent on Rossetti, 94
Kerr, Fred
in *Mr and Mrs Daventry*, 362 n
Kerr, Mr Commissioner
Indians' conversation reminiscent of, 37
Kiosks
recommended for London, 97; W wishes he could see Rothenstein's work on, 328
Kipling, Rudyard
W will never again out-Kipling Henley, 310; Fabulet's translation of, 343 n; his introduction to d'Humières' book, 243 n
Kitten, *see* Harding, Reginald

Klein, Dr
called in by Turner, 368; District Doctor ignores certificate of, 369
Knave of Spades
W's walking-stick removed by, 357
Knight, Joseph
buffaloes resemble, 39
Knowles, James
W sends Lady Wilde's pamphlet to, 28
Koolapoor, Rajah of
his bust at Florence, 17
Kropotkin, Prince Peter
his life praised, 216

Labouchere, H. du P. (Labby)
one of W's heroes, 37; on plagiarists, 80 n; prints part of Douglas's letter in *Truth*, 178 n
Lady of Wimbledon, *see* Schuster, Adela
Lady Windermere's Fan
W can't get grip of, 90; alterations in discussed with Alexander, 102–103; produced, 102; alterations explained, 104; burlesque of licensed, 105; and great Celtic School, 112 n; taken from W by the Law, 235; possibility of Strangman's translating, 297; Alexander buys acting rights and makes payments to W, 361 n
La Jeunesse, Ernest
W fascinated by *Napoléon* of, 289; his recollections of W, 289 n; more intolerable than ever, 345
Lamartine
the cry of Marsyas in, 218
Lane, John
told binding of *Salome* quite dreadful, 115; W's *Poems* (1892) first book to carry imprint of, 115 n; W's contempt for, 115 n; *Sphinx* published by, 123 n; wicked and routed, 114; breaks with Mathews, 122 n; and publication of "Mr W.H.," 122–124; his ignorance of French, 123
Langtry, Lily
at tea with W, 25; W would have married with pleasure, 25 n; the adored and adorable, 37–38; her second American tour, 54; W tells of his engagement, 54
Language
W once a Lord of, 186; should be tuned like a violin, 231, 291
Lawson, Edward (Lord Burnham)
W writes to, 90 n; Reggie Turner illegitimate relation of, 247 n

Leadville
  W's visit to, 41–43
Leclercq, Rose
  original Lady Bracknell, 128 n
Le Gallienne, Richard
  gives W poems in MS, 74; sent first-
  night seats, 103
Lemaitre, Jules
  W wishes to know his opinion of
  Salome, 140
Leo XIII, Pope
  W blessed by, 356; artist as well as
  saint, 356; makes W admire Bernini,
  358; W's mussel-poisoning cured by
  blessing of, 358; W sees again, 360
Leslie, Mrs Frank
  marries Willie Wilde, 16 n
Leverson, Ada (the Sphinx)
  the Sphinx of Modern Life, 112; her
  meeting with W, 112 n; and *The
  Green Carnation*, 124; binds *Intentions* for W, 125; her *Punch* article
  praised, 125; suspected of keeping
  W's diary, 125; her skit on *Ideal
  Husband*, 127 n; her brilliant article
  returned, 127; told of visit to Monte
  Carlo, 130; homage sent to, 130; W
  writes to from Holloway, 133; W
  deeply touched by kindness and
  affection of, 134; and MS of *Sainte
  Courtisane*, 134 n; writes to W in
  Holloway, 135; sends books, 136; has
  W to stay during bail, 137 n; has
  some of Douglas's letters to W, 141;
  visits W at Headlam's and describes
  the scene, 265–266; W writes to on
  first day of liberty, 267; her open
  secret, 276; her account of Ross's
  canonisation, 278; and Ernest Leverson's involvement in divorce suit,
  284; to pay extra at chalet, 292;
  named on laurel wreath, 370
Leverson, Ernest
  husband of the Sphinx, 112 n; regards sent to, 130; lends W £500,
  130; W writes to from Holloway, 133;
  W deeply touched by kindness and
  affection of, 134; charming note from,
  135; Adela Schuster's gift of £1000
  handed to, 140 n; asked to fetch W's
  belongings from Oakley Street, 140;
  visits W at Reading, 140 n; to hand
  over balance of money, 251; W's
  hopes of money from, 262; visits W
  at Headlam's, 265; W sends regards
  to, 267; the open secret of the Sphinx
  276; his divorce suit, 284

Levy, Edwin
  warns W against Douglas, 190
Lewis, George
  W plans to consult, 168; W begins to
  lose esteem of, 169; "the one great
  safeguard of my life," 169; grotesque
  idea of W's fighting, 243; tells Constance of W's friends, 319
Lewis, George, Junior
  W sends pencil-case and drawing to,
  27
Lewis, Mrs George
  W describes American successes to,
  31, 35; Indians described to, 37; W
  sends Indian fan to, 44
Lewis, Kate Terry
  "Decay of Lying" described to, 77
Lewis, Katherine (Katie)
  W sends love to, 38; "that trenchant
  critic of life," 44
Liber Conformitatum
  unnecessary in assessing St Francis,
  215
Lincrusta-Walton
  and Dadoes, 292; at 16 Tite Street,
  292 n
Linnæus
  mentioned by W, 237
Lippincott's Magazine
  publishes *Dorian Gray*, 81 n
Lipton's tea
  Athenaeum advertisement makes W
  feel like, 334
Lloyd, Constance, *see* Wilde, Constance
Lloyd, Otho Holland
  his letter to Mary Lloyd, 138 n;
  Constance's letter to, 105 n
Lockwood, Sir Frank
  his denunciation of W, 230
Loftie, Rev. W. J.
  proposes W for Savile Club, 73 n
Lombroso, Cesare
  referred to by W, 142; more expert on
  perversity than Douglas, 183
Longfellow, H. W.
  W breakfasts with, 33
Lonsdale, Lady
  at tea with W, 25; *A Woman of No
  Importance* dedicated to, 25 n
Lorne, Marquess of
  W lectures to on Dadoes, 44
Los Angeles
  a sort of Naples, 40
Loti, Pierre
  La Jeunesse's parody of, 289 n
Louÿs, Pierre
  W meets in Paris, 96; his letter to W,

Louÿs, Pierre—*cont.*
97 n; *Salome* sent to, 101; his corrections to *Salome*, 101 n; rebuked for not acknowledging *Salome* dedication, 110; sympathises with W, 134; his success, 148; tells W he must choose between Douglas and, 148; compared favourably with Douglas, 155

Loverde, Giuseppe (boy)
W meets at Palermo, 355–356

Lugné-Poe, A.-M.
W's gratitude to, 139; produces *Salome*, 139 n; W would like book by, 252; W invites to breakfast, 268; and W's next play, 287

Lumley (solicitor)
enquires for Douglas, 22

Luther
quoted by W, 93

Lytton, Earl of
and Shakespearean production, 62

Lytton, Lady Betty
enjoys "Decay of Lying," 77

Machines
more wilful than animals, 360

Mackail, J. W.
backs W for Savile Club, 73 n

Macmillan, George
accompanies W to Greece, 15 n; backs W for Savile Club, 73 n

Macmillan, Malcolm
disappears on Mt Olympus, 15 n

Mademoiselle de Maupin
Beardsley's illustrations for, 340 n

Maeterlinck, Maurice
W wants books by, 248

Magdalen College, Oxford
W wins Demyship at, 2; W rusticated from, 15; Douglas and Johnson at, 89

Mahaffy, Rev. John Pentland
his influence on W, 2; leaves W at Milan, 4; W sees every day, 11 n; W corrects proofs for, 11 n; takes W to Greece, 14–15; "raging" at W's rustication, 15; backs Lady Wilde's claim, 75 n; "my first and my best teacher," 111

Malebolge
W in lowest mire of, 159

Mallarmé, Stéphane
thanked for *Le Corbeau*, 92–93; W meets in Paris, 49; W loses inscribed books by, 179; would understand W's meaning, 303

Mallock, W. H.
his *New Republic*, 9

Mansfield College
W at Berneval treated as President of, 283

Marbury, Elisabeth
the best chance in America, 314, 315

Margate
nom-de-plume of Ramsgate, 330

Marillier, H. C.
the artistic life described to, 64

Marlowe, Christopher
cited by Whibley, 83 n; W in prison asks for works of, 145 n; W wants works of, 248

Marshall, Mrs
to type *De Profundis*, 241; reliable, 300

Marsyas
W's references to legend of, 75–76, 209, 218, 328, 333; in much modern Art the cry of, 218

Martin, Thomas (warder)
W's prison notes to, 248–249; his contribution to Sherard's *Life*, 248 n; and children in prison, 260; his dismissal, 260 n, 269–271; mentioned to Nelson, 282; Davitt's questions in House about, 269 n, 339 n; W's gift to, 295

Marvell, Andrew
quoted by W, 355

Massingham, H. W.
W plans to write to, 279; W sending postscript to, 282

Matchless mine
W's visit to, 41–43

Mathews, Elkin
publishes English *Salome*, 115 n; breaks with Lane, 122 n; and publication of "Mr W.H.", 122–124; W suggests giving plays to, 124

Mattos, A. Teixeira de
difficulties of bust in theatre, 112; marries Lily Wilde, 112 n; visits W in last illness, 366; sends wreath to W's funeral, 370

Mattos, Henri Teixeira de
and bust in Haymarket Theatre, 112 n

Maturin, C. R.
W's great-uncle, 266 n; W's alias taken from, 352 n

Maupassant, Guy de
cited by Whibley, 83 n

Maurice, *see* Gilbert, Maurice

Max, *see* Beerbohm, Max

Maypole soap
W suggests giving away *Ballad* with, 342

Meilhac and Halévy
  W's heroine reads *Frou-Frou*, 119
Mellor, Harold
  to visit London, 347; W stays at Gland with, 348–349; W turns against, 349; tedious, 349; refuses to pay, 350; invites W to Italy, 354; takes W to Sicily, Naples and Rome, 355–357; leaves Rome, 357; in Paris, 362; drinks and talks mineral waters, 362; sends wreath to W's funeral, 370; named on laurel wreath, 371
Melmoth, Sebastian
  W's adoption of as name, 266; suggested by Ross, 266 n; W still registered as at death, 369
Melmoth the Wanderer
  W takes name from, 266 n, 352; loved by Rossetti, 246; Ross and Adey's introduction to, 266 n
Mentone
  Douglas's behaviour at, 334; Ross moves his mother to, 368
Mercure de France, Le
  Douglas's article intended for, 137 n, 223, 239; ridiculous, 182; compared by Douglas to *Fortnightly*, 183, 187; founded by Vallette, 331 n; Davray reviews *Ballad* in, 331 n; to publish French translation of *Ballad*, 331 n, 340; send wreath to W's funeral, 370
Meredith, George
  W charmed by *Amazing Marriage*, 246
Meredith, Miss
  Adey's housekeeper, 279
Merrill, Madame Stuart
  attends W's funeral, 370
Merrill, Stuart
  sympathises with W, 134; corrects *Salome*, 101 n; draws up petition for W's release, 134 n; Ross asked to write to, 139; W would like book by, 252
Meynell, Alice
  and the Laureateship, 191
Milan
  W visits, 2–4, a second Paris, 4
Miles, Frank
  sketches Lady Desart, 5–6; W stays with, 7; with W at Moytura, 10; W goes rowing with, 20; shares rooms with W in Salisbury Street, 23; draws Mrs Langtry, 25 n; shares rooms with W at Keats House, Tite Street, 26–29
Millais, J. E.
  W attends his ball, 24; "that splendid fellow," 40

Miller, Joaquin
  his letter and W's reply, 34–35
Millward (prisoner)
  sent money by W, 279; letter possibly to, 280
Milner, Alfred
  invited to W's wedding, 55
Milton
  quoted by W, 206, 207
Mods
  W's First in, 6
Mommsen, Theodor
  his *History of Rome* sent to W in prison, 139 n
Monte Carlo
  W visits with Douglas, 130 n; "of all revolting places," 159
Monticelli, A. J. T.
  W's sorrow at loss of picture by, 179; picture rescued by Rothenstein and sold for W's benefit, 304
Montreal
  W's drawing of poster at, 42
Moore, George
  Max's caricature of, 348; *Importance* not to stand near anything by, 348
Moréas, Jean
  sympathises with W, 134
Mormons
  W describes and draws, 40–41
Morny, Duc de
  colour of coats altered by, 92
Morris, William
  W loses inscribed books by, 179; Christ and, 210; at 16 Tite Street, 292 n
Morse, Col. W. F.
  suggests W's American tour, 31; asked to buy fancy dress for W, 33;
Mount-Temple, Lady
  and lease of Babbacombe, 107
Moytura House
  W at, 10
Mozart
  Douglas's sonnet on, 310
Mr and Mrs Daventry
  plot outlined by W to Alexander, 118–120; told to Miss Schuster, 146 n; sold to Sedger, 349 n; written by Harris alone, 362 n; W's dispute with Harris about, 362–364; its London production and reception, 362 n; W's grievances about, 365; W could always have raised £100 on, 365
Mulierast
  Ross's immortal phrase, 294

Orleans Club
Queensberry's remark at, 179
O'Sullivan, Vincent
pays W's fare to Naples, 307; coming
to Naples, 313; appearance of his
book approved, 324–325; his *Aspects
of Wilde* quoted, 221 n, 307
Ouida
the only *lionne* left, 71
Outlook, The
Henley reviews *Ballad* in, 330 n
Oxford
W undergraduate at, 1–21; W rusticated from, 15; Ruskin W's dearest
memory of, 71; "Oxford temper" not
acquired by Douglas, 155; W visits
Douglas at, 156; Douglas's early
trouble at, 154, 163, 169, 184, 222; as
turning-point in W's life, 197; W
remembers reading Pater at, 199; W's
hopes at, 203; W dubs himself Infamous St Oscar of, 334

Padua
W visits, 3
Paillard's
W and Douglas sup at, 164; £85
spent at, 172
Palermo
W describes, 355–356
Pall Mall Gazette, The
Besant and the obvious in, 96; re-
buked for review of *House of Pome-
granates*, 99; interview on banning of
Salome, 105; Archer's letter to, 106 n;
W denies authorship of *Green Carna-
tion* in, 125; describes Douglas as W's
shadow, 173; W on Alfred Austin in,
191 n
Panthers
W returns to fight with, 130; feasting
with, 220
Paris
W stays in, 49–50; W's honeymoon
in, 55 n; W stays in, 92–93, 96–101;
W's thoughts in train to, 162; W with
Douglas in, 164, 172; W takes Atkins
to, 180 n; W unwilling to live in, 286,
291; W anxious for rehabilitation as
artist in, 288; W leaves Dieppe for,
306; described by O'Sullivan in, 307;
W lives in, 327–369; Ross recalled to,
365; W dies in, 369; expensive to die
in, 369; W reburied in, 371
Parkinson, Rev. Thomas, S.J.
W breakfasts with, 12

Pascal
works of sent to W in prison, 139 n
Pater, Walter
his letter on W's Grosvenor Gallery
article, 19; portrayed in *New Republic*,
9 n; praises *Happy Prince*, 72; his
review of *Dorian Gray*, 85 n; books
by sent to W in prison, 139 n; W
reads in prison, 148 n; quoted by W,
159; strange influence of his *Renaissance* on W's life, 199; *Marius* and
religion, 204; his words attributed to
Wordsworth, 204; wrongly quoted by
W, 357
Patience
first productions of, 31
Patmore, Coventry
and the Laureateship, 191 n
Payne, Ralph
and book in *Dorian Gray*, 116
Peel, Willy
W breakfasts with, 101 n
Pentonville Prison
W imprisoned in, 133; W transferred
to Wandsworth from, 138 n; W to be
transferred from Reading to, 261; W
released from, 265
Percy, *see* Douglas of Hawick, Lord
Percy, Bishop
W in prison asks for *Reliques* of, 145 n
Père Lachaise Cemetery
W jokes about, 367; Ross hopes to
transfer W's remains to, 370; W re-
buried in, 371
Petitions
Merrill's, 134 n; W's to Home Secretary, 142, 251, 252; Adey's, 146 n
Pharaoh
possible reference to, 287; W plans to
tackle at Posilippo, 310
Philistines
Henley seized on by, 78; in *Scots
Observer*, 86–87; fury in the honest,
91; newspapers written by prurient
for, 95; English journalists are, 106;
banning of *Salome* a great triumph for,
107; Douglas treats brother as, 162;
Christ's war against, 214; the Philistine element in life, 220; W in heart
of Philistia, 221; Ross and W plan to
rescue Shakespeare from, 242; W's
struggle against hideously Philistine
world, 308
Picture of Dorian Gray, The
published in *Lippincott's*, 81 n; the
story only fit for C.I.D., 81; defended
against *Scots Observer*, 81–87; de-

Prison—*cont.*

Daily Chronicle interested in reform of, 279; Nelson man who could change system, 282; W could write three articles on, 282; Davitt's question on, 269 n; influence of *Salome* production on W's treatment in, 287; W not ashamed of having been in, 296; all sensitive on leaving, 295; difficulty of describing artistically, 312; Prison Reform Bill debated, 334; lack of sanitation in, 336; lack of books in, 336–337; brutality of doctors in, 338

Prussia, Queen Louisa of
and Goethe's lines, 201

Publisher
no objection to his reading books he publishes, 123; best method of printing name of on title-pages, 316, 324; untrustworthy look of, 328

Pugin, A. W. N.
Ballad dedication to avoid looking like tombstone by, 317

Puritanism
W in false colours as champion of, 221; Queensberry representative of, 266

Pusey, Rev. E. B.
believed still alive by *curé*, 292

Queensberry, Marchioness of
W writes to about Douglas's future, 113; W's conversation at Bracknell with, 156; her letters to W, 162, 163, 224–225; W's regard for, 164; her grief for Drumlanrig, 168; Douglas complains to, 189; Douglas advised to show letter to, 224; puts blame on W, 228; W denies conditions attached to £200 from, 332 n

Queensberry, eighth Marquess of
his marriage and divorce, 113 n; given dinner by Hawtrey and Brookfield, 105 n; on the rampage, 118; refused ticket for *Importance*, 128 n; his plot for first night, 128–129; W finds card of, 129; arrested and charged, 130 n; W's unwillingness to put Douglas in box against, 131; Douglas's belief he could discredit, 131 n; acquitted, 131 n; W thought but to defend Douglas from, 133; debt unpaid by family of, 149–151; his triumph, 150; and W's bankruptcy, 150, 171; begins attack on W, 164; invades Tite Street, 167; Douglas's

attacks on, 172–173; pursues Lord Rosebery to Homburg, 174; drunken, *déclassé*, and half-witted, 174; Douglas's telegram to, 175; his passion for notoriety, 176; his letters to *Star* on W's trial, 178 n; his pleasure at W's bankruptcy, 179; Bauër on, 184 n; ape and buffoon, 184; his appearance in Court described, 220; W's lawyer's letters to, 221; his correspondence with Douglas, 221; outdone by Douglas, 222; his wish for a scandal, 225; twice divorced, 225; W's false position with, 243; possibility of his making scene at Dieppe, 298; any member of his family deemed disreputable, 319

Queensberry, seventh Marquess of
his death, 164 n

Quilter, Harry
W accused of dressing like, 36 n, accusation rejected by W, 37; abused by Whistler, 66 n

Radley College
Wilkinson writes from, 346, 352; had nothing left to teach Wilkinson, 352

Raffalovich, André
and scansion of tuberose, 60–61; supports Beardsley, 60 n; his book on homosexuality, 327 n

Ramsgate
Margate *non-de-plume* of, 330

Ranee (of Sarawak), *see* Brooke, Lady

Rankin, McKee
Leadville miners resemble, 41

Ravenna
quoted, 3 n; copy sent to Marion Willett, 19 n; awarded Newdigate Prize, 20 n

Reading Gaol (*see also* Prison, Prince, Nelson, and *Ballad of Reading Gaol*)
W imprisoned in, 138–263; Constance Wilde's visit to, 139; W's transfer to, 186, 219; Martin improves W's lot in, 248; W leaves, 265; W's talk of, 267; W's letter to *Daily Chronicle* about, 269–275; W's number in, 279; many good fellows in, 281; chaplain at a good-natured fool, 315; W's doctor in *Ballad* not portrait of doctor at, 315, 318, 321; *Ballad* based on execution in, 317 n; goodness of warders to W in, 318; Adey's visit to W in, 319; colour of W's hair unaltered by, 366

Referee, The
W's ironical reference to, 104

Ross, A. G.—*cont.*

354; unfortunate incident with, 354; his sightless eye and terrible smile, 355; Robbie's imagined treatment of, 362; visits W in last illness, 365

Ross, Robert

at Cambridge, 74; W's meeting with, 74 n; his share in "Mr W.H.", 78; and *Scots Observer*, 86; friendship with Adey, 114 n; lame and bearded, 114; told of Queensberry's card, 129; asked to fetch MS of *Sainte Courtisane*, 134; visits W at Reading, 140; asked to retrieve W's letters to Douglas, 140; at the sea with his mother, 146 n; his wit and satire, 146; and MS and publication of *De Profundis*, 152 n; and origin of "Decay of Lying," 157; and Douglas's translation of *Salome*, 161; his noble action in Bankruptcy Court, 188; his regular letters to Reading, 191; the symbol of affection, 196; W's delight at visit of, 200; pays for W's books, 223; his comfort and help to W, 223; W plans to go abroad with, 236; appointed literary executor by W, 240; his bad handwriting, 241, 248; his delightful literary letters, 246; and list of books for W's release, 247–248; his painful visit to Reading, 252; Turner defends and praises, 261 n; describes W's arrival at Dieppe, 266; suggests W's alias, 266 n; W suggests alias for, 267 n; takes W to Berneval, 276; stern with W at Dieppe, 276; W wants no other friend but, 278; canonised by W, 278, 283, 334; the best half of W, 280; his Catholicism questioned, 283; W's chalet described to, 285; coins word "mulierast," 294; severe, 294; receives three letters from W in one day, 296; thanked for ties, 297; wished a happy Jubilee, 299; Douglas's assumption of social superiority to, 300; told to bring *Esmond* and Queen Anne chairs, 301; W's return to Douglas explained to, 308; typescript of *Ballad* to be sent to, 310; to see Smithers and Pinker, 310; W distressed by letters of, 309; his letters to Smithers quoted, 316 n; on dedication of *Ballad*, 317 n; can ride anything except Pegasus, 318; blamed for showing W's letter to Smithers, 318; Douglas no more disreputable than, 319; blamed for

agreeing with lawyers, 319–320; blamed for letter to Smithers, 322–323; W broken-hearted by attitude of, 323 n; natures like his not found twice in a lifetime, 324; accused of being a *low-Church* Catholic, 329; his phrase "home-made paper," 340; sends W £5 by stealth, 341 n; offers W new suit, 343; W asks permission to dedicate *Importance* to, 344; thanked for clothes, 344; W threatens to alter dedication, 345; his account of James amuses Harris, 347; his inscribed copy of *Importance*, 349 n; W gives false names and addresses for, 358–359; his letters in style of Jane Austen, 362; imagined as Cinderella of his family, 362; called to Paris by telegram, 365; on W's last illness, 365; his final interview with W, 365–369; leaves for Nice, 368; calls Fr Cuthbert Dunne, 368; sleeps at Hôtel d'Alsace, 368; describes W's death, 368–369; follows W's coffin, 369, 370

Rossetti, D. G.

guyed in *Patience*, 31; his works at Babbacombe, 108 n; his letters dreadful, 246; his wife's poem, 248; his lovely line, 293

Rossetti, W. M.

accused of suppressing his brother's poem, 293

Rothenstein, Will

and banning of *Salome*, 105–106; quoted on Conder, 290 n; his Pilgrimage to the Sinner, bringing lithographs, 296; W's letter of welcome to, 296–297; W's importance in career of, 297; W sends note on Henley to, 303; W's note rejected by, 304; editor of paying magazine, 304; rescues Monticelli and sells for W's benefit, 304; his praise of *Ballad* appreciated, 328; with W in France, 344; named on laurel wreath, 370

Rouen

reunion of W and Douglas at, 305; W stays at, 306

Royal Literary Fund

its grant to Lady Wilde, 75 n

Royalty Theatre

Mr and Mrs Daventry produced at, 362 n

Rugby game

Harris talks, 348

Schwob, Marcel
    his corrections to *Salome*, 101 n; *Sphinx* dedicated to, 101 n
Scots Observer, The
    attacks *Dorian Grey*, 81–87
Scott, Gilbert
    proof of *Ballad* dedication like bad brass by, 317
Scott, Walter
    W reads in Glasgow, 64
Scribe, Eugène
    W asked to adapt his *Verre d'Eau*, 301
Sculpture
    no longer a representative art, 188
Sebastian, St
    Keats compared to, 17; W's alias probably referred to, 266 n
Second Mrs Tanqueray, The
    London production of, 116 n; in Australia, 117 n
Sedger, Horace
    no truth in advertisement of, 349; his option on *Mr and Mrs Daventry*, 362 n
"Selfish Giant, The"
    praised by Pater, 72 n
Shakespeare
    Hamlet at Verona, 3; *Aurora Leigh* ranked with *Hamlet*, 9; W on costume in, 62 n; at Oxford, 62, Lytton on, 62 n; W speaks on at Stratford, 74; W's essay on sonnets of, *see* "Portrait of Mr W.H."; Keats quoted on, 82; Mamilius entirely delightful, 99; W condemned to speak language of, 100; not to be confused with his creations, 101; *Lear* quoted, 169; W's letter compared to sonnet of, 169; *Hamlet* quoted, 193, 291, 321; nothing to equal Christ's Passion in works of, 206; effect of sonnets of, 209; Christ and plays of, 210; *Dream* quoted, 211; Hamlet's madness discussed, 233; Rosencrantz and Guildenstern analysed, 232–233; *Macbeth* quoted, 242; Ross and W plan to rescue from Philistines, 242; Douglas's sonnet to, 242 n; Border ballads true predecessors of, 288; Harris thinks of at top of voice, 348
Shallowness
    the supreme vice, 197, 198
Shannon, C. H.
    his friendship with Ricketts and their work for W, 79 n; his designs for *House of Pomegranates* defended, 98; does not draw for blind, 99; to design cover of *Importance*, 345; named on laurel wreath, 370
Sharp, William
    W finds motto for, 76 n
Shaw, Bernard
    praised for opposing censorship and for book on Ibsen, 108–109; popularises Jaeger clothing, 56 n; on Pigott, 105 n; *Salome* sent to, 108; his answer, 109 n; thanked for *Widowers' Houses*, 112; and the great Celtic School, 112 n; his attack on Nordau in *Sanity of Art*, 142 n; possible drafter of Adey's petition, 146 n
Shelley, P. B.
    read in Nebraska prison, 43; quoted by W and Raffalovich, 60–61; of Christ's company, 205; W wins bet on Arnold's phrase about, 350
Sherard, R. H.
    W sends Rodd's poems to, 50; his failings as W's biographer, xii; dedicates poems to W, 51; W defines friendship to, 51; cheers W in Holloway, 134; his fine chivalrous friendship, 135; fails to persuade Bernhardt to buy *Salome*, 135 n; Ross asked to write to, 139; a friend of Bauër, 140; his indiscretion, 146 n, 148; the bravest and most chivalrous, 181–182; his kindness to W, 223; attacked by Douglas, 223; W's confession to, 230; his contribution from Martin, 248 n; and Dowson, 290 n; accused of censuring W at Authors' Club, 312–313; quoted, 312 n; in his grenadine at Berneval, 313; creates scene in Campbell's Bar, 343; his deterioration, 343–344; Dowson dies in house of, 353 n
Shone, R. V.
    told to refuse Queensberry ticket for *Importance*, 128
Sibleigh, Charles
    calls after W's death, 369
Sicily
    W at Taormina, 327 n; W visits and describes, 355–356
Sickert, Helena
    W sends Matthew Arnold's poems to, 23; W writes to from Nebraska, 42; invited to write for *Woman's World*, 69; contributes, 70 n
Sickert, W. R.
    Leadville suitable subject for, 43

Wilde, Constance—*cont.*
illness of, 302; Blacker prevents W
from seeing, 302 n; W plans to visit,
308; result of her refusing to let W
see children, 308; her letter too late,
311; stops W's allowance, 319; horrified at Adey's visit to Reading, 319;
her violent letter, 320; thinks *Ballad*
exquisite, 332 n; her letters to Blacker
quoted, 332 n; explains her financial
position to Blacker, 332 n; her horror
of Douglas, 332 n; her death, 338; W
visits grave of, 349

Wilde, Cyril
his birth, 63; essentially Wagnerian,
63; promised chocolates, 93; "better
not come up," 129; W's love for and
hopes of seeing occasionally, 151;
"my friend," 151; W's misery at
separation from, 181, 207; Adrian
Hope guardian of, 193, 227; Constance must be father and mother to,
227; W deemed unfit to be with, 249;
W's idolatrous love of, 257; his advice
as good as Ross's, 260; his photograph sent to W, 282; W anxious to
see at Dieppe, 282 n

Wilde, Isola
W's sister, 1; W's poem on not
typical of his work, 121

Wilde, Lady
early history, 1; disgusted at W's
rustication, 15; her pamphlet sent to
Knowles, 28; her grant from Royal
Literary Fund, 75 n; her Civil List
pension, 75 n; W stays with on bail,
136; her death, 139 n, 186; Leverson
asked to retrieve her copies of W's
books, 140; W's affection for, 143;
her memory brings remorse, 192;
quotes Goethe, 200–201; compared to
Mrs Browning and Madame Roland,
224; died broken-hearted, 224; her
Sidonia loved by Rossetti, 246; compared to Constance, 254; W dreams
of, 278

Wilde, Lily
her marriage, 16 n; her second marriage, 112 n; tells Constance of Adey's
visit to Reading, 319; visits W in last
illness, 366; sends wreath to W's
funeral, 370

Wilde, Vyvyan, *see* Holland, Vyvyan

Wilde, Sir William
his career, 1; his death, 7; Moytura
House built by, 10; his anecdote of
Irish landlord, 258

Wilde, William (Willie)
mystified by W's rustification, 16; W
sends cheque for cirgarettes to, 113;
writes W monstrous letters, 135;
could compromise a steam-engine,
135 n

Wilkinson, Louis
invents dramatic society to gain epis-
tolary access to W, 346; Radley had
nothing left to teach, 352; sends
wreath to W's funeral, 370; named on
laurel wreath, 370

Willett, Marion
W sends poem to, 19

Willis's Rooms
Douglas enquired after at, 127;
Douglas taken to supper at, 155, 231,
235

Wills, Mr Justice
judge at W's second trial, 133; on
Douglas, 227 n

Wilson, Dr Henry
W disappointed by will of, 18

Wimbledon, Lady of, *see* Schuster,
Adela

Winter, John Strange, *see* Stannard,
Mrs Arthur

Woman of No Importance, A
binding designed by Shannon, 79 n;
produced at Haymarket, 111 n; and
great Celtic School, 112 n; W quotes
from, 158, 196, 198; cancelled speech
in, 226; W refers to Mrs Daubeny in,
297

Woman's World, The
W's editing of, 67 n, 69; and Arthur
Fish, 83 n

Wood, Alfred
blackmail his sole source of income,
222

Wooldridge, C. T.
Ballad dedicated to memory of, 317-318

Wordsworth, William
quoted by W, 67, 157, 195, 202;
Pater's words on attributed to, 204;
Arnold not healed by, 218

Wormwood Scrubs
press wrongly announce W's release
from, 261

Worthing
W'a stay at, 118–125; *Importance*
mostly written at, 118 n; Douglas
interrupts W at, 165

Wyndham, Charles
suitable for *Importance*, 126; his dress
in *London Assurance*, 90–92; visits W
at Berneval, 301

Wyndham, George
  sent to propose W should drop Douglas, 225; Douglas visits in House of Commons, 131 n

Yates, Edmund
  and the *World*, 66 n
Yeats, W.B.
  quotes W on Sharp, 76 n; his review of *Dorian Gray*, 85 n; told to choose from W's poems for anthology, 121; his choice in two anthologies, 121 n; records W's remark on Willie, 135 n; Max's caricature illustrates letter by, 348 n
Yellow Book, The
  Beardsley art-editor of, 115 n; his drawing of Mrs Patrick Campbell in, 116 n; first appearance: dull and loathsome, 117
Young, Dalhousie
  visits W at Berneval, 290; his courageous pamphlet, 290 n; the best of fellows, 290; and W's Monticelli, 304–305; named on laurel wreath, 370
"Young King, The"
  the note of doom in, 204

Zola, Emile
  W meets in Paris, 49; cited by T. E. Brown, 84 n; *Dorian Gray* classed with *La Terre*, 86